On the Edge

The Spectacular Rise and Fall of COMMODORE

Brian Bagnall

VARIANT PRESS

VARIANT PRESS
143 Goldthorpe Crescent
Winnipeg, Manitoba
R2N 3E6

Copyright © 2005 by Brian Bagnall
All rights reserved,
including the right of reproduction
in whole or in part in any form.

Photographs courtesy of R.J. Mical,
Dave Haynie, Chuck Peddle, and Bil Herd.

Designed by Mike Newton

Manufactured in Canada

Library and Archives Canada Cataloguing in Publication

Bagnall, Brian, 1972-
On the edge : the spectacular rise and fall of Commodore /
Brian Bagnall.

Includes bibliographical references.
ISBN 0-9738649-0-7

1. Commodore International--History.
2. Computer industry--Canada--History.
3. Computer industry--United States--History. I. Title.

HD9696.2.A2B33 2005   338.7'61004'0971
          C2005-904402-0

Thanks to everyone who helped make this book better: Cameron Davis, Denny Atkins, Gareth Knight, Henry Makow, Ian Matthews, Jim Brain, Jim Butterfield, Martin Goldberg, Robert Bernardo, and Winnie Forster.

Contents

Introduction	vii
Prolog: The Rise of Commodore	ix
1. MOS Technology – 1974 to 1976	1
2. The Acquisition – 1975 to 1976	26
3. The PET – 1976 to 1977	37
4. Releasing the PET – 1977 to 1978	63
5. The Trinity – 1977 to 1979	86
6. Business is War – 1979 to 1980	113
7. The Color Computers – 1979 to 1980	129
8. The VIC-20 - 1980	157
9. Computers for the Masses - 1981	188
10. The Race to a Million – 1981 to 1983	206
11. The Secret Project - 1981	224
12. The Commodore 64 - 1982	243
13. Selling the Revolution - 1982	261
14. Commodore Mania - 1983	282
15. TED - 1983	304
16. Dismissing the Founder - 1984	327
17. The Sequel - 1984	349
18. Brawling for the C128 – 1984 to 1985	370
19. The Savior of Commodore – 1982 to 1985	394
20. The Amiga – 1985 to 1986	426
21. Dropping the Ball – 1985 to 1987	458
22. The New Amigas – 1986 to 1987	482
23. A Radical New Direction – 1988 to 1992	510
24. The Fall of Commodore – 1992 to 1994	536
Epilogue	549
Bibliography	558

Introduction

"Do you remember? I do."

- Bouncing Souls, '87

Commodore Business Machines ended operations on April 29, 1994. A decade has now passed. What has Commodore meant to the world?

Amid the chaos, infighting, and excitement, Commodore was able to achieve some remarkable industry firsts. They were the first major company to show a personal computer, before even Apple and Radio Shack. They sold a million computers before anyone else. The first true multimedia computer came from Commodore. Yet with all these firsts, Commodore receives almost no credit as a pioneer.

The history of early computers has tended to focus on Microsoft, IBM, and Apple, snubbing contributions made by Commodore. "There is a lot of revisionism going on and I don't think it's fair," says Commodore 64 designer Robert Yannes. "People wanted to ignore Commodore."

An early-popularized story of the microcomputer revolution was *Accidental Empires*, by Robert X. Cringely (born Mark Stephens). The former Apple employee perpetuated a select view of the microcomputer revolution, a view that not everyone accepts as accurate. In *Infinite Loop*, Michael Malone writes, "The pseudonymous Cringely is notorious for his sloppy way with facts."

In his book, Cringely said, "Commodore wasn't changing the world; it was just trying to escape from the falling profit margins of the calculator market while running a stock scam along the way." In reality, Commodore employees worked tirelessly to deliver state of the art technology to their customers at a price far lower than Apple's.

PBS adapted Cringley's book as a popular TV series, *Triumph of the Nerds* (1996). The adaptation ignored Commodore completely.

Turner Network Television produced a movie called *Pirates of Silicon Valley* (1999), based on a more credible book, *Fire in the Valley*, by Paul Freiberger & Michael Swaine. Regrettably, the producers ignored much of the book and focused on Steve Jobs, Bill Gates, and IBM.

"The PC came out, we changed players, and the whole early history just got lost," says PET designer Chuck Peddle. Peddle deplores the emphasis on IBM, Apple, and Microsoft at the expense of earlier developers. "None of that is true. It's not fair that the stuff that happened earlier has been so badly ignored."

"I'm not sure it's intentional, it's just the West Coast mindset that everything happens on the West Coast, so we don't even need to pay attention to what happened everywhere else," says Yannes. "Most of the revisionist stuff I read was coming out of California and Commodore was mostly successful after it left California."

When writers are not ignoring Commodore, they often get their facts wrong. In *The Silicon Boys and their Valley of Dreams*, David Kaplan describes the Apple IPO in 1980 and then adds, "But Apple soon bred competition. Radio Shack and Commodore and even Atari, among others, started selling their own personal computers." In truth, Commodore and Radio Shack began selling personal computers in 1977, and Atari followed in 1979.

This rosy picture of Apple starting the microcomputer industry could not be further from the truth. Apple had a very slow start and eventually climbed to first place sometime in the early 1980's, only to lose their lead to Commodore once again. In the very earliest days, Commodore was pioneering the consumer microcomputer industry.

While IBM pushed business computers and Apple pushed style, Commodore put computers into the hands of ordinary consumers. Throughout the eighties, Commodore consistently had the best prices, often with the best technology. The Commodore 64 is the Model T of computers, selling more units than any other single computer model, according to the *Guinness Book of World Records*.

In the summer of 2004, I began interviewing Commodore insiders. We traveled back to the seventies, eighties, and nineties and relived the Commodore experience. I am thankful to each of the participants for taking me on that journey, something I will never forget.

The journey has ended for me, but for you it is about to begin. I hope you enjoy reading this book as much as I enjoyed writing it.

Brian Bagnall
May 22, 2005

Prologue: The Rise of Commodore

Hailing a taxi in New York City in the early 1950's might have put you in the company of future business titan Jack Tramiel. As you sat in the back seat, two large, bulging eyes would appraise you through the rear view mirror, determining if you were worth anything to him. At the time, Tramiel was positioning himself for riches and glory. It was a humble beginning, but driving a taxi was a blissful step up from the work camps of Poland during World War II.

In July 1947, a 19-year-old Idek Tramielski proposed to and married a fellow concentration camp survivor named Helen Goldgrub in Germany. While there, the Hebrew Immigrant Aid Society (HIAS) contacted Idek and helped him emigrate from Europe by paying for his passenger liner ticket to New York City. Idek changed his name to Jack Tramiel.

In 1948, Tramiel enlisted in the U.S. Army and served as a cook at Fort Dix. Later, he joined the *First Army Office Equipment Repair Department*, which was responsible for maintaining and repairing almost 25 thousand pieces of office equipment. Jack served two tours of duty in Korea in 1950 and in 1952.

After his service ended, Jack worked for a typewriter repair company called *Ace Typewriter*. There, he met a German named Manfred Kapp, and the two started their own repair company called *Singer Typewriter*.

In 1958, Jack, Manfred, and their families moved to Toronto, Canada and formed a typewriter manufacturing company called *Commodore*. The company quickly grew until a scandal rocked the Canadian financial scene, with Commodore at the center. After an embarrassing public inquiry, Commodore was finished; or so it seemed.

In 1966, a Canadian Investor named Irving Gould purchased Commodore and redirected Jack Tramiel into the burgeoning calculator business. By 1973, savage competition from Texas Instruments and Japanese calculator manufacturers began hurting Commodore's profits. Jack began to look elsewhere for cheaper calculator parts.

CHAPTER

1

MOS Technology

1974 to 1976

Hi-tech companies need three players in order to succeed: a financier, a technology-God, and a juggernaut with a type-A personality. Commodore would require these three ingredients to take them to a new level. They had Irving Gould, with his financial expertise and deep pockets. They had Jack, so aggressive people sometimes referred to him as the scariest man alive. All Commodore needed was a visionary engineer to take Commodore into a new field of technology.

The Grey Wizard of the East

In the 1970's, the image of a computer genius was not in the mold of the young hacker we are familiar with today. Teenaged tycoons like Bill Gates had not filtered into the public consciousness, and *WarGames* (1983, MGM) was not yet released, with the prototypical computer hacker portrayed by Matthew Broderick. The accepted image of a technological genius was a middle-aged man with graying hair and glasses, preferably wearing a long white lab coat.

Chuck Peddle was the image of a technology wizard, with his wire-frame glasses, white receding hairline, and slightly crooked teeth. At two hundred and fifty pounds, the five foot eleven inch engineer always struggled with his weight. Peddle describes himself at that time as "totally out of shape," but he was characteristically optimistic and never without a joke or story to tell.

Peddle possessed the ability to see further into the future than most of his contemporaries and he obsessively searched for the next big innovation. His mind was always active, sometimes to the point of causing sleep deprivation. "I don't sleep much," says Peddle. "Never did." In fact, the pattern of sleeplessness went back to his earliest days.

Peddle's father was one of 21 kids. His family originated in the Canadian Maritimes but the poor region made it difficult to support a family. "The whole area is very depressed," says Peddle. The family moved to the United States in search of a better economy.

Charles Peddle was born in Bangor Maine in 1937, one of eight children. "My mother said that when I was young I used to lie awake in my crib. I would cry and fuss and didn't sleep as much as the other kids," he says.

Peddle was raised in the state capital of Augusta, Maine, with a population of just over 20,000. Unfortunately, the move from the Maritimes to Maine only marginally improved the family prospects. "There is a tremendous amount of leakage across the border [from the Maritimes]," he says. "People are willing to work for nothing because they are starving to death at home. So it keeps wages down [in Maine] and it's always been a poor state."

In his senior year of high school, Chuck thought he found his calling. "In high school I worked in a radio station," he says. "I really wanted to be a radio announcer. For you, now, that really doesn't mean very much, but back then that was pre-TV and radio announcers were big."

Nearing the end of high school, Chuck traveled to Boston to try out for a scholarship in broadcasting. For the first time in his life, he saw his competition and realized he did not have enough natural talent. With a sense of relief, he recalls, "I failed as a radio announcer." Returning to Augusta, Chuck talked things over with the radio station owner, who told him, "I'll employ you as a radio announcer, but you will always be stuck in Maine because you are not good enough."

Peddle spent some time in the military as he contemplated his future. "I went into the Marine Corps just before I got out of high-school in 1955 and I went in active reserves in 1960," he recalls.

During this time, Peddle's former science teacher recognized a gift in Peddle and encouraged him to enter engineering. Peddle listened to his advice, but was unsure he wanted to enter the sciences.

"I didn't want a pick and shovel job," he says. "I wasn't sure what I was going to do and I was dirt poor. Luckily, in Maine you can be dirt poor and still get by." Unable to earn enough to pay for tuition fees, he applied for student loans.

At the end of summer, Peddle entered the *University of Maine* and enrolled in engineering and business courses. "When I started, I didn't have a clue what I wanted to do. I just knew I didn't want to do pick and shovel jobs anymore," he says. Partway through the first year, the university required students to choose a discipline. "I really loved physics, so I took engineering physics with an electrical minor."

Peddle remembers the dismal state of computing. "There wasn't a computer on campus, nor was there anyone on the campus who was computer literate," he says. In his final year, things began to change. "On the entire campus, there was one analogue computer, which had been bought in the last four months," he recalls. "The analogue computer was so primitive and they didn't know how to use it. There was zero knowledge about computers on that campus."

Peddle received a standard education in engineering, devoid of computers. Over 200 miles away, at the Massachusetts Institute of Technology (MIT), a revolution was occurring which would soon change his situation.

Chuck Peddle's main influence was the legendary inventor and mathematician, Claude Elwood Shannon. Though virtually unknown to the world, Shannon was the founding father of the modern electronic communications age. Shannon was an eccentric, who terrified people by riding his unicycle through the hallways at night while juggling.

Shannon also built a reputation for inventions that were of little practical value to anyone. Over the years, he filled his beachside house with juggling robots, maze-solving robot mice, chess playing programs, mind-reading machines, and an electric chair to transport his children down to the lake.

In 1948, while working at *Bell Labs*, Shannon produced a groundbreaking paper, *A Mathematical Theory of Communication*. In it, Shannon rigorously analyzed the concept of Information Theory and how we transmit pictures, words, sounds, and other media using a stream of 1's and 0's. Chuck Peddle was enchanted with Shannon's theories. "Today, you take this for granted, but you have to remember that someone had to dream all this up," he says. "Shannon was one of those guys that dreamed up from nothing the idea of the way information goes back and forth. Everyone else's work stands on his shoulders and most people don't even know it."

In 1958, Shannon returned to MIT at Lincoln Labs as a lecturer and Artificial Intelligence researcher. While there, he spread his concepts on Information Theory. "He changed the world," says Peddle. "Shannon was not only a pioneer but a prophet. He effectively developed a following, almost like a cult." One of Shannon's cultists would soon spread the word to the University of Maine.

During Peddle's senior year, the University of Maine accepted a lecturer from MIT who studied under Claude Shannon. According to Peddle, "He had a nervous breakdown, so he left MIT. The University of Maine was so happy to get him because he was so superior to the type of instructor they could normally get. They gave him the opportunity to teach only four classes per week between the hours of eleven o'clock and noon. The guy was being totally babied and should have been since he was a great instructor. He decided to put together a class to teach people about Information Theory."

Chuck Peddle, father of the 6502 (Das neue P.M. Computerheft).

At the time, Peddle was enrolling for his final year and the Information Theory class happened to fit into his schedule. As Peddle recalls, "It changed my life."

The class began with the instructor discussing the eyes and ears as the primary sensors for receiving information. "He started teaching us about Boolean algebra and binary logic, and the concept of Information Theory," recalls Peddle. "I just fell in love. This was where I was going to spend my life."

"The whole thing about how information moves back and forth is essential to almost everything I've done," he says. However, the topic that interested Peddle the most was computers. "You have to understand how exciting it was," explains Peddle. "Information Theory was interesting, and I've used it from time to time, but the computer stuff this guy taught me was life changing."

Though this new revelation came late, Peddle immersed himself in computer theory for his final year. "I got an A on my senior paper in physics class by giving a discussion on binary and Boolean arithmetic. I was trying to build an and-gate in my senior class [from early transistors] and the top electrical engineers on campus couldn't help me figure out the structures and why my and-gate didn't work," he recalls. Peddle and a friend even tried growing a transistor crystal but soon gave up.

As graduation approached, Peddle began searching for a place of permanent employment. He had married while in College and already had a family. "I came out of college and I had three kids; two and a half, actually. I had the third one right after [graduation]." The new responsibilities motivated Peddle to find a better life.

Peddle knew he wanted to live in California and he wanted to work in computers. "I only interviewed computer companies," he recalls. "At all of the companies of any size, like GE and RCA, you went to work on a training program for a year or two. You really were just interviewing to join their training program."

Of all the companies, GE made the best impression on Peddle. "I kind of fell in love with GE," he says. "When I got my offer, I thought I would take it, because they had such a good training program."

Peddle and his young family moved to California to start a new life with General Electric. Before long, Peddle was working at GE's computing facility in Phoenix, Arizona. Peddle worked with massive mainframe computers, similar to those seen in the 1965 film *Alphaville*. The first computer Peddle used was a GE-225, which he describes as a "very old, very slow machine with small capacity."

Peddle entered programs into the GE-225 computer by feeding a stack of punch cards into a card reader. Peddle recalls, "I would set up long six or seven hour runs, drive across the city and go to bed with the instructions, 'If this breaks, call me.' People would wake me up in the middle of the night, I would find a solution in ten minutes and go back to sleep."

In 1961, Peddle and two of his coworkers developed the concept for variable sector disk formatting. They even filed a patent for their idea. Years later, Peddle would use this idea to give Commodore disk drives more data storage than the competition.

In 1963, John G. Kemeny developed the *Basic* computer language at Dartmouth College in New Hampshire, along with Tom Kurtz. They developed Basic for the GE-235 mainframe computer, and as a result, Peddle was almost immediately aware of it. "I taught Basic the day after

6   THE SPECTACULAR RISE AND FALL OF COMMODORE

it was invented," claims Peddle. "I got one of the original Basic manuals from a guy in Dartmouth and taught my people in Phoenix."

A year later, Kemeny and Kurtz created the revolutionary *Dartmouth Time-Sharing System* (DTSS) for the GE-235. With the time-sharing system, multiple users could interact with the mainframe computer simultaneously using terminals. General Electric immediately recognized the value of this new system and used it to form the basis of a new multi-million dollar business. "Two years later, GE goes into the time-sharing business," recalls Peddle. "They're selling time-sharing to everybody and GE was selling more computers than they could build. It was a big goddamned deal."

GE-225 Mainframe Computer System (photo courtesy of GE).

With the time-sharing business suddenly ballooning, General Electric sent Peddle to their largest computing center in Evendale, Ohio to set up time-sharing systems for General Electric's jet engine business. The massive computer facility contained ten IBM-7094 mainframe systems, five GE-600's, and 25 GE-225's. Peddle recalls, "We were running time-sharing for about 4000 engineers and programmers." The refrigerated computing facility seemed futuristic in the mid-sixties, with white tiled walls, raised floors, and rows and rows of mainframe computers.

Setting up the time-sharing systems was time consuming, and Peddle often stayed at the computer facility around the clock. During this time, Peddle picked up a habit originated by GE founder Thomas Edison. "I stole the idea of cots from him," he says. "Everyone understood that if I'm tired, I go to my office and take a half hour nap."

After Peddle set up the time-sharing systems, he became administrator for two of the systems. The experience gave Peddle valuable knowledge that he would later use to develop his own computers. "I got a really good understanding of what worked on time-sharing and what didn't work, and what people wanted," he says.

While working with GE, Chuck met John Pavinen and Mort Jaffe, computer pioneers who would later become involved with him at Commodore. "John Pavinen was my manager at GE. He's the guy who put GE in the computer business," says Peddle. "A lot of the pioneers in the computer industry came out of GE."

Peddle also remembers some darker moments in the computer scene. "People used to be able to get their hands on computers," he recalls. "Then, in the late 60's and early 70's, there was a big revolt against technology. People were attacking computer centers with axes, claiming computers were taking over our lives. We're talking about serious hippy-type stuff. So all of the computer rooms locked the doors."

The need for security drastically reduced the freedom people previously enjoyed. "If you wanted to get a computer run, you walked up with your punch cards and left them on someone's desk," says Peddle. "They went from these time-sharing friendly, I-can-do-everything systems to having zero access to the computer." Peddle detected a strong demand from users to own their own computers.

The time-sharing business Peddle helped develop at GE was phenomenally successful, but in the late sixties, it started failing due to increased competition. By this time, Peddle had risen to a high-level management position. GE sent him to Phoenix to start another time-sharing company. Suddenly, "Time-sharing crashed; out of business; goodbye," says Peddle. "Companies started figuring out how much money they were spending on these time-sharing services and it was millions. GE was just cleaning up, but it just wasn't cost effective the way it was being done, so companies kept cutting it off and they moved the computers internally."

GE gave Peddle an assignment to work on cash registers, which made Peddle start to think about the concept of distributed intelligence. At the time, shared computing kept the brains of the computer at one central location and people could only interact with the computer system using dumb-terminals (a keyboard and monitor).

Peddle envisioned distributed intelligence, where he would transform the dumb-terminal into an intelligent-terminal that could have a printer connected to it, or other peripherals and data entry devices. "I sat down and derived the principles of distributed intelligence during a four-month period," says Peddle. "There was a focus on five or six stations around a minicomputer in a centralized architecture. My concept was you moved the intelligence to the place where you used it." It was a step towards networked computers.

"Then I started trying to teach GE about it," says Peddle. Unfortunately, in 1970 GE decided they were no longer interested in computers. "I was getting nowhere with GE because they were getting ready to sell the computer business. Two months later, they sold the company to Honeywell."

Peddle had the option to receive a severance package or move elsewhere in GE. For Peddle, the decision was easy. "Myself and two other guys took the termination agreement. We said, 'This is found money, so we're going to start our own business.' We had already started on the cash register business, and I had a deal with *Exxon*."

The three partners immersed themselves in their intelligent-terminals. "We got it all done and actually built the electronics that demonstrated the concepts," says Peddle.

During this time, Peddle devised many concepts that would have made him wealthy if he chose to patent them. "We invented the credit-card driven gasoline pump, the first credit verification terminal [i.e. credit card scanners] and the first point of sale terminal [i.e. computerized cash registers]." Peddle now laments, "It's too bad we didn't patent the shit out of it because we could have been very wealthy as a result of that."

Peddle realized the intelligent terminal needed a fundamentally new component to make their ideas work. "We needed our own microprocessor," he says. This realization would lead Peddle on an extraordinary journey that would change millions of lives.

At first, Peddle tried to develop the technology within his fledgling company but it was hopeless without funding. "We had everything going for us, but we didn't know how to raise money," he says. It was time for Peddle and his team to move on.

Chuck Peddle and his wife now had four children, but the stresses of Peddle leaving his secure job at GE caused the marriage to disintegrate. They divorced in 1971. "I put a bag of clothes in my [Austin-Healey] Sprite and drove away," he says. Within weeks, in what Peddle terms a 'planned transition', Peddle remarried a voluptuous blonde with two children from a previous marriage.

"I took some time out, because there was a change in life; going through the divorce and all that," says Peddle. In 1972, Peddle tried to start a Word Processing company using *Digital Equipment Corporation* (DEC) time-sharing systems. "We actually did the first on-line text processing system, setting type for newspapers," he says. Peddle was too early. "That company couldn't make it either."

The experience gave Peddle valuable knowledge he would need to develop the next generation of microprocessors. "I had done all the microelectronics and knew why a microprocessor needed to happen, and how to make a microprocessor, and how to make things that used microprocessors," he says. "But I didn't have a microprocessor because they weren't around yet."

In 1973, Peddle spotted an employment ad from *Motorola* for their new microprocessor program in Mesa, Arizona. He recalls, "I went down and talked to the guy who was running the program, who was a calculator guy." Peddle's experience at GE won him the job. "He basically hired me to finish the program."

Chuck started work at Motorola in 1973, around the time when Large Scale Integration (LSI) of semiconductor technology allowed the circuitry of a calculator or computer to fit onto a single chip. As the Intel 4004 and 8008 processors were gaining popularity, Motorola decided to enter the microprocessor market with their own chips.

A Motorola designer named Tom Bennett created the original architecture for the 6800, but Peddle felt it needed some changes. "They kind of muddled their way through the architecture for the 6800, which had some flaws in it. I was able to fix some of those flaws but it was too late for others," says Peddle. The final 8-bit microprocessor had 40 pins, 4000 transistors and an instruction set of 107 operations.

Peddle also made a major contribution to the project by designing the support chips for the 6800. Computers had to interact with peripheral devices like disk drives and printers, so Peddle designed a specialized support chips for this purpose. One chip to emerge was the 6820 Peripheral Interface Adapter, which most people just called the PIA chip. The 6820 became a major reason for the eventual popularity of the 6800.

Although Motorola engineers grasped the importance of what they had created, the management and salespeople knew very little of microprocessors. According to Peddle, some managers at Motorola even tried to kill the project. "So I built a demo of the chip using some of the hardware for my cash register to show everybody that microprocessors really did work," he says.

The salespeople at Motorola required an education on microprocessors but there were no courses. "They didn't know how to sell it, so I put together a training class for their applications engineers," says Peddle.

Peddle was instrumental in making some of the first deals for Motorola, including *Tektronics*, *NCR* (National Cash Register company), *Ford Motor Company*, *Unisys*, and *Burroughs* (makers of calculators). "I wound up going into the field presenting the architecture because I was the only one in the company who could intelligently talk to customers and have architectural discussions," he says.

The presentations usually ended the same way. "The guys would sit down, we would explain the 6800, and they would just fucking fall in love," says Peddle. However, the $300 price tag for a single 6800 processor prevented engineers from adopting the 6800 microprocessor in low cost products.

According to Peddle, someone would invariably say, "You're charging too much for it. What I want to use it for is not to replace a minicomputer. I want to use it to replace a controller, but at $300 per device it's not cost effective."

Armed with this knowledge, Chuck Peddle had an epiphany. He recognized the vast market for cost-reduced microprocessors. Both Intel and Motorola were overlooking an important market. Peddle slavered at the possibilities.

In August 1974, Motorola publicly introduced the 6800 chip for $300. The 6800 would eventually become successful for Motorola, in no small part to the efforts of Chuck Peddle. It almost became too successful and Motorola saw no reason to attack other markets.

Peddle pushed Motorola for a cost-reduced microprocessor. According to Peddle, "One week I returned to Motorola after one of these trips, and I had a letter there, formally instructing me Motorola was not going to follow a cost reduced product. I was ordered to stop working on it," recalls Peddle. Undeterred, Peddle wrote a letter (which he still owns today) saying, "This is product abandonment, therefore I am going to pursue this idea on my own. You don't have any rights to it because this letter says you don't want it." From that moment on, Peddle stopped working on microprocessors for Motorola. He continued teaching classes and finished the 6520 PIA chip he was developing, but his true focus was finding a way to make his low-cost microprocessor.

While still employed at Motorola, Peddle tried raising money to fund his microprocessor. He visited *Mostek* (not to be confused with MOS Technology) and talked to prominent venture capitalist L.J. Sevin of Sevin-Rosen[1], but he was not interested in Peddle's idea. Peddle continued talking to people in the semiconductor business.

One day, Peddle ran into an old friend from GE who now worked at Ford Motor Company. His friend mentioned John Pavinen, another ex-GE employee who was now running a semiconductor company near

---

[1] L. J. Sevin is responsible for funding startups like Compaq, Lotus, Cyprus, and Mostek.

Valley Forge, Pennsylvania. "When I started looking around for partners, I knew Pavinen was a killer computer guy," he recalls. "I called him up. He said, 'Come on down. Let's talk about it.'"

Peddle flew to Pennsylvania to examine MOS Technology. The facility was located at 950 Rittenhouse Road, a 14-acre site in an industrial park, called the *Valley Forge Corporate Center*. Peddle was impressed with the small firm. It had good credentials and many customers, among them a calculator company named Commodore.

Satisfied, Peddle sat down to discuss his new project with John Pavinen. "Pavinen immediately loved the idea of doing the product," says Peddle. The two discussed the specifications for the microprocessor, but MOS Technology was only capable of manufacturing chips using the P-channel process. Peddle wanted the more advanced N-channel process.

Pavinen felt he could deliver the N-channel process. "He had taught himself process development when he was working at General Instrument, and was really good at it," says Peddle. "He considered himself to be a competitor to [Andrew] Grove [of Intel]. He was convinced he could do a five-volt N-channel process in the same amount of time it would take me to develop the microprocessor."

The partnership between Chuck Peddle and John Pavinen seemed to hold promise. For his part, Pavinen badly needed a new product to replace the shrinking calculator market. MOS Technology engineer Al Charpentier describes the situation that caused MOS Technology to accept Chuck Peddle's proposal. "Here's a company that is somewhat dying, and the calculator margins are shrinking," he says. "They wanted market share."

Pavinen told Peddle, "Move your people and we'll set up a second group within the company. You run your own show."

As Motorola publicly unveiled the 6800, Chuck Peddle and seven coworkers from the engineering and marketing department left Motorola to pursue their own vision. The team included Will Mathis, Bill Mensch, Rod Orgill, Ray Hirt, Harry Bawcum, Mike James, Terry Holt[2], and Chuck Peddle. The departure of several of Motorola's top engineers seriously drained the company of much needed expertise on the eve of the 6800 debut.

Pavinen gave Peddle and his team a stake in the company. "The deal was, if the microprocessor took off, we would have a piece of the company," he recalls.

---

[2] Terry Holt later became president of S3, a semiconductor company that supplied a popular all-in-one chipset for IBM PC compatible computers.

On August 19, 1974, the team started work on their new processor at MOS Technology. With Chuck Peddle and his band of engineers, MOS Technology would radically change the market for computers.

MOS Technology

In 1969, a large industrial manufacturing company called *Allen-Bradley* wanted to enter the new semiconductor business. They financed the creation of MOS Technology. The three men who founded and operated the new startup had previously worked with Peddle at GE. They were Mort Jaffe, Don McLaughlin, and John Pavinen.

For the first five years, MOS Technology supplied calculator chips and other semiconductor parts to the electronics industry. Then Chuck Peddle and his team of ex-Motorola employees began working on a revolution within the microprocessor industry.

This revolution would occur at Valley Forge, Pennsylvania on the East Coast, approximately 100 miles inland from the Atlantic Ocean and 20 miles from Philadelphia. It was an appropriate place for a revolution. Almost 200 years earlier, Valley Forge was the turning point in the American Revolution when General George Washington's tired and bloodied troops retreated to Valley Forge for the winter, only to emerge with an unwavering offensive. Chuck and his band of engineers would also retreat for the winter, and in the following summer, they would unleash a powerful new weapon.

In the seventies, Valley Forge was a small, dispersed town with a population of about 400 people. MOS Technology headquarters resided in the peaceful setting, along a lone country road surrounded by wildlife. Street names like Adams Avenue, Monroe Boulevard, Madison Avenue, and Jefferson Avenue celebrated the revolutionary past. Directly across the road from MOS was a beautiful golf course, *General Washington Country Club*, tempting the MOS executives to squeeze in a round of play. Less than a mile away was the *Audubon Wildlife Sanctuary*, a park filled with serene trails where Canadian geese gathered in the fall while migrating south. Horse trails snaked in and out of the surrounding countryside. Riders would often emerge from the bushes and stare at this out of place high-tech firm. They could scarcely understand what was going on inside.

The headquarters hearkened back to the 1950's. It was a box-shaped two-story building with glass windows along the front and sides. Stray golf balls frequently bounced off the front windows, occasionally leaving small bullet sized holes that no one ever repaired. To the side and rear of the building were two huge parking lots, largely deserted since most people preferred to use the circular driveway out front.

The engineering lab on the second floor was the fountainhead of ideas for the company. This was where engineers invented the semiconductor chips. The engineers subdivided the lab into a maze of smaller rooms, each with a specific task. It was in this environment that Chuck Peddle would plan the centerpiece of his revolution.

Although Peddle envisioned a true microprocessor, it is a delicious irony that he did not design it for computers. "It was never intended to be a computer device. Never in a million years," he reveals. Instead, he envisioned the microprocessor for home electronics, home appliances, automobiles, industrial machines – just about everywhere except personal computers. "If we were going to do a computer, we would have done something else."

Price was the key to achieving widespread use of his microprocessor. Peddle envisioned a series of processors of varying size and complexity. The full featured microprocessor would sell for between $20 and $25. This meant the actual production cost could not exceed $12; otherwise, it would be unprofitable.[3]

With microprocessor economics, MOS desperately needed to sell high volumes of chips to overcome their design costs. According to Al Charpentier, the burgeoning microprocessor industry was having problems establishing itself. "You've got a new technology that everybody is interested in but it's not taking off," he explains. "The numbers back then were tiny. They were scientific curiosities because they were so expensive. So [MOS] wanted to drive the interest level way up, and that's how the $20 price tag got hammered in."

The price seemed unreasonably low compared to Motorola. "We wanted to own the market," says Peddle. "If you want to own a market, you take a price point that you make good money at, and you make sure nobody else can play with you. You build big, fast companies that way."

When asked why he did not chose a slightly higher price, say fifty dollars, Peddle says, "Because then I don't get the design in. At twelve bucks and fifteen bucks and twenty bucks I get design-ins everywhere." Peddle was after widespread success. "We wanted people to put microprocessors everywhere. We were trying to change the world."

The ex-Motorola employees split into three groups, each with their own areas of expertise. "We came in and effectively took over two or three rooms, and operated totally independent of the rest of the company for a long time," says Peddle.

---

[3] Generally, the manufacturer doubles the manufacturing cost when selling to a dealer, who then doubles the price again to sell to the consumer. Since MOS Technology would sell the microprocessor directly without an intermediary, they only doubled the manufacturing cost once.

Making Chips

Chuck Peddle, Will Mathis, and Rod Orgill would collaborate to design the initial architecture for the new microprocessor. "It was just the perfect product, the perfect time, the perfect team," says Peddle.

The architects' task was similar to designing a small city, except the streets in this city would be paved with metal. Electrons would inhabit their city, traveling the streets until they reached a transistor. Timing within this little city would be critical, otherwise traffic would halt, causing the chip to lock up.

Peddle and his group intentionally numbered their chips starting with 6500, so it would sound similar to the Motorola 6800. "It was a cheaper version of the 6800 and there was intended to be a whole string of them," he explains. "In hindsight, with many years and lawsuits behind us now, it was designed to sound like the 6800."

The first chip in the series was the 6501, which could drop into a 6800 slot. "It was definitely not a clone," says Peddle. "Architecturally it's a 6502. The only difference is it plugs into Motorola socket."

Peddle explains the 6501 strategy. "We were competing in a market where we were selling to people who might have bought the 6800," he says. "Having a plug-in compatible version was just a marketing game." Unfortunately, socket compatibility would later provoke Motorola.

The centerpiece of their project was the 6502 microprocessor. "The 6502 was what we were driving for," he says.

To create the architecture of the chip, the three engineers created a simple diagram to represent the structure of the chip. "We would start with a basic block diagram," says Peddle.

Some of the most important design work took place away from MOS Technology. "We put some of the more significant stuff in while drinking booze at Orgill's house one night," says Peddle. "The way to do really creative work is to work on it and then sometimes you've got to let it alone. If somebody gets a bright idea at a party, you take time out and you go argue about it. We actually came up with a really nice way of dealing with the buses that came out of a discussion at Orgill's."

Al Charpentier was one of the calculator chip designers at MOS Technology. He witnessed Peddle driving his team to build the new processor. "Chuck was an interesting character," he recalls. "He could be a bit pompous, but he had a vision and he was pushing that vision. Chuck was the visionary."

Peddle created a concept called *pipelining*, which handled data in a conveyor belt fashion. Instead of stopping while the microprocessor performed the arithmetic, the chip was ready to accept the next piece of data right away, while internally it continued processing data. This feature would make the chip faster than anything produced by Intel or Motorola at the time. A one-megahertz 6502 was equivalent to a four-megahertz Intel 8080.

The semiconductor team not only developed a microprocessor, they also developed the supporting chips. The first was the 6520 PIA chip, which was a clone of the Motorola 6820 PIA. One chip, called the 6530, contained 1 kilobyte of ROM, 256 bytes of RAM, a timer, and two IO ports. This allowed engineers to assemble a complete computer using only two chips. The team also developed 128-byte 6532 RAM chips.

One by one, the architects passed their designs to the layout people.

The layout team consisted of two main engineers: Bill Mensch and Rod Orgill. A third engineer, Harry Bawcum, aided the layout artists. It was their task to turn an abstract block diagram into a large-scale representation of the surface of the microprocessor. Orgill was responsible for the 6501 chip, Mensch the 6502.

Chuck Peddle originally hired Mensch at Motorola after Mensch graduated from the *University of Arizona*. "Mensch was literally right out of school," says Peddle. One of eight children, Mensch grew up in a small farming community in Pennsylvania. According to Mensch, "I lived on a dairy farm, got up at 4:30, milked the cows, and went off to school."[4]

At Motorola, Peddle was impressed with Mensch's natural talent. "He was just spectacular doing N-channel design and layout. He was the worlds best layout guy," raves Peddle.

Mensch was dependable, which made him a favorite with MOS engineers. "Bill was a good guy," says Charpentier. "He was very knowledgeable and knew what he was doing."

Rod Orgill, the youngest member of the team, worked at Motorola on the fabrication process of the 6800. Out of everyone on the team, Orgill had the most diverse set of abilities. Peddle relates, "Rod was a combination of chip designer and architect." For the first time in his life, Orgill would acquire layout abilities as an understudy to Mensch.

Peddle claims the 6501 was a marketing game, but Rod Orgill believed the 6501 would be more successful than the 6502. According to Mensch, "We made a bet and said who's going to have the highest volume and Rod says, 'There's no question: following Motorola's marketing, the

---

[4] The quote is from an interview with William Mensch by Rob Walker, *Silicon Genesis: An Oral History of Semiconductor Technology* (Atherton, California, October 9, 1995)

6501 will surpass your [6502] design and yours won't even have a chance.'"

The small group of young engineers worked in a small room on the second floor containing several large art tables. Here, Mensch and Orgill brooded over thick sheets of vellum paper. The layout consisted of thousands of polygons, each a specific size and shape. Thin lines called *traces* connected the polygons, creating a complex circuit. Incredibly, the engineers created the layout in pencil, one component at a time. The task was formidable, with a completed diagram containing approximately 4,300 transistors.[5]

Near the end of the design process, disaster struck. The engineers realized their architecture would not fit within the allotted area of the microchip. "When we sat down to optimize the system, we discovered we were 10 mills too wide," says Peddle. "The design was almost done. Mathis and I put a big piece of paper down on a table and sat there and optimized every line until we got rid of 10 mills."

The engineers were on a tight deadline to have the product ready for the upcoming *Wescon* show in September. They obsessively searched for ways to recycle lines in the schematic, thus reducing the area. Peddle grimly recalls, "Mathis and I had to keep redoing the architecture to make sure they stayed within that area."

To print the microchips, the engineers used a process called Metal Oxide Semiconductor, or simply MOS. This process used six layers of different materials, printed one on top of the other, to build the tiny components on the surface of a silicon wafer. This meant the layout artists had to create six different diagrams, one on top of the other.

The process required incredible precision because the layers had to line up exactly. The surface of the chip was necessarily dense in order to fit everything into a small area, so the artists squeezed transistors and pathways close to each other. If a single layer deviated by more than a few microns, it could touch another pathway and create a short circuit.

After the layout was completed, the engineers faced the soul-draining task of rechecking their design. The most sophisticated tool in this process was a small metal ruler, or more accurately, a scale. Herd recalls, "They would take their scales out of their pocket - don't call them a ruler – and they would measure for months! They would measure each transistor and make sure it was two millimeters by point seven."

Mensch, Orgill and Bawcum sat bleary-eyed over their drawings, sometimes for 12 hours a day, painstakingly measuring every point on the layout. They measured the size of components, the distance between

---

[5] In contrast, the Intel Pentium 4 released in 2000 has 42 million transistors.

components, the distance between traces, and the distance between traces and components. With a touch of sympathy in his voice, Herd explains, "You could be a really talented designer but if you couldn't check your design with the mind-numbing repetitiveness, your stuff didn't work and you would get a bad reputation."

Mensch and Orgill kept small cots in the room so they could work for long uninterrupted periods followed by a few hours rest. "With the semiconductor guys, that tends to be something you do when you are doing that at a certain level of design," recalls Peddle. "You tend to just keep going."

Even today, Peddle is still in awe of Mensch's ability as a layout engineer. "Bill has this unique ability to look at the requirements for a circuit, and he can see how it is going to layout in his head," he says. "He's just totally unique. Nobody matches Mensch."

In June 1975, the chip design was ready. It was up to the process engineers to imprint the design onto tiny silicon wafers. Months earlier, Pavinen promised Peddle he would have the N-channel process ready. Pavinen was true to his word. "He gave me everything I wanted," says Peddle.

The procedure to shrink a large, dense design onto something smaller than a thumbtack is both mysterious and under-appreciated. In many ways, it is also the most important step and, if intelligently planned, it can reduce the cost of a microchip dramatically. Engineers simply call this step the *process*.

When Pavinen and his two partners founded MOS Technology, it was their explicit goal to be the best process company in the business. "MOS Technology's business premise when they started was that they knew how to process better than other people," says Peddle. Engineers at the time documented very little of what they did, and most process engineers stored the process in their heads.

In order to print the transistors and other components to a silicon chip, the engineers had to create a *mask*. The mask blocks out everything except for the parts of the chip they want, much like a stencil blocks spray paint to produce letters. The mask relied on the principles of photography and light.

To transform the circuit diagram into a mask, the engineers used a material borrowed from the graphics industry called *Rubylith*. Rubylith is a sheet of acetate film with a red base covering the surface. Since the semiconductor industry was in an early stage of development, the tools to transfer the diagram were outrageously primitive. According to Bil Herd, "They were doing chips by cutting Rubylith with razor blades. They would kick their shoes off, push some tables together, and jump up on them." It was up to engineers Mike James and Harry Bawcum to perform the tedious task of cutting out pieces from the Rubylith to form the mask.

According to Bob Yannes, who arrived at MOS just after the Rubylith years, "I can't imagine using that stuff. You're looking at this huge red plastic thing in front of you and you're supposed to peel off the parts that are supposed to stay and leave the parts that are supposed to go away. Unless you were very careful, you got the two confused and you ended up peeling off the stuff that is supposed to go away. Then you start taping it back down again."

With engineers crawling all over the huge sheets of acetate film, it was vital sharp toenails were not exposed; otherwise they would drag over the surface and slice into the acetate. Engineers were not known for they attention to their appearance and it became vital to keep pairs of fresh socks available. "Everyone would wear fresh socks with no holes in the toes for getting on the table," explains Herd with some amusement.

Orgill and Bawcum created six Rubylith masks for the 6502 chip, one for each layer. Once completed, the engineers photographically reduced each of the large sheets of Rubylith to create a smaller negative. Engineers chemically etched a tiny metal mask using this negative. The technicians would eventually use this mask, almost like a rubber stamp, to create thousands of microprocessors.

Precise robotic machines used the tiny metal mask to duplicate the pattern over the entire surface of the silicon wafer. In the early seventies, the metal mask made contact with the surface of the silicon so the electrons could flow through the mask, imprinting the design to the surface. "People used to have what they call contact masks, which were pretty destructive on the mask," recalls Peddle. "They actually put the mask on the chip and it got worn out very quickly." Every time a mask wore out, the designers had to go through the laborious process of making a new mask.

At MOS Technology, John Pavinen pioneered a new way to fabricate microprocessors. "They were one of the first companies to use non-contact mask liners," says Peddle. "At that time everybody was using contact masks."

With non-contact masks, the metal die did not touch the wafer. Once the engineers worked out all the flaws in the mask, it would last indefinitely.

Pavinen and Holt handed off the completed mask to the MOS technicians, who began fabricating the first run of chips. Bil Herd summarizes the situation. "No chip worked the first time," he states emphatically. "No chip. It took seven or nine revs [revisions], or if someone was real good they would get it in five or six."

Normally, a large number of flaws originate from the layout design. After all, there are six layers (and six masks) that have to align with each other perfectly. Imagine designing a town with every conceivable layer of infrastructure placed one on top of another. Plumbing is the lowest layer, followed by the subway system, underground walkways, buildings, overhead walkways, and finally telephone wires. These different layers have to connect to each other perfectly; otherwise, the town will not function. The massive complexity of such a system makes it likely that human errors will creep into the design.

After fabricating a run of chips and probing them, the layout engineers usually have to make changes to their original design and the process repeats from the Rubylith down. "Each run is a couple of hundred thousand [dollars]," says Herd.

Implausibly, the engineers detected no errors in Mensch's layout. "He built seven different chips without ever having an error," says Peddle with disbelief in his voice. "Almost all done by hand. When I tell people that, they don't believe me, but it's true. This guy is a unique person. He is the best layout guy in world."

With the mask complete, mass fabrication of the microchips could begin. Fabrication occurred in an alien-like environment on the second floor of the MOS Technology building called the clean rooms. These hermetically sealed rooms produced a nearly dust free environment. The precautions were extreme, since a single grain of dust during the etching process could cause a miniature short circuit.

To enter the clean rooms, lab technicians were required to don hairnets, beard nets, moustache guards, gloves, paper booties, and white jumpsuits. "It makes you look like a bunny," says Peddle. "We used a lot of them." As a final measure, the technicians walked over a sticky-mat to remove the last traces of dust before stepping into the airlock.

Within a crimson-tinted darkroom, technicians replicated print after print of the 6502 circuit. They coated the round silicon wafers with thin layers of metallic substances. After each layer, technicians placed the wafer into a special machine that copied the circuit from the metal mask to the surface of the silicon wafer. Electrons flowed through the mask, causing a thin layer to harden in the shape of the circuit. Each wafer had the chip pattern imprinted approximately fifty times.

In another room, bathed in yellow light, technicians developed the microchips. This process was almost exactly like developing a photograph. A studious technician carefully washed each wafer with chemical solutions that removed all but the hardened circuitry. The industrial strength solvents went by names like trichloroethene, trichloroethane, dichloroethene, dichloroethane, and vinyl chloride.

The technicians repeated the process six times for the six layers, each time using a different set of chemicals and metallic substances. According to Peddle, "You put this mask on the device and do whatever step you are going to do, and then you take it off, put another mask on, and do another step."

The top layer was aluminum, which was the best conductor. Beneath the aluminum were various semiconductors such as Germanium. Each layer went by a different name, such as diffusion layer, buried contact, depletion layer, polysilicon, poly-metal contact, and metal. With all six layers applied, the wafers entered an oven to bond the circuitry.

Technicians then added a passivation layer[6] to protect the fragile metallic circuitry from oxidation. After applying the passivation layer, a machine sliced the wafers into individual chips, each smaller than a fingernail.

The chemical etching process used dangerous industrial solvents. Inevitably, the solvents evaporated into the air, which worried some of the staff. Robert Russell, an early Commodore employee, chuckles about the general indifference regarding this threat. "MOS had a little cafeteria at the back alongside the production line," he explains. "They had a chemical release in the production line that turned all your blueprints that were hanging on the walls different colors. You would come in and they would all be yellow or green. You kind of hoped that wasn't happening when you were breathing it."

"The production of semiconductors produces all kinds of nasty byproducts," says engineer Bob Yannes. Inevitably, accidents occurred. "I remember things happening like occasionally we'd have a gas leak in the front end and you'd have people walking through the building saying, 'Hurry! Get out of the building!'"

Most people were ignorant of the dangers posed by the semiconductor industry. "This is a time in history when everybody looked at the clean rooms and the guys all wearing their bunny suits, and how sterile it was, and everybody wanted a semiconductor company in their hometown," says Peddle. "It was high tech, big money, and clean as opposed to a foundry or something like that. What they didn't realize was these guys

---

[6] This final layer, called the passivation layer, was difficult for Pavinen to perfect. For mysterious reasons, small pinholes appeared in the passivation layer. After a year or so, the areas on the chip around these tiny holes would begin to oxidize and the chip ceased functioning.

were dealing with the most poisonous, noxious shit in the world, and they had to put it somewhere."

The semiconductor industry was still new in 1970 when John Pavinen and his partners created MOS Technology. "Nobody in the semiconductor industry had a clue about how to deal with the stuff they were making for years," says Peddle. "John did the best he could and he actually did pretty well."

The industrial solvents drained from the chip fabrication line into a 250-gallon concrete holding tank. "They built these double tanks and they stored it underground. But you know, we just didn't have the technology," says Peddle. "Let me just make a point; John Pavinen was a very meticulous guy, and he absolutely designed his tanks the best he could given the environment at the time."

In early 1974, a serious disaster occurred. Technicians monitoring the tank realized the tank was emptier than it should have been. During the cold Pennsylvania winters, the concrete tank developed a small crack. "Some of their storage tanks leaked and it leached into the ground," recalls Yannes.

Pavinen kept the spill quiet, even from Peddle. "We didn't join him until the summer of 1974, and they wouldn't have told us about it anyhow," says Peddle. "With all due respect, they keep that stuff a lot quieter in Silicon Valley. There's been a whole bunch of stories about breast cancer being much higher in Silicon Valley, and there's a bunch of other anomalies."

As the Environmental Protection Agency later determined, the leak was the source of groundwater contamination in the area.[7] The Valley Forge Corporate Center bordered a residential development that relied on well water, so there was cause for concern. Fortunately, water tests at the time indicated the solvent had not yet entered the water table. Pavinen replaced the faulty tank with an unlined steel tank.

After the chemical solvents etched the chips, the technicians inserted the flecks of silicon and metal into an easy to handle package.

---

[7] According to EPA reports, in December 1986, the EPA performed a site inspection in which they collected soil samples, surface water, and water from nearby residential wells. Tests revealed low levels of trichloroethene and other volatile organic compounds in the soil and shallow bedrock underneath 950 Rittenhouse. Furthermore, the EPA found traces of volatile organic compounds in the well water supply, but they did not approach dangerous levels. MOS Technology began a soil-cleaning program to extract the dangerous solvents, and in 1996, the residents received public water lines from an outside water source.

Today, semiconductor companies typically place their chips in black plastic shells with silver pins. Back in 1975, MOS Technology placed their microprocessors in distinctive white ceramic shells with forty gold plated pins.

As if a price drop from $300 to $25 was not radical enough, Peddle and his team planned to release an ultra-low cost microprocessor called the 6507. "Our goal was to do a $5 processor," Peddle states flatly. "The 6507, which was a subset of [the 6502], could be made at a cheaper price. It was designed to be a really small package."

The packaging determined how cheaply Peddle could sell his chips. "Packaging costs money and pin outs cost money," explains Peddle. "Back in those days, those big 40-pin packages were very expensive." The 6507 contained only 28 pins.

In a perfect world, every single chip would work. If they fabricated 10,000 chips, they would ideally have 10,000 working chips. However, imperfections snuck in from every imaginable source. Inconsistencies in the etching process caused flaws. Small particles of dust getting in the way of the mask caused flaws. Even impurities in the silicon wafer produced flaws. The number of flaws the engineers could defeat determined the *chip yield*.

Technicians methodically tested every single chip to determine if it worked. In 1975, most chipmakers considered a 30% yield to be quite successful. The industry simply discarded the remaining 70%. The process was inherently inefficient and resulted in monumental chip prices. If Pavinen wanted to achieve low cost microprocessors, he would have to use every trick available to raise the yield.

In the seventies, most semiconductor houses tested their chips with a *Fairchild Century* system. The huge machine occupied almost an entire room and cost almost a million dollars. As Bill Mensch explains, "We couldn't afford them at MOS Technology." Instead, Mensch constructed a small handheld chip tester that resembled a computer motherboard covered in IC chips. Every single chip from MOS Technology was hand tested by the homebrew device for the first year and a half of 6502 production.

Through careful planning and innovation, MOS Technology achieved a chip yield of 70% or better. Peddle attributes this success to Pavinen and his non-contact mask process. "Because they could afford to spend a lot more money making a perfect mask, they got much better yields," he says. The low production costs meant Peddle's vision would come true.

Selling the Revolution

The team now had hundreds of working microprocessor chips, but their battle was just beginning. "We brought it out on schedule, on cost, and on target," says Peddle. With almost no budget for advertising, it would be up to Peddle and his team to create as much fanfare as possible.

"We wanted to launch the product in a spectacular way because we were a crummy ass little company in Pennsylvania," explains Peddle. At first, he attempted to garner free publicity from newspapers. "Some people liked the story and put us on the cover of their newspaper, which hyped us up," he recalls.

Prior to launching the 6502, MOS Technology hired Petr Sehnal, a friend of Chuck's from his days at GE. "Petr was a Czechoslovakian intellectual who came over to this country," recalls Peddle. "He was kind of acting as a program manager and getting everything ready for the show, and he was the West Coast sales manager."

To reach their target audience, Sehnal wanted to take the 6502 to the masses. The annual *Western Electronic Show and Convention* (Wescon) was showing in San Francisco in September. Sehnal knew the show would be the best place to launch Peddle's revolutionary new product.

The microprocessor would be useless to engineers without documentation. Peddle recalls, "We were coming down to launching, and my buddy [Petr Sehnal] kept telling me, 'Chuck, you've got to go write these manuals.' I kept saying, 'Yeah, I'll get around to it.'" Peddle did not get around to it.

With Wescon rapidly approaching, and no manual in sight, Sehnal approached John Pavinen and told him, "He's not doing it."

"John Pavinen walked into my office with a security guard, and he walked me out of the building," recalls Peddle.

According to Peddle, Pavinen gave him explicit instructions. "The only person you're allowed to talk to in our company is your secretary, who you can dictate stuff to," Pavinen told him. "You can't come back to work until you finish the two manuals."

Peddle accepted the situation with humility. "I wrote them under duress," he says. Weeks later, Peddle emerged from his exile with his task completed. The 6502 would have manuals for Wescon.

The team planned to sell samples of the 6501 and 6502 microprocessors at Wescon, along with the supporting chipset. "We then took out a full-page ad that said, 'Come by our booth at Wescon and we'll sell you a microprocessor for twenty-five dollars.' We ran that ad in a bunch of places," recalls Peddle. The most prominent advertisement appeared in the September 8, 1975 issue of *Electronic Engineering Times*.

Things were going well until his team arrived for the show. Peddle recalls, "We went to the show and they told us, 'No fucking way you're going to sell anything on the floor. It's not part of our program. If we had seen these ads we would have killed you.'"

Having come so far and worked so hard, Peddle and his team were not ready to give up. "They told us this just enough in advance that we took a big suite, the *McArthur Suite*, at the St. Francis Hotel," says Peddle. MOS Technology would sell their contraband microchips from booth 1010 by redirecting buyers to a pickup location, much like drug dealers.

"People would come by the booth and we'd say, 'No you can't do it here. Go to the McArthur Suite and we can sell you the processors," recalls Peddle. "We became so popular people would get on the bus at the convention center and ask, 'Is this the bus to the McArthur suite?'"

The promise of low-cost microprocessors caused a sensation. Many people thought the $25 chip was a fraud or assumed it performed poorly. Peddle was confident these questions would resolve themselves once people started using his chips.

Eager hobbyists and engineers lined up in the hall outside the McArthur Suite. Chuck's wife Shirley greeted the engineers, collected their money, and handed out chips. "My very pretty wife was sitting there, and we had this big jar full of microprocessors," recalls Peddle. "You walked up, we would take your microprocessor off the top, and she would put it in a little box for you."

The large jars full of microchips seemed to indicate MOS Technology was capable of fabricating large volumes of the 6502 chip. This was subterfuge. "Only half of the jar worked," reveals Peddle. "The chips at the top of the jar were tested and we knew the ones on the bottom didn't work, but that didn't matter. We had to help make the jar look full."

Shirley Peddle also sold manuals and support chips. Peddle explains, "You could buy this little RAM/ROM I/O device for another $30 and we would sell you the two books we wrote, which turned out to be very popular."

The manuals gently introduced readers to the concepts of microprocessor systems, explaining how to design a microprocessor system using the 6500 family of chips. It was a bible for microcomputer design. "Everyone told us how good they were to use," he recalls. "We were very proud of that."

After completing their purchases, customers entered the suite. Here, Peddle demonstrated the 6501 and 6502 chips, along with tiny development systems such as the TIM and KIM-1 microcomputers.

"They would go around the suite and they would see the development systems, and they would find out how to log onto the timesharing systems so they could develop code," he says. "Then they would wander away."

The purpose of selling the chips at Wescon was not to raise money. It was to cultivate developer interest in the chip. If all went well, the engineers and hobbyists would go out into the world and design products with the 6502. Waiting in line outside Chuck's hotel room was Steve Wozniak, who thought he might be able to use the chip for a homebrew computer project. Peddle's documentation undoubtedly influenced Wozniak.

In the months that followed, engineers and hobbyists began reporting success with the MOS microprocessors. Thanks to a review in the November issue of Byte magazine, the chips soon gained a larger following. Dan Fylstra, founder of the company that would someday sell the legendary VisiCalc spreadsheet, wrote an article titled, 'Son of Motorola'. People soon became convinced that the 6502 chip was a legitimate microprocessor.

The 6502 did not immediately improve MOS Technology's finances, but it had a major impact on the computer industry. "It spawned a whole class of users, called hackers back then," says Charpentier.

"It changed the world," says Peddle. In September 1995, as part of their 20th anniversary edition, Byte magazine named the 6502[8] one of the top twenty most important computer chips ever, just behind the Intel 4004 and 8080.

---

[8] Even pop-culture recognizes the 6502 chip. The animated television show *Futurama* revealed that one of its characters, a robot named Bender, has a 6502 microprocessor for a brain. *Futurama*, "Fry & the Slurm Factory" (Season 2, Episode 4).

CHAPTER

2

The Acquisition

1975 - 1976

The calculator wars of the mid seventies damaged MOS Technology. Many of their most important customers had fallen and only Commodore remained. John Pavinen needed to do something to save MOS Technology. He gambled on Chuck Peddle's 6502 proposal. Now he would find out if the 6502 was enough to save his company.

First Customers

After Wescon, Chuck Peddle and Will Mathis began traveling across North America. "We started getting all kinds of phone calls from people wanting to know what was going on," recalls Peddle. Many of them were calling because they were unable to attend Wescon.

Chuck Peddle and Will Mathis agreed to handle the most promising twenty percent, while marketing sent literature to the other eighty percent. "I was just flipping through them and I spotted this Grass Valley, California address," explains Peddle. The address was for *Cyan Engineering*, owned by *Atari Incorporated*. "I picked up the phone and the guy that answers is Steve Mayer. He was on the research team doing the Atari programmable game system."

Peddle agreed to meet with Steve Mayer following the Wescon show in San Francisco. Peddle recalls, "We did the Wescon show, got in a car, and drove up to Grass Valley."

The engineers gathered and began thinking of ways to design the game console using the cost reduced 6507 chip. "In two days, we put together the architecture using my microprocessor and my cheap I/O device, and [the Jolt Computer] developed by [Microcomputer Associates], all under Mayer's direction," recalls Peddle.

During two days of intense work, the engineers discussed price. "We literally put together the plan and agreement," recalls Peddle. "They came back and said, 'This is the price I need for the chipset.'"

Atari wanted to pay an incredibly low twelve dollars – not just for the 6507 microprocessor but also for the supporting chipset. Peddle and Pavinen mulled over the proposition. Atari already had some early success with a standalone Pong arcade machine and they were about to release their home version of Pong to the mass market. According to Peddle, he and Pavinen concluded that, "If we can make some money at it, let's do it, because these guys have a chance for some volume."

Two days after the chip was unveiled at Wescon, Mayer had a deal. "He was truly an early adopter," says Peddle. "We sold a microprocessor, RAM, ROM, and I/O chip all for twelve bucks, at a time when nobody could do a product for under 150 dollars."[1]

Peddle learned Atari was not developing one game console, but three. One used the MOS Technology 6507, one used a Motorola microprocessor, and one used an Intel microprocessor. Neither team was aware of the others. "They thought they were the real design teams, up until the time they had the architecture done for the chips," recalls Peddle. "So Motorola told their management they had Atari locked up." It was a premature conclusion.

Atari required a semiconductor company to fabricate their custom chips for the game console. Chuck Peddle and John Pavinen suggested Synertek. "The guy who was the president at Synertek was the project engineer in a computer lab in GE several years before, by the name of Bob Schreiner," recalls Peddle.

In a move that seems strange today, Peddle and Pavinen wanted other companies to produce the 6502 microprocessor. They did not want MOS Technology to be the only semiconductor company producing the 6502. "If you want to be a big player in the microprocessor business you have to have a second source for your chips," explains Peddle.

Peddle was more than happy to sell manufacturing rights to Synertek. "Schreiner didn't have a microprocessor, wanted one, and wanted the Atari business," explains Peddle. "Atari gave him the contract for doing the custom layout for the game chip."

When asked why MOS Technology did not hold on to a 6502 monopoly, Peddle quickly replies, "People won't give you a monopoly.

---

[1] Atari initially sold their game console for a suggested retail price of $199.95.

They want a second source. Atari would never have signed with us if we didn't have a second source."

From Atari's point of view, a small company like MOS Technology could easily fail, which could interrupt the supply of microprocessors. A second supplier gave Atari confidence their supply would remain uninterrupted. "Schreiner was actually with us when we were doing the development," reveals Peddle. "It turned out to be good for both of us."

For months, the engineering teams worked on their respective Atari consoles. A former Synertek engineer named Jay Miner (who would later work for Commodore) developed the custom chips responsible for graphics and sound. "That Atari team was full of red hot people," reflects Peddle.

In October, Atari informed the other Atari engineering teams that they had decided to use the MOS Technology chipset. Motorola was furious. "They sued us a week after Atari announced they were using our product," recalls Peddle.

On November 3, 1975, Motorola filed a lawsuit against MOS Technology alleging patent infringement. "They claimed we had stole all their intellectual property. We didn't steal anything," contends Peddle. "It didn't look like the 6800, it didn't smell like the 6800, we didn't want it to be like the 6800."

Motorola knew they could have had the 6502 themselves when Peddle offered it to them a year earlier. Now, in the face of losing a valuable contract with Atari, the magnitude of their error became apparent. "They sued us because their pride was hurt," claims Peddle.

In the meantime, Peddle continued traveling the country, putting his microprocessor into everything from printers to entertainment devices. "If I wanted to sell my microprocessor to a printer company, I had to go help design the product for them," says Peddle. "I would pack my development system up and we would go somewhere. In a week, I would design a microprocessor system. That's how I built my sales up."

Peddle also met with *Allied Leisure*, which at the time was larger than Atari. "I was flying around the country doing designs," recalls Peddle. "I went to Florida because this guy from Allied Leisure said he had a fun application. He had knocked-off Pong when it was in the arcades and bars, and he had been very successful. He actually out-Ponged Atari as far as the games go."

However, Allied-Leisure did not want Peddle to help design a Pong game or an arcade game. "They were into electro-mechanical games in a big way," he says. "We got into a discussion and I volunteered to build them a pinball game."

Peddle saw pinball as a good opportunity to demonstrate the capability of the 6502 to control multiple mechanical devices. "I wanted to do the game because it was a fun thing and it used lots and lots of I/O devices," he recalls. "We could do some fun stuff and we could keep up with the speeds. I wanted to prove to everybody that you could make the microprocessor to do all that stuff well."

"In the course of designing my game, I used to work all night and sleep on a mat at their place," says Peddle. He completed the design and showed it at the National Computer Conference. It was the first pinball game to use a microprocessor.

While in Florida, Peddle also spent time designing a photocopy machine for a company called *Saxon*. "I worked on both while I was there," says Peddle. "I sold one of the copier companies on the idea of doing a copier using my microprocessor."

More than any other engineer at MOS Technology, Chuck Peddle contributed the most to achieving market acceptance of the 6502. As Peddle recalls, "Every electronic engineer in the world said, 'I'm going to stop designing with discrete logic and I'm going to start designing with the microprocessor.'"

"We changed the world," says Peddle.

Peddle helped anyone with an interest in developing for the 6502, including two kids working out of their parents garage. "While we were out visiting Atari, my West Coast [sales] manager [Petr Sehnal] said, 'Hey, there's some kids working on a machine in his garage and it's not working. We have a development system with us, so why don't we go over and help them?'"

Steve Wozniak, the young man who visited Chuck Peddle in his hotel suite, was a smart, inquisitive, impish young man with a penchant for electronics. Wozniak worked for Hewlett-Packard at the time and he began designing a computer while at work.

Other engineers undoubtedly influenced Wozniak when he created his first computer. Rod Holt claims Wozniak purchased a 6502 based JOLT computer from him, which Wozniak undoubtedly studied. He also learned from the MOS Technology manuals, included with the 6502. "My books had a lot of influence on him," says Peddle.

Both Peddle and Sehnal visited the young entrepreneurs. For Steve Wozniak, it must have been a thrill to meet the designer of his favorite microprocessor. "These guys were in the Bay area and their product didn't work, so we took my development system over and spent an afternoon with them in the garage helping them bring up their system," recalls Peddle.

Peddle used a system called ICE (In Circuit Emulator) to program the ROM code in real time. "It was a great big bulky thing with a big old heat sink on the back," says Peddle. "You plug it into the board you were working on and you could program it right there."

Peddle finished his work and the two kids promised to keep in touch. Surprisingly, Peddle and Steve Jobs formed a lasting friendship, despite Jobs' lack of engineering background. "Steve [Jobs] is a hustler. He was a hustler back then and he's a hustler now," comments Peddle.

In February 1976, Wozniak brought his 6502 based computer, the Apple I, to the Homebrew Computer Club. The reception was lukewarm. Without a printed circuit board, the computer looked even less user friendly than MOS Technology's KIM-1 computer.

Wozniak attempted to interest Hewlett-Packard in his design, but they were not interested. In April 1976, Wozniak obtained official release of the technology from Hewlett-Packard. In July 1976, after refining the Apple I to include a keyboard connector and display adapter, Wozniak and Jobs made their sales pitch for the Apple I at the Homebrew Computer Club for $666.66. The price included just the circuit board alone, and did not include a case, a keyboard, or even a power supply. In all, Apple sold about 200 Apple I computers; far less than the KIM-1.

The Acquisition

In early 1976, Allen-Bradley, the financial backers of MOS Technology, began to reconsider their investment. "Somewhere about the time we launched the 6502, we spent a lot of money fighting Motorola," recalls Peddle. "Allen-Bradley decided to part ways partially because of the Motorola lawsuit and partially because they were in a very unhappy working relationship with some of management at MOS Technology, who were difficult to work with from time to time."

Furthermore, the decline of the calculator business made Allen-Bradley nervous. "[Texas Instruments] was in the process of just fucking the calculator business big time," recalls Peddle. "A lot of the customers for MOS Technology were dying. Allen-Bradley looked at it and said, 'One of the reasons we got into this business is we thought there would be some synergy. There's no synergy.'"

Inconceivably, rather than liquidate MOS Technology, Allen-Bradley gave the company to the three founders for almost nothing. "They decided to just not be involved anymore," says Peddle. "Allen-Bradley basically handed the company back to the founders six months before the acquisition."

Why would a large corporation like Allen-Bradley give away a company that just launched a hot microprocessor? "Nobody at Allen-Bradley thought about microprocessors being hot," explains Peddle. "It was just not even in their mind. Microprocessors became strong because we made them strong over that time. But six months before, right after we launched it, it wasn't a big deal in terms of the volume."

With Allen-Bradley out of the picture, the three founders now owned a company largely built with other people's money. John Pavinen, Mort Jaffe, and Don McLaughlin must have felt giddy. "The founders knew they had a winner on their hands with the microprocessor," says Peddle. "They figured if they could get the thing back for free, they would do that. I suspect they paid a little bit for it, but effectively free."

Without Allen-Bradley, the financial backing suddenly stopped. "Now they had the company in their hands, but they didn't have the financing," explains Peddle. "The semiconductor business tends to eat money even though it generates a lot of money. All the things, like the KIM-1 and all that stuff were coming along. And the Motorola suit had hurt."

The three owners attempted to solve the problem of financing. "I knew during that time they were thinking about raising money by some kind of public offering," recalls Peddle. Unfortunately, their efforts to put together a public offering failed. As a result, "they were ripe for some kind of a deal," says Peddle.

Commodore began purchasing calculator chips from MOS Technology in 1972. By 1976, they were MOS Technology's largest customer by virtue of having survived the calculator wars. Peddle recalls, "Jack effectively saved their bacon that year, because they weren't doing that well, and Jack basically just bought processing time for his own designs." This made MOS Technology dependant on Commodore for revenue. As the three owners would later learn, being dependant on Commodore also made them susceptible to Jack's will.

According to Chuck Peddle, Andre Souson was responsible for instigating the MOS Technology acquisition. "Souson spotted two things," explains Peddle. "One, they were the right partner for them to make the calculator stuff. Two, Andre felt I was on the right track with the microprocessor."

Jack was an easy sell, since the acquisition of MOS Technology would help achieve his master plan. "His primary drive was he needed vertical integration," says Peddle. "So in effect, what started out as 'Gee, we'd like to buy a bunch of chips and then maybe you can process some chips for us,' went to, 'How would you like to just let us buy you?'"

Bob Yannes, a MOS Technology engineer, speculates how Jack took control of the company. "He ordered a bunch of calculator chips from

MOS and apparently there was a bug in it," says Yannes. It was not a major bug. "I think they did one calculation wrong. You took the cosine of some bizarre number and it came out 0.000001 off."

Yannes continues, "Then MOS got sued by Motorola for possible design infringement with the 6502 over the 6800. So they were embroiled in that, spending money on lawsuits. Then, as I understand it, Jack came in and said, 'Okay, well I'm not going to pay for those chips. If you want, I'll buy your company from you for almost nothing.'"

The questionable methods Jack used to obtain MOS Technology have become legend, making it difficult to separate fact from fiction. But is the legend true? "Having met Jack and dealt with him on a low level, I would not at all put it past him," says Yannes.

Peddle gives a similar explanation. "Jack is the kind of guy that will look for any lever," he says. "It is undoubtedly true he was squeezing them on payables. Whether they found a bug or didn't find a bug, whatever. As a standard practice, Jack would rack up a bill and then squeeze people."

If Jack was doing business with your company, he needed your parts and supplies. However, he also wanted vertical integration, so he wanted not only your parts but also your whole company. Normally, if Commodore became beholden with debt to a supplier, the pressure was on Commodore to repay it. However, Jack did not play by normal business rules.

"If Jack owed you a lot of money, you were in trouble," says Peddle. Jack realized the best way to acquire MOS Technology under his terms was to hold back payments, making MOS Technology starved for cash. With money running out, MOS Technology would be unable to pay their employees, making them amenable to almost any deal. "He would sometimes use it for leverage," recalls Peddle. "He's a very clever, very ruthless businessman."

In September 1976, Commodore fully acquired MOS Technology. "He basically bailed them out by buying the company out from under them," says Yannes.

"Jack bought the company for stock and some cash," recalls Peddle. "The founders actually got reasonable amounts of Commodore stock, which were very depressed at the time."

Did the MOS Technology owners receive a bad deal from Jack Tramiel? "Beauty is in the eye of the beholder," says Peddle. "Considering the financial state they were in, and their inability to pursue what they needed to do without a significant amount of outside financing, they got a good price."

The stock was not worth much at the time. "It wouldn't have been much because it didn't need to be much," says Peddle, estimating that it would have been worth a few hundred thousand dollars in 1976. "They got an intangible for their intangible. They had a processing capability, they had a factory, they had everything else, and Jack had a company that was public. In effect, he offered them a way to exit from their investment in a public way."

Over time, the few hundred thousand dollars turned into millions. "I think one of the reasons they all held it was because they did not get registered stock," ventures Peddle. "They were forced to hold it for two years, which turned out to be highly, highly advantageous to them."

The engineers at MOS Technology did not fare as well as the owners. Some of the ex-Motorola employees received the promise of stock when they first joined MOS Technology. "They cashed out all of us that might have had some ownership in the company," explains Peddle. "We just got cash. I was not a real owner of the company, except for a deal that we were going to get paid off."

According to Peddle, the deal with Commodore occurred without their knowledge, which caused some friction between the engineers and the owners. "This was done effectively without all of us who were working in the business having a clue," he says.

Under the deal, MOS Technology would retain their current headquarters. Commodore continued leasing the building at 950 Rittenhouse Drive from Allen-Bradley until 1978, at which time Commodore purchased the entire building.

Soon after the acquisition, MOS Technology fell under a subdivision of Commodore called *Commodore Semiconductor Group*, along with Frontier Semiconductor. "They were the same thing. Commodore acquired other companies and put them all under that umbrella," explains Al Charpentier.

When Jack bought MOS Technology, he could not have imagined the riches it would bring to him and his company. The acquisition had been undertaken solely to achieve vertical integration of calculator products, but it was about to transform Commodore into a true computer company.

The Commodore Curse: Part I

The previous years with Chuck Peddle had been exhilarating for the entire 6502 team. They made headlines when they departed Motorola for MOS Technology and they even had their group picture featured on the front page of *Electronics News*, which they put on the wall in the MOS Technology lab. The 6502 had revolutionized the microprocessor industry. Anything that came after was bound to be anticlimactic.

Chuck Peddle recalls the high of working with the 6502 team. "It was the best project team I have ever worked with and it was the best product I've ever worked on," he says. "All the other guys who worked on it feel the same way."

Unfortunately, the success created a dilemma. "The problem was, it was a very successful project, with all kinds of hype," explains Peddle. "Then – and I went through this with my second wife - there's a time when that's over and all you've got to do with life is business."

After the product launch came the tedious legal issues with Motorola. "We went from there into what most of the guys saw as the lawsuit and all the shit we had to go through for that," recalls Peddle. Suddenly engineers were spending time giving affidavits to lawyers and gathering information, usually accompanied by excruciating explanations to educate the lawyers and the courts on microprocessors. "It was a big fucking lawsuit and ended up costing us a million dollars."

Peddle also blames some of the management for not valuing their engineers enough. "Pavinen is a wonderful guy but he's not a people guy at all," he explains. "He had his favorites and everyone else he treated badly."

"There were serious problems within management too," recalls Peddle. "McLaughlin and Pavinen didn't like one another very much."

Peddle believes the three owners made the engineers feel they were not integral in the direction MOS Technology was taking, especially with the Commodore acquisition. "The top three guys got very self-focused as a threesome," Peddle explains. "They were so focused on getting the company back [from Allen-Bradley]."

While Peddle busily promoted the 6502, his engineers were without a goal. "I went from driving the program to marketing and things like that," explains Peddle. "Some of us were busy and very much focused, but the rest of the team had assignments that weren't as exciting."

In all the hype, Peddle had little time to get his team started on a follow-up project, such as a 16-bit version of the 6502. "I wasn't driving them," says Peddle. "We didn't have a concrete 'This is what we are going to do next, let's go get them,' plan because we were so busy trying to get the first thing circled."

"When Commodore took over, that was kind of like the end of the road because Commodore was really buying it for the calculator business," explains Peddle.

It was anticlimactic to go from microprocessors back to calculator technology. "The calculator guys had real assignments, but these guys didn't want to fool around with calculators," says Peddle. "They had done that earlier in their lives, so it was just easy for them to melt away."

The first engineer to melt away was arguably the most valuable: Bill Mensch. "Fundamentally Bill was a very young guy at Motorola, right out of school, but he was a real talent," recalls Peddle. "At MOS Technology he definitely took bigger and bigger pieces, and he had matured, if you will. He picked up a lot of the things he wanted to do with his life and he had proven to himself he could do almost anything."

Unsatisfied at MOS Technology, Mensch resigned and returned to Phoenix. Shortly after his departure, someone used a felt-tipped marker to black out Mensch's picture from the group photo on the wall.

Others soon followed. "Most of them just said they missed the West Coast," says Peddle. "The whole thing was coming apart. Effectively the microprocessor team vanished all at one time. Mathis went to DEC. Orgill went to HP in Colorado. [Harry] Bawcum went somewhere. All of the people just went away."

One by one, the remaining employees blacked out the faces from the photograph on the wall. "All of them left in a period of about three months," says Peddle. Soon, the picture began to look eerily black. The very people who would be capable of taking Commodore microprocessors into the 16-bit era were disappearing.

No one in Commodore management really understood how vital the engineers could be to the continued success of the company. Unfortunately, Commodore would repeat this pattern many more times. Commodore engineer Dave Haynie later dubbed this pattern the *Commodore Curse*.

Peddle looks back at the 6502 project as one of the best experiences of his life. "It was a unique time in history," recalls Peddle. "You only get to do one of those in your lifetime, I think," he muses.

With most of his coworkers gone, it was up to Peddle to help resolve the lawsuit with Motorola. Today, the courts would dismiss the lawsuit immediately, but high-tech matters were unknown to the legal system at the time. MOS Technology did not have money to spend on a lawsuit, so they settled with Motorola.

Chuck Peddle explains the settlement. "They never were able to prove any trade secrets [were stolen] but they found our N-channel device violated one of their patents," he says. "In order to get the license to the patent, we had to settle the suit." MOS Technology agreed to drop the 6501 processor from their product line.

Peddle was reluctant to go along with the settlement. "We settled in such a way that implied we had done more than we had," he says. "It was a good business decision but it just pissed me off."

In the end, Bill Mensch won his bet with Rod Orgill when Motorola squashed the 6501. According to Chuck Peddle, the cancellation meant nothing to MOS Technology. "I didn't mind throwing it away," he says. "If they had called up and said we want you to kill the 6501, we would have killed it. They didn't need to sue us."

CHAPTER

3

The PET

1976 - 1977

The idea for a personal computer came to Chuck Peddle while he was in Florida at Allied-Leisure, working on his pinball game. While there, a scruffy young engineer from Iowa befriended Peddle. "There was this kid – ponytail, shorts and everything," recalls Peddle. "He kind of got involved and hung around while I was doing this development."

The young engineer's name was Bill Seiler. At the time, Seiler also designed devices for Allied-Leisure. "He was designing analog circuits that made gaming noises," says Peddle. "Cars would sound like cars, airplanes would sound like airplanes and that sort of thing."

Seiler purchased a computer kit from a Dr. Sooting in Colorado. "[Seiler] was the first guy I actually saw bring up a personal computer," recalls Peddle. "He was all proud of it."

Seiler programmed his computer to play the Star Spangled Banner but soon ran out ideas. "Basically, he didn't have a clue what he was going to do next," says Peddle.

Weeks later, Peddle traveled to the West Coast to unveil the 6502 at Wescon. While there, he visited the Homebrew Computer Club. "In the computer club, you could get a copy of Basic stolen from Bill Gates for this machine," he recalls. "The Basic was pretty ugly."

Upon returning to Florida, Peddle gave Seiler a copy of Basic. Seiler thought nothing of the pirated copy because in 1975 there was a weak concept of software ownership. "Bill Gates wrote some kind of open letter to some magazine and Bill [Seiler] read it," explains Peddle. "Gates was saying, 'You guy's are taking my livelihood. I developed this thing and you're stealing it. I'm not making any money and we're going to go out of business.' Bill Seiler felt so bad he sent Gates the money for the copy he stole."[1]

A picture started forming in Peddles mind. "Seiler triggered in me that people who were building this stuff didn't have a clue what they were going to do with it, and when they were all done they didn't have anything that really worked," explains Peddle. "The programmers said, 'I don't want to build my own kit.' Lots and lots of people said, 'I don't know how to build my own kit. I can't get anyone to build one for me, and when they work they don't work very well.'" It was as if Henry Ford introduced the world to the automobile by selling a box of parts.

"I realized that we were selling KIM-1's because a lot of people didn't want to build their own kit," explains Peddle. "But the KIM-1 didn't do enough. It just wasn't a strong enough product for anything and wasn't intended to be. It was supposed to be a way to play around with my processor."

Peddle believed he might be able to construct a personal computer at MOS Technology due to his earlier agreement. "I had a commitment from the company that as soon as I got to a certain point I would get to go do my computer," he recalls. "It was obvious they were not going to keep their word on that. They called me in one day and said, 'We don't have the money.'"

Allied-Leisure expressed interest. "I talked to the guy who was the president of the company, showed him Bill's computer and said, 'I'm convinced that we need to build a complete product and I know how to build it.' This guy said, 'If you want to do that, come down here.' So I basically finished up what I was doing [at MOS Technology]."

Peddle was now committed to Allied-Leisure and began restructuring his life around Florida. "My youngest daughter moved from Phoenix back east with me with the promise that we would move to Florida," recalls Peddle.

"I was getting ready to bail and go to Allied-Leisure to make my own computer when Commodore bought the company," says Peddle. To Peddle's surprise, his old acquaintance Andre Souson now worked at Commodore as head of engineering. "We had known each other from that period, although we were not bosom buddies or anything."

Peddle recalls the soft-spoken Souson. "He was a really gentle, intelligent Frenchman," he says. "He had long wavy hair and a moustache. He was an older guy with a stunningly beautiful wife and they lived in Palo Alto."

---

[1] Peddle had a chance to ask Bill Gates if he remembered receiving the check. Gates replied, "Yeah, and we really noticed it because almost nobody did."

"Andre called me up and asked some questions," explains Peddle. "I said, 'I have to tell you Andre, I'm not sure I'm going to be around here very long.' He said, 'Look, don't make any decisions. Get on an airplane, bring your wife out, come out to the West Coast, and let's talk about it.'"

"So we flew out and I told Andre my idea for the computer. Andre said, 'I'm convinced we can go do this product. Oh, by the way, we have our hands on a spec from Radio Shack for a similar product.'"

Radio Shack wanted a computer system for hobbyists and they sent a specification to some of their suppliers. They hoped one of them could design and manufacture a computer for them. According to Peddle, "The Radio Shack sales manager came down and said, 'Sign us up for a whole bunch of calculators for the Christmas season. By the way, we're going to give you a bid at CES for the computer.'"

Tramiel was understandably wary of the unproven market. He saw it as an opportunity to sell more calculators. "The plan was, we would make this computer for Radio Shack and that would get us instant distribution to sell calculators," says Peddle. "So I met with Jack Tramiel."

Peddle had met other tycoons in Silicon Valley, but none so magnificently cold hearted as Tramiel. "Jack was a terribly smart guy," says Peddle. "He picked up a lot of things that the rest of the world didn't. He was one of the best minds I've ever met, but totally ruthless."

Both Peddle and Souson described a computer small enough to fit on a desktop, yet with more than enough power for an individual user. "Souson was pretty persuasive that we should go do that," recalls Peddle. The idea appealed to Jack and he listened attentively. Undercutting the competition was in Jack's blood, and this was an opportunity to undercut the biggest competitor of them all: IBM.

"They basically told me, 'We'll set you up in the computer business. It's your business and you can run it, because it's not part of our calculator business. If it goes, it's yours. We want to own it, but depending on how well you do with the computer, we will give you significant stock.'"

Before shaking hands, Peddle made a special deal concerning his wife, Shirley. "She got to travel with me. That was one of my deals when I went to work for them," he explains. Under the deal, Commodore would pay for her transportation and lodging. "She was totally involved with everything I was doing at MOS Technology and early Commodore. She was free help for Commodore and Jack didn't pay her anything."

"I said to Jack, 'Okay, we got a deal.' We shook hands on the deal. They moved me across the country and gave me a loan so I could buy a house in California," says Peddle. Chuck Peddle would now build computers for Commodore.

It was a meeting of minds with a similar philosophy. Both Jack and Chuck believed it was better to sell low-cost products to the masses rather than inflate prices and sell to the elite. Other companies claimed to have this philosophy, but it would take Commodore to fulfill the promise.

Jack Tramiel, founder of Commodore (photo courtesy of Ian Matthews).

Peddle returned to the East Coast to inform his employers he was leaving for Commodore. He knew they would not be enthusiastic, since they had lost almost the entire 6502 team already. "I went back to MOS Technology and said, 'I'm going to the West Coast to do a computer.' By this time Jack owns the company, so they're not going to tell him to fuck off," he says.

Chuck's fellow engineers at MOS Technology remember the move. "Chuck went to the West Coast because that is where the power was at," explains Al Charpentier. "Jack lived in California, so where would Chuck go?"

Unfortunately, Peddle had to break his promise to his youngest daughter to live in Florida. "She gets in my house in Pennsylvania and I tell her, 'No, we're moving to California.'"

In October 1976, Peddle, his family, and his three cars traveled to California. "I just packed up, put one car in a van and put another car behind it and my wife and daughter drove another one. We packed up and drove across the United States."

Bill's Basic

Based on Chuck Peddle's experience with the Dartmouth Timesharing system, he believed users needed the Basic computer language to do anything useful with a computer. Peddle recalls, "These people wanted a computer they could use to write Basic because they loved doing it."

When corporations began locking the doors to computer rooms, users had nowhere to program. "There was no way they could do it at work so they went out and bought their own machines just for that purpose," recalls Peddle. "I knew there were at least two million people that had been trained that I could sell this machine to."

Today, the inclusion of a built in programming language might seem quaint, but in 1977 it was perhaps the most important aspect of a personal computer because there was no software industry. Users had to develop their own software, and Basic was the simplest path.

To acquire Basic, Commodore would make a deal with a small company called *Micro-Soft*. At the time, Micro-Soft was a much different company from the Microsoft of today. They owned no operating system and sold programming languages, principally their highly regarded version of Basic.

A young Bill Gates led the company. Many people mistakenly believe Bill Gates invented Basic, but John Kemeny and Thomas Kurtz invented it in 1964 at Dartmouth College. Peddle finds the misconception amusing. "I knew Basic when Gates was still in God-damned grammar school," he says. "They were all hobbyists and amateurs."

Bill Gates and Paul Allen were still new to business. Their company had grown to five employees and their Basic language was quickly becoming the industry standard. Micro-Soft was located in Albuquerque, New Mexico.[2]

In late 1976, Peddle received a call from Micro-Soft. "A guy calls me up from this place Micro-Soft and says, 'I've got a Basic for the 6502 and we're not finding any customers. Would you like to start marketing it for me?' It turned out this guy's name was Rick Wyland," he says.

---

[2] Micro-Soft resided at Ed Roberts MITS, which manufactured the Altair computer. The two companies were so close Roberts believed MITS actually owned the Basic language, since Paul Allen was an MITS employee and director of software. In 1977, Micro-Soft painfully separated from an angry Ed Roberts.

Wyland had taken the original Intel 8008 code created by Bill Gates and, just for fun, converted it to the 6502 microprocessor. "He had done it on his own because the place that Bill had built up was kind of loosey-goosey," explains Peddle.

When Wyland showed his ad-hoc project to Bill Gates, he did not receive an enthusiastic response. According to Chuck Peddle, Gates general reaction was, "That is such a shitty [microprocessor] because of the stack. I don't want us to waste any more time on it. Get some money out of it and get out of it."

Wyland and Peddle continued talking back and forth until Peddle and his family began their trek to the West Coast. "I was taking the Southern route because it was getting ready to snow up North," recalls Peddle. "So I organized to come through Albuquerque and sit down with Gates and Wyland in their two-room office over a bank. It's late October and just starting to snow as we come across the panhandle in Albuquerque."

Peddle had a positive first impression of the young Gates. "Gates is a tough competitor and he's been pretty ruthless about stuff, but down underneath he is a real good guy," he says.

Peddle told Gates and Wyland the features he wanted in his Basic language. According to Peddle, he said, "I'm building a computer. I want to build Basic into ROM. I want to make it very user friendly and there's some things in Basic I have to extend: I need an I/O structure and I need the ability to draw characters on a screen."

Gates replied, "If you can afford it, we'll do it." Peddle was impressed with Gates. "Gates is a very honest businessman," he explains. "He made a commitment that we would have a working Basic." With an informal agreement between Micro-Soft and Commodore in place, Peddle and his family continued their journey.

In California, Peddle reunited with his West Coast 6502 sales manager, Petr Sehnal. "We decided how to make the Basic have I/O capability and we made several changes that we could get in on time [for CES]," explains Peddle. "Some we couldn't get in on time but we could get them in later before we went into production."

With their general specification for the Basic language completed, Commodore brought in Micro-Soft. "We flew Rick [Wyland] out and he did the deal," recalls Peddle. "We negotiated a one time paid up license for the thing. Wyland was all happy because he got money enough to cover all of their development expenses. So he did what Gates told him to do: he got rid of it."

Commodore paid very little for the rights to use Micro-Soft Basic. "The price was actually negotiated by Souson," recalls Peddle. "He just took a flat deal and a negotiated price that wasn't very heavy because we were selling zero computers. Apple is selling 10 or 20 [Apple I kits] a month. The industry is totally in its infancy. Numbers like twenty-five and fifty thousand dollars are big numbers. So we bought Basic with a one time license, paid up."

According to the deal, Micro-Soft would keep the modifications made to 6502 Basic and sell it to other companies. "The deal was, we would extend it but he had the rights to sell whatever we did," says Peddle.

Peddle was not worried that other companies might use his innovations against him. "I was going to support that because obviously I was still a MOS Technology guy. His [6502] Basic was going to be available to other people," he says. "They liked the extensions I put in, they thought they were a good idea, so they agreed to them in as part of their normal Basic."

At first, Bill Gates was not very involved with the 6502 Basic project. "We really didn't work with Bill hardly at all on the product," says Peddle. "It wasn't until after we got going and started doing some stuff that Bill started getting involved, although he actually did write some of the code for the final product. Bill wrote good interrupt driven code that really worked."

In a 1993 interview with the Smithsonian, Bill Gates recalled his early start with Commodore. "…they started with us from the very beginning. Because we helped Chuck Peddle, who was at Commodore at that time, really think about the design of the machine," he says. "Adding lots of fun characters to the character set, things like smiley faces, and suit symbols. That was the first machine we did that had this wild extended character set."

Peddle explains the origins of the character set. "One of my specs was that I had to be able to do card games because that's one of the things people did with computers."

According to Peddle, Micro-Soft was not the main creative force behind Commodore Basic. "Micro-Soft was crucial to our program and very supportive, but they weren't driving the program; we were," he says. "It was our ideas and our concept. Bill, other than writing a little bit of code, was not involved in those discussions."

Bill Gates is famous for his shrewd business style, but in 1976, he was still learning his craft. The deal for Basic would ultimately turn into one of the biggest missteps of his early career. From the moment Commodore purchased Basic from Micro-Soft, Commodore could include it in all computer models they happened to make in the years to come, without paying royalties.

"As far as I know, Jack Tramiel was the only one who ever got the upper hand on Bill Gates," says engineer Bob Yannes. "They wanted to charge him a per-unit fee and Jack would never agree to a licensing fee. He would only buy stuff right out, because that way he knew what it would cost him and he didn't have to worry about what it was going to cost him in the future. I guess Micro-Soft didn't think that Jack was likely to be very successful, so they agreed to it, and he bought Micro-Soft Basic."

According to Jack's son, Leonard Tramiel, the Basic programming language remained the same for years to come. "It was a one time, royalty free purchase," says Leonard. "The ROM's went through different versions, and there were changes in the operating system, but I don't think there were any changes to Basic itself. The Basic part was identical."

The license allowed Commodore to improve the operating system, however. "As far as new features and functions [to the operating system], I don't think those came from Micro-Soft. Those were done internally at Commodore," says Leonard.

Bob Yannes believes Micro-Soft overestimated Jack Tramiel. "I think, probably in the back of their mind, Micro-Soft was thinking, 'This is a primitive form of Basic. Two years from now he's going to need a new version anyhow, so who cares.' Well, Jack didn't care what kind of software his machines had," laughs Yannes. "He was putting the same Basic in every machine, even though it was obsolete."

How much did Commodore pay Micro-Soft for the incredible unending license? "I've never told anyone the number because it's kind of a polite thing between me and Gates," says Peddle. "It's a very low number."

Commodore employee Bob Russell learned the exact amount. "We had bought it outright for ten thousand dollars originally," he reveals.

The Commodore-Apple Merger

Peddle had very little time to complete his prototype computer. "We've got just enough time to do the computer before the Consumer Electronics Show, which is in January," he recalls. "But we have to start with some equipment and we have to kind of hack our way to it." To complete the computer in two months, they would need to start with an existing piece of hardware.

Peddle called on Steve Wozniak and Steve Jobs. "We kept in contact with them because they were a 6502 customer," he recalls. "One of the ways to get it done quickly was to start with the Apple I and do our own version of the machine that met my criteria."

Through 1976, Wozniak gradually improved on the Apple I. Chuck Peddle explains, "His definition of a machine appealed to the people that

Woz knew; the hobbyists and the guys who were excited about doing something better. Graphics was one of the main things."

In September, Wozniak improved the display to allow color graphics. Color was nothing new at the time and even the lowly Altair had a color display adapter called the *Dazzler*. Steve Wozniak's color graphics adapter could display four colors at once – two colors better than black and white. The text was muddy, with color pixels seeping into the white characters.

Wozniak also created six expansion slots for his improved Apple. This brought it up to date with the functionality available to other computers, including the Altair and the KIM-4 expansion module.

In October, Chuck Peddle approached Apple in the hopes of acquiring Wozniak's technology. "We tried to get them to sell us the Apple ... as the basis for our PET," says Peddle.

The person negotiating on behalf of Apple was Steve Jobs. The two partners came to Commodore headquarters with the intention of selling their fledgling company.

"Andre sets up a meeting with Apple to have a discussion about how we could get to the CES show together," recalls Peddle.

According to Peddle, he and Souson told the two Steve's, "If you work with us we can put together a deal, we can go to CES, and we can have a product that meets our new spec."

During their discussions, Peddle and Wozniak had several disagreements over the design. "There were two fundamental things that blocked it," explains Peddle. "One, Woz had written this really nice little thing called Sweet-16, which made it real easy to program in machine language." Peddle liked the machine language assembler, but he believed it was too complex for ninety percent of computer users. Peddle believed users needed a Basic programming language. "Woz and I had a big argument about it."

"They felt the thing that their customers wanted was some music, audio, and color graphics," recalls Peddle. Their instincts were accurate, but Peddle felt the machine should be simpler. "My argument was, color graphics are wonderful, but people can't just instantly pick up and use it. If I do character graphics and teach them how to use it, everybody can do their own pictures in a hurry."

Although there were disagreements, Wozniak and Jobs were still willing to sell, as long as the price was right. According to Wozniak, "We went to Commodore and talked primarily with Andre Souson. Steve Jobs was trying to talk Commodore into buying the Apple II for a large amount, like hundreds of thousands of dollars. ... Steve Jobs also wanted

Commodore to hire us along with the proposed deal. The deal was never on paper and never concrete, as to how much."

"The discussions never got beyond a meeting with Jack and Steve," says Peddle. "Jack's view was that Steve wanted much too much for the company and in the fall of 1976 he was right. I remember him laughing about Steve Jobs and his view of his company's position."

Jack was willing to purchase Apple, but he wanted the lowest price possible. To do that, he put pressure on Jobs by refusing his initial offer. "Basically Jack decided to go along with it but he tried to squeeze Steve," explains Peddle.

Steve Wozniak tells a different story. "We were told that Chuck wanted to do his own thing and that he could do better than us at reaching the cheap needs of customers. Jack Tramiel, the Commodore president, was talked by Chuck into shooting for cheapness. We were told that Chuck Peddle was the instrumental force in passing on this deal."

However, Peddle denies turning down Apple. "Petr and I were more interested in our short term problems of getting prototypes done," says Peddle. "I was never asked nor gave an opinion except that using the existing Apple I board would help us get the original prototypes done."

As it turns out, a retired Intel executive and millionaire named Mike Markkula had his eye on Apple. "What Jack didn't know is that right about that time Mike Markkula had fallen in love with the idea of doing his own computer," explains Peddle. "He effectively came out of retirement from Intel and he threw money at them at the same time Jack was trying to squeeze them, so Jobs just walked."

If the transaction had gone through, the world would be a different place today. "The incident didn't change either company, but had they merged, it would have changed the industry," says Peddle. Commodore possibly would have released the Commodore Apple and Wozniak would have become one of Peddle's engineers.

More importantly, Commodore would have eliminated an early rival at the bargain price of only $100,000. However, Apple did not look like a formidable rival at the time. "At this time Jack was only tire kicking in [the computer] business. His focus was on turning around his calculator company," says Peddle.

Prototype

Without the Apple computer to use as a foundation, Peddle had to look elsewhere. "My buddy on the West Coast [Petr Sehnal] was working with a customer designing some piece of equipment that was small enough to fit in the case we wanted," recalls Peddle. "It had a 6502 in it and enough other stuff in it that we could hack it around and make it drive the screen and run the keyboard."

What kind of hardware was it? "I don't remember," says Peddle. "We started with a card that they were selling for something like a machine controller, I think. We just adapted it." When pressed further, Peddle thinks it was, of all things, a computerized sprinkler control system. "It may have been controlling solenoids for watering your lawn. It was a little general purpose thing that was designed for that kind of control application."

Peddle had been nurturing his idea of a computer system since his days at GE. He wanted to build a microcomputer system with all the elegant functionality of the Dartmouth system. "I'm trying to build a product people will perceive as professional, as opposed to hobby," says Peddle. "I wanted them to be proud of what they bought." He wanted a mainframe computer without the mainframe. Physically, the computer would resemble a mainframe terminal.

Peddle also received inspiration from Hewlett-Packard. "HP was selling a Basic computer for $5000 or something like that with an IEEE interface[3] on it," recalls Peddle, who decided he would put an IEEE-488 interface on his computer. "I was trying to make everybody believe we were an HP but at $500."

"The definition of the product was lots of capability from a user standpoint; Basic in ROM and some demonstration software and manuals," explains Peddle. "It was a system that worked when you plugged it in and you never had to think about it. That was totally different from what anyone was shipping at that point in time."

Peddle and Sehnal worked out of the tiny Commodore office building at 901 California Avenue in Palo Alto. "Jack and Andre had an office there," says Peddle. "Jack was pretty broke when we started. The calculator business had gone to shit." They quickly assembled a makeshift lab.

Petr Sehnal, who was most familiar with the sprinkler system controller, was crucial in assembling the prototype computer. "Petr had really good mechanical skills, because he was an ex-mechanical engineer as well as an electrical and computer science engineer," says Peddle.

Rounding out the team were two Japanese calculator engineers, Fujiyama and Aoji. "I always called him Mr. Fujiyama because that's what Jack called him," says Peddle. "Fujiyama was more of a

---

[3] At the time, Hewlett-Packard called it the GPIB (General Purpose Interface Bus). The IEEE later accepted the interface as a standard for minicomputer peripherals, such as printers and disk drives.

mechanical guy than an electrical guy, though he had both skills. He helped me with the packaging a lot. [He was] just a spectacular little Japanese guy. Fujiyama just made things happen."

"Aoji was the technician," says Peddle. "Aoji was a great tech and really dedicated; just really nice guys to work with."

Peddle knew it would take time to develop a case for the computer, so he contacted Larry Hittle, the man who fabricated the KIM-1 line. In early November, Hittle created some prototype cases. "We knew an industrial designer and we had a couple of buddies who did some sketches and helped put the thing together," says Peddle. "We ordered two wooden prototypes of the product we wanted, nicely shaped; a real pretty box."[4]

A *Courier* terminal inspired the shape of the computer case. "If you look at it pretty carefully, it's a knockoff of a terminal," admits Peddle. "I would say it looked a lot like a Courier system. It has very similar lines."

Commodore attempted to associate their computer with the future. Using 2001 in the name was part of this strategy, but the proposed case styling went even further. Molded-plastic epitomized the future in the 1970's. This look is evident in everything from the *Jetsons*, to George Lucas' *THX-1138* and Woody Allen's *Sleepers*.

One of the most controversial design decisions originated with Jack Tramiel. "I'm having trouble making a regular keyboard fit in the case," explains Peddle. "I'm wandering around and Jack is talking to the Japanese engineers. I wandered in and showed Jack the problem."

According to Peddle, Tramiel asked him, "How do you know they really want a typewriter keyboard?"

Peddle replied, "Well, I really don't."

Jack said, "I've got a calculator here that we built that's not going anywhere. You can have that keyboard. It's done and it's yours."

Tramiel clearly wanted to use Commodore's vertical integration to supply a keyboard, rather than purchasing a professional keyboard from another supplier. "It's very indicative of Jacks thought process," says Peddle. "He was willing to gamble on a new idea."

Against his better judgment, Peddle decided to follow his boss. "I shut up and built it the way he suggested," he recalls.

Jack delivered a rubberized 69-key keyboard. It used the popular QWERTY layout, along with uppercase and lowercase characters, plus a

---

[4] The fate of the original wooden prototype is unknown. Leonard Tramiel comments, "I wish I could find that machine. I'm not quite sure what happened to that one."

numeric keypad on the right side. "It was very calculator like; you couldn't touch type on it, but it fit in our case," says Peddle. From an ergonomic standpoint, the keyboard was impractical for prolonged typing. Since the plan was to market the computer to businesses who would undoubtedly want to use it for typing documents, the decision seemed misguided.

Peddle also decided the computer would have a built in monitor. "We made the decision independent of Radio Shack that building the monitor in was the only way to sell the product," he says.

Unfortunately, no one at Commodore knew anything about television electronics. "We'd never done that," says Peddle. "I had a guy who was kind of kicking around Commodore at the time and I gave him the assignment."

"We walked out and bought a *Sony* [television] that was the right size and we crammed it into the box," explains Peddle. "Thanks to my buddy Adam Osborne's book on how to make a TV, we got it to work. He read Adam's book and we just hacked. We took the TV board apart and we built something up so we could demonstrate the TV."

In December 1976, Commodore leaked information and photos of the mockup computer to *Electronic Engineering Times*. The same month, Commodore's stock rose from 4 ½ to 7. It was a sure sign the personal computer could help offset Commodore's financial woes in the calculator business.

To help motivate Peddle, Jack offered him one dollar for every computer Commodore sold. Peddle accepted, though he seemed unsure if Jack was sincere about the deal.

In spare moments, Andre Souson tossed around potential names for the new computer. It would be three letters, as the TIM and KIM had been before it, and it would sound friendly. Souson might have pulled some inspiration from a Commodore calculator. The box for the 776M called it a Personal Electronic Calculator. Souson might have thought Personal Electronic Computer also fit in with this scheme, but the acronym PEC did not sound like much of anything. He needed to contemplate the name further.

Souson soon received inspiration from a fad. Peddle explains, "In the fall of 1976, a guy in Los Gatos, California started packaging rocks with cute sayings called the *Pet Rock*, and he sold tons of them." Legendary Californian advertising man Gary Dahl had caused an inexplicable mania by selling Pet Rocks. He packed a simple Beach Stone in a gift box shaped like a pet carrying case, accompanied by an instruction book titled 'Pet Rock Training Manual'. In just a few months, Dahl sold over a million rocks at $3.95 each.

Souson loved the name. "Both he and I used the words *warm and fuzzy*. I gave quotes about how computers are supposed to be warm and fuzzy," says Peddle. To Souson, the Pet Rock was warm and fuzzy. "That was absolutely the image we were trying to get. Once we picked it, we tried it on some people and they kind of liked it."

The designers had an acronym, but it had no meaning. "I was making the words mean something so that we didn't get caught up in arguments about stealing the Pet Rock," recalls Peddle. Unfortunately, there were not many T-words in computer vernacular. Typewriter was a candidate, but it would mislead buyers into thinking it was an electric typewriter. Terminal was another candidate, but Chuck disliked the name since it strictly implied a brainless keyboard and monitor.

Peddle finally hit upon *transactor*. "The Personal Electronic Transactor is because I was in the intelligent terminal business and transactions were something we used there," he explains. "So the Personal Electronic Transactor doesn't really fit, but it fit my company background." It was a vague description, but it worked.

Souson also wanted a futuristic name. The movie *2001: A Space Odyssey* (1968) seemed to epitomize the future. "If you think about it in 1977, that was the futuristic thing people talked about," recalls Peddle. "That set a tone of futuristic. There wasn't a *Star Wars* movie yet and there wasn't a *Star Trek* [movie]. Go back in that time and you'll see that 2001 implies a successful future."

Souson appended the number 2001 to the PET name. "2001 was absolutely picked because of the movie. It wasn't inspired, it was absolutely ripped off," says Peddle, proving Picasso correct that good artists borrow, great artists steal. The computer now had a name.

The Demo

With CES nearly upon them, Peddle and his team had little to show. "We are fucking hacking," recalls Peddle. "We had two months to do something and make this absolute hodge-podge. We stuffed it into a case and nothing worked."

It was an anxious situation. "Jack had made it clear that if I didn't perform he was going to kill the project," says Peddle. "This was wonderful, after I moved my family to the West Coast and everything. But I love challenges, and usually if you start insulting me you just piss me off and I work harder."

The team boarded an airplane for CES, without a working computer. Jack hoped to display the PET on the show floor, along with his calculators, but a bug prevented the PET from booting up properly. As Leonard recalls, "When the machine was hooked up to the development system it worked great, but when you plugged the processor in, it didn't work."

John Roach of Radio Shack would view the computer and make his assessment on the last day of the show. With only days remaining, there was intense pressure to eliminate the bug. Peddle recalls, "We got a suite, and I worked two groups of engineers 24 hours a day. I slept maybe one or two hours a day."

Jack toured the CES show floor to see if his competition had beaten him to the personal computer. The disco era was almost at its peak and throngs of attendees with trendy bell-bottom pants waded past the display booths. Companies used disco-balls and colored lights to attract attention while playing current hits like the Bee Gees *You Should Be Dancing*. Jack sweated his way through the displays and was relieved there was no other competition for the personal computer.

As the show progressed, the increasingly strung-out engineers searched for the source of the bug. In the midst of this turmoil, Peddle found beauty. "I remember a vision that I will carry with me until my death," says Peddle. "I was sitting there, getting the computer sort of working, looking across the Chicago lakefront. It was 50 degrees below zero outside and there was this ice fog all over the lake, and the sunrise on it was just spectacular. I will always have the image from that hotel in my mind."

The sunrise was a good omen. Leonard Tramiel recalls, "It took a while to find that error, and unfortunately it was found the last day of CES. It turned out there was just a microscopic technical issue that was absolutely trivial to fix that took a surprising length of time to find." The computer booted up, but the image horrified the engineers.

"To give you a feel for how dumb we were about TV's and everything, the day before we were supposed to show it to John Roach we got the God-damned thing working but the image was upside down," recalls Peddle. "We didn't know how to fix it so we go back and read the Osborne book. We were really not very sophisticated about some of that stuff. We finally got it kind of hacked together."

The Radio Shack meeting could make or break the PET. "On the last day of the show, Jack brings John Roach up to the room," recalls Peddle. "It's the first time I met John Roach."

Roach was about to see his star rise in the business world, but he was an unknown in 1977. "John was not the head of Radio Shack at that time," explains Peddle. "He was an operations guy. He just happened to wind up with the assignment of getting a computer to work."

Nervously, Peddle revealed the PET computer to John Roach. "I show him this thing, sort of working and kind of interesting. John basically

52   THE SPECTACULAR RISE AND FALL OF COMMODORE

says, 'Well it's obviously not totally working but you've got people that sound pretty smart. I know your company and I know you'll make it happen. Let's sit down and talk about a deal.'" The deal would have given the PET computer immediate and massive distribution all over the world in Radio Shack outlets.

Sensing interest from Roach, Jack went ahead with his plan to ask for a larger order of calculators. "Jack wanted a big commit on calculators if he did it," recalls Peddle. It was a big mistake, and Roach started to have second thoughts.

"John was convinced that he could do it himself because he knew we hadn't worked on it very long," says Peddle. "He kind of looked at it and said, 'You know, if those guys can do it that quick, I can probably get a team to do it.'" Commodore would not supply computers to Radio Shack. It was a devastating blow to Peddle.

"So he basically went back to Dallas and commissioned a team to design the Radio Shack machine," explains Peddle.

Peddle thought his dream was lost. Fortunately, the rapid rise of Commodore stock made Jack take notice. "We came back from the show," he recalls. "Jack said 'I saw you bust your ass. I saw you get something done. I've decided we are going to spend the money and make this happen.'" It was an uplifting moment for Peddle, who had worked so tirelessly the past few months.

Refining the Design

In January 1977, Commodore became the first computer company to announce a personal computer for the mass-market. Commodore would unveil the PET at the upcoming West Coast Computer Faire in April. The features surpassed everyone's expectations, with a built in keyboard, monitor, cassette storage unit, Basic programming language, and four kilobytes of programmable memory, all for only $495.

The announcement sent shockwaves through the nascent microcomputer companies of the time. Some microcomputers sold for several thousand dollars. The *Cromemco Z-1*, an S-100 compatible computer, was selling for $2495 without keyboard or monitor. No company could offer such a complete system at the same price.

The hobbyist market had anticipated and dreaded this moment ever since Commodore acquired MOS Technology. Dan Fylstra, a KIM-1 and eventual PET owner, described the reaction in the February 1978 issue of Byte magazine:

> ...Commodore Business Machines Inc, a well-known maker of pocket calculators, startled everyone in the personal computer industry by announcing its PET

computer. ... The announcement was greeted with considerable enthusiasm and skepticism, for Commodore obviously was stretching the state of the art in technology, manufacturing and mass distribution.

Jack wanted Chuck and his team to have the final production model ready for the June CES show. He gave Peddle the resources to expand his team. Commodore was about to create their first computer systems division.

Peddle knew he wanted Bill Seiler, the inspirational hardware hacker from Florida who created sounds for electronic games. "Bill Seiler was a hippy - long hair, drove a crummy little car, worked in rock band," says Peddle.

Aside from his Sooting computer kit, Seiler was involved in other hardware projects. "He was a blue boxer," adds Peddle, referring to the illegal practice of using an electronic speaker device to hijack telephone calls. "He even got busted for having a blue box. He was everything the hobbyists were and he was an absolute loner. No friends; nothing."

When Seiler arrived on the West Coast, he signed up for the Homebrew Computer Club, an acclaimed nexus for early computer hobbyists. "That was the one that was meeting up at SLAC [Stanford Linear Accelerator Center]," explains Peddle. "Woz was in that, Gordon [French] – a whole bunch of people were in that." Seiler's only acquaintance on the West Coast was Peddle, so the Homebrew Computer Club was a welcomed activity outside of work.

The other new addition to the PET team was Leonard Tramiel, Jack's second son who had attended CES in January. Leonard was now 23 and had just earned his physics degree at Columbia University. "I graduated from the university in the spring/early summer of 1976," recalls Leonard. "I took a year off from the middle of 1976 to the middle of 1977."

During this time, Leonard decided what he wanted to do with his life, and it brought him into a major disagreement with Jack. "[Leonard] loves his dad, but it's kind of funny because there was a time when his dad didn't love him," says Peddle.

Leonard fell in love with physics and now wanted to earn a PhD. "His father thought he was making a mistake," explains Peddle. "Jack didn't want him to do that, so he was squeezing him economically because Leonard was going off to be an astrophysicist. But it's okay. Fathers do this to their kids all the time."

Jack adamantly refused to pay for Leonard's tuition. "Leonard is a very funny guy; very docile and very inventive at that time in his life, but a very mild mannered person," says Peddle. "Jack was definitely not mild mannered. This was kind of like his first rebellion, and I helped him."

Peddle recognized Leonard as someone who could evaluate and test the project. "Leonard was involved in the QC [quality control] work," explains Peddle. "He was very critical about what we did and he was very fair about it. He would run tests and figure out what we were doing wrong, bring it to our attention, and demand we fix it. I put him in that role of being the in-house critical user."

"Jack threatened to fire me because I hired Leonard," says Peddle. "Jack didn't hate me, but he gave me shit for it." Although Jack could no longer exert financial pressure on Leonard, he was probably also grateful to see his son in the company. "I put him on the payroll and he managed to get through the summer, so Jack couldn't squeeze him."

Chuck assembled his team and began planning a better design for the PET. "It was a very small group," recalls Leonard. "Chuck was a real bright guy who knew what he wanted the machine to do and explained it pretty well. We got together and did what he wanted. It was a pretty simple design and we made it work as best we could."

The engineers would be designing a circuit board, jammed with integrated circuits and processors. "We started building up two or three prototypes," says Peddle.

Like the KIM-1 before it, the PET circuit board would contain a MOS 6502 CPU running at 1 MHz, situated in the center of the board. To one side were 8 sockets for the RAM chips. Peddle used MOS Technology 6550 Static RAM (SRAM) chips, each containing 512 bytes of memory.

Unfortunately, MOS Technology was having very little luck producing reliable memory. "We tried to design RAM's but that's a true specialty. They could never do it well," says Peddle.

From the start, Peddle designed the PET as a closed system without expansion slots. Additional peripherals, such as printers and disk drives, would connect to an IEEE-488 slot at the back of the computer. "It was designed to be a self contained unit, and it had the IEEE interface to control all the peripherals," explains Peddle. "That's what made Commodore so much money." Users could connect up to 15 peripherals through the IEEE-488 interface.

It was up to Bill Seiler to refine the video electronics hacked together during CES. He would need to conceive new circuits to control the cathode ray tube and display text to a screen at 60 times per second.

The PET would contain all 128 characters defined by the ASCII standard, plus an additional 128 graphical characters, which allowed users to create pictures. Users later whimsically dubbed the character set PETSCII. "I never really liked that term since it was never much of a standard," reveals Leonard. "The part of PETSCII that coincides with ASCII is standard but the rest of it is not."

Leonard created the symbols through experimentation. "While the PET was being developed, I designed most of the graphics character set," says Leonard. "It was a joint effort, but I put most of that together."

The biggest test for his character set was a graphical version of a popular KIM-1 game. "What Leonard worked on, which he should take a lot of pride in, was Lunar Lander," says Peddle. "It was the program we put in every book on the PET."

The graphical symbols contained arrows, lines, corners, curves, card suits, and screen control codes - over 50 graphic symbols in all, most of them accessible from the keyboard. "It turned out to be a very useful and flexible way to do graphics," says Leonard.

The PET would require 2 kilobytes of memory to store all the characters. Peddle included a second text mode, which did not have many of the character graphics but supported upper and lower case text. This required another 2 kilobytes for the text mode definitions. Chuck used a Commodore Semiconductor Group 6540 ROM chip to store the characters. "One of the things that made my personal computer work was that ROM's had just come into real strong being, and MOS made good ROM's," says Peddle. "We took advantage of the fact that ROM had made a breakthrough in density. We were able to make a full operating system and a full Basic and everything else and stuff it into ROM, just like today everybody uses flash [memory] for that function. Nobody had done that before."

For months after CES, the Commodore engineers refined Basic with Micro-Soft. "Micro-Soft did the debugging, we did the testing," says Leonard. "I did more testing and not much interacting with the people at Micro-Soft. That was done largely by Chuck." Ray Holt, designer of the SYM-1 and JOLT computers, also acted as a beta tester for Micro-Soft Basic.

Peddle chose a nine-inch Sony picture tube at random but it fit the case so well, he decided to strike a deal with Sony. Jack Tramiel relied on Mr. Fujiyama and Aoji. "They were the Japanese leads and contacts," says Peddle. "They helped negotiate the deal with Sony."

The two engineers also helped choose the Sanyo cassette unit for the PET. "We went out and bought a reasonably decent Japanese cassette," says Peddle. "We took it apart and looked at the signals."

Peddle programmed his code for the cassette unit using the same ICE development system he used to make the Apple I operational. "It was a very powerful tool," recalls Peddle.

According to Peddle, "I literally sat there with a development system and a scope and wrote the code." He throws all modesty aside when describing his code. "There is really some smart shit in there," he says.

"It worked much better than anyone else's cassette. It had error recovery and lots of stuff."

Lack of memory forced Peddle to leave his code undocumented. "The problem was that the development station that I was using didn't have enough space in the memory to write line comments for the code I was writing," he explains. "I wrote them down somewhere, but ultimately, this code was literally written on a machine with a scope and it wound up being undocumented." The undocumented code would haunt Commodore engineers for years to come.

The final PET design had a simple, modular design. The main board had a video signal connector, which allowed the nine-inch monitor to plug right into the board. The cassette recorder and keyboard also had connectors on the motherboard, making it easy for users to upgrade the keyboard. However, before the final product release, the hand of Jack Tramiel would change much of the design.

The Birth of an Industry

Leonard Tramiel unveiled the PET 2001 to the world. "The first showing of the PET was at the Hanover Faire in Germany in March 1977," recalls Leonard. "It was shown first at the Hanover Faire in that hand-carved wooden case."

Though Peddle wanted to show off his computer, Jack wanted him to continue development at home. "Jack felt I didn't have time to do that," he says.

Leonard was unhappy taking the PET to Hanover. "We stuck him with a product that didn't work very much and stuffed him in a booth with the calculator guys. He was never happy with that assignment," says Peddle. A month later, they would unveil the PET in the United States.

Sometime after the January CES, Jim Warren, the editor of *Dr. Dobbs Journal*, contacted Chuck Peddle. 'Big' Jim Warren, a tall bearded computer hobbyist, had an idea for a computer show just for microcomputers. "Warren is a funny guy," recalls Peddle. "He dreamed up the idea of the show. He went to a whole bunch of us and charged us relatively little money to set up booths, because he knew all of us were just getting started."

Warren would make his profit on admission fees. "He was charging everyone twenty-five bucks to come by and look at what was effectively a computer store," explains Peddle.

In mid-April 1977, the West Coast Computer Faire was upon the engineers. The three-day event took place over a weekend. This was to be the first major gathering of hobbyists and microcomputer companies, and many saw it as finally legitimizing the nascent microcomputer industry. "That is a landmark decision in the world of personal computers," says Peddle. "Jim Warren deserves all the credit he ever got for dreaming that thing up." There were no large computer companies in attendance; no IBM, DEC, or Hewlett Packard. Commodore was the heavyweight of the show and rivals eagerly awaited a glimpse of the much talked about PET-2001.

In the months leading up to the West Coast Computer Faire, 'Big' Jim Warren became a promotion machine. He created a flyer proclaiming, 'You can be a part of it'. He copied the advertisement on bright yellow paper and handed fliers out to anyone who would take one. The same flyer also appeared in full-page ads in computer publications like Byte and Dr. Dobbs Journal.

The gathering took place at the Civic Auditorium across from City Hall in downtown San Francisco. On Friday, April 15, the doors to the underground *Brooks Hall* opened to the public. "There were important moments in history, and that was one," says Peddle.

Hobbyists flocked to the event. "The fucking lines outside of the building signing up for the show were phenomenal," recalls Peddle. Attendees received a tantalizing 42-page black-and-white program with heavy gloss covers packed with descriptions of exhibits and presentations. They also received a brown paper bag with string handles to carry paraphernalia.

Warren fulfilled his promise of 'You can be a part of it'. "He was right, people wanted to be part of it," remarks Peddle. "By that time, everybody in the Bay area wanted a part of the action. It had been talked about and written about, and everybody wanted something to happen."

The auditorium was gleefully chaotic. Warren expected seven to ten thousand enthusiasts to attend, a figure many thought overly optimistic. Instead, 13,000 attended. Saturday was the big day for the convention and the isles were jammed with people. The floor overflowed with tables and booths, separated by yellow-orange curtains. People crowded around the booths waving dollar bills for products.

"It felt a lot like Woodstock. Everybody was there in fucking jeans and there was not a suit in the place," recalls Peddle. "These were the guys with the thick glasses and the slide rules in their pocket. This was their thing."

Peddle was clad in a leisure suit, which was considered stylish in the seventies disco era. Peddle's picture would later appear in *Personal Computing*, much to his embarrassment today. "There's this article inside and I'm wearing this really hokey leisure suit," he recalls. "I weigh about 250 pounds, totally out of shape."

Above the din of the crowd, attendees could hear strange sounds they had never heard before. These were early demonstrations of computer music and sound effects. The perfect, unerring rhythm captivated early listeners even though the buzzers producing the sound were primitive by today's standards. There were even early demonstrations of speech synthesis, slurred almost to the point of incomprehension.

Other booths featured a chance to have your picture digitized and printed on computer paper. One young artist attempted to sell computer-produced artwork for the outrageous price of six hundred and fifty dollars per printout.

Compared to industry gatherings today, the first West Coast Computer Faire was pandemonium. It was about the money, but it was also about learning and exploration with a distinctly fun element. Organizer Jim Warren wore roller skates to get around the show. If a new complication arose which demanded his attention, Warren would press the walkie-talkie to his ear, give a quick reply and skate off in a new direction.

Computer users brought their nerdy science fiction enthusiasm to the convention. There were at least three unlicensed *Star Trek* games displayed in various booths. The games were unsophisticated, but they gave onlookers a chance to understand the potential of computers in a fun way. Attendees would type in commands and most of the time received the response, 'Captain, I'm afraid your last command made no sense'. Despite the shortcomings of these early games, people received a distinct thrill from interacting with a computer.

Around the edges of the auditorium were side-rooms, where presenters gave unorthodox presentations. Among them was Ted Nelson, author of *Computer Lib*, a book hailed as revolutionary for the time. The book, written in 1974 before the KIM-1 and Altair 8800, envisioned networked computers with libraries of information linked together. At the conference, Nelson gave an impassioned speech about software, criticizing the current state of affairs.

In the center of the auditorium were the larger microcomputer companies, including Commodore (with their *Mr. Calculator* booth), *Processor Technology*, *IMSAI*, *MITS*, *Sphere*, *Cromemco*, *Digital Research*, and *Byte Publications*. Attendees glided from booth to booth, watching demonstrations and stuffing their brown paper bags with product handouts. Many of the attendees used the show to decide which computer they would eventually purchase.

In the center of the anarchy was Chuck Peddle with his PET, which had increased in price from $495 to $595. "We kind of got the prototypes working at the West Coast Computer Faire," says Peddle. The PET could power up and run Basic programs, but it was not the final design.

The PET – 1976 to 1977

Physically, the PET computer impressed spectators. Other computers were a tangle of wires and cables. Wires ran from the keyboard to the computer, from the monitor to the computer, and from the cassette recorder to the computer. As well, every device had its own power cord. It was wire spaghetti. In contrast, the PET had one single power cord. Spectators loved the beautiful, smooth styling of the case. Many commented that it was exactly how a computer should look.

Every half-hour, Peddle gathered spectators around and began his presentation. "We had to develop the market for computers and tell people why they wanted a computer," says Peddle. "We told everybody they could checkbook and all that shit."

Peddle boldly predicted something that even computer fanatics had a hard time believing. He said, "You're not going to stop with one computer. Most everybody is going to have two or three." The prediction came at a time when most people did not own one computer. "They thought I was fucking crazy," says Peddle. Today, people commonly use a computer at work, a notebook computer, a pocket computer, a desktop computer at home, and maybe one for the kids.

He concluded his presentation with a memorable comparison. "The idea was to plant ideas in peoples minds. If you get a big audience you try to leave them with things they don't forget," explains Peddle. "I used to tell people that computing was an urge. It was a need, the same as the hierarchy of oxygen first, water second, and all that stuff. And computers fit in there."

Where did computers fit in Peddle's hierarchy? "Right about sex," says Peddle. "Once you are hooked on computers, you will get back to using your computer whether you like it or not."

Between presentations, Peddle had time to tour the show floor and inspect other products, such as the Apple II from his friends, the two Steves. Peddle liked what he saw. "Steve [Jobs] was focusing on a really neat package," says Peddle. "It was done very cleanly."

The Apple II did little to stand apart from other computers. It lacked lower case characters, which made it unsuitable for word processing, one of the major uses of a computer. Furthermore, the Apple II had no cursor keys. Users were required to hold down the control key with a letter combination to move the cursor, such as Esc-D.

Spectators who turned on the Apple II saw a screen full of random alphabetic characters and symbols, and possibly some colored blocks. Users had to press a reset key in the upper right hand side of the keyboard to get things started. After this, an asterisk would appear in the bottom left-hand corner of the screen, indicating the computer was in monitor mode. To get into Apple-Basic, the user had to press Ctrl-B, which would bring up a different prompt indicating BASIC was ready. Compared to the PET, it was not user-friendly.

Peddle received free publicity from the show. "Magazines were just starting to happen," recalls Peddle. "You know this argument that rock music and all that stuff was pulled together by Woodstock. That show kind of brought together the suppliers, the customer, and the reality that this was going to be a real business."

One writer for *Personal Computing* magazine produced a series of articles detailing the beginnings of the personal computer industry. "He was covering the West Coast show," says Peddle "This guy did a really good job."

Peddle was interviewed and, along with others, gave predictions for the industry; some realistic and some far fetched. "I had made certain statements of where the industry was going and what the computer was going to do," says Peddle. "This guy went off and he talked to a whole bunch of people, who later on came into the business, asking, 'Is this going to be a real business?' Everybody's saying, 'Yes, it's going to be a real business. It's going to happen.'"

Personal Computing later published the story. "It's called the *Birth of the Personal Computer*," says Peddle. "The picture on the cover was literally an operating room with a doctor giving birth, and he's pulling this personal computer out of this blanketed form, and it's the PET." Inside, along with a photograph of Peddle, resplendent in his leisure suit, is an article naming Peddle as the father of the personal computer.

Years later, Apple revisionists attempted to paint the West Coast Computer Faire as Apple triumphing over the competition.[5] This depiction could not be further from the truth, according to author Michael S. Malone. In *Infinite Loop*, Malone claims most attendees remember other companies such as Commodore making a stronger impression. Magazines from around this time strengthen this viewpoint, with Byte completely failing to mention Apple in their July 1977 coverage of the West Coast Computer Faire.

Computer buyers in 1977 had a difficult choice to make. Among the deciding factors was price, where Commodore was poised to dominate their rivals. In contrast, Apple wanted $1298 for their 4-kilobyte computer. Those lured in by Steve Jobs sales pitch would have to invest even more money to obtain a cassette recorder and monitor. The Commodore PET sold for less than half the cost of an Apple II. For most people, the PET was an easy choice over the competition.

---

[5] The TV movie *Pirates of Silicon Valley* (1999) inexplicably shows everyone flocking around the Apple booth, while all the other booths are deserted.

Three personal computer titans were about to rise from the West Coast Computer Faire and dominate the computer scene for the remainder of the seventies and into the eighties. "I wasn't sure if Jack was going to screw me about the computer before we got to the West Coast Faire," says Peddle. "Jack goes to the show, he sees the people lining up, and he says, 'This is a business and I am going to play in it.' He backs the program."

"John Roach [from Radio Shack] comes around scouting the show and says, 'I am going to make a business out of this'. He goes back and finishes his machine, and launches his machine at the East Coast show in New Jersey later that year."

"Apple had their prototype there, I had prototypes there, and that's really and truly the genesis of the personal computer," says Peddle. "Before that, we were all trying to get there. All of a sudden, here's this guy [Jim Warren] proving to everybody that there is a real market by bringing the technical people together. It was a really, really important deal."

The Commodore Curse: Part II

In the midst of success, the Curse of Commodore was about to strike again. Andre Souson had spotted MOS Technology and the 6502 processor, instigated Commodore's first personal computer, enticed Chuck Peddle to stay with Commodore, and named the PET computer. It was time for the curse to take effect.

According to Peddle, it was inevitable Andre and Jack would part ways. "Andre was a Jack loyalist," says Peddle. "But Jack had a way of eating up people like Andre because Andre was relatively straight. A lot of guys around Jack had their shifty side."

According to Peddle, Souson played fair. "He had a good mind and always used his mind well, in spite of his association with Tramiel," says Peddle. "I'm sure a few times, because he was associated with Tramiel, he got on the odd side of deal because Tramiel did that."

Trouble began in early 1977 over a seemingly insignificant disagreement. "Andre and Jack got into this fight over something that was going on in the calculator business, and Andre was defending his position one day," says Peddle. "Basically Jack said, 'Get out.'"

It was the end of the line for Souson at Commodore. "This guy had been totally loyal and built his life around him," explains Peddle. Now he would end up helping Commodore's rival achieve success.

Peddle explains, "Andre basically walked across the street [to Apple] and said, 'I want to be in the personal computer business but I'm not going to get to do it with Commodore.'"

Steve Wozniak later recalled the meeting in an interview with *Failure Magazine*: "His head of engineering, Andre Souson, talked to us for a while. He believed in us and left Commodore to come to Apple."

At the time, Apple was looking for investors and they had no firm plans for marketing products in Europe. "They didn't have a clue how to do Europe," says Peddle. "Markkula didn't know anything about it. Nobody knew anything about it and Andre did."

According to Peddle, Souson had ample wealth from his Commodore days. "He was making serious money," says Peddle. "He went to Apple and said, 'Listen, I will invest a bunch of money in the company. What I want is European distribution rights.'" Apple gave Souson full distribution rights to all of Europe for Apple products.

"It was at a very appropriate time for him with Apple because Apple was just getting started and they loved having a guy to take over Europe. It was a perfect match," recalls Peddle.

Years later, the situation changed due to the upcoming Apple Initial Public Offering in 1980. "Apple is coming down and getting ready to go public," recalls Peddle. "They took a look at the company and discovered that this one guy has all the rights to all the machines ever for the rest of his life in Europe. They basically said, 'We don't want that on our prospectus.' So they went to Andre and they said, 'What does it take to get you to go away?'"

Souson knew what he wanted: Apple stock. "I think he wound up with as much stock as Jobs and Markkula," recalls Peddle. "He had them by the shorties and he'd earned every penny of it. He absolutely put money into them when they needed money, he backed them, and he made Europe happen."

In the end, the departure from Tramiel was the best thing that could have happened to Souson. "Jack screwed him and this guy just made fucking millions - hundreds of millions," says Peddle. The dismissal also hurt Jack, who was never able to penetrate the French personal computer market with the P.E.T. computer.[6]

---

[6] The word *pet* means something else entirely in French. "Andre, who is a Frenchman, knew that pet in French is [fart]," explains Peddle. "So in France, it was always P.E.T., with dots." The association probably did not help Commodore's marketing effort.

CHAPTER

4

Releasing the PET

1977-1978

The West Coast Computer Faire awakened Jack to the possibility of a new personal computer business. Commodore was barely surviving the calculator wars and he was ready to use every tactic he knew to dominate this new industry. He would use resourcefulness, cunning, flexibility, secrecy, speed, positioning, surprise, deception, and manipulation. Any company not prepared to match Jack would find themselves slowly fading into oblivion.

Final Design

As the hardware design of the PET neared completion, Peddle realized he needed a software engineer. "I had to have somebody who could write the fundamental architecture," says Peddle.

Finding a skilled engineer in the wild, like Bill Seiler, was rare so Peddle tapped into a steady source of engineers. "When I was at Motorola doing the first computer class, there was this balding guy sitting at the back of the room," explains Peddle. "He introduced himself afterwards as Dr. Roger Camp from Iowa State University."

After Peddle's class ended, the two talked. According to Peddle, Dr. Camp told him he was on sabbatical. "It's a fucking professor!" exclaims Peddle. "He and I got to be friends somewhat at that point."

After Peddle left Motorola, he maintained contact with Dr. Camp, who continued to teach at Iowa State University. "I call him up and tell him I'm working on this personal computer," says Peddle.

Camp had already heard of the PET project when Peddle asked for a software architect. "I've got the perfect guy for you," replied Camp.

"He calls this guy up, but this guy says, 'I'm packed to go to IBM and I'm leaving this weekend,'" recalls Peddle. "Roger said, 'Listen, don't go until you've flown out to see this guy. He's crazy but I think you might like what they're doing.'"

When Feagans arrived in California, Peddle and Seiler tried to convince him not to go to IBM. "Bill Seiler and I sat down with him and we told him what we are doing," explains Peddle. The sales pitch worked, and Feagans ended up staying far longer than a weekend. "I think he stayed in that hotel for about three weeks," says Peddle.

"It was funny because about three weeks later IBM calls Dr. Camp and they said, 'We are really worried about this young man John Feagans because he was supposed to leave on this weekend to come and see us. We think he's been kidnapped!' Roger said, 'Well, he sort of has been,'" recalls a bemused Peddle.

Feagans was a brilliant addition to the PET team. "Every year after that, Roger would pick the smartest, weirdest kid in the class and send him to me," says Peddle.

Even though Feagans was reclusive, he was everything Peddle wanted in an engineer. "Feagans was an absolute loner," recalls Peddle. "He absolutely got into his code and spent all his time doing that. He stayed friendly with everybody but was really and truly distant."

Feagan's task was to write the code that resided in the ROM chips. "He wrote the system," explains Peddle. "He was the guy who wrote the glue." In essence, Feagans was creating the operating system.

The PET had many more functions than the KIM-1. As a result, the ROM was an enormous 18 kilobytes stored on seven 6540 ROM chips. It was up to Feagans to fuse the Basic editor, file commands, character set, and other sub-systems into a seamless operating system. The operating system would accept keyboard commands such as LOAD, RUN and SAVE in order to get and retrieve programs.

Feagans was determined to do things right. He even inserted a 1-kilobyte diagnostic routine into the ROM. Commodore technicians on the factory line used the routine to identify errors and validate the operation of newly assembled PET computers. The diagnostic routine ended up squeezing out the machine language monitor, which Peddle planned to include in ROM, but that was fine since Peddle believed machine language was beyond ninety percent of his users anyway.[1]

Contrasted to the random characters of the Apple II startup screen, Feagans' operating system was friendly as soon as the user turned on the

---

[1] Peddle included the machine language monitor on a cassette tape in North America.

power switch. The PET started up by communicating to the user that Basic was ready, with the message, '*** **COMMODORE BASIC** ***'. It then listed the available memory, told the user it was '**READY**', and presented a flashing cursor.

During this hectic period, Peddle encountered health problems. "Every so often I would go into what was the equivalent of a kidney stone being passed. It paralyzed me," recalls Peddle.

Peddle visited a physician, who informed him he was having gallbladder problems caused by the formation of large gallstones. "I had to have my gallbladder out," explains Peddle. Unfortunately, the doctor would not operate unless Peddle lost weight. "The doctor diagnosed me and said, 'I'm not going to touch your body until you lose 50 pounds.' He got me running and changed my life."

Peddle began a strict regimen of jogging, accompanied by the athletic Bill Seiler. "I took up running seriously because of the [impending] operation," says Peddle. The two jogged through the nearby Stanford University campus, where students saw two men out of breath as much from running as from their animated PET discussions.

One day, Peddle learned there was very little money to develop the PET. "Commodore was having serious, serious financial problems when we started off with the PET," explains Peddle. "The calculator stuff wasn't doing well and they were getting killed all the way around. Jack smartly never admitted he was broke."

One of the most expensive parts was the molded plastic case. "Even though he had made all these brags to me, he really couldn't afford the money to go tool a case that looked as pretty as [the wooden prototype]," says Peddle. "But he wouldn't admit it at the time."

Jack tried to sell Peddle on the idea of using a folded-metal case. "I said, 'I want to build the case out of plastic,'" recalls Peddle. The rounded, molded plastic case would have easily made the PET stand out from their competitors. It was a chance to take the lead and cultivate a reputation for Commodore as a stylish innovator.

"He said, 'Listen, we're going to build the case out of metal.' I said, 'But Jack, it doesn't fit what I'm trying to do at all.' He said, 'You don't know what people will buy, but I'm the boss, and we're going to build it out of metal.'" It was a difficult change to accept but there was little Peddle could do.

"Jack owned a company in Toronto, Canada that made file cabinets," says Peddle.[2] "We get on an airplane, go up to Toronto, and sit down

---

[2] Commodore was also producing low cost office furniture in the factory.

with these guys. They start tooling the metal, and they convinced Jack and Jack convinced himself that they could make something that looked almost as good as my pretty one. But it didn't."

Jack and Chuck also worked with the Canadians picking out color schemes for the computer. "The guys in Canada said, 'What color do you want?' I said, 'Fuck, I don't know. I think I want light colors.' Jack said, 'You know, we can paint them anything we want.' So we actually built 25 of about 10 different colors."

"There were black ones, and red ones, and yellow. I don't think we ever did pink ones," recalls Peddle. Yet another featured wood-panel trim around the monitor and keyboard; a popular look for seventies electronics. "The vote came down on the light blue with the light white."

For Jack, the move fit in well with his strategy for vertical integration. "His file cabinet business wasn't doing that good," explains Peddle. "So he got some business for that, and that's why the original PET was metal."

Peddle had already compromised once on the keyboard. Now he was giving up one of his principle design goals. "[I wanted] something friendly; spend the night with it; cuddly. That's why we didn't like the metal very much." Secretly, Peddle was becoming frustrated.

Although Peddle believes similarities between the PET 2001 and *2001: A Space Odyssey* are incidental, the look of the new PET case was very close to the production design of the film. The fictional ship, *Discovery,* is stark white, with trapezoid shapes, including the computer monitors. This matched the trapezoidal profile of the new PET case.

The associations of the PET 2001 and *2001: A Space Odyssey* became even more apparent when the Japanese designers presented their final keyboard. In the film, the buttons on the Discovery are mostly of blue and red, exactly the same coloring as the PET keyboard. The PET keys are also in a perfect grid, just like the button panels in the film. During the scene where HAL ejects astronaut Frank Poole into space, the screen displays the words 'computer malfunction' in upper case surrounded by a red background. Other displays, such as the vital signs of the astronauts, are in white surrounded by either red or blue rectangles. This is identical to the look of the space, shift, and return keys on the keyboard. Even the font of the keys is identical to the fonts used in the movie. The similarities seemed too coincidental.

The effect it had on buyers was undeniable. Richard Mansfield, an early PET 2001 owner and editor of Compute!'s Gazette, later described the PET as "a lovely, futuristic piece of work: a sleek gray cabinet, a glossy keyboard, and a nine-inch black-and-white monitor jutting above like the entrance to a space station."

However, Chuck Peddle believes no one intended to emulate the look of the film. "We were not copying 2001. We hadn't seen it for a long time," he says. "Probably we just both picked a popular font."

However, it seems improbable the similarities could have occurred by chance. Since the keyboard design went to Japan, it seems likely the designers noted the number 2001 in the name and decided to use the film for inspiration.

PET-2001 Keyboard.

Although the final metal PET case was not what Chuck Peddle wanted, it was still a remarkable design. Much like the hood of a car, the case lifted open on hinges to allow easy access to the interior of the computer. To hold the case open, a rod folded out to support the open case. It was simple and functional. In contrast, both Apple and Radio Shack had seals on their cases, and breaking the seal voided the warranty.

June CES

The West Coast Computer Faire was a show for hobbyists, allowing Commodore to connect with the grass roots of the computer movement. However, for mass-market penetration, Jack would take the PET to the summer *Consumer Electronics Show*.

The Consumer Electronics Show first debuted in 1967. Crowds at the show consisted largely of electronics manufacturers and dealers, and it was all business. The manufacturers created elaborate displays to highlight their latest electronics and set up orders, while the retail distributors walked the floors looking for exciting new products. No one had ever displayed a microcomputer at CES.

Commodore entered the video game market at CES. Pong machines were popping up in living rooms and basements all over the country, and Jack hoped to capture a part of this market. Commodore released two Pong consoles, the *TV Game 2000K* and *3000H*, both manufactured in Hong Kong. "All that gaming stuff was from [Al] Charpentier," says

Peddle. The systems were slightly ahead of others at the time since it included four-player pong complete with four controllers.[3]

Peddle wanted to transform the microcomputer into a true consumer product, right beside televisions and VCR's. By attending CES, Jack would do more to popularize the image of personal computers than any other figure in the industry.

Attending CES was no small expenditure for Commodore. The West Coast Computer Faire cost Commodore about $100,000 in flights, registration fees, and displays. In contrast, attending CES would cost close to half a million dollars. Unknown to everyone except for Jack and his inner circle, Commodore was almost out of money. "He never admitted it to me," reveals Peddle. "Chris [Fish] finally admitted it later. He said, 'Jack was absolutely broke! We were just dead broke. We needed every penny just to stay alive.'"

Unfortunately, Peddle and his team did not have a production model ready for June as they had hoped. "We took the computer to CES in June with just a prototype working," recalls Peddle. "It really wasn't ready to go." He also brought the different colored steel cases from Canada. Anyone who attended the show saw a rainbow of PET computers, including the wood-paneled PET.

On June 5, 1977, as *Three's Company* made its television debut in North America, the doors to CES opened. Most of the Commodore booth displayed calculators with a small section for PET computers. Commodore was the only microcomputer company at CES.

The PET was a curiosity at the show and garnered attention from the crowds, if not sales. The show also generated publicity for the PET. During the course of the show, Commodore's stock rose to 9 ¼. This was another signal to Jack and Irving that the personal computer held promise.

Being the first microcomputer company to explode onto the scene, Commodore was the key beneficiary of attention directed at microcomputers. Within a short period after CES ended, the press began generously covering the PET. Small news items appeared on local television shows, radio stations, and in newspapers and magazines.

However, for all the interest generated, the PET was still just a curiosity. Most of the large retailers were unsure if it was a marketable product and were unwilling to risk their careers by ordering shipments of the computer. "We had shown the product at CES but the computer dealers weren't really there, and the other guys weren't sure," says

---

[3] The Pong systems did not catch on. Pong fell out of favor following the release of the Atari 2600 and Commodore ended production.

Peddle. "It didn't get a great response." However, the interest they received from one person inspired Jack to survive the cash crisis.

"There was a guy in the Midwest who used to sell used computers. Big stuff," says Peddle, referring to bulky mainframe computers. "He saw the [PET] computer at the West Coast Computer Faire." Later, the same man approached him at CES. "The guy walked into my booth and said, 'I want to be the first customer. Here's a check for 25 thousand dollars. When you ship me that many, I'll give you another check.'"

The man was Rick Inatome, who later founded the pioneering *Inacomp Computers*. "Rick was one of the major players in the Midwest computer business," says Peddle.

The check stunned Jack. Normally, retailers placed orders and only paid when Commodore delivered the product. Here was someone who would pay large amounts of cash up front for a non-existent product, just so he could ensure his supply. The transaction caused Jack to reformulate his business plan.

Days after the show, Jack approached Peddle with his new idea. "Jack comes to me one day and he says, 'We're going to be like HP.' I said, 'Yeah, Jack, that's what I'm trying to do.'" However, Peddle misunderstood Jack's words.

"He said, 'No, you don't understand. Listen to me. When HP first came out with their calculator, they took advance sales where people had to send the money in and then they shipped to them within 90 days. That's what I mean about being like HP.'"

Peddle now laughs at the misunderstanding. "I've got this image I want to be like HP and I want my product to be professional," explains Peddle. "He doesn't mean that at all! He means the selling technique like HP. It doesn't matter to him what the product looks like. None of that matters to him."

Jack noticed the high demand, so he instigated a policy of advance payments, with a promise that customers would receive their computer in 90 days. The advertisement read, "Shipments of 8K units will begin in September 1977. Price $795." To make the contract legally binding, it included the phrase, "I attach my check for $795 in full payment. I understand that delivery will be within 90 days or I will get my money back." In truth, many would wait for up to six months for delivery, but few if any requested their money back.

Jack's idea saved the company. "We were so broke we could not bootstrap the company without that money," says Peddle.

The Death Knell of the Big Computer

A week after CES, Peddle was in Dallas, Texas for another exhibition. This time it was the *National Computer Conference*, held on June 13, 1977. The conference took place at the *Dallas Convention Center*, which had the equivalent of five football-fields worth of floor space for the 300 exhibitors. Displays were extravagant. The Data General exhibit comprised an entire planetarium capable of seating 50 people. The conference was three times the size of the West Coast Computer Faire, drawing in over 36,000 attendees.

The very first National Computer Conference was four years earlier, in New York City. The conference regularly attracted such distinguished speakers as Douglas Engelbart, the inventor of the mouse. Normally the conference was the domain of the larger computer companies. The industry commonly referred to the big eight computer companies as 'IBM and the seven dwarfs', which included Univac, Burroughs, Scientific Data Systems, Control Data Corporation, General Electric, RCA and Honeywell. Other major attendees at the show included Memorex, National Semiconductor, Datapoint, and Sperry.

Peddle remembers the experience. "It was in the middle of summer in Dallas," he recalls. "The first two floors of this big convention center are set up for all the big computer guys. It's a dog and pony show with IBM limousines and all that shit."

This year, however, the conference was trying out something new. "The guy came up with this idea for what he called the personal computer boutique," explains Peddle. Organizers created an exhibition hall just for microcomputer companies, which they called the *Personal Computing Fair*, held in a separate area below the main floor and away from larger computer companies. "He stuffed us down in the basement of this center," says Peddle. If the big computer companies had not been aware of microcomputers before, they would surely take notice now.

Peddle created a PET with eight kilobytes of memory. The new model was identical to the 4-kilobyte model, except for the additional four kilobytes. It would sell for a suggested retail price of $795.

Before the show, Jack had instructed Peddle and his wife Shirley to take preorders for the PET. It was the first trial of Jack's idea. "We were down in the basement and I've got four machines working literally the day before the show," recalls Peddle. "I finished them at the show."

Peddle also managed to persuade an editor from Electronic Engineering Times to cover the show. "We had gotten a lot of good publicity when we did the 6502," says Peddle. "I knew one of the editors real well and he said, 'What are you doing?' I told him about the computer and he

Releasing the PET – 1977 to 1978

said, 'It doesn't exactly fit with what we are doing but why don't I do an article on it?'"

"So he comes out and he takes this picture of my wife," explains Peddle. "She is built like Zsa Zsa Gabor. She's holding the computer and it wasn't intended to be a pinup, but it was."

The magazine later published the picture, which became popular with computer users. According to Peddle, "She would have people come to the show and ask her to please sign this thing, saying, 'I keep it in my office. Everybody will be totally jealous.'"

"She used to love it when people would come up," recalls Peddle.

The Commodore display was a simple counter with a white tablecloth surrounded by blue curtains. "We've got these four machines lined up on this counter top," recalls Peddle. "I had three or four people all operating the same program on the machines." Curiously, Commodore was still displaying the wooden PET prototype.

"We were just talking about the things you could do, and would give some easy demos," says Peddle. "I had Leonard there and people like that who were showing what you could do while I was giving the pitch."

Software was non-existent in 1977. "We had nothing; just trivial stuff," recalls Peddle. "We would show them you could program in Basic. This was way before software."

Although the PET had an IEEE-488 interface, Commodore had yet to make any peripherals such as printers and disk drives. Instead, Peddle connected the interface to an oscilloscope.

By the time he attended the National Computer Conference, Peddle had refined his sales pitch to an art form. In many ways, the engineer felt more like a performer. "In the beginning we just kind of showed them how the machine worked and they had to gather around," explains Peddle. "I'm giving these demos, standing up giving these pitches and getting them all excited."

The attendees saw the opportunity to own their own computer. "You've got to understand the hysteria that had built up over time," recalls Peddle. "They saw a packaged machine they could use."

At the end of his pitch, Peddle enacted Jack's preorder plan. "This is just like a medicine show. I would say, 'If you want to buy one, the pretty lady over here will take your money and we will ship to you in 90 days or we'll send you your money back.'"

To Jack's surprise, the crowds surged forward. "These people are five deep, handing checks forward, saying 'Put my check in first!'" recalls Peddle. "Jack was absolutely right. These people just fought to give my wife their checks. She would give them a receipt with a number on it that said that was the order in which we were going to ship to them."

72   THE SPECTACULAR RISE AND FALL OF COMMODORE

One of the first orders came from *Personal Software* founder Dan Fylstra, who ordered his PET at the National Computer Conference. Months later, Fylstra received unit number 17 and wrote a positive piece for Byte magazine.

"The crowd is so big and she's taking so long to collect the money that I got a half-hour break," recalls peddle. "So I take this opportunity to walk upstairs on the last day of the show."

The third floor contained the exhibits for the big computer companies. Peddle was shocked at what he saw "The entire floor above me was empty of customers," says Peddle. "All the big computer guys are sitting there talking to one another. There is nobody on the fucking floor."

"Meanwhile, you can't get into the boutique. Downstairs the guys who are supposed to be at the show are fighting one another to give me a check so they can get in queue. It was the death knell of the big computer."

Early advertisements of the period show Commodore going directly after the big computer companies. One brochure reads, "In a league with IBM, HP and Wang minicomputers. The PET should not be confused with game products that hook up to household T.V.'s. It is a minicomputer."

"If you had taken a snapshot at that show you knew what was going to happen to the computer industry. I was walking among the dinosaurs while they were dying. They had lost the momentum, and the momentum was building under their feet and they didn't have a fucking clue."

In September, with PET production beginning, stories of the PET filtered through many influential magazines. Byte magazine featured a write-up on the PET by Jeff Raskin. The fully integrated design of the PET must have influenced Raskin. Years later, he went on to design the Macintosh computer for Apple, one of the few desktop computers to include a built in monitor.

Peddle gave interviews to the media, along with his wife Shirley. "She got totally into this being a movie star," recalls Peddle. "We were interviewed on TV and all kinds of crap. We were like movie stars."

Peddle also noticed a subtle attack on computers from the media. "I had made a statement that computers were going to change the way the classroom worked and that they were going to be a very important part of the classroom," says Peddle.

A San Francisco station heard the comments and decided to create a controversial news story. "The local news channel in San Francisco found out when I was arriving from Toronto and met me at the airport with a camera," says Peddle. "They wanted to discuss this comment about schools. He said, 'Are you on record that computers are going to replace teachers?' I said it will augment teachers but not replace them."

The news station turned the story into a conflict between teachers and computers. "It turned out to be total bullshit," says Peddle. "They wanted to pick up on the line, so they took some pieces out of my quote. Then they ran this old school teacher saying kids still need the warm, loving attention of a school teacher to teach them how to do things."

The story provoked animosity against computers. "This was at a time when people didn't believe in computers very much," says Peddle. "They would take the piss out of computers on television. It was a hot topical comment."

The PET received better coverage in *Popular Science*, the magazine that launched the Altair 8800. The editors ran a feature listing the most popular microcomputers of the day, including the Altair 8080, the IMSAI 8048, the Processor Technology Sol, the CompuColor, and even the upcoming Radio Shack TRS-80.[4] The editors were impressed with the appearance of the PET and featured it on the cover. The image showed the PET sitting on a kitchen counter, with a recipe for Oriental Salad on the screen.

Jack's preorder strategy worked better than anyone could have imagined. In the months that followed, orders from magazine advertisements poured in, along with personal checks. According to *Fortune Magazine*, "The ads appeared, and a hugely encouraging $3 million in checks came back."[5] Commodore had survived another brush with death.

In early 1977, there were approximately 250 computer stores[6] and the number was rapidly growing. Commodore wanted to tap into these dealers to sell the PET.

Commodore had been receiving a measured number of dealer calls, mostly from those who attended CES and received Chuck's business card. After the Popular Science article, Commodore began to experience massive interest in the PET. On some days, the receptionist handled between 40 and 50 dealer inquiries. This was much more than Commodore had planned for, and soon Commodore could only promise shipments in four or five months.

To join the Commodore dealership program, dealers were required to have a service technician, a retail storefront, and a good credit rating. Once again, Jack hoped to leverage money any way he could in order to

---

[4] The virtually unknown Apple II was missing from the article.
[5] *Fortune* magazine, "Jack Tramiel is Back on the Warpath" (March 4, 1985) p. 46.
[6] Based on the number of Byte magazine's direct dealer sales outlets.

produce the PET computers. Dealers were required to send a cash deposit for their computers. Likewise, dealers collected prepayment for PET computers from their customers, just like Commodore. As a result, money flowed into Commodore before they assembled and shipped a single computer.

Manufacturing

With the production design finalized by July, Peddle and his team began manufacturing PET computers. Despite the incredible demand, there would be no large manufacturing plants dedicated to PET construction. Neither was there high-profile advertising. Irving would not allow it.

The prepayment plan allowed Commodore to survive but Tramiel wanted more than to survive. He wanted to dominate. Jack wanted large loans to quickly ramp up production, which would have satisfied both the customers and the ever-important dealers. Unfortunately, Irving did not hold the same philosophy.

Peddle recalls, "He was one of the things that frustrated Jack more than anything else in the world because Irving wouldn't let Jack go out and raise money." Without short-term capital, Commodore would limp out of the starting gate.

With a little advertising, Commodore could raise demand to incredible heights. Instead, Irving's restraint slowed down production. Commodore could not attain market share fast enough compared to their rivals. Irving Gould was about to lose Commodore's chance to grab a massive early lead in the North American market.

Perversely, Gould seemed to take pleasure in exerting control over Tramiel. According to a 1983 Forbes article, "He kept Tramiel on a very tight financial leash. 'I wouldn't give them enough money to take any real risks,' Gould says."[7]

According to Peddle, "Jack was not really justifying it. Jack was just saying, 'You know, you need to give me more money.' Irving's thought was, 'You've always done better when you didn't have a lot of money.'"

After a hard battle, Jack convinced Irving he needed a loan for a minimal factory setup. Gould signed for a $3 million loan. The loan funded three factories: one for Japan, one for Germany, and one for the United States. Since the Commodore US sales force had the lowest profile within Commodore International Limited, they would receive a bare minimum. "We basically took a little factory over on Reid Street just down near the airport in San Jose," says Peddle.

---

[7] *Forbes* magazine, "Albatross" (January 17, 1983) p. 48.

Releasing the PET – 1977 to 1978

To meet the low price-point, it was vital to get the best prices on all the parts going into the PET. The buyer for these parts was John Calton, who had been with Commodore since arriving as Irish immigrant in 1954.

As the longest-serving employee at Commodore, aside from Jack himself, Calton knew Commodore inside and out. He had absorbed Jack's philosophy and had risen to one of the most important ranks in the company. Calton's strategy for buying from outside vendors was simple: know their manufacturing costs before negotiating. Calton would meticulously research a company before even beginning to talk about price. As a result, Calton knew exactly how low the supplier could go. Calton was a key part of Commodore's ability to undercut their competitors' prices while remaining profitable.

In the 1970's, the manufacture of computers was not the same as the computer-automated assembly lines of today. Sitting on the clean, white tile factory floor were rows and rows of workbenches. Each bench had tool-racks filled with pliers, screwdrivers, and other equipment.

Here, workers sat hunched over circuit boards, stuffing them full of components. Parts came from all over the world. "He had a couple of manufacturing guys there," recalls Peddle. "We went into that building and started getting the cases out of Toronto and building the boards one at a time."

The process of printing a printed circuit board, or PCB, was similar to making a chip. A special light shone through a stencil, hardening a surface coating on the board. Peddle's team then washed the board with special chemicals, dissolving all the copper except for the designated electrical paths. Workers then drilled hundreds of tiny holes into each board, into which they would insert resistors, transistors, and IC chips. "We slowly set up a small production line," recalls Peddle.

Most of the factory workers were either Mexican or Korean immigrants, chosen because they worked for cutthroat wages. Workers would grab a resistor, bend it to shape, and insert the two wires into the appropriate holes on the circuit boards. Once the boards were full, they went to a flow-soldiering machine, which quickly bonded the parts.

According to Peddle, the cheap manufacturing budget caused problems. "We bought all these boards that had not been properly short tested," he recalls. "I remember we spent Christmas sorting our way through these shorted boards with low resistance ohmmeters. It was me, Seiler and a couple of other guys."

After each board was assembled, it was placed into one of the metal PET cases from Toronto, along with the monitor and tape unit. Then the lengthy testing period began. Workers placed each machine on a table with dozens of power outlets. The worker turned the machine on and executed the built in diagnostic routine. If any part failed, the worker opened up the case to hunt for the problem.

Once the technician confirmed the machine was working properly, the machine remained on for a period of 24 hours, known as the burn in period. If it lasted 24 hours, it was likely to last for dozens of years since the machine was solid state with no moving parts. Peddle was determined to earn Commodore a reputation for quality, even with such a limited budget.

In 1977, there was no need for a warehouse yet. "We weren't really in very heavy production until the next year," recalls Peddle.

By the end of 1977, Commodore was able to produce less than 30 machines per day using this technique; far below the demand. With frantic dealer calls coming in every day, it was an excruciating situation for everyone.

Not Enough to Go Around

In the summer of 1977, *Star Wars* appeared in movie theaters across North America. Suddenly, computers were cool and the public was primed for the PET 2001.

PET computers started trickling out of the small factory on Reid Street sometime in September 1977. It had taken Peddle and his small team less than a year to conceive, design, and manufacture their computer. The release coincided with much of the press coverage that had been building for the PET, since there was a three-month delay after CES for magazines to publish their coverage of the event.

Although there had been many orders for the 4-kilobyte PET, it became clear the memory was severely limiting. Commodore wisely began discouraging orders for the 4-kilobyte version and started pushing the $795 8-kilobyte version.

The opportunity to purchase a computer for personal use seemed incredible. Years earlier, the Pentagon had paid millions for their computer systems. Now, ordinary people could afford a $795 PET 2001 with similar capabilities.

Bill Gates, in a 1993 Smithsonian interview, saw the PET 2001 as a landmark machine for the pricing as much as the technology. "The Commodore machine, the PET, was actually the most aggressively-priced machine," he recalls. "It had some very innovative things."

One of the major questions of the period was what to name these new computer systems. They were definitely not *kit-computers*, nor were they *hobbyist computers*. The term *microcomputer* was no longer adequate to describe these easy to use, fully integrated computers. Some writers felt there was no distinction between the more expensive minicomputers from DEC and IBM, so they used the term *minicomputer* to describe the PET. Byte contributor Dan Fylstra tried the term *television-typewriters*, which he used to differentiate between computers with a picture tube and computers with simple lights.

Another early name was *appliance computer*, which gained some early acceptance due to a Popular Electronics cover of a PET 2001 sitting on a kitchen counter. Byte began using the term *personal systems*, which came close to describing the new computers. All these terms referred to the same thing, and eventually the term *Personal Computer* became accepted.

People were also not sure what to call people who used microcomputers. Byte magazine frequently used the word *computerist*, a clunky word that never caught on. Others used *computer hobbyist*, *enthusiast*, or *hacker*. Eventually *computer user* or simply *user* came to signify anyone who used a computer.

Technical publications were having their own problems understanding the technology. Popular Science, a magazine that should have known better, was sometimes comically wrong. The author of one of the earliest PET reviews (October 1977 Popular Science) did not understand the function of the cassette unit. He believed the tape player was for audio cassettes to teach the user how to use the computer. He also thought the black and white PET monitor would display photos, something that would only be possible years later on far more powerful computers.

The gadgets section of Playboy magazine (February 1978) featured an entire page dedicated to the PET. It included seven PET photos, and one photo even included the Playboy bunny logo in PETSCII characters. Playboy titled their article, 'Your Own PET Computer'. The friendly name by Andre Souson was having the desired effect.

Though reviewers universally praised the PET, they also noted the lack of a proper keyboard. It was obvious to the reviewer from *Electronics Today* that it would be difficult to type on the PET for sustained periods. The calculator keys did not produce enough tactile feedback, and users had to watch the screen carefully to verify input. The lackluster keyboard left an opening for competitors like Apple.

Despite the keyboard, Commodore clearly had momentum over the competition. The PET boasted a built in monitor, a built in data storage device, lower case characters and clear text. Users received everything they needed right out of the box. The PET was the first totally assembled, totally integrated computer with all the necessary components for software distribution and development.

Reviews for the PET and Apple II appeared in the March 1978 issue of Byte magazine. Future Personal Software founder Dan Fylstra wrote an in depth, nine-page review of the PET. Fylstra was impressed with the ease of use of the PET 2001 and gave it a favorable review.

In contrast, editor Carl Helmers labeled the Apple II a 'proof of concept' of the idea of a personal computer, but clearly thought the design needed to evolve further. In his ten-page review, he criticized the case, Steve Jobs only contribution to the Apple II, for its poor design. Helmers noted several mechanical problems that caused the fasteners of the top cover to break after a few uses. He also noted a problem keeping the keyboard moored to the case. Helmers also noted strong interference patterns on the television caused by radio frequencies inadvertently generated by the Apple II.

However, the review hinted that high-resolution capabilities held potential, once users began purchasing more memory. With memory prices so steep in 1978, most users did not equip their Apple II with enough memory to take advantage of the high-resolution graphics. If memory prices dropped, the Apple II could become a promising video game machine.

Commodore print advertising was conspicuously absent from many of the leading computer magazines of the time. MOS Technology had previously placed advertisements in all the leading computer magazines for the KIM-1, but following the acquisition by Commodore, advertising stopped. The lack of advertisements made Commodore look less substantial than Apple.

The slight must have angered the publishers, who relied on advertising to remain profitable. Instead, Jack expected free publicity from reviews. The misstep would soon cause magazines to ignore Commodore. In the early stages, however, Byte continued to cover Commodore products.

Despite some early problems, the PET was destined for success, and the stock market took notice. "Commodore's stock was running because people were starting to catch on that this is going to be a big deal," recalls Peddle. "Two or three months later, we're having trouble shipping and we're not shipping on time." Commodore began defaulting on their 90 day delivery guarantee, and Jack and Chuck became worried people might demand their money back. To Peddle's relief, "Nobody ever asked for their check back. Never."

However, some customers became impatient and aggressive. According to Peddle, "This guy comes wandering into the company and says, 'I'm an investment analyst. I'm going to go back to New York and tell the world you are lying about shipping computers. You are just a stock fraud.'"

"He says, 'You are another Viatron[8].' I said, 'Well gee, it's really not just for show. Let me take you to the factory and I'll show you I'm shipping machines.'"

The distraught analyst had ordered a PET and he gave Peddle his queue number. "His order was another two or three weeks away," recalls Peddle, who had become nervous about bad publicity. "I figured it out. I said, 'I'll tell you what. I'll put your number on this machine.'"

The gesture caused a sudden reversal in the demeanor of the New York analyst. "Suddenly he was the sweetest guy in the world! He was just there to give me shit so he could get his machine," says Peddle.

The analyst was satisfied and returned to New York. "The guy ultimately gives us a great recommendation and the stock runs," says Peddle. "*And* he goes and signs up as a dealer with us."

By the end of 1977, Commodore had only managed to assemble a meager 500 machines. "That's a funny volume level compared to today's world," remarks Peddle. In their review, Byte magazine commented on the poor availability of the PET. Commodore was not making the best of a good situation.

A New Kind of Market

Soon after PET computers started appearing in Mr. Calculator stores, an unexpected phenomenon began to occur. Kids and teenagers instinctively drifted towards the new PET. At first, this irritated the store managers, who thought the kids were preventing adults from using the machine.

However, Jack was quick to recognize this phenomenon and exploit it to sell more computers. As word began to filter back to Commodore, the marketing people formed a new sales tactic: get to the parents through the kids. Now, advertisements read, "Until now, parents interested in expanding their children's educational experience, turned to expensive encyclopedias. With the advent of the PET personal computer a new avenue of visual learning is now available for your youngsters for as low as $595." The advertisement concluded, "Your youngster will think he's playing, you'll know he's learning with the remarkable PET."

---

[8] In 1968, a company called Viatron tried to market personal computing with a product called the *Viatron Everything Terminal*. Viatron offered consumers access to a shared computer system for $39 a month, and like Jack, they began taking preorders for their service. By 1970, the company had $100 million in back orders, yet they had failed to deliver a product. The company soon folded with charges of fraud.

Chuck Peddle had little doubt his computer appealed to ordinary people. "These were people wanting a machine so bad they could taste it," explains Peddle.

Back in 1977, as a new user sat staring at the blinking cursor, the question was not, 'What can the PET do for me?' but more appropriately, 'What can I do for it?' Software was non-existent, so it was up to users to create software.

Perhaps the single standout came from Peter Jennings, creator of MicroChess for the KIM-1. "He was a very early developer and he wrote MicroChess, which was very important to us when we were selling the PET," explains Peddle. "Jennings was one of my first partners. We did shows together. We had dinners together. He was a very important guy in our lives."

Shortly after Commodore released the PET, Jennings ported MicroChess over to the PET. This was easy to do, since the PET used the same 6502 chip as the KIM-1. As an added advantage, the PET was swimming in memory compared to the KIM-1. Now, Jennings had access to four times the memory, giving him room to improve his chess-playing algorithm, as well as provide a graphical interface so the player could see the chessboard.

The first PET computers lacked a proper manual. This omission is surprising, considering the excellent documentation included with the KIM-1. The documentation included with the PET was scarcely a few photocopied pages with instructions for turning on the PET and some rudimentary BASIC programming commands. "We did a small manual immediately," recalls Peddle. "We taught them how to write the code and bring up Lunar Lander."

Chuck Peddle explains the reason for this omission. "We had a guy by the name of Gordon French who was supposed to write a better manual, but he didn't do a good job," reveals Peddle. Apple exceeded Commodore with their manual. "Jef Raskin wrote this absolutely great book for the Apple. That was one of the ways Apple got ahead."

A proper manual appeared in 1978. "We finally wrote some decent manuals by bringing in outside people to do the writing," says Peddle. Commodore eventually included Adam Osborne's 430-page manual with every PET.

The lack of documentation was distressing to most users, but user newsletters soon appeared, with names like *The PET Gazette*, *The Computerist*, and *The PET Paper*. The newsletters focused on Commodore, with news, hints on hardware, tutorials, and even full programs for users to type in and save. These early publications did not last long, but larger magazines later supplanted them.

Commodore International

Back in 1976, Commodore created Commodore International Limited (CIL) in the Bahamas. Underneath CIL were the divisions that made up the Commodore International army: Commodore Germany, Commodore Canada, Commodore Switzerland, Commodore Japan, Commodore Hong Kong, Commodore Business Machines (US), and Commodore UK. A general manager headed each country.

"Commodore was a European company when I joined them," says Peddle. "They were not doing that well in North America from a calculator standpoint but they were the definitive player in Europe."

Commodore employee Dave Haynie explains the company structure. "Commodore was run like a cellular company," he says. "Each cell did its thing, and ran fairly independently of the parent, CIL. This is why every company did marketing differently."

The international general managers met four times a year with Jack in order to discuss Commodore products and strategy. They enjoyed almost complete autonomy in their efforts to market products. Each country had control over their product distribution system, advertising, and packaging.

The cells were so autonomous they decided which products they would market. If Commodore made a product and the cells did not feel strongly about it, they could ignore it. "To get their product, each marketing company places orders, and Commodore fills them as best as they can," explains Haynie. "Commodore says, 'Here's a new product!' The marketing departments would order it or not order it. It was survival of the fittest and I think it worked well."

In the United States, the general manager was a tough executive named Dick Sanford. Sanford began his career as an accountant with *Arthur Anderson* until Commodore hired him. Sanford worked closely with Jack and pushed for the Commodore move into the Bahamas in 1976.

Dick Sanford started at Commodore as Company Controller. It was his job to act as the company hatchet man, laying off employees or management when the need arose. Sometimes he would ask managers if they wanted to resign, sometimes he would fire them outright if they were incompetent, or if there was a personality clash and Jack just wanted them to go, he would "prepare them" for a layoff. This meant setting them up for a fall, or as one Commodore employee put it, 'giving him enough rope to hang himself'. One way or another, if Jack wanted someone out, Sanford could arrange it in a legal manner.

When Jack promoted Sanford to General Manager, he controlled Commodore US in theory. In truth, that would be nearly impossible when Jack Tramiel was around. However, even among the General Managers, everyone recognized Dick Sanford as the second in command at Commodore.

After the release of the PET, Commodore took a clear early lead over the competition in Europe. "Commodore was just destroying Radio Shack and Apple," recalls Peddle.

Leading the charge into Asia was Commodore Japan, where Commodore owned a factory for building PET computers. "We also launched it in Japan because we built the product in Japan at the beginning," says Peddle.

The PET 2001 received acclaim at the Hanover Faire, winning Computer of the Year in 1978. "At the Hanover show in Germany, we had really incredible booths in the early days," says Russell. However, Germans were not as aware of the Commodore name as other countries. This created more of a challenge for Commodore West Germany's general manager, Harold Speyer.

Speyer ultimately brought success to Commodore with the PET computer. According to Peddle, "The Germans always pay more for their machines than anybody." Speyer increased the price and marketed the PET to the industry rather than home consumer users. Jack did not attempt to curtail this strategy, since in 1978 he was still feeling out the real market for microcomputers. Germans accepted the PET as a serious business machine.

The treasure of the Commodore empire was the British division, known as Commodore UK. The headquarters were located in an industrial estate 35 kilometers East of London in Slough, Berkshire at 675 Ajax Avenue. The offices were old and worn, with walls painted a dull yellow. Many offices had windows that pointed not outward to the English countryside, but inward towards storage aisles and calculator assembly lines.

Despite the drab workplace environment, Commodore UK was teeming with enthusiastic, motivated people. Their motivation came not from large benefits and material goods, but from the privilege of working for one of the Commodore's best managers, Kit Spencer. "He started in the sales and advertising area," says Leonard Tramiel.

Christopher Spencer, known as Kit to those around him, was the sales and advertising manager of Commodore UK. Born during the height of World War II, Kit was hard driven, competitive, charismatic, and loved by his employees.

With his slim, athletic build, Kit took his natural desire to compete into sports. "He liked to play tennis," says Leonard Tramiel. Spencer played at a competitive level, holding trophies at several levels and even competing in the Junior Wimbledon tournament.

Spencer had been with Commodore since 1974, when the brutal calculator wars threatened Commodore's existence. At the time, he was in charge of the UK marketing operation. While Commodore watched most of its calculator market shrink in the U.S. and Japan, Kit steadily built up market share in the UK. His brilliant dealer promotions and retail advertising were largely responsible for the success.

Kit's secret was his unwavering work ethic. The manager worked side-by-side with his employees, using his experience to formulate the UK marketing strategy. Kit did everything, including the creation of presentations, advertising slogans, press releases, interviews, and newsletters. He did it all and he did it fast, resulting in a steady increase in market share.

There was a sense of youthful fun in the UK offices, something not present in the US offices. Commodore UK employees derived a large degree of satisfaction from what they were engaged in, and this was no accident. Commodore UK had a strategy of hiring hobbyists. The young staff loved to come into work each day, since Commodore paid them for doing something they would do without pay.

The Commodore brand name, which Kit had steadfastly built up over the years, was a significant asset in the UK. Commodore had an excellent reputation for quality, innovation, and low prices from their calculators. In fact, most people either owned a low cost Commodore calculator or knew someone who did.

Jack knew the PET demand was high and predicted that in the UK, demand would outstrip production. As a result, Jack decided to raise the price of the PET 2001 for the European market from $795 to the equivalent of $1295. Jack hoped the English would be amenable to the increased price. As Peddle comments, "The English are poor but they buy decent products."

Commodore UK would rely on PET computers assembled in the US, Germany, and Japan. In April 1978, the first machines began arriving on British soil.

The Commodore PET was an immediate success in the UK. Britons loved the PET computer. Among them was British science fiction author Douglas Adams who later wrote, "I remember the first time I ever saw a personal computer. It was at Lasky's, on the Tottenham Court Road, and it was called a Commodore PET. It was quite a large pyramid shape, with a screen at the top about the size of a chocolate bar. I prowled around it for a while, fascinated."[9]

---

[9] Douglas Adams, *Salmon of Doubt* (Harmony, 2002) p. 91.

Because of the aggressive marketing campaign and well-oiled dealer relationships, Commodore was able to capture close to 80% of the microcomputer market in Britain. Spencer actually sold more computers in the United Kingdom for a higher price than Jack could in the much larger US market. Germany also managed to capture 80% of their microcomputer market using similar tactics.

Forbes magazine pinpointed the key to success in Europe. "...Commodore did better in Europe, where it had a ready-made distribution system from its adding machine days. Priced at $1,295 in Europe – vs. the $795 price in the U.S. - the PET had sufficient margins to be supported aggressively."[10] With a heavy advertising push, Spencer sold over 30,000 machines in the first year. Since Peddle designed the PET 2001 to sell for only $795, the profit margin was astronomical.

Although the immediate success in Europe benefited Commodore, it actually hurt Commodore US, since Jack decided to channel their resources away from the US market. "In North America, Jack wasn't pushing as hard, because we had limited ability to make product and we sold them for more in Europe," says Peddle. "If you've only got limited resources, which we always had, you focus on where you make the most money."

Even in the midst of success, Irving Gould was not willing to raise money on the stock market to reinvest in Commodore. "Commodore went public, the stock really just kept running, but Commodore never picked up any of that money," says Peddle. Instead, Irving made Jack rely on profits and occasional loans to run the company.

"We had US presence but no where near what we had in Europe," concludes Peddle. Although the US did not have the same success, the PET continued to sell well in the United States and dominated the competition in the first year or two.

One of the biggest successes turned out to be the stock analyst from New York. "He became one of our biggest dealers in the United States," says Peddle. Peddle saw the extraordinary sales figures of this one dealership and decided to investigate the secret of his success.

"I just wanted to drop in on him in New York. He's selling them in a basement right off Wall Street," recalls Peddle. To his surprise, the first thing he saw in the basement was his competition. "They've got Apples stacked everywhere. People are coming in and buying Apples."

"I said, 'You're moving a lot of Commodore's. Where are they?' He said, 'Well, I keep them out back,' or something like that. It turns out he wasn't selling any Commodores in the United States. He was getting

---

[10] *Forbes* magazine, "Albatross" (January 17, 1983) p. 48.

them at a cheaper price than they could in Europe and he was bootlegging them into Europe."

As Peddle later found out, the dealer began selling PET computers exclusively in the United States but soon discovered a grey market in Europe. "He worked that scam out later," says Peddle. The dealer began ordering extra PET computers just for the European market, and then stopped selling PET computers in the United States altogether. The situation hurt Kit Spencer, since dealers in the United Kingdom began ordering computers from American dealers rather than Commodore UK.

Commodore also introduced the PET into other European markets, but not all. "The Spanish weren't a big market at that point, although later on they became an enormous market," says Peddle. However, Commodore was able to penetrate into most of the smaller Western European nations. "The Scandinavians absolutely paid good prices," says Peddle.

One of the most interesting battles in Europe was in France between Commodore and their former ally, Andre Souson. Souson established Apple in Europe by creating *Euroapple*. He tried to win over customers by attending the same trade shows as Commodore but Commodore dominated the small Apple booths. According to Peddle, "One of the reasons they didn't do better against us is that Andre wasn't playing with the kind of money we were willing to play with."

Apple was an unknown name in Europe, and it would take serious resources to compete against the already established Commodore name. As a result, the Apple II had to compete with technology and price alone. Price conscious buyers saw it for what it was: an overpriced computer lacking many of the most important features present in the Commodore PET. The only region Apple was able to defeat Commodore was in Souson's home country of France.

CHAPTER

The Trinity

1977 - 1979

For a brief period, it seemed as though Commodore might dominate the personal computer industry. The PET 2001 easily surpassed the first generation computers from MITS, IMSAI, Ohio Scientific, and Processor Technology. However, in the same year Commodore released the PET, the competition released the Apple II and the Radio Shack TRS-80. Byte magazine later dubbed the competitors the *1977 Trinity*.

Engineer Bob Yannes witnessed the dawn of the personal computer while working in a computer store. "The big breakthrough, which came with the PET and the TRS-80 (and to some extent the Apple II, although I won't give them as much credit as they want), was the fully assembled computer," remarks Yannes.

Chris Crawford, an early game designer and PET owner, summarizes the 1977 Trinity. "A lot of people don't realize that the Apple got off to a slow start. In the early days, the horserace was between the PET and the TRS-80," says Crawford. "The Apple was nowhere to be seen. It was too expensive to sell."

The first two years of personal computer sales marked a period of slow production for all three companies. Even Byte magazine, the largest computer magazine at the time, had difficulty obtaining computers to review in a timely fashion. Even though Commodore and Apple began taking orders in June 1977, the reviews both appeared in March 1978.

Growing an Apple

At Apple, chairman Mike Markkula, who had already invested $250,000 of his own cash in the company, began transforming

Apple into a professional company. "Mike Markkula is a marketing genius," says Peddle, who credits Markkula over Steve Jobs with Apple's initial success. "He was the guy that was tying the company together and he brought in Regis [McKenna]."

Regis McKenna, a former Intel advertising executive, was responsible for Apple's early advertising. "Regis hit on this great idea of making these two guys in the garage and how wonderful they were," explains Peddle. "Mike Markkula and Regis McKenna created the Apple legend in a very careful, controlled, PR way."

Without the two former Intel executives promoting Apple, Jobs and Wozniak did not stand out from other computer hobbyists of the time. "There were six guys who did kit computers at the same time or ahead of them," says Peddle. "Woz and Steve would have wandered off into the sunset and you never would have heard of either one of them except Mike Markkula fell in love with them."

Of the two founders, Steve Jobs was easy to sell to the public. "Steve [Jobs] is a very, very charismatic guy," recalls Leonard Tramiel. However, the mediocre sales of the Apple I computer, a period before Markkula and McKenna, testifies to his lack of results compared to other kit computers. "It's really easy to get carried away with what he is saying, but as far as actually producing sales and making money and selling machines, Commodore did a far better job than Apple," says Leonard.

Although Steve Jobs was a natural, Steve Wozniak lacked a compelling persona. "If you were to read the literature during that time, you will discover that [McKenna] probably took Woz to two places and then dumped him because Woz just didn't come across as smart and interesting," recalls Peddle.

In May 1977, Apple moved into their first company headquarters in Palo Alto, close to Commodore. McKenna launched Apple's first advertisement in Byte magazine in July 1977, a month after Commodore sold their first PET computers. In comparison to the amateurish advertising of other computer makers in the 1970's, early Apple magazine advertisements are clean and refined.

Apple's marketing impressed Leonard Tramiel, who today recognizes Apple as the pioneer in personal computer marketing. "As far as I'm concerned, Apple invented marketing," says Tramiel.

The Apple II manufacturing process was comically stone aged compared to Commodore. "They didn't have funding," explains Peddle. Since Apple did not have the money to set up a factory line, workers assembled Apple II motherboards from their homes. An enterprising woman named Hildegarde Licht stopped by Apple in her white van to pick up boxes of parts and components. During the day, she drove around Silicon Valley dropping off the boxes and picking up completed circuit boards. This haphazard system probably accounted for the high failure rates of early Apple computers.

In August 1977, Byte had a full cover picture of Isaac Newton sitting under an Apple tree. Unfortunately, it had nothing to do with Apple computers. When people mentioned Apple and computers together, they were usually talking about the APL programming language, which many people just pronounced Apple. In 1977, customers greeted the debut of the Apple II with silence.

While Commodore was receiving dozens of dealer inquiries per day, Apple was selling less than five computers per day. In the months that followed, Apple received about three hundred orders for the Apple II. The results were promising compared to the sales of the Apple I but disappointing compared to Commodore and Radio Shack.

Part of the reason for the lack of Apple II sales was due to the unfinished state of the Apple II. Bob Yannes explains, "The Apple II was fully assembled but it did not have a TV output because they couldn't get around the FCC emissions problems." The Federal Communications Commission regulated, among other things, radio signals. Unfortunately, the Apple II emitted strong radio interference signals, which the FCC does not allowed in consumer devices.[1]

To get around the rules, Apple pretended they did not intend the Apple II for the home market. According to Yannes, "They basically said, 'Okay, this is a data processing device and therefore the Class A FCC rules apply to it (the more relaxed rules) because this is going to be used in an industrial environment and not in a home.' They couldn't put an R/F modulator in it to hook to your TV set because obviously that was something for the home."

Without an R/F modulator, the Apple II was too complicated for inexperienced users. "The PET and the TRS-80 both came with their own monitors, so they a more appropriate solution for most people than the Apple II was," says Yannes.

The original design by Steve Wozniak also had several flaws. "Right after the Apple II came out, Electronic Engineering Times wrote a story about the three major design flaws that Woz made on the Apple II,"

---

[1] The FCC has two requirement levels, *Class A* and *Class B*. A computer that meets the FCC Class A requirements may be marketed for use in an industrial or a commercial area. A system that meets the more stringent FCC Class B requirements may be marketed for use in a residential area in addition to use in an industrial or a commercial area.

reveals Peddle. "He didn't understand the ways the [6502] chipset worked and some other electronics stuff."

In response to these problems, Apple hired an engineer to redesign Wozniak's motherboard. "There was a guy who was hired at Apple to redesign the Apple II and make it real engineering without offending Woz," explains Peddle. "He basically went through and redesigned the product. Woz was a technician; he wasn't a real engineer."[2]

The other disappointing feature of the Apple II was the lack of a decent Basic programming language. The Apple II relied on Integer Basic, which was inadequate for business use. "Three months after we are both in production, Markkula comes up and they buy Apple Basic from Microsoft," recalls Peddle.

"Gates again got a fixed price but higher [than Commodore]," explains Peddle. How much did Apple pay for their Basic? "Gates at this point effectively took our number and doubled it for Apple." [i.e. $20,000]

Peddle believes the computers appeared at roughly the same time. "Both of us were in similar timeframes. They had to redesign and put the Apple Basic in after that," he says. Perhaps most telling is Byte magazines conclusion in a November 1982 article, which credits the PET as the first personal computer.

By the end of 1977, Apple had sales of $775,000 for the fiscal year, which included sales of the Apple I. This clearly put Apple in third place, after Radio Shack and Commodore.

Despite their third-place standing, Regis McKenna was determined to promote Apple as the clear winner. "Apple did a great job of promoting the success of their product, whether it existed or not," says Leonard Tramiel. "I know that through that entire time, Apple had ads claiming that they were number one, where in fact they weren't. Every month, they had an ad asking the question, 'Why is Apple number one in the world of Personal Computers?' And the answer of course was because they were number three, behind Radio Shack and Commodore. They just lied."

Through 1978, Apple continued gaining sales. One of Apple's earliest breakthroughs, and one of Commodore's earliest errors, occurred with the largest computer dealer in the United States, *ComputerLand*.

ComputerLand stores initially sold mainly hobbyist computer systems, such as IMSAI, Proc Tech, Polymorphic, Southwest Tech, and Cromemco. The release of the 1977 Trinity should have brought both

---

[2] Wozniak flunked out of the University of Colorado. He later went back to university and became a full-fledged engineer.

Commodore and Apple into ComputerLand stores.[3] However, an early misstep by Jack Tramiel prevented the PET from receiving wide distribution in their outlets.

ComputerLand ordered all computers for their franchises. Their business model required favored pricing to remain profitable, but Jack refused to give them a deal. ComputerLand was not happy.

As a result, ComputerLand decided to promote Apple II computers instead of the PET. In December 1977, ComputerLand advertised the Apple II computer with 4 kilobytes of RAM for $1,298 or $1,698 with 16 kilobytes of RAM. The franchise eventually became a hit, and success for the franchise meant success for Apple. As ComputerLand spread across the continent, so did Apple. Though ComputerLand could not hope to match Radio Shack's proliferation, it gave Apple a solid market from which to build.

Between Mike Markkula at Apple and Jack Tramiel at Commodore, it was clear Apple respected the computer retailers more. In a 1993 interview, Bill Gates identified this strength. "Apple ... really went out to computer dealers and did a good job, far better than people like the MITS guys and the IMSAI guys. They really thought of this as a market where they had to develop the channel and do new things."

The Trash-80

The undisputed leader for the first several years was the TRS-80 from Texas based *Tandy Corporation*, owners of the Radio Shack chain of stores. John Roach, the man who viewed Chuck Peddle's PET 2001 prototype at the January 1977 CES, led Radio Shack into computers.

According to the official Radio Shack history of the TRS-80, a Radio Shack employee named Don French initially conceived the idea of selling computers through Radio Shack in 1976. By December 1976, the designers had the official go-ahead to develop a computer for Radio Shack. This version of history seems peculiar, since Roach gave Commodore a bid for the computer contract at the January 1977 CES. Perhaps John Roach had not intended to use the PET at all and just wanted to evaluate the competition. According to the history, engineers finished their handmade prototype by January 1977.[4]

---

[3] ComputerLand could not sell Tandy machines because Radio Shack stores sold TRS-80 computers exclusively.

[4] At least two other companies received bids for the Radio Shack computer: Sphere Corporation and Microcomputer Associates. In later years, Michael D. Wise of Sphere claims Radio Shack lifted parts of his design. Ray Holt of

The prototype ended up costing Radio Shack less than $150,000 to develop, including case tooling. The marketing department assigned the computer an overly optimistic $199 price tag and conservatively predicted sales of 3,000 units annually.

The Radio Shack computer had similar features to other computers of the day. The microprocessor was a Z-80, an 8-bit microprocessor made by a company called *Zilog*. The computer featured 4 kilobytes of RAM (expandable to 16 kilobytes), 4 kilobytes of ROM, a 53-key keyboard, a 12" black and white RCA video display, and a cassette recorder.

According to Chuck Peddle, the design was lacking compared to the PET due to the ROM size. "We built in a big enough ROM to get all the Basic, the operating system, and all that stuff in ROM which was one of the key things to make it work," says Peddle.

Commodore achieved early success with their ROM chips and outclassed the competition. "We could get some really high density ROM's, so we gambled on a much bigger ROM than Radio Shack did, which ultimately caused them a lot of trouble." As a result, the TRS-80 lacked many features in the PET, such as lower case characters.

Radio Shack increased the price of the TRS-80 to $599.95. Unlike the integrated PET, the TRS-80 was modular and buyers could purchase the components individually; the microcomputer for $399.95, the video display for $199.95, and the cassette recorder for $49.95.

On Wednesday, August 3 1977, company president Lewis Kornfeld unveiled the TRS-80 Model I in New York City's Warwick Hotel. "The TRS-80 wasn't a bad computer. It had a number of nice features," says Yannes.

By the time Radio Shack released the TRS-80, Peddle had enjoyed sales since June 1977 and even had some software to demonstrate for the PET. "We showed Microchess at the east coast faire when Radio Shack launched their computer," says Peddle.

At the time of the introduction, Radio Shack had only managed to build 25 TRS-80 units, which was fine since they had predicted annual sales of only 3000 units. Radio Shack planned to release the computer to a third of their 3,500 company owned stores. Although there was virtually no press coverage of the release, the marketplace responded overwhelmingly. More than 10,000 orders came in within a month of the introduction. Radio Shack had a hit on their hands.

The response to the TRS-80 not only surprised Tandy, but also Commodore and Apple. Apple had always thought it was in a race with

---

Microcomputer Associates (who wrote the ROM software for the KIM-1), also believes the prototype he offered was reverse engineered.

Commodore. Commodore thought it was a race against IBM. Radio Shack showed both companies it was a race for mass distribution. "Radio Shack [success] was understandable because they had Radio Shack stores to sell them through," explains Yannes.

Radio Shack was in every city and mall in North America where the entire population of North America could see it. Once shoppers caught a glimpse of the curious new machine, they could not resist dipping into the Radio Shack store to learn more. After a few minutes at the keyboard, many walked away dazzled by the promise of computers. It was a powerful marketing tool.

Bill Gates, in a 1993 interview with the Smithsonian, concludes, "Radio Shack, with its distribution and its name, set the market on fire."

Though Commodore started strong in North America, any advantage they had was soon lost. By the end of 1978, they had managed to sell approximately 4000 PET computers in North America (according to Byte magazine). In contrast, Radio Shack sold over 55,000 TRS-80 computers in their first year of production.

All Commodore had to compete with Radio Shack were Mr. Calculator stores. Mr. Calculator was not really working out for Commodore and they could not hope to match Radio Shack in both distribution and expertise. The only good news for Commodore was that Radio Shack was also having problems manufacturing the systems fast enough to match their orders. For a long period, each Radio Shack store received only one TRS-80 to sell.

Users affectionately called the TRS-80 the Trash-80 for some of its quirks and limitations. The tape system was a horror to use and the Z-80 microprocessor was not even running at full speed. The monitor also displayed incredible static due to a lack of proper shielding.

The Basic language in the Radio Shack computer was also inferior to the PET. "John Roach introduced his computer with Tiny Basic [a free Basic developed in California] because his ROM wasn't big enough," says Peddle.

John Roach soon decided he needed to improve the Basic language in the TRS-80. "He was trapped and he actually went to Gates," says Peddle. "We were kicking his ass, and Apple was kicking his ass because Basic was what people were buying."

"Now [Bill has] got John and he sees that things are going so he figures he's worth more, because he knows John has got to compete with us," recalls Peddle. "So he doubles the [Apple price]. Roach basically says 'I don't want to pay you that number. I don't know how many of these we are going to sell. Why don't you take a piece of the action.' Gates said, 'No, I want a fixed price.' That was the last time Bill took a fixed price."

Although Gates missed lucrative royalties, he was triumphant nonetheless, having sold his premier programming language to all of the 1977 Trinity. "These machines drove the market and eventually, a year after they were out, all of them had our BASIC built-in," recalls Gates.

Radio Shack continued to dominate both Commodore and Apple for the remainder of the seventies. They later refined their design and delivered the TRS-80 Model II on May 30, 1979, which was state of the art for the time. By the end of 1979, Radio Shack had sold over 150,000 TRS-80 computers, giving them approximately 35% of the personal computer market. With new peripherals like disk drives and printers, users could spend as much as $4,000 for a complete system. In 1979, computer equipment sales were over $100 million according to Tandy, or approximately 12.7 percent of Radio Shack's North American sales. It seemed like Radio Shack was unstoppable.

A Real Keyboard

After the surprise success of the PET, it was clear Peddle had done much to reverse Commodore's ailing revenues. He was justly walking confidently through the hallways of Commodore and people took notice. "The official inside Commodore joke is that [PET] stood for Peddle's Ego Trip," says Peddle.

Commodore encountered problems almost immediately after the introduction of the PET into Europe. Improbably, another company reserved the PET name. Electronics behemoth *Philips*, based in the Netherlands, was just about to release a professional computer, which they called the *Programm Entwicklungs Terminal* (Program Development Terminal). Though it would not pose a threat to the Commodore PET, Philips legally held the rights to the acronym PET. Jack picked his fights carefully and he was not about to tangle with a massive company like Philips. Commodore changed the name to CBM, hoping to elicit comparisons to IBM.

Peddle was determined to transform the PET into a serious business machine. "The product took off, except the universal response was, 'We want a regular keyboard,'" he recalls.

Peddle convinced Jack to replace the calculator keyboard with a full sized keyboard. "He was reactive enough and we said 'Okay, that didn't work. We'll put another one out,'" says Peddle.

Peddle also added a simple speaker to the new PET design, giving it the same sound capabilities as the Apple II.

The larger keyboard took up more space, so Peddle removed the cassette unit. Instead, Commodore introduced a separate product, the *CBM C2N Cassette Drive*, for a retail price of $95.

94   THE SPECTACULAR RISE AND FALL OF COMMODORE

To Peddle's horror, the original PET 2001 had a bug which the engineers had been unable to isolate. "Every so often the machine would go off into Never-Never Land because it would be doing a computation," explains Peddle.

Leonard Tramiel, who used a PET computer for his studies, finally solved the mystery. Peddle recalls, "Leonard found it by virtue of being bored while he was living at Columbia University."

Leonard diligently tried to reproduce the reported bug and finally cornered it. He explains, "I diagnosed it down to a sample program that [reproduced the bug.]"

Surprisingly, the bug originated in code written by Bill Gates himself. "Bill wasn't that familiar with the 6502 architecture," says Peddle.

Microsoft corrected the bug and Commodore released a new version of the ROM code, called Upgrade Basic[5] (later renamed Basic 2.0). The most important aspect of BASIC 2.0 was that it allowed a disk drive. Even though Commodore did not yet produce a disk drive, it was something they intended to release shortly.

In late 1978, Commodore began churning out upgraded PET computers. There were two models: a non-business version with PETSCII characters on the keys and a business model without PETSCII characters. Commodore released them as the PET 2001-N and the PET 2001-B series.

The new models were expandable to 32 kilobytes. Users could purchase models with 8, 16, or 32 kilobytes of memory. As a result of Peddle's changes, the PET and CBM line became the most business oriented computers of the 1977 Trinity.

Made in Japan

Peddle planned to make use of the IEEE-488 interface. "I was trying to build a machine that could be used for business and I also knew people who needed word processing," explains Peddle. "I wanted a cheap printer."

If Peddle could dominate the Word Processing market with the PET, he could take a dramatic lead over the competition. "Apple wasn't playing in the printer market," recalls Peddle. Since the PET 2001 had lower case letters (something the other two computers in the 1977 Trinity lacked) it would give the PET a clear advantage as a business computer.

---

[5] Basic 2.0 contained an Easter egg that caused the word MICROSOFT! to be printed on the screen. According to Jim Butterfield, when Leonard Tramiel heard this he said, "Those bastards! I told them we need every byte of memory we could get and they throw in junk like that!"

Peddle approached *Centronics*, a North American printer manufacturer. "There's a Centronics port on your machine," explains Peddle, referring to the parallel port on many modern PC's. "The printer port is called a Centronics port. It was defined by this company called Centronics, who was at that time the leading minicomputer printer supplier."

"I went to the guy who was in charge of the company," recalls Peddle. "I remember sitting with him in New York and talking about the fact that personal computers are going to sell millions and they were not going to sell millions at the price he was charging for printers. If he wanted to make things that sold in the millions, he had to reduce his costs."

Peddle offered Centronics a deal. "We were willing to sit down with him and design a new printer, along with him, using our [6502] microprocessor," explains Peddle. Microprocessor technology, especially using a 6502 chip, would drastically reduce the price of Centronics printers. "At that time, he may not have even had a microprocessor; he might have had discrete control. We could go in and make some serious cost reductions for him and get him a lot of volume."

However, the response was not what Peddle hoped. "He basically looked me in the eye and said, 'I don't need to do that. I've got the world, I've defined a standard, and I know what I'm doing. I don't need to be any more competitive than I am now. Everybody will come to me and pay my price.'"

Centronics missed a deal worth millions. "I specifically said to him, 'What you just did was to force me to ruin you. I'm going to go find a supplier that wants to be a player in the millions market. He's not one of the guys you are playing against today but he's going to eat you. Are you sure you don't want to reconsider?'"

Peddle's dramatic prophesy had no effect. "He was clear. 'I don't have to, I don't want to, and I'm not going to.' It was an American company, an American product, and all the flag waving you want," he says.

Peddle was incensed that a company would turn down a lucrative offer. "I'm pretty ticked off because we really need a low cost printer if we want to make the market really take off," he says. Peddle had no option but to align with the Japanese and teach Centronics a lesson in free market competition.

Jack called on his Japanese contacts to find an appropriate manufacturer. Commodore had a long history with Japanese partnerships. "We were using Japanese [cassette recorders] and we were using Japanese monitors so Japan was a real important part of our program," explains Peddle. "Jack knew the people at Epson/Seiko pretty well because they had been buying calculator stuff from them."

The two Japanese engineers in California once again proved their worth. "[Mr. Fujiyama] set up the meeting and we met the guy who designed the LCD watch; a really, really wonderful guy from Japan," recalls Peddle. The two talked, and Peddle proposed the Japanese would supply the printer head mechanism while Peddle would design the electronics.

"He basically supported me on the program in terms of getting a mechanism," says Peddle. "They had a 20 or 30 column adding machine printer." Twenty columns was fine for calculator output on rolls of paper, but Peddle needed something to print to standard paper up to 8 ½ inches wide. "He agreed to make an 80 column carriage."

Peddle made sure his business dealings with Epson-Seiko would not create additional competition for Commodore. He requested a promise from Epson to stay out of the personal computer business. "They told me they weren't going to go into the computer business," explains Peddle.

The Japanese were enthusiastic to strike a deal compared to the reluctant Centronics. "So I sat down and designed the electronics using my microprocessor," says Peddle "I handed him the design and an order for a large number of the printers."

Commodore allowed Epson freedom of access in Japan. "During this time they had been working with us, they had been going into our factories," recalls Peddle. "They had understood what we were doing and the way we made the computers. We were meeting with these guys and they were charming, smart, and really supportive." It was too good.

"At this point, we want to start talking about how we are going to do some volume business," says Peddle. "It was an early product and there were some issues we wanted to deal with, so we scheduled a trip to the factory which was out in the mountains outside of Tokyo."

Months later, Peddle arrived in Tokyo to visit the factory. "You go out on this little train," recalls Peddle. "We're staying at this Japanese inn where you go in and your bath is a dip bath; there's no shower. We're eating Japanese food, and they've got the karaoke bars."

"Two things happened that day. One, in the railroad station I had bought a handheld computer made by Seiko, after they told me they weren't going to go into the computer business." The discovery surprised Peddle, who believed Epson/Seiko had promised not to compete with Commodore for the personal computer. "So here they have a handheld computer running Basic. It's not a direct competitor, but you know, it's kind of a pretty good indicator they were thinking about it. I said, 'I want to sit down and discuss this.'"

"I'm ready to go in and visit the factory," continues Peddle. "Well, they wouldn't let me into the factory building my printer." Peddle found the refusal humiliating. "They said, 'There's company rules against anybody coming in and visiting our factory.' I was very upset. I'm dealing with this guy who is one of the worlds biggest patent holders. He's a very straight guy, but he just basically said, 'I talked to my Japanese people and they had made the decision that the Americans weren't going to steal from them, they were going to steal from the Americans.'"

Although Peddle's treatment in Japan left a bitter taste, Epson delivered exactly as promised. "The people at Epson did in fact build a low cost printer and did help us to develop the market," concludes Peddle. "We shipped a lot of Epson printers."

Commodore used an OEM arrangement with Epson. This meant Commodore purchased the printers from Epson and branded the printers with the Commodore insignia. The first printer was the CBM 2020 printer, released in 1978, which was almost as tall and as heavy as the PET computer itself. The 2020 printed upper case, lower case, and PETSCII character graphics. In 1979, Commodore released the CBM 2022 and 2023 printers, which sold for $795.00 and $695.00 respectively. These were true dot matrix printers, allowing text and graphics output, much like inkjet printers.

Epson decided to expand their market for computers beyond the IEEE-488 interface. "They did a version with the Centronics interface," recalls Peddle. The cheaper Epson printers dominated the costly Centronics printers. "We absolutely put Centronics out of business[6] and we put Epson in the business because the guy at Centronics wouldn't cooperate."

Epson also released a personal computer system on the international market in 1982. "They went into the business of competing with us," says Peddle. Were their actions a little duplicitous? "What do you mean a little duplicitous?" laughs Peddle. "Absolutely! That's not a new story."

In the end, the Epson deal benefited Commodore more than it hurt them. "It was one of the keys that made Commodore work very well," concludes Peddle. "Commodore created the whole market for printers with personal computers. If you look at Apple, the printing and the business stuff was not as important."

With the printer, increased memory, speaker, and professional keyboard, Peddle felt his computer could compete for the business market better than Apple or Radio Shack. "We had better peripherals, we had a bigger machine, and it was stronger," says Peddle.

---

[6] When IBM released their personal computer in 1982, Epson benefited enormously. "For a long time, Epson was the leading supplier to the PC market," says Peddle.

A Change in Jack

While Commodore struggled with the PET, a palpable mood overtook Jack Tramiel. "Jack changed his character during that time," recalls Peddle. According to Peddle, the change resulted from a personal tragedy in the Tramiel family.

During 1976, Jack's oldest son found the love of his life. "Sam had married a girl they approved of," explains Peddle. "There was this very close tie between Jack and Helen and the daughter." As Peddle recalls, Sam and his wife also had a baby during this time.

In 1977, Jack's daughter in law became ill. "She gets this cancer and they take her to a whole bunch of treatments and everything else," says Peddle. "It's supposed to get better."

During her treatments, Sam refused to voice hope for a cure. "Sam says that he never told anybody that because he didn't believe it," recalls Peddle. Sam had good reasons for his belief, since he had discussions with the doctors that others had not participated in. "He thought, from what the doctors had said, that the stuff they did was going to make her well for a year and then she was going to die."

"Jack and Helen went through this big depression with the daughter," says Peddle. "I mean, it was a big God damned deal to them."

In late 1977, it seemed like there was hope for the family. "There was a period of time when she suddenly popped back, and everybody believed that she was going to make it," explains Peddle. "When she got better, there was this big celebration and they took them all over the world. There was this whole thing of joy."

The world travels took place sometime in late 1977 and 1978. Curiously, Sam refused to believe his wife was safe. "Sam, apparently, totally believes that all he was doing was making sure she lived the last year of her life as well as she can," says Peddle.

In mid-1978, the cancer returned and put the Tramiels through even more anguish. "All of a sudden, she reverses and dies painfully over about a six-month period," concludes Peddle. "Their personal life was just shit during that time for them. It was like God had given them a present and then took it away."

The loss of his daughter in law changed Jack. "Jack came back from that whole experience just never the same person," reveals Peddle. "It really soured him on a whole lot of life. There was a piece of him that died with her, and it was a nice piece."

Jack seemed to pass through the normal stages of grieving. "For a long time he was just totally depressed basically," says Peddle. "You didn't walk into his office and find him weeping, but he was just an angry person. Everything made him angry."

Jack never passed through the anger stage. "Jack never really recovered from that in my opinion," says Peddle, who noticed Jack's despair changing into something worse. "Maybe five years later or ten years later, but during that time he was much more ruthless."

The Race for the Disk Drive

Peddle had evolved his PET 2001 into a serious business computer. "We started off making a $595 computer for the general masses," says Peddle. With an improved keyboard, a larger monitor, and more memory, the CBM computers were legitimate business machines. "The Europeans were basically putting us into competition against Hewlett Packard and all the others making that level of computing device."

By the end of 1977, it was apparent cassettes were not the ideal form of data storage. "Everybody is thinking we need to go to a better storage device," recalls Peddle, referring to disk drives. An IBM engineer named Alan Shugart invented the first floppy disk drive in 1971, which used eight-inch disks. In 1976, Shugart invented the 5¼-inch floppy disk, which soon became standard.

"Now I'm too smart," Peddle states sarcastically. "I've done a bigger version of the PET and put a keyboard in it, and we're ready to go into business computing. Now I know that if you want to do real business computing on a computer, you need two floppy disks." It was a belief Peddle carried from his days at General Electric.

"I hired this team to come in and build a dual floppy disk controller that works on our IEEE bus," recalls Peddle. As with his previous hires, Peddle turned to Roger Camp at Iowa State University.

"Every year, Dr. Roger Camp fed me the brightest and best out of his class, who were weird," says Peddle. "They were guys who were not going to fit in other places but were really sharp."

Peddle interviewed and hired a young engineer named Glen Stark to build the electronics for the dual disk drive. According to Peddle, Stark did not start out at Commodore as a 'weird' engineer. "Stark came west with his girlfriend. He was a much more of an open guy than Seiler or Feagans," recalls Peddle. "Then his girlfriend left him and broke his heart. For about two years, he also became a recluse."

Peddle preferred recluses on his team. "I had these three loners," says Peddle. "The nice thing about having loners who are really smart working for you is they bust their ass working 24 hours a day."

The new hire impressed Peddle. "Glenn was brilliant when he got going in the right direction," says Peddle. "You give him an assignment and he would get it done."

Peddle hired another Iowa State graduate named Scott Paterson to program the disk drive. "Scott Paterson was hired around the same time [as Glen]," recalls Peddle. Patterson was a fitting addition to the team due to his perfectionist attitude. "He was the guy who was trying to drive us into doing pure things, like the Kernel and stuff like that."

Besides Peddle, Scott Paterson was the only family man on the team. "Scott has got a wife and kids," says Peddle. "She was always important to him. They are the image of an Iowa couple: both really nice people, hardworking, industrious; all the things that made the Midwest work."

Paterson and Stark formed a close relationship while working on the disk drive project. "They were a team for years," says Peddle. "It was kind of funny having this one happily married guy in this team of loners. Scott was exactly the opposite from Glen."

With his team assembled, Peddle and his engineers began working on the dual floppy disk drive.

Meanwhile, Apple was losing out to their competitors because, compared to the Commodore PET, loading programs with the Apple II was slow and unreliable. "Woz was bored with how slow his cassette loaded his program," says Peddle. "In fact, he used to get errors because his coding for his cassette was not robust."

"Steve [Jobs] knew that they needed to go to floppy because everybody was working with floppies at that time. So he told Woz, 'You have got to get a floppy done by the Consumer Electronics Show.'"[7]

After months, the Apple II disk drive failed to materialize. "They had committed that product for a show and Woz wasn't doing it," says Peddle. "I think he hadn't figured out how to do it and he was just thinking about it, trying to make it happen."

"Finally everybody in the company puts pressure on him," says Peddle. "Steve cajoles him, sits with him, and does everything he can."

Wozniak studied an IBM floppy disk drive to inspire his own design. Finally, just before CES, Steve Wozniak came through. "Woz invented redundant coding for disks again - GCR," says Peddle. "It was a brilliant piece of work. He made it work and got it ready for the show."

When Apple attended their first CES in Las Vegas in January 1978, they were able to demonstrate a crude prototype of the disk drive. Chuck

---

[7] Most accounts of this story say Mike Markkula pushed Apple to develop a disk drive.

and Jack were not happy to learn the competition had developed the technology ahead of them.

Prior to CES, political maneuvers within Commodore conspired against Peddle. "The first problem happened in the Fall of 1977," recalls Peddle. "Jack wants to replace Chris Fish, the CFO of the company, with Dick Sanford because he thought Chris wasn't capable of doing his job."

At the same time, Jack was growing weary of Peddle running the computer business. "Jack decides he wants me to focus on engineering," explains Peddle. "In order to keep Chris off his high horse, Jack tells him Chuck's going to be too busy and the only guy Chuck will work for is you. So I go to CES show in January, being told for the first time I'm not running the business."

It was a devastating blow to Peddle. "It's the first time he and I are not buddies," says Peddle. "The personal computer business, which I set up, was supposed to be mine." Peddle's close friend, Chris Fish, convinced Peddle to continue forward with his work.

When CES arrived, Commodore had no disk drive. Peddle's over-ambitious dual floppy design slowed down the project. Furthermore, the dual drives were largely unnecessary, since the IEEE-488 interface allowed multiple disk drives to connect together. It would be simpler to sell individual disk drives and allow users to choose how many they wanted to purchase.

Peddle also believes the inexperience of his new hires slowed down the disk drive project. "The problem I had was I just barely had hired Scott Patterson and Glen Stark and I didn't have any horses," says Peddle. "They came out of school and they were supposed to do this job. They got tangled up on the hardware and I didn't have time to go fix it."

In the middle of Peddle's technology push, he found out he would require major surgery on his gallbladder. "I took up running seriously because of the [impending] operation," recalls Peddle. "I started running marathons and lost 60 pounds. I thought I was cured because my body totally changed."

According to Peddle, "I went back to the doctor and he said, 'You don't understand. You have to have your gallbladder out.'"

Peddle had his operation. "They took six great big stones out of my gallbladder," recalls Peddle. "He said any one of them could have caused me just nothing but trouble."

During recovery, Peddle received visits from family and friends in the hospital. "I go into the hospital and Leonard came by," recalls Peddle.

Though he was back in University, Leonard Tramiel continued his association with Commodore. "I came back and worked the summer of 1978, and did a fair amount of unofficial consulting for several years after that," recalls Leonard.

Peddle's closest rivals also paid him a visit in the hospital. "One of the people that came by wasn't anybody from my company, but it was Steven and Steve," says Peddle. "We had always kept in touch and we had always stayed friendly during that period."

After his release from hospital, Peddle continued pushing the disk drive project forward. "We signed up for a set of [disk drive heads] sold to us by Simon Connors, from *Shugart Associates* after Alan [Shugart] had been forced out," recalls Peddle. The disk drive head was a crucial mechanism in the disk drive, allowing it to physically read and write to a floppy disk. Apple also relied on Shugart.

In July 1978, Apple delivered the disk drive at the introductory preorder price of $495, and $595 after that. It was an incredible price breakthrough for a company that had the costliest microcomputer of the 1977 Trinity. "The single floppy made Apple take off," says Peddle. The company Jack once declined to purchase and perceived as little or no threat to Commodore was becoming a force.

Wozniak's disk drive was much simpler than the PET dual disk drive, but it suited most users' needs. "The [Apple] single floppy didn't do anything like [handling complex] data, but it let you store and load programs much faster," says Peddle.

Jack Tramiel was unhappy his competitor beat Commodore to the market. "Jack Tramiel almost killed me," laughs Peddle. "He said, 'You've been fucking around making this high-end dual machine and you let them eat your lunch.'"

Peddle received his first Jack Attack. "The guy was just kicking my ass because I deserved it," recalls Peddle. "There was no shouting and there was no hate. I fucked up and he was telling me I hurt the company really bad."

Jack was clear about his reasons for punishing Peddle. "His view was that I spending too much time on other things and didn't do the disk drive right," explains Peddle.

What came next crushed Peddle. "Jack punished me and, to get me focused, he took me totally out of management of the computer business," recalls Peddle. "He said, 'You are not going to do management anymore. You are only going to do development.'" Peddle was no longer in control of the computer systems division he had built for Commodore.

A Defection

After his demotion, Peddle felt cheated. "We started out with an agreement that I would run the systems business," says Peddle. He also had complaints about some of Jack's business decisions.

During this time, Jack was focusing resources on creating memory at MOS Technology, which Peddle thinks was at the expense of his computer systems program. "My view was that he had not given me the resources because he had all these other guys fooling around with the memory business," says Peddle.

Unfortunately, MOS Technology was unable to keep up with the Japanese. "The Japanese changed the way memory worked and got more density over the Americans," recalls Peddle. "It was just obvious that they were going to kick our ass for a while."

Commodore wanted to make DRAM memory chips for the PET computers because they could fit more memory in fewer chips. "We started Commodore with static-RAM memory and discovered it didn't work," explains Peddle. "We had to go out of the memory business because we fucked it up big time."

Jack's habit of using unproven managers in positions of power also frustrated Peddle. "Jack always had the hero of the day," explains Peddle. "He would bring people in who would tell him that he was the greatest guy in computers and that he could make them more money. Jack would say okay, and he would hire him. Then, instead of me being in charge of them, I'd be working for them for a week. That wasn't my deal."

Commodore soon gained a reputation for the constant turnover of management. "They came and went pretty fast," says Peddle. "Sometimes I would hire someone and all of a sudden Jack would see what they were doing, fall in love with them, promote them, and give me another assignment. It was like he couldn't leave it alone."

Jack constantly stirred around Peddle's projects before anything could congeal. "Most of the time I was doing the right things for him," says Peddle. "I messed up with the floppy, but the rest of the time I was doing the right things. So it had me in an unhappy frame of mind."

The constant interference by Jack predictably took a toll on Peddle. "Our personal relationship got screwed up during that time," recalls Peddle. "He was in a bad mood and he was playing with my life in ways in which he played with everybody's lives."

At first, Peddle tried to work through the problems at Commodore. "Some of the time when you were there you just put up with it," he says. Gradually, Commodore was losing Peddle's loyalty.

At the same time, Apple was desperately seeking a new head of engineering because of their dissatisfaction with Steve Wozniak. After the difficulty in motivating Wozniak to develop the disk drive, Apple management wanted more stability. "They suddenly realized that their entire company was dependant on this one petulant 26 year old," explains Peddle. "Markkula, Jobs, and particularly Mike [Scott] said, 'We're not going to be in that situation again. We're going to go hire technical people that are better than Woz.'"

Apple came to Peddle at just the right moment. "Jack fucked me up and Steve [Jobs] came to me with a great offer," recalls Peddle. And what was the job offer? "To replace Woz and be the technical guru for the company."

Apple used everything in their power to lure Peddle. "I met with [Mike] Scott and Steve [Jobs]," recalls Peddle. "Basically the guys at Apple offered me a deal that would have made me one of the top five stockholders at Apple." The offer was too attractive to decline.

In the summer of 1978, as the *Commodore's 'Flying High'* hit the top 40 on the music charts, Peddle walked out on Commodore. Leonard Tramiel recalls Peddle leaving. "I assume it was because he thought he could do better there or had more flexibility," says Leonard.

Incredibly, Peddle walked away from a fortune in Commodore stock. "Terrible decision on my part," says Peddle. "I left Commodore without sorting out my life with them from a financial standpoint."

As might be expected, the sales pitch made by Steve Jobs was better than reality. "Going to Apple was a terrible decision," says Peddle. The Apple executives had no real plan for Peddle. It soon became apparent to Peddle he would not enjoy the same status he had at Commodore.

"It turns out they had, through a totally independent channel, hired this HP guy that Woz had worked for," recalls Peddle. The engineer was John Couch. "Woz loved him and they thought he was the greatest guy in the world."

Peddle was still new to Apple and trying to concentrate on engineering, so it took him a while to see the true picture. "I walked through the door, and it was obvious they didn't expect both of us to accept," says Peddle. "They basically hired both of us for the same job."

Peddle found himself in competition with John Couch. "The problem was, this guy was very good politically," explains Peddle. "He was a typical HP builder type who wants a good desk and all of the perks. I don't have fancy offices and stuff like that; it's not what I do."

While Peddle concentrated on engineering, Couch played politics. "This guy effectively went in and started playing power games," recalls Peddle. "He consolidated his position, ran his position up, hired more people, and became head of engineering. I wound up working for him, which was not the deal at all."

Peddle's first task at Apple was to help Steve Jobs on the new Lisa project. At this point, Jobs had not yet visited Xerox and raided their best ideas. "I worked closely with Steve through the time of the Lisa," recalls Peddle. "We were close. We used to go to lunch together and go for walks in the woods."

Peddle claims he was at Apple when they first began thinking of using a graphical user interface. "Jobs and I spent all this time doing architecture work on what was then the Lisa," recalls Peddle. "I clearly remember Jobs went to see these guys [at Xerox PARC]. He and I had lunch and he was just totally in love. He said, 'This is what we have to do', and he put it in the Lisa."

"The Lisa was going to be the *Xerox Star*," says Peddle, referring to the minicomputer Xerox introduced in 1981, before Apple. "The Xerox Star was a tremendous product. It had a very high-resolution screen and a tremendous word processor. The Lisa turned out to be the Star but it wasn't hard disk-drive oriented."

Peddle predicted Lisa would be a marketing disaster. "I basically walked out on Lisa when it was obvious that they were going to make it a ten thousand dollar box," explains Peddle. "My words were, 'Apple doesn't have the ability to sell a ten thousand dollar box, nor does the market need one.' They got all huffy about that so they reassigned me to the Apple III."

After management removed Chuck Peddle from the Lisa project, and later Steve Jobs, it fell to Peddle's rival John Couch to complete the project. "He's the guy that ultimately led to the Lisa fiasco," says Peddle.

In the meantime, Peddle concentrated on the Apple III architecture. "I sat down and defined it as a bridge product, which wasn't the product they came out with," says Peddle. "I wound up hiring two or three guys and we kind of set off in a corner and started doing some work."

As the months went by, Peddle realized it had been a mistake to leave Commodore. "The most important thing that was in my heart was that I felt I had left the thing I created," says Peddle, choking up slightly. "What we were doing [at Apple] was interesting and all of that but my heart just wasn't in it."

Peddle decided to leave Apple. "When we parted, Steve [Jobs] said, 'You never looked happy here. You just never looked like you liked it.' And he was right."

With almost no hesitation, Peddle gave up a major stake in Apple that would have been worth millions. "I wanted to go to Commodore," says

Peddle. "If I had been money oriented, I would have sucked it up, skated through all this bullshit, and been a very rich guy."

The decision still seems to trouble Peddle. "Leaving and coming back from Apple without getting a major stock position was another stupid decision, but I really wanted to come back," he says. In the end, the Lisa turned out to be the marketing disaster Peddle predicted.

The Apple III project also turned into one of the biggest disappointments for Apple, largely because of poor engineering and faulty assembly that caused the chips to seat improperly in the motherboard (something that had nothing to do with Peddle's contribution to the project). "It turns out that the guy who did it wound up making some pretty bad mistakes," says Peddle.

Steve Jobs realized Peddle was no longer any use to him and the friendship ended; a characteristic often noted by people who have worked with Jobs. "We parted ways after I left Apple," says Peddle. "We never looked back, either one of us at that point. He wouldn't give me the time of day now because Steve is Steve."

"He turned into something that he wasn't, and maybe it was always under there," muses Peddle. "Steve was a friend at one time. Steve lost most of his redeeming characteristics. He got rich and ugly and arrogant and a whole bunch of other things."

Coming Home

At the end of 1978, Peddle discovered a way to return to his beloved PET. While Peddle was away at Apple, Jack progressed with his vertical integration strategy by acquiring two more technology companies. "He had bought this CMOS company and an LCD company," recalls Peddle.

Commodore began producing a product no one expected: digital watches. The digital watch was a popular fad in the late seventies and Jack wanted a piece of the market. He acquired a watch-making company called Micro Display Systems Incorporated (MDSI) from its founder, Tom Hyltin. However, the digital watch market threatened to go the same way as calculators and soon watches were so cheap it was no longer profitable for the majority of companies, including Commodore.

Jack had previously sold LED or Light Emitting Diode watches and calculators on the consumer market. However, the Japanese found a way to undermine these markets with a new technology called Liquid Crystal Display (LCD). "Commodore was making LED calculators and LED watches, and they got killed by the LCD," recalls Peddle.

Jack's first reaction was to attempt to purchase LCD parts from Japan. "That was when they first discovered how clever the Japanese were," says Peddle. "The Japanese basically told them that there was too much internal demand and that's why they wouldn't sell them the LCD's or the parts for it. Then they hammered into the market, Seiko being the primary driver."

Jack found a potential source of LCD technology in the United States. "That's when Jack went out and bought himself an LCD company and a CMOS company," says Peddle.[8] Commodore acquired LCD manufacturer *Eagle Picture* in Pennsylvania and CMOS manufacturer *Frontier* in Southern California.

According to Peddle, Commodore hoped to create a synergy between the two companies by creating CMOS semiconductors for LCD systems.

Commodore relied on a man named Bud Fry to make the program work. "Jack had hired a marketing guy who knew semiconductors pretty well," explains Peddle. "Bud Fry had this idea he wanted to do something in calculators. He basically got Jack to give him permission to come and pick me up to go do this thing."

Peddle knew exactly who he wanted on his team to help him design the CMOS microprocessor. "We wanted Bill [Mensch] back in the fold," says Peddle. "He talked to me about it and I told him about Mensch and what he could do. They put me and Bill into a deal at the same time."

Since the meltdown of the 6502 team, Mensch had been consulting. "Mensch was working in Phoenix with a design center house," says Peddle.

Jack Tramiel lured Mensch back to Commodore. "In effect, the deal with Bill was we would set him up in a thing called the *Western Design Center*," explains Peddle. "He would get rights to use the [6502] technology. In return for that, he would develop most of the semiconductors." It was a remarkable deal for Mensch, who now had his own technology lab and a degree of autonomy. Mensch established the Western Design Center at 2166 East Brown Road in Mesa, Arizona.

Peddle negotiated with Jack to reinstate his previous financial agreements. "They promised me that they would finish my stock option deal," reveals Peddle. However, Peddle could not get every agreement reestablished. "I had a deal that I would get a dollar for every computer they made and I lost that deal, which is okay. I never expected him to honor it anyway."

Although Peddle was able to mend his financial situation, it would take more time to earn back Jack's trust. "Jack didn't forgive me for leaving

---

[8] According to Peddle, Commodore wanted to use the LCD technology in the ChessMate product. "It was supposed to be an LCD also, but apparently the LCD never got started," says Peddle. Instead, ChessMate used red LED digits.

for a while – maybe ever," recalls Peddle. "We developed a personal relationship again for a while but there probably was not the degree of trust between us that would have been there if I had stayed."

Peddle and Mensch had made a breakthrough for microcontroller devices with the 6502 chipset and now they hoped to create something similar for the LCD market. "We were making a small microcomputer that was LCD oriented," explains Peddle.

Commodore hoped to sell the semiconductor devices to manufacturers of calculators, meters, and anything that used an LCD screen. "The idea was to have a product that could be used to sell intelligent LCD products," says Peddle. "It would be highly programmable and easy to adapt to a bunch of applications."

In a 1995 interview with Stanford University, Bill Mensch claims the LCD project was not an original idea. "The first project I did was copied," reveals Mensch. "Toshiba had a five function calculator. We reverse engineered and designed ... it had the same function when the dust cleared. LC5K3 is what it was called."

Jack wanted the chip to compete with the Japanese counterpart, so price was foremost in the design. "I designed a calculator chip and then Jack Tramiel got the - he called it the Japanese price, which was one half the U.S. price," says Mensch.

Although Mensch's chip had the same function, it was superior to the Japanese designed counterpart. Not only was it 50 percent smaller than the Japanese chipset, it also contained 64 bit architecture – a first for 1979. "That little chip in here could do four-bit operations, eight-bit all the way up to 64-bit in one op code," claims Mensch.

Unfortunately, the engineers discovered Frontier was incapable of manufacturing the CMOS chipset. "We went to the manufacturing place that was supposed to be able to build the CMOS, and they didn't stand a chance of building it," says Peddle. "They had been overrated when they came into the company."

Commodore was unable to nurture their investment. "To get CMOS built took a significant investment," explains Peddle. "At that time, the Japanese told everybody what the rules were. If you didn't go out and invest $100 million in good process equipment, you couldn't play."

Irving Gould was partly responsible for the failure of Frontier. "Jack tried to back door it by buying this company," says Peddle. "Every time he would try to go out and raise money to make that kind of investment, Irving would tell him no."

The failure of Frontier meant Mensch would not collect from Commodore. "All the things we got Bill started on died, not because of anything he did," says Peddle. "When that fell apart, Jack basically decided he didn't need a design center. He threw Bill to the wolves."

The abandonment by Jack surprised Mensch, but he persevered. Mensch comments on Tramiel, "He put more companies out of business than probably anyone in the electronics industry, with great pride. He put me into business. I figured if I could survive with Jack Tramiel for two years, I could survive anywhere."

The Killer App

By 1979, Apple was not faring well compared to the rest of the 1977 Trinity. "Apple was getting into serious trouble," says Peddle. "Their sales were dropping off, they didn't have market share, and we were kicking them. Radio Shack had come out with two or three models and was doing pretty well and the CP/M machines were starting to come along. Apple almost went away."

Despite poor sales, Apple continued to claim Apple was number one. "That was the kind of stuff they did," says Peddle. "Markkula turned McKenna loose and said, 'Any lie McKenna tells, as long as I don't tell it, I don't give a fuck.'"

In December 1978, Apple computer ads began calling the Apple II, 'The World's Best Selling Personal Computer'. Despite the lofty claim, the TRS-80 was far outselling the Apple II. By the end of 1979, Radio Shack had sold over 150,000 TRS-80 computers, giving them approximately 35% of the personal computer market. In contrast, Apple sold only 35,100 units in the 1979 fiscal year, their most successful year yet.

"They kept building on that image and just kept telling lies," says Peddle. "McKenna has always been good at that. He can make you believe any lie he wants. Clearly, during that time, that whole revisionist thing started." Soon, the lies would become truth.

The story of VisiCalc starts with Peter Jennings, the genius programmer who created Microchess in one kilobyte of memory for the KIM-1. By the summer of 1978, Jennings had ported Microchess to all the most popular machines; namely the PET, TRS-80 and S-100 machines. The Apple II version would come later.

Jennings sold his software under the name *Micro-Ware*. Packaging was amateurish but standard for the time, with the cassette tape and printed instructions sealed in a plastic zip-lock bag. Jennings sold Microchess at computer shows, personal computer dealers, and through mail order.

At one such computer show, PC-78 in Atlantic City, Micro-Ware went in a new direction. Jennings met with Carl Helmers, editor of Byte

Magazine, who wanted Jennings to meet Dan Fylstra, an MBA student at Harvard and a knowledgeable programmer of the 6800 microchip. Fylstra was also a writer for Byte and had previously written a review of Microchess.

Fylstra was just beginning a new company with the sole purpose of selling software. His plan was to sell third party software under the *Personal Software* banner.[9] Personal Software was the first company to publish the legendary *Zork* adventure game, developed by *Infocom*.

Fylstra and Jennings eventually decided to merge the two companies under the name Personal Software. "[Peter] Jennings had a partner, a young guy from Harvard," recalls Chuck Peddle, referring to Dan Fylstra. "I've got this memory of him at one of the shows, of him taking four machines and saying we're going to go out and write a bunch of code for these, which they did."

Peddle helped Fylstra any way he could because he saw Personal Software as symbiotic with the PET computer. "[Fylstra] is hooked on Commodore," says Peddle. "Jennings is hooked. We're personal friends and we're helping them sell product in Europe. It's a really good relationship."

Personal Software owned at least four PET computers for software development but decided to try the Apple II market. "They had bought one Apple, but they decided they would back Commodore because we had other things going for us," says Peddle.[10]

Personal Software eventually became interested in distributing a software program from a fellow Harvard student, Dan Bricklin. Bricklin had an idea for an electronic calculating ledger that would allow real-time manipulation of numbers in rows and columns. "One day, a couple of guys from Harvard wander in and say, 'We've got this idea for something we want to write,'" recalls Peddle. What happened next would change the face of computing. "[Fylstra] says, 'Well, the PET's are all tied up. Why don't you take that Apple there and see what you can do with it. It runs the same Basic.'"

The PET computer was the leading business oriented personal computer, with users perceiving the Apple II as a games machine. Despite this, the Apple II would receive VisiCalc, a business oriented application. "It was just absolute blind-assed luck," says Peddle. "These

---

[9] The third-party developer plan was ahead of its time and is now the common model used by the console and PC gaming industry.

[10] Peter Jennings says it was just salesmanship. "Of course we told Peddle that," says Jennings. "We told Steve Jobs that we supported Apple above all the others and we told Tandy that Radio Shack was our favorite."

guys had the idea for the architecture and they didn't care about the machine."

"It is true that Dan Bricklin *prototyped* the first spreadsheet on an Apple II because it was the available machine at that moment," says Jennings. However, he adds that he and Dan Fylstra had discussions later and decided to release the first version for the Apple II.

Fylstra and Jennings immediately liked the idea and agreed to pay for development costs of $4,000 to $5,000 per month, spent mostly for access to a timesharing system. Jennings agreed to defer his royalties on Microchess for the development of VisiCalc. In effect, profits from TRS-80 and PET software were about to fund an Apple II application.

VisiCalc impressed those who saw it. "It was one of the most creative software packages ever written and the only true piece of software that went on PC's without ever having a parallel on mainframe computers," says Peddle. "Word processing, we were doing on timesharing systems. Everything you did on a [personal] computer, we were doing on big computers, except for VisiCalc."

When Personal Software released VisiCalc on October 17, 1979, it became an instant hit. Sales of VisiCalc directly drove the sales of Apple II computers, even more so than the sales figures indicated due to software pirating of VisiCalc. "VisiCalc saved Apple," says Peddle. "People were buying Apple's and taking them into work to do VisiCalc work. The Apple II became the definitive VisiCalc machine."

In the first month alone, VisiCalc sold over one thousand copies at $100. Soon, Personal Software raised the price to $150 but sales only increased. Personal Software became a software giant, with Microsoft a distant second place.

Though everyone knew VisiCalc was a winner, it took a while for VisiCalc to gain popularity. Chris Crawford summarizes the growth of VisiCalc and Apple. "It wasn't until VisiCalc set in in 1980 and 1981 that the Apple really got going."

Even with the boost in sales provided by VisiCalc, Apple remained in second place. Tandy sold close to 300,000 TRS-80 Model I computers by the end of 1980, due to their massive distribution that now amounted to almost 8000 stores worldwide. This resulted in $150 Million in computer sales, compared to Apple with $75 million, an incredible increase from $10 million the previous year. Considering Radio Shack equipment cost even less at retail than Apple II computers, this puts Radio Shack total sales far higher than Apple.

However, 1980 was the year Apple finally surpassed Commodore, which had sales of only $55 million. This marked an incredible increase for Apple of 650% from the previous year, compared to Commodore and

Tandy, which had increases of 150% and 131% respectively. The aberration was a direct consequence of VisiCalc.

VisiCalc was a clear turning point for the Apple II. As a game machine, it was too overpriced to compete with the Atari 2600 VCS. VisiCalc transformed the Apple II into a business machine and Apple did almost nothing to make it happen. "It made Apple the definitive computer in the US market," says Peddle.

In 1980, Apple took their company public. "Apple was not a particularly successful company until the second or third year," says Leonard Tramiel. "When Apple went public, they were the first, just incredibly over hyped initial public offering. They had just an incredible amount of money that they raked in as a result of that IPO, which carried them through until they actually started making boatloads of money, after the Mac came out."

With Apple and Radio Shack dominating the US marketplace, there was little hope for the PET computer in North America. "It was never a planned activity to screw up in the United States," says Peddle. "We just couldn't get ahead of the curve fast enough. It wasn't that we weren't trying."

CHAPTER

6

Business is War

1979 - 1980

The PET and CBM computers had made Commodore exceedingly profitable. In early 1979, Jack relocated from his offices in Palo Alto to a much larger building in Santa Clara. "They had a building which was the production facility and the engineering lab," says Bob Yannes. The high-tech building, located at 3330 Scott Boulevard (next door to *AMD*), would serve as Commodore headquarters and manufacturing.

The new headquarters had angled windows along the front and large solar panels on the roof. The futuristic building could deal with life in a region renowned for its seismic activity. Giant metal springs and steel cables helped dampen the effects of tremors.

Commodore executives took the prime offices under the glass windows along the front. "Jack's office was way over in the front corner," says Robert Russell. The corner office gave Jack more window space than anyone but it was also the most dangerous in an earthquake.

Jack had a unique penchant for courting disaster. "There were huge 20 foot glass panes running up to the [solar array]," says Russell. "During an earthquake, when those front panels flexed, everybody was running towards the [walls] because they didn't want to get toasted. When the earthquake started, it was flexing up and down and the windows were actually bowing. Of course, the only one that ever broke was in Jack's office." Luckily, Jack was not hurt when the windows shattered.

Beside him was the conference room where executives and managers laid out their battle plans. Jack placed the administrative people near him, in a large area crammed with desks and cubicles. These were the Commodore foot soldiers: accountants, the purchasing department, and sales people. Their area was the most chaotic in the entire building.

Behind the administrative and technical areas was the factory, which produced PET computers. Tom Mitchell, one of Jack's trusted executives, oversaw manufacturing.

The warehouse section was at the back of the facility. It had a high roof to accommodate boxes that were often stacked to the ceiling. Here, a surly group of workers loaded shipments into delivery vans that pulled up to the large doors. Sometimes they ran out of space. "When product backed up it piled up in the hallways in engineering," recalls Russell.

The building also housed the engineering labs, where Commodore engineers devised new products. "Engineering had a hardware lab in one corner and the drafting people were up in the front under the windows," says Russell. In 1979, the engineering projects were in trouble.

Disk Drives at Last

While Bill Mensch was working on the LCD project at the Western Design Center, Chuck Peddle visited the new Commodore headquarters to check out the progress on his beloved PET. He was not impressed with his successor. "While I was away at Apple, this engineering manager, Tim Kennedy, was brought in to replace me," he says. "I was only gone for a short time and this one guy totally fucked things up."

The dual disk drive project was still not completed, and worse, the team had deviated from Peddle's original plan. "Management had let these guys get totally off track on what the disk drive was supposed to do," says Peddle. "I discovered that the machine was going to be a serial read/serial write device; effectively two tape drives. Well, that's not what you use floppies for."

Peddle used the opportunity to ingratiate himself back into Commodore. "I managed to convince them to cancel it," recalls Peddle. "I jumped in on the disk drive and then effectively forced Kennedy out and took over all engineering."

The engineers started the project over from the beginning. "We sat down and redefined the whole product after I came back," recalls Peddle. The redesign meant the disk drive would not appear for several more months, but Peddle was determined to do it right.

To gain a lead over the Apple disk drive technology, Peddle used an innovation he developed back in 1961. "We took my patent, which had run out, and used it to double up the code," says Peddle, referring to the amount of data that could be stored on a single disk. The Apple disk drive could only store 150 kilobytes on a 5.25-inch disk. Peddle's 2040 disk drive could store 170 kilobytes.

The 2040 was also useful for more than just loading and saving programs. "It was a real honest-to-goodness file management device," says Peddle. "You could read and write records, you could go in and sort records, and you could do all the things with that product that you could only do with computer systems dramatically more expensive."

The 2040 was a massive unit, almost as large as the PET itself. It even had a hinged lid for easy access, much like the PET, with a support arm to hold the lid open.

The 2040 drive was suited for low-capacity computers of the time. The 2040 dual drive had two processors, a 6502 and a 6504, as well as its own RAM and ROM chips. In effect, the 2040 drive was a standalone computer. "We went to distributed intelligence peripherals, so there really was no operating system level of activity," says Peddle.

In contrast, the Apple II stored the disk operating system (DOS) in RAM, which taxed the memory and CPU cycles. "The [Apple] disk drive wasn't really extensible and never did get extended," says Peddle. With CPU speeds of one megahertz and memory often less than 32 kilobytes, computing power was at a premium. Chuck Peddle's design philosophy left memory and CPU cycles to the computer.

The original PET 2001 computer with the built in cassette recorder could not read or write data to the disk drive because BASIC 1.0 had not been designed to work with disks. Only the later releases with BASIC 2.0 and above could use the 2040 drive.

It was up to John Feagans to improve the operating system. "He wanted to get out of Basic because the original code inside the PET was just all spaghetti," says Russell. "John said, 'Let's break up all this stuff that deals with the hardware and get that into its own section of the code,' rather than here's a routine that runs the cassette and here's a routine that runs the keyboard and here's a routine that runs the display."

Feagans planned to implement something called a *kernel* for the next generation of computers. "John Feagans was the architect of what became the kernel concept, which was a separate operating kernel versus the Basic interpreter," explains Russell.

The word kernel is a synonym for nucleus, as in 'the kernel of truth'. In computers, the kernel is essentially the nucleus of a computer operating system that provides basic services for all the other parts of the computer. These services include things like getting a character from the keyboard when the user hits a key, loading and saving memory from external devices, and moving the cursor position on screen.

Before Feagans, the hardware engineers gave the operating system very little thought. Engineers tended to combine the kernel, the shell (the actual commands to access the kernel, such as LOAD, SAVE, and

PRINT) and the programming language into one mixed-up creation. Feagans was on a quest to separate these parts of the operating system into modular pieces.

In May 1979, Peddle received another programmer from Iowa State, Robert Russell. By the time Russell graduated, he was well aware of Commodore technology. "I was in charge of the labs where the original PETs were installed in the University," says Russell. "We used the 6502 emulators and programming devices that existed at that time to actually design classes around them."

Russell knew most of the Commodore engineers, including Glen Stark, Scott Paterson, and John Feagans. "I actually argued against them in college in the computer labs about some of the processors they were pushing," he recalls. "I was an Intel man and they were Motorola and MOS Technology pushers at that time."

In University, Russell purchased a Sol computer kit from Processor Technology. "I put one of those together on my dorm desk in my first year of college. It basically took over my desk," recalls Russell. The new technology was fraught with peril. "I had to build my own power supply, which caught on fire," he says. "I was typing away and it was burning right in front of me, but I was looking at the TV screen. Luckily my roommate noticed."

When it was time for Russell to graduate, Dr. Roger Camp felt he had another weird engineer for Chuck Peddle. "[Camp] got the other guys into Commodore and was well hooked up to the 6502 community," recalls Russell. "He really pushed me through and also John Feagans."

Russell soon decided to leave Iowa. "What do you do in the Midwest? You go someplace else to get a job," says Russell. "I had good job offers but they were cold places. All of a sudden, I had an offer from Commodore to go work in Santa Clara with my old friends. California definitely looked a lot more appealing than my other options at that time, which was to go work in Minneapolis."

Compared to the other reclusive engineers, Russell was strikingly normal. "If you've ever seen a picture of Russell, he's pretty round," says Peddle. "He looks like a corn fed Iowa farmer."

Russell enjoyed working for his new boss. "I really liked Chuck Peddle personally," says Russell. "He treated the engineers well. Honestly, they were part of his family, though obviously the other guys were more favored than me. I remember going over to his house and looking at the car he had taken apart in his garage. It was a Triumph or Stag or some sort of import British car that was in pieces. I always wondered if he ever put it together."

In August 1979, approximately one year behind the Apple disk drive, Commodore introduced the 2040 drive. At $1,295.00, it was priced for the high-end business market.

In the initial release, Commodore experienced a high failure rate from some of the early 2040 disk drives. "There were lots of times we had to solve drive problems, whether you were a drive guy or not," explains Russell.

Russell says the factory workers dumped non-working disk drives onto the engineers, hoping for a solution. "They wanted us to give them software that would actually make the drives so they wouldn't fail," says Russell. "At Scott Boulevard, we used to pile the 2040 dual drives up in the hallways until they reached the ceiling, and then you were like, 'Okay, we better find a solution for whatever is wrong.'"

As with the early PET computers, Jack preferred selling the costly disk drives on the European market. "We used to turn out tons of PET's and floppy disk drives, but they were all going to Europe because he could get twice the money for them," says Russell.

New Competition

In 1979, two more competitors met Jack Tramiel on the battlefield. One was a major customer of Commodore and the other was a bitter rival that once almost destroyed Commodore.

Through the years, Commodore continued to sell the 6507 microprocessor to Atari. "MOS shipped a lot to Atari," recalls Al Charpentier. "Apple wouldn't deal with MOS for some reason, but we shipped a ton of those 6502's."

Atari was desperate for ROM chips, since each game cartridge contained a four-kilobyte ROM chip. MOS Technology produced some of the best ROM technology at the time. "We were their biggest supplier of ROM for their games," reveals Bob Yannes.

When Atari 2600 games began to lose their edge, Commodore came through with a technological breakthrough that gave their games new life. "The Atari VCS could only address 4K of memory in a game ROM, and they wanted to be able to address more than that," recalls Yannes. "I actually ended up designing a custom chip for Atari. We custom designed them an 8K bank switch ROM. It looked like a 4K ROM [to the VCS] but it would trigger into another bank when you accessed a particular address. We jumped through hoops to get that done on time for their Christmas season."

In January 1979, at the Winter CES, Atari announced the Atari 400 and Atari 800 home computers, code-named Candy and Colleen. These were legitimate computers with keyboards and the ability to display powerful color graphics on a television.

Not only did Atari now have superior technology in their systems, but they also had an established distribution channel. In December 1979, *Sears* began selling the Atari home computers. The low end Atari 400 sold for $549.95 and the higher-end Atari 800 sold for $999.95. Commodore's customer was now a direct competitor.

By June 1979, the company that put Commodore out of the calculator business was poised to enter the computer market. Texas Instruments launched the TI-99/4 for $1150, which also included a 13" color monitor.

Tramiel was particularly weary of Texas Instruments, since they were his only competitor with vertical integration. Texas Instruments used their own microprocessor, called the TMS9900, running at 3 MHz. However, much like other computer companies of the day, production problems meant Texas Instruments was unable to produce sufficient quantities until almost a year later. The TI-99/4 also received very little software support. In March 1980, the TI-99/4 had fewer than 30 programs available, all made by Texas Instruments. This time, Jack held the high ground over his old enemy.

Losing North America

In 1979, Jack clashed with Irving Gould over Irving's refusal to raise money using Commodore stock. "Irving was fucking with his head. I remember when [Jack] was really pissed about that," says Peddle. "He was one of the things that frustrated Jack more than anything else in the world, because Irving wouldn't let Jack go out and raise money."

Gould spent much of his effort in New York promoting Commodore. "Irving is a businessman," says Peddle. "He went out and sold the idea of how smart we were to pump up the stock."

As the eighties approached, Commodore stock climbed even higher. Since Commodore introduced the PET, they had doubled and sometimes tripled their revenues each year at a time when most companies were happy to increase revenues by ten percent. The stock market reacted accordingly. By June 1979, Commodore stock climbed to $41.63 per share; almost 10 times the 1976 price.

Jack tried to convince Irving to raise money for Commodore to pay off debts, expand production, and promote the PET in the United States. "We've got the company starting to move and Jack doesn't have the money," recalls Peddle. Unfortunately, Irving still thought Jack should slowly grow Commodore with profits from the European market.

Jack and Chuck visited Irving to plead their case. "We went back to New York," recalls Peddle. "Jack goes back to the board of directors and says, 'You guys are just fucking with my life. Go raise me twenty million dollars. The stock's moving so you can borrow against it.'"

The demand was reasonable. "This was stock that was worth thirty times more than it was when I joined the company," explains Peddle. "They could have easily raised a whole bunch of money and put legs under the company."

Jack's prostrations had no effect on Gould. While Apple used their stock offering to grow the company, Irving Gould refused. "Irving Gould was such a tight son of a bitch that he told him no," says Peddle.

Even more incredible was Gould's reason for not using Commodore stock to raise money. According to Peddle, "Irving said, 'The stock is going to keep running and I don't want to give away the cheap stock.' He just kept doing that." Gould had forgotten the reason for the stock market.

"Jack came out of that meeting and he was so fucking mad," recalls Peddle. "Irving had cost him market position in the U.S. because he couldn't do it with very little money. He was so pissed and he had every right to be."

Europe consumed the entire supply of PETs at elevated prices, so it would be foolish to do anything except send PET computers to the European market. Nevertheless, to ignore the United States was long-term suicide. "We were in California and there was no place you could buy a Commodore computer," explains Russell. "Early on, there was lots of demand [in the United States]. We asked him, 'Why aren't there more machines available?' Jack said, 'Listen, we're getting twice as much money for them in Europe.'"

The lack of success in North America frustrated Jack. In England and Germany, Commodore enjoyed an 80% market share, despite higher prices than the United States. Robert Russell explains, "You see these price lists in Europe and you say, 'My God! No wonder Jack doesn't want to send any product to the distributors in the States.'"

With Commodore almost failing when they introduced the PET, Jack had little choice but to ignore the less profitable U.S. market. "When you are trying to grow a company, you respect certain things Jack did," explains Russell. "Jack wasn't a big corporate guy but he helped drive the growth by a lot of the shrewd moves he did."

Ignoring the U.S. market inevitably hurt Commodore. "On the other hand, it's short term growth. It's not long term, IBM type of growth," says Russell. "With certain things like that, he plays for the short term."

The lost opportunity to dominate North America consumed Jack. "It was a tremendous pressure on a guy who was starting to see things work for him," explains Peddle. "They always said 'Jack, you'll find a way to make it happen.'"

While Apple enjoyed proper funding for long-term success, Jack relied on short-term tactics. "We were never really allowed to go to the board and have discussions about how you get to be a real technology company," says Peddle. "We did tons of shortcuts. Almost every shortcut we did worked but none of them had legs."

The lack of proper funding by Irving Gould had other consequences on Commodore, including the potential to fall behind the competition technologically. "We got out in front of Apple and companies like that but didn't maintain it," explains Robert Russell. "You say, well why didn't you maintain it? Well, they had a lot more engineers than us and a lot more for product development at times when there were only ten or twelve engineers [at Commodore]."

Peddle feels the death of Jack's daughter in law coupled with the unreasonable pressure from Irving Gould changed Jack Tramiel during this period. To Peddle, it seemed like Jack was now going out of his way to hurt other people. "Before, Jack was ruthless to survive," says Peddle. "His view was, 'I'm a survivor, I worked in the camps, and I'll do anything I can to keep my company alive.' He was really good at it but it went to being something else."

Bob Yannes recalls Jack's philosophy. "His motto was, 'Business is war'. You didn't win by competing with your competitors or outdoing them; you won by *destroying* your competitors and putting them out of business."

One of Jack's shortcuts made it difficult for Commodore partners to survive. "He had suppliers make a bid on something and he would say, 'That's too much. This is what I want it for,'" recalls Yannes. "They would say, 'But we're going to lose money if we sell it to you for that.' He would say, 'Do you want the business or not.'"

Surprisingly, many suppliers accepted Jack's offer. "They would sell him stuff at a rate where they were going broke," says Yannes. "They would go out of business and Jack would go find another one. That's just how he did business. Everyone knew he did business that way so it's their fault if they got burned by him."

One person caught off guard was Bob Schreiner of Synertek, who collaborated with MOS Technology on the 6502 project. "I went out and cut a deal to get Synertek to do something for me on memory," recalls Peddle. "We promised we'd buy more memory from them."

Tramiel seemed to have no qualms about breaking agreements. "It was a signed deal," recalls Peddle. "Jack then said, 'I know it's a signed deal, I know I agreed to do it, and I know these guys really helped me. But I don't have to do it now and I'm not going to.'"

"Jack's attitude was, if he didn't think it should be paid, he would just rip the check up and tell them to sue him," says Peddle.

Jack's aggressive policies might have helped Commodore in the short term, but they alienated beneficial allies in the electronics industry. "They survived it and we survived it," says Peddle. "But [Bob] Schreiner said, 'I will never trust Jack again.'"

The broken agreements placed Peddle in an awkward position, since he was often responsible for making the deals in the first place. "It was just obvious Jack was not going to keep his word, and it was my word because I had cut the deal," says Peddle.

"I quit cutting deals for Jack," reveals Peddle. "I told him one day, 'When I cut a deal, I mean it. You can cut the business deals and if people want to go along with you that's fine but I will not cut a business deal.' And I never did."

Jack continued to break agreements, despite Peddle's rebellion. "Jack didn't keep his word whenever he felt it was in his interest not to keep his word," says Peddle. "I saw him do it to about five people."

Peddle was most hurt when he saw his own friends at the receiving end of Jack's tactics. "He took my buddy who helped me do the original PET [Petr Sehnel], and then gave him a promotion and then broke him out of the company. He took my buddy [Larry Hittle] in Phoenix who helped us with the KIM-1 and effectively broke him after cutting a deal. Some people would say he broke the deal with Bill [Mensch]," says Peddle, referring to Jack's abandonment of the Western Design Center.

Did Jack ever ruin people for no reason? "It's not *not* true," responds Peddle cryptically. "Jack destroyed some people because he could. Jack wasn't as bad as [some people] painted him later but he wasn't an angel."

Jack's ruthless style earned him a reputation akin to a high-yield nuclear weapon in a business suit. A visit from Jack to your section of the company could easily leave behind a trail of devastation, often in the form of sudden layoffs. As these visits became common, Commodore employees began calling them Jack Attacks.

"The Jack Attack thing got to be routine," says Peddle. "When Jack spotted people fucking up, he came at them hard, and he usually found people fucking up most of the time."

Despite Peddle's disapproval of some of Jack's methods, he admired his ability to unearth incompetence within Commodore. "Jack, for a long, long time, signed every check the company wrote," explains

Peddle. "The Jack Attack was instigated by Jack seeing something in a check he was supposed to sign that would piss him off and he would call people in and beat the shit out of them."

To survive without proper financing from Irving Gould, Jack studiously monitored costs. "I used to ask him why he did it, because it was pretty tedious," recalls Peddle. "It gives you a pulse of what is going on. Anytime a company is a little bit successful, a whole lot of people start empire building. It lets you figure out who is spending your money when they shouldn't be."

The unorthodox method allowed Jack to keep a tight reign on his company, but it also resulted in unhappy visits to Jack's office. "About once every two days he would find somebody doing something either fraudulent or stupid," recalls Peddle. "Then he would go jump all over them."

Peddle blames the frequent Jack Attacks on Tramiel's policy of giving almost anyone a six week trial. "Jack would hire these truly incompetent guys and he would give them a chance to do something, and then they would go off and really screw something up," explains Peddle.

Robert Russell was amazed by the chaos of his first year at Commodore. "I was the mouse in the corner for a lot of interesting shit early on," recalls Russell. "I came out in a time when there got to be a lot of turmoil as far as managers."

Perhaps most incredible to Russell was the lack of a chain of command at Commodore. "It just so happened that Jack came directly to the engineers and impressed us with, 'I want you guys to get the job done no matter who your boss is,'" says Russell.

Russell has fits of laughter at the thought of the top person in the company giving orders to a junior engineer. "Yes sir! We knew who the boss was," says Russell.

The constant rotating door of management at Commodore sometimes made things confusing for the engineers. "I don't know how many managers I had," says Russell. "I would go home on vacation and come back to have a different manager. I think there were almost ten managers in the very first year I was there that were supposedly my manager."

Jack also stopped development of calculators. "All the calculator people [in MOS Technology] went away," says Peddle. "I think the only people left were the game guys."

Jack continued his practice of listening to new recruits. In late 1979, Jack hired a marketing graduate named Michael Tomczyk, who told Jack outright he thought Commodore marketing was the reason for the lackluster success of the PET. A thirty-megaton Jack Attack was imminent.

In late 1979, Jack fired his entire marketing department, including four marketing managers. Only two marketing people remained in Commodore: Dick Powers, whom Jack hired for conventions and trade shows, and Michael Tomczyk.

PET Software

When Commodore released the PET in 1977, there was little effort made to encourage software development. Only Chuck Peddle courted software companies, such as Personal Software. Despite this, a software industry spontaneously developed around the PET.

In 1980, Personal Software finally released a version of VisiCalc. Personal Software was concerned with piracy, so they included a unique copy protection in the form of a special 'dongle' chip that plugged into a spare socket on the PET motherboard.

According to Peddle, the PET version of VisiCalc was superior to the original Apple version. "We had an 80 column screen by that time and Apple was still limited to 40 characters," remarks Peddle. "You could do those tables in a heartbeat."

If Personal Software had created VisiCalc for the PET first, Commodore would likely have dominated both the North American and European markets. "It would have put it everywhere," says Peddle.

Commodore UK recognized VisiCalc as an important application for the business market and later sold PET computers bundled with VisiCalc. The availability of genuinely useful applications for the office allowed Commodore to dominate the European business market.

The word processor was the other killer-app for the business market. The PET had two heavyweights: *WordPro* and *Wordcraft*. The software sold for as much as £400.

Businesses also relied on database software to keep track of payroll. The PET received at least two database packages. The first, written entirely in Basic, was Compsoft's *DMS*. Commodore could not resist the lucrative market and released a database program called *The Manager*.

Users also found programs listed in magazines like Byte, Dr. Dobb's Journal, and user group publications. One such publication was the PET Gazette, started in April 1978 by Len Lindsey. From the beginning, growth was incredible. During the first year, Lindsey sent the newsletter to as many as 4000 people. Len Lindsey later merged the PET Gazette with *Compute! Publications* and helped develop the popular 8-bit magazine *Compute!*.

For the home user, games were always the most potent killer-app. Many of the first PET games originated on the KIM-1. These included

Lunar Lander, *Hunt the Wumpus*, *Tic-Tac-Toe*, *HorseRace*, *Maze*, and *Nim*.

Some of these early games were surprisingly fun. *Nightmare Park* challenged players to find their way through a labyrinth park. As the player walks through the maze, random events spawn mini-games.

The PET also had the requisite Star Trek game. In many ways, unlicensed Star Trek games were the killer-app of the game world, though not killer enough to sell computers in the millions. The most popular form of the Star Trek game had players searching for Klingon ships in a simple universe represented by a grid.

Adventure games were some of the most interesting and unique games for the PET. Scott Adams, an early adventure game pioneer, released a game called *Adventureland* for the PET in 1978. The game was similar to the legendary *Colossal Caves Adventure* for mainframe computers.

One of the most popular genres, the Role Playing Game, began life on the PET. A young programmer named Jeff McCord developed the game while attending at Henry Clay High School in Lexington, Kentucky. The school purchased a few PET computers and McCord learned Basic and began developing a game he called *Gammaquest II*. McCord developed the game on a four-kilobyte PET and allowed his fellow classmates to play the game after school.

In his first year of college at the University of Tennessee, McCord submitted his game to a company in Sunnyvale, California called *Automated Simulations* (later known as *Epyx*). The company gave McCord $2000 in advances on royalties and McCord promptly moved to California to become a programmer.

Automated Simulations released the game as *Temple of Apshai*. An interesting feature of Apshai was the use of the manual as an integral part of game play. Since the PET had only four-kilobytes of memory, the player could look up the room number in the manual for a more complete description, such as "A shallow pond fills most of the room. The surface of the water is covered with a white mold, except in the northeast corner where a clump of golden-brown seaweed is visible." RPG's quickly became more complex, with some games taking weeks or months to explore.

One of the first multiplayer networked games was *Flash Attack*, written in 1980 by Ken Wasserman and Tim Stryker. The game used a special cable to connect two PETs together, rather than using a true network.

Though the games were fun and captivating to those who played them, graphics were not outstanding on the PET compared to the Apple II or Atari 800. Graphics were composed of black and white PETSCII symbols. Despite the limitations, playing these games into the early morning was a magical experience at the time.

The Inner Family

At 48 years of age, Jack Tramiel was no longer the compact, muscular scrapper of his youth. He was now a rotund, balding, middle-aged man with wild grey hair. However, the passion that drove him showed no signs of diminishing. "Jack didn't really run his business like a business," says Yannes. "To him, business was war, and his employees were troops, and if you got close enough, you were like family."

Jack had spent a lot of time away from his three boys, mostly because of the frequent travels he endured. "Jack comes out of the camps, comes to the United States, gets something going, gets the company started, loses the company, then builds it back up again," recounts Peddle. "His whole life was that company. He kind of sacrificed his relationship with his kids. Other than gambling and some other things, Jack worked."

His sons were now mature and Jack felt a strong need to bring them into the Commodore business. He even shared his dream with some of his most trusted executives in the early eighties. Jack felt so strongly about his sons he even considered placing a clause in his will to make it more profitable for his sons to work together.

The oldest child in the family, Sam, was now 32 years old. While living in Canada, Sam received economics training at York University. He was the businessman of the family, who apprenticed under Jack. Of Jack's three sons, only Sam was involved in the day-to-day operations at Commodore.

In the late seventies, Sam incensed Jack and Helen Tramiel with his actions following the death of his young wife. "Sam started fooling around quicker than they thought he should," recalls Peddle. "He was a healthy young man, and he had been effectively cooped up with a wife who was dying for some time, so he went out and started partying."

Jack and Helen felt Sam had not allowed enough time before moving on with his life. "They got pissed and threw him away for a while," reveals Peddle. "Jack got mad at Sam and sent him off to Hong Kong."

In Hong Kong, Sam attempted to save the digital watch business for Commodore. With digital watch prices dropping so rapidly, it became more lucrative to manufacture them cheaply overseas using LCD technology instead of power-hungry LED technology. Sam found a new manufacturer to maintain their digital watch business.

Leonard, the middle child, was the scientist and intellectual of the family. "Leonard was different," says Charles Winterble, an engineering manager at Commodore. "Leonard and Sam were like night and day. Leonard was a software guy and didn't really have a lot of interest in running the company." For the moment, Leonard was out of the picture completing his PhD at Columbia University in New York.

Gary, the baby of the family, was the moneyman. In the early eighties, Gary Tramiel was an undergraduate studying for a career in finance. Incredibly, at this early stage in his life, he managed the Tramiel family's multi-million dollar investment portfolio. After graduating, Gary became a stockbroker for *Merrill Lynch*.

Al Charpentier liked the Tramiel sons, but felt they might not have the same potential as Jack. "None of the Tramiel sons were like their father," says Charpentier. "They all had reasonable skills and they weren't bad guys but Jack had that drive and desire to succeed."

For the time being, Jack continued mentoring his sons and guiding them towards a career at Commodore. Perhaps someday, they would learn enough from their father to run the company.

Aside from his immediate family, Jack also kept a circle of close associates. "There was a term called the Inner Family," explains Charles Winterble. "The inner family extended beyond his own family. He cared about those people in the inner family. You went to the ranch, you met his wife, and you sat down for drinks after all the business was over."

Jack's Inner Family was composed of Commodore employees from all over the world. Some were general managers and some were rookie engineers. "Each country had a few people," says Winterble. "Just because you were a GM didn't mean you were part of it. You were sometimes in and sometimes out."

Jack only allowed those who earned his trust into his inner circle. "That was just how Jack was," says Yannes. "Jack had a very small group of people that he trusted. As far as I know, he rewarded them well. The people who were in the Inner Circle were very wealthy."

Belonging to the Inner Family meant a lot to those who were a part of it, including Charles Winterble. "He asked about you; about your goals, about your family, and what you wanted to do," says Winterble. "You had special privileges and he would care a little bit more about you."

Jack educated members of his inner circle on how he wanted them to do business. "When you worked with Jack, as I did in my job, you had to learn the business parts of it," says Winterble. "In his words, he told me he wanted to teach me two things: he wanted to teach me to be Japanese and he wanted to teach me to be Jewish. That was his training program for me, and he did it! I learned about business and a lot of things in the consumer marketplace from him directly or indirectly. He sent me to

Japan and had me working with a bunch of these people to learn. It was interesting."

Although inner circle members received reprimands, Jack rarely gave up on them. "If Jack would get pissed off at you for something and you were a loyal employee and you were going to be there forever, what he would do is he would send you away on these long extended journeys around the world with some kind of an assignment," explains Peddle, who refers to the sabbaticals as *punishment tours*.

"Chris [Fish] had one of those," says Peddle. Fish was running the personal computer business after Jack demoted Peddle in 1978. "Chris got to do that for about six months to nine months, and the next thing you know, Jack said, 'You're not doing a good enough job at this so I'm sending you to set up distributorships.'" According to Peddle, the task was a punishment tour. Jack had given these to others over the years, including his own son Sam. The tours were the business equivalent of work tours from the WWII labor camps.

"Chris had been assigned to effectively fly around the world and set up distributorships," says Peddle. "There were all these stories of being literally ostracized from his family for a long period of time."

At the June 1980 CES show, Fish came back into favor. "Jack had sat down with him at CES and basically told him that his purgatory was over," says Peddle. "[He said] he was going to give Chris European management. That was his comeback into the fold."

Longtime employee John Calton also received a punishment tour. Calton had worked for Jack since he opened his typewriter repair shop in New York in the 1950's. "He had been with Jack since he was an Irish kid and he was totally loyal to Jack," says Peddle.

Now, Calton was the corporate buyer for the company, just a few doors down from Jack's office. With cost cutting so central to Jack's strategy, Calton held a key position at Commodore. "John wasn't the sharpest guy in town, so every so often he would screw up," says Peddle. "The next thing you know, you hear about John, and he would be here for three months; then he would be over there. Sometimes he would leave the United States and leave his family for a year. He was on these punishment tours for Jack."

The banishment concept was similar to a Japanese business practice called the 'window seat'. When a Japanese employee made a mistake, the executives sent him to a less important role in the company until he learned from his mistake. The banishments were also similar to the deportations Jack witnessed in Polish work camps. Whatever Jack's inspiration for this concept, he used it regularly.

"The idea was that they were getting punished for not doing what they were supposed to do," says Peddle. "It was an interesting punishment. You weren't fired; you weren't sent off into the corner; you were actually sent away from your family and sent away from everybody. Sam got some of that, too."

Robert Russell, the young engineer hired in 1979, also entered Jack's Inner Family. Russell worked out of an office at 3330 Scott Boulevard, in the same building as Jack. This meant Jack often dropped in on his engineers to monitor the progress of his projects.

"When I got some things done, he liked me," says Russell. "He kind of dragged me around. It was real exciting for a young guy out of college being dragged around by the president of a company to shows in Vegas and meeting people who were going to be presidents of the company and flying around in the jet."

Russell was surprised at the things he witnessed around Jack. "I would listen to them singing their German marching songs. I thought, 'That's pretty bizarre,'" recalls Russell. "That's what he admired about the Germans when he was a young kid in Poland. He remembered the songs."

"Jack told me when he was a young child and the Germans invaded Poland, where he was at, that he was impressed with the German army because they were all in shiny uniforms marching in sync, singing the German songs," says Russell. "As a child, he thought that was great when they came into Poland. Apparently it was quite a grand parade marching through."

Russell also noted the tight bond between Jack and his wife, Helen. "She was a very motherly type of person," says Russell. According to Russell, Jack would playfully say, 'Mama, cut my food for me,' and Helen would slice his food and feed him. "It was kind of embarrassing as a twenty-one year old but still kind of funny," says Russell.

Jack had conquered Europe, temporarily lost ground to Radio Shack, and matched Apple. As the new decade began, Jack would look for ways to dominate the North American personal computer market.

CHAPTER 7

The Color Computers

1979 - 1980

Although the PET had the Apple II beat in many areas, it conspicuously lacked color. "We had pretty much drawn a barrier for Apple at the higher end stuff in Europe," recalls Peddle. "We were doing very well, but the Americans were buying the color story. Apple had color and we didn't. We were getting ready to do color."

VIC

With Commodore exiting the calculator and RAM memory business, MOS began looking into other types of semiconductor chips. A young engineer named Albert Charpentier began work on a video game chip. "It was the last shot they had at trying to make a game computer," recalls Peddle. "They were trying to make a game computer to compete with Atari and everybody."

Al Charpentier was born in Philadelphia in 1952. Since his youth, Charpentier wanted to be an engineer. "I was fascinated from the age of seven about how the picture on the TV arrived in my home," he recalls. "I wanted to understand how you control a TV and that ultimately led to the video chips I designed."

Charpentier attended the University of Pennsylvania in the early seventies, but there were no courses in semiconductor design. "There was semiconductor physics and stuff like that but nothing like VLSI [Very Large Scale Integration]. It was all being developed as we did it," explains Charpentier. In 1975, Charpentier graduated with a Bachelor of Science in Electrical Engineering.

Immediately after graduation, Charpentier began work at MOS Technology as an engineer. Engineers John May and Don Schneider mentored Charpentier in semiconductor design. "The engineering staff at MOS continued my education. They basically taught me how to go about the process," he says.

Charpentier spent his early years at MOS Technology designing calculator chips, always veiled in his own cloud of tobacco smoke. "He always had a cigarette in his mouth, even if it wasn't lit," recalls Bob Yannes. "Sometimes he'd have lit cigarettes in three or four ashtrays scattered around the office."

His boss, Charles Winterble, was impressed with the chip designer. "Charpentier was a rail-thin guy and a chain smoker. He was just a hyperactive kind of guy," says Winterble. "He was also a clean-cut guy. Charpentier would show up frequently wearing a tie to work."

During the Pong videogame fad, MOS Technology helped companies develop semiconductor chips. "MOS Technology had made videogame chips for a couple of companies, like Coleco," says Yannes. At the time, most of the electronics resided in the game cartridge. "They looked like game cartridges that you plugged into the game [module], but in fact the game module itself was just a power supply and an R/F modulator. The game cartridges weren't software; they were whole custom chips to play that particular game."

Charpentier found the game design inefficient. "Al basically thought that was a pretty crazy way to do that," recalls Yannes. "Why not have a microprocessor and a video chip in the box, and the cartridge could just be software, which is where Atari ended up."

After the MOS Technology acquisition, Charpentier worked for Jack Tramiel. "I liked him," says Charpentier. "He had a tough way about him and he was gruff. He had some pretty big flaws. If you could look past those flaws, he had a lot of things he could teach you."

When the calculator market crashed, Charpentier suddenly had the freedom to pursue his own projects. "At the time, MOS Technology had just had a big layoff," says Yannes. "As a result of the layoff, Al ended up as the head of the chip department. He told me the reason he did [a video] chip is because he wanted to learn how TV's worked."

Charpentier offered to design a video chip for Commodore. "When Commodore took over in late 1976 or early 1977, that's when I basically made the proposal," says Charpentier. "I started on the chip in 1976 and didn't have it working until one year later." The video chip would become part of the 6502 family of chips, so Al gave it the numerical designation 6560. He called it the Video Interface Chip, or VIC.

The VIC displayed eight colors: black, white, red, cyan, purple, green, blue, and yellow. It could also display bitmapped graphics if the chip had eight kilobytes of memory available. The chip even had the ability to work with a light gun or light pen. Charpentier planned to add sound synthesis to his video chip too.

According to Chuck Peddle, he knew Atari was developing a more advanced chip at the time. "We kind of kept telling them, 'Don't bother because you're not going to be able to compete,' because we had a relatively good insight into the Atari infrastructure," says Peddle. Unfortunately, a non-disclosure agreement with Atari prevented Peddle from telling Charpentier what he knew. "We weren't allowed to communicate it to them." It was for the best.

The design process for the VIC 6560 was similar to the process used by Peddle to design the 6502. "There was a team of people involved," says Charpentier. "There was a logic designer, a circuit designer – generally, they would be the same person – and then a layout designer."

Much like the 6502 design process, the methods were primitive. "With today's capabilities, it seems so crazy what we were doing 30 years ago," recalls Charpentier. "There wasn't the computing power, so it was all done by hand."

As usual, once the design was completed, Charpentier spent weeks measuring to make sure the different layers lined up. "After the layout was done you had to check it by hand and make sure all the interconnects were correct," recalls Charpentier. "I had that chip operational in 1977."

Charpentier impressed Winterble with his dedication to the semiconductor craft. "It was amazing, the number of things he could carry," recalls Winterble. "Back in those days, we slept on cots to get some of this done. These were very serious guys. Charpentier was probably close to genius."

The 40-pin chip worked exactly as Charpentier hoped. "We had the full palette of colors," recalls Charpentier. He even added a feature that allowed programmers to redefine the character set. On the PET, programmers could not change the fonts and character graphics, but the VIC chip allowed users to change all the characters. This feature would allow diverse graphics in video games.

With the work completed, MOS Technology hoped to sell the chip to other electronics companies, as they had with the 6502. "The original intent was that we were going to sell it as a standard piece of silicon and sell it to somebody who would want to make a product," says Charpentier. "A videogame was the intent at the time."

Charpentier unveiled the VIC chip at the January 1978 Consumer Electronics Show. Programmers created a small, colorful demo that showed a ball bouncing around on the screen. They also handed out literature encouraging manufacturers to use the chip in low-cost CRT terminals, biomedical monitors, and control system displays.

Apple attended the same show for the first time. "Steve Jobs and Wozniak came by," recalls Charpentier. "They were very impressed and really liked it a lot. Woz was wondering how we did the colors. Woz must have come by three different times and I wouldn't tell him," laughs Charpentier.

Charpentier also brought the chip to the Hanover Fair in Germany. As things turned out, no one was interested. "We were trying to sell it into the merchant market as OEM and it never went anywhere," recalls Charpentier.

The biggest detriment to the VIC chip was the character display. Charpentier designed the chip around video games, which is clearly visible in the thick, blocky characters produced by the VIC chip. The chip could only display 22 characters per line, compared to 40 characters for the PET. It was clear to Charpentier that his VIC chip was in danger of fading into oblivion.

Moore Park R & D Labs

In late 1979, Chuck Peddle had an opportunity to change the simple computer systems division at Commodore into his vision of a technology company similar to Hewlett-Packard. "We had some good gains and Commodore was doing pretty well by that time," recalls Peddle. "We were trying to expand the company at that point."

Peddle planned to create three research and development labs, all operating out of separate buildings far from Commodore headquarters. Surprisingly, Peddle met with no resistance from Jack Tramiel.

"These were nothing expenses," says Peddle. "If anything, Jack used to get shit from Irving because we didn't show up good on analysts' screens. They said we weren't spending enough on engineering." Commodore even resorted to artificially pumping up the number of engineers on the stock reports. "We used to throw everybody and their dog into engineering just to try to get their numbers up," reveals Peddle.

With Commodore's appetite for engineers increasing, Peddle developed a second source by creating a small research lab at the *California Polytechnic State University* in San Luis Obispo. "We set that up because we were looking to get people out of the colleges there like we had at Iowa State," says Peddle.

Peddle also developed a research center using former acquaintances from his GE days. "I knew a bunch of guys in Phoenix who were really smart guys, working out of this company called Courier," explains

Peddle. "They had spun out of Courier because Courier had been bought and sold, and they were not happy. So a friend of mine [Larry Hittle] offered to set up a design center, similar to the one Bill had, which would be owned by Commodore."

Peddle wanted his Phoenix team to focus on high-end business systems. "It would be an advanced technology center for Commodore," explains Peddle.

The team began looking at data storage devices to handle mainframe data from the business world. Peddle wanted an eight inch floppy disk drive that would be compatible with the IBM 3740 disk format, as well as Peddle's efficient GCR format.

The Phoenix team developed several different models of eight-inch floppy drives with different storage capacities. The first drive, the 8060, was a single drive that could store 750 kilobytes. Later drives included the 8061 with 1.6-megabyte storage capacity and the 8062 dual-drive with 3.2-megabyte capacity.

In 1980, Commodore was selling the 2040 dual disk drive for $1,295.00. Cables cost another $80. Later, Commodore released the 8050 dual disk drive, which doubled the storage capacity (double density) from the 2040. This drive sold for $1,695.00. "We did things with densities on floppies at Commodore that put us way ahead," recalls Peddle.

Peddle also set up a California lab that would become the crown jewel of Commodore's research program. Here, Commodore engineers would develop secret weapons that would give Commodore long-term technological superiority over their rivals.

Peddle loved the vibrant microcomputer scene in Silicon Valley, so he wanted a research center to take advantage of the synergy with other companies. Peddle chose *Moore Park*, a lush industrial park in San Jose. The name of the industrial park was in honor of Gordon Moore, the cofounder of Intel and author of Moore's law.

The Moore Park lab was about ten minutes away from Commodore headquarters in Santa Clara, California, near the bizarre 160-room *Winchester Mystery House*.

Peddle wanted his key engineers to concentrate on the future of Commodore technology. "The idea behind Moore Park was to get away from the day to day factory stuff," says Peddle. "During that time we came up with the idea of splitting the group up and leaving guys like Russell to hand-hold the factory while we were off designing what was going to happen next."

The engineers at the Moore Park facility were all young, recent hires who had proven their abilities at Commodore. "They took away all the first rank engineers," says Russell. "It was kind of a way to give all the senior guys their own office, because we couldn't really do that in the other building." The team included Bill Seiler, John Feagans, Glen Stark, Scott Patterson, and recruits Peddle would hire in the following months. Robert Russell was only recently hired and too inexperienced to join.

The research center was modest by most standards. "It was a second story office building and not a big office building," says Russell. "It was all broken into offices or labs. They had a hardware lab, a software lab, and they had a conference room."

According to Peddle, the research cost Commodore very little. "We didn't spend a lot of money on things," he recalls. "We had a discretionary budget where we could get toys. We had to read books for that time and we had to buy some competitors' equipment. It was a well-funded development center by Commodore standards, but certainly nothing very astounding; ten people or something like that. We were using people's minds rather than Jack's money."

Both Chuck and Jack appreciated the relative isolation of the research centers. Jack believed marketing people slowed down the design process and exasperated engineers, and he even forbade his own marketing people from visiting the Moore Park labs. This provided an ideal, free setting for Commodore engineers to develop elegant technologies.

The charter for Moore Park was clear. "The idea behind Moore Park was to be on top of every one of the technologies that were starting to explode," explains Peddle. "To understand them and decide how we were going to integrate them into the next products we were doing."

Peddle expected Moore Park to deliver consumer products for the coming year, while the Phoenix Research Center developed technologies with no definite goal. "[Moore Park] was both a technology center and an advanced development center, whereas in Phoenix they were just an advanced development center," says Peddle.

At any given time, Moore Park had up to a dozen different projects. "Moore Park had somebody working on everything a computer could do," recalls Peddle. "We were doing voice in/voice out. We were doing voice recognition. We were doing all kinds of communications stuff. We actually did some primitive networking work." Some of the technology seemed exotic for the early eighties, including a working prototype of a touch screen. "We were using LED's [light emitting diodes] along the sides [of the monitor]," says Peddle.

Incredibly, Moore Park developed digital camera technology similar to a webcam. "We were trying to find what you do with computers," recalls Peddle. "One of the things we wanted to do was have a computer where you can call up people and talk to them, and they can see you and you can see them."

In the late seventies, the digital camera revolution had not yet begun, so Moore Park had to pioneer the work using a technology called CCD (Charged Couple Device). "CCD allowed it," says Peddle. A CCD is an array of receptors in a grid. When a photon of light hits one of the receptors, it releases an electron. The CCD device has a grid of pixels, almost like a monitor, except the CCD pixels receive light instead of emitting light.

"Basically we had one guy who was just totally in love with CCD and what you could do with vision, and that was his charter," recalls Peddle. "He was a very weird guy but he was making that happen. I think they were the first people to show a CCD camera on a personal computer."

Peddle wanted to use the CCD camera and his computer to revolutionize personal communications. "We did some work on communications that could support it," explains Peddle. In the pre-Internet era, phone lines were the only infrastructure capable of transmitting data across the world. The team researched modems for data transmission.

"We had some pretty good communications guys," says Peddle. "We had a clear understanding that we would get nominal speeds. I don't think we projected 56 [Kilobaud] but we had certainly projected 20. It isn't screaming fast, but in the kingdom of the blind, the one eyed man is king."

To gauge the public interest in video communications, Peddle demonstrated the primitive technology behind closed doors. "What we did were these nice little hokey demos, making them look better than they were; knowing that we had to have some more speed in the modems," reveals Peddle.

In mid-1980, Commodore released the 8010 modem. "The modem stuff was a direct result of the work that was going on at Moore Park," claims Peddle.

The 8010 was an acoustic coupling modem, which meant the user was required to manually dial a number to the connecting computer and then place the receiver in a specially designed coupling device. The modem retailed for $395.00 and was capable of delivering groundbreaking speed of 300 baud or approximately one line of text per second on a 40-column screen.

The vast array of projects led Peddle and his team to wonder how a single computer could use multiple peripherals elegantly. They began to think of the operating system. "The problem was, if you are going to do all this shit, you had to have some kind of an operating system, and you had to have some way of tying it all together," explains Peddle. "Johnny [Feagans] and some of the software guys were trying to keep it all under one umbrella. We had some interesting questions about that."

Their questions eventually steered them towards developing the next generation computer for Commodore.

The Apple Killer

In late 1979, Chuck Peddle and his team began focusing on a next generation product for Commodore. "As soon as we had the printer and other stuff done for the Commodore PET, we started focusing on what's next," says Peddle.

It was hard to ignore the growing influence of computer games. "Computing was going a couple of places," says Peddle. "It was going to good games, because at this point in time Atari is a very successful gaming company. It was obvious graphics were going to go someplace they hadn't been. Color was going to be very important in that market."

The Apple II, along with VisiCalc, began gaining momentum in late 1979, and Jack Tramiel took note. "The instructions from Jack were that he wanted a product to compete with Apple," recalls Peddle. "It was intended to be an Apple killer." Jack wanted Peddle to show his Apple killer at the January 1980 CES.

Robert Russell saw early plans for the computer. "It was like the Apple II and Atari 800, which were out at that time and doing quite well," says Russell. "The whole idea was to give more options and expansion, and a more integrated package. It was a bigger box with slots."

As plans for the Apple killer took shape, Peddle came to the realization that the 6502 was not up to the task of serious computing. He needed two computers: an expensive, high-end computer for the business market and a cheaper home computer based around the 6502 architecture. "It started out as the Apple killer," says Peddle. "Then we changed its direction. What we needed was a totally different machine for the high-end: higher disk space, lots of memory, and a much better processor."

To Jack's dismay, work on his Apple killer virtually stopped while Peddle and his engineers regrouped. "We kind of abandoned the idea of doing what would be an Apple II look alike," says Peddle. "I suspect it is one of the things that Jack got mad about."

Between the high-end business machine Peddle had in mind, and the low-end games machine, it was apparent Jack favored the latter. "We were looking effectively at both," says Peddle. "We were spending more time on making sure we could do the low-end because that is what Jack wanted first."

The Color Computers – 1979 to 1980

Bill Seiler, the loner Peddle befriended in an arcade in Florida, took the development lead on the low-end games machine. "Seiler had some interesting, clever thoughts in him," says Peddle. "He was really good with kids. He was really good with games. He had a good understanding of that sort of thing. He had a good understanding of video."

Seiler dubbed his game machine the TOI. "Bill Seiler came up with it," recalls Peddle. Seiler intended the name to convey a sense of playfulness. Meanwhile, Peddle gave meaning to the TOI acronym, calling it *The Other Intellect*.

"The TOI became focused around a low-end machine," says Peddle. "The little machine was all focused around the best graphics game-playing computer you could build."

Seiler began working with the MOS Technology engineers on the East Coast to develop an improved color graphics chip. "We wanted a good, low-cost color chip," says Peddle. "Effectively MOS Technology were being sponsored by us to get their chips done. One group had the role of defining a new next generation computer system, and the other guys had the role of building the chips for it."

Seiler designed his own circuit boards to test his ideas. "Bill Seiler did some really interesting display stuff, none of which ever made it out," says Russell.

Seiler worked primarily with Al Charpentier. "The architecture of the chip was done by Charpentier," recalls Peddle. "There were multiple conversations between Seiler and some of those guys and Charpentier and his team."

Moore Park was limited in what they could work on while MOS Technology developed the new chips. "Once we concluded we needed a high-end graphics controller, we were at the mercy of MOS Technology," says Peddle. "There was no reason to draw schematics, because they weren't ready." Instead, Moore Park focused on building smaller prototypes to test different aspects of the new system, such as DRAM. "We did all kinds of prototypes," recalls Peddle.

Bob Yannes recalls the scaled back design of the TOI. "There were no card slots," says Yannes. "I think it was 16K/32K memory."

Rather than a monitor, the TOI would use a household television. "The TOI was taking the concept of a color PET and [building it] around using a color television," says Russell. "It was more a forerunner to the Commodore 64 as far as its ambitions."

Moore Park also continued developing advanced projects, such as the digital camera, modems, and networking. Unfortunately, Jack Tramiel did not like what he was seeing. "Jack definitely felt that we were spending too much time screwing around with all these different things and not getting done what he told us to do," says Peddle. "His impression was correct; we weren't getting it done, but we weren't getting it done because the product that we had chosen to do was dependent on a chip that we didn't have yet."

The PET Jet

Jack had known wealth during his typewriter days, but his personal fortune had never been as high as it was in 1980. Commodore sales reached $125 million for 1980, compared to $79 million for 1979, and Commodore had a net income of $16.2 million. As a result, Commodore traded publicly at over $90 per share - and that was after splitting two for one and three for two many times since 1976! Jack was now worth over fifty-million dollars.

Although Jack lived a modest lifestyle, he indulged his love of expensive automobiles. "He had quite a car collection," recalls Russell. "He had a flashy red 308-style Ferrari. Jack had some weird cars. He had things with expired Canadian plates sitting around and a junker that was probably a nice car at one point in time."

The pride of Tramiel's collection was his V-12 Jaguar, which required expert maintenance. "He had the Jag that he had special mechanics to keep in tune," explains Russell. Despite his wealth, Jack drove himself to work everyday.

During one visit to the Tramiel ranch, Jack offered Russell an unusual deal. "I was out admiring his Ferrari one time and he said, 'Don't take salary for the next few years, and it's yours,'" recalls Russell, who politely declined the offer.

In contrast to Jack, Irving lived an expensive lifestyle. "Everybody was complimenting [Irving] on what a great job he was doing," says Peddle. "He was having a lot of fun. He was doing it the way he wanted to do it. He engaged in a lot of vices all his life; smoking, drinking, women. He lived life to the fullest."

Peddle respected the company director. "Irving was an important part of my life and he always treated me fine," recalls Peddle. "He was always willing to sit down and talk to me. I learned a lot from Irving."

Irving split his time between New York, Toronto, and the Bahamas, where he owned a massive 70-foot yacht. "We're talking about a *Trimaran*; a big, fucking wonderful yacht," says Peddle. "If he wanted to go somewhere in the yacht, he would tell the captain, 'Go sail it into here and I'll fly in and meet you.'"

The frequent trips using commercial airlines became tiring for Irving. "Irving had an office in Toronto that he worked in part of the time and an office in New York. For a long time, he would travel back and forth with commercial airplanes," says Peddle.

With his reams of valuable Commodore shares, Irving could easily afford his own jet. However, he was not interested in spending his own money. Gould, the man who would not allocate the funds to expand the PET market into North America, insisted Commodore purchase a jet for his own use.

Corporate benefits and status symbols were not something in Jack's character. When he used commercial airlines to get around, Jack insisted on flying coach. He felt first-class tickets were a waste of company money. Irving had a different view. "Irving basically said, 'My lifestyle needs a private jet,'" recalls Peddle. "Jack was actually looking at a turbo-prop, but Irving wanted a real jet."

Eventually, Commodore purchased a seven-seat *Westwind IAI-1121*, making them the first microcomputer company to own a corporate jet.[1] In recognition of the product that made it possible, Irving and Jack dubbed it the *PET Jet*.

Jack allowed his engineers to use the Pet Jet for trade shows. "It was convenient for us to go to shows because we could load it up with all our equipment and go to Germany or Switzerland with it," says Charles Winterble. "This way everything was with us."

"Jack flew whenever he could," recalls Peddle, even though Irving dominated its use. "It used to piss Jack off, because Jack knew he built the company; he made all this money, he bought this jet and everything else, and ninety percent of the time Irving was using it to go on this lifestyle that he had."

The Color PET

The VIC 6560 chip was the first color chip by Commodore. The next chip to reach the public was the 6566 VIC-II chip, which appeared in 1982. In between the 6560 and the 6566 were some curious gaps. Unknown to the public, Commodore made two failed attempts at more advanced color chips before a usable video chip finally emerged.

In late 1979, Jack sensed his engineers were not doing enough to create a color computer for the upcoming CES show. Jack decided he would make the color chip happen through his own will.

---

[1] Israel Aircraft Industries manufactured the Westwind IAI-1121 jet. Coincidentally, IAI dubbed their jet the Commodore Jet in 1963 when they began work on the project. Some people still refer to this model as the Commodore Jet.

"Jack really wanted to do a 40-character color computer," explains Yannes. "We began working on a 40-column version of the VIC chip, the 6562, in late 1979 when Jack told his group he wanted to show a color PET at the January 1980 CES. He was always coming to people a few weeks before a show and telling them he wanted something new for the show!"

Al Charpentier recalls the origins of the 40-column computer system, which he refers to as the VIC-40. "The VIC-40 was originally proposed to Jack as new video game project that would require the 6562 chip," says Charpentier. "Jack read the proposal in '79 and blessed the project."

With the deadline less than a month away, Al Charpentier decided to modify his VIC chip to produce 40-columns. "The only thing we had time to do was take the VIC-I chip and double its speed so we could do twice as many characters," explains Yannes.

The engineers also decided to improve the number of colors that the chip could display in high-resolution mode. "Al redesigned the color generator to produce better colors, and I redesigned the video output to provide the multicolor mode that would allow us to produce a bit-mapped display with more than two colors," says Yannes.

Doubling the speed of the VIC-chip was not easy, especially with the slow memory that existed in 1979. "That created some real timing problems because – this is kind of a laugh today when you think about it – the fastest memory chips you could get were 450 nanosecond access times, and this video chip would have required 200-nanosecond parts," explains Yannes.

Though new, Yannes was a quick study. "The 6562 was the first chip design work I had ever done," recalls Yannes. "I joined Commodore right out of college in June of 1979, and although trained as an electrical engineer, I had no training or experience in chip design. I remember thinking it wasn't such a great idea to put me on a project that needed to be done quickly and correctly the first time."

Yannes found time to experiment with sound synthesis. "I also redesigned the sound generator to add new waveforms," explains Yannes. "The 6560 had step-approximations of sine waves, which sounded pretty bad. Al didn't know much about sound synthesis."

Instead of merely generating the same types of sounds using sine waves, Yannes added several different types of sound waves. "Sine waves are pure tones with no harmonics, which makes for pretty uninteresting sounds, and the steps in the waveform made it sound pretty noisy," explains Yannes. "I changed the waveform generators to provide a saw tooth wave, a square wave, and either a triangle wave or a pulse wave."

Normally, it takes over a year from the initial conception of a new chip to the time it exists in silicon. Since Charpentier and Yannes started with the original VIC design, it only took them a week to produce the new layout and another week for the MOS technicians to deliver a working chip. "We had a turnaround time on a custom chip of two weeks, which is absolutely unheard of," says Yannes.

MOS Technology was Commodore's ultimate weapon. "We had to redesign it, simulate it, get it laid out, and get it through the front-end processing to get functional chips out in time for the show," recalls Yannes. "If Commodore had not had MOS Technology as an in-house resource, there was no way [to get it done]. There is no chip manufacturer that would jump through hoops like that to make prototypes for a show."

Despite the rushed effort, Charpentier and Yannes made surprisingly few errors. "It turns out we had only one layout bug in the chip on the first pass, and we corrected it and got new wafers processed through the MOS fabrication in one week," says Yannes.

With less than a week before the CES show, Bill Seiler inserted the new chip into a modified PET motherboard. Meanwhile, Robert Russell changed the ROM code to allow the PET to work with the new chip. Externally, the prototype resembled a regular PET computer. "It was actually in a PET case with a color screen," says Russell.

Jack had willed a 40-column color computer into existence in time for the CES show. It was a shortcut using the outdated VIC chip, but it was there nonetheless. This raised questions in Jack's mind: if he could make the color chip happen, why could Chuck Peddle not?

The G-Job

With the Apple killer awaiting a new graphics chip, the Moore Park engineers realized they would not have anything to show Jack at the upcoming CES show. However, the team had access to jars of unused, unwanted VIC chips. "Soon after we started, we took the VIC color chip and started playing with it," recalls Peddle.

Bill Seiler came up with the idea for an alternate low-cost computer. He told Peddle, "I can make this really self contained unit with the VIC chip. We can't get what we want, so let me build this thing and see if we can get people interested."

Even in the late seventies and early eighties, Seiler stood out in a crowd because of his massive, unkempt beard and long, blonde ponytail that stretched all the way down to his waist. "He had the body of a gymnast; relatively small, like a gymnast would be," says Peddle. "He had a long ponytail forever and always wore cutoffs and sandals."

Not only did Seiler look distinctive, but he also had a distinctive philosophy. "When he first moved to California, he came in this little Honda," recalls Peddle, referring to the original *Honda Civic* that did not compare favorably to Chuck Peddle's *Porsche*. "I asked him about it and he said, 'I'm like a turtle. I don't want to own anything I can't put in the Honda.' He wanted to pack up and go anywhere. That was his view about life."

When Seiler first came to California, he stayed with Chuck Peddle and his family for a few months. "He lived with me in my house," says Peddle. "Of course, the kids loved him. All of us loved him."

While not at Commodore, Seiler enjoyed the unique California culture. "He swims, surfs, body surfs, wind surfs, and runs," says Peddle. "I probably got him into running more than anybody. We used to run together a lot."

Seiler took computer graphics seriously and attended computer graphics conferences. "Seiler was into this show called *Siggraph*, which is about graphics," says Peddle. Siggraph, a gathering of computer users searching for ways to improve computer graphics, held the first conference in 1973. "Seiler had been going to Siggraph since the time it started. He was a true pioneer. He walked the walk and talked the talk."

Seiler was a curious man by nature and often became so engrossed in technology he forgot his surroundings. At a family gathering of Commodore employees at *Disneyland* in California, a laser beam captured Seiler's attention. While other Commodore employees had fun on the rides, Seiler studied the blue laser beam attached to the Disneyland Hotel. Lasers were all the rage in the early eighties and Seiler was fascinated. He purchased a silver Mylar helium balloon with a long string and floated the balloon in front of the laser, studying the way the balloon scattered the light. Those who attended the gathering remember seeing him playing with the light all night. Four hours later as everyone departed, he was still playing with the laser.

Seiler was also a competent programmer and wrote a software package called *Basic-Aid* for the PET, which added some useful Basic commands to the existing Commodore Basic. He also wrote *Extramon*, a machine language monitor program used by developers to create high-level machine language programs for the PET. Seiler was also the lead designer of the PET 8032, which allowed 80 columns years before it was available on Apple computers.

Now, Bill Seiler was Peddle's number-one engineer at Moore Park. Seiler called his low-cost project a *G-job* because it was the type of fun project engineers created in their garages around Silicon Valley, usually on their own time.

The Color Computers – 1979 to 1980   143

Unfortunately, the other engineers at Moore Park were unenthusiastic. "It was really Seiler carrying the ball on his own," says Peddle. "To some extent, Seiler had to put up with his partners in the lab thinking that it was too low-level, because most of the focus was on bigger, better, faster. Everybody pooh-poohed it because there was only a [22]-character screen. A bunch of people that argued nobody would buy it."

Peddle tentatively supported the idea, hoping it might appease Jack. "What we were trying to do was to not stop any good ideas in the lab," says Peddle.

Seiler designed his computer for kids. "He was the greatest guy in the world with kids. That's one of the reasons that some of the stuff we did turned out so well. Bill thought like kids did," says Peddle. "Seiler visualized a machine that would play great games. The major thing he did was keep us focused on warm and fuzzy and friendly."

Instead of redesigning a complete computer system, Seiler used a standard PET motherboard as the basis for his computer. He carefully sawed the motherboard in half, removing the video section of the board, and replaced it with a VIC chip. The result was a messy but functional tangle of multicolored wires.

"It was effectively a PET under the table running the screen," says Peddle. "It was a VIC chip and it was color, but to make it work he just basically hacked together a regular PET." The engineers knew the prototype was not in a final form. "We'd make some kind of product that would work, but it wasn't necessarily producible, if you will."

The original PET ROM's only worked with the CRTC chip, not the VIC chip. To make his color display work, the ROM code required changes. Seiler turned to his friend and co-worker, John Feagans.

Feagans was born on the West Coast in Oregon. Since an early age, he had an affinity for electronics and creativity. At the age of eleven, Feagans tried to build his own electronic organ. While still in high school, Feagans published a pictorial book on trains called, *The Train that Ran by the Sea*. He also built his own high-quality furniture and brewed his own beer and wine. Now he was one of Commodore's key developers.

"John is schoolmasterly," says Peddle. "He's the sort of guy you would think of as a high school science teacher or a schoolmaster. He's kind of tall, kind of slim, very mild-mannered, and wears glasses. He has a studied, quiet voice."

"He was a sharp, young guy," says Winterble.

Although the hardware engineers are more often glorified, software engineers like Feagans were equally important in making the system work properly. "He was as close to a software engineering manager as we had," recalls Peddle. "He really formalized that position. I'm not sure that people would have necessarily seen John as much of a manager, but on the other hand, he could be considered a leader."

Compared to Peddle, Feagans was introverted and quiet. "He was very private," recalls Peddle. "He didn't socialize very heavily. He was just John. Generally, you could trust him to get done whatever he said he could commit to do. He was a very serious guy."

Bil Herd, one of Commodore's most extroverted engineers, concurs. "He was regarded as something of a kook, but I think he always got his part of the job done," says Herd.

One of Feagans' closest friends at Commodore was his fellow programmer, Robert Russell. "He went to College at Iowa State University," recalls Russell. "That's where I ran across him because he used to argue for the 6502 and I would tell him he was full of shit."

When Russell was new to Commodore, he shared a house with Feagans and the two became a sort of odd couple. "John was kind of tough to get along with at points in time," says Russell. "He was kind of a perfectionist; a clean guy. When I lived with him, I cooked sauerkraut in his pans. He freaked out because it boiled over, and it was going to etch the copper. We supported each other and remained friends, even though we had our differences about how things were to be done."

At Commodore, Feagans pushed for better architecture in software and wrote much of the early code for the PET computers. By the time Russell joined Commodore, Feagans passed much of the low-level coding to him. "He was an architectural-type of guy, not a down and dirty guy," says Russell.

Feagans was also instrumental in creating tools for his computer programmers. "He wrote the compiler we used," says Bil Herd. "You have to remember, during this time, they're writing the code on PET's, and it would take overnight to compile. There were no Vaxes at Commodore at that time."

Feagans patched the existing Basic 2.0 ROM's in order to make the VIC chip work with Seiler's G-job. Because it was only a fun project, the two kept their goals to a minimum. Seiler's computer could not output high-resolution bitmapped graphics, but users could still make color pictures using PETSCII.

Seiler needed a case for the motherboard. As it turned out, a ghost from Commodore's past would provide the solution. Seiler discovered some of Commodore's old printing calculators lying in the trash. He realized the bulky device was just large enough to house his prototype motherboard. Seiler removed the bowels of the device and modified the case by cutting away plastic and drilling holes in the sides for connectors. He also enlarged the keypad opening to accommodate one of the early rubber PET keyboards. Moore Park now had a prototype to display at the upcoming CES show.

CES Las Vegas

Just after the start of the new decade, companies gathered in Las Vegas to display their latest technology. "You always do your R & D stuff for the January show," explains Peddle. "The January CES show was – and to some extent still is – the place where everybody goes to get ideas for what might happen that year. Then we go to the June CES show to sign orders for what they are going to buy that year."

Chuck Peddle brought some of the cutting-edge technology he and his engineers developed at Moore Park. "One of things we decided to do was a backroom suite of Commodore capabilities," recalls Peddle. "We did a show-version of the big disk drive, we had some speech going, and we had the CCD [digital video camera]."

Commodore unveiled their three competing systems: the ColorPet, the TOI, and Bill Seiler's G-job, which the engineers presented as a bridge towards the TOI.

The ColorPet was the most complete product in appearance. "I believe what was shown at CES was literally a PET with a color display," recalls Yannes. The ColorPet demonstrated the new sound features of the 6562 chip. "I recall helping John Feagans with some of the music stuff for a demo," says Yannes.

Bill Seiler's G-job was also functioning at the show. "He built it up a little bit more and showed what you could do with it from a graphics standpoint," says Peddle. "We hadn't supported it with very much software, but he did demonstrate it."

Although the VIC-based computer was working, Peddle views the demonstration as something of a deception on their part. "The thing in January was just a demo," explains Peddle. "We were trying to make something that was going to be potentially real, but it was strictly all fake. You can do a lot of things if you put stuff on top of tables, and under the bench you have a lot of crap. That's part of the business."

The TOI – the Apple killer Jack was waiting for – was nowhere in sight. The engineers had to rely on pamphlets to describe the TOI. Peddle described his goals for the machine and then showed the G-job, hinting that the final product would be similar but better. The demonstration worked. In April 1980, Byte magazine described the system:

> Heading the list was the prototype of the TOI ("The Other Intellect") color computer. Aimed at the low-end market, the TOI is designed to interface with your home color television

set. The displayed image will feature 16 colors, 160 by 192 resolution (with three colors in the high-resolution mode), Microsoft BASIC, and a standard keyboard. The price could be under $700.

The engineers were disappointed they could not display an actual TOI prototype, however. "We missed the show because there was nothing from MOS Technology that we could use," says Peddle, although he acknowledges that some blame for the delay was due to the architecture designed by Peddle's engineers. "Their argument might be that the architecture they were working on at that time was wrong and they had to change it. That's probably true too. But it was them driving the architecture, and we were just writing the specs for that product."

Peddle knew Jack would not be impressed. "He would have expected something that was further along," he explains. "What he wanted us to have at the show was a product that he was going to take to market."

When Peddle returned from Apple, he had repaired his relationship with Jack by successfully releasing the new PET computers and disk drives. Unfortunately, it did not last. "The personal relationship was very good and then it got bad again, which happened to almost everybody with Jack," says Peddle.

Peddle tried his best to demonstrate something without a proper video chip, but Jack viewed it a different way. He came to the show to expecting to see the Apple killer he had asked for. "Jack went through and reviewed the things at the show," recalls Peddle. "It was the first time he had a chance to see all of it himself. He went around and talked to everybody."

The reaction was not what Peddle hoped. "He was basically pissed at me because we weren't moving fast enough on the Apple killer," recalls Peddle. "Jack turned [Seiler's VIC computer] down in an angry way. Jack said, 'This isn't what I told you to do. You're failing.' He's right, we were."

Jack believed Peddle was trying to placate him with Bill Seiler's G-job. According to Peddle, Jack said, "Listen, what you're trying to do with this VIC computer is to cover for the fact that you haven't done what I told you to do, which is create a product that we can put out this year and wipe out Apple."

"He thought we were screwing off, because we didn't have it done," recalls Peddle. Jack felt he had good reasons to believe Peddle was not working hard enough to deliver a color chip. After all, Jack himself had rushed in at the last minute and persuaded MOS Technology to develop the 6562 color chip and the ColorPET.

Peddle felt he had done everything he could have. "The bottom line is our definition of the product involved us having a chip," he explains. "If we wanted to be cost competitive, we needed a chip rather than trying to do it in standard stuff. So we built our future around a chip which was delayed a few times. The chip didn't happen on schedule."

Jack refused to acknowledge that it takes time to develop new technology. "Jack didn't like excuses," says Peddle. "He had very little patience with us."

Rather than blame MOS Technology for the delays, Jack blamed Chuck Peddle. "Jack chooses to get angry at whoever he wants to get angry," says Peddle. "There are a lot of messengers with spears in their bellies." Peddle agrees he was the logical person to blame. "It was my responsibility."

After the show, Peddle dropped all plans of continuing with the low-cost VIC-based computer. "I told Seiler, 'Okay, we had a chance to show it, Jack said no. Let's go ahead and focus on getting the TOI done.'"

Although the 6562 chip was good enough to demonstrate a ColorPET at CES, it was inappropriate for a personal computer. "We got through the show, but when Jack found out that it required 200-nanosecond RAM, he freaked out because that's very expensive," recalls Yannes. "He said we've got to change that."

Plans for a ColorPet also disappeared. "It was just too hard to get anything working well," says Yannes. "I think the product just kind of went away, because it was clear it needed to be designed from scratch and not pieced together from existing junk."

After Peddle's rebuke from Jack, he began pushing harder for the Apple killer. "We started putting some serious pressure on the guys to get a better chip," recalls Peddle. "We also started talking about how we would come to market without the full implementation. In other words, there were some things we could do to effectively work around the fact that we didn't have a chip."

MOS Technology began work on the 6564 chip, which they intended to use for the Apple-killer computer. "That's what necessitated the 6564/65 chip, which was a 6562 re-designed to work with slower DRAM memory," explains Yannes. The 6564 was a moderate improvement on the VIC chip. "Resolution was 320 x 200 with the same colors as the VIC-20. In all cases, we were talking about a 40-character line."

Peddle's engineers pushed for dynamic RAM, or DRAM, rather than the more expensive static RAM, or SRAM. "Chuck Peddle's group wanted to use DRAM to get more memory in less chips," recalls Yannes. "We had to come up with a video chip that would do 40-character lines but would work with slower memory and refresh the memory. That's what went into the TOI, but it was a nightmare, because we were trying to shoehorn stuff onto the original VIC chip that it just wasn't meant to do. It was a real kludge."

Charpentier and Yannes ran into problems due to the slow DRAM chips. "The system design became a timing nightmare as we tried to accommodate the VIC timing to a slower, multiplexed memory bus, which also needed to be refreshed periodically," says Yannes. "I actually have schematics for the TOI prototype and it was pretty messy. I remember Chuck's group was having trouble with memory reliability as the system heated up."

The time limit facing the engineers was demoralizing. "We had between January and June to try to design a chip that can do a 40-character display and they had to try to design a system that would use it," says Yannes. "It was just – eww."

Once again, the unreasonable schedule ended up hobbling the engineers rather than spurring them on. "There wasn't enough time for a proper redesign, where the video chip would have generated all of the DRAM timing strobes, which is why the TOI prototypes weren't reliable," says Yannes. "As the parts heated up, the critical timing parameters would drift apart."

Robert Russell also watched the second attempt at a color chip fall apart. "The big problem [with the TOI] was they just couldn't make it work," says Russell. "The chips and stuff they were using just didn't hang together."

The Next Generation Computer

While the 6564 floundered, Chuck Peddle began to evolve ideas for a business computer. "Our job was to guess where things were going," he says. Peddle believed computer architecture would center around permanent data storage devices. "I tried to convince Commodore that the future of the world in computing was hard disks," says Peddle.

The Phoenix team began developing a new product for Commodore in 1980. "We started a hard drive," reveals Peddle. Unfortunately, the technology was unreliable. "I think we chose *Memorex* or one of those guys and I don't think they ever finished the drive we selected."

Commodore also manufactured two external hard drives for the PET. The first drive, the CBM D9060, was capable of storing five megabytes of data, an incredible amount back in the early eighties. Commodore also later released the CBM D9090 with 7.5 megabytes of storage.

"We had done a lot of really pioneering work on how we were going to do the disk drive and what the disk drive meant to us," says Peddle. "We were considering putting a bunch of disk management stuff out in the hard drive controller, but you start getting too divorced from the central processor."

Peddle felt the PET/CBM computers were limited by the 6502. "The higher-end CBM machines were absolutely running out of gas with the 6502," explains Peddle. "We couldn't develop the languages and we really couldn't put a proper disk-operating system on it."

The disk drive work at Phoenix led Peddle to some difficult realizations. "The hard disk effectively forced us to believe the analysis we had done," says Peddle. "We concluded that we got the wrong microprocessor. It's a big tough conclusion when you've built your whole business around a microprocessor."

While work progressed on the TOI computer at Moore Park, the Phoenix team developed a more advanced business computer. "We had basically decided it had to have much better graphics but not necessarily color," reveals Peddle. "We thought there was a tradeoff to be made there. You could make an 80-column plus screen relatively easily if you didn't have color. It had to have bigger floppy disks, and it had to be extensible into a hard disk."

The biggest concern was how to create a computer that could handle several different applications, such as his CCD digital video camera. "We had concluded that we had to get a totally different operating system, with totally different memory capabilities than we had in the 6502. It wasn't a contender at that point," explains Peddle. "We had to make a decision on what was going to be a contender." The Intel 8088 microprocessor seemed like the best candidate.

More than anything, Peddle wanted Jack to take his next generation, business computer seriously. "We were trying to convince Jack and the rest of the company that there was a serious business opportunity in going up-market; a new machine, new architecture, new everything for the business computer market," says Peddle.

Jack was not enthusiastic about another business computer. "He didn't see it as something that would have been a natural jolt to the company that would greatly enhance his stock position," says Peddle. Jack still wanted an Apple killer for the consumer market. Peddle recalls, "He had taken a position that, 'Okay, we've had fun in the business computer stuff in Europe but we're going to go focus on what we know best, which is consumer electronics.'"

Peddle tried a new tactic. "That was when we proposed that we split the company," says Peddle. "Jack would set up a separate division and let us go off and pursue the business market. We would help him get his consumer business going until he could bring in a new team."

Jack was not happy with Peddle's suggestion. "I don't think he ever really responded to us," recalls Peddle. "The thing that got Jack seriously upset with us is he viewed myself and two or three other guys as leading a rebellion against him within the company. I think it really gnawed at him that we would propose breaking his company into two sections in more or less direct defiance to his position."

Jack had good reasons to see the proposed split as a rebellion, since Peddle received a lot of support for his idea. "The Europeans believed it," says Peddle. "There was clearly a major faction of a third to fifty percent of the company who said, 'Look, we've been very successful at this other thing. If we can see a clear direction to get there lets go do that, but we can still do the consumer product.' There was never anybody who said no, we don't want to do a consumer product. It was more a recognition that there were two separate markets and two separate technologies that needed to be addressed independently. The proposal to split the company was a very sound one."

The plan bordered on insubordination. "We were really proposing a massive change to his company, and it was a direct disagreement with him," Peddle explains. "We were being polite to him, but it was clear we were leading a rebellion - but it wasn't a palace coup."

The split would clearly undermine Jack's control of the company. "His whole life was that company," says Peddle. "For him to be threatened in the thing that was his life was probably pretty scary for him, particularly when you look at his background. He had some pretty scary things happen to him in his life, so he wouldn't have been a very secure person."

Soon, Jack began mistreating and ignoring Peddle. "It wasn't just me he treated like that," says Peddle. "He treated me like that more than anybody else, but there were other people he treated in a somewhat similar way."

Worse still, Jack began to look for someone to replace Peddle. "There's a whole bunch of management theories that say you shouldn't have anybody who is irreplaceable," explains Peddle. "Jack was always looking to do that. At Commodore if you would ask the stockholders, they would say the same thing: 'Get this guy backed up. You should always have two of them.'"

Jack turned to MOS Technology for a replacement for Peddle. "I think it was around April of 1980 that Jack told us he wanted to show a PET with a color display at a big European show, which was only a few weeks away, of course," recalls Yannes. "I think basically he was getting kind of unhappy with the West Coast group. Either they couldn't make the products that he wanted or they were taking too long."

The Color Computers – 1979 to 1980

Yannes feels the request was merely an exercise to test the East Coast group. "I don't think Jack had any real interest in the product. He simply wanted to see if the engineering group at MOS Technology, Charlie [Winterble], Al [Charpentier], and I, could deliver what he demanded when he wanted it."

"He said, 'I want you to do this, and you've got two weeks to do it in,'" recalls Yannes. "At the time I was thinking, 'He's got to be kidding. Does anyone really want this product? When are they planning on producing it?' I really think that all Jack intended to do was to see if we would jump through hoops for him and give him what he asked for, regardless of what he asked for."

With weeks to go before the show, the team could not even contemplate creating a new silicon chip. Instead, they created a circuit board. "There was just no time to do anything," recalls Yannes. "I hacked together a simple color board that connected to the existing PET, and we put together a few units for the show. It was just a quick slap-together of stuff to get a color screen on the PET."

The result was a PET computer that could merely display bitmapped color graphics. "There were no changes to the system at all," explains Yannes. "All you had to do was, instead of writing one bit into memory to turn a white pixel on, you would write red, green, or blue. It didn't have intensities or anything. It was just either red, green, blue, yellow, cyan, magenta, black, or white."

Yannes also programmed a simple demonstration for the show. "There was no software for it," he recalls. "I think we scanned a color picture and had it throw it up on screen."

Although the team questioned the usefulness of the product, they built it anyway. "I don't think Jack had any intention of producing it," says Yannes. "He just wanted to see if he could come in, disrupt our schedule, say, 'Drop whatever you're doing. You've got two weeks to do this - do it.' And we did it. I don't think Jack really trusted anyone except his family. So you really had to prove yourself with him."

Charles Winterble also believes Jack did not intend to sell the product. "It was nothing," he recalls. "Part of the problem is that it wasn't really well-integrated. It was obviously an add-on. I'm sure Chuck's ideas would have been the right way to do it."

Jack was impressed with the three East Coast engineers. "That gave him the confidence that we would perhaps be able to pick up some of the design aspects of their products if the West Coast group either wasn't doing it or left," says Yannes. "I don't know what kind of politics were going on over there, but it was pretty clear Jack was trying to find some other group of people in the company to design products. Once he saw that we could deliver and given that Chuck Peddle and his team were getting rebellious, Jack gave us control over system engineering."

Commodore showed the Color PET at the massive Hanover Fair to unenthusiastic attendees. "We went to the show and showed it," says Charles Winterble. "I remember doing a lot of scrambling around trying to get RGB monitors and stuff like that from Germany." After the show, Jack gave up plans for a ColorPet product.

The Roundabout in London

In April 1980, Jack held an international meeting in London. "Jack brought a bunch of us to Europe to set up a dual planning session," recalls Peddle. Before the meeting, Jack surveyed the computer scene in Britain and was surprised to see his old calculator competitor, Sinclair, in the computer market. Jack knew low-cost computers were beginning to appear on the computer scene and he was familiar with the Atari 400, released the previous year for only $600. What he saw in Britain was a revelation.

The remarkable Clive Sinclair filled the roles of both Jack Tramiel and Chuck Peddle in one person. He ran the company and designed their products, while carrying on high-profile relationships with an ever-changing line of beautiful women. Sinclair developed a computer similar to the KIM-1 called the MK-14, with modest success, and in February 1980 released the ZX-80, which was designed for economy. It lacked color and even sound, but the sub-£100 price made it a success.

"The Sinclair was directly responsible for Commodore doing the VIC-20," explains Peddle. "He saw that it was taking off. Fundamentally, Jack always was into the market, and the market was buying the Sinclair machine."

On the first day in London, Jack held several private meetings with top Commodore executives. "He and Irving had a meeting in downtown London," recalls Peddle. "Dick [Sanford] and I went to dinner with Irving and Jack, and we had this nice conversation, and everything went fine. It was a very pleasant meeting."

After the dinner meeting, Jack had a small run-in with the London police. "We had a little too much to drink and he got busted on the way home," recalls Peddle. "He went the wrong way around a roundabout, which is the reason the cops busted him, but the cops were nice enough to let him go home."

Jack rented a beautiful English country club called Burnham Beeches to host the conference, complete with waiters in tuxedoes. "We drive back to Burnham Beeches, which is out in the woods somewhere," says Peddle.

The next day, the major players within Commodore convened in a meeting room at Burnham Beeches. Sitting at the table were Harald Speyer of Commodore Germany, Kit Spencer and Bob Gleadow of Commodore U.K., Tony Tokai of Commodore Japan, Yashi Terakura, Chuck Peddle's Japanese counterpart, Jim Dionne of Commodore Canada, and Ernst DeMuth of Commodore Switzerland. The top executives of Commodore US also attended, including Chris Fish, Dick Sanford, Dick Powers, Chuck Peddle, Jerone Guinn, and Jack Tramiel's personal assistant, Michael Tomczyk.

"Jack's late for the meeting the next day, so we start the session off," recalls Peddle. "All of the team had agreed that we really needed to have a really good business product as a follow-on product [to the PET]."

The executives felt comfortable starting the meeting without Jack. After all, Jack was not really part of the computer business. Until recently, Jack was involved in calculator products. Chuck Peddle, Chris Fish, and Dick Sanford ran the computer business.

Peddle began his briefing on the business computer. Later in the morning, Jack finally appeared. "Jack walks into the room after having studied the Sinclair thing," says Peddle. "In that moment, he decided that he was going to take back control of the company from those of us that were off doing the business stuff. Here was his chance to go back into the consumer electronics business, which he felt he could do better than everybody in the room."

Some time after CES, Jack quite correctly surmised that his head engineer was no longer listening to him. When calculators fizzled, all the power at Commodore was with computer products. Jack was in danger of losing relevance in his own company. When Jack asked for an Apple killer, Peddle did not deliver it. It seemed like Peddle was making his own decisions rather than listening to Jack. Even worse, the rebellion was spreading among his own executives. Jack knew he would have to do something to get his rogue engineer under control.

Predictably, Jack had no enthusiasm for Chuck Peddle's business computer proposal. "We had a business plan and the whole management team had put it together," says Peddle. "Jack walks in and says, 'Forget it. This is where the company is going.'"

The new plan was the low-end market. "He blocked out that we were going to do something and compete against the Sinclair," says Peddle, who found it ironic that just months before at the January CES, Jack had turned down Bill Seiler's low-cost computer angrily. "He expected us to then have the follow-on Apple product as soon as we could get it. That was his discussion in that room."

The executives had mixed reactions to his announcement. Executives thought a low-cost computer would undercut sales of Commodores keystone computer, the PET. Others questioned whether it would be possible to make a profit on something that sold for so little. Jack was not worried. He saw the same thing happen with calculators and believed the same would inevitably happen with computers. Commodore now had impressive vertical integration and he was confident this would give him an advantage over the competition.

Only a handful of people supported the idea: Tony Tokai, Yashi Terakura, Kit Spencer, and Jack's personal assistant, Michael Tomczyk. Some executives who initially supported Peddle's business computer now abandoned him as soon as they realized Jack did not support it. "Spencer was the consummate politician, so he was pushing it until Jack walked in and Jack said something else, then he was immediately on Jack's side," says Peddle. "Of course, all of the local managers jumped in and told him what a great idea it was."

Jack instructed his managers to discuss the idea further and departed. He would return the next day to review their plans.

Chuck Peddle was devastated. He was a purist when it came to computers and he wanted elegance and power in computing. Now he was supposed to get behind a computer less powerful than what Atari, Apple, and NEC currently produced.

Once Jack left the room, he began formulating a counter-proposal. "I had the whole European sales staff on my side, because they had built their reputation on business computers," says Peddle. "Our response, which was put together that same day, was, 'Jack, we accept that that's where you want to go, but the company is big enough to handle both. You go off and drive that and let us go build the business computer business.'"

That night, as Jack slept, his idea for a low-cost computer crystallized. When he awoke, he had a clear goal for Commodore. Jack returned to the meeting and asked the executives to discuss the strategies they came up with the previous day. Instead, Dick Sanford suggested the idea to create a new division, and Peddle championed the idea.

Jack felt Peddle's suggestion was open rebellion. "There is no question that he viewed that as a direct insult to his idea that we are going to go back into the consumer electronics business," says Peddle. "He put all of us on a short leash that day."

The counter-proposal landed many of Commodore's top executives in Jack's cross hairs. "He was unhappy with Chris [Fish]; that's why he screwed around with Chris. He was unhappy with Dick Sanford; that's why he ultimately forced Sanford out. He was unhappy with Mitchell.

He was unhappy with all of them, because he perceived that we didn't see his vision," says Peddle.

According to Peddle, they were more than happy to carry out Jack's plan. "The problem was, we did see his vision," says Peddle. "We knew what he needed to have done, and we could see how he could get between here and there. But we had a different vision. We had a vision of what ultimately became the PC business and he didn't share that vision."

The discussions eventually deteriorated into small groups of executives talking together. Jack allowed the discussions to continue for a while, then stood up and banged his palm on the table. Conversation stopped, and everyone faced Jack. With all eyes on him, Jack announced, "The Japanese are coming, so we will become the Japanese." The statement had everyone pondering the meaning of his words.

Jack identified the Japanese as his main competition early on, just like other companies such as Apple. In the early eighties, Japan was firmly on the minds of many North Americans. Since the late sixties, Japan had taken over American industries one at a time: small electronics, household appliances, televisions, radios, stereos, and automobiles. Now they had their sights set on the personal computer market.

Jack knew their primary advantage was their ability to deliver low-cost products. To become the Japanese, Jack wanted to undercut *their* prices. "I think he originally set some price goals that left them aghast," recalls Robert Russell.

As a master tactician, Jack took the battle to his enemy. "Jack wanted to fight the Japanese in their home market with a low-cost machine rather than the Japanese come over with a low-cost machine and fight us in the US," says Russell. Jack had seen calculator prices drop dramatically and almost put him out of business. Now he wanted to be the one driving prices down.

Although Jack had previously introduced his new products to the North American market, he decided to release the low-cost computer to Japan first. North America would follow. "It wasn't exclusive to Japan, but Jack wanted to scare the Japanese right on their own home ground and sell it there," says Russell.

Tramiel discussed the Japanese in a March 1986 interview with German magazine *Data World*. "The Japanese can only be successful in the computer industry if there are no longer people like me," said Tramiel. "The Japanese think on a long-term basis and need a three-year plan. They are not innovative and can only be successful if innovative people disappear from the industry."

Ironically, Jack was more like the Japanese than he was to his contemporary North Americans. The Japanese lived and breathed the philosophy of *Sun-Tsu's Art of War*. To Jack, business was war.

Jack's announcement meant Commodore would not wait around for the Japanese to take over yet another industry pioneered in the western world. One of Tramiel's most famous quotes is, "The minute you're through changing, you're through." Now Jack was going to change Commodore. Appropriately, the 1979 hit song, *Turning Japanese* by the Vapors summed up the new philosophy for Commodore's employees.

Commodore would now radically change direction and produce a fun computer. Jack had diverted Commodore on tangents before, producing everything from watches, thermostats, Pong machines, and office furniture. Now he was putting major resources into a new product and effectively halting further advances on the business computer.

Jerone Guinn, the tall, quiet Texan who now ran MOS Technology, volunteered his engineers to build the low-cost computer. Having the prototype built on the East Coast was Jack's way of showing Chuck he was not entirely dependent on him. If Chuck would not support his idea, other engineers would.

Chuck could not help but be feel resentment as he watched Tramiel chip away at his lead engineer role. He knew the fundamentals of computers and wanted nothing more than to design the next great machine. Now he was supposed to sit back quietly while Jack decided Commodore's next generation of computers.

CHAPTER

8

The VIC-20

1980

On the surface, Commodore computers look like friendly, innocuous little machines. Behind the scenes, however, the first consumer level computer from Commodore caused a civil war within the company. Jack orchestrated the war intentionally, playing one faction off the other. "Jack pitted people against each other," says Peddle. "He played those games with everybody all the time."

Al Charpentier witnessed Jack breeding animosity between his employees. "He created an environment of competition within his organization, and I'm not sure that is good or bad," says Charpentier. "At the time I felt it wasn't. You actually had competing engineering groups in Japan, Pennsylvania, and California. Literally, Jack would play us off on each other. He would send my work to Japan to have them critique it and have me critique their work. That's not a bad thing to do, but he would do it in a way that set us up as adversaries."

Jack used intense competition to bring out the best in his people. The biggest rivalry occurred between the systems group at MOS Technology and Moore Park in Silicon Valley, which some East Coast engineers called *Silly Valley*. Would the Commodore engineers come together when it came time to deliver their next computer?

The MicroPET

Commodore's next product came from Bob Yannes, a product of the seventies. At 22 years of age, he looked more like a teenager, resembling Luke Skywalker with glasses. "Bob was kind of a thin, young guy with blonde sandy hair," recalls Charles Winterble. "[He was] just the nicest guy in the world."

In 1979 MOS Technology was running out of engineers. "I was looking to hire some people because when Commodore took over MOS Technology, there was an exodus that happened over a year or so," recalls Al Charpentier, referring to the departure of the 6502 team and the calculator engineers. "There were only a few people left in the semiconductor design department, so I wanted to hire some people."

Charpentier went to the local universities in the Philadelphia area. "Bob was a senior at Villanova, so I interviewed him," explains Charpentier. "When he came in for the interview in our office, he saw the VIC-I chip that I was working with and he got really interested in it. He wanted to know if he could do his senior project on the chip."

Yannes remembers the incident. "When Al told me about the VIC chip he had worked on, I was like, 'Great! Tell me about it.' I got him to send me some samples and I built my senior project for school around that," he recalls. "I made a color video card that plugged into the S-100 computer that would give it graphics and sound. That was the Altair 8800 bus that eventually got adopted as an industry standard."

While other people his age were playing videogames at the local arcade, Yannes intently studied a videogame chip. "I worked on my senior project in my bedroom and at the lab at school," says Yannes. "It wasn't that complicated a project because the VIC chip did so much of the work. All I really needed to do was add memory to it and then design a bus interface."

Yannes was pleased with the results but the project was too advanced for his instructor's level of expertise. "A lot of the stuff was pretty much beyond them," says Yannes. "This was state of the art back then, and I was hand-assembling code."

Yannes graduated from Villanova University in May 1979. In July, Commodore hired him as a full-time engineer. Yannes became a protégé of Al Charpentier and quickly learned semiconductor design. "Once he joined the company, he was working on various projects on calculator stuff with me," recalls Charpentier.

Yannes fell in love with the VIC chip but was surprised that hardly anyone was interested in using it. "MOS Technology was a merchant semiconductor house," explains Yannes. "They were selling to the outside world, and here they had a chip they spent a lot of money developing and they were trying to get people interested in it."

"There were samples being given to places like Japan," recalls Charles Winterble.

The VIC-20 – 1980

Unfortunately, most companies turned down the VIC chip. "There was one Japanese company that was using it in an arcade game," says Yannes, referring to an arcade clone of *Space Invaders*.

"It was really frustrating. I thought this was a great chip and hardly anyone seemed interested in using it," says Yannes. "My job was to try to figure out how to get people interested in using the VIC chip."

Yannes created a video card for developers by extending his school project. "I designed a board which I called the ACE board that would attach to either a KIM-1 or an S100 bus to give you a video interface," says Yannes. "That was going to be sold as kind of a development system to let people see what this thing was capable of."

"We were just looking for things to do and trying to get ways to sell the VIC chip to the OEM market," says Charpentier.

Yannes saw his opportunity to produce a VIC based computer when Sinclair released the ZX-80. "It was in the spring of 1980 that the Sinclair ZX-80 came out, and all the great press about it was really frustrating to me," recalls Yannes. "I thought the Sinclair ZX-80 was just terrible. [The video display] was black-and-white. Every time you typed on the keyboard the display went blank, because they were doing the display update in software."

Yannes felt he could offer more value for a lower price. "Here's this crummy little Sinclair computer out there for 250 bucks, and we can do a real cool one for 200 bucks," explains Yannes. "To hear all this good press about all these people being excited about it, I just said, 'This is crazy. We have this little video chip here that can make a great little color graphics computer for less than the Sinclair. We can even put a real keyboard on it and make a nice product instead of that horrid thing.'"

Yannes began forming a picture of a Commodore computer using the VIC chip. "I had sort of come to the conclusion that no one in the outside world seems to be interested in this chip for whatever reasons. Fine, why don't we do something with it?" recalls Yannes. "It would have color graphics and the screen wouldn't go blank when you typed on the keyboard. You could play games and things."

"Bob said he would put this prototype together that might show more capabilities," recalls Charpentier. "Using the knowledge he gained doing his senior project, he was able to put his prototype together."

Yannes was aware of the one weakness in the VIC chip. "All we needed was to get over this mentality that a 22-column display was not good enough," says Yannes. "That's when I made the first prototype of what would ultimately be the VIC-20."

The VIC chip also received new features from the failed 6562 and 6564 chips. "Meanwhile, since we had already finished the work on the new video section, we dropped that back into the 22-column 6560 VIC, still hoping to generate some outside sales interest in the chip," says Yannes.

Yannes also wanted to improve the sound capabilities of the chip. "The tone generators that were in the original VIC-I chip when I first started working there were not really very good," explains Yannes. He copied the improved 6562 tone generator. "Although that chip never went into production, those design changes were put into the original VIC-I chip."

The prototype had modest goals. "The prototype I did on my own was literally two or three day's worth of work," recalls Yannes. "It was hardly anything because I just slapped together some boards that were lying around in the junk bin."

Bil Seiler's prototype was a G-job, but Yannes' project came together in his home. "There's a story going around about how I built the VIC-20 prototype in my garage," says Yannes. "It wasn't my garage, it was my bedroom. I didn't have a garage."

Yannes did not even use a soldiering iron to connect the wires. "I wire wrapped the thing," says Yannes. "I just took an old memory board from a KIM-1 and put a perf board on the side of it, then hooked up a processor and the VIC chip. Then I built a little case out of some sheet plastic that I had lying around, and I put the old PET calculator-style keyboard on it."

After three days, Yannes had a computer that connected directly to his television set. "I called it the MicroPET," says Yannes. "I said it was a pico-computer. If the PET was a microcomputer, then this was a pico-computer."

Yannes showed his MicroPET to Al Charpentier and Charles Winterble. "He's tinkering around, and he comes in one day, and Al grabs me and says, 'You need to look at this thing.'" recalls an amazed Winterble. "What Bob had done was jury rig a character memory ROM and put some interface chips into it, so the VIC could put characters on the screen. He demonstrated it and we said, 'Holy mackerel.'"

Although Yannes was just interested in making a competing product for the Sinclair ZX-80, he believes the management at MOS Technology saw his computer as a way to bring system's design to the East Coast. "I guess when Al and Charlie saw it, they thought, 'Hmm, this is interesting.' I was pretty naïve about politics and stuff. I was just doing my job. What we decided to do was build up a much nicer prototype and when Jack Tramiel was going to be at MOS Technology for the general managers' meeting, it would be presented to him."

Charles Winterble and Al Charpentier became involved with the development of the new prototype and showed it to their boss, Jerone Guinn. "Then the issue became, 'Well, what have you got here?' The idea was you put Microsoft Basic on here and we've got ourselves a little Basic computer," says Winterble.

Winterble decided to produce a more refined case. "We went to a local shop, and we had a little case molded," recalls Winterble. "It wasn't even injection-molded, it was a vacuum-formed case; the kind of thing where you take a sheet of plastic and it's vacuum formed into a shape. Then we put metal on the bottom of it and we put a keyboard in there."

The MOS Technology team decided they would not tell the competing Moore Park engineers about the MicroPET. "They were being secretive about us working on it before the meeting so Chuck's team wouldn't catch on and deliver," explains Yannes.

Without experienced programmers like Robert Russell or John Feagans, there was no way Yannes could modify the Basic ROM to work with the VIC prototype in time for the show. As a result, the prototype lacked an operating system or Basic. "It was an extremely minimal prototype," remembers Leonard Tramiel. "It did its job to demonstrate what the machine could do."

Without an operating system, Yannes could not load programs into memory from disk or tape. Instead, he created a demonstration program and put it in a ROM chip. "I wrote this little software routine that would tell the features of the machine and scroll these screens up," recalls Yannes. The VIC chip's scrolling effects were impressive. Messages popped onto the screen, then slid off the top as background music played. They could even slide down, left or right.

Yannes considered the MicroPET a concept machine rather than a production machine. "It was just for show," explains Yannes. "It was never a functional computer. There was no functional operating system or anything."

In May, Jack stopped by West Chester for a general managers' meeting. "On his way back from New York, he goes to see those guys, and they show him this architecture which they had created on their own," recalls Peddle.

"Charlie [Winterble] was the one who engineered this presentation to Jack," recalls Yannes. "Jack didn't know it was coming, and none of the people at the meeting knew it was coming except for Charlie and Al."

Chuck Peddle believes their manager, Jerone Guinn, saw an opportunity to take over systems design. "Yannes didn't understand that his boss [Jerone Guinn] was off pumping Jack up that he could do all that work on the East Coast," explains Peddle.

Peddle viewed Guinn as more of a politician than a leader. "[Jerone] came in from Texas, originally to help Jack with the LCD business," recalls Peddle. "He discovered that wasn't a good place to be, so he retreated into taking over MOS Technology from [Mike Canning]. He was a great politician."

Going into the meeting, Jack was already unhappy with Peddle and looking for an alternative. "I don't know the politics involved, but I guess Jack had been trying for some time to design an inexpensive home computer, and they kept turning out things that were too complicated and too expensive," says Yannes.

Jack took his seat at the meeting, and Charpentier and Winterble revealed the MicroPET to Jack. The demonstration program showed off all the capabilities of the VIC chip. The smooth scrolling went over well with Jack. "It ended up looking very impressive, because you didn't normally see that, even on high end monitors," says Yannes. "I kept the whole demonstration in black-and-white, and then the very last thing said, 'Oh and by the way, it has color,' and then it went into this color kaleidoscope program. It was a pretty dramatic demonstration."

Although Yannes only intended to demonstrate the potential of the VIC chip, Jack loved the entire computer. "I was not at the meeting, but apparently it blew Jack away," recalls Yannes. "He wanted to do something with this right away. When he saw this, he said, 'We want this. We want to do this.'"

According to Charpentier, the conversation with Tramiel went something like this:

    Charpentier: "Here's the chip. What do you think?"
    Jack: "All right, ship it."
    Charpentier: "You mean the chip?"
    Jack: "No, no, no. I mean that!" (pointing to prototype board)
    Charpentier: "This?"
    Jack: "That."
    Charpentier: "This?"
    Jack: "That."
    Charpentier: "Really?"
    Jack: "That."

Despite the limited ability of the computer, Jack was impressed. "The Sinclair didn't do much either," says Peddle. "That was one of the reasons why it didn't bother him as much when those guys showed him what they showed him."

Jack wanted his low-cost color computer released by the end of the year; an ambitious goal considering the time it takes to design a computer and set up production lines. In order to expedite the prototype phase, Jack planned to show the prototype at the June CES in Chicago, a mere two weeks away.

After the meeting, the managers called Yannes in to commend him. "They called me into the meeting," recalls Yannes. The rookie engineer felt intimidated by Tramiel. "He was a formidable figure. He just looked like someone you didn't want to mess with."

Jack offered to give the nervous Yannes a PET computer. "I already had a PET though," recalls Yannes. "I was so naïve when he asked me if I had a PET computer I said, 'Yes, I do.' Later on Charlie told me, 'He was going to give you one so you should have said no.'"[1]

When Chuck Peddle and his group found out the East Coast prototype was going to CES, frustration reached a new level. "The West Coast guys got a little bent out of shape," recalls Yannes. "It definitely created some issues with the West Coast group and MOS Technology."

Yannes feared the West Coast engineers might be upset with him personally. "I wouldn't be surprised if Peddle's group thought we had sabotaged them by giving them a bad 40-column chip [the 6564], then blind-siding them with the VIC-20 prototype," says Yannes. "I had no agenda other than to beat the pants off the ZX-80 and get the 6560 chip used in *something*! Charlie Winterble and Al may have seen this as a political opportunity, but I was fairly naive at the time and was just trying to help the company I worked for."

According to Peddle, afterwards Tramiel said, "I wish my team in Moore Park had done this." Peddle felt insulted, because his team had done a VIC based computer and shown it in January, but Tramiel had rejected it. "Jack finally listened to our idea of doing the VIC-20," he laments.

The issue proved volatile. "Jack's point was, 'I always wanted one of those.' My answer was, 'We showed you one of those and you didn't want it. You wanted something that was Apple like.' But when he saw the Sinclair, and he saw that it was selling well, he wanted one of those," says Peddle.

Peddle watched helplessly as the power shifted away from his group. "All of a sudden, they are the new corporate heroes, and they are going to build this thing that ultimately became the VIC-20," says Peddle. "Jack is approached by [Guinn] about how his team could develop this stuff and said, 'We don't need Moore Park anymore,' because his team could do all these things." Peddle was seething with resentment. His team's ideas were being ignored and then only accepted when someone more favored showed them to Jack.

---

[1] Jack later showed his gratitude to Yannes. "We gave Yannes, from Tramiel, a $5,000 check a couple of months later, which was a lot of money for a kid," recalls Winterble. "What's really cool is that he used a good deal of it to buy his mother a kitchen."

Peddle believed Jerone Guinn led Jack to believe the MicroPET was a complete computer system. "Guinn shows this hacked-up thing that Yannes does and tells Jack it's ready to go," says Peddle. "It wasn't ready to go. Yannes should have admitted that he didn't know how to make it go. The only one who knew how to make it go was Seiler."

After the meeting, Peddle and Jack quarreled some more. "Jack and I had a fight," recalls Peddle. "Jack was going to show it at the Consumer Electronics Show, and I said, 'Look, I don't want us to look stupid because we built a pretty good reputation. I don't want us to get screwed up by showing something that doesn't work.'"

"Jack said, 'You just have sour grapes, because you guys didn't do it.' This wasn't true. Obviously, we had initiated it." Peddle departed Pennsylvania back to California on the PET Jet.

Jack had made an impressively quick decision. Prior to the morning meeting, Jack had no idea his East Coast engineers had a prototype. "Right after the original prototype was shown to Jack at the managers' meeting, he just basically said, 'Do it,'" recalls Yannes. "I have a feeling he probably came down hard on the California guys, knowing Jack."

After the general managers' meeting, MOS Technology had to prepare more prototypes. "When Jack said, 'Okay, we want to show these at CES in June of 1980,' we quickly built a few more prototypes to bring to the show," says Yannes. "Literally we had two weeks to do it."

Before Yannes could begin work on the prototypes, he received an animated phone call from Peddle. "As I recall, Chuck Peddle called back from the flight back to California," says Yannes. "This was back before they had cell phones in airplanes. He wanted to call in with a problem he found in the design with it, which I kind of chuckled at, because this was just a prototype that I threw together. It never was intended to be a production design. He was trying to shoot it down as quickly as he could."

Peddle views the call differently. "I was trying to tell his boss that what he did wasn't a production thing," says Peddle. "It was to try to get him to tell his boss that it really wasn't a complete unit."

When Peddle landed, he broke the news to his Moore Park engineers. However, Peddle did not accept defeat. Instead, he resolved to bring a better prototype to the show. "We went and hacked together a prototype of what would ultimately be the VIC-20," recalls Peddle. "We worked all night to get it done. We had two days to do it in."

There was now a horse race within Commodore, fueled by egos, to see which prototype would dominate CES. The PET group at Moore Park had skilled programmers and could incorporate an operating system, but they had little time. The East Coast group was ahead, but all they had to show was a colorful demonstration program. The attendees at CES would ultimately decide.

Chicago CES

The day before CES opened their doors, Commodore employees descended on Chicago. Among them was Jack's son, Leonard, who flew in on a commercial flight from New York. Everyone stayed at the elegant *Conrad Hilton* in downtown Chicago.

Bob Yannes attended the show, a rare treat for the rookie engineer. "The reason I went there was just in case it broke. I was the only one who knew how to fix it," says Yannes.

CES was an expensive show. It cost between $100,000 to set up a smaller booth in June and up to $1,000,000 for larger two-story booths used in January. These booths were so large they even housed offices on the second floor. For this show, Jack went low end, purchasing a single-story booth located at the back-lot portion of the convention hall.

Every year CES introduced the latest in consumer electronics. This year Mattel introduced the Intellivision, which received intense interest. The big item at the show, however, was still the Atari 2600 VCS. Atari displayed their systems and games in a huge two-story booth located in prime territory on the show floor.

Radio Shack also attended with a large booth displaying their TRS-80 computer and other products. Apple was not present, since they relied on computer stores to sell the Apple II, rather than retail stores.

In 1980, Commodore's booth looked almost insignificant compared to others on the floor. The Consumer Electronics division of Commodore was really the main reason to attend CES. The booth prominently displayed calculators, digital watches, and their newest product for 1980, the digital thermostat. Ken Hollandsworth and a small group of salespeople were responsible for this division.

The Commodore booth housed product displays and an information desk with brochures and price lists. There were a pair of small meeting rooms, each with a desk and a pair of chairs, used for signing new accounts to distribute Commodore products. On average, Commodore signed a dozen new accounts each hour.

The June CES show was a curious venue to display the prototypes. Normally, manufacturers displayed production models and took mass orders from retailers. Jack wanted to gauge how distributors and the press reacted to his low-cost games computer. Commodore did not have a reputation for fun and games in 1980; they were CBM, the business machine company.

A large meeting room with tinted glass walls housed the MicroPET prototypes. "I think we had half a dozen there," recalls Winterble. "They break and they are sabotaged. You've got to watch who is touching them."

The MOS Technology team had tried hard to undercut Moore Park with their secrecy, but Moore Park succeeded in developing a prototype in time for the show. "We went out to the show and the guys from the West Coast were there too: Chuck Peddle, Bill Seiler, and John Feagans. They had come up with their own thing using a VIC chip," recalls Yannes. "I didn't even know it was going to be there. I'm not sure that Al and Charlie knew either. I think they got that built literally hours before they left for the show."

Yannes was impressed with the Moore Park prototype. "Theirs was fully functional! Actually, it was very close to what the VIC-20 finally was because it was based on the PET architecture," remarks Yannes. "The one that the West Coast group had done actually had Basic running on it, but it didn't have any applications or anything."

Of the two, Peddle obviously favored his team's prototype. "Yannes had one machine and Seiler had another machine," recalls Peddle. "He just showed something that was more computer-like than what Yannes was showing. We were trying to make something potentially real."

Although Yannes was impressed with the rival computer, the presentation was less refined. "It didn't look like the VIC-20 at all," says Yannes. "I think it had the old PET calculator keyboard. They didn't have time to get a case together for it, so they used this old Commodore desktop calculator case, and they shoved it in that. I remember it had a Commodore bumper sticker stuck over the front of it to hide the fact that it was a calculator." The modified calculator case was tiny, at about five by nine inches and three inches deep.

"We had these two machines there, one of which looked pretty good and didn't do anything and another one which was actually functional but looked pretty horrible," recalls Yannes. "The other one was clearly built out of parts scavenged from a scrap box somewhere. No one would believe for a second that that was what the final product was going to look like."

As the show began, Peddle was still upset with Jack and Jerone Guinn. "Only because they were there with something that didn't work," says Peddle. "We kept telling everybody, but Guinn was so fucking stupid he was telling Jack it was something else. I had a right to be upset." Peddle was correct about the incompleteness of the East Coast computer. It lacked an interface for a cassette unit, disk drive, or other peripherals.

With no operating system, there was no way to type commands. It was not a real computer.

Despite the tensions, once the show began, the two engineering groups came together. For the first time ever, Yannes met Chuck Peddle. "I talked to Chuck Peddle once at that CES show, and he was cordial to me," recalls Yannes. "I was worried that he was going to be upset, and for all I know, he was upset with everyone else, but I think he just said, 'Well, this guy is just an engineer. He's not actively trying to undermine my empire.' He was very nice to me."

Commodore made no formal announcement of the MicroPET, though they printed up a stack of leaflets with a product description. "It wasn't shown out on the floor," recalls Yannes. "It was in a little room in one of the booths. I think the only people that were getting to see it were people that were invited. They may have showed it to the press, too."

Outside, scores of people trafficked by, stopping to press their noses up to the smoky glass. What they saw was a four-foot high counter with a row of small computers, each with a small glowing color television set.

Yannes stood by his machine like a proud father. Charpentier gave a quick rundown of the VIC features and hoped-for features of the machine and asked people to excuse the faults, promising that the real version would be much better.

Jack was jubilant that he now had a physical embodiment of the computer he desperately wanted. He stood off to the side, carefully noting the reaction of those who saw the computer and occasionally asking how many they might be interested in ordering.

As word spread, curiosity in the MicroPET began to mount. Soon, people began pleading to go inside, and some even got a little testy when the marketing people turned them down. "Everybody seemed to be pretty excited," recalls Yannes.

As it became more apparent the low-cost color computer would be a hit, competition between the East and West Coast dissolved into cooperation. During breaks, Yannes, Seiler, Charpentier, Feagans, and Winterble spent much of the time comparing the benefits of each prototype and discussing possible features they could include in a final product. Together, they could develop something special.

During lunch, several Commodore employees gathered in the cafeteria. Jack broached the subject of giving the machine a better name than MicroPET. In keeping with friendly three letter names, Jack suggested calling it the VIC, since the video chip was the main feature of the new computer. VIC would stand for Video Interface Computer.

Japanese companies often used CES as a chance to examine the inner workings of new products months or even years before the actual product release. While the meeting room was unattended, a pair of Japanese engineers slipped in to get a closer look at the prototypes. One had a small notepad ready to jot down specifications, and the other held a small screwdriver set. "That actually did happen," recalls Charles Winterble. "They came in and started taking it apart." Before they could begin their study, someone noticed movement inside the office and chased away the rival engineers before they could open the lid. To Jack's relief, the Japanese would not have the advantage this time.

On the final day of the show, Peddle noticed Jack Tramiel courting a new engineer. "Jack was always looking for a hero to replace me," says Peddle. "It always pissed us off when he did it."

The attempts to replace Peddle seemed like ingratitude on Jack's part, considering the success Peddle brought to Commodore. However, Peddle believes Jack's apparent enmity towards him stemmed from insecurity. "Jack really did not want to be dependant on anybody," says Peddle. "The more successful I was with helping him, the more that feeling of dependency increased rather than decreased."

After the meeting in London, Tramiel wanted an engineer who would take orders. "Jack convinced this guy by the name of Tom Hong to leave Apple and come to work for Commodore," explains Peddle. "Hong had a really good stock position at Apple, and he walked away from it, because Jack had promised him some serious stock options at Commodore in return for coming over. He was hired to replace me. Tom was given the assignment of getting the VIC-20 ready for production."

"The reality was that Hong was overrated," says Peddle. "Jack got sold on a bill of goods, which he often did."

Codename Vixen

After CES, Jack gave his engineers one month to create a production model of the VIC computer. Despite the tight schedule, the Moore Park engineers ignored the project. "They didn't want to have anything to do with the VIC project," says Russell. "They were busy on the TOI."

The VIC computer would be a physical departure from the familiar design of the PET. The new design was a computer in a keyboard, relying on users to provide a television.

Instead of starting with the more advanced prototype from Bill Seiler, management wanted to use Bob Yannes' prototype as the basis of the new design. "The original one from the West Coast ended up in my hands," says Russell. "It was a chip demonstrator board."

Commodore management believed Yannes created a more advanced prototype than it actually was. "It kind of was dumped on me," recalls

Russell. "They were kind of like, 'Okay, Bob, take this hardware and put the software on it.' It was like, 'Argh! You've got to be kidding me.' It had none of the peripheral ports figured out and not enough ROM to sneeze in."

Jack and the other managers were calling the new computer the VIC ever since CES, but the engineers were unenthusiastic about the name, which sounded like a plumber. The engineers made a play on the word VIC, calling their computer by the codename *Vixen*. "That was the codename really early on," says Russell.

Russell was virtually the only person who supported the Vixen on the West Coast, aside from Jack Tramiel. "I was a big staunch supporter of the VIC," explains Russell. "The other people on the VIC team were Andy Finkel and the marketing guy, Michael Tomczyk."

Most of the support for the VIC computer was with Yannes, Charpentier, and Winterble on the East Coast. "The VIC-20 wouldn't have happened without the guys on the East Coast pushing for the thing and championing it, but they didn't give us anything we could build a computer out of," says Russell.

Russell found very little support from Chuck Peddle and his team, who remained focused on the TOI project. "They obviously wanted to kill the VIC project," says Russell. "I kind of had to choose sides and I supported the East Coast guys, because I was enjoying working with the Japanese people. I kind of took it as my project to make sure it got done."

Although Russell worked out of Commodore headquarters at 3330 Scott Boulevard, he often paid visits to Moore Park. "I'd go over there and hang with those guys in the conference room when they would talk about the project, because they wanted me to do stuff on their [TOI] system, too," says Russell. "Chuck Peddle was not a VIC-20 supporter at all. He wanted the TOI, and that's what all those meetings were about."

Russell did his best to push the VIC computer into the meetings. "I was in the meetings that they were holding, trying to sort out the TOI and also at the same time trying to do the VIC on the side," says Russell.

According to some Commodore employees, Chuck Peddle was not happy when his Moore Park engineers helped with the VIC project. "They really were competing for resources against each other," says Russell. Peddle hoped the VIC project would die a natural death.

Russell was primarily a software engineer, leaving him to beg and cajole Bill Seiler into furthering the hardware development of Vixen. "Bill Seiler was really the top notch hardware guy who really made all the original hardware hang together," recalls Russell. "I needed him to help me keep that alive, because I pretty much got abandoned on VIC."

The lack of enthusiasm by Moore Park was evident. "They kind of helped me as a fellow engineer," says Russell. During the meetings, Russell made fun of the TOI computer. "There was the acronym first, and then there were people who added meaning to it. I was throwing Tool of Idiots at them all the time and that wasn't going over real well," laughs Russell. "Of course, they called the VIC something totally degrading too."

The ambitious engineering cycle for the Vixen and TOI created a pressure cooker, but the Silly Valley engineers enjoyed the experience. The Silicon Valley community respected Chuck Peddle, and he used his status to bring in outside engineers to educate his team on the latest advancements. Peddle brought in an engineer named Bob Metcalfe to lecture the team on a new technology called Ethernet. Commodore engineers previously experimented with networking PET computers but Ethernet had serious potential.

Russell had almost complete freedom working on the Vixen. "Most of the time there was no real head of engineering. There were just engineers who had the responsibility to get things done. That was how it worked with the VIC-20," says Russell. "Chuck was kind of head of Moore Park, and he may have had the title of head of engineering, but he never came and told us what to do in our building. It was much more likely that Jack came in and said these things needed to be done."

As the lone West Coast VIC supporter, Robert Russell began to receive favoritism from Jack Tramiel himself. "I was working on VIC-20, standing in the middle of the engineering cube area," recalls Russell. "I had cubes with the VIC stuff out in front, and [Jack] came into there and said, 'I need someone to carry my bag to the airport to go to Vegas.' And he pointed at me!" says Russell. "I carried this little duffel bag that weighed maybe three pounds or something."

Although Russell had planned a day of engineering, he soon found himself aboard the PET Jet bound for Comdex. "We flew out with the guy who later became the Commodore president, and [Jack] was doing the interview and carrying on with that guy in the PET Jet to Vegas," recalls Russell.

Upon arrival, Jack gave Russell permission to tour for as long as he wished. "He gave me a handful of casino chips from the Sands Casino," says Russell. "He told me, 'Tell the pilot when you want to go back, and have a good time.'"

It was a surreal experience for the young engineer from Iowa. To this day, Russell is unsure why Jack wanted him along for the trip. "Who knows? I think Jack just wanted to be nice to me," ventures Russell.

Deal-making seemed to be in Jack's blood, even when he spoke to his engineers. Sometimes, Jack offered his engineers deals in exchange for lower salaries. "He was trying to see what he could get," says Russell. "He was always doing that. Serious or not serious, it was one of those things that you never called Jack on. He would shake your hand, and it would be a done deal."

Tramiel offered Russell the same deal he offered years earlier to Peddle for the PET. "Jack Tramiel offered me a deal that I didn't take, because I didn't think it was going to pay off," explains Russell. "He offered me a buck on each VIC-20 if I didn't take salary. At the time, I was like, 'How can I live?' So I turned it down." The deal had the potential to make Russell a multi-millionaire.

Russell found Jack's favoritism advantageous when he needed to get things done. "Once people knew that you were a Jack favorite, you could do pretty much anything you wanted," explains Russell. "I had meetings, and I said, 'Well, Jack told me to do it.' I played the Jack card all the time. I could bullshit my way through anything, because people were scared to go up against Jack. They were like, 'Yes, sir! Open the doors.' Jack would back you up, even if he hadn't told you to do it."

Russell used his Jack card frequently, which gave the VIC project the momentum it needed. "That was when I rode Jack's dissention," says Russell. "I conned Seiler into helping me rebuild stuff and design things like the memory add-in board, so you could actually have enough memory to do something on it."

Despite having Jack's full support, Russell had problems locating equipment. "Moore Park on the West Coast was kind of where the top notch, original engineering team went to," explains Russell. "So they ended up with most of the equipment. I actually had to go over and debug the VIC-20 stuff on their prototype."

Unfortunately, the Moore Park equipment was in use during the day. "I would work in the office over on Scott Boulevard during most of the day, and then I would drive over there and work most of the night," recalls Russell.

The VIC-20 was a games computer, but it only contained a single joystick port. One joystick was limiting, compared to the Atari 400 computer, which had four joystick ports. However, the oversight was understandable since most current games like *Asteroids*, *Sub-Hunt*, *Night Driver*, and *Pong* used paddles. *Pac-Man*, which Namco had not yet released in North America, popularized the joystick.

The single port supported two analog paddles. "The paddles were on the VIC chip," says Yannes. "It could support either an X-Y analog joystick or two conventional rotary knobs." Curiously, Commodore never released an analog joystick for any of their computers.

Commodore copied the same connector used on the Atari 2600: a standard D-shell connector with nine pins. The connector was not proprietary to Atari, which meant Commodore could copy it without fear of a lawsuit. Other computer makers, such as Sinclair and a line of Japanese computers, also used the D-shell connector, establishing a standard for joysticks.

Since the PET did not have a cartridge port, Seiler had to design one from scratch. Vixen cartridges were easy to distinguish from Atari 2600 cartridges because of their size. Since the Vixen would use the slot for memory expansion as well as games, the slot required more address lines. This resulted in massive game cartridges compared to other systems.

One of the unique aspects of the Vixen was the serial port, which allowed multiple disk drives, printers, and other peripherals. The concept was similar to the IEEE-488 connector of the PET but less expensive. The idea for the serial port originated with the TOI project.

"The serial bus was meant to be much lower cost," explains Russell. "On the IEEE, we always needed a second processor to run the interface on the peripherals. On the serial bus, the whole idea was to do it with one processor that could run the interface and the drive." As a result, Commodore could manufacture cheaper disk drives and printers.

Although the serial interface cost less, it was slower. "Obviously IEEE was a heck of a lot faster because after all, it has this big parallel stream," says Russell.

The new interface was also smaller, reducing the size of the computer. The IEEE-488 connector was 5.5 centimeters in width, versus a 1.5-centimeter diameter for the round serial connector. "The cables alone cost a fortune, so that was a big reason we didn't want to do that anymore," says Russell.[2]

The designer of the serial interface was Moore Park engineer Glen Stark. Peddle recalls, "He was the guy that defined the interface that was patented for Commodore that allowed it to fake the IEEE interface over a single wire cable."

---

[2] The IEEE-488 cables were available from only one source, a company called *Belden*. According to Jim Butterfield, "In the year preceding the VIC-20, these cables became unavailable for some reason. Commodore found itself in the position of building disk drives and printers for their computers, but being unable to hook them up."

While Glen Stark designed the interface and the concepts, Russell implemented the code. "He was the guy that helped Glen and got things done," says Peddle.

According to Russell, he was given the objectives of the serial interface and told to make it happen. "I was left as the implementer," says Russell. "I had to figure out how to make the whole serial port system work."

Russell also had to modularize the cassette code written by Peddle years earlier. "About eight people went back and tried to document it," says Peddle.

He went in blind since the code was undocumented. "This cassette code had this bizarre frequency domain nonsense without comments," recalls Russell. "Chuck Peddle had to give me a lot of [his] time to help document the cassette code because nobody had a clue how that worked. I remember sitting up in the corporate side in an office with Chuck Peddle, who was over at Moore Park by that time, going over the code with him and him trying to remember what the heck he had done."

Russell liked working with Peddle, despite his ambivalence towards the VIC project. "He impressed me, because he had personally done things like the cassette code on the PET even when he was leading the project," says Russell. "I really admired his work ethic."

Once he completed the TOI serial interface, Russell decided to include it in the VIC computer. "That's something I did on my own," says Russell. "I wanted to have serial communications, so I wrote a software serial interface for the VIC. If I hadn't have done it, nobody would have cared, and it wouldn't have been in the computer."

Seiler also added a strange proprietary port called the user port. This expansion port allowed companies and hardware hackers to create additional peripherals for the VIC computer.

Memory was the most important consideration in order to meet Jack's target of a three-hundred dollar computer. MOS Technology had a surplus of one-kilobyte RAM chips, which engineers no longer used in PET computers. Jack made sure his designers used these one-kilobyte RAM chips in the new computer to clear out inventory.

The VIC computer would also benefit from advancements to the TOI operating system. "John Feagans was the architect of what became the *kernel* concept, which is the separation of the actual operating kernel versus the Basic interpreter," explains Russell.

Although John Feagans originated the kernel design, Russell ended up programming the kernel code for the TOI and Vixen. "He wanted to move on to other things, so I picked it up," says Russell.

The VIC 6560 chip was capable of high-resolution graphics up to 192 by 200 pixels. This required a lot of memory, so high-resolution was only available if the user purchased a memory expansion unit. Without it, there was not enough memory to contemplate a bit-mapped screen.

Video was the most important aspect of the VIC code. "I had one guy working with me in the [Scott Boulevard] building working on the display code," says Russell. "Some of the toughest stuff that had to be cleaned up was the display [code]. That was kind of a modular piece, because we had already split it off to do an 80-column version [for the PET]."

The VIC character set was stored in a four-kilobyte ROM chip. Each character was eight pixels wide and eight pixels high. Perhaps the biggest improvement of the Vixen over the PET was the robustness of the character graphics. On the PET, programmers were limited to building their graphics from the PETSCII character set. With the Vixen, programmers could now modify each character. For example, the letter A could become a stick man.

Since Commodore was not supplying a monitor with the Vixen, the engineers had to be wary of the different types of televisions that existed. Engineers had to accommodate the different border sizes around television sets, so they began using the famous Commodore border. As a bonus, users could change the color of the border to one of 16 colors available on the VIC chip.

Televisions standards were different around the globe. North America and Japan used the NTSC standard, which the VIC 6560 chip used. European television sets used the PAL standard, so Commodore Semiconductor Group created an alternate VIC chip called the VIC 6561. Jack loved the different television standards because North American Vixen computers would not work on European television sets. This meant he could charge different prices for computers and software in different regions with no risk of importers taking advantage of the price difference, as they had with the PET.

With the computer-in-a-keyboard concept, there was no room for an internal power supply. This meant engineers had to design an external power supply. The power brick made the Vixen look less refined, which is why marketers rarely showed the computer with the cables and power supply in the same photograph. Heat was a major concern in the VIC-20 design. As Russell recalls, "The original VIC-20 prototype would get so hot that the heat sink would rot off the motherboard, so we put in a huge, over-designed regulator in that."

Through the month long design, Chuck hoped the project would die before it made it to production. While visiting the headquarters, Chuck would try to convince Jack to go with the TOI as a low-end alternative and concentrate on a business computer. When this happened, executives would hear Jack's voice roaring through halls, causing many to wonder if Chuck was suicidal. "He made it clear he wanted the [VIC] to succeed," says Russell. "That was crucial."

After a month, a production computer emerged. "We had really tight time schedules and we pretty much did that to our time schedule," says Russell.

The result was closer to Seiler's prototype than the East Coast prototype. "There should be no question in anyone's mind that the primary architect behind the VIC-20 was Bill Seiler," says Peddle. "We didn't have to go back and invent all kinds of new things except for the I/O stuff."

"Seiler had most of the hand in what was really the design," says Russell. "Seiler was the guy who made sure there was production hardware."

Bob Yannes affirms that the final design of the VIC-20 was nothing like his prototype. "If you look at the VIC-20, it is a PET, except instead of the 6845 video controller, it has the VIC chip in it," says Yannes. "It has the same I/O structure and the same processor, and the kernel code that was running in there was the PET operating system kernel."

"We didn't have to go back and invent all kinds of new things except for the I/O stuff," Peddle concurs. "We were just basically putting it all together to make it work."

Jack had hired Tom Hong from Apple to make the VIC computer happen, but Chuck Peddle believes Hong had very little to do with the project. "He was hired as a stud from Apple who was going to come in and make the VIC-20 happen," says Peddle. In reality, Peddle's own engineers made the VIC-20 happen.

Jack Attack

Robert Russell enjoyed favoritism from Jack because of his support for the Vixen, but he was not immune from Jack's wrath. "I was supposed to bring prototypes out for the meeting where the TOI and the VIC were shown to the analysts in New York City at the *Four Seasons*," says Russell. "This was a very important thing."

Although meetings among Commodore managers were important, meetings with investors were more important. A poor presentation could cause investors to lose confidence in Commodore.

Russell knew the importance of presentations, so he intended to ride with the prototype on the commercial airliner. Unfortunately, one of his managers gave him different instructions. "My managers on the West Coast wouldn't let me hand-carry the stuff on," recalls Russell. "It got put in luggage, and of course the box got lost. It didn't show up."

Jack gave an embarrassing presentation without the TOI prototype. "I went with them to the introduction to the analysts," says Russell. Afterwards, things seemed normal. "I got a beautiful dinner at the *Tavern on the Green* in New York with the engineers and Jack."

After the meeting, everyone traveled from New York back to Pennsylvania and MOS Technology. Russell was about to receive his first Jack Attack. "It actually happened in the president of MOS [Technology's] office," says Russell. "Jack called me into the office and chewed me to within an inch of my life."

Although Russell was just following orders, he felt the full impact of Jack's displeasure. "He was just very much angry, very much frustrated, and wanted to know why I had screwed up," says Russell.

Despite explaining that his manager would not allow him to carry on the prototypes, Jack felt Russell had erred in his judgment, telling Russell, "Why did I put you on a jet to fly you out here? I didn't want to see you, I wanted the product here, and I wanted it to be working!"

Jack Attacks were intensely personal, and every word came straight from Jacks heart. "You're just kind of like, wow, sensory overload," says Russell. "The guy is really calling you an idiot and who knows what else. He could definitely make you feel like you were a pretty small pimple on his butt." To invoke a Jack Attack, you had truly risked causing the company damage, and Jack took that personally.

The 22-year-old Russell feared the worst. "I thought I was getting along and going places in this company, and here it looks like my career is over," recalls Russell.

Russell listened to Jack's words and began to make sense of it. "To Jack, it was like, 'You don't follow the stupid thing your boss is telling you to do; you do what is right.' Use your own common sense is what he was really saying."

After the verbal thrashing ended, Tramiel asked, "Do you have anything to say?"

Russell replied meekly, "Yes, sir. I understand completely. I will never ever let you down like that again."

The effect of a Jack Attack was electric. "If you understood the concept you could walk out his office alive, which I did," says Russell. "I've suffered a Jack Attack or two, but I always said I understood and never made the same mistake twice. He had no patience for fools."

"The president of MOS's secretary was outside and couldn't believe I walked out of there alive," recalls Russell. "She said, 'I was so sure you were fired.'"

Even today, Russell seems incredulous about the event. "It was just because I followed my boss's instructions," he says. "It wasn't under my control."

Russell looks back on his Jack attack with humor. "It's a badge of honor, especially if you were one of the survivors," says Russell. "He said a lot of things like that to people and a lot of people didn't get the message. They thought he was attacking them."

Russell witnessed other Jack attacks that did not end happily. "If you got confrontational, I'm sure it could end up with you getting fired," says Russell. "I saw a lot of people leave that way."

Russell noticed his managers rarely survived Jack Attacks. "I used to see my managers come out of there, and you were like, 'Okay, is he going to come back to make the turn and come into the office? Nope! He's going out the door. Okay, I guess he's no longer my boss.'"

As managers routinely fell victim to Jack Attacks, it became difficult to find anyone willing to work for Commodore. "They just didn't have a director of engineering, because we couldn't hire them after a couple came and went," says Russell. "It was so bad that we ended up putting our high-speed printers in the head engineering manager's office because it was usually empty."

The stressful work environment sometimes produced casualties, even within Jack's inner circle. At one trade show in Germany, an inner circle member experienced a dangerous mental breakdown. "We were at a trade show in Germany, and we were all going to head someplace as a group and we wondered, 'Where's Jack?' Nobody could find Jack or figure out what's going on," says a former Commodore employee.[3] "Then a couple of people took us to the side and we went up to his room. Jack was in his room with his wife Helen, John Calton, and a woman who was a manager, and they were being held at knifepoint by an employee."

The tense standoff lasted hours. "We were sitting in a room, trying to get updates as to what was going on," he says. "It went on all day long. Eventually, he was occupied in one room, and they all ran out of the room. They came down the stairs, and he chased them down into the lobby, and they went running through the lobby."

"When this guy was running through the lobby, he was noticed fairly soon, because he was nude," he recalls. "He was subdued."

For the second time in his life, Jack had survived a near death experience. As it turned out, Jack and John Calton were not the only

---

[3] The employee wished to remain anonymous.

executives the manager wanted to kill. "Apparently he had a list, and on the list were the five or ten people in the company he intended to kill."

Jack made sure his manager received proper care at a local hospital. "In Germany, if you are convicted of a mental health issue, you could have very serious consequences at that time. You wouldn't be able to get out of the country, and you would be locked up. So before he got out too fast, Jack arranged to pick this guy up out of the hospital and took him out of the country on a plane."

Despite the personal attack, Jack felt compassion for the man. "Jack made sure he took care of this person. He went out of his way to do everything he could do to make sure this person was taken care of. There was no grudge or anything like that. This was an inner family kind of guy, and Jack took care of him."

Rising Sun

Bob Yannes remembers the day Commodore U.S. found out what Jack's famous statement really meant. "People were saying the Japanese are going to take over this market just like they've taken over every consumer electronics market," recalls Yannes. "Jack's quote was, 'We will become the Japanese.' No one quite really understood what that meant, but it sounded good, and you really didn't question Jack anyhow. But I guess what he really meant was that we were going to use the Japanese to produce the [VIC computer]."

The VIC project was going to Japan where general manager Tony Tokai would launch the product. "It wasn't targeted to [North America]," recalls Russell.

Jack had a clear vision of how to defeat the Japanese in the personal computer market, and he planned to meet them on their home ground. "I heard it very early on in the project that that was the goal, that that's why it was so important that it get done for the company," says Russell.

In July, 1980, Jack sent Bill Seiler's designs and prototypes to Tokyo. Jack only allowed Michael Tomczyk, his personal assistant, to communicate with Japan. All questions and instructions on the VIC project now passed through Tomczyk. This indirectly gave him a degree of control over the project.

Tomczyk communicated using a Telex machine, which was similar to a FAX machine except it handled text only. Tomczyk sent a flurry of costly telexes to Japan, which caught Jacks attention. One day, as Tomczyk was standing in the hall, he was surprised to feel someone kick him from behind. When he turned around, it was Jack.

Over in Japan, production of the VIC computer began. Like many of Commodore's overseas operations, the premises of Commodore Japan

The VIC-20 – 1980

were unimpressive. Commodore Japan headquarters were in downtown Tokyo in a small four-story building where Commodore was one of many renting tenants. Land was at such a premium that cars used a special car-elevator to get into the underground parking.

With the motherboard already completed by Seiler, the Japanese merely redesigned the layout of the circuit board. "The Japanese were doing the layout stuff, working on keyboards and case work and stuff like that," says Russell.

The head engineer of Commodore Japan was Yasaharu Terakura, whom people referred to as Yash or Yashi. According to Commodore engineers, he was a hard-working, hands-on engineer with an amusing personality. Terakura was popular with all the North American engineers and was supportive of the VIC proposal from the start.

Chuck Peddle knew Terakura from his earlier visits to Japan and saw him become more westernized. "Yash at one time was a very Japanese guy," says Peddle. "He was involved with the work we did with Epson. He taught me a lot about Japanese culture. I learned to stop and admire my plate of food from him. He's just a straight guy; a serious, intelligent, hard-working, very focused guy. I don't recall him ever getting caught up with anybody's politics."

Bob Yannes fondly remembers his time spent with Terakura. "He was a great guy," recalls Yannes. "Great English. He was always very humorous and always poking fun at people. He was a great buddy of mine. I really loved Yashi."

Commodore Japan had a modest engineering department, which included a small band of technicians. Over the years, they had become an important component of Commodore. "Japan was the source of our disk drives and some of our chip stuff," says Russell. When the VIC prototype arrived, the Japanese technicians descended on it.

The engineers opened the machine and pored over the circuit board, documenting the layout of circuits within the machine. The production design was literally a redesign of the prototype, which they could then produce using assembly line equipment. The Japanese engineers excelled at the task. "Most of production engineering was done in Japan," says Yannes. "They took the PC board from the West Coast and redesigned it for their insertion equipment."

One of the least friendly aspects of the VIC-20 was the operating system. The prototype sent to Japan used Basic 2.0, with decidedly unfriendly commands. In order to list the contents of a disk, users had to type **LOAD"$", 8** and then type **LIST**. On other operating systems, such as CP/M, users merely typed **DIR** to see a listing. However, Commodore engineers predicted most users would use cartridges and cassette drives, so there was no pressing need for commands to copy, delete, or list files.

The disk drive would be the most severe test of the new serial interface design. One of Russell's co-workers at Commodore had been responsible for developing the disk drive code. "Bob Fairborne was supposed to write the drive interface," says Russell. Fairborne was a competent programmer and delivered good code, but the hardware contained a problem. "[Fairborne] had done all his work, but when it came down to the final thing, it didn't work. The 6522 chip had a glitch."

The VIC was supposed to use the 6522 Peripheral Interface Adapter chip to attain fast disk drive access. "We were originally supposed to use the 6522 high speed lines, but they didn't work right," explains Russell. "Unfortunately, Bob Fairborne wrote all this code and spent all this time, and it wasn't reliable and would lock up the computer and the peripheral. When it was all 'done', none of it really worked."

The engineers struggled with the chip problem, but eventually time ran out. "Jack came into my office and said, 'We're shipping on time in ten days,' and he wanted to close the code," says Russell.

Russell now had no option but to implement a quick fix, regardless of performance. "They didn't care how fast it was, so I just wrote code that worked," recalls Russell.

Every time Russell revised his code, he had to burn the code into a chip to place it into the VIC computer and test it. "At the time, we were [burning] EPROM's to meet ship dates, which were costing a fortune," says Russell. "Luckily we had MOS Technology. We could do ROM's as fast as we could get the mask layer to them."

Russell's engineers were impressed with his hurried solution. "I attribute the serial bus to him as a heroic effort when the [PIA chip] was found to have a glitch," says engineer Bil Herd.

One feature made the Vixen stand apart from the competition. "The smartest thing - and I think this was Jack's idea - was putting a full-sized keyboard on it," says Yannes. "What you had on the market in the price range at the time were things like the Ti-99/4a, which had a calculator keyboard, and the Atari 400, which had a membrane keyboard. I don't think those companies realized that people didn't take those products seriously, particularly because of that keyboard."

Chuck Peddle believes the keyboard decision was a result of the earlier blunder with the PET 2001. "That's why the [VIC] is built around a regular keyboard," says Peddle. "We knew that you needed a regular keyboard because we got punished by the market until we put one into our product."

Although the VIC computer was not very powerful, the keyboard made it look legitimate. "Its graphics weren't as good, it didn't have as many characters per line, it had much less memory than either of those machines, but the real keyboard on it just made it look like a real computer whereas the others looked like toys," says Yannes.

Although the final design took place in Japan, the North American engineers developed the character set and keyboard layout. "The original keyboard layouts were done in Japanese," says Russell.

The opportunity allowed Michael Tomczyk to take command of the project. "I remember at one point Mike Tomczyk came in on the VIC-20 and said, 'Okay, well I'm in charge of marketing this thing,'" recalls Yannes. "We had never heard of him before or seen him before, and we were like, 'Okay.'" Yannes appreciated Tomczyk's support on the VIC project. "He was very enthusiastic," says Yannes.

To design the character set, Commodore Japan sent a worker to North America to help Robert Russell. "I worked with a Japanese girl to do the keyboard layouts because I don't know anything about creating Japanese symbols," says Russell.

Russell produced a special Japanese ROM chip capable of displaying Japanese Kanji characters. It could also display regular upper case alphanumeric characters, making it one of only two Japanese computers capable of displaying Kanji and the western alphabet.

Chuck Peddle attributes the success of the final design to Yashi Terakura. "Yashi Terakura deserves enormous amounts of credit for the work he did," says Peddle. "Yash was the one who made the keyboard stuff work on time. Success has many fathers, and in this case, it did have many fathers."

The general manager of Commodore Japan was Taro Tokai, known as Tony by westerners. He had loyally served Commodore since 1968, when Commodore moved into calculators. Tokai was one of the most important general managers because of his ability to negotiate with parts suppliers in the Far East, and he was skilled in setting up and operating manufacturing plants. "He was also getting the stuff out of Korea, and he was overseeing Korea and Taiwan until they built up the Hong Kong operation," says Russell.

Tokai gave Commodore access to the same chips Japanese electronics companies relied on. "If you went over to Japan you would find they had ten thousand chips that weren't available in the United States," says Russell. "At that point in time, the chip technology was already shifting to Japan. The NEC's of the world were catching up with what they were doing in the U.S., especially peripheral chips and integrated chips."

When the RAM chip shortage hit the world in the early eighties, Tokai continued supplying Commodore. "We were really scrounging to buy RAM's and stuff like that," says Russell. "He was a big supplier of parts for the computers."

Tokai spoke formal English, and just as important, blended into Western business culture. Like the other general managers, Tokai was always present at meetings in London and trade shows such as CES.

Physically, Tokai was startlingly thin. When he traveled to North America, his fellow managers were worried about his health and encouraged him to eat more. He had a long face with a pencil-thin moustache and spoke in a soft, deep voice.

Tokai was the first Japanese businessman Russell met. "Not knowing much about the Japanese, I was really impressed," says Russell. "Then I found out he was the wild maverick of Japan. He had a huge reputation in Japan for being this bright, non-traditional Japanese manager."

Russell was in awe of Tokai's ability to market American electronics in Japan. "He was a sharp guy," says Russell. "He was marketing things like the VIC where he's going up against Japanese products in their own market, and he was selling PETs. I mean, my God, how did he do it?" says Russell. "All those other guys had specialized keyboards with all different types of shift keys to generate all the character sets."

Russell soon learned that Tokai was an exception compared to his Japanese contemporaries. "Most Japanese managers, and even people below them, were company men," says Russell. "Tokai wasn't like that at all; he was his own man. He was going to be successful on his own. Commodore was a great vehicle early on, but you could tell he was independent of that."

Tokai's unusual style earned him praise in the Japanese press. "They ran articles on him in Japan that said this is the type of person the Japan manager needs to become," says Russell. "Honestly, when I meet the Japanese managers that I'm impressed with, they are still all the Tony Tokai types. There are a lot of mild-mannered ones that I've run across in my time in Japan, but the ones who blow you away are like Tony Tokai."

Tokai was one of the rare Commodore managers receptive to Jack's low-cost VIC computer. He had seen the market share of the PET in Japan plummet from 50% to only 15% in the space of three years and was eagerly awaiting a new product to reverse the trend.

His most ferocious competitor in Japan was NEC. In 1976, NEC released the *TK-80*, the first Japanese home computer. TK stood for training kit, and it was similar to the KIM-1. Next, NEC released the *Compo BS/80* in 1978, which included a keyboard and television output. In 1979, NEC released the *PC-8001*, a more sophisticated entry with eight colors and high-resolution graphics of 160 x 100 pixels, plus upper and lower case text. By the early eighties, the PC-8001 owned 45% of the Japanese personal computer market.

As general manager for the Japanese region, Tokai could market Commodore products as he saw fit. He decided to call Vixen the *VIC-1001* to retain continuity with the PET 2001.

The VIC-1001 case was a unique design. "All the plastic design, all the case work, and all the molds that had to be cut were being done out of Japan," says Russell. "Whether your product came out or not was dependent on Tokai." Unlike the metal PET case, the Japanese created the case using injection-molded plastic.

Commodore Japan had a small drafting group for their designs. "They had a big design bureau inside where they had the drafting people," says Russell.

The Japanese drafting people produced a memorable case. Other computers, with their right angles and sharp corners, seemed not quite as friendly. The VIC-1001 case, with smooth rounded edges, looked like a cozy pillow with a CPU inside.

With the internal electronics reorganized for manufacturing, the final design was ready for production. In only two months, the Japanese had produced a clean, small, easy to manufacture, reliable machine. By September, Tony Tokai had a minimal production process ready, and VIC-1001 computers began rolling off the assembly line.

Tokai contracted a third party company to develop games for the VIC-20. He chose a new company called *HAL Laboratory*. The three Japanese founders liked *2001: A Space Odyssey*, and they decided to name their company after the computer HAL.

Tokai purchased home computer rights to several of the most popular arcade games of the day: *Space Invaders*, *Galaxian*, *Night Driver*, *Rally-X*, *Lunar Lander*, and *Pac-Man*. With the rights secured, he sent several VIC-20 computers to HAL Laboratories and hired them to develop the games. HAL Laboratory pushed the graphics and sound of the VIC-20 to the limit, producing accurate reproductions of the original games.

In late September 1980, the VIC-1001 debuted in the *Seibu Department Store* in downtown Tokyo. Seibu was the Japanese equivalent of Bloomingdales and sold high-end products on several large floors. At the time, the store hosted a small computer show exhibiting products from approximately one hundred companies.

Tony Tokai and Michael Tomczyk hosted the small Commodore booth in the store. The competition must have felt threatened by the low price of the VIC-1001. "[Jack] named a price of $300 and they were like, 'Oh, you're nuts', but he scared them," says Russell.

That evening, after the close of the show, Tokai called Jack long-distance to report the results of the convention. Through the static filled phone line, Jack could barely hear Tokai's soft voice, but he managed to hear orders of over 1000 computers on the first day. This was a success, considering there were probably only a few hundred thousand personal computers worldwide. Jack slept well, knowing his low-cost computer might drive back the Japanese competition.

Demise of the PET Jet

There have been infamous accidents involving corporate jets - infamous because usually only famous people own corporate jets, so accidents tend to receive a lot of publicity. Commodore was about to join the list. "There was a disaster with the [PET Jet] that was very dramatic," recalls Charles Winterble.

In September 1980, Jack Tramiel boarded the PET Jet along with company controller Dick Sanford, Commodore U.S. general manager Dick Powers, and consumer division manager Ken Hollandsworth. They had just picked up two software authors in Chicago. Jack hoped the flight to California would impress the pair, but instead it ended up terrifying them.

The flight was normal to begin with. Takeoff and landing in smaller jets was always the most nervous part for passengers and crew, since small jets were more susceptible to runway vibrations and gusts of wind. As they bumped and rattled down the runway, the two programmers gripped the armrests a little tighter. Soon, they were on their way home.

Whoever sat closest to the on-board kitchen was responsible for serving food and beverages aboard each flight. Today, Ken Hollandsworth happened to be closest to the kitchen so he began brewing a fresh pot of coffee for everyone.

Dick Sanford and Jack were sitting together with the programmers discussing their deal when Jack sensed a change in the cabin. It smelled as if something was burning. He mentioned it to Sanford, who reasoned it was most likely a heating coil used to keep the temperature constant at higher altitudes. The two agreed and rejoined the negotiations.

Jack continued nodding and talking with Sanford, but he remained uneasy. He had not been a survivor for so many years without being a keen observer. Soon the smell was so powerful no one could deny something was wrong. Sanford got up from his seat and headed to the cockpit to consult with the pilot. The pilot was equally unsure. According to the indicators, everything was normal with the aircraft. Nevertheless, there was no denying the strong smell.

When Sanford returned to the cabin, he noted a visible haze illuminated through the port windows. It seemed to be emanating from to the coffee maker. This was a relief, as it meant something was probably burning on the heating coil. However, when he got closer he noticed the fumes were puffing out of cracks in the cabin wall. They had an electrical fire and they could not even get to it.

Soon, all six passengers were studying the wall, hoping the fire would consume itself by running out of combustible material. One of the programmers from Chicago unclipped a fire extinguisher from the wall and handed it to Sanford, who pressed it up to the narrow crack and squeezed the handle. Unfortunately, the extinguisher was dead. Nothing but light mist of powder seeped from the nozzle. Perhaps one of the previous occupants of the jet had been playing with the extinguisher.

Jack placed his hand on the plastic wall and noticed the heat was extreme, almost as hot as a boiler. Suddenly, everyone noticed a wavering orange glow. Sanford peered behind the counter and could see flames quickly spreading.

Jack had been concentrating on the wall and he glanced up towards the cockpit. Thick, black smoke now covered the top third of the cabin, with an eerily straight line demarcating breathable air from non-breathable air. At this rate, the pilot would not be able to see out of the windshield for much longer.

Sanford notified the pilot there was an uncontrollable fire. The pilot immediately reported an emergency. The airport authorities arranged for an emergency landing strip for the jet.

The opposite wall was now engulfed in flames. As they reached the ceiling, the intense heat melted the light metal trim and it began dripping. Images of how the passengers would soon meet their end became apparent.

In the cockpit, the pilot noticed the electrical systems no longer functioned. When he landed he would be unable to reverse the engines for a quick stop, which meant they would require a longer landing strip. With all electrical systems out, the pilot relied on manual controls.

The closest suitable landing strip was too far away, and the pilot knew they did not have enough time. "He was ordered to put this thing down on a runway," says Winterble. Instead, the pilot took control of the situation and requested a closer runway, even if it was dangerously short. "That was very admirable," comments Winterble.

In the enclosed fuselage, the air became toxic. Not only did the synthetic materials give off horrible fumes but the flames quickly ate up what little oxygen remained in the air. For the six passengers, it was now a desperate fight for breathable air.

People now crouched down low to stay out of the dark, black smoke creeping to the floor. Jack was kneeling down with his face close to the ground, fighting for each breath of air. The heat was oven-like in the small cabin, and all the men's faces were dripping with sweat. Combustibles were burning violently, causing the plastic to sizzle and bubble. Suddenly, Jack found himself laboring for air, as though he was suffocating. Dick Sanford noticed and propped Jack up so he could hold his face next to an air-vent.

Sanford believed they were all dead now and accepted their fate. His only regret would be hearing the screams of the two programmers from Chicago as the hot metal dripped on them from the ceiling.

Jack turned to Sanford and saw the look of serious resignation on his face. There was no mistaking the look. They were finished. Knowing it was his last few moments on earth, Jacks thoughts turned to his family.

By now, the fire had spread to the inside of the wing, consuming insulation and other synthetic materials. It was rapidly closing in on one of the two wing-mounted engines, and the passengers feared it would hit a fuel line, instantly turning their plane into a ball of fire.

Jack and the passengers were severely weakened and delirious from lack of oxygen. Several blood vessels in Jack's bulging left eye had burst, giving him a grotesque appearance. The lack of oxygen was a blessing in disguise, however, because without oxygen, the progress of the flames slowed down dramatically.

The pilot had managed to get them over Des Moines, and they were now approaching the airport. The pilot knew the runway was not quite long enough, but it was the best they could do. The plane came in hard due to the lack of power controls and continued down the runway. One the wheels touched down, the pilot rammed down the manual brakes, but the plane continued. It reached the end of the runway and continued onto the grass field. The pilot noticed a metal post sticking out of the ground and sharply veered the jet to one side to avoid it. Had they hit the post, fuel likely would have gushed out of the plane right onto the flames. Eventually, they came to a stop. They had been on fire for 45 minutes.

Hollandsworth forced open the side door and the occupants lunged out onto the grassy field, tasting clean air once again. The emergency vehicles met the plane almost as soon as it stopped. The rush of fresh air into the cabin reignited the smoldering flames, but the firefighters quickly had everything extinguished in a spray of foam.

Winterble believes the pilot's quick thinking and refusal to follow his original orders saved the lives of his passengers. "The pilot was a hero," says Winterble. "If the pilot hadn't taken control of the situation and gone beyond the call of duty, they would never have made it."

One paramedic attempted to fix an oxygen mask over Jack's mouth, but Jack waved him away. The fresh air felt too good in his lungs. After a few minutes, he was able to catch his breath.

After the harrowing ordeal, all six passengers and the pilot retired to the airport lounge for drinks. Travelers who saw the motley group of soot-covered, disheveled, red-eyed men must have thought they were street people who somehow made it into the airport. Jack did not care. It was the third time in his life he had narrowly avoided death.

News of the incident shocked the Commodore engineers who had flown in the PET Jet many times. "We were in the plane a couple of weeks before then, and all of a sudden this thing nearly goes down," says Winterble.[4]

Different people take different meanings from the events in their lives. According to Michael Tomczyk, Jack told him, "It was a message. God was telling me, 'Don't fly so high.'"[5]

---

[4] Gould replaced the PET Jet with a British made Hawker-Siddeley HS-125.

[5] Michael Tomczyk, *The Home Computer Wars* (Compute! Publications, 1984), p. 186.

CHAPTER

9

Computers for the Masses

1981

With the success of the Vic-1001 in Japan, Jack felt Commodore now had a chance to capture a share of the North American market. Success would depend on how widely Commodore could distribute their computer and how well they could advertise.

Jack hoped Chuck Peddle and the rest of Commodore would support the VIC-20 project when it became clear he wanted to conquer the consumer market. Unfortunately, most of his executives and engineers did not support his vision. The disagreement was a festering wound and continued to worsen. A power struggle was taking place.

The Commodore Curse: Part III

At the heart of the struggle was the failure of Jack's calculator business and the rise of Peddle's computer division. "We've got a pretty good business going and Jack discovers that he's out of the calculator business," says Peddle. "The Japanese put him out. He bought this LCD company and it's not working out. He bought this CMOS company and it's not working out. So he doesn't have a calculator business anymore."

Since he began talking about the low cost color computer, Jack developed a saying, "We will make computers for the masses, not the classes." Since the low cost PET-2001, the PET computers evolved into high-cost CBM business machines. "In Jacks mind, and it's true, we drifted away from the original entry level concept," says Peddle. "The business computer stuff was never his thing."

Jack felt like an outsider when it came to selling business computers. "We were all having meetings and talking about business computers and everything else, and Jack wasn't very interested," explains Peddle. "All these guys are effectively conspiring to take away his company. It's his company."

Jack's son Leonard saw both sides of the conflict. He was friends with Peddle, who was something of a mentor to him, but he also clearly understood the agony Jack endured from the rebellion. "I'm not sure that [Peddle] liked taking instructions very well. He had this idea of where things should go and how they should be done," recalls Leonard. "Chuck was a pretty self centered person; not in negative way, but he just had a strong image of himself."

Leonard understood why Peddle was pushing for a more advanced business computer. "Chuck Peddle was not a go with the flow kind of guy, but you can't really develop anything new if you are a go with the flow kind of guy," he explains.

Perhaps the biggest obstacle was the language barrier between engineers and management. Although Peddle was part marketing person and part engineer, he seemed to have an inability to explain his ideas to Jack. "Other people didn't agree, and he was not very good at convincing them," recalls Leonard.

Peddle admits he did not try hard enough to convince Jack. "We had a pretty good team that could see ahead architecturally and we didn't really explain this very much at Commodore," says Peddle. Instead, Peddle focused his conversations on executives who already agreed with his business concept. "We basically just went back to the management, and management at that time was Dick Sanford, Chris [Fish] and these other guys more than it was Jack." Leaving Jack out of the discussions was a mistake.

According to Peddle, Jack came to him to discuss the VIC-20 project. "You came to me to make a cheap machine for the masses," said Jack. "What you've done is started doing a machine for the classes."

Peddle replied, "No, that's not really true. What we're doing is we're letting the architecture take us where it should take us."

Unfortunately, the language barrier prevented Jack from agreeing with Peddle. "That wouldn't have been something he would have even understood," comments Peddle. "He was a smart guy, but computer architecture would have been beyond him."

Instead, Jack was convinced his low-cost computer was the future of Commodore. "He had fallen in love with the Sinclair stuff and he just wasn't listening," laments Peddle.

Peddle continued pushing for two separate computer divisions. "It was obvious that the company needed to go in two totally independent directions," says Peddle. "Commodore could have absolutely been a dominant world player in the high-end market (which ultimately came to be the PC market) and the game oriented fun computer market."

According to Peddle, Jack told him to stop work on the business machine. Peddle contemptuously ignored his employers instructions. "I didn't stop the work," reveals Peddle. "It was an R & D group."

Peddle had caused a rebellion, turning Jack's executives against him. He was threatening Jack's position at Commodore, and Jack knew he had to do something. It was not difficult for Jack to identify the managers he would have to deal with. "Sanford is a problem. Fish is a problem. I'm the biggest problem," says Peddle.

Peddle's unhappiness with Jack began when he hired Tom Hong. He believes Jack gave Hong more credit for the VIC-20 project than he deserved. "Jack had taken off for some reason during that period," explains Peddle. "He gave this guy Hong the assignment of coming up with the design and getting it ready for production. When he came back, it was done, and I think he really felt this guy had done it."

At the time, Peddle believed the VIC-20 was going to be a failure. "We had suggested to Hong that he take credit for it because we didn't want to get into an argument," says Peddle. "We frankly felt we were secure enough that we didn't need any credit."

In September 1980, Peddle confronted Jack by surprising him after a flight into California. "I picked him up from the airport one day because I wanted to talk to him about the design center," says Peddle. "He wasn't happy because he told somebody else to pick him up. So he felt I had him trapped, which I did."

"Jack and I had this conversation about the things we needed to do," recalls Peddle. "I told him some stuff I wanted to get done. I almost told him I had finished VIC-20 for him."

Peddle also held a long-time grievance that he was no longer running the personal computer business, which he was promised when he first came to California. Peddle told him, "Jack you're not taking care of me. You're not working with me the way we agreed on."

As Peddle drove on, their discussion turned into an argument. Peddle felt emboldened, and said, "Jack, every time you haven't listened to me something has gone wrong. Instead of arguing with me, you should be treating me better."

The conversation did not help Peddle's cause. "I could tell he was pissed when I dropped him off," says Peddle. Jack was now certain his engineer had defied his orders to stop work on the business computer. He felt his engineer was out of control.

It is easy to see why Tramiel was unhappy with Peddle. Without Jack, Peddle would not hold an influential position in the computer industry designing future products and running several R & D labs. Peddle simply wanted too much freedom. He wanted to run his own company within Commodore, without Jack. It was a disdainful attitude towards the man who gave Peddle so many opportunities.

"The next day he announced he was breaking up Moore Park," says Peddle. The memo told his Moore Park engineers to report to the Santa Clara offices. Peddle would be on his own assignment.

"I was reassigned to Pennsylvania," says Peddle. "If you want to talk about Jack Attacks, he came in the morning and gave orders to [lawyer] Richard [Blumenthal] and they disbanded Moore Park in an hour. There wasn't even a chance to wrap it up and document it or anything. It was a very abrupt decision."

Jack also closed the other research centers in Phoenix and San Luis Obispo. The latter was not a big loss, according to Peddle. "I never really got them going," he says. "Commodore trashed it so soon."

Peddle believes Jack closed the centers in anger. "I don't think that happened because of Jerone Guinn. I don't think it happened because of Tom Hong. I think it happened because I pissed Jack off that night," says Peddle, referring to the drive from the airport. "Was he already unhappy? Yes. Was he upset with me because I was pushing him into a separate business? Yes. Were those all triggers to what happened? Yes. He decided to show me, 'It's my company and I'm going to make it what I want it to be.'"

Jack named Peddle's rival, Tom Hong, head engineer of Commodore. "When they disbanded Moore Park, all those guys went to work for Hong," says Peddle.

The closure of the R & D centers hurt Peddle. "I felt really bad about Moore Park," says Peddle. "It was something that we did very well."

Jack also broke his promise to Chris Fish, possibly because Fish supported the business computer. "Jack hired this president, Jim Finke as European President," says Peddle.[1] The broken promise discouraged Fish. "Effectively, Chris took the attitude, 'Screw this, Jack. Just as you are promising me that I'll be head of Europe, all of a sudden you bring this guy in.'"

Fish now held enough Commodore stock that he could easily resign. "Chris was just capable of cashing out his shares, which at that time were worth about three to four million dollars in 1979," says Peddle. A week

---

[1] Curiously, Jack seemed to want Finke to replace himself. According to Peddle, "Jack told everybody he was bringing Finke in and grooming to take over presidency of the company, which he never did."

after Jack closed down Moore Park, Fish decided he had taken enough and left Commodore. "I think Jack thought he would go away and come back after a while," recalls Peddle. Fish never did.

In the middle of 1980, Commodore began a migration to the East Coast. Jack was tired of losing employees to other companies in Silicon Valley. Jack was also looking for ways to reduce his taxes, likely from his observations of Irving Gould. "I think he wanted to get out from under California taxes," explains Peddle. "He wants to spend more of his time in New York. He was also thinking about some way to get dual citizenship as a Canadian." As a Canadian citizen, Jack would be exempt from taxation when selling Commodore shares.

In August 1980, Jack asked Chuck to begin preparations to move back east, presumably for a punishment tour. "He wasn't trying to fire me," says Peddle. "He was just sending me back to work for [Dick] Sanford in Valley Forge."

"He fully expected me to take my punishment and hang around for a little bit until I got back into favor," says Peddle. Chuck did not intend to leave the West Coast. He had grown accustomed to the warm climate of California and more importantly, he wanted to remain close to the strong technology environment.

Peddle talked with Jack and Dick Sanford about his impending move. "The only option for me was I had to move to Pennsylvania and go into purgatory like those other guys," recalls Peddle. "I basically told them, 'Hey, that's not our deal. I don't want to go.' Sanford basically said, 'Well, then I've got to terminate you.' I said, 'Okay, terminate me.'"[2]

Chuck Peddle, the man who saved Commodore by creating their computer business, was gone. "I'm sure it was a total surprise to [Jack] that I wandered out the door," says Peddle.

It took Peddle many years to figure out why Jack mistreated him at Commodore. "Why, after I've done all these things for him, why does he force me out?" asks Peddle. "It's because I effectively stole his company without ever intending to. ... The guy whose name is on the door has a real hard time letting go. Jack felt his name was on the door at Commodore."

Sirius Stuff

When the conversation to terminate Peddle took place, Peddle was already planning to leave Commodore. "I had already talked to

---

[2] In court, Sanford later denied having this conversation.

Chris [Fish] and [John] Pavinen about starting a new company," recalls Peddle. "The two of them approached me at the same time and said, 'Why not go do this yourself?'"

"Chris and I actually started the idea. We decided to do it over drinks at the *Buena Vista* after running a marathon," says Peddle. "Chris had been part of this discussion on spinning out the company. John [Pavinen] came up with the idea that the world was ready for a new computer."

The trio planned to build a personal computer using some of the work developed at Moore Park. "I was working on all these pieces, most of which either indirectly or directly got incorporated into our PC machine," says Peddle.

In a move that was sure to antagonize Jack, Peddle began recruiting Commodore employees for his new company. First up was Tom Mitchell, a Commodore production executive. "We were very careful how we recruited people out of Commodore," says Peddle. "We expected to get sued so we developed this paper that people had to sign."

Most of the engineers at Peddle's former research labs were disappointed with how Jack had so casually discarded their hard work. Peddle approached Bill Seiler, Glen Stark, John Feagans, and Robert Russell to join his new company. Both Seiler and Stark accepted almost immediately, but Feagans and Russell had reservations. "[John] Feagans was approached," says Peddle. "John turned us down."

Russell felt there were some bad feelings between Feagans and his defectors. "They acted as if they didn't want John and they kind of thought he wasn't on their side," says Russell.

Contrary to Peddle's assertion, Robert Russell remembers the Commodore engineers getting together for discussions. "I went out and did a whole bunch of offsite super-dooper secret meetings," recalls Russell. "We were at a Japanese place eating shabu-shabu that night. The whole bunch was there."

At first, Russell felt it would be best to leave Commodore because the West Coast was losing its importance. "It was pretty clear that it might have been a good idea to leave and go join up with those guys," he says.

At the time, Russell was working on an advanced Basic for Commodore. "[It] was designed to do high accurate math for business stuff, and it had all the Microsoft bugs expunged from it," recalls Russell. "They said, 'Can you bring that with you? Nobody's going to notice.' It just struck me wrong. As much as I liked Chuck and his team, I really didn't want to go."

Jack temporarily moved the remaining engineers, including John Feagans, into the company headquarters in Santa Clara. Meanwhile,

Peddle and his defectors formed *Sirius Systems Technology* in Scotts Valley, California.

The closing of the Moore Park R & D center and Peddle's departure from Commodore also marked a change in his personal life. Peddle's second wife, Shirley, had been involved with Commodore. Without Commodore, sometime was missing. "We had done all these wonderful things," recalls Peddle. "She turned forty and decided that she wanted to try other things. I was starting a new company, so she went her way and I went mine. We tried to get back together but it didn't really work out."

When Jack found out Peddle was stealing Commodore employees, he became vengeful. "I take [almost] the whole team and go out and start another company," says Peddle. "He was really pissed about that." It was an open declaration of war.

Tramiel felt even worse when he realized the man who replaced Peddle was inadequate for the task. "He thought Hong had done the [VIC-20] design so he thought he had me replaced," says Peddle. "Jack turns around and looks at this guy, and gives him some other assignment, which he screws up. He wasn't as capable as Jack thought he was, so Jack fired him."[3]

Since his return from Apple, Peddle had accumulated approximately three million dollars worth of Commodore stock. A month after Peddle left Commodore, Jack sued both Sirius Systems and Chuck Peddle personally. Jack claimed Peddle was in possession of stock certificates that he had not earned. "There were two suits," explains Peddle. "One was to fuck me personally and the other was to just screw us up."

Peddle maintained Sirius Systems had not infringed or used any intellectual property from Commodore. "There was no way we were possibly infringing on anything we did at Commodore," says Peddle. "What we were doing was totally different." He decided to hit back at Commodore. "I countersued them for $10 million for spurious lawsuits," says Peddle. "My $10 million countersuit had some merit because they were just persecuting me."

Even though the two sides attacked each other with lawsuits, Peddle and his partners maintained a friendly demeanor in the press, for a while. "We didn't say anything bad about him," says Peddle. "If you read the press, we said only complementary things."

Unfortunately, one of the Sirius partners did something Peddle now regrets. "This is now getting real serious and we made a real bad screw-

---

[3] Hong later sued Commodore. "This guy wound up with zero stock in Commodore and zero stock in Apple," explains Peddle. "He was pretty desperate. He actually sued Commodore, but I don't think it worked out. Jack was pretty clever about how he did those things."

up - a seriously, seriously, dumb-assed, stupid screw-up," says Peddle. "My partner [Chris Fish] got all mad because he sued us, and he said, 'I've got information that can put Jack and Irving in jail and I'm going to put it on the line.'"

Fish attempted to intimidate Jack and Irving out of the lawsuit. "In order to keep it from getting into the legal system, but to send a serious warning, we gave an interview to a guy who published effectively a bunch of stories about Jack in *Barons*," recalls Peddle. The articles chronicled Jack's past with the Atlantic Acceptance scandal and Irving's dealings in the Bahamas.

"So at this point we had taken a relatively bad situation and made it infinitely worse," explains Peddle. "Now we had thrown down the gauntlet and said this is really personal between us and Tramiel."

Unfortunately, the allegations had no substance. "It turned out my buddy was just blowing fucking smoke," says Peddle. "He didn't have hard evidence. He had his speculation, which ultimately he recanted. So all it did was to really inflame these guys with no benefit."

The court case was to take place before a 12-member jury. "I was supposed to meet with Tramiel because the courts wanted us to settle the case two weeks before that time," says Peddle. "But they scheduled it during the same time I was launching our new company in Vegas."

Tramiel and his lawyers showed up for the settlement hearing with no one to talk with. "I think Jack went to that settlement conference, having his lawyers telling him he was never going to win the case, and that we hadn't stolen anything from him," says Peddle. "I think he went to that settlement conference to make up."

Peddle admits he could have attended the meeting. "The real truth probably is that I was so fucking confident I was going to win I was telling him to stuff it," reveals Peddle. "I think not showing up for that - insulting Jack - was the worst thing we did."

"I could have settled it probably by paying their legal expenses," says Peddle. "It would have been like a quarter of a million dollars or half a million dollars. I had four million dollars worth of stock that day. That deal was on the table, and I never even went in and looked at it because I was so sure I was going to win."[4]

Peddle blames his mistakes on his righteous attitude at the time. "I was legally right and I was morally right. When you are that right you get your judgment fucked up," says Peddle. "Right doesn't matter. I made

---

[4] Peddle alternates between two, three, four, and in one interview even five million dollars, presumably because of the fluctuating price of Commodore stock throughout the trial period.

terrible judgmental decisions about how I dealt with the law and I dealt with Jack because I was so convinced I was correct."

Peddle's disrespectful behavior towards Tramiel made Tramiel determined to win the case. Commodore lawyers began using every legal tactic in their arsenal against Peddle. "The day we were getting ready to go into [the courts] with the jury trial, they changed the whole case," says Peddle. All the money spent on Peddle's lawyer for close to a year was now for nothing. "After they bled us as much as they could bleed us, they burned us by just dropping the suit."

In place of the jury trial against Sirius, there was now only the single case against Peddle for all of his Commodore stock. A single judge would determine the outcome of Peddle's case. "The minute they changed the case, I should have just gone back and said, 'Okay, how do we settle now?' They were in a mood to settle," says Peddle.

Somehow, the lawyers convinced the judge that Peddle was holding onto stock he had not yet earned. "Their representation was they gave me the shares but I agreed to give them back, even though there was no document to back that up," says Peddle.

The trial went poorly for Peddle. "We were just totally out-lawyered," recalls Peddle. "They jerked us around ten different ways and my lawyer was too naïve. We were so sure we had won. We lost." Another judge later turned down Peddle's appeal.

"I lost everything. I had effectively two or three million dollars worth of stock. Everybody else in the company had cashed out two or three million dollars worth of stock and Jack cheated me out of everything I ever made," says Peddle. "It was everything I own."

In the wake of the judgment, Peddle was unprepared for the devastation it would personally cause to his family. Both his ex-wife and his daughter fell into a severe depression. "My wife was with me every step of the way when we built the computer business," explains Peddle. "Jack Tramiel had made promises to her just like he made promises to everybody. She knew exactly the sacrifices we made as a family and everything else to make that happen."

"For him to go into court and be able to reach in and deprive us of every penny we owned after they knew how much we had done and sacrificed, they just basically said that the world is totally unfair," says Peddle.

Today, with the tragedy far behind him, Peddle retains his sense of humor about the decision. "Do you know what the definition of ten thousand lawyers buried in chains in the bottom of the ocean is?" he asks. "A good beginning."

The Product Manager

The few Commodore employees who supported the VIC project gained power within the company beyond their official title. On the West Coast, rookie engineer Robert Russell gained influence by supporting the VIC. Michael Tomczyk also supported the VIC, and soon took charge of the unwanted project. In a short period, he suddenly eclipsed senior marketing executives due to Jack's unequivocal backing.

Although working closely with Jack had advantages, it was also potentially dangerous. Tomczyk was inexperienced and it was likely he would make mistakes, and Jack did not tolerate mistakes lightly.

Tramiel and Tomczyk, who had both served in the army, had good chemistry. "Michael Tomczyk and Jack had this great relationship," says Russell. "Jack kind of wanted to rattle the whole marketing organization, because he wasn't really happy with marketing."

Jack used Tomczyk as a tool against his own marketing executives, pitting one against the other. "Tomczyk was kind of this rogue marketeer," says Russell. "Jack would let him put whatever he wanted to on his business card."

Commodore was a loosely structured organization, so Tomczyk used a printing service to create ever-improving business cards. "He kind of let Tomczyk choose whatever title Tomczyk wanted to, just to threaten the other marketing people. So some guy would say, 'I'm VP of marketing,' and Tomczyk would have a business card printed that said he was *Executive* VP of marketing," laughs Russell.

"[Tomczyk] had a lot of ego and Jack used that Ego," says Russell. "Jack kind of thought it was funny."

When injured executives complained to Jack, he refused to intervene. "Jack said, 'You've got to fight it out for yourselves,'" says Russell. "I was always ending up on the other side of Tomczyk in these fights. The other marketing guy would corner me [and say], 'Oh, we've got to watch out for this Tomczyk character! He's a big threat to the company.' I didn't give a shit because I was an engineer, but because I went to the shows they knew I was in good with Jack. They would always try to get me involved in their schemes."

Although Tomczyk held influence, he really wanted the product manager title for the VIC computer. The product manager is responsible for tying together marketing, advertising, engineering, product support, production, packaging, and distribution. Unfortunately, product manager was the one title Jack would not allow Tomczyk to print on a business card because he did not believe in product managers.

When Tomczyk became the central communications node for Japanese-American discussions on the VIC project, he took the lead. "I interacted a heck of a lot with Tomczyk," says Russell. "He was kind of always there when the VIC was real. When it went to the West Coast, Tomczyk showed up soon afterwards. Really, he was kind of the marketing guy for the VIC."

In his new role, Tomczyk attempted to steer the development of the VIC computer. "I don't think he really had anything to do with the design of the VIC-20," says Yannes. "He had some overly optimistic ideas of what the VIC-20 could do. It was a very primitive computer."

One of Tomczyk's biggest contributions was giving the computer a name. Commodore engineers wanted to call it Vixen, but Jack overruled this because it sounded too sensual. Tomczyk wanted to call it the *Commodore Spirit*, but the name had a negative meaning in Japan. "It became ghost in Japan," says Russell. "That was something that Tomczyk wanted to call it but it was a big no-no once it got to Japan."

According to Tomczyk, he finally decided on the name VIC-20 for the North American market. Since then, there has been endless speculation on why the number 20 is used. Some thought it was 2001 with the 01 dropped. Others thought it might be the sum of the ROM memory: 8 kilobytes of Basic 2.0 plus 8 kilobytes kernel plus 4 kilobytes character set ROM. However, Tomczyk maintains the number has no meaning and he chose it because it sounded friendly.

In October, Dick Sanford held a meeting of the regional sales managers in Valley Forge, Pennsylvania. After Sanford addressed the group, Jack announced Tomczyk as the new director of marketing for the United States. Jack had fulfilled nearly all of Tomczyk's ambitions. As director of marketing, he could make a difference. He had risen very high very fast.

In late 1980, Dick Sanford sent one of his assistants to help Tomczyk develop a business plan for the VIC-20. To Tomczyk's surprise, there was no schedule for the release in North America. Tomczyk saw this as an opportunity to solidify his position as the VIC-20 product manager. He set an introduction date for the second quarter of 1981.

Tomczyk needed some business cards printed for the upcoming CES, so he casually asked Sanford if he could use the title of VIC-20 Product Manager. Sanford did not object, so Tomczyk printed them up. Tomczyk's plan was to allow the idea of him as product manager to sink into everyone's consciousness until no one could deny it. He hoped Jack would either not notice or not care enough to revoke the title.

Computers for the Masses - 1981

In early January 1981, Commodore was in full force at CES Las Vegas. Sam Tramiel was temporarily home from his punishment tour in Japan and he brought several different digital watches for display. Some had a black leather wrist-strap with a silver body and a black face with the Commodore logo. Others had adjustable metal wristband and gold, oval shaped bodies. Some models had built-in lights and automatic alarms, which were state of the art in the early eighties.

Commodore was pushing hard to sell the watches, and dealers had to purchase them in large quantities. The Commodore name was not one people associated with watches, however, and the products were not selling as well as Jack wished.

One of the big surprises of CES came from the Japanese, or rather the lack of Japanese. The North American computer industry fully expected the Japanese companies to enter the personal computer market in 1981. However, as Commodore employees visited the NEC booth, there were no computers on display. Many believed the VIC-20 release in Japan a few months earlier caused the Japanese to withdraw their plans in the face of such cheap American computers.

Commodore boldly displayed the VIC-20 computers, which were in fact Japanese VIC-1001 computers with different labels. "We showed it to everybody," says Charles Winterble. "We had crowds lined up. [It was] just phenomenal."

In the back room, Jack talked with potential customers with his cigar in hand, bellowing smoke like a steam-powered CEO. "Jack would frequently talk," says Winterble. "There would be a crowd brought into the back room - investor types, the key retailers, the key sales guys, key customers." Jack frequently repeated his mantra, "Computers for the masses, not the classes."

Jack relied on his East Coast engineers to describe the product. "Jack would do an introduction and then frequently me and Bob [Yannes] would put on a dog and pony show," says Winterble. "I would give an overview of the technology, and if there was an engineer asking about bits and bytes it went to Bob."

The computer was a hit with retailers, but Commodore did not accept retail orders for now. Instead, they only allowed orders from authorized dealers in the new Commodore dealer network, which Dick Sanford reorganized in October 1980.

After CES, a few thousand VIC-20 computers began arriving from Japan in plain blue and white boxes with manuals that John Feagans' wife had roughly translated. The Japanese had sold all the VIC-1001's they could manufacture for the Christmas season. It was time for Tomczyk to put his skills to work.

Jack allowed his executives to formulate their own plans but he regularly visited them to monitor their progress. "When Jack was in, the whole place was chaos," says Winterble. "He was a terrific hands-on manager. Some people liked it and some people hated it." Jack walked down the hall, popping into one office after another while leaving a trail of cigar ashes.

Most executives enjoyed their interactions with Jack. "Jack has a way of making everybody feel extremely important," says Winterble. He could also just as easily tear employees down in a Jack Attack.

"If you didn't deliver, it was Jack's way of getting your attention," says Winterble. "I doubt if there was ever a Jack Attack for somebody who delivered what they said they would deliver. You were allowed to screw up. If you screwed up stupidly or screwed up multiple times, that is what he reacted to. Just making an honest mistake would not get you a Jack Attack."

Michael Tomczyk had risen too high, too fast. As a result, he did not possess the proper experience to perform his job at the high level it required. Jack often gave blunt criticism, and later told Tomczyk, "I talk to you like this because I know we're friends."[5]

At the close of CES, Jack put Commodore in high gear to get the VIC-20 ready for North America. The task was immense. A factory would need to produce them in quantity. The computer needed a box design. Someone would have to write a proper manual. A library of launch titles would need to be prepared, with peripherals such as disk drives and printers. Commodore would have to fulfill thousands of dealer orders and someone would have to design an advertising campaign.

It would be up to Tomczyk to develop advertising. Jack gave him two weeks to develop a presentation. Under the pressure, Tomczyk managed to contract pneumonia but decided to work through the illness. Two weeks after CES, Tomczyk entered Jacks office to present his marketing plan. Despite the sickness, he was upbeat and eager to receive Jacks approval. His day was about to turn into a nightmare.

Typically, a professional ad agency is present in the room and gives part of the presentation. The director of marketing also usually brings along some of his staff to suggest alternatives. Tomczyk's inexperience showed. He went in alone, with no one to support him or his ideas. To make things worse, his illness made it appear to Jack that he was indecisive. Jack smelled blood.

---

[5] Michael Tomczyk, *The Home Computer Wars* (Compute! Publications, 1984), p. 226.

Tomczyk started his presentation by showing a picture of a proposed box cover, with the theme 'Lightning Strikes Twice' (referring to the previous PET success). The proposed box cover borrowed the famous image from Stanley Kubrick's *2001: A Space Odyssey*, showing the earth at the bottom of the frame with the VIC-20 floating in space. A bolt of lighting shot through the VIC-20.

Jack found the box derivative and amateurish, saying, "It's not friendly! What's friendly about lightning? People get struck by lightning."[6] Jack thought for a moment, and said, "I want to show people on the box, enjoying their computer. That, to me, is friendly."

Jack suggested the possibility of a spokesman for Commodore. "I haven't given it much thought," was Tomczyk's reply.

This seemed to set Jack off, who proceeded to criticize Tomczyk for failing to prepare. "You couldn't bullshit him at all, and particularly in areas of marketing and sales, which he knew cold," says Winterble. "He expected results."

He then asked Tomczyk to continue with his presentation. Tomczyk showed the rest of his advertising images, which were all based around the lightning concept, which Jack had already dismissed. Jack was growing impatient.

In Vietnam, Tomczyk had never encountered anything as ferocious as the Jack Attack he was about to receive. The door was open for everyone to hear. Charles Winterble often heard Jack attacks echoing through the offices of Commodore. "A guy had to listen a lot," says Winterble. "He didn't get a lot of chances to talk. He would suffer the indignation of being told how poorly he was doing and he'd have to listen to it for a while." Just down the hall, around the corner, the newly hired marketing people stopped their work to listen to the booming tirade.

After what seemed like an eternity, the meeting ended. Though Tomczyk felt relieved to be out of the room, it was not over. This was just day one of his Jack Attack.

As Tomczyk entered his office, several of his new employees asked if Jack would fire him. Tomczyk smiled reassuringly and told them, "No, I'm not going to be fired. It's only a Jack Attack. It happens to the best of us." He was correct on all counts.

Day two of the Jack Attack was even more depressing for Tomczyk. Jack threw him out as marketing director and sent him on a mini-punishment tour by banishing him from the company headquarters. Jack took away his office and sent him to work in the crowded consumer

---

[6] Michael Tomczyk, *The Home Computer Wars* (Compute! Publications, 1984), p. 195.

products division. Compared to his old office, it was like working from a boiler room.

Preparing for Launch

After the January CES, Commodore slowly began the rollout of the VIC-20 to North American Commodore dealers. "They started out selling them through computer stores like ComputerLand and places like that," explains Yannes.

With Tomczyk no longer in charge, Jack assigned Ken Hollandsworth the task of overseeing the massive June CES launch, where Commodore would begin taking retail orders. Commodore would attempt to sell the VIC-20 in the same markets they sold their watches and calculators.

A few days after his Jack Attack, Tomczyk moved into his new workspace at the cramped *Consumer Products Division*. There, he squeezed into a small desk near the sales order clerks. Hollandsworth gave Tomczyk the task of creating a manual and launch software for the VIC-20.

In early February, Tomczyk hired Neil Harris, a Cornell University dropout who worked at a PET computer dealer in Philadelphia. Harris would become a key player in the push to get the VIC-20 into retail stores. Soon after, Tomczyk hired Andy Finkel, a close friend of Neil Harris who also attended Cornell University. Without any office space, the programmers crammed into the service manager's office.

The new group had difficulty obtaining VIC-20 computers for development. "They were always in my possession in the early days," says Russell. "When there got to be a few more we gave some to Tomczyk and Andy [Finkel] and guys like that."

The programmers also worked on a VIC-20 programmer's manual. Their technical information came directly from the VIC-20 engineers. "We did all the documentation that ended up in the programmers reference manual," says Russell. "Andy Finkel and those guys pretty much took all our charts, diagrams, memory maps, and all my folders and notebooks, and that's what became the reference guide."

Russell misspelled the word kernel in his documentation, which inadvertently resulted in every Commodore programmer using a special variation of the word. "The Commodore version of it was because I misspelled it on my big banner heading on the top page," says Russell. "So that's how it became known as the *kernal*."

The programmers were under tremendous pressure to deliver a manual quickly, but they succeeded. "[Tomczyk] had people like Andy who were clever, smart people who saved his ass by actually making sure that some things got done that he was trying to do," says Russell.

The VIC-20 would require a software library before the product launched at the upcoming CES. At present, there were no professional software titles. "We had translated some PET games and just put them in color," says Russell. "Some of the stuff was written in Basic."

Commodore translated two PET games, *Cosmic Jailbreak* and *Draw Poker*, and enhanced them with better sound, color, and graphics. Commodore UK originally developed Cosmic Jailbreak, an engrossing game with a twisted sense of humor. In the game, some determined aliens are trying to break their fellow aliens out of a prison by taking it apart one brick at a time. The player has to shoot them before the prisoners escape.

With the manual completed, the VIC-group transformed into a software house. Charles Winterble believes it was a mistake to have Tomczyk controlling a software group. "It's being run by a marketing guy who's really not even a marketing guy," says Winterble. "He was certainly not a software manager."

When Ken Hollandsworth saw the success of the manual, he asked Jack to give Tomczyk more resources for software development. Jack gave the group a new workspace in King of Prussia, Pennsylvania, a ten-minute drive from MOS Technology. The group moved into an open bay with walls and shelves around their work area. In the cubicle-like environment, each person had a four-foot wide desk to work on.

As the trio improved their programming skills, they began producing reasonable software titles. Neil Harris developed two tape-based games called *VIC-21* (Blackjack) and *Super Slither*. Another programmer named Duane Later developed *Space Math* and worked on other cartridge games such as *Blue Meanies* before leaving Commodore.

Andy Finkel stood apart from the rest of the group. He would later become a programming guru, but for now, he was building his skills. He developed *Loan-Mortgage Calculator*, *Car Chase*, and *VIC-20 Music Composer*.

In the ensuing months, Tomczyk's group grew even larger. He hired at least four new people, including programmers Bill Hindorff, Rick Cotton, David Street and Lee Ancier. "Within that group there were about six young guys," recalls Charles Winterble.

The programmers initially developed all of their software in Basic, with graphics using simple PETSCII characters. They looked like PET games with color and sound. Surprisingly, none of the games used a joystick. Tomczyk's inexperience as a software manager was showing.

None of the titles approached the quality of games found in arcades. "When they started the software group they didn't do very good work," says Winterble. "The fact of the matter is most of them, except for Andy, had no knowledge about how to do software architecture and how to put together a plan from beginning to end to develop it. They thought they could just sit down there and start coding. What they developed was product you would expect without a knowledge of how to truly develop software at the time."

The programmers developed a fun atmosphere, away from management interference. "They were over in this little building separate from the engineering organizations and marketing organizations," explains Winterble. After work, the group attended science fiction conventions and played board games. They also took long lunch breaks at the local arcade, teasing others that it was all for research.

Others in the company soon noticed the group's antics were out of proportion to the work they delivered. "They were kind of tucked away, living this life of Riley," explains Winterble. "The idea was we should treat these guys like superstars. They really don't have to come to work if they don't want to. Things like that."

The VIC-20 had a head start in Japan, so it had the largest software library. Tony Tokai sent his lineup of games across to North America. When Tomczyk saw them, he could not resist adding the dubiously legal games to his software lineup, even though Commodore did not own the North American rights. Tokai also sent some original games from Commodore Japan, such as *Mole Attack* and *Super Alien*.

The Japanese and UK games impressed Robert Russell. "In those days, to see that stuff on that little VIC, and the fact that they were actually playable, was pretty much blowing me away," says Russell.

Tomczyk negotiated the first game licensing deals for Commodore. He licensed five Scott Adams text adventure games: *Adventure Land*, *Pirate's Cove*, *Mission Impossible*, *Voodoo Castle*, and *The Count*. Andy Finkel used Adam's code and reprogrammed it for the VIC-20. It was an impressive feat, since he had to trim the 24-kilobyte games to fit onto 16-kilobyte cartridges. He also programmed the games to work with an add-on piece of hardware called the *Type N Talk*, which gave the games speech capability.

Tomczyk also licensed *Sargon II Chess* from Hayden publishing. Andy Finkel, who was rapidly becoming the software guru of the Vic group, once again adapted the code to fit into a 16-kilobyte cartridge.

Tomczyk sent shipments of games to Commodore dealers as soon as they were ready. Commodore distributed the software in two ways: major games on cartridges and lesser applications and games on cassette tape. Tomczyk packaged the tapes in six-packs, making them ideal discount products.

The cartridges were easy for Commodore to produce because they were already producing cartridge ROM's for Atari.[7] "Commodore was building almost all the VCS ROM's," says Russell. "MOS Technology was the cheapest ROM producer at that point in time."

With the software library ready, there were only a few more things to contend with before the consumer release. The original Japanese design of the VIC-20 had one major problem: the heat sink was in contact with the cartridge port, which made it so hot people sometimes burned their fingers inserting cartridges. Engineers solved the problem by moving the heat sink slightly.

A major problem occurred when the FCC realized computers emitted radio frequency waves, sometimes enough to disrupt a neighbor's television or radio reception. They immediately imposed restrictions on the emission of radio waves and required computers to use metal shielding. The PET never had these problems because Jack selected a heavy metal case.

The FCC requirements surprised Russell. "Nobody had to meet the FCC requirements before, which was a gigantic roadblock all of a sudden near the end of the VIC," says Russell. The engineers modified the VIC-20 design by adding metal shielding around the video circuitry. The solution added to the cost to manufacture the computer, but Russell says there was no option. "We'll hire or spend whatever money we have to; otherwise we won't be able to sell any computers."

At the National Computer Conference in May 1981, Harald Speyer of Commodore Germany and Kit Spencer of Commodore UK showed up with unique box design for the VIC-20. Commodore Germany designed an eye catching silver-gray box with a colorful rainbow logo. Commodore UK translated the German text and added the phrase, "The Friendly Computer," which Michael Tomczyk had trademarked earlier. The VIC-20 now had a box.

By the end of May, a large number of VIC-20 computers had been sold by Commodore dealers. As a result, customers were frequently calling with questions. In response to this, Tomczyk hired six college students for the *Commodore Hotline*. This was the first official technical support provided by Commodore. The VIC-20 was now ready for the North American public.

---

[7] Commodore employees could even play the Atari games before anyone else. "We had all the early stuff before it was released, and we played all these Atari games," says Russell.

CHAPTER

10

The Race to a Million

1981 - 1983

Before 1980, the personal computer industry had sold less than a million computers worldwide. By 1981, Apple was beginning to take the lead. With computers gaining popularity, it became a race to see who would be the first to sell a million computers.

CES Chicago

In June 1981, Commodore was ready to take retail orders for the VIC-20 at the Consumer Electronics Show. The Commodore booth was the best yet, with a large pillar and five VIC-20 computers arrayed around it. With all the game cartridges available for demonstration, the product generated a lot of excitement.

Robert Russell was excited to unveil the computer he helped develop. "I sat by that baby 24/7 when the VIC-20 came out," he says. "I went out with [Michael] Tomczyk to buy the big screen monitor and told the little old ladies in the booth all the bullshit stories to tell the press."

A year earlier, Commodore had released the CBM 8032 computer system for the equivalent of $5,000, including printer and disk drives. Now Commodore was offering a color and sound computer for only $299. The price left the competition stunned.

The biggest draw at CES was the Atari 2600. According to Russell, it was easy to convince people to buy a VIC-20 instead of the Atari game console. "We were pushing the whole computer angle, which they couldn't," says Russell.

When Russell told retailers the VIC-20 could play games *and* run applications software, they asked him, "What do I need a computer for?"

The Race to a Million – 1981 to 1983

Why would I buy it? Why would I spend $300 for it?" They were good questions, since games were the VIC-20's strength.

The cartridge lineup for the VIC-20 was impressive. It included *Invaders, Avenger, Super Alien, Pac-Man, Jupiter Lander, Night Driver* (renamed Midnight Drive), *Mission Impossible, Mole Attack, Rally-X* (renamed Car Race), *The Sky is Falling, Slot, Star Battle, Sargon II Chess*, plus the five Scott Adams' adventures. The software library was large enough to satisfy the retail marketplace for months.

Pac-Man received the most attention, since Pac-Mania was sweeping North America. Commodore surreptitiously used his image to promote the VIC-20 at CES.

VIC-20 Pac-Man was identical to the official Namco Pac-Man. It had the same music, the same sounds, the same maze, the same yellow Pac-Man, and the same ghosts that changed blue when Pac-Man ate a power pill. "On the VIC-20 I liked playing Pac-Man. That was done very well," says Yannes. It was probably the best home-version of Pac-Man for any computer or console in the world. It was also illegal in North America.

Atari had already purchased the North American rights from Namco. At the same CES show, Atari displayed the Atari 2600 version of Pac-Man. There was much anticipation around the release and Atari expected strong sales. Unfortunately, attendees universally disliked their version.

When Atari saw the VIC-20 games on display, they must have had two reactions. The first would have been respect for the programmers who produced such excellent copies of the originals. The second would be outrage at the obvious copyright infringement.

There were other unauthorized games too. VIC Invaders was a clone of *Space Invaders* by Taito. Midnight Drive was a clone of *Night Driver* by Atari. Car Race was a clone of *Rally-X* by Bally-Midway. Star Battle was a clone of *Galaxian* by Bally-Midway. Jupiter Lander was a clone of *Lunar Lander* by Atari.

Shortly after the Commodore booth opened, Atari lawyers informed Tomczyk and Tramiel of the infringements. Tomczyk felt the blood drain from his face as he realized the VIC-20 launch titles were in jeopardy.

The name VIC Invaders infringed on the name Space Invaders. This was easy to remedy because other companies had emulated Space Invaders and Taito had not properly defended the game, so everything but the name became public domain. Commodore could retain the same game play.

Midnight Drive was too close to the original Night Driver name and Atari objected, so Commodore changed the name to Road Race. The game play could remain the same because there were many similar 3D racing games.

208   THE SPECTACULAR RISE AND FALL OF COMMODORE

Jupiter Lander was fine, because the 1979 Atari Lunar Lander was a copy of the Lander game going back to shared mini-computer systems. Even the PET had a version of Lander earlier than Atari.

Following CES, Commodore faced legal problems with two companies: Atari and Bally-Midway. In Britain, Commodore released the Pac-Man clone and renamed it *Jelly Monsters*. They also released another Pac-Man clone called *Cosmic Cruncher*, which featured a Commodore chicken-head logo running through a maze with space ships. Atari sued for copyright infringement on both games.

At the same time, Atari sued Magnavox, which had produced a Pac-Man clone for their Odyssey game console. Atari won the lawsuit in 1982 and as a result, Commodore decided to settle their lawsuit out of court.

Bally-Midway also had legitimate legal claims against Commodore. Rally-X was a shameless rip-off of the game Rally-X by Bally-Midway. Even the text instructions were identical. Bally-Midway lawyers put a stop to the game.

An investor relations consultant named Steven Greenberg, who represented both Commodore and Bally-Midway, spotted an opportunity. Greenberg acted as an intermediary and arranged a meeting between the companies. Jack, Irving Gould, Steven Greenberg, and Michael Tomczyk flew to Chicago to discuss licensing.

The Bally-Midway executives were surprisingly amicable towards Commodore. Jack purchased the rights to produce *Omega Race, Wizard of Wor, Seawolf, Clowns,* and *Gorf.* Under the deal, Commodore in-house programmers would develop the games and Bally-Midway would collect royalties for each game sold.

Of the games, Seawolf and Clowns were the oldest and simplest to program for the VIC-20. Even in 1982, Seawolf was an older title, first released in arcades in 1975. Clowns was an aging but entertaining game originally released in arcades in the late seventies. Commodore later touted both of these games as arcade classics in their advertising material.

Surprisingly, Bally-Midway did not insist on Commodore licensing the Rally-X game from Hal Labs in Japan. However, Sid Sheinberg knew Commodore was inviting trouble so he insisted the game undergo a superficial makeover. Bill Hindorff, one of the software programmers working under Tomczyk, took the game and changed the cars to mice, the barrels to cats, the flags to cheese, and all of the in-game text. Commodore re-released it in November 1981 under the new name *Radar Rat Race*.

The Transformed Man

The dramatic success of Commodore in the United Kingdom was largely the result of Kit Spencer. Advertising was much stronger in the UK than their North American counterparts. In Britain, Kit Spencer was the well-known spokesman for Commodore.

Jack wanted to make sure Commodore launched the VIC-20 properly in North America. After Tomczyk failed to impress him with his advertising plans, Jack began looking for a new director of marketing. He decided to bring Kit Spencer to North America. In October 1981, Jack asked Spencer to move to Pennsylvania where he could no longer enter the annual Junior Wimbledon tennis tournament.

Kit was one of the few early supporters of the VIC-20 ever since Jack announced his plans. To launch the computer successfully, Kit's first goal was to convince Jack to create a worthy multi-million dollar advertising campaign. This was no easy task since Tramiel was notoriously thrifty. However, Tramiel respected Kit's judgment because of his wild success in the UK and he authorized the campaign.

Kit's advertising would bring the VIC-20 to the minds of customers across North America through television and magazines. Jack suggested a company spokesman months before to Michael Tomczyk and now Spencer picked up the idea again.

In the early eighties, most computer companies had a spokesman named Bill. Radio Shack had Bill Bixby and later Bill Gates in a stunning pink-collared shirt and white sweater. Texas Instruments had Bill Cosby. Commodore would also have a Bill.

Spencer made an inspired choice for company spokesman. Almost every computer nerd in the 1980's was a Star Trek fanatic. A sure sign of this was the number of early computer games that focused on Star Trek. The characters from Star Trek even routinely appeared on the cover of early Byte magazines.

The two lead roles of Star Trek belonged to William Shatner and Leonard Nimoy. Initially, Kit considered Leonard Nimoy, who portrayed Spock, the authority on science and technology aboard the Enterprise. However, Nimoy was already representing a Magnavox computer, so Spencer approached Shatner.

Shatner had lived an uneven life since the cancellation of Star Trek in 1969. He released an album of offbeat renditions of popular, psychedelic songs called *The Transformed Man*. In the seventies, between guest spots on network television shows, he performed in stage plays across the United States, touring in a small pickup truck and sleeping in the back under a fiberglass shell. His low point came in 1978 when he released a two-album set of songs, poetry, and book readings titled *Captain of the Starship*.

Shatner came into favor again in 1979 with the release of *Star Trek: the Motion Picture*, which led to one of the most popular movie franchises in history. In 1981, when Commodore contacted him, he was about to begin filming *Star Trek: the Wrath of Khan*, which would elevate him to superstar status. It was fortunate timing on the part of Spencer.

Like most companies, Commodore did not produce the commercials or print advertisements. Instead, they hired an ad agency called *Kornhauser & Calene*. The ad agency was responsible for many high-profile brands including *Arm & Hammer* baking soda (with the boxes wearing scarves and earmuffs and chatting with each other inside the freezer), *Head & Shoulders* (the man with two different dandruff shampoos on each side of his head saying, 'This side tingles'), and *Black Flag* insecticide. The agency would film the Shatner commercials and shoot the print photographs in New York.

At the first photo shoot, Spencer introduced Shatner to the VIC-20. The Commodore staff, including Michael Tomczyk and a marketing employee named David Rogers, was mildly curious to see how the captain of the Starship Enterprise would react to the latest in technology.

Shatner sat down in front of the demonstration VIC-20, which Tomczyk had connected to a color television, and began slowly typing. As the Commodore crew stood around, they heard a click, then another click, then a couple of clicks, then a few seconds later another click. The captain of the Enterprise had just typed hello using the index fingers of both hands. He quickly filled up the screen with random gibberish, amazed that a television could display things other than television shows. It was obvious it was the first time he had used a computer. Their spokesman was not very knowledgeable, but he was enthusiastic.

As a smiling Shatner posed in a grey business suit from Bloomingdales, the photographer took hundreds of photographs in a variety of poses. Kornhauser & Calene would later incorporate his image into future ads. The first ad showed Shatner presenting the VIC-20 with a sweep of his arm, with a quote from Shatner saying, "The first honest-to-goodness full color computer you can buy for only $299.95."

Kornhauser & Calene also produced life sized cardboard cutouts for Commodore retailers to use for in store promotions. In these, Shatner is wearing a blue pin-stripe business suit while holding a PET computer.

In the television commercials, Shatner emerges from behind a star-field before reciting the slogan, "Why buy just a video game? The wonder computer of the 1980's. Under $300."

Using Shatner as the spokesman was genius. Now people would associate the high-tech image of Star Trek with Commodore and the VIC-20. "They did some great commercials," recalls Robert Russell.

Shatner also attended conventions on behalf of Commodore.[1] "I met him when he came by some shows," says Russell. "Shatner was certainly a hoot."

For the first time, Commodore surpassed Apple's marketing, which lacked high-profile television advertising. In the space of a few months, Kit Spencer gave Commodore the most high-profile campaign out of any computer company.

Commodore received an unexpected surprise when Paramount Pictures released Star Trek II: the Wrath of Khan on June 6, 1982. In an early scene with James T. Kirk and Doctor McCoy, a Commodore PET 2001 is clearly visible in the background of Kirk's residence in San Francisco. In the scene, Bones appropriately discusses Kirks 'relics', so presumably the PET is part of Admiral Kirks prized collection of late twentieth century antiques.

Spencer also produced VIC-20 product literature for Europe. "At that time, almost all the literature came out of the US," says Russell.

Unfortunately, the literature they produced for Commodore Germany was unintentionally obscene. In German, the name Vic sounded like a swear word. "It was the shorthand for fuck," says Russell. "It became the VC-20 over in Germany." VC-20 stood for *Volks Computer*, or 'the people's computer'. The name was significant for Germans, since it sounded similar to the much-loved Volkswagen.

When Spencer sent over a stack of glossy posters to Commodore Germany, Speyer had no option but to print up small VC-20 stickers and replacing the existing print with them. Speyer had to phone Spencer and tell him, "Don't call it the VIC-20!" When engineers came to Germany for trade shows, Speyer warned them not to repeat the same mistake.

In Commodore UK, British users affectionately called the VIC-20 the breadbox computer[2] because of the unusual shape of the case. The VIC-20 faced stiff competition from Sinclair, but the lack of color and sound in the ZX-80 made the VIC-20 a winner. Commodore UK soon began using the factory in Cornby, Northants to produce VIC-20 computers locally.

Commodore brand name recognition increased dramatically over the Christmas season. Before Christmas, the average North American did not

---

[1] In 2003, Commodore/Shatner fan Robert Bernardo asked Shatner if he remembered Commodore. The movie star asked, "Are they still around?"

[2] In Germany, they also called it the breadbox, or Brotkasten.

recognize the Commodore name. Now, everyone knew Commodore. In a few short months, Kit Spencer had turned Commodore's situation around dramatically.

Attention K-Mart Shoppers

All of Spencer's advertising would be for nothing unless the mass consumer market could obtain VIC-20s easily. Jack was no longer content to sell computers from specialized computer stores and wanted to sell computers everywhere people shopped.

A marketing executive named David Harris brought in Commodore's biggest retailer. In late 1981, Harris arranged a meeting between Jack Tramiel and Fred Shimp, the electronics buyer for K-Mart. During the meeting, a grateful Tramiel promised Shimp he would remember K-Mart as 'our first wife' in mass marketing. Shimp commented that some men go on to have other wives, but Jack promised, "We won't forget you were first. Our first wife will always be special."[3]

K-Mart soon became the world's largest computer retailer. The stores contained a computer center with demonstration VIC-20s. This was a great way to attract shoppers and many stopped to try out the new devices. Shoppers could also browse an excellent display of software and hardware peripherals in glass cabinets.

Retail distribution was much different from specialized computer stores. At ComputerLand, a store employee would approach new customers, test them to see how much they would be willing to spend, and then steer them towards an Apple II if at all possible. After all, ComputerLand stood to make more money if each customer bought a $1200 Apple II rather than a $299 VIC-20. [4] However, at retail giants like K-Mart, there was no one to steer customers. They just researched the product as best they could and bought one. It was the perfect venue for Commodore.

Jack sold VIC-20 computers cheaper to K-Mart than they did to regular computer dealers and K-Mart soon began selling the computers for under $200. Suddenly, Commodore dealers were stuck with overpriced VIC-20 computers they could only sell at a loss. "Jack burned ComputerLand," says Yannes. "When he introduced the VIC-20 it was $299. Then he started selling it in K-Mart for one hundred some bucks."

---

[3] Michael Tomczyk, *The Home Computer Wars* (Compute! Publications, 1984), p. 235.

[4] According to author Jim Butterfield, ComputerLand also routinely steered customers away from the less profitable PET computer. Later, when word traveled back to Commodore, they severed relations with ComputerLand.

The sudden price drop alienated every single Commodore dealer. Yannes recalls, "ComputerLand said, 'How could you do this to us?' Jack's replied, 'That's business.'"

When asked if Jack offered the computer chains a rebate to make up for the difference, Yannes laughs. "You've got to be kidding me! Jack Tramiel? No. No he would not." Surprisingly, Jack saw no long-term value in maintaining good relationships with his Commodore dealers. "Long term value is not something Jack understands," says Yannes. "It's, 'What can you do for me now?' It's all driven by greed."

Christmas 1981 was a turning point for Commodore. K-Mart sold VIC-20s all across the nation and manufacturing plants turned out thousands of VIC-20s each day.

Once K-Mart began selling computers, their competitors came to Commodore. Retail giants such as *Sears*, *Toys'R'Us*, *Musicland*, and *J.C. Penny* signed up to distribute Commodore computers. The VIC-20 was now a guaranteed success.

Commodore was a force in North America. Jack had lost the early momentum of the PET due to a lack of distribution. Now, Commodore had more distribution channels than any other computer company, including the mighty Radio Shack. The new retail strategy would help them eclipse all other computer makers.

Sometime in 1981, Jack made the decision to stop production of calculators. He also phased out the old KIM-1 computer. The VIC-20 gave him the courage to bet the future of Commodore on the microcomputer.

VIC-20 Peripherals

From his experience with the PET, Jack knew he could sell several peripherals for every VIC-20 computer he sold. Financially, the peripherals were as important as the computers.

Commodore anticipated that the most important VIC-20 peripheral would be the cassette unit. Since the VIC-20 used the same cassette interface and code as the PET, Commodore continued selling the same cassette unit for a cost of $75.

Robert Russell designed an expansion device to allow PET peripherals to connect to the VIC-20. "I did IEEE cards for the VIC-20 and the IEEE kernel because we were trying to use the drives," says Russell. "I don't think any of those things made it as products for Commodore."

Russell also helped develop VIC-20 memory expansion units. "I was working on VIC peripherals under the Commodore brand, like the memory board," says Russell. By inserting more memory, users could load larger programs into memory. The VIC-20 was theoretically capable of up to 32 kilobytes of total memory. At the VIC-20 launch, three memory cartridges were available: three kilobytes for $39.95, eight kilobytes for $59.95 and a special three-kilobyte cartridge for $69.95, which allowed high-resolution graphics and additional Basic commands.

Memory expansion became an integral part of owning a VIC-20 and Commodore sold almost as many expansion cartridges as they did computers. Eventually, Commodore sold a 16-kilobyte expansion cartridge for $109.95.

The field of computer telecommunications was building momentum in the early eighties. Michael Tomczyk was aware of this and wanted the VIC-20 to have the ability to get users on-line. Completely on his own, he began seeking manufacturers to develop a Commodore modem.

An engineer named Dennis Hayes invented the personal computer modem in 1977. It was a critical piece of technology that allowed telecommunications industries to grow. "He had all the patents on the original modem stuff," says Russell. Hayes compatible modems soon became the industry standard.

"Tomczyk got Hayes involved with us to get the modem going," recalls Russell. "I worked with Hayes on the modem to work with my serial bus design."

At the time, modems were selling for $400. Tomczyk knew this was too high, considering the cost of the VIC-20 was under $300. He wanted Commodore to sell a modem for under $100. In order to remain profitable, the manufacturing cost had to be one third of the retail price, or $33 in parts. "We wanted the simplest, cheapest thing," says Russell.

"We were basically building a prototype card hanging off the back of a VIC-20 prototype in Santa Clara," says Russell. Occasionally, Tomczyk dropped by to check on the progress of the modem. "He might have come by and bothered us in that little cubicle."

The modem was the first big test of Russell's serial interface. "I was sweating whether we could figure out how to make it work with my serial implementation," says Russell. "That was the first time anybody tried to do something other than just running a stupid serial port off it. That required some serious hand shaking."

Russell was impressed with the engineering ability of Dennis Hayes. "That guy was a genius," says Russell. "He was putting stuff together that blew me away."

Most modems at the time had a special device that clipped to the phone receiver, called an acoustic coupler. The Commodore modem omitted this device to save money. "It was straight to the phone jack," says Russell. "I don't know if it was the first one but I know that he was trying stuff out that hadn't been tried before." Russell and Hayes were able to shrink the circuitry to fit into a three by six inch case.

To give users something to do with the modems, Tomczyk approached the leading on-line services of the day and requested free subscriptions and trial offers. It was a brilliant marketing strategy other on-line services would later emulate.

Each user who purchased a modem received a free subscription to *CompuServe* and an hour worth of on-line time. *The Source* and the *Dow Jones Information Service* also gave one free hour, but they stubbornly would not waive the subscription free.[5]

Commodore also teamed up with CompuServe to produce an online magazine called the *Commodore Information Network*. It included helpful computer advice, troubleshooting tips, and the latest news.

Commodore unveiled the VIC-1210 modem at the January 1982 Winter CES. Retailers were enthusiastic about the latest peripheral. Later, Byte magazine wrote a favorable three-page product description in the March 1982 Byte issue. In it, Tomczyk said, "We think this modem may sell as many VICs as the game cartridges." Compute!'s Gazette also gave the VIC Modem a favorable review, noting it was the least expensive method for telecommunications on the market.

Commodore released the VICModem in March 1982 for a price of $109.95. The product information, written by Tomczyk, fancifully proclaimed, "Science fiction is now reality. Science fiction writers used to speculate that one day we'd be able to use 'electronic libraries' in our home or office...Your Commodore computer gives you tomorrow's world of electronic communications today.....You've stepped into the next era of technology, the Computer Information Age!"

VIC-20 owners wondering what the user port was for now had their answer. The modem quickly became the number one use for the user port. By 1983, Commodore sold over 100,000 VIC modems, making it the largest base of telecommunications in the computer world. Within months, the Commodore Information Network became the most popular portal on CompuServe. According to Tomczyk, Commodore eventually sold over a million modems for the VIC-20.

The release of a floppy disk drive was less successful. A senior executive named Alan Fink grossly underestimated demand. Kit Spencer compiled a sales forecast, which estimated 15% of VIC-20 owners would purchase a drive. Fink ignored this forecast and created his own, which predicted only 1.5%.

---

[5] After Commodore released the VIC-20, CompuServe outpaced The Source.

The disk drive was virtually identical to the PET 2031LP disk drive, except it used the new Commodore serial bus. Inside the disk drive was the original ROM code by Scott Patterson. "I did the modifications to make the serial stuff work inside the 1540," says Russell.

The new drive also required less processor power. "The original [Pet] drives were written for two 6502 processors," explains Russell. "One did the GCR encoding and a second dealt with the IEEE interface. Basically the 1540 drive was getting one processor to do all that stuff."

Although the PET 2031 was a fast disk drive, there was no way to make it perform fast on the VIC-20. Russell was shocked to discover the VIC-20 had a devastating bug in one of the IO chips. "We were sitting there looking at the 1540 drive, and the units were locking up," recalls Russell. "Neither one was doing anything."

Jack was growing impatient. "Jack came in and said, 'It's going to be working 10 days from now,'" recalls Russell. "It was like, 'Yes sir!'" To make matters worse, Russell's fellow software engineer was leaving Commodore. "Bob Fairborne was leaving town, going back to the Midwest," explains Russell.

Russell needed a quick solution. "I just did the slowest, surest thing that I thought would work," explains Russell.

Since the timing of the IO chip was off, the only way for him to make the disk drive work was to slow down the transfer speed by four times. "That's when I wrote the really slow code," says Russell. "I wasted millions of people's hours I was told later."

A company called *Alps Electronics* manufactured the drive heads. Unfortunately, due to Alan Fink's estimates, Commodore manufactured very few drives. As it turned out, close to 15% of VIC-20 owners eventually purchased 1540 disk drives. The demand caught Commodore by surprise. Alan Fink survived Commodore until the summer of 1982.

Migrating East

After Jack closed his R & D centers, he wanted to move Commodore closer to New York. Robert Russell believes necessity was part of his reason for moving. "He couldn't hire people on the West Coast because of his reputation," claims Russell. "People didn't want to work for Jack."

Intense competition for engineering talent made California unattractive. "In those days, if you were pissed off you could walk across the street and get $5,000 more," says Russell. "At Commodore, you could earn $18,000, but once you had been there a year and people knew you, it was easy to get more money."

Jack resorted to another tactic to hold his employees captive. "A trick of Jack's was to give people stock options that he knew they couldn't afford to exercise," explains Yannes. "Then he lent them money to exercise the options, so they became indebted to the company until they were permitted to sell the stock."

Jack's shortcuts could only last for so long. "In 1981, he said, 'I want to move the engineers out [to Pennsylvania],'" recalls Russell. "It was one of those things where I didn't really want to move but I was asked."

Russell tried his best to remain on the West Coast. "People came and went in those two years, but they were trying always to consolidate people on the East Coast," recalls Russell. "I was saying, 'No, no, no,' and the movers were sitting outside my house for two days saying, 'Yes, yes, yes. The company says you're moving and we can't leave until we move you.'" Finally, Russell relented and moved to the East Coast.

The few engineers who made the transition moved in with the semiconductor engineers. "We spent a couple of years at MOS Technology in that building," says Russell.

Although Russell migrated, many engineers resisted and stayed on the West Coast for a few more years. "There were some, like John Feagans, who didn't want to move and wouldn't move," explains Russell. "There were some good engineers that just didn't move and we lost them. We lost some like Bob Fairburn who went back to Illinois." The Japanese engineers, Aoji and Fujiyama, also quit Commodore.

Charles Winterble felt it was a mistake to lose their California presence. "You needed to have a California connection," says Winterble. "There are a lot of creative people in California working on exciting things. The cross-fertilization in California when you are sitting down for lunch with other people is an important interaction."

Arcades in the Home

In the months following the Bally-Midway licensing deal, Commodore programmers began their VIC-20 arcade conversions. This time, instead of Basic, they programmed in machine code, using a CBM computer to compile the code.

One of the most successful conversions was Omega Race, a relatively new title released by Bally-Midway in 1981. Andy Finkel, now a programming guru, was responsible for coding an almost exact clone of the arcade game. Omega Race became an instant favorite.

Gorf was an elaborate Space Invades style of game with diverse game play on each level. One level consists of dive-bombing aliens in the same vein as Galaxian, while another level has a large space ship, which a player must shoot full of holes until the alien inside is destroyed.

Gorf was an ambitious game for the VIC-20, so Tomczyk divided the project among six programmers, including Bill Hindorff, Andy Finkel, Jeff Bruette, Eric Cotton, Mike Scott, and Jimmy Snyder. Finkel saved time by recycling some of his code from Omega Race. Surprisingly, VIC-20 Gorf was an almost exact translation of the arcade game.[6]

Bob Yannes believes the VIC-20 was more than adequate for the task. "The VIC-20 had pretty much the resolution and graphics capability of the arcade games at that time," says Yannes.

The VIC-20 already had a large user base and the Commodore games were a huge success. Each game sold for $29.95, with Gorf, Omega Race and the Scott Adams Adventures selling for $39.95. Jack and Irving Gould were pleasantly surprised when each game went on to make Commodore millions of dollars. Since most games had only small groups of one or two programmers, it one of the most profitable divisions.

Michael Tomczyk also negotiated with Nintendo to purchase the North American rights to their arcade games for Commodore computers. At the time, *Donkey Kong* was very popular, and it would have been a profitable game for the VIC-20. The contract was ready for Nintendo to sign but Jack cancelled the deal because Commodore already had an agreement with Bally-Midway. The sudden cancellation humiliated Tomczyk.

In the spring of 1982, Tomczyk wanted to take the Commodore games division in a new direction and start creating games based on original ideas from their programmers. He also wanted to give his programmers royalties from the games they designed. The deal would give the programmers more incentive to create a hit. Tomczyk prepared a royalty structure and scheduled a meeting with Jack.

Unfortunately, Jack was not happy with Tomczyk's handling of the software group. The only real successes came from the Japanese arcade games and the Bally-Midway agreement. Tomczyk's latest request for royalties only added to Jack's unhappiness.

Charles Winterble saw Jack's dissatisfaction with the group. "They're not putting anything out and Jack's getting a little ticked off about the whole thing," recalls Winterble.

Charles Winterble paid a visit to the group. "I wanted to see the work they're doing," says Winterble. "A guy is working on a piece of software for a rocket game and he demonstrates the thing for me. He's been working on it for four months and on the screen there are a couple of

---

[6] The final game of the Bally-Midway deal, *Wizard of Wor*, would never appear on the VIC-20, although Commodore announced and advertised the title. Development began on the game, but it eventually fizzled away when Commodore began concentrating on their next computer.

lines. If you look very carefully, it might look like the stick figure of a rocket with some little dots coming out the front of it. He's explaining to me what's going to be there. It's like selling land in Arizona. 'Here's where there's going to be the swimming pool.'"

The only person in the group who seemed able to produce exceptional results was Andy Finkel. "Andy was very sharp guy," says Winterble. "If he was managed properly at the time, I'm sure he could do anything."

For the second time in a year, Jack turned Tomczyk's world upside down. The decision seemed incredible to Tomczyk, who had hired and mentored most of his staff. Jack moved Tomczyk to public relations director for Commodore, a function he found unsatisfying.

Jack asked Winterble to bring the division under control. "So I inherited the group," says Winterble.

Commodore was not the only company to produce software for the VIC-20. The rapidly growing user base made it irresistible to game publishers.

In total, the VIC-20 attracted over 100 publishers, including Avalon Hill, Broderbund, Cosmi, Creative Software, Epyx, HES, Imagic, Parker Brothers, Sega, Sierra On-Line, and Sirius. From Britain, the VIC-20 lured developers like Llamasoft, Anirog, Romik, Mastertronic, Ocean, Firebird, Thorn EMI, Virgin Games, and Rare. In Germany, a developer named Kingsoft dominated the games market. Most European publishers cheaply distributed their games on tape.

Popular games from other computer systems were also ported to the VIC-20, including Choplifter!, Lode Runner, Miner 2049'er, and Shamus. Even Atari eventually released official ports of their best arcade games to all major computers, including the VIC-20. Unfortunately, many of their ports were substandard and Atari took a lot of abuse over these lackluster games.

The VIC-20 received impressive but short-lived commercial software support. In total, companies released 530 commercial games, 35 applications, 30 educational titles, and 15 programmer utilities. Of these, Commodore produced 106 software titles. Most commercial development ceased by the end of 1983.[7]

---

[7] Tape releases far outweighed cartridge releases, with 182 cartridge titles released and 428 tape based titles. There were no commercial disk-based releases for the VIC-20, owing to the limited quantities of disk drives produced by Commodore.

Big Blue Emerges

In the early eighties, personal computers were starting to catch the attention of Fortune 500 executives. These companies relied on mainframes and minicomputers supplied by IBM, but they started to see the benefits of on-demand computing in applications like VisiCalc, which were impossible on shared systems.

Jack ignored Chuck Peddle's ideas for a business computer. After Peddle departed, an executive named Bill Robinson tried to convince Jack to attack the business market. Robinson came from the minicomputer industry, and as such, he knew microcomputers had the potential to replace minicomputers.

However, Jack once again ignored his executives. He told Robinson he felt Commodore was not ready to attempt to break into the business market. Instead, Jack wanted to wait a year to get everything in place first. Robinson became frustrated and departed Commodore. As it turned out, IBM got there first.

In September 1981, IBM released the new IBM PC 5150. It was exactly what the industry was looking for at the time. It was modular and offered great expansion capabilities. As Byte magazine said, "It has a number of interesting features and a few flaws, but it is easily the best-designed microcomputer to date." The IBM PC sold with a color graphics adapter (CGA) which produced 16 colors, including high-resolution graphics and a programmable character set like the VIC-20.

The IBM PC contained Microsoft Basic in a 40-kilobyte ROM chip, very similar to the PET and VIC-20. Like Commodore BASIC, it contained the commands NEW, LOAD, SAVE, LIST and RUN.

Bill Gates, who learned his most valuable lesson at the hands of Jack Tramiel, made sure to specify that Microsoft would receive royalties for each copy of the operating system sold. Since MS-DOS was not ROM based like Commodore computers, Microsoft could continually upgrade the operating system. Microsoft would go on to release new versions and amass a fortune.

The very first IBM PCs had only 48 kilobytes of RAM. Like the VIC-20, it used cassettes to load and store programs.[8] The entire package sold for $1745.

VIC-20 sales were unaffected, but the IBM PC was an Apple killer. With a floppy drive, the IBM PC sold for $2575, compared to $2788 for an Apple II plus with an 80-column board and floppy drive. IBM sold more than 250,000 personal computers in the first year. It took Apple five years to sell 500,000 Apple II computers.

---

[8] The cassette commands remained in the operating system until MS-DOS 5.

The release of the IBM PC turned out to be the defining moment for personal computers. The world wanted a standard for computer software just as it had wanted a standard for VCR's and audio cassettes. Now they had one.

The Finish Line

Jack accomplished his goal and of computers for the masses and not the classes. The VIC-20 became the most popular computer for middle class computer users.[9]

By late 1983, Apple had sold 700,000 computers.[10] As they watched their sales slowly creeping near the magical one-million mark, the VIC-20 began gaining momentum. "The VIC-20 was the first computer to sell more than a million units," says Yannes. "It did that months before Apple sold their millionth Apple, even though the Apple II had been on the market since 1977.[11] The VIC-20 hit a million units after not even a year of production. That gives you an idea of really how slow their sales were. That's not exactly a fantastic sales rate."

Sales of the VIC-20 were impressive compared to the other big entry in 1981, the IBM PC. In fact, IBM only shipped 13,000 computers between August and December 1981. This compares to Commodore shipping up to 9,000 VIC-20s per day at their peak.

By 1984, Commodore dropped the retail price of the VIC-20 to only $79.00. According to Compute! magazine, Commodore sold 2.5 million VIC-20 computers before they discontinued it in January 1985. The same year, *Computer Chronicles* credited the VIC-20 with starting the home computer phenomenon. "It was a cool little computer and it was the first computer to sell over a million units so a lot of people must have liked it," says Yannes.

In the midst of success, Robert Russell felt sick for turning down Jack's offer of a dollar per VIC-20. "They sold a million of them! I'm an idiot," says Russell. He was about to learn something else that would make him even more unhappy.

---

[9] One of these users was Linus Torvalds. In 1981, a nine-year-old Torvalds received a VIC-20 from his grandfather. Torvalds used his VIC-20 to learn Basic programming. He was taking his first steps, which eventually led him to create a revolution with Linux.

[10] Time magazine, "The Hottest-Selling Hardware" (January 3, 1983), p. 37.

[11] Steve Wozniak still occasionally tries to claim the Apple II was the first to a million. On BBC World's *Most Powerful*, aired December 2003, Wozniak claimed, "Sales shot sky high. Apple was the first company to sell a hundred thousand computers; a million computers."

To motivate his employees, Jack created a bonus plan. "Commodore had put together a profit sharing plan for the employees where they had put a chunk of stock aside," explains Russell. "What they would do is take the increase of the value of the stock and then divide it up among the employees proportional to their salaries."

The success of the VIC-20 surprised even Jack. "When they designed that plan, they didn't expect Commodore was going to go from a $50-million company to a $500-million company in a couple of months," says Russell. "The stock shot through the roof."

Employees in the plan were ecstatic. "The stock plan made so much money that every person would have received double their salary as a bonus," recalls Russell.

Unfortunately, Jack did not offer the plan to the entire company. He had been so impressed with MOS Technology, whom he credited with starting the VIC-20, that he only offered the plan to them. "It was just the people at MOS," says Russell. "Nobody else had a bonus plan."

Until the migration to the East Coast, none of the West Coast engineers knew of the plan. "When I moved out there, everyone saying, 'We're going to get a mint because the VIC-20 has driven up our stock price so much.' We were like, 'What the hell are you talking about? How come we didn't get offered that?' The guys from the West Coast were hugely pissed off."

The bonus plan seemed unjust to Russell, who had designed most of the VIC-20 with Bill Seiler. "That was one of the issues that hurt," says Russell. "They did double their salary, but it was all because of the VIC-20 success. You know, I thought I deserved a hell of a lot more."

When it became apparent Jack underestimated the bonus plan, he began to back out of the agreement. "I don't think Jack could deal with giving away that much money," says Yannes. "They started playing some shenanigans about the stock plan, 'No, no, no. You misunderstood us. This is what we really meant.'"

Russell believes Jack had no option. "The inequality between them and the rest of [Commodore] would have torn the whole company apart," says Russell. "Those guys maybe didn't realize that, but it would have."

Jack called a meeting at MOS Technology to explain the revised bonus plan. "I remember going to the meeting where it was rescinded," says Russell. "They had all the guys down in the cafeteria room at MOS."

Jack and MOS Technology president Jerone Guinn delivered their version of the bonus plan. "There were lots of unhappy people there," recalls Russell. "These guys had posters and charts on the wall that said what they were going to get."

The Race to a Million – 1981 to 1983

Jack had made a promise to his engineers and it seemed inconceivable to take it back in the midst of wild success. To keep his promise to the engineers, he could have retroactively offered the plan to the few remaining West Coast engineers to satisfy everyone. Instead, he chose to hold back most of the promised bonus.

After delivering a convoluted explanation about the revised plan, Guinn asked his employees to sign a new agreement. "They had a complicated explanation of what they 'really meant'. They handed out these forms where they told you how much money you would get, which was nothing at all like twice your salary," says Yannes. "In fact, it was a fraction of your salary."

Jack applied pressure on his employees to manipulate them into signing. "You had to sign this form that you understood and agreed to it, and if you didn't sign the form then you didn't get anything," says Russell. Under duress, the engineers had no option but to sign.

Yannes and his fellow engineers at MOS Technology felt outrage. "Every MOS employee got cheated out of what they had been promised," says Yannes. "It was still a sizable amount, but when you've been promised a bonus of twice your salary and receive less than half your salary, it led to hard feelings."

Yannes was surprisingly accepting of the new agreement. "He wasn't one to make a big fuss," says Russell. "He was upset, but he wasn't an outspoken guy."

"Getting into a lawsuit against your employer is a bad thing to do for your career," explains Yannes. "I just signed the form and said, 'Fine, I'll take whatever you want to give me.'"

After the meeting, Morale at MOS Technology was at a new low. "There were a lot of people that were really bent out of shape and there were people talking [about a] class action suit," recalls Yannes.

Yannes had some consolation. "I was fortunate in that Jack actually gave me a separate bonus for the VIC-20," he says. However, the meeting left him weary of Commodore. "It was pretty clear that unless you were among Jack's elite circle of friends and trusted people, you weren't going to make much money at Commodore, no matter how hard you worked and no matter what you contributed to the success of the company."

The revised agreement failed to satisfy West Coast engineers like Robert Russell. "They did do something different, but those guys got a bonus nobody else got," laments Russell. "I always got screwed on Commodore bonuses. Believe me, it was not the first or last time that it happened."

CHAPTER

The Secret Project

1981

In early 1981, Commodore began planning a new line of computers without the genius of Chuck Peddle. "As far as Jack was concerned, the future of product development was going to come out of the East Coast," says Robert Russell.

The VIC-20 had unexpectedly turned into a gold mine for Commodore and now Jack needed to follow it with something more powerful. "The VIC-20 had not achieved the kind of success that it eventually did. It was just coming to market, so it was time to do another project," says Charpentier.

A TOI Story

The departure of Peddle left the TOI in a lurch. Many of the key engineers working on the TOI were now gone and there were no executives pushing for the computer. With so much emphasis on the VIC-20, the TOI project became less important to Commodore. "Once [the VIC-20] was shown to Jack prior to the June 1980 CES, I think it was all over for the TOI," says Bob Yannes. "It was having too many problems, it was too expensive, and it wasn't really what Jack wanted."

Although Charpentier struggled with the 6564 chip through most of 1980, the problems remained. "It was absolutely technical issues," says Russell.

Bill Seiler had previously attempted to overcome problems with the chip through hardware hacks, but nothing worked. "If Seiler could have solved it with hardware fixes, I'm sure he would have but they couldn't really make it work because of the core chip," says Russell.

Eventually, MOS Technology gave up on the 6564 chip. "There was really little we could do to help Peddle's group," says Yannes. "We had already told them the proper solution was to design a new chip, but there simply wasn't time or budget to do that."

The TOI is a story of failure, where the engineers pushed too close to the limits of RAM speed. "They were up against the edge of technology," says Russell. However, Al Charpentier was not defeated. He would soon begin a redesign of his graphics chip, and it would be even more ambitious than the 6564.

Doing it the Right Way

After the departure of Chuck Peddle and the subsequent dismissal of his replacement, Tom Hong, Commodore needed someone to design computers. They needed someone with vision.

The success of the VIC-20 threatened to kill innovation within Commodore. "The VIC-20 is now being sold. It's a pretty good success story making lots of money, and it's got a hugely established software base of games and applications," says Charles Winterble. "So now all of a sudden we have an establishment for the VIC-20."

Winterble and his MOS Technology engineers wanted to develop a sequel with 40-characters per line. They provisionally dubbed this idea the VIC-40. Unfortunately, some executives so adored the VIC-20 they were hostile anything else. "You had to be careful where you mentioned the VIC-40 because somebody would shoot you," explains Winterble.

Flush with the success of the VIC-20, the sales organization wanted nothing else. "There was a real controversy about the idea of coming out with a product that would displace the VIC-20," says Winterble. "Talk about crummy strategy! We're hearing from the marketing guys that we can't have another product; we can't have a VIC-40. 'Don't even talk about it because you'll kill our business.'"

Commodore marketing was intent on duplicating the longevity of the Atari 2600, which sold well for over half a decade without improvements. "It was typical short sighted, sales oriented [strategy]," says Winterble.

The engineers at MOS Technology knew they could not rely on the technologically inferior VIC-20 for long, so they began to discuss an improved 40-column color computer. "We said, 'Okay, let's talk about the VIC-40, quietly,'" says Winterble.

Winterble and Al Charpentier discussed their plans away from Commodore. "Al and I were close friends and we would go to a little restaurant, Friday nights particularly, and drink too much wine," recalls

Winterble. "When we went there, we said, 'What are we going to do? We've got this fantastic design area and we're doing nothing with it.'"

Winterble was trying to figure out a way to make MOS Technology profitable. "We couldn't get MOS Technology sales to take off, so we needed some great stuff," he explains. "Out of that came a bunch of chips."

The first chip was a new 6502 processor. "We took the 6502 processor and made it into a core, and we could drop that into a whole bunch of different processors. Those were pretty much just cookie cutter designs," says Winterble. The 6510 processor emerged from their talks. "The 6510 was just a 6502 with I/O on it."

They also proposed a more advanced chip to handle peripherals. "We did a 6526 chip, which was the CIA," says Winterble. The CIA chip controlled peripherals, much like the PIA chip. "We called it Charlie's Interface Adapter because I did the architecture on it. It was later the Complex Interface Adapter. I started it, and Yannes finished it and did it right."

The most exciting discussions were about sound and graphics. After two previous attempts, Charpentier and his team had failed to deliver a workable 40-character color chip for the ColorPET and the TOI. Now Winterble was going to give Charpentier a chance to do it right. He told Charpentier, "The time has come for us to do a 40-character VIC-chip."

The engineers wanted to target the entertainment market. "It was to be a game chip," says Winterble. "It would also be a computer, no problem, but games were hot back then. We said, 'Let's do the world's greatest game chip.'"

Winterble presented the project to Jack Tramiel. "I asked Jack if we could talk to him," says Winterble. "I'm sitting in my office, which is on the second floor of MOS Technology." Winterble heard Jack's familiar voice in the hallway. "All of a sudden he's in my office sitting down. He's got this great big cigar and he's flipping ashes on my floor. I always hated that damn cigar, but you didn't complain."

Winterble took a breath and presented his case. He told Tramiel, "Look, we've got an idea. We want to do a 40-character game chip and it can also be a computer. We want to organize a project to do it."

"I didn't even really finish talking and he said, 'Do it,'" laughs Winterble.

Winterble was still stinging from the failure of two previous graphics chips. This time, he wanted to make sure they planned the project. "I said, 'Well wait a minute, Jack. We want to do a study on this thing. What I'd like to do is really dig into it, look at the competition, come up with an analysis, and do a business-plan. You know, do the whole thing the right way."

Jack realized his engineer was serious about the project. "He looks at me and says, 'Okay, how much time do you need?' We talked about it and he said, 'I'll give you ten days.'"

Charpentier realized if he wanted to create an appealing chip for the marketplace, it would need to surpass everything else available. To study the competition, Charpentier and Bob Yannes played video games on the best game systems of the time. "We bought every computer we could get our hands on. At that time, it was game systems: *Mattel Intellivision* and all the Atari stuff," says Winterble.

Surprisingly, the Intellivision was their biggest influence. They also studied the Texas Instruments 99/4A and the Atari 800. During this time, they compiled a list of all the features they wanted their chip to incorporate. "The entire resources of our little facility there at MOS [were occupied] for ten days," recalls Winterble. "We took everything we could apart and tried to analyze the capabilities and project the capabilities [into the future]."

Charpentier was very interested in developing a graphical capability called sprites. Sprites are two-dimensional moving objects used in games. The process is fundamentally similar to cartoon animation, where artists create an object on cellophane and then overlay the object on top of a background. Programmers can create sprites without any specialized hardware, but the results are often slow and flickering. Charpentier wanted to create hardware-accelerated sprites.

The engineers studied sprites in other systems. The Atari sprites, called *player-missile graphics,* failed to impress Yannes, "They are terrible," Yannes says. "They don't have enough color, they aren't big enough, and they don't do what you want."

In contrast, Yannes was impressed with the sprite capabilities of the Ti-99/4A with the Texas Instruments Extended Basic cartridge. Their sprites could smoothly move to any point on the screen, and once set in motion, the sprites continued to move without any further program control. However, Yannes saw room for improvement. The Texas Instruments sprites were only one color and they were small.

The MOS Technology engineers realized they had to improve on the sprites or else they would merely have the same technology as their competitors but two years behind. They would have to predict the next step in graphics technology.

Al Charpentier originated most of the ideas and discussed them with Winterble and Yannes. "Al was really into video architecture," says Winterble. "We had many a late night discussing the architecture of that

VIC chip. We'd talk in the abstract about sprites; how many sprites, how the sprites would work, and how the interrupts would work."

The two quickly decided their chip would support multi-color sprites, which could move independently with minimal programmer intervention. They decided to better Atari and include eight sprites, compared to four. The engineers also devised some ingenious features to enhance sprite capability. Automatic collision detection would help programmers, since most games relied on collisions. They also wanted to make it possible for each sprite to double in size.

Winterble compiled a massive report. "We put together great color photos and this thick report," says Winterble. "We had gotten two hours sleep in ten days."

Their report was a proposal for a video game console. "The project that we presented to Jack for the VIC-II chip was actually to do a high-end video game system," says Charpentier.

Ten days after their meeting, Jack returned. "He sits down in exactly the same chair with another damn cigar, and I go through [the proposal]," explains Winterble. "It's an inch thick and he's paging through the pictures, looking at it, looking up at me, looking at it paging through it at about a page a minute. He reads about one sentence, looks up at me, and says, 'Ok, damn it, now will you do it?' He was just appeasing us." Although Jack barely acknowledged the report, the research gave the engineers a clear goal for their next set of chips.

Jack instructed Winterble to keep the project a secret within the company. "No one was to be told about it," recalls Winterble. "In particular, marketing was not to be told about it. Jack's statement to me was, 'You're marketing. It's engineering driven and when it's done we'll tell marketing about it.'"

Jack allowed Winterble and his team complete freedom. "It was kind of funny, because I wanted to work with a budget," says Winterble. "I had this business training and I wanted to use it for something."

When Winterble asked for a budget, Jack told him, "I'm not going to give you budgets because budgets are a license to steal. I'll watch you, and if you spend too much money, I'll stomp on you."

Winterble knew it was a once in a lifetime opportunity, free from marketing and management interference. "This guy turned over the company to us. It was amazing. He gave us the keys," says Winterble.

VIC-II

Charpentier's previous failures made him more determined to succeed. He was responsible for the architecture of the video chip, dubbed the VIC-6566. The biggest limitation to the design was the number of transistors that could fit onto a microchip. At the time, designers created their chips using components and pathways that were 5-micrometers in width.[1] "Back then, you're probably talking under 10,000 transistors, with maybe 100 capacitors on a chip," says Charpentier.

Charpentier had the freedom to pack as many features as he could fit on the surface of the chip. To accommodate this limitation, he developed a prioritized wish list of features. He would layout the most important features first and when he ran out of room on the chip, his design was complete. "The decisions that were needed at various points became fairly automatic," says Winterble.

Because of memory limitations, Charpentier decided to use a screen size of 320 pixels wide by 200 pixels tall, or 64,000 pixels total. With each pixel represented by a single on-off bit, this meant it would only require 64,000 bits, or 8000 bytes of memory to represent a screen. Since the chip must refresh every pixel on the screen fifty times each second, the chip had to draw an incredible 3,200,000 pixels per second.

Charpentier designed the video chip to use 16 kilobytes of memory. This left 8 kilobytes for displaying the background, and the rest of the memory for character sets and sprite data. Charpentier allowed several different modes of display, allowing programmers more freedom. At 320 x 200 pixels, a game programmer could display images with only two colors on the screen. If the programmer wanted four colors at once, then they would use a resolution of 160 x 200 pixels.

Charpentier was most excited about generating color. "I put in a pretty complex color generation scheme that was way ahead of its time," he says.

Charpentier knew scrolling games would be popular, so he included functions for shifting the screen by one or more pixels in each direction, just like the original VIC chip.

Video chips can display bitmapped graphics pixel by pixel. Charpentier allowed bitmapped graphics, but not much beyond plotting individual dots. He included no hardware routines for drawing lines, curves, or filling in polygons. If a programmer wanted to create wire frame objects or polygons, the 6502 processor would have to perform the calculations, resulting in slower 3D games.

Charpentier dedicated two-thirds of the chip surface to sprite functions. With the architecture complete, it was time to begin the layout. The tools available to the engineers had improved since the days of the VIC chip.

---

[1] In contrast, the chipset built four years earlier for the Atari VCS (2600) used 6-micrometer technology.

"They were using computers to do the layout, but they were still checking plots by hand," says Yannes. "They were still drawing the chip layouts on Mylar and then digitizing them."

Yannes witnessed the evolution of semiconductor design tools. "Originally it was a real drafting area with big tables, pencils, and T-squares," recalls Yannes. "They had only one station for the computer, so that's why they would draw them by hand and then the guy working at the computer station would digitize them. Then they would go in and edit them if they needed to. Eventually they all had their own computer stations."

Charpentier worked with two draftsmen and a CAD operator (Computer Aided Design). The CAD operator sat in front of a special purpose *Applicon* system and created a blueprint for the chip. The two draftsmen would then use his schematics to lay out the surface of the chip, hunched over large pieces of vellum paper. "The chip work he did by hand with his team was phenomenal," says Winterble. "It was all hand layout work."

The most difficult part of the process was checking the layout, which most engineers found mentally draining. "No matter how brilliant you were as a chip designer, if you couldn't take months of tedious work, you could not be a chip designer," says engineer Bil Herd.

For hours at a time, Charpentier hovered over his diagrams, bellowing smoke and measuring distances. "He always had a cigarette in his mouth," says Yannes.

Charpentier was able to progress quicker than other semiconductor design-houses because he had one tool no other had: an on-site fabrication facility. "Having the fab area was such a key," says Winterble. "We had people coming in at all hours to make sure that this stuff could be passed from hand to hand to hand to get a very fast turnaround in our chip area." Normally it took a few weeks to manufacture a chip, but in an emergency, the fabrication facility could produce a new batch of chips in just four days.

For debugging purposes, Charpentier sometimes created a test chip. "We didn't have emulation tools to speak of for the time," recalls Winterble. "What we would do is we would build certain parts of the circuit on a special test chip."

The system worked wonders for development. "Once it's in the whole chip system, you can't get at stuff," explains Winterble. "You take five or ten of the different key circuit areas, put them on a test chip, and run it through fab real fast. Then you bring out the [test] pads so we could probe and make sure things worked properly."

When time allowed, Winterble and Charpentier left the offices to visit the local *Valley Forge Golf Club*. "We'd try to sneak out in the late afternoon sometimes and catch nine holes," says Charpentier. "We were just hacking around and having some fun."

Soon, the engineers barely left the offices at MOS Technology. "We were working just ungodly hours of 16 hours days. A couple of times I put in 24 and 36 hour days," says Charpentier. "When you are cutting edge, it takes a passion."

Without management interference, the engineers focused everything on their task. "We were just kind of doing what we thought was the right thing to do," says Charpentier. "We were having fun. It was during that time I call the Wild West era in that we were cutting new ground and no one knew where it was going."

Once his team finished the layout, it was time for the first pass of the complete chip. It was a nervous time because so much could go wrong. "The one thing you don't want to have happen when you first come out with a chip is you don't want a data bit to be dead on a data bus or an address line to be dead inside the chip because then you can't do anything," says Yannes.

Winterble had to modify the MOS process to produce a workable chip. "We played around with our processing just to get the speeds up," says Winterble. "We kept making our oxides thinner and thinner so it would make it."

Normally, chips are full of bugs on the first pass and rarely work properly. Incredibly, the 6566 VIC chip worked on the first pass. "I've heard Charlie say everything worked except one sprite," says Yannes.

The engineers wasted little time in connecting the chip to a makeshift computer to see the display. "Our first pass of silicon, enough of that video chip worked that we were able to jury rig a computer that day," says Winterble. "It was a phenomenal effort to get that much working on that pass."

The SID

While Charpentier worked on his video chip, Bob Yannes designed the architecture for a new sound chip. The 24-year-old Pennsylvania native had been dreaming of creating a sound chip since he joined MOS Technology years earlier.

Yannes' fellow engineers at MOS Technology liked and respected the quiet engineer. "He did his work and wasn't pushing to get his name on everything and take credit for things," says his best friend at the time, Robert Russell. "Bob was a fair haired, bright, sharp young puppy."

Throughout his early life, Yannes looked far younger than he actually was. "I think probably everyone just thought I was a little kid," says Yannes.

Yannes took an early interest in electronics, using what little money he had to purchase parts and kits from the local Radio Shack store. "Being a child of the sixties, I was into pretty much any technical stuff," says Yannes.

"One of the first electronic things I built was a digital clock," he recalls. Using instructions included with the clock chip, Yannes acquired the parts and wired them together on a perforated board. "I remember it had a really big LED display and it would overheat and then lock up. But for a first project, it worked at least."

Yannes was also into photography and built his own darkroom. He merged his two interests by creating electronics to help with the development process. "I built my own darkroom timer," says Yannes. Instead of an amateurish perforated board, Yannes created his own etched circuit board for the project. However, the naïve hobbyist made a few mistakes. "One thing I didn't realize was the etchant that they used, ferric chloride, reacts with aluminum very violently. I was using an aluminum foil pan to hold it, so suddenly it started frothing and foaming and smelling really bad. I learned my lesson with that and went to glass dishes for etching circuits."

Yannes was lucky to experience computing at an early age. "The first computer I ever played with was in junior high school, which was a time sharing system," he recalls.

In the early 1970's, while in high school, Yannes became infatuated by the new sounds of electronic music. The innovative movement was full of pioneers exploring the musical potential of technology. The sounds influenced the direction Yannes' life would take.

One song influenced Yannes more than any other. "*Lucky Man* from ELP [Emerson Lake and Palmer]; the synthesizer solo in that," says Yannes. "When that came out we all asked, 'What made that sound?' That drove a lot of people to find out what it was, and when they found out what it was they developed an interest in it."

As his interest in electronic music grew, Yannes began listening to electronic music pioneers from Germany and Britain, like *Kraftwerk* and Mike Oldfield. "I listened to all of them," says Yannes. "I had their albums."

In 1974, Yannes discovered he could order analog music synthesizer kits and build them himself. Due to his severely limited budget, Yannes settled on a company called *PAiA Electronics* in Oklahoma. "I had no money at all," recalls Yannes. "The PAiA kits were kind of crude but they were very inexpensive, which is why I could afford them. There were a few other companies making kits, but they were thousands and thousands of dollars."

The first synthesizer Yannes built was unimpressive. "They had their little *Gnome* synthesizer, which was forty bucks. It wasn't really a music instrument but it made some interesting sounds," says Yannes. Crude as the kits were, Yannes was learning valuable lessons about sound.

After high school, Yannes attended *Villanova University*. The same year, MITS released the low cost Altair 8800 microcomputer. "When the first Altair 8800 computer came out back in '75, a friend of mine got one and that really got me into microcomputers," he says.

Yannes began devouring computer magazines like Byte. "Byte was a great magazine," says Yannes. "In the early days, it was pure hackers and hobbyists. It wasn't a mainstream magazine but it was published like one. It was big and thick on shiny stock but it was hardly polished. The early days were like the Wild West frontier."

In college, Yannes earned his tuition by assembling computers. "One of the things I would do to earn some money was to build computer kits for the science lab or the computer lab," he recalls. "At a local Byte Shop, I built these systems and get them working. There were a lot of people coming in who wanted computers but they weren't interested in building their own and particularly debugging it because a lot of them weren't very reliable designs back then."

Using some of his earnings, Yannes purchased a more expensive Synthesizer kit from PAiA. "I ended up getting one of their modular systems when I was in college," says Yannes. "That one was actually a useful musical instrument. I made some recordings with that."

Yannes was somewhat disappointed with the course material in university. "I was really interested in microprocessors and most schools are fairly behind the curve when it comes to technology," he explains. "In one of our classes, we were studying the Intel 4004 processor. I was just so far ahead of that already, so I negotiated with my professors to do independent study courses and independent project courses."

Yannes favored the 6502 processor over the others. "It was one that I could actually afford, which was great. You could get an 8080 for $200 or you could get a 6502 for $25," recalls Yannes. "Back then, you tended to develop a particular fixation with a processor. You had your [Intel] 8080 people, you had your [MOS] 6502 people, and your [Motorola] 6800 people and they would get into violent arguments over which one was the better processor. Kind of like Ford and Chevy."

Music led Yannes to experiment more with computers. "I'm not a good musician at all, but I was very much interested in making synthesized music," says Yannes. "I hoped to have a computer with a multi-track sequencer that I could play the information into and then edit it to correct my mistakes. I was also just interested in computer graphics. I thought it was really cool what you could do on a computer screen."

In 1978, his final year at Villanova, Al Charpentier visited Yannes on a recruiting drive. "He interviewed me on campus," says Yannes. "I was aware of MOS Technology because I had been playing with the 6502 processor for a couple of years by then."

Yannes could not turn down the opportunity to work for the company that made his favorite microprocessor. "I basically said, 'Okay, I want to go work for these guys,'" says Yannes. "Al said one of the reasons he hired me is he figured someday my knowledge of music synthesis would be beneficial to the company. Al is a very smart man."

Yannes quickly learned some harsh realities about working in a competitive environment. "The first day I went to work at MOS Technology, I walk in and I have my own office and my own desk, and I went, 'Wow!' I opened up my desk drawer and in it was a letter laying off the person who previously had the office," says Yannes. "I really didn't know what I was getting into, to be honest, but it's what I wanted to do and I certainly have no regrets."

Yannes never thought of himself as a Commodore employee. "I always kind of viewed that I was working for MOS Technology, which was fine to work for," says Yannes. "Mostly, working for Commodore was fine. Probably they didn't reward their employees as well as they should have."

For the next few years, Yannes' mind soaked up knowledge of semiconductor design. Because of his youthful appearance, Yannes was sometimes mistaken for a teenager who had mistakenly wandered into Commodore. "It certainly doesn't help earn respect," says Yannes.

According to Russell, the work at MOS Technology was not what Yannes wanted. "He was a frustrated musician," says Russell. "He wanted to do sound stuff so bad, but he was basically working on the other stuff because he had to."

Yannes had an opportunity to use his knowledge when he improved the sound capabilities of the 6560 VIC chip. Then, in early 1981, Winterble finally proposed a sound chip for Commodore. Yannes felt like his whole life had been building up to this one project.

Charles Winterble remembers the dedication Yannes had to the project. "The most important thing in Bob's life at the time was the sound chip. He always wanted to do a sound chip," says Winterble. "The engineers called the chip SID, which stood for Sound Interface Device.

The friendly three-letter name was in the same tradition as TIM, KIM, PET, and VIC. They also gave it the product number 6581.

Winterble wanted to make certain Yannes could meet the aggressive January 1982 CES deadline. "The most common problem is the engineers just get too many creative ideas and lose track of the priorities, and the result is you get nothing done," he explains.

Winterble told Yannes, "I'm not going to tell you what you can and can't put in your sound chip, but you know we've got a date, and we've got a cost issue. Within those constraints, you be as creative as you want to be."

Yannes and Winterble created a list of features. "He wanted something very elaborate," recalls Winterble. "I put together a die size for Bob, and made a prioritized list of must-haves and might-dos."

Yannes had the freedom to include as many features as he could fit onto the surface of the chip. "As a little team, we worked out pretty damn good methods," says Winterble. "That's why we got so much done in so little time."

Unlike Charpentier, Yannes did not look to the competition for inspiration. "I thought the sound chips on the market, including those in the Atari computers, were primitive and obviously had been designed by people who knew nothing about music," says Yannes.

The biggest difference between Yannes' chip and other sound chips would be the precise frequency control. "With most of the sound effects in games, there is either full volume or no volume at all," explains Yannes. "That really makes music impossible. There's no way to simulate the sound of any instrument even vaguely with that kind of envelope, except maybe an organ."

A sound synthesizer was the right strategy for producing sound on low memory computers. Today, most sounds in games are prerecorded and digitally stored, resulting in files larger than several megabytes each. With only 64 kilobytes to work with, the SID had to be capable of creating great sound from very little data.

Most people look at a tiny fingernail sized chip and wonder how it could possibly generate sound. The secret was in a tiny mechanism on the chip, built from transistors, called an oscillator. The oscillator produces an electronic signal, which travels to a signal amplifier and finally the speaker.

The number of voices a chip can produce is important for the quality of music and sound. Each voice can produce a different instrument, so a chip with only two voices will produce dull music compared to a chip with eight voices. Yannes initially planned to support an astounding 32 voices on his chip.

Yannes would have to build special circuitry to share the oscillator, called a multiplexer. No one had ever attempted a multiplexing sound chip before. "I wish I had done it because it would have been the first chip implementation of a wave table oscillator," says Yannes.

Unfortunately, multiplexing was too low on the list of priorities. "We just didn't have the time to get the design and layout done, so once we got one voice working we just replicated it three times in the layout," says Yannes. "If you look at a SID chip under a microscope you'll see three chunks that look the same."

The SID chip could produce four base sounds. Yannes included four waveforms he called saw tooth, noise, pulse, and triangle because of the shape of the waveforms.

His fellow engineers were under the impression he was designing a sound chip exclusively for computers and video game consoles. "That's what Al and Charlie thought!" reveals Yannes. "I really wanted to do a multi-track, polyphonic music synthesizer."

Yannes even snuck in some features that had no relevance to computers. One of the input pins on the SID chip could receive signals from another source, such as an electric guitar. "We were working so fast on the VIC chip and the SID chip that no one was looking over my shoulder to see what I was doing," recalls Yannes.

Yannes even included a lookup table in the chip to convert data from musical notes into the equivalent frequencies. However, Charlie Winterble objected to the extra silicon it would use. "Charlie axed that, and he was totally right," says Yannes. "It would have been a big waste of silicon just for a minor convenience."

After only four or five months, the design was finished and ready for production. Yannes was able to include most of the features he wanted. "He got about two-thirds or even three-quarters of the list done," says Winterble.

The sound chip used 7-micrometer technology, compared to 5-micrometer technology for the VIC-II chip. This ensured each silicon wafer produced a high yield, which reduced costs.

Yannes nervously waited for his first chips. He knew what the SID would look like, but he really did not know how it would sound. "The SID chip came out pretty well the first time," says Yannes. "It made sound. Everything we needed for the show was working after the second pass."

Yannes was not fully satisfied with the SID chip. One of his disappointments was the poor signal-to-noise ratio, which produced an audible hum when the SID was quiet. However, most programmers dealt with this by stopping the oscillator when the note was completed, making it difficult for the listener to detect the noise.

"So many things in the SID chip don't work as well as they could have because there just wasn't time to make them right," says Yannes. "If I had taken the time to do the multiplex oscillator and timing design, I don't think we ever would have gotten the product out in the timeframe."

Yannes was a perfectionist, and the problems with the chip weighed on him. "We were so close to the thing we were worrying about every little detail," says Yannes.

However, Charlie Winterble put Yannes' achievement in proper perspective, telling him, "This thing is already 10 times better than anything out there and 20 times better than it needs to be."[2]

Nine months after Winterble spoke with Tramiel about a new project, Charpentier and Yannes had their chips ready. "I look back on that and I'm still amazed," says Charpentier.

Compared to other semiconductor development cycles, the VIC-II and SID chips took about half the time to complete. "I don't think anyone had ever done that before and I don't think anyone at Commodore could have done it again," says Yannes.

Charpentier credits the speed of the project to the freedom given to the engineers. "Part of it was we were just left alone," he explains. "There weren't a lot of people in our face during the chip design process. We were in control of the design. Bob, myself, and Charlie knew what we wanted to accomplish and just did it without much fanfare or debate."

Like true artists, the engineers signed their work by placing their initials right on the chip, along with the MOS Technology logo. "Hidden in the layout were the people's initials," says Winterble. "It was something I didn't know about until it was done."

Yannes recalls early attempts to market the chips to other companies. "We were seeing if anyone was interested. In the early development phase we actually went to a couple of set top box companies to promote these chips in their systems," reveals Yannes. "You had people making boxes for cable TV companies that needed graphics capability to put menus up on the screen."

Yannes goal of selling the SID chip to synthesizer manufacturers also went unrealized. As Yannes recalls, "At one point, *Sequential Circuits*, which was a well known synthesizer company at the time, had called with some interest in the chip. They never really did anything with it."

---

[2] In September 1995, as part of their 20th anniversary edition, Byte magazine named the SID as one of the top-20 most important chips ever.

Efforts to market the chips ended when Jack gave new orders. "Once this thing started going on, I remember that Jack sealed it up," says Winterble. "We're not going to tell anybody, we're not going to show it to anybody, and it's going to be strictly a Commodore product."

Although Yannes hoped to see his sound chip adopted by other companies, he took the news in stride. "You pretty much knew up front that Jack was in charge and he called the shots," explains Yannes. "Therefore don't get flustered when the totally unexpected happens because that's the nature of how he runs his business."

The Porsche Pets

Now that Chuck Peddle was gone, Jack proposed a line of high-end business and personal computers to compete with IBM and Apple. Development of the computers occurred in parallel with the chip design. "We were designing the chips in tandem," explains Yannes. "We were working hand in hand to try to come up with something that would work in these systems they were designing."

Rather than one computer, Commodore developed several different computers around the new chips. "There was going to be a whole line of computers based on that whole product," says Charpentier.

The new systems would replace the aging PET line. "We had plans for taking the same architecture, putting in additional memory through banking, and creating a whole series of computers essentially to take the place of the PET," explains Winterble.

The black and white B256 business machine used the 6545 CRTC chip for video display and the SID chip for sound. The machine would have 256 kilobytes of memory, which required a 6509 processor to access the additional memory. The engineers included a slot for an optional Intel 8088 processor running at 5 MHz, or customers could purchase a BX256, which included the 8088 chip.

The engineers also developed a personal computer for the home, which they dubbed the P128. The 128-kilobyte machine used both a SID chip and a 40-column VIC-II chip, making it appealing to home users.

For the moment, Yannes had no input into the computer designs. "I wasn't in the systems design group," says Yannes. "I was still in the chip design group so I really wasn't that involved in designing the computers, other than whenever they needed to know about how the chips worked."

Jack chose Charlie Winterble to lead the new systems development. "By that time, Charlie was the head of engineering for Commodore," recalls Yannes. "Al was the head of Systems Design and Chip Design."

However, Winterble and his MOS Technology engineers were inexperienced with systems design. It was an entirely new field for them.

"Al and I were chip people, and we only really became systems people during this project," says Winterble.

Winterble and Jack wanted a memorable computer case. "We wanted to do a really exotic case design for the personal one," recalls Winterble. "His instructions were for me to use Porsche. I remember him saying, 'You can get the best design center in the world.'"

Winterble traveled to the *Porsche Design Center* in Stuttgart, Germany. The grandson of Professor Ferdinand Porsche started the design firm in 1972. Porsche prided itself on its 'disciplined aesthetic that refines objects down to their basic function'. Over the years, Porsche has designed everything from pens to auto-bodies.[3]

"I went over to Porsche design facilities over there in Stuttgart and worked with them and they designed a beautiful case that, really when you looked at it, was reminiscent of the 928 Porsche," recalls Winterble. "I met all the Porsche people, and that was really great for me because I happened to own a 911 at the time."

The computer earned a new name because of the anticipated Porsche design. "At one point they were being referred to as the Porsche Pets," says Yannes. The case design was exotic, but it was also impractical. "The Porsche PET was just a blue-line concept sketch that looked like a space helmet. I remember it had a CRT monitor that was suspended on a swivel and would have been ridiculously expensive to produce."

Commodore dropped the concept and sought a US firm. "The packaging had been designed by a house in Boston, headed by Ira Velinsky, who was later hired by Commodore," says Yannes. The engineers were more enthusiastic about the practical Boston designs. "The guys in Boston had done a really nice job making them. They were very curved."[4]

Although Commodore abandoned the Porsche concept, they surreptitiously continued using the Porsche name to promote the Boston designs. "People assumed that these new cases were the Porsche Pet's and there were those at Commodore who tried to promote that false impression," says Yannes.

The task to design the computers before CES was immense for the small team of engineers. "We tried to do them simultaneously with a handful of people. It was quite a job," recalls Winterble. "Along with each of these were the peripherals to go with them. You had to have a

---

[3] The Porsche Design Center has continued to design computer cases, but Commodore was the first.

[4] Velinsky later won the German *iF Product Design* award in 1983 for his cases.

240 THE SPECTACULAR RISE AND FALL OF COMMODORE

disk drive. You had to have a modem. You had to have all these things, and they had to be ready at time-zero."

Robert Russell began creating code for the new computers. "I was starting up with what became the P and B series," recalls Russell. "We worked on Basic 4.0 which was the extended Basic. We called it Business Basic."

A Radical Course Change

After completing the final design on the VIC-20, Japanese engineer Yashi Terakura decided he liked his North American engineers so much he would join them. The charismatic and effective engineer moved to Pennsylvania.

When Charpentier and Yannes first proposed their chipset, they intended to use the chips for videogames. "Originally, we first started out designing those chips to build the next generation of video game [consoles] and we were also going to use them in these two computers," says Yannes. Sometime during 1981, they lost the idea of using the chips for video games.

When Yashi heard about the next generation chips, he decided he wanted to create a dedicated video game console, which he called the *Ultimax*. "He wanted to do a game machine," recalls Russell.

Although it seemed obvious for Commodore to build a game machine using their new chipset, no one at Commodore proposed the idea before Terakura arrived. "There was no intention at that point of us producing something like the Commodore 64 or even anything like the Ultimax," says Yannes.

Soon after Terakura began work on his project, the machine underwent a strategic name change. "It was originally called Ultimax until somebody noted it sounded like a feminine hygiene product," explains Yannes. Soon, engineers began calling it the *Max Machine* instead.

Although the other Commodore engineers aided Terakura with the SID and VIC-II chips, Terakura drove the project himself. "We had Yashi Terakura working on trying to do the Max technology stuff," says Russell. "He was coming to us and asking us what to do to try and get the Max thing done."

During development, the engineers discussed how much memory to include in the Max Machine and could not agree on the proper amount. "When we were developing the Max architecture, we only put 4K of RAM in it to keep costs down," says Yannes. However, Robert Russell knew it would not be enough. "The software group wanted 8K of RAM so that they could produce a full bit-mapped display."

The Secret Project – 1981

Jack learned of the disagreement and decided to help his engineers resolve the argument. "It was a big fight until Jack stepped in," recalls Yannes. Acting like a modern day King Solomon, Jack listened to their positions and gave his judgment. "He decreed that we should put 6K of RAM in as a compromise and then left."

The engineers stood in shocked silence, since the solution helped no one. "6K cost more than 4K and it still wasn't enough to do a bit map display," says Yannes. "We all just stared at each other."

As 1981 progressed, the attitudes of Commodore employees towards the VIC-20 changed from scorn to respect, partly because the VIC-20 was now covering a significant portion of everyone's paychecks. "When the chips were working, it was clear that the VIC-20 was becoming a successful product," says Charpentier. Low-end computers began to look more promising.

Meanwhile, the engineers continued development of the high-end computers. "We were supposed to be doing the P series and B series," says Russell. However, the engineer's faith in the new line of computers was beginning to falter. "Bob Yannes and I went to Al, and I think we all approached Charlie and said, "We really don't like this P series machine. We want to do just the simplest thing possible."

Russell added, "We can even make it support what Yashi wants to do with the Max Machine."

The engineers discussed their concept in an impromptu meeting with Tramiel. "Jack would hold court, if you will, at various times," explains Charpentier. "He was the emperor. Sometimes it was the marketing people, sometimes it was the engineering people. He would sift the information and make a decision."

The engineers proposed a true sequel to the VIC-20. "We basically had a meeting with Jack and said, 'Gee, why don't we put this into a VIC-20 case and do a VIC-40.' That was the original name we had used," recalls Charpentier.

The biggest decision with the VIC-40 was the memory size. "When you are laying out the groundwork, you know that you want to be able to have [lots of] RAM, but the fact is RAM was still very expensive," explains Charpentier. It was obvious to the engineers that the machine would need more memory than the VIC-20. "The original game concept was to put 16K into it."

Commodore was never successful producing reliable memory, making Jack's vertical-integration strategy incomplete. The inherent cost of memory would make the machine too costly to be a true VIC-20 sequel.

With such a small amount of memory, the engineers knew the computer would not directly compete with the new 48-kilobyte Apple II plus.

Surprisingly, Jack insisted on more memory for the machine anyway. "Jack felt we should design it with 64K," says Charpentier. Tramiel predicted the price of memory would fall by the time the computer was ready for mass production.

Yannes felt Jack's decision was correct. "It was really a brilliant move because 64K RAM's had just come out and it meant that you could introduce a machine that had 64K of memory when everyone else had at most 48K," says Yannes.

Winterble assumed Jack would want the new computer for the June CES, only seven months away. Normally, engineers require at least a year to design a computer, but Winterble knew if he put his engineers on high alert, they might get it done.

Instead, Jack wanted the new computer sooner. "Jack decided he wanted to show a machine with 64K of RAM at the January 1982 CES," says Yannes. It was already November, and CES was less than two months away. "I don't even know that he intended to put it into production."

Tramiel expected miracles from his engineers. "Every time before a show he would come to someone and say, 'I want something for the show.' You had to jump through hoops to have something," says Yannes. Faced with this goal, the engineers could either throw their hands up in disgust or do their best to meet his seemingly unrealistic target.

The aggressive deadline took all his engineers by surprise. "We didn't start working on that until Thanksgiving of '81," recalls Yannes.

Winterble assigned Bob Yannes, Robert Russell, and a technician named Dave Ziembicki to complete the project. "Charlie approved us to go ahead and pursue that with our own little team," says Russell.

CHAPTER

12

The Commodore 64

1981 - 1982

With less than two months to build a complete computer system, the engineers rarely left the MOS Technology building. "In the middle of the building lab, we took over one corner of the room and worked 20 hours a day, 7 days a week to get the prototypes running," says Russell

As managers, Charles Winterble and Al Charpentier did not perform hands-on work on the VIC-40. "It was Bob Yannes, me, and Dave Ziembicki the technician who really went off and did the Commodore 64," says Russell. "Luckily we had a guy like Charlie Winterble who let us go off and do that when we were supposed to be making the P and B stuff work."

Designing a full computer system was a new challenge for Bob Yannes. "I was still in the chip group so I wasn't really supposed to be working on systems," says Yannes. "The only reason I ended up doing the C64 was because I was the only one who knew enough about the chips and how to put them together in a timely fashion."

With such a tight schedule, Yannes and Russell began laying out the architecture of the computer. "Bob [Yannes] and I sat down and came up with the hardware architecture," recalls Russell.

Yannes was an assiduous engineer by nature. For two short days, Yannes worked in his office and the drafting area to design the architecture for the VIC-40. "It was a pretty easy architecture," says Yannes. "I just designed the most minimal system I could with the fewest number of components. There's not a whole lot of stuff in there. There's the VIC chip, the SID chip, and there's 64K of DRAM."

Almost none of the design came from the VIC-20. "There were very few chips that were used in the C64 that had ever been used before," says

Yannes. Only the serial port, cassette port, and user port remained the same. It also used the same joystick connecter, except there were two.

Rather than use the same bulky cartridge system of the VIC-20, Yannes decided to borrow technology from the Max Machine. "Since the Max Machine was already in progress, I decided to make one of the C64 memory configurations match the Max so that it would be able to use Max game cartridges," explains Yannes. "When you plug the game cartridge in, it would automatically collapse the memory map of the Commodore 64 to look like the Max Machine."

The VIC-40 was essentially a computer with a game console built into memory. The engineers wondered how they could create such a complex memory layout before CES. They found their salvation in the Programmable Logic Array chip (PLA). According to Russell, "I remember finding that chip and saying, 'Oh, that will do exactly what we want!'"

The PLA chip acted like glue to hold the different parts of the system together. Yannes could simply insert the PLA chip and program it later. "I didn't have time to design all the logic before they laid the PC board out, so I just took a PLA and named the signals I needed and told them to lay that out," recalls Yannes. "While they were laying it out I could figure out the coding for the PLA. That got us to the show."

When engineers need to build a circuit quickly, they use thin wires and a special wire wrap tool to connect the chips together. However, Yannes believed it would be inadequate. "You really couldn't do a wire wrap with dynamic RAM because the timing was too tight," says Yannes. Instead, the engineers would fabricate a printed circuit board.

To allow time to develop software, Yannes left nothing to the last minute. "We had to have a working circuit board practically a month before that to get the software working because we wanted to show it running with Basic," says Yannes.

"It was going to be perfect," says Russell. "We made it simple and clean. We cut boards and everything in one month."

Since Russell's move to the East Coast, he and Yannes developed a close relationship. "We worked hand in hand on the C64. We spent all that time in the lab," says Russell. "We were best friends."

Bob Yannes also looks back fondly on the friendship. "We hung out a lot together back then," he recalls. "He was transplanted from Iowa to California to Pennsylvania so he was probably [alone]; at least I was always in my environment."

According to Yannes, in between work, the two engineers took in science fiction films from the early eighties. "We were going to movies together and all kinds of stuff," says Yannes. "We were both single geeks without any social life." Yannes remembers seeing two groundbreaking films employing state of the art computer graphics, *Tron* and *The Last Starfighter*.

The VIC-40 schedule destroyed the two largest holidays of the year for Yannes and Russell. "It had us jumping through hoops to try to get some totally new thing that we hadn't even intended to work on and try to get it done between Thanksgiving and early January with Christmas break in the middle," says Yannes. "I remember checking the PC board layout over Thanksgiving weekend. That's how tight the timeframe was on that."

Although the new assignment would cause Yannes to miss the holiday season completely, he did not think of Jack as a Scrooge. "It didn't matter," he says. "I was living at home and I wasn't married or anything. I thought this was great."

Throughout the development of the project, the engineers kept the project a secret from others at Commodore. "We didn't talk to marketing," recalls Winterble. "We bounced ideas off Jack, but he didn't really care about the specifics of it."

Not even John Feagans knew about the project, even though the computer used his kernel code. "He didn't do code work on the C64 at all because he never even knew it existed until it came out," says Russell. "It's his architecture and it's me building on what I did on the VIC-20."

Out of all the engineers at Commodore, Yannes' philosophy of low-cost computers was the closest to Jacks. "I tried to design the cheapest possible thing I could because that was just my nature," he explains. "I didn't like expensive things, I didn't have very much money, and I didn't see any reason why this stuff needed to be expensive."

Although the P and B computers had specialized cases, no one tried to design a new case for the VIC-40. "If you've ever wondered why the C64 has the same case as the VIC-20, it's because we didn't have any time to tool anything up," says Yannes. "We just put it in a VIC-20 case and spray painted it. Everything about the Commodore 64 is the way it is because of just an unbelievably tight time constraint on the product."

In retrospect, Charles Winterble believes the decision to use the VIC-20 case ended up wasting more time. "One of the design criteria which we chose, which was a mistake, was we said, 'Gee, let's put this all into VIC-20 plastic.' That was wrong because we didn't have enough room," explains Winterble. "We spent so much time and resources trying to make the motherboard fit inside that stupid VIC-20 case."

The engineers also had to choose colors for the text and background. "Blue and white is what we used, because that gave you the best color contrast, other than black and white, which was too boring," says Charpentier. "We wanted the people to see those colors."

Problems with the chips remained well into December. According to Charpentier, "We literally had gotten the video chips a couple of weeks or a weekend before the [CES] show."

By the end of December, after slightly more than a month, the design was complete. Commodore now had a computer they could show to the world at CES. Yannes was understandably proud.

Russell began developing demonstrations of the VIC-40 computer. "All that stuff was originally Basic with just a million poke statements," says Russell. "You didn't write assembly language for those early demos; you poked in assembly language. We're talking some ugly old Basic code for the original demos."

A Commodore engineer named Fred Bowen helped create a playful demo of a small man who walked out onto the screen and showed off all the features of the VIC-II and SID chips. "Freddie Bowen wrote a lot of the stuff," says Winterble.

"We had a sprite guy with some music playing," says Russell. "We had the transparency and stuff like that to show the sprites. ... I can remember doing the coding with Yannes trying to get stuff to work."

John Feagans, who remained on the West Coast, also developed some demonstration software. "I remember John Feagans had done some music stuff to demonstrate some of the sound," says Yannes. "They had different music programs for various PET's along the way. I think he just converted them to play whatever library of songs they had."

Working together in the small lab, the two engineers passed time creating new music using Yannes' SID chip. "I remember sitting in the lab with a prototype and Yannes is there and it's the day before Christmas," recalls Russell. "We couldn't get good radio reception in there, so we're creating music with the SID to listen to."

Surprisingly, Robert Russell had a disk drive functioning with the VIC-40 in time for CES. "We loaded them in from a 1540 drive," says Russell.

By the end of December, the team had multiple VIC-40s. "We had built two or three at that point in time that were running pretty good," says Russell.

It was a remarkable achievement to have working computers for CES, especially considering the engineers had not even started the VIC-II and SID chips until April of 1981. "Nine months later we had enough working prototypes and we were able to go to the show," says Winterble.

"So much of the Commodore 64 was just the way it was because of the constraints of time, and I think it actually made it a better product to be honest," says Yannes. "We didn't have time to fiddle with things and change it around too much." The final verdict on the computer would come at CES.

Winter CES

The Winter CES rolled around on the first weekend of January. "When you worked for Commodore, you always had to have something for the Winter CES," says Yannes.

The night before departing for Las Vegas, the engineers prepared to transport their delicate prototypes. "We were putting the things together and packing them up to ship them," recalls Yannes.

Once in Las Vegas, the engineers hauled their prototypes to Jack Tramiel's suite. He would determine whether it was worth showing to the crowds. The tired engineers took up a corner and readied their prototypes. "We were pretty burned out just from getting this stuff ready for the show," says Yannes.

Robert Russell remembers overhearing Jack and his inner circle discussing their plans while he worked. "I was in Jack's hotel suite preparing a demonstration," recalls Russell. "There was some strange stuff I saw. He would be going over things with the European and Asian cronies about them getting things in and out of countries. I don't know how legal a lot of it was. I didn't want to know some of that stuff because it sounded like you might end up in a barrel someplace."

It was clear to Russell that Jack and his inner circle were prepared to do almost anything in the name of business. "They were so bad," says Russell, laughing so hard he can barely speak. "There were times they were pissed off at certain people. Customs and duties were a lot more complicated in those days than they are these days. Every country in Europe was different. They made certain threats because they were having problems with some of the European countries as far as how they were handling product and dealing with all the issues."

Although the young engineers worked hard on the VIC-40, there was no plan to display the computer. "It wasn't even planned to be on the floor or anything," says Russell. No one except for Jack and his small group of engineers were aware of the project. "We actually took it and showed it to him and some of his cronies in his suite in the hotel. Those guys didn't know about it at all until we showed it."

The nervous engineers displayed the result of over a month of compressed labor. "We told him what it was, how simple it was, and what it could cost," recalls Russell. "He said, 'Put it on the floor.'"

As Winterble predicted, marketing was not happy to hear about the secretive project. "When these guys found out about it, and found out that they were not involved in it, then right away you can imagine: *it* hit the fan," says Winterble. "It was turmoil."

With no advanced warning of the product, Kit Spencer had to work non-stop to prepare print material for the prototype. "The marketing guys ended up claiming it was going to do everything under the sun on the charts," says Russell. For the most part, the engineers dictated the content of the advertisements. "We told the marketing guys what to write down and made up signs."

The VIC-40 name lasted through most of the production design. However, marketing wanted to change the name to match the other computers in the Commodore lineup. They already had the P128, which was a personal computer with 128 kilobytes. They also had the B256, which was a business computer with 256 kilobytes. Now they had a consumer computer with 64 kilobytes, so naturally it became the C64. Most people just called it the Commodore 64.

Compared to most prototype demonstrations, the Commodore 64 was remarkably complete. "Almost all the stuff that was put together quickly for the show was not anything that was real," says Yannes. "They were smoke and mirrors. Part of it was just to get some press at the show and to gauge people's reaction to things. The Commodore 64 was probably one of the most real things that showed at a show."

Yannes was too inexperienced, too quiet, and too much of an engineer to become involved with demonstrating his prototype. "The only reason I was there was in case it broke and needed to be fixed," he explains. "I was pretty much off to the side, but I think there were a few times when I was called upon to explain some of the features and capabilities, particularly when it came to the sound."

There was not much competition at the 1982 Winter CES. Commodore's main rival, Atari, was still showing their Atari 400 and 800 computers. Mattel introduced the *Aquarius* computer, and a company called Spectravideo introduced the *SV 318*. Both of these machines were similar to the VIC-20 in specifications, but both were doomed largely because of their calculator-style keyboards.

Yannes also spied on potential competitors. "One of the things I was supposed to do at that show was to case the competition and check what was going on at the other places. Charlie or Al asked me to do it," he recalls. The competition was weak. "There wasn't really anything out there. It really was a coup because Apple and Atari and everybody else were just pretty much showing what they already had with a few little additions here and there."

The Commodore 64 was also able to demonstrate a full line of peripherals, including the disk drive. "It used the VIC-20 disk drive and the VIC-20 printer and all the peripherals that had been designed for the VIC-20," says Yannes. "We didn't have time to design new peripherals."

The engineers also brought prototypes of the P and B series computers, as well as the Max Machine. Commodore hid these in a small office within the booth and showed them to journalists, software developers, and sometimes even trusted acquaintances from competing companies. "We had a couple of backroom things going on for special customers," says Winterble.

Although marketing created the Commodore 64 presentation at the last moment, it was an impressive demonstration. "It was a rather fancy booth," recalls Winterble. "We had a bunch of stations showing different aspects and different parts with a skilled person at each space. One guy was showing a game demo, one guy was showing something else. We had them scattered all around this booth."

One Commodore 64 demonstrated the capabilities of the SID chip using John Feagans music program. The beautifully strange music filled the air, acting as a siren call for technophiles. "They were lined up," says Winterble.

Mostly, the presenters just let Fred Bowen's demonstration program show off the features. "It was really impressive for only having the machine in his hands for a short period of time," says Winterble. "He wrote a 'Welcome to Commodore 64,' that came out with a big splash. Then this little man walked across the screen, turned around, and started doing things. It was a great little demo using the sprites."

As Robert Russell recalls, the burgeoning computer press industry helped fuel interest. "There was starting to be a whole press industry around personal computing," says Russell. As word got out about the new computer, the lines to enter the booth grew longer. "It was a huge sensation. Everybody and their brother were stopping by."

Yannes was also thrilled at the positive reception of his computer. "The C64 just kind of blew everybody out of the water because it came out of nowhere," says Yannes. "There was no expectation of it, it was very reasonably priced, and it had 64K of RAM which was a magic number at that point in time because nobody else had 64K of RAM."

The computer even impressed Chuck Peddle, who never missed a CES show. "The C64 was an enormously successful machine," says Peddle. "It was a great game machine; not because of the 6502 and not because of the memory that was in it. It was a great game machine because of the work Charpentier did."

Perhaps the most impressive aspect of the computer was the proposed price by Commodore. Before the show, Jack decided on a retail price of $595. Competitors reacted to the announcement with skepticism and shock. "We got their attention," says Winterble. "The guys from Atari came by to look at it and said, 'They can't do that. It's impossible for the price.'"

From the reactions, Charles Winterble felt the new computer might even outsell the VIC-20. "When we left CES, we knew we had a fantastic product," says Winterble.

It was an incredible leap in computing power from their previous efforts. Never before had a computer company gotten everything so right in one package. "It was such a big hit at the show," says Yannes.

Press was good but not as prominent as Commodore received in earlier years. David Thornburg of Compute! magazine mentioned the VIC-40, reporting, "For sheer impact, Commodore stole the show with the announcement of two new color computers!"

However, Byte magazine reported nothing on Commodore. By now, Commodore had a reputation of announcing products such as the ColorPET and TOI and not releasing them, so Byte was weary. Byte seemed far more interested in the low cost VIC modem, which made its debut at the Winter CES.

The meaning of the Commodore 64 debut was obvious to Jack: he finally had his Apple II killer. Now all he had to do was deliver the crushing blow. He wanted to get the machine into production quickly.

Marketing Battles

After CES, Jack wanted the Commodore 64 sent to the assembly lines. Unfortunately, the prototypes could not be mass-produced. "We weren't ready to go into production," says Winterble. "After the show, we had a great deal of work to do to really turn it into a production product."

Although the MOS Technology engineers had no experience in production engineering, it would be up to them to design a production model in record time. "We wanted to be in production in three months," says Russell.

To launch the product, the marketing team also had plenty of work to do, since they were unaware of the project until CES. "It wasn't even handed to marketing until after that show," says Russell.

Winterble suspected there would be some resentment within Commodore due to the secrecy of the project. "Commodore was a company that had friction a lot of times," explains Winterble. "One of the big friction areas was between marketing and engineering. There was a long standing... animosity is probably too strong of a word, but marketing and engineering at Commodore did not get along. And from our point of view, why did we care?"

Michael Tomczyk, like most marketing people, still clung to the success of the VIC-20. "Tomczyk was fighting the C64," reveals Peddle. "I've written him a note two or three times saying, 'I don't know why you did that at the time.' The VIC-20 did exactly what it was supposed to do, which is to pave the way for the C64."

Part of the animosity was probably due to the favored position of the engineers in Jack's eyes, and the powerlessness of marketing to influence engineering. "The engineering side had an easier life because everybody is an expert in marketing, but if you're going to be an expert in engineering you have to know the technology," says Winterble.

Kit Spencer wanted the engineers to modify the C64. "When we met with the marketing people and went through it all, there were a number of issues that they wanted to change right away," says Winterble.

Spencer raised some legitimate issues with the Commodore 64. First, the operating system was horribly antiquated. It was no different from the PET released almost five years earlier. Second, the computer had no backward compatibility with VIC-20 software. The VIC-20 was a huge market and Spencer did not want to lose the established software base. Third, the Basic language had no support for sprites, sounds, or graphics. This forced programmers to use difficult POKE statements.

Winterble opposed Spencer on every change. "One of my jobs was to fight the battles," says Winterble. "I had relatively strong opinions about things and I was willing to fight."

Spencer recognized the importance of DOS to the new IBM PC computers. He wanted Commodore computers to have the same high-level operating system, so he tried to push the engineers into adopting the CP/M operating system. CP/M was an important and popular operating system at the time with hundreds of business related applications.

One of the key features of CP/M was the ability to create directories. Without them, disks with more than one program often contained a disorganized jumble of files.

To allow an alternate operating system like CP/M to load automatically, the engineers would have had to include a feature to load a program from disk as soon as the user turned on the computer. "All the routines that need to be there are there, but there should also be a facility for automatically reading the first track of the disk and booting a more sophisticated operating system into memory," says software developer Brian Dougherty, who later created the GEOS operating system.[1]

---

[1] *IEEE Spectrum* journal, "Design case history: the Commodore 64", (March 1985), p. 48.

Winterble disagreed with Spencer over CP/M. "One of the battles that came up was CP/M," says Winterble. "They were pushing for, 'We've got to have a computer that will run CP/M.'" Winterble felt the CP/M operating system was not worth including.

As a compromise, the engineers developed a CP/M cartridge using the Z80 microprocessor. "We designed it right from the beginning [of the production design] to take a Z80 module," says Russell.

Since the engineers believed the computer would use CP/M, Russell made no effort to improve the native operating system. Memory limitations also prevented the Commodore 64 from using the new Basic 4.0, intended for the P and B computers. "Why did we have [Basic 2.0]? That's how much room the ROM could fit," says Russell.

Time was the overriding factor for Russell and the engineers. "We were trying to get it out the door," he says. "We could see the computers coming that had better Basic and real operating systems but we wanted to do the simplest, most straight forward, cheapest and quickest system possible."

Yannes acknowledges Basic 2.0 was antiquated by 1982. "It was a very primitive Basic," he recalls. "It had no graphics expansions or sound extensions or anything."

Basic 2.0 was the antithesis of user friendly. To delete a file, the user had to type:

OPEN 15,8,15:PRINT#15,"S0:*filename*":CLOSE15

In contrast, Basic 4.0 users merely typed:

SCRATCH *filename*

Another quirk of the Commodore Basic operating system was the memory designation. Commodore engineers chose to identify the size of files and disk space using blocks as opposed to bytes or kilobytes. Few users understood what a block was. They knew their computer had 64 kilobytes, but it was hard to say how much memory each program occupied on disk.

Spencer appealed to Jack, but he was unsupportive. "Jack didn't care what kind of software his machines had," says Yannes. "He was putting the same Basic in every machine, even though it was obsolete and had very few features."

Jack had no concept of how crucial the operating system was to the success of a computer. His views were rooted in mechanical devices like typewriters and calculators, so he placed an emphasis on hardware. In effect, he had a blind spot when it came to the invisible software in the ROM chips. "Commodore was an extension of Jack Tramiel, and to him software wasn't tangible," says Charpentier. "You couldn't hold it, feel it, or touch it, so it wasn't worth spending money for."

The extra ROM chip would have added approximately three dollars to the cost of the Commodore 64 in 1982. Though this was by no means a small amount to add to the cost, it would have improved the system significantly.

Spencer also lobbied for backward compatibility with VIC-20 software. Backward compatibility was on the drawing board ever since John Feagans implemented the kernel. Now that Commodore was designing their next computer, they had the option of following Feagans plan and making their next computer backward compatible.

However, Russell had an insurmountable obstacle preventing him from achieving backward compatibility. The VIC-II video chip was not capable of displaying the same resolutions as the original VIC-I chip. As a result, it could not display 22 characters per line. Without this native capability, there was no point in even attempting backward compatibility.

Robert Russell remembers discussing backward compatibility in the VIC-II chip. "We wanted a compatibility mode, but that would have taken up too much of the chip," he explains. "We would rather have sprites than compatibility mode."

Winterble also took part in the discussions. "Al originally had compatibility built into the chip, but realistically you are talking two totally different machines," he says. "When you are that price sensitive, every penny counts. You really don't want to put a lot of hardware in there for backward compatibility. It's better to rewrite the software and use the new features."[2]

Spencer also found little support from Jack Tramiel. "He couldn't care less if anything was compatible at that point in time," says Russell. "When you would talk to Jack, he was like, 'Don't worry about compatibility. We'll sell them a new computer for cheap, so who cares about compatibility.' As far as we were concerned, if it ran Basic it was compatible."

In the end, Spencer had no option but to defer to Jack's decision. "The marketing people obviously really wanted backward compatibility because that was big to them," says Russell. "Kit was definitely marketing at that point in time. We got beat up [by Spencer] but Jack silenced them when he said he didn't care about compatibility. The engineers won that battle."

---

[2] Al Charpentier does not recall considering a VIC-I mode for the VIC-II chip.

One of the biggest omissions from Basic was the lack of programming commands for sound and graphics. Under the original Microsoft deal, Commodore could have added commands to Basic for the SID and VIC-II chip but they chose not to because of Jack's reluctance to invest in software. As a result, Basic programmers found themselves faced with complicated POKE and PEEK commands, which required a comprehensive knowledge of memory locations. This dampened the enthusiasm of many beginners who hoped to homebrew Basic games.

The extra commands would have required costlier ROM chips. "It would have been quite a bit more money because there would have been a second chip," says Russell. "At that time, our process only allowed us to make a certain sized chip."

Winterble blames the lack of manpower on the lack of features. "We talked about putting in macros and the ability to do some of these things, but we just didn't have the resources to do it," says Winterble. "We didn't have the people. It was such a small software group. The idea was we would try to go back and do some of that stuff later on."

Commodore later released a special cartridge with more commands, but it found little success in the marketplace. "The *Super Expander* cartridge added a bunch of extensions to Basic to let you access the features of the Commodore 64," says Yannes.

With the limited ROM space, Russell barely had room to insert his own initials. "In those days we didn't even dream of putting in Easter eggs because in the C64 I had 5 bytes left when I was done," says Russell. "I was going to put in, 'BYRSR', but Bob Yannes but didn't think that was a good idea so we just put RRBY in it."

Winterble began to feel annoyed when the marketing people went straight to his engineers to request features in the VIC-40. "We had things like the marketing guys trying to call the engineers directly and lobby for changes," he says.

The relationship between Winterble and Spencer continued to deteriorate until the two had an explosive argument. "I remember one time we bumped heads," says Winterble, who was growing tired of marketing people disturbing his engineers. "I tried to keep the guys isolated so they could do their job." In one heated exchange, Winterble chided Spencer, saying, "You don't talk to these guys. Leave them alone." After that, the engineers were free to complete the design without interference.

Although the Commodore 64 was not truly software compatible, Commodore paid lip service to backward compatibility. Their marketers promoted limited backwards compatibility, meaning VIC-20 hardware like joysticks, modems, disk drives, and printers would still work on the

C64. Additionally, the Basic 2.0 ROM meant very simple Basic programs that did not use POKE commands would technically run on both systems. Commodore hoped the ambiguous statement might entice VIC-20 users to buy the new C64.

It was probably wise to drop backward compatibility, given the limitations of the VIC-20. Unfortunately, it seemed to set the pattern for later years.

Delay of Game

Jack expected his engineers to complete their design in three months, but by the end of March, it became clear the target was overly optimistic. Bob Yannes blames the unrealistic goal on the seemingly refined state of the Commodore 64 at CES. "After the CES show everyone was thinking that it was a real product because it looked real, because we used the VIC-20 case and just painted it," says Yannes. "It looked like it was ready to go into production."

If Commodore had more engineers, they would have been able to divide the tasks. "I think maybe there were 10 or 12 engineers in the whole company that were true engineers, including software, hardware, and chip design," says Russell. "Including people in Japan, the total number of engineers in the company was 15 when the Commodore 64 was built."

Most of the engineers were working on other diverse projects for Commodore. "That includes people working on the PET, and a couple of guys down in Texas doing the whole cash register business," says Russell. "They ended up with us on the C64 in later days, because they were some of the few resources that existed within the company."

One of the most obvious changes made to the Commodore 64 post-CES was the screen color. "Even though it had good contrast, the transition from blue to white produced kind of an ugly edge," explains Yannes. "We ended up having to make it light blue on dark blue so the color didn't change. Just the intensity changed."

Now that the final design was underway, the determination to meet a low cost target grew stronger. Charpentier says, "We agonized over every transistor." For his part, Winterble vetoed ideas for added features.

Although the case would become as distinctive and loved as the Volkswagen Beetle, Charpentier himself was never a big fan. "I always thought the VIC-20 case looked clunky," he says.

Winterble also had his own reasons for disliking the case. "If we had made the case bigger to begin with, we would have made the design much more manufacturable," he says. "It was hell for those poor guys in manufacturing. We squeezed things to the limit to fit all this crap on the board. This was a product that was manufacturing hostile."

Yannes had plans to substitute the case with a new design in eight to ten months. "We always wanted to design a new case for the Commodore 64," says Yannes. "It was never our intention that it would go into production with the VIC-20 type case. I would have liked to have seen much better styling on the case."

Charpentier describes the proposed design. "It was thinner in front and had more of a wedge shape to it," he says.[3]

The production design seemed to be going smoothly until the engineers decided to try to improve the video chip. "We took the time to make a design change in the video chip, which I think both Al and Charlie would agree that we probably shouldn't have done," says Yannes.

The engineers wanted to improve the color on the chip. "It was the same thing with the Apple and Atari computers," explains Yannes. "You would get interaction between the luminance signal, which is the black and white information, and the color signal. So you would end up with these various colors on the screen that weren't really what you wanted, but it was just the nature of the NTSC video standard that the luminance and chrominance signals interact with each other."

To purify the colors, Charpentier made a risky last minute change. "Al had the idea that if the two clocks were independent from each other then that interaction wouldn't happen," says Yannes. "We separated the clock generators on the VIC chip so that the color crystal was a separate clock from the video shift rate."

The results were impressive but flawed. "We didn't get the false colors anymore, but unfortunately because the two clocks weren't phase synchronized at all, so there was this waviness in the screen which was really objectionable," says Yannes. The engineers required a Texas Instruments chip to fix the problem. "We ended up having to throw in this phase-lock loop circuit to lock the two clocks together, which added cost to it."

According to Yannes, Jack was not happy using the extra chip. "It was particularly messy because the only [company] who made this chip was Texas Instruments, and we were going up against their Ti-99/4A computer with the Commodore 64," says Yannes. "So here we are dependant on one of our major competitors for a critical component."

Commodore regained control over their chip supply by using MOS Technology to clone their competitor's chip.

---

[3] Many years later, Commodore adopted this design in the revised Commodore 64c.

When the production design was completed, the total cost to manufacture one unit came out to $130. Even Jack must have been impressed. His strategy of setting unrealistic goals for his engineers paid off.

"The reason we could is because of vertical integration," says Winterble. "We put so much in just a couple of chips." Without vertical integration, the custom SID and VIC-II chips would account for a much more significant portion of the costs. Atari and Apple lacked the in-house expertise to manufacture their own custom chips, which meant they had to hire costly outside companies (often MOS Technology) to come up with designs. As a result, Apple and Atari computers were both costlier and not as technologically sophisticated.

The low production cost meant Commodore could sell their computer for under $600. "You could basically take the suggested retail price and divide by four," explains Yannes. "The typical thing to do was for you to have a raw cost, then double it to sell it to the dealer, and then have the dealer double it to sell it to the consumer. That was the model."

In June 1982, the production design was completed enough to send to production. "It took us six months, and we all got crap over that," says Russell.

Falling Behind Moore's Law

Moore's Law, created by Intel's cofounder Gordon Moore in 1965, predicts the number of transistors per square inch doubles every 18 months. This results in massive gains in computing speed proportional to the number of transistors. A less known feature of this law is that the price of computing power halves every 18 months. While Commodore and their customers were reaping the benefits of cheap products, MOS Technology was failing to keep pace with Moore's Law.

The main processor for the C64 was not a 6502, but rather the newly minted 6510. This chip was a minor revision over the 6502. Today, we measure the advance of computer technology by the speed of computing, but the microprocessor at the heart of the C64 was no faster than the VIC-20, the PET, or even the Kim-1 released in 1975. In fact, the C64 was imperceptibly slower than the VIC-20.

Although MOS Technology was very competitive with Motorola and Intel with the 6502, they were weak in the key area of microprocessor research. Engineer Bill Mensch attempted to develop a 16-bit sequel to the 6502. "When it came to next-generation, we were thinking 16-bit in 1976," says Mensch.[4]

---

[4] *Compute!* magazine, "New Life For The 6502?" (February 1986), p. 26.

Robert Russell discovered evidence of the 16-bit project developed in partnership with Synertek. "I found a September 1978 description of the SY6516, which was a 16-bit 6502," says Russell. "Synertek was the company that was supposed to be designing it. I have a specification sheet on it with timing and temperature settings. Reading this, it looks absolutely real."

Unfortunately, Synertek became a victim of the competitive semiconductor industry. "I think Synertek got into financial problems right around that point in time," says Russell. "There were some rough years."

MOS Technology's financial problems hampered development of a 16-bit version before the Commodore acquisition. "Nothing happened for the longest time," says Winterble. "I think part of it was the financial resources of MOS Technology. They just simply couldn't afford it. I have no doubt that if they had the resources they would have done a spectacular job because the 6502 was a phenomenal architecture."

The 16-bit project eventually faded away at MOS Technology. "It just never got any kind of support in the organization," says Charpentier. "To be in the microprocessor business, you have to sell microprocessors into the OEM market. Commodore had never developed an OEM semiconductor market. They were a systems house that developed computers with it. It just wasn't a focus in the company."

After Mensch developed a calculator chip for MOS Technology, he wanted to produce a special low-power 6502 chip. However, MOS Technology turned him down, so Mensch approached other companies such as Rockwell, GTE, Synertek, and Mitel but they rejected his proposal.

Mensch designed the processor anyway. Charles Winterble believes many of the features developed at MOS Technology went into Mensch's chips. "A lot of the ideas that were in that went down to the Western Design Center probably because it was the same people," he says.

Mensch wanted to design a CMOS 6502 chip. The CMOS process was more efficient than the outdated NMOS process. The NMOS process, or N-Channel Metal Oxide Semiconductor, required 13 layers to form a chip. CMOS, which stood for Complimentary Metal Oxide Semiconductor, used only six layers. CMOS also used less current, and it was faster.

In early 1981, Mensch began designing the low-power 6502 chip using CMOS technology. "Ultimately, they came out with a CMOS version of the 6502," says Peddle. Mensch called his new chip the 65C02.

Mensch went back to the companies that previously rejected him and offered to license the technology. GTE, Synertek and Rockwell purchased a license, but Commodore decided instead to sue for theft of trade secrets since the 65C02 used the same instruction set as the MOS owned 6502 design. Mensch settled out of court and agreed to grant rights to the 65C02 at half the standard license fee. Jack relished the deal.

Without the knowledge and experience of Peddle and Mensch, MOS continued to fall below the expectations of Moore's law. While other companies like Intel and Motorola were making strides with 16-bit and 32-bit processors, MOS focused on custom semiconductor chips like the VIC and SID.

In 1982, MOS Technology began working on a 16-bit processor once again. "There was a 16-bit 6502 program," reveals Charpentier.

In August 1982, Byte printed rumors that Commodore had working prototypes of their new family of 16 and 32-bit microprocessors. Then in November 1982, they began calling the new chip the 65000. The article even speculated Commodore would use initial production runs of the processor in a new computer of their own. "We tried to do the same thing at MOS with a few people there," says Winterble. "We didn't start until '82 or so. Probably as they started working on it they let it leak out for publicity sake."

Leading the design of the chip was one of Chuck Peddle's engineers. "It was Will Mathis," says Charpentier. "He was part of the original [6502] team."

Although Winterble was the head-engineering manager of MOS Technology, he had little enthusiasm for the project. "It was at a difficult time, now that the C64 was done," says Winterble. "We hired back the architect who did the original 6502, who was local up there, and we brought in a couple of other guys and we put together a team to do that. But about then was when Al and I were less enthusiastic, and we started thinking about where our future's going to be."

Winterble felt the team should keep the 16-bit 6502 as simple as possible. "We allowed the creative people to go ahead and do their free-wheel thinking about fancy new architectures and stuff like that," says Winterble. "[They discussed] different approaches to doing a processor. I was not in favor of this too much. I just wanted to do essentially the same thing [as the 6502], but just 16-bit. Then the issue became, well why bother doing that?"

According to Winterble, the project team lost focus soon after forming. "It got to the point where they were doing some layouts, but the guys who were doing the architecture were sort of undisciplined people," he explains. "After a certain point it became, 'This is not going to fly.'"

Normally, if Jack pushed for a product, his engineers became highly motivated and completed the product. However, Jack seemed indifferent to a 16-bit processor. "There was no push at all," says Winterble. "We weren't getting anywhere and it never really got going." The lack of a 16-bit processor severely hurt Commodore's chances of remaining competitive in the future of computing.

Although Commodore ran their computers at 1 MHz, Charles Winterble claims they were able to achieve faster speeds with the 6502. "We thinned the oxides down and we intentionally did some very high speed versions of that," says Winterble. "One thing MOS [Technology] had going for it was a really good quality oxide. By thinning these gates down, we were able to drive it faster and faster. Then we did selection, in terms of our testing, to pull out the fast ones. We actually made a couple of really hot processors for a chess tournament for somebody. He literally water-cooled it, and he ran it at something like 8 MHz. It was just ridiculous how fast he ran it."

Even though MOS Technology could theoretically produce faster chips, Bob Yannes claims they could not use them in the Commodore 64 because of RAM memory limitations. "That would never have worked," he states. "The speeds we had to operate at had to be a multiple of the video rate. The RAM timing wouldn't hold up at that. With the video and the processor alternating on the bus, you're basically running the memory at twice as fast as it would normally be run."

In addition, the costs of producing parts for a 2 MHz Commodore 64 would drastically raise the price to customers. "The other problem is that the cost goes up exponentially because not only does the processor have to run faster, but the RAM and the ROM have to run faster," explains Winterble. "It isn't even linear; it's exponential. It would be too expensive."

Surprisingly, the lack of microprocessor speed did not immediately hurt the Commodore 64. In 1982, consumers were generally not aware of processor speed since most were taking their first steps in the computer world. To them, it was much more valuable to be cheap than fast.

CHAPTER

13

Selling the Revolution

1982

In 1982, Commodore was on the verge of releasing a technologically superior computer for the masses. Their timing could not have been better. Computers were about to go mainstream and the marketplace was ready for a breakthrough product.

Summer CES

As the June 1982 Consumer Electronics Show rolled around once again, the engineers were finalizing their production design of the C64. Commodore brought their entire lineup of new computers to the show, including the C64, P128, B256, BX256, and the Max Machine.

As usual, the C64 attracted the most attention. This time, Commodore had more than simple demonstration programs for the computer. "The Japanese converted some of their VIC-20 games to the Commodore 64," says Yannes. He quickly adds, "They were not particularly well done."

The Japanese programmers rigidly adhered to preliminary specifications for the SID chip. "That was one of my definite peeves with them," he says. "They were so hung up on the specs of things that they would write stuff according to the specs, even if it didn't work."

As a result, the games shown at CES did little to show off the true potential of Yannes' SID chip. "They had games where you couldn't even hear any of the sounds on them," says a dejected Yannes.

Yashi Terakura brought his Max Machine to the show. "There were different variations of it," says Robert Russell. "One was just a stripped C64 without a keyboard and with a cartridge slot in it that pointed upwards." Another variation included a membrane keyboard.

Although Kit Spencer did not support the Max Machine, he produced a color pamphlet that read, "Commodore announces the third-generation game machine: a true computer and music synthesizer that will out-zonk, out-zap, out-sing, out-think, out-program, out-teach and out-sell the competition."

The Max Machine met with little enthusiasm. Jack hoped the Max Machine could compete against the Intellivision, Atari VCS, and ColecoVision for the console market. As a console, the Max Machine had the best sound and graphics capability of any competing console at the time. However, it seemed uncomfortably positioned somewhere between the computer market and the console market.

A Basic cartridge was available for the system, which seemed to indicate it was a computer. If it was a computer, it was glaringly inadequate, with only four kilobytes of RAM and a membrane keyboard. The future of Max was in question.

A Troubled Production

Already three months behind schedule, Winterble's team submitted their C64 design to the production group. Many problems remained.

The lead production engineer for the C64 was David Ziembicki.[1] His first task was to create a printed circuit board (PCB) for production. According to Charles Winterble, Ziembicki did not have much area to work with. "We didn't have the experience at the time to design manufacturability and we made a lot of mistakes," he reveals. "We squeezed things to the limit to fit all this crap on the board."

After the departure of Chuck Peddle and most of his team, Commodore lacked systems engineers who understood manufacturing. "We weren't board people," admits Winterble. "We made mistakes trying to save money, like trying to use the same tooling as the VIC-20 case." In the end, Commodore ended up spending more money than they would have if they retooled a larger case.

In April 1982, the reckless production schedule resulted in a costly error. The production facility was on the West Coast, so Robert Russell sent his ROM code before validating the code. Once he validated the code, he would sign off on it and the facility could begin mass production without having to wait for delivery from the east.

The temptation to begin production proved too great.

Russell continued testing the ROM code on the East Coast and realized there was a serious bug. "I made a mistake and a shifted character wasn't

---

[1] David Ziembicki later invented a sensor to detect obstacles in the path of vehicles while backing up. As of this writing, he is in lawsuits over the patent.

correct on the keyboard. If you did shift-some character it was still lower case," he says.

When Russell contacted the West Coast technicians, he was horrified. "They went ahead and started manufacturing them and made a million of them," he recalls. "I came in and said, 'Whoops! Stop everything. Don't release that part.' They said, 'It's too late.'" As a result, Commodore had hundreds of thousands of worthless, unsalvageable ROM chips that cost over a million dollars to manufacture.

Russell expected retribution from someone at the top but management treated the situation with humor. "The president of the company shows up in my office," recalls Russell. "He said, 'That's going to be a buck a day for the rest of your life that you are here at Commodore.'"

Chip shortages threatened the C64 production schedule. "The industry was building a few thousand computers and all of a sudden you're talking a million," says Russell. "People never heard of the volumes we wanted. We ended up trying to buy parts from Russia because you just couldn't get them [anywhere else]."

The C64 seemed to have a congenital defect with the video chip. "You would see light blue sparkles on dark blue, especially after it heated up," says Bil Herd. The bug became so pervasive users began calling it the sparkle bug. Though it sounded like a friendly insect, it was not so harmless.

With the hardware unchangeable for the immediate future, it was up to Robert Russell to attempt to fix the problem in software. "They rewrote the code so that the unused characters were changed to dark blue. It was sparkling dark blue on top of dark blue so you couldn't see it," says Herd.[2]

Russell also blames the Federal Communications Commission for adding to their difficulties. "They also ran into the whole FCC requirement which really made things a lot more complicated," explains Russell. "The FCC is a whole other nightmare with prima donnas."

In June, the C64 entered production. The production facility developed comically primitive testing procedures for the computers. "We had to come up with our testing techniques," explains Winterble. "How do you verify color back in those days? For a while there, we had operators standing there in front of test sets looking at the colors saying, 'Oh yeah, that's blue. Oh yeah, that's blue.'"

Al Charpentier read early reviews of the C64 and was surprised to hear it criticized for its garish colors. This seemed odd to Charpentier, who

---

[2] According to Herd, "Russell was later rewarded with a $20,000 bonus for coming up with this solution."

thought the C64 colors were vibrant and well chosen. He looked further into these criticisms and found out the assembly line workers were adjusting the color output on the circuit board until they saw color. As a result, many just turned up the color saturation all the way, resulting in overpowering colors.

The inadequate testing of the C64 soon became apparent to others outside Commodore. As an Epyx programmer later reported, "I've opened up brand-new Commodores and found traces cut. They obviously use a power screwdriver to assemble the C64, sometimes miss the screw, and chop the traces. How, you might wonder, could that have passed the final inspection? Well, those traces are hooked up to the disk-drive connectors, which they obviously don't test."[3]

According to Bil Herd, when production lines encountered a shortage of VIC-II chips, technicians went to the bin labeled 'defective chips' and took the sign off it. "The idea we had was trying to make it stick under the tree," says Herd. "Meaning that we could sell all we wanted in December but they came back in January."

Volume shipments started in August 1982. "They started out selling them through computer retail stores like ComputerLand and places like that," says Yannes.

Adding to Commodore's woes were house fires started by the Commodore 64. Robert Russell saw the results of the fires first hand. "I had to go do fire investigations as part of my career," says Russell. "It wasn't the VIC-20 so much as the Commodore 64 that I investigated. The Commodore 64 was much worse because the power supply was much more overloaded. It burned down buildings and houses because people had managed to put their draperies over top of the power supply."

The sparkle bug continued appearing in some computers, even as Commodore shipped. Charpentier focused his search on the VIC-II video chip, but it appeared to be working fine. Finally, he went to his logic analyzer and eventually tracked the bug down to a ROM chip.

With so many problems, it looked like the Commodore 64 would be a disaster. However, the team had managed to work through the challenges. As Ziembicki later recalled, "The key is to be able to solve your problems while you're running." It seemed like they had defeated their last major problem, but there was another devastating blow to come.

---

[3] *IEEE Spectrum* journal, "Design case history: the Commodore 64", (March 1985), p. 48.

Driving in the Slow Lane

Jack knew the value of selling peripherals. On the VIC-20 and C64, peripherals relied on the serial port, first developed for the TOI. Unfortunately, the intense pressure to release the Commodore 64 ended up hurting the final quality of the product. "What you ended up with on the Commodore 64, to a large extent, was whatever tricks we had to pull to get stuff ready to show for [CES] being put into production because there wasn't time to do anything else," says Yannes.

Robert Russell was disappointed with the slow speed of the VIC-20 serial bus and planned to improve the speed dramatically with the C64. "The slowness has to do with the serial bus," says Russell. "It has nothing to do with the disk drive."

Russell designed an improved mechanism for the C64. "I had a high speed method already set up in hardware," he explains. Russell modified the design of the serial bus on the C64 by adding high-speed lines and replacing the 6522 IO chip. "On the Commodore 64 we had the 6526 chip, and that had working high speed lines on it. On the schematics that I did, I had those lines connected to the serial port."

Russell also wanted to release an improved 1540 drive called the 1541 drive, which also used the 6526 chip. "The original plan was to use the 6526 in what was going to be the 1541 drive and the Commodore 64," he explains.

The changes would increase speeds dramatically. "It would have been 20 or 30 times faster," claims Russell. "It would have run at the limit of the drive rather than the limit of the serial bus."

Russell had not yet upgraded the ROM code as the release date neared. "The 1541 would have been high speed even on the early C64s but I couldn't get the code done in time because we were busy fighting other problems with the chipset," says Russell. Russell planned to change the ROM code once he received production samples of the C64.

The East Coast engineers sent their completed design to the West Coast and waited for the production circuit boards. "Our final schematics and all final production drawings were being done in Santa Clara because we had no people that did them on the East Coast," says Russell.

Unfortunately, no one at Commodore was prepared to take the time to inspect the final production units thoroughly before mass-producing them in the thousands. "When we released something, they built as much as they could of it," explains Russell.

Bob Yannes offers some insight into the immense pressure to deliver the new computers. "The bottom line is, look at the rate the VIC-20s were selling. They were doing 1000 per day at one point. They would say, 'If this takes you two extra weeks, how many millions of dollars is that?' We were like, 'Yep, you can't argue with that.'"

Russell finally received a C64 circuit board and began examining the finished product. "I'm doing the tests and everything is working fine because we hadn't written the high-speed code yet," recalls Russell. "Then I looked at the board and said, 'Where are the high-speed lines?'"

Someone on the West Coast had changed Russell's schematic. "The production guys took them off when they did the production boards. I put high-speed lines on and they deleted them," says Russell.

When Russell realized what happened, he was livid. "I threw a hell of a fit," he recalls. He was determined to find out why someone had neutered his high-speed serial bus. "I tracked it down and it was the production engineers in California who cut it off."

Ironically, the engineers thought it was more efficient to remove his high-speed lines. "The guys that actually did the production board layout cut off the signals to save some money," explains Russell. "They thought, 'Why are these extra lines running to these signal pins?' so they chopped them off and screwed us." It was like building an eight-cylinder engine with eight fuel lines and cutting off seven of them.

Russell was determined to rescue the disastrous situation. "I ran down to Charlie, throwing a total fit. He says, 'Well is it still functional?' I said, 'Yeah, it still works as a 1540.'" Winterble looked into the situation and found out the production facility had manufactured too many circuit boards already. "We couldn't change it after hundreds of thousands of PCB's were in production," laments Russell.

Stopping production on the C64 and restarting it with a new design was out of the question. "Technically it would have been possible, but you've got to realize, they were already moving their production and going to ship," says Russell. "If I had done that, it would have been several weeks until I got a finished unit for evaluation."

If Russell attempted to make changes now, early customers would be extremely unhappy. "There would have been a bunch of machines out there that would have been incompatible," explains Russell.

It was now pointless to design a faster 1541 drive. "We never bothered spinning another drive," says Russell. "The 1541 became just a 1540 with minor software changes." The deletion of a few metal circuit traces ultimately resulted in millions of wasted hours for C64 owners.

Incredibly, the drive became *even slower* when they attempted to make the 1541 compatible with the VIC-20. "The biggest compatibility pain in the butt was that stupid VIC-20 disk drive," says Charpentier. "We didn't want to do it but marketing really forced us into it."

Russell originally intended the C64 to interface with an improved 1541 disk drive that used the 6526 chip. Instead, he had to make the 6522 in the VIC-20 talk with the 6526 chip in the 1541. "We thought it was a rather straight forward redo using the new I/O chips rather than the 6522, and it wasn't," says Winterble. "He had a lot of difficulty getting the disk drive to work using the 6526."

Russell struggled with the problem, but soon began feeling intense pressure from Jack Tramiel. According to Bil Herd, "Jack said, 'It's going to be working Monday and you're going to set it right here.' He showed him where on the desk it would be sitting and working. Bob [Russell] wrote the serial bus over a weekend in software."

Russell had almost no time to address the problem properly. "It started out slow and we made it even slower," says Yannes. "So much of the processor's time was being interrupted by the video chip and the drive couldn't keep up with it, so they had to slow it down even more."

To maintain backward compatibility, Russell intentionally slowed the 1541 drive speed by four times to work with the VIC-20, even though the C64 used an improved 6526 controller.

The new 1541 literally took over two minutes to load a 64-kilobyte program into memory. Compared to the competition, the C64 now had the slowest drive.

The solution made every engineer at Commodore shudder. "Of course it's slow because it makes up for broken hardware," says Herd. "Things like this were done to make the date, to keep their jobs, and most of all to keep Jack happy."

Charpentier expresses his frustration at the marketing people at Commodore. "The unfortunate problem was, the marketing and sales people really didn't understand what computers were about," he says. "To them it was just another thing and the world says make it compatible, regardless of whether or not you are going to cripple the machine, which they did."

Charpentier believes the decision to remain backward compatible was ultimately shortsighted. "They had inventory on the shelf," says Charpentier. "If we make a change to the C64 and bring out a new disk drive, we've got unsold inventory. There are issues like that that clouds people's judgment."

Yannes, a perfectionist by nature, felt the mentality to ship at all costs hurt the final product. "It was like, 'Well, you have something that works. Ship it.' We were like, 'But it doesn't work very well.' They would go, 'It doesn't matter because it doesn't need to work well. It just needs to work so we can ship it.'"

Al Charpentier also believes it was a mistake to use the antiquated 1540 design. "It was an interesting problem because Kit was there at the same time as we were trying to convince the marketing crew not to use that terrible disk drive," he recalls. "We wanted to come out with a new disk drive with higher speed, and we didn't win that argument. It was never clear to me if the marketing guys believed that or that was what Jack was telling them."[4]

Third party companies soon eliminated the C64's slow loading times. "Later on they came out with software revisions that allowed it to run much faster," says Yannes. Several ingenious companies released fast loader cartridges. Epyx released the most popular cartridge, which increased speeds by five times.

Aside from the slow speed, the 1541 disk drive was a unique piece of technology. The internal memory and 6502 processor allowed programmers to reprogram the 1541. Users could even load a program into the disk drive, unplug the disk drives from the computer, and the program would continue running. Users could then copy programs by inserting and removing disks without using the Commodore 64 at all.

The C64 could also load programs while performing other tasks. Games like *Mars Saga* loaded game data while playing music, a feat that caused other systems to bog down. For all the criticisms, the 1541 did amazing things no other system could do.

Hackers also realized amazing feats with the 1541 drive. Sometimes their accomplishments were just plain weird, such as playing quiet, audible music with the 1541 drive. Since the head could rattle at different frequencies, an intrepid hacker found a way to play different notes. No other computer owner could brag that their disk drive could play *Amazing Grace* or *Daisy Bell* (A Bicycle Built for Two).[5]

Kit Spencer predicted 70% of users would purchase a disk drive for the Commodore 64. It was a bold prediction given the low number of VIC-20 owners who purchased one, and it could potentially leave Commodore with a costly surplus of product. Consequently, 90% of North American Commodore 64 owners purchased a drive. "I suspect they sold a printer for every five or six computers and they probably sold a floppy disk [drive] for every one," says Chuck Peddle. "Low cost peripherals were very important for the success of Commodore during that time."

---

[4] The 1540 drive was not fully compatible with the C64. A bug in the VIC-II chip caused the C64 to freeze when using the 1540.

[5] HAL in 2001: A Space Odyssey sings Daisy Bell while a crewman unplugs him. It was the first tune played by the Altair at the Homebrew Computer Club.

Commodore experienced supply problems very early with the 1541. In August and September 1983, 1541 drives all but disappeared from store shelves because Commodore was unable to meet demand. "At the peak of Commodore 64 popularity, we weren't able to ship disk drives," says Russell.

Robert Russell sheds light on why Commodore had problems delivering. "They weren't working," he says. "I had written a real simple production test early on to validate that the drives were good and aligned. It basically beat them around and validated them."

Either Russell's validation test was too strict or the drives were unreliable. "At that time, the drive company was Japanese and the drives were assembled in Japan," says Russell. "One time they quit running my software test to validate 1541 disk drives because it failed too many drives, according to the Japanese."

Soon, users began reporting high failure rates with the disk drives. The drive heads were becoming misaligned. Tom Halfill, editor of Compute!'s Gazette, complained that four of the seven drives owned by the magazine failed in this way.

Robert Russell remembers the masses of disk drives that began piling up at Commodore headquarters. "We had an employee parking lot in the back of the company, and half of it was semi-trailers hauling stuff in from overseas," recalls Russell. "We had 30 semi-trailers full of 1541 disk drives in the back parking lot sinking into the asphalt. I don't know how many hundred-thousand drives were out there."

Disk drives began mysteriously disappearing. "The worst thing that happened was when guys were stealing stuff from the production floor," says Russell. "They would basically re-consign whole truckloads out of there."

I Adore My 64

With the engineering job complete (or at least good enough), Winterble's team reluctantly stepped away from the Commodore 64. "We accepted the fact that our job was done for a long time," says Winterble. "I don't in any way fault the fact that the marketing teams and the sales teams and those people had to come in and do their jobs. It's like a relay race, and it was time to hand off the baton."

Kit Spencer had proven himself by making the Commodore PET the most popular business computer in Britain and then spectacularly launching the VIC-20 in North America. Although the engineers had largely excluded him from shaping the C64, he was determined to bring the masses to Commodore.

Kit was now a seasoned advertising executive and he realized the importance of building brand recognition. He wanted to make Commodore the Coca-Cola of computers. To do this, he would use familiar sounds and images that people would learn to associate with Commodore. First, he would need to get through Jack.

Al Charpentier witnessed the pains endured by marketing people at Commodore. "One of the things that was difficult for anybody who claimed to be a marketing guy at Commodore was that Jack felt he was the premier marketing guy," he explains. "I think Kit knew more than Jack would let him do. It was tough, because Jack had a sense of what he wanted to accomplish and the people around him just had to execute that rather than being able to leave their own mark on things."

Kit wanted a major advertising campaign, and that meant a big budget. Jack did not believe in budgets. Spencer laid out a proposed advertising campaign that would cost the company twelve million dollars.[6] It would be the most expensive advertising campaign in Commodore history. Perhaps impressed with Spencer's success with the VIC-20 launch, Jack uncharacteristically approved the budget.

As usual, Jack kept a close watch on all of Spencer's decisions, adding to the pressure of carrying such a massive project. To Spencer, it seemed like everyone in the company had something to say about the proposed campaign. Executives suddenly became frustrated writers and directors who foisted their ideas on Kit in the hallways. All eyes were on Spencer to make the campaign a success.

It was obvious to Spencer that the best spokesman would be William Shatner, who contributed to the launch of the VIC-20. Unfortunately, Shatner's contract with Commodore ended in September 1982 and Commodore could no longer use his image to promote their computers. Shatner had also become a super-star.

With the success of *Star Trek II: Wrath of Khan* and the popularity of *T.J. Hooker*, Shatner's agent wanted a significantly higher rate. Jack refused, mostly because he was used to paying less for each new deal. With no high profile spokesman, Spencer would have to approach the advertising campaign from a different angle.

With the VIC-20 going into its second Christmas season, Spencer produced several VIC-20 commercials to keep sales moving. Spencer used his imported British sense of humor to reach the young target audience.

---

[6] The $12 million figure is from Michael Tomczyk's book, The Home Computer Wars. However, Byte magazine (February 1983) claims the budget was $22 million. Since Tomczyk was an insider, his figure is likely more accurate.

Selling the Revolution – 1982

He devised a series of diverse and wickedly funny commercials around the concept that you could buy a real computer for the price of a video game machine. The target was obviously the Atari VCS, with commercials pointing out that it was not a real computer (despite the name Video Computer System).

Each of the ads stressed the educational aspects of the VIC-20. In one commercial, a thirty-year old burnout sits in front of a fish bowl pretending to play a video game, staring eye to eye with his goldfish. The meaning was clear. Many parents feared video games did little to expand intelligence.

Spencer knew the Commodore 64 measured favorably against the competition in nearly every aspect. He decided to go head to head with each of the most popular computers of the day: Apple II, IBM PC, Atari 800, and TRS-80. Because the engineers gave the C64 so much power, he could remain truthful and straightforward.

Spencer hired advertising agency *Ally & Gargano* to film the commercials. They used the sardonic voice of Henry Morgan, whom the Internet Movie Database describes as a "Radio and TV personality possessed of excruciatingly sarcastic wit." Morgan was a perfect spokesman to taunt the competition and his voice instantly became identified with Commodore.

The first thirty-second commercial to introduce the C64 stressed memory and price. The ad presented the computer on a black pedestal while the narrator informs the viewer it contains 64 kilobytes of memory for only $595, compared to the IBM PC with 16 kilobytes for $1565, the Apple II with 48 kilobytes for $1530, and the Atari 800 with 16 kilobytes for $899. It ends with the prediction, "The Commodore 64 could be the microcomputer industry's outstanding new product since the birth of this industry."

Spencer also created a series of short but potent commercials targeted against specific computers. These commercials were cheap but allowed Commodore to stay in the public consciousness without much expenditure. The first ten-second spot against Atari claims consumers would have to buy four Atari 800 computers for $899 each to get the same amount of memory as one Commodore 64.

The commercial against Apple was simple but visually effective. It showed a green apple that gradually disintegrates as someone takes bites out of it. The soothing voice of Henry Morgan says, "There's a new personal computer from Commodore. With a third more built in memory than the Apple II at half the cost." By the end of the commercial, all that is left is an apple core, which falls over.

The IBM ad was much in the same vein as the Atari ad, only it used animation. It shows a lone cartoon elephant while the announcer asks, "If this is the memory of the IBM PC for $1565, then what's this?" Three more elephants squeeze into frame, jostling for position. "The memory of the Commodore 64, for under $600."

One humorous ad shows a poor college freshman whisked away on a train. Seconds later, he returns to the same train station. The announcer suggests things could have worked out if only he had a Commodore 64. "They were guilting the parents into buying a C64 because their fat kid came home from college and didn't know what he was doing," says Commodore engineer Dave Haynie. "They were extremely well done commercials."

Bob Yannes approved of the educational angle. "Part of Commodore's marketing program was, 'Do you really want to buy your kid a computer game that is going to rot his mind, or buy him a computer, which by the way can play video games too.' That was a very successful marketing campaign," recalls Yannes.

Given the climate of uncertainty towards computers in the early eighties, and the unproven record of computers in education, some California educators felt the commercials were disingenuous. "A lot of people objected to them," says Haynie.

In the final thirty-second commercial for the series, Spencer turned the other computers against their own companies. It shows a Basic code listing from an Apple computer, and the announcer explains, "We asked the computers which was better on the basis of price and memory." Of course, the Apple II, IBM PC and TRS-80 all choose the Commodore 64. It concludes sardonically, "That's what we like about our competition; they're so honest."

Perhaps the most memorable part of the Commodore commercials was the background music. Spencer licensed music from *Switched on Bach* by Walter Carlos[7], which featured Two-Part Invention #13 by Johan Sebastian Bach. Today, people are more likely to identify it as the Commodore theme song. The catchy tune presented the perfect impression of technology, sophistication, and playfulness. Viewers who heard the commercials could not stop thinking about the tune and ultimately could not stop thinking about Commodore.

Spencer also produced radio jingles, creating the famous 'I Adore my 64' theme song. The commercial jingles were as memorable as those by *McDonalds* and *Coca-Cola*. The first song sounds suspiciously like a Beatles tune:

---

[7] Walter Carlos also composed the score for the movie *Tron*.

I adore my 64, My Commodore 64.
I sing with it, write with it,
figure my path to flight with it,
My Commodore 64.
I rate with it, create with it,
telecommunicate with it,
My Commodore 64.

The other jingle is slightly edgier:
I adore my 64. My Commodore 64.
I cook with it, steam with it,
educate the team with it,
My Commodore 64.
I pitch with it, catch with it,
count my chicks before they hatch with it,
My Commodore 64.

None of the advertising touted the superior sound and graphics capabilities of the Commodore 64 since the in-house software from Commodore in late 1982 did little to exploit the abilities of these chips. Consumers would have to discover these capabilities themselves.

Spencer also produced print advertisements for magazines. The first advertisement ran the headline, "When we announced the Commodore 64 for $595, our competitors said we couldn't do it. That's because they couldn't do it."

In contrast to the television and radio advertising, the print advertising contained technical details. Spencer emphasized price, memory, software, peripherals, games, graphics, and sound. The advertisements also promised an optional CP/M cartridge, a promise that would eventually land Commodore in trouble.

In total, the advertising campaign produced over 12 different television commercials, radio spots, and magazine ads. Commodore ran the ads intensely before Christmas and then played them occasionally over the next year. "Commodore may have been the first one to run television ads for a computer in Prime Time," claims Yannes.

Spencer's advertising campaign was critically well received. "They won Clio's for some of those early Commodore ads," says Dave Haynie. The Clio Awards are the premier advertising awards. In 1983, they presented Ally & Gargano with two awards for the television commercials and the radio campaign.

Kit Spencer's campaign did exactly what it was intended to do: it got the message out. Spencer had chosen an effective strategy with his bold comparisons against the competition. His commercials, and Commodore's pricing, would soon bring Atari, Radio Shack, and even Apple to their knees.

It was a golden age for Commodore 64 advertising. Unfortunately, they would never recapture the same level of media saturation attained by Spencer.

The Commodore Curse: Part IV

After the departure of Chuck Peddle, Jack was uncertain if he had capable engineers to design his computers. These fears quickly dissipated when his East Coast engineers created the most successful Commodore product yet.

Unfortunately, the engineers felt strong dissatisfaction within Commodore. Bob Yannes still felt bitterness from the reneged bonus. "That was just something that stuck in everybody's craw," he says. "It was one of the points that helped me realize that being at Commodore wasn't likely to get me very far up the ladder of financial success."

Due to the success of the Commodore 64, the engineers expected a bonus for their work. Despite delivering an exceptional product, Jack was not happy with the engineering delays. "We were supposed to have it done in three months and it took us six," recalls Russell. "I don't even think any of us got a bonus for the C64 because it was late according to Jack."

No one needed a bonus more than Yannes. "My salary wasn't particularly high," he says. "They did give me a bonus for the VIC-20 concept, which was pretty nice, but I never got any kind of bonus for the Commodore 64 for all the extra work I put in. That was a little bit of a slap in the face."

Jack compensated Charles Winterble and Al Charpentier well, but they began wondering what to do after the C64 project. "We weren't dissatisfied," says Winterble. "Quite the contrary, we were all excited over the fact that now [the C64] was going to be sold, but our role was no longer as important as it was before. Our role was more like fixing production problems. Who wants to do that? We were a creative design team and we wanted to continue with the creative design stuff."

Both Winterble and especially Charpentier knew what they wanted to do next, but they no longer had the freedom they once enjoyed. "Jack wanted us to do a handheld CMOS computer," recalls Winterble. The engineers had no enthusiasm for the proposal. "There was nothing lined up that was going to be as exciting as what we were working on."

Charpentier's approach to engineering was fundamentally different from Jack's philosophy. "The real market to develop was the business market," he says. "Jack always felt that low-end was more appealing. That's where he lived."

Charpentier approved of the low-end market, but he wanted to go after the high-end market where technological innovation occurred. However, Jack wanted an even cheaper computer like the Sinclair. "I wanted to take aim at Apple, but Jack saw it as a different market," says Charpentier. "He felt [a cheap computer] was going to be more appropriate. It was just a disagreement of where things should go." The disagreement between Jack and his engineers was eerily similar to the earlier disagreement with Chuck Peddle.

Charpentier put forward a plan for Commodore's next machine. "After the Commodore 64, my next proposal was a C80, if you will," reveals Charpentier. "A *Commodore 80* with 80 columns to compete head on with the Apple II. Jack Tramiel and I had many, many, many discussions on that."

As a video chip designer, Charpentier knew which features he wanted to add to the next VIC chip. "The next thing I was going to do was create variable sized sprite structures," he explains.

The Commodore 80 would be unable to connect to a standard television. "Since TV's can't do 80 columns, it would have had to have been a separate CRT monitor," says Charpentier. "It was going to use a higher speed floppy, an 80-column display, and up to 256K of RAM."

Charpentier would have attempted to make the computer backward compatible with the C64. "It probably would have been a sensible thing to do but it never got to see the light of day," he says.

Despite the recent success of his engineer's designs, Jack overruled him. "It was clear that Jack was going to be calling the shots," says Charpentier. "He did a reasonable job in his own company, but he didn't understand what was going to happen with the computer market. I knew that the [cheap computer] was the wrong choice. I tried to convince him otherwise, he didn't agree, and that was his shekels."

Charpentier believes Commodore was lacking top-level executives who knew about computers. "The only people that were computer users were the engineers and the geeks, and they weren't in management," he says.

Bob Yannes also felt management did not give the design team much respect for their past successes. "It was pretty clear that in the future, any products we did were going to be predefined for us by marketing," he says. "We wouldn't have any freedom to do what we wanted."

The worst insult to the engineers came in the midst of financial success for Commodore. With his yearly performance review approaching, Yannes expected a raise for his efforts on the C64. "They were having such an enormous growth in their earnings and stock value," he recalls.

"When we were to have our reviews and get our salary increases, they announced that salaries would be frozen."

It was too astonishing for the young engineer to believe. The explanation was even more astonishing. "If they paid us more money, it would weaken the curve of the profit growth of the company, and they didn't want the financial analysts to see the curve leveling off," explains Yannes. "They wanted to keep it looking like it was going up and up."

Yannes is unsure who decided to freeze their salaries. "I wouldn't be surprised if it came from Jack," he says, but given Irving Gould's past obsession with the stock price, it seems more likely it came from him. Whether it was Jack or Irving, the shortsighted attempt to help the stock undoubtedly weakened the long-term prospects of the company.

The financial success of Commodore was due in no small part to the efforts of their engineers. Now, because of their astonishing success, the engineers received financial punishment. It was intolerable. "We were supposed to understand that? 'Oh yeah, that's great! No problem,'" says Yannes. "That helped motivate me to leave."

When Charpentier called Yannes in for his review, he presented a new opportunity. Charpentier said, "Here's the bad news: your salary is frozen. Here's the good news: I'm starting another company. You want to come join me?"

Yannes was ready to accept. "I think we all realized we were instrumental in the Commodore 64," he says. "We were the marketing team and the design team and everything. We really didn't have any outside influence over us and it was pretty much a home run. So we felt, 'Why are we doing this for someone else?'"

Winterble initiated the plan to leave Commodore. "I had an idea for a product and I talked to Al," begins Winterble. "Al and I joked over wine about the million-dollar idea. We talked about what we could do in the way of a product that we could do independently [of Commodore]."

With the Atari VCS still popular in 1982, Winterble conceived of a new product to expand the system. "We had an idea to turn that into a computer, called *My First Computer*," explains Winterble. "It was essentially a membrane keyboard that fit into the VCS slot and we put Basic in a little ROM. For $29.95 instead of buying a ROM cartridge, you buy a little computer. It was a great idea."

Winterble brought his idea to Atari. "All we had was this vague idea," says Winterble. He presented his idea to Atari CEO Ray Kassar, who agreed to purchase the product for a million dollars. Atari would develop the software themselves.

Charpentier barely hesitated when he left Commodore. "Once Jack had said he wanted to do the [cheap computer], I said I'm out of here," recalls Charpentier. "I felt very good about our decision. Opportunities were presenting themselves and it was a pretty exciting time back then."

Bob Yannes found it difficult to leave Commodore. "I actually had a lot of angst in leaving," he says. "I enjoyed working there. It was a lot of fun." Yannes eventually decided his opportunities were greater with Charpentier and Winterble. "We were gone in late August, early September of 1982," he recalls.

To avoid the wrath of Jack Tramiel, the engineers made their escape while Jack was away on a business trip. "We intentionally did it when he was in Japan," recalls Winterble. "One of the concerns was whether they would beat up on Yannes. We figured, 'We need some breathing room. Let's do it without people being able to jump all over us.'"

Winterble attempted to recruit other Commodore engineers. "They asked me to go along with them," recalls Russell. He was willing to go along. "They basically got their million dollars if they got that thing done," he says.

As Russell recalls, the plan called for the engineers to develop the hardware while Atari would deliver the computer software. Russell realized there was little need for a software engineer like himself. "I would have gone with them if I thought they needed me," he says.

Reluctantly, Russell declined the offer to join their startup, saying, "I'll come join you sometime in the future. Let me know when you're doing software." Despite the promise, he never joined.

Russell felt devastated at losing contact with his best friend. "You've got to realize, Bob Yannes and me were really good friends," he says. "We'd go out for lunch together practically every day." In total, five of the six key members of the C64 project joined Winterble, including production engineers David Ziembicki and Bruce Crockett.

The sudden departure of Al Charpentier left many of the VIC-II chip features undocumented. "We knew that eventually we would want to get more of that [information] out, but we ended up leaving before I could write the definitive manual on how to do some of the tricks," he says.

The former Commodore engineers worked modestly at first. "After we got out we worked out of my basement and we worked with no money," says Winterble.

Soon after forming *Peripheral Visions*, the former Commodore engineers heard from Jack's lawyers. "Jack hears we're doing something and he wants to know what it is, and he sues us," recalls Winterble. "We've got papers coming in and it's like, 'Well, for what?' 'For stealing trade secrets.' 'Well, what exactly did we steal?'" The lawsuit did not even specify the supposed trade secrets. It was obvious Jack did not know anything about their project.

Winterble made an agreement with the Commodore lawyers to disclose the details of the project. "If we told him what we were working on, if it was not anything that Commodore was working on, they would drop the lawsuit," explains Winterble. "So we said cool. We told them what we were working on. He said, 'Sorry, that's my product. You can't have it. I'm going to sue you anyway.'"

The lawsuit made little sense to Winterble. "We didn't work on it at [Commodore] or anything like that," he says.

Although Jack may not have had legal justification to sue Winterble, he had good reasons to be angry. Winterble, who was one of Jack's trusted inner circle, quite obviously looted some of his best engineers from Commodore. Furthermore, the engineers went straight to their primary competitor, Atari. "There was a little revenge in there because he was mad, and I know he was mad about this," admits Winterble. "He was probably pissed at me because we executed this while he was not there."

The seemingly frivolous lawsuit disappointed Winterble. "We helped Commodore, and our reward is this?" he says. "It just hurt our feelings. I mean, you are allowed to leave a company! Slavery was outlawed long ago, so why should we be punished for something we had a right to do."

During meetings with their lawyers, Jack let his ex-Commodore engineers know exactly how he felt about them siding with Atari. "If you left, you were a traitor and Jack could be very vengeful even to the detriment of his company," says Yannes. "I have a vivid memory of him sitting across the discovery table from us and growling how 'this troika had betrayed him'. If I had still been employed by him, I would have been frightened, but it was almost comical. It reminded me of Nikita Khrushchev banging his shoe at the UN."

Robert Russell found himself in an awkward position, torn between his loyalty to Commodore and his former coworkers. "I heard that [Jack] wasn't happy and that there were some lawsuits they were trying to pursue," says Russell. "I kept my head down about that whole thing because they were personal friends of mine."

The case should have been simple to decide but in 1982, law courts were unfamiliar with technology issues. "If anyone was knowledgeable about technology it wouldn't have lasted a second," says Winterble. "In other words, if this had been filed out in California where you had people who were used to dealing with technology issues everyday, it was a non-issue. The difficulty was that we had to educate a court system and that's an expensive proposition for a couple of little guys."

Surprisingly, managers at Commodore helped Winterble prove that Commodore never had an Atari VCS computer project. "Their management, Elton Suthard and a few other people, said that's baloney," recalls Winterble. "We had their deposition saying this was never worked on. Their people were agreeing with us."

Commodore lawyers even tried to claim that the Atari VCS project was infringing on intellectual property merely because the keyboard contained a 6502 processor. "We designed a product that used the 6502 and Commodore owns the 6502, therefore we're infringing on them," laughs Winterble. "The 6502 is sold publicly to anyone who wants it. The data sheets are available to anyone in the world who wants to design with it. This is a good explanation that takes about five minutes; it takes three years in court."

Winterble eventually won, but it had the desired effect of slowing down Peripheral Visions. "By the time we educated the court system and worked our way through, it cost us about $300,000," he reveals.

Despite the harsh treatment from Jack Tramiel, the engineers still valued their time with the company. "I enjoyed it a lot," says Charpentier. "Jack was tough to work for but in the engineering area he really gave the engineers a lot of freedom to be creative. I had a lot of fun there."

Charpentier still values the lessons he learned from Jack. "He was a hard charging guy who I learned a lot from," he says. "I learned a lot of things not to do. I certainly wouldn't want to emulate the way he did some things but in terms of building a company, it was a good training ground for me."

Charles Winterble has equal praise for his former boss. "Even today, I look back at Jack Tramiel and I thank him," says Winterble. "I learned a lot from him. It's unfortunate the terms we separated weren't the best in the world, but it was a great experience."

The Death of Max

After the successful debut of the C64, Commodore planned to release the Max Machine. Jack hoped it might ride some of the success of the C64 due to the similarities. "When we first designed the Commodore 64, it was going to be a $600 computer and the Ultimax was going to be a hundred-something dollar computer that was going to use the game cartridges that were developed for the Commodore 64," says Yannes.

Once Yashi Terakura completed his design, Jack passed the project to Japan. "We had put together the architecture for it," says Winterble. "Japan grabbed that and worked on the [production] design."

Jack was attempting to duplicate the success of the VIC-20 by releasing the low-cost computer in Japan first. He set a target price of $179. Once again, he was trying to meet his Japanese competition on their home ground. Once the machine had a foothold in Japan, he would launch it in the United States.

The Max Machine outclassed the other leading game consoles. In technical specifications, the Max Machine would have had approximately the same graphics and sound capabilities of the hugely successful Nintendo Entertainment System, released years later.

As a computer, the machine was lacking. With the Mini Basic cartridge, only 510 bytes of memory were available for programming. This was obviously not useful to anyone. Another Basic cartridge included an extra two kilobytes of RAM; only nominally better.

The decision to push the product despite objections within his company showed Jack had not yet made the transition from calculators to computers. He believed the low price would make up for a weak product.

Back in North America, Jack placed Kit Spencer in charge of preparing an advertising campaign for the Max Machine. Kit began preparing his advertising campaign with the New York ad agency Ally & Gargano. Michael Tomczyk would help design the packaging and manual for the machine. Both men saw the obvious but they dutifully went to work anyway.

According to product literature of the time, Commodore intended the Max Machine as a third generation game console. To become a true console, the engineers needed to take a stand and eliminate the keyboard. Without the manufacturing cost of a keyboard, Commodore could release a cheaper console with superior graphics and sound. Instead, it remained a poorly defined computer.

Commodore Japan manufactured and released the Max Machine in their home market alongside the Japanese Commodore 64. As many had predicted, the Max Machine was a monumental flop.

By November 1982, Commodore was still planning to go ahead with the North American release. The situation had changed during the development of the machine. When the project began, the VIC-20 was selling for $299. The $179 Max made sense until the Price Wars (as the press called them) began. By the time the Max Machine was ready for release, the VIC-20 was selling for under $200.

By early 1983, even the Commodore 64 was closing in on the Max Machine price. "It wasn't long after the introduction of the Commodore 64 that it was down in the $300 range and then it was down in the $130 range," says Yannes. "There just wasn't any reason to produce the Max Machine. Why buy the Max with its membrane keyboard and tiny amount of memory when you can buy the C64 for [nearly] the same price and get a whole computer?"

Jack handed off the North American product release to Bill Wade, who clearly saw the product had no future. He convinced Jack to abandon it and this time Jack agreed. The price of the VIC-20 was now lower than the Max Machine price, making the Max irrelevant.

Epilogue of the P & B computers

After the release of the C64, Commodore planned to release the P & B computers to replace the antiquated PET line. The P series were personal computers (with no monitors), while the B computers were for business with 80 column displays and monochrome monitors.

Commodore handed out demonstration units to select dealers. In November 1982, Byte magazine announced the P128 for $995, the B128 for $1695, and the BX256 for $2995.

Charpentier feels the P128 was of little value to anyone. "The whole problem with them was that they didn't have sufficient graphic information when you looked at the Apple doing 80-columns," says Charpentier.

In Europe, Commodore created an elaborate naming scheme for the P & B series. They dubbed the new line the CBM-II. The CBM 505 and 510 were the personal computers, with 64kb and 128kb respectively. The CBM 610 and 620 had 128kb and 256kb memory. They also planned to sell high-end 710 and 720 computers, which included detachable keyboards and swivel monitors.

The design group came up with a revolutionary look for personal computers. The 700 series were the best-looking computers in the early eighties, far ahead of their time. They used rounded moldings reminiscent of the rounded look Macintosh monitors would use decades later. The CBM-710 and 720 models even housed two floppy disk drives.

Byte magazine viewed the computers at the National Computer Conference in Texas. They remarked, "Commodore gets the prize for the wildest styling of any computers we saw at the show."[8]

Although Kit Spencer had little impact on the design of the C64, he made marketing suggestions for the P & B series. Spencer targeted the computers against the IBM PC. He pushed engineers to develop an optional CP/M expansion board, which included a Z80 microprocessor.

Commodore produced limited numbers of the computers and released them to dealers. Users had little reason to purchase the computers, which received almost no software development. Soon, dealers sold off their stock at below cost. The success of the C64 overshadowed the P & B series.

---

[8] *Byte* magazine, (Vol. 7, No. 9, September 1982), p. 61.

CHAPTER

14

Commodore Mania

1983

Christmas of 1982 was a turning point for Commodore. The Commodore 64 had a massive advertising campaign with regular television commercials, distribution through thousands of dealers, and demonstrations in stores. It was now up to the consumer to decide if Commodore would become a success.

Media Madness

In 1982, Disney gave the image of computers a face-lift when they released a groundbreaking film about the world inside a computer called *Tron*. It was the perfect climate for Commodore to promote their new computer.

Commodore's own Michael Tomczyk expressed his thoughts on Tron and videogames to Compute! magazine in October of that year. "The concept of TRON, when you are really the computer - and the computer is you - is definitely going to happen. That's the ultimate. The trends of the pricing and power and technology indicate this is really going to happen. The physics of the fantasy expressed in that movie are probably impossible, but we are moving in that direction. We are moving toward the ultimate TRON."

Through 1982, Commodore sold the C64 through computer dealers. In the first two weeks of the August release, Commodore sold 12,000 C64 computers; a new record for a two-week period. Between September 1 and December 1, 65,000 systems sold.

C64 buyers had their expectations exceeded because Kit Spencer's television advertising stressed memory and price but said little about its superior sound and graphics. Commodore began to earn fierce brand loyalty.

Magazine reviews for the C64 were unanimous in their praise. Byte contributor Stan Wszola applauded the C64's sound and graphics, though he mentioned the lackluster Basic 2.0. He also pointed out the poor quality control of Commodore manufacturing, since he had to return two computers before he finally obtained a working system.

Creative Computing's Ron Jeffries appreciated the amount of computing power available for under $600, though he found problems with the video display, which appeared blurry.

Christmas sales surpassed expectations, but 1983 was really the year of the C64. On January 4, 1983, Time selected the Computer as their man of the year for 1982. A generic computer graced the cover, making it the only year in which a human failed to win. Public interest in computers surged.

To their credit, Compute! magazine was one of the first publications to recognize the potential of the C64. In January 1983, publisher Robert Lock announced a Commodore only spin-off magazine to be titled *Commodore Gazette* (later renamed *Compute!'s Gazette*).

The same year, North American television realized the value of computers in society and began airing *Computer Chronicles*. This weekly TV show was dedicated to computer news and helped increase public awareness about computers. The show frequently mentioned Commodore and occasionally featured Tramiel and his sons as guests.

Hollywood also continued exploring the field of computers for drama. In June 1983, MGM released *WarGames* starring a young Matthew Broderick. The film glorified computer hacking, a subject briefly touched upon in Tron. With a strong cold war theme, it went on to gross almost eighty-million dollars in the United States alone. It was a reflection of the mainstream acceptance of computers. A golden age for Commodore had begun.

In January 1983, Commodore began selling to retail giants like K-Mart and Sears. Once again, Jack dropped the retail price of the C64. Bob Yannes recalls what happened next. "He went to ComputerLand with the Commodore 64 at $595 and they said, 'You're not going to do what you did with the VIC-20, are you?' and Jack said, 'Oh, no.' And then of course, he did. A couple of months later he's selling them in Kmart for $399." The move left dealers with overpriced stock.

Curiously, Yannes blames ComputerLand for doing business with Commodore in the first place. "You know, how stupid could ComputerLand be? Jack didn't care if his dealers made any money on them," he says. "He would cut his profits as much as he could to try to take over the market."

The move alienated both large and small dealers. "Commodore made some blunders there," says engineer Dave Haynie. "The classic story was that the local mom and pop dealer could buy the C64 for less at the local K-Mart than they could buy it from their local distributor, which gave Commodore a really bad name." Jack could have warned his dealers of the upcoming price drop and given them a chance to sell off their inventory. Instead, he undercut his own distribution network.

In response to complaints, Commodore encouraged their dealers to concentrate on the new P and B series, which did little to placate anyone. In one move, Jack had virtually destroyed Commodore's reputation with their dealers.

"Charlie [Winterble] told me this joke, in relation to Jack," says Yannes. "There was this turtle that was going to cross the river and there's a scorpion there. The scorpion asks the turtle if he'll take him across the river. The turtle says, 'No, you'll sting me and I'll die.' The scorpion says, 'I'm not going to sting you. We'll both drown.' So the turtle says, 'Okay.' The scorpion climbs up on the turtle's back and the turtle goes across the river. Suddenly he feels himself being stung. He turns to the scorpion and says, 'Why did you do that? We're both going to die!' The scorpion says, 'It's my nature.'"

Sears soon became a major computer distributor. The stores had a separate area for computer sales, with about five demonstration C64 computers complete with floppy drives, tape units, printers, and monitors.

Though sales of the Commodore 64 were on an upward trajectory through 1983, it took time to build the market. In fact, sales of the VIC-20 continued to dominate for most of 1983, largely due to faster production and an ever-decreasing price.

Commodore sold a million C64's sometime in the first half of 1983 and the engineers decided to flaunt their success at the upcoming CES show in June. According to engineer Bil Herd, "We were going to a show and somebody said, 'You know what? We need to see the millionth one.'"

Unfortunately, no one was waiting on the assembly line to pull out the millionth C64. "I just happened to walk back into the lab and Gayle Moyer was back there rooting through this big pile of trash that accumulates in these labs," recalls Herd. "I asked, 'What are you looking for?' He said, 'I'll know when I find it.' Then he goes, 'Aha! Here it is!' He pulls out of this pile of junk the millionth Commodore 64!"

"In reality, it was a random one," says Herd. "He took it, sprayed it with gold, and put it in the display at the CES show."

Microsoft watched as the computer with their Basic achieved new sales records. "The Commodore 64 must have really rankled Microsoft because I don't think they made a dime on it, even though there were millions and millions of Commodore 64's sold," explains Yannes.

Jack was still using the same contract written in 1977 for the PET. "There was a negotiated contract with Gates, and it called for unlimited use," recalls Winterble. "I'm sure that the people who were on the other side of that contract weren't real happy. The relationship between Commodore and Microsoft wasn't that great."

Building a Software Library

One of the biggest criticisms the Commodore 64 had to overcome was the lack of software on release. Today this seems incredible, given the unmatched software library that eventually developed, but software development was slow for the first year, mainly because of the lack of volume disk drive production until late 1983.

"The people who bought Commodore 64's didn't buy them because there was lots of applications software," says Yannes. "They bought them because if they didn't get a computer they were going to be left out and fall behind."

Commodore advertising initially promised CP/M compatibility and the massive CP/M software base. Unfortunately, due to engineering difficulties, Commodore was unable to launch the CP/M cartridge alongside the C64.

An unnamed engineer dubbed 'Shooting Star' was in charge of the CP/M cartridge. Robert Russell hoped to speed up development of the cartridge by analyzing the competition. "I gave him the [Apple II] schematic and the documentation and said, 'This is what we want.' I didn't care whether he copied it or not, but I'm sure he did because he wasn't that great an engineer," says Russell.

The CP/M cartridge remained plagued by technical problems. "It took him a long time to even make it somewhat functional," says Russell. "There were some serious timing problems with that card that kept it from really coming out and succeeding."

The Federal Trade Commission noticed the false advertising and promptly cracked down on Commodore. According to Byte magazine, "Commodore Business Machines signed a consent agreement in Aug-84, under which Commodore agreed not to advertise capabilities that don't yet exist. Commodore had advertised CP/M capabilities for its

Commodore 64 computer long before the optional Z80 coprocessor was available."[1]

The Commodore software division in North America had an uneven record at producing marketable software products for the VIC-20. "Even early on, we had software teams doing games for the VIC-20, but they always had weak managers," says Russell. "They did a few games but they were not very good." The most marketable games came from Commodore Japan.

Although Robert Russell developed system software for the ROM chips, he initially had nothing to do with the software division. "The software group was applications and gaming support in [those] days," says Russell.

After Jack relieved Michael Tomczyk of his duties, the software division bounced around from one manager to another, including Robert Russell. "It ended up me being in charge of them after their manager [Charles Winterble] left," says Russell. "They were doing games that were really pretty good based on the VIC-20 and then translating them to the C64. For the amount of people they had, and I don't think it was ever more than ten or so, they were pretty impressive."

In late 1982, Jack decided software was a serious business and he appointed his friend Sigmund Hartmann to establish and operate the software division. Robert Russell first met Hartmann in Germany. "I was at the Hanover show, sitting up in the booth in case anyone needed specifics," says Russell. "Jack came to me and said, 'Hey, take this friend of mine Sig around and show him what you find interesting at the show, Bob.'"

Hartmann, a likeable yet shrewd businessman, was born in Germany and educated in Belgium. For 18 years, Hartmann worked at *TRW Automotive*, which included managing engineering projects for *NASA* and *GM*. With his thick German accent, Hartmann frequently apologized when Commodore employees could not understand him and often spelled out words to make sure people understood what he was saying. Under Hartmann, the newly structured software division would operate as an independent software company within Commodore.

The software division contained three sub-divisions: games, business productivity software, and educational titles. The VIC group became the games division while the PET software division became the business division.

---

[1] *Byte* magazine (October 1984), p. 9.

In organizing the division, Hartmann shrewdly hired former software managers Michael Tomczyk and Bill Wade, allowing the division to build on their previous experience. Hartmann also named Andy Finkel, one of the original VIC-20 games developers, technical manager for the group. Jack gave Hartmann a mandate to create a full Commodore 64 software library for the June 1983 CES show.

To lead the educational software division, Hartmann hired Dr. Dan Kunz, who was formerly responsible for selling PETs to schools. Some of the first C64 software titles came from the *Educational Software Program*. Hartmann recognized there was not much of a market for selling educational software, so he released the software as public domain to boost the educational image of the C64.

The Educational Software Program mostly converted BASIC educational titles from the PET and VIC-20. In total, there were 96 educational titles created between 1982 and 1983. In early 1984, with the C64 established, Commodore closed the Educational division. Their last game was *Lemonade*, a copy of the popular educational game *Lemonade Stand*.

The games division had greater success with their software sales. With the exception of the smash hit *Choplifter* by Broderbund, Commodore dominated the C64 software sales charts, not merely because of their obvious head start but because of the surprising high quality of their games.

The ever-reliable Hal Laboratories of Japan produced many of the early C64 games. Commodore now understood the rules of copyright so there would be no repeat of the infamous Jellyman/Pac Man legal disaster. Hal Laboratories produced early 1982 classics like *Night Driver*, *Le Mans*, *Avenger*, and *Jupiter Lander*.[2]

Robert Russell feels Hartmann's greatest strength was going outside of Commodore to acquire game titles. "He could deal with the outside companies," says Russell. "That's what made him effective."

One of the most lucrative relationships for the C64 continued from the VIC-20 days. Hartmann continued the licensing deal with Bally-Midway for their popular arcade games. Under the agreement, Commodore programmers turned out credible versions of *Sea Wolf*, *Clowns*, *Kickman* (originally titled *Kick* in the arcades), *Blueprint*, *Lazarian*, *Omega Race*, *Gorf*, and *Satans Hollow* through 1982 and 1983.

Robert Russell remembers his envy of software programmers like Andy Finkel who played games on a daily basis. "They had a game room over on the software side," says Russell. "They had all the latest arcade

---

[2] These were the last games Hal Laboratories made for Commodore.

games. I don't even know if I ever played any games in that thing, but I always wanted to."

Bob Yannes was thrilled to see a software library building up around the machine he designed. "I used [a 64] all the time," says Yannes. "I enjoyed playing Omega Race."

Although most game conversions were of high quality, Commodore still had problems maintaining consistency. The first version of *Wizard of Wor*, released in 1982, did not live up the quality of the arcade game. Commodore was determined to get it right, however, and they released an improved version in 1983, which became an admired classic. Like the arcade game, it even included speech when used with Commodore's *Magic Voice Speech Module*. Commodore's relationship with Bally-Midway ended in 1983, after which *Sega* began converting Bally-Midway games for the C64.[3]

Commodore also experimented with third party developers. One of their early attempts was with a company called *Fahrenheit 451 Software*, which produced *Arctic Shipwreck* and *Quark IX*. Both of these games met with lackluster success, however, and the relationship did not continue.

Hartmann also orchestrated a lucrative partnership with Infocom to distribute many of their most popular text adventure games. Commodore distributed *Deadline*, *Starcross*, *Suspended*, and the complete *Zork* trilogy. Of these, *Zork* was the most popular and spawned a dedicated following. In early 1983, Infocom ended their relationship with Commodore when they established their own distribution channels.

Commodore extended their relationship with Scott Adams and Adventure International, who had previously produced games for the VIC-20. In 1983, Commodore published seven Scott Adams adventures, which met with mediocre success.

In an attempt to regain interest in Scott Adams adventures, Commodore and Adventure International teamed up with *Marvel Comics* for the Questprobe series of adventure games featuring *The Incredible Hulk*, *Spiderman*, and the *Fantastic Four*. Curiously, Hartmann also released the games for the IBM PC, Apple II, and Atari 800. In an interview with RUN magazine, Hartmann said, "If we were to sell it for only one system, we'd be missing the boat. That's why we're pushing to get maximum exposure in the marketplace."[4]

Advertisements for the Questprobe series proclaimed, "You'll see why Commodore is quickly becoming a software giant." However, the game

---

[3] Sega turned out hits like *Tapper*, *Up 'n Down*, and *Spy Hunter*.
[4] *RUN* magazine, "For Gamesters Only" (December 1984), p. 24.

lacked true innovation and fared poorly in the marketplace. Traditional adventure games were having a hard time competing against action games and the Questprobe series proved to be the finale for Scott Adams Adventures.

Commodore had their first legitimate hit with *International Soccer*, developed by Andrew Spencer of Commodore UK in 1983. The game was a landmark game for sports titles. Aside from being very playable, it featured nice touches such as players running onto the field at the beginning of the game, a trophy presentation to the winning team, and an animated crowd. Fans around the world, and especially Europe, embraced the title.

Andrew Spencer followed with *International Basketball* in 1984, which used much of the same code from his International Soccer game. This time the game featured a random crowd, a scoreboard, and courtside advertisements for Kellogg's, Coca-Cola, and of course Commodore. He followed up the game with *International Tennis*.

Chuck Peddle credits games for allowing Commodore to stay ahead of the IBM PC. "The games on the PC were not very good for a long time," says Peddle. "You didn't buy it as a game machine. Commodore [was] an adequate outlet for games for a long time."

According to Robert Russell, Commodore was concerned with software piracy even before the VIC-20 days. "We were trying to figure out how to do things protection wise," says Russell. "The problem was, we'd come up with a scheme and then we'd sit down and figure out in an hour how to bust that scheme."

In an ironic twist, Commodore turned out to be its own worst enemy when it came to piracy. Even game cartridges were not safe from illegal copying. "Someone at Commodore would hack the game cartridges and put them on a floppy disk," says Yannes.

With the release of the 1541 disk drive in late 1983, software became much easier to distribute, for both publishers and crackers. "Here's a little known fact: Commodore was probably the biggest source of cracked software," reveals Bil Herd. "The worst thing you could do was submit a copy of something to the games and applications group."

According to Herd, a cracker who used the name *The Giant Clam* actually worked in the software group. "The rest were good people, don't get me wrong, but there were a few nefarious types that would generally make sure a cracked version of the game was available within a week," says Herd. "The Giant Clam worked at Commodore."

Robert Russell was also aware of The Giant Clam. "That would have been one of the guys over there in [Andy] Finkel's team," confirms Russell. "There were a lot of weirdo's in that group."

The Giant Clam remained undetected for a time until Commodore received a preview copy of International Soccer. "It was the soccer game produced by Commodore England," says Herd. When pirated copies of the game began appearing in North America, it was clear the pirate was an insider. "Later the FBI got involved because the only people that had even received the game were from Commodore West Chester," says Herd. It is unknown whether the FBI apprehended The Giant Clam.

The Commodore 64 received early software development by the top game publishers of the day, including Broderbund, Epyx, Electronic Arts, and Sierra Online. Other publishers came along and disappeared just as quickly, such as Spinnaker, Sirius, Hesware, Creative Software, Synapse, and Tronix.

With the release of the Commodore 64, game publishers quickly shifted away from the Apple in favor of Commodore. The Apple II and TRS-80 dominated a 1982 catalog from Eypx, with some support for Atari and IBM games, and a handful for the VIC-20 and PET. By 1983, the situation changed dramatically, with games like Pitfall and Jumpman Junior exclusively for Commodore and Atari computers. In 1983, TRS-80 games all but disappeared. By 1984, the Commodore 64 was receiving first releases such as the classic *Impossible Mission*.

Commodore engineers often indulged their need for games. "My favorite game was *Kennedy Approach*, an air traffic controller game," says Herd. "It was good enough that I would come out of my office with sweaty palms and a slight shake. Later I would have dreams in which I could hear the screams of the people going down in the mountains outside of Denver due to my not being able to get them vectored for approach fast enough."

Commodore engineers also found time to play Epyx's first hit. "Jumpman was probably the most popular game with some staying power throughout engineering and I assume some of the other departments," says Herd.

Commodore even published a game submitted by two young Canadian programmers called *Jack Attack*. It was a joke most Commodore employees could appreciate. "You would have to be an insider to know what that meant," says Charles Winterble.

By the early eighties, it was already common for companies to have their own publication, such as *Atari Age*. Commodore started two magazines: a 'serious' computing magazine and an entertainment magazine called *Power/Play*. Former VIC-20 software developer Neil Harris acted as publishing manager and frequent contributor.

Commodore started Power/Play in mid-1982. From the beginning, Commodore used the quarterly magazine to promote in-house games. They also accepted advertising and promoted third party games, though they favored their own creations. Commodore games like Jack Attack received cover status and eight page treatments while they overlooked popular titles like *Frogger* and *Q-Bert*.

As the popularity of the magazine increased, Commodore began publishing bi-monthly and then monthly. By late 1984, the magazine also began giving more coverage to third party hits like *M.U.L.E.* and *Archon*.

Commodore's other computer magazine had its origins as the PET User Club Newsletter in 1981. A Commodore employee named Dennis Barnhart[5] merged the newsletter into a magazine called *Interface*. "Dennis started it when he was at Commodore," says Peddle. "It was just another marketing thing."

Interface was too close to another early computer magazine called Interface Age. In mid-1981, Commodore changed the name to *Commodore the Microcomputer Magazine*, and then in July 1984 they changed to *Commodore Microcomputers*. The magazine was the counterpart to *Power/Play*, promoting Commodore productivity titles.

Surprisingly, the publishing division of Commodore produced significant revenues. For every five computers Commodore sold, one customer purchased a Commodore manual. As a result, Commodore sold 600,000 books in 1983.

On the business software side, Commodore produced an uninspired line of business software. The applications included *Easy Calc 64*, *Easy Finance* I through V, *Easy Mail*, *Easy Spell*, and so on. They also produced a series of small business applications with names like *General Ledger*, *Accounts Payable*, *Accounts Receivable*, and *Inventory Management*. The titles met with limited success.

John Feagans, who still resided on the West Coast, initiated the most successful productivity application by Commodore. In the early eighties, computer enthusiasts near Silicon Valley were taking notice of graphical user interfaces developed at *Xerox Palo Alto Research Center*. The idea of a graphical user interface (GUI) intrigued Feagans and he began developing his own project for the Commodore 64.

---

[5] Dennis Barnhart later worked for Chuck Peddle, then became famous when he started a company called *Eagle Computer*. On the same day as the IPO, he purchased a Yacht, went for lunch and celebrated over drinks, then smashed his $70,000 Ferrari into a guardrail. He died from his injuries.

Feagans designed a word-processing application and a system to manage files using a GUI and a joystick-controlled pointer. Feagans called his application *Magic Desk*. "John was the type of guy who liked to design things," says Russell. "He did some really interesting graphics stuff later on for the C64; the Magic Desk. If you look at it, that is the architecture people copied later on *GEOS*."

Feagans was in a rush to have his product ready for the June 1983 CES show. He called on Michael Tomczyk to fly down to the West Coast to help with the design. Tomczyk hastily drew up the first screen on graph paper during the flight, which showed a desk with a clock, a door, a wastebasket, and other office accoutrements. It was user-friendly, but it took the GUI metaphor too literally. Though it was primitive, it was a preview of next generation user interfaces.

Due to the success of the Commodore 64, 1983 was a surprisingly successful year for the Commodore software division. According to the Wall Street Journal, Commodore was the third largest software producer for 1983.[6] "That was when our software group was peaking," says Russell. "Sig Hartman was responsible."

Path of Destruction

By 1983, there were too many computers in the market and it was time for another shakeout. As Byte magazine noted, "System suppliers have tried to become much more aggressive in their marketing, but only the better-financed and established companies are succeeding. Add to this the current recession, and it's no surprise that industry pundits are predicting a shakeout among personal computer manufacturers in the very near future as marketing becomes more important than the products themselves."[7] Byte later dubbed the event the *Great Shakeout*.

Commodore entered into the war with the single greatest weapon they had ever devised, the C64. For the next few years, it would be the central piece of artillery on the battlefield, with the VIC-20 in a supporting position. Between 1982 and 1984, the C64 left a smoldering path of destruction in its wake.

Jack knew that to eliminate the competition, he would have to take Commodore places others could not survive. With his lean company and vertical integration, Commodore could decrease the price of their computers to a point where others would not be able to follow. Of his

---

[6] *Wall Street Journal* (February 23, 1984).
[7] *Byte* magazine, "Shakeout Predicted" (February 1983), p. 433.

competitors, only Texas Instruments had vertical integration down to the semiconductor level, but their product was not as strong as the C64.

In late 1982, Jack dropped the price of the VIC-20 below $200, and Commodore soon began shipping 70,000 units per month. Many were sold at *Toys'R'Us*, which recently opened computer sections in their stores. In retaliation, Texas Instruments offered a $100 mail in rebate on the $300 Ti-99/4A in August 1982. Texas Instruments was attempting to follow the same path they used to dominate the calculator industry. In December, with the C64 dominating the Christmas season, Atari dropped the price of the Atari 800 to under $500.

In January 1983, with the C64 now selling at K-Mart, Jack lowered the price from $595 to $399. "He planned to reduce the cost of the Commodore 64 but he wanted to wait until after Christmas to get the last bit of money," says Dave Haynie.

In February, Texas Instruments further reduced the Ti-99/4A to $150. They were going head to head with the VIC-20. Commodore responded in April by cutting the prices to all their peripherals, which allowed dealers to lower their VIC-20 price to under $100, in the hopes of making their profits back on peripherals.

In the same month, Commodore instigated a strange offer that literally removed the competition from homes. "Right about the time I started working there Jack had come up with this great marketing scheme," says Dave Haynie. "He had an offer, strategically delivered as Tramiel always did, that said, 'Send in any sort of computing device and you can get $100 off your Commodore 64.'"

Commodore soon had a warehouse full of competitor's computers. "We had a lot of junk around there," says Haynie. "I remember looking through that, and there was a Sol-20. That was the computer I wanted when I was a kid."

With the storage space filling up with computers, Commodore employees began topping up their salaries by bartering with the computers. According to Bil Herd, employees could go shopping for stereo equipment and other electronics using the computers, if you were willing to sneak past manager row with a computer under your arm.

Commodore employees speculated that the offer actually increased sales of Timex-Sinclair computers. Customers sometimes purchased $50 Timex-Sinclair computers just to take advantage of the $100 rebate offer. The excess Sinclair computers became a running joke within the halls of Commodore. "We had all these Sinclairs," says Bil Herd. "I started using them as doorstops."

In May 1983, Atari offered a $100 rebate on the Atari 800, bringing it to the same price as the C64. In June 1983, at the CES show, Jack announced he would reduce the price of the C64 from $360 to just $200, one-third the original price. Intense free market competition had produced a computer buyer's paradise.

The price cuts hurt Texas Instruments and the company predicted they would lose $100,000,000 in the second quarter of 1983 alone. Meanwhile, Commodore showed a profit of $25,000,000 in their third quarter. It was clear Commodore could outlast their strongest competitors.

On Friday, October 28, 1983, Texas Instruments announced they were pulling out of the computer market. Jack had defeated his former nemesis from the calculator wars. Within two days of announcing their withdrawal, Texas Instruments stock surged 30 percent.

In the middle of 1983, Jack abruptly terminated the PET sales organization, a clear indication he wanted to focus exclusively on the consumer market. Commodore also weeded out their smaller computer dealers. Now, instead of thousands of small computer stores, Commodore only dealt with approximately 65 major distributors.

Atari had no vertical integration to compete with Commodore and often bought their parts from Commodore. After selling two-billion dollars of product in 1982, sales dropped abruptly to $1.1 billion and Atari lost $538.6 million in 1983. Atari owner Warner Communications saw the trend and wanted out before Atari bled them to death.

Jack's 'business is war' philosophy was effective. "Jack always wanted to drive the price down so that no one could compete, and he succeeded," says Yannes. "The C64 was a steamroller. No one could really go up against it."

Radio Shack, once a potential reseller of the PET, also failed against the C64. The TRS-80 initially benefited by distribution in almost 7000 Radio Shack stores, but this seemed more like a limitation as time went on. Radio Shack was unable to penetrate into the wider market. Owners also dubbed the TRS-80 the Trash-80, owing to its poor quality. Tandy eventually dropped the TRS-80 line and started making IBM PC clones.

By 1982, the Apple II was starting to look dated. There had been updates, but they were not fundamental. With the release of the C64, potential Apple customers became dismayed when they compared it with the C64. The Apple II was too expensive and un-cool for games.

Apple's fear of Commodore went back to 1977, when they realized Commodore's ownership of MOS Technologies could give them an unbeatable advantage. With the C64, Apple's worst fears came true. The Apple II now looked sad with its poor sound and muddy graphics. Commodore, using its own graphics chip, sound chip, and microprocessor, was able to sell an incredible computer for a fraction of their price.

Apple could have charged their customers less for the Apple II. Between 1977 and 1982, there were many opportunities to decrease the price, since the cost of components fell yearly. Instead, Apple was intent on overcharging their customers. In contrast, Jack routinely lowered his prices as soon as components became cheaper.

Apple released the Apple IIe in January 1983 to strike back against the C64. The main selling point was 64 kilobytes of RAM, up from 48 kilobytes in the old Apple II+. Apple charged an excessive price of $1395, which did not include a disk drive or monitor. There was no real technological advantage over the C64 with the exception of expansion slots. The unreasonable high price made any positive points irrelevant.

In 1984, Apple released the Apple IIc, which no longer had any expansion slots. Now, nothing separated it from the C64 except price and inferior technology. Customers complained that Apple was losing touch.

Through the price wars, IBM remained implacable because they stayed out of the home market. Businesses continued buying their computers and IBM quickly established itself as the office standard.

In late 1983, IBM wanted a piece of the home market and made plans to release a $700 home computer called the *IBM PC Jr.* to compete with the Commodore 64.

Jack responded to the IBM announcement with disdain. The Wall Street Journal quoted him as saying, "There are far more people with $200 than $700 for a computer." Jack reaffirmed his strategy of conquering the market with low prices. In the end, Jack was right and the IBM PC Jr. failed.

The great shakeout reaffirmed Commodore's strengths compared to the competition. Jack had all but destroyed Atari, Texas Instruments, Timex, Radio Shack, Osborne, Coleco, and Mattel, while weakening Apple. Only IBM remained untouched by the mighty C64. Jack had patiently built up a company with unbeatable vertical integration and now he was reaping his rewards.

For the first time in years, Commodore surpassed Apple in yearly sales. Commodore sold $681 million worth of products in 1983, and increase of 124 percent from 1982. It seemed like Jack had answered any lingering questions about his leadership.

Are you big in Japan?

By the time Alphaville released their hit song *Big in Japan* in early 1984, Commodore had already lost the Japanese market. Even the potent C64 was not having an impact. A new type of computer dominated Japan and threatened to spread to other parts of the world.

The winning strategy for Japan came from Dr. Kay Nishi, whom Chuck Peddle first met when he launched the PET. "There was this 19 year old kid who wrote a magazine called ASCII," says Peddle. "The first time I met him was at the Hanover Faire. He was just gaga. He took pictures, goes back home and sells them."

In 1981, Nishi was working for IBM. The 26 year old witnessed the increasing popularity of home computers and decided to design one. "He and [Bill] Gates formed this team," recalls Peddle. "They were both about the same age and he moved to Seattle. He's pushing Gates to design a computer with the Japanese."

Nishi was familiar with the story of how the *Sony Betamax* format failed. He saw personal computers as home electronic devices, like VCR's. Likewise, he quickly identified software as the media of computers (like VHS tapes in VCR's).

Nishi envisioned a computer where competing companies would build computers that used the same software. "It was called MSX and all the Japanese companies standardized on it," says Peddle. Dr. Nishi claims MSX stood for Machines with Software Exchangeability.

All computers using the MSX standard would have the same specifications: an 8-bit Zilog Z-80 microprocessor at 3.58 megahertz, a Texas Instruments video processor, 16 kilobytes of video memory, a General Instruments AY-3-8910 audio chip, Atari style joystick ports, and at least 8 kilobytes of memory (though most included 64 kilobytes).

Sony and Matsushita (Panasonic) were the first companies to take notice of Nishi's concept and designs. The two giants contacted each other to discuss plans to implement Nishi's vision. Soon, 11 other companies joined, including Sanyo, Hitachi, Canon, Mitsubishi, Toshiba, Fujitsu, Kyocera, General, Yamaha, Pioneer, and JVC.

The MSX standard included Microsoft Basic on a 32-kilobyte ROM chip. "They gave Gates a paid deposit against 'per machine' royalties," says Peddle. "Kay Nishi thought they were going to kill the market. His theory was to come in under us with a packaged machine that could be sold using Japanese style and Japanese customs."

Tony Tokai released a Japanese version of the C64 in early 1983, just before the MSX computers appeared. The machine had Japanese Katakana characters in place of many of the PETSCII characters and it booted up to black text on a pink background as opposed to the familiar blue colors. It sold for a price of 99,800 yen (approximately $400 US). Commodore users in Japan received support from a magazine called *Vic! The Magazine for Computer Age*. The computer met with initial success.

The first MSX computers appeared in autumn 1983. As promised, they were the VHS of computers. Although the computers were technologically inferior to the C64, and cost more, the promise of a universal standard won out. Japanese buyers knew software makers would rush to support MSX.

The C64 withered against the might of the MSX standard. There was no conceivable way for Commodore Japan to compete against the combined advertising might of Sony, JVC, Panasonic, Canon, and Yamaha. Through the course of the MSX lifetime, developers released approximately 70,000 different MSX software titles worldwide. Commodore Japan gave up and sold off their remaining C64 inventory at below cost to cut their losses.

In 1984, Japan attempted to enter the North American market with their MSX standard. Microsoft even organized a lavish launch party at the June 1984 CES in Chicago, but the MSX met with a lackluster reception. "The Commodore 64 just killed MSX," says Peddle. "Atari and Ti were fighting at the same time, so MSX just never got anywhere."

Although the C64 was unable to dominate the Japanese marketplace, it was responsible for keeping Japanese computers from dominating the rest of the world. In a December 1982 broadcast of the Computer Chronicles, Jack Tramiel told his hosts, "As far as the Japanese are concerned, I was able to keep those people out of the US market and almost the world market for the past seven years. ... What I'm trying to do is come out with the best product, the best quality, and the best price and by doing so, I keep those people out. Thanks to God, I've been successful so far."

Host Gary Kildall agreed, saying, "The C64 was definitely one of those devices that kept the Japanese machines out."

Battlefront Europe

The European market was a completely different scene from North America and Japan. The IBM PC had not yet reached Europe and the Commodore PET and CBM computers continued to dominate the business market. Furthermore, Europe had an embarrassment of computers the rest of the world had never heard about. Many of these exotic computers came from Britain.

One of the earliest 8-bit computers was the *BBC Micro*. The name BBC comes from the British Broadcasting Corporation, which to North Americans would be like buying a PBS (Public Broadcasting Service) computer. In the early eighties, the BBC ran a televised series on computers. The BBC wanted to demonstrate a computer with advanced features, so they created a specification and contracted a company to build and market the computer. *Acorn* took up the offer and built the BBC Micro, which users dubbed the Beeb. The Beeb was very popular as an educational computer with schools and homes, and Acorn sold more than a million Beeb's.

The Sinclair Spectrum ZX-81 (known to North Americans as the Timex Sinclair 1000) sold briskly until the introduction of the VIC-20 and C64. The ZX-81 was a basic personal computer with very few features, and did not have longevity due to the lack of sound and graphics capabilities.

In April 1982, Sinclair released an improved computer called the ZX Spectrum. It came with either 16 or 48 kilobytes of memory and a built in Basic programming language. The Spectrum, or Speccy as users affectionately called it, was an instant hit.

Compared to the C64, the Spectrum had few technical advantages. It had a poor calculator style keyboard (which Sinclair upgraded in 1984), beeper sound, and only eight colors.

When Commodore released the C64 in the UK, it almost immediately overtook the Spectrum. Commodore UK continued the strong tradition in advertising set by Kit Spencer and featured televised commercials emphasizing education.

One major difference in the UK marketing plan was the inclusion of a cassette unit with every C64. This meant the cassette unit became the standard for software distribution in the UK. Software makers distributed all their games and applications on cassette and ignored disks for a time. As a result, disk drives did not succeed as widely in the UK as elsewhere.

Commodore dominated Germany and the Scandinavian countries. According to Robert Russell, no one adored Commodore more than the Germans did, especially near the Braunschweig factory. "Those people still remember it with great pride," says Russell.

Harold Speyer, General Manager of Commodore Germany, continued his success. "He was the guy who drove the C64 in Europe into being such an important product," says Peddle. "Harald drove Commodore to the top of the pyramid with the work he did with sponsorships. He sponsored an around the world race and two or three things that put Commodore on everybody's lips all over Europe."

Russell agrees. "He made the whole business thing," he says. "We were bigger than IBM for a long time in Germany as far as product sales, volume, and reputation. We were fighting with HP for quality reputation."

Speyer was in high demand in Europe, but he remained loyal to Commodore. "IBM was killing themselves trying to get him in the early PC days to come over to their side because he was a smoking marketing guy," recalls Russell. "He wouldn't even go work for IBM in Germany because he considered it a step down from Commodore."

Russell occasionally visited the Braunschweig factory. "One time we flew over with my engineers in the corporate jet carrying all the prototypes for the Hanover show," recalls Russell. "They didn't have enough fuel to fly there so they diverted to Hanover."

Unknown to Russell, the townspeople of Braunschweig made plans for receiving the Commodore jet. "The jet had never been in Germany before," explains Russell. "They thought Jack was coming."

The diversion to Hanover saved Russell and his engineers some potential embarrassment. "The thing that killed us was the pilot came on and said, 'Oh, you just lucked out because they had the mayor, some dignitaries, and a band thinking Jack was going to be on the plane.'"

Jack wanted to exploit the eastern European market during the Cold War. "Jack flew around in the jet and went to Eastern Europe, and they flew an escort fighter alongside him when they were over Hungary or one of the eastern European countries," recalls Russell. "It was still the Iron Curtain."

Russell often felt nervous crossing borders into Eastern Europe. "We got held up in customs because we had all these strange boxes with computers that the customs guys didn't have a clue about," he recalls. "All the early computer prototypes, they wanted to know what the Hell they were. I couldn't speak their language and they had machine guns, so I didn't want to pick a fight."

During one border crossing into East Germany, Russell and two of his coworkers almost met with disaster. "It was extreme paranoia," says Russell. "We were a weird group because Frank [Hughes] was a big old Southern guy, I'm a Midwesterner, and we had an oriental girl Madeline Shaw who was in the back of the car. They were kind of wondering what the Hell we were in [East Germany] for."

Unfamiliar with border crossing procedures, Hughes inadvertently alarmed the border guards. "The guards were motioning to him to come over and show them his papers and Frank thought he was supposed to go in the booth," recalls Russell. "He's there trying to open the door and the guard freaked out. All of a sudden all these guns swing around at us. The guy almost machine gunned the bunch of us."

From the car, Russell recalls screaming, "Frank, don't open the door!" Although the tense situation resolved itself, Russell was not eager to return to Eastern Europe.

The MSX computer also gained popularity in many parts of Europe. *Philips*, based in the Netherlands, was working with electronics giant

Thomson on a European standard from 1982 to 1983. The project did not make sufficient progress and Philips instead decided to join the MSX standard. Philips became the largest supplier of MSX machines in Europe, but made little headway in the UK. "The thing that screwed [Nishi] up was Clive Sinclair did his junk machine which moved the price point down," says Peddle. However, the MSX computers succeeded in many smaller markets, including France, Spain, the Netherlands, Korea, and even the former Soviet Union.

Since the days of the PET, Commodore remained a fixture in Europe. Jack could always rely on strong sales of Commodore products, especially in Britain and Germany. Years later, Europe, Australia, and Canada were the only markets that kept Commodore afloat.

The Commodore Curse: Part V

At any other company, Kit Spencer would be highly valued after his successful launch of the VIC-20 and C64. At Commodore, however, it seemed like his record meant little. "If you were in marketing at Commodore, you had a tough job," says Winterble. "You had to deal directly with Jack, you took abuse, and you didn't last very long."

During the C64 advertising campaign, Spencer had his plan questioned by everyone, including Jack. According to Charles Winterble, Spencer never attained status in Jack's trusted inner circle. "Spencer was in and out," he says.

Robert Russell believes the success of the VIC-20 and C64 had much to do with Spencer's efforts. "Real early on, Kit Spencer was key," says Russell. "Kit was really an important person." Despite his success, Jack kept Spencer confined to sales and advertising.

When Spencer attempted to act as marketing director for Commodore, Jack refused to back him up and sided with his engineers. "Back at that time, prior to 1984, marketing as a term or concept didn't exist," says Leonard Tramiel. "You had sales and advertising and product development, and they were done by separate groups."

Leonard Tramiel believes his father was correct in allowing his engineers to lead product development. "In my opinion, they were better off for it," says Leonard. "I never understood why an advertising person should be involved in product development. They don't know how products work, they don't know what can be done and can't be done, so I don't know how they can design new products."

Despite being at odds with Spencer, Commodore engineers held a genuine fondness for the Englishman. "They liked Kit because he had a good personality," says Russell. "He'd get along with the new folks and he'd get along with the old folks."

Spencer likely would have remained vice president of sales and advertising had Commodore not lost their president, Jim Finke. Finke found it difficult working for Tramiel, who ruled with absolute authority. "The president made a decision at a press conference and announced it," says Yannes. "Jack called him later and said, 'What are you doing making decisions?'" It soon became clear to Finke that even the president of Commodore held little power with Jack around.

In June 1982, after serving for 18 months as Commodore President, Jim Finke resigned. After his departure, he made a cryptic statement about his cigar smoking CEO to the Philadelphia Enquirer. "[Jack] comes in like a lighted flare in a darkened room. He illuminates the scene with such brilliance that you're almost blinded. But his vapor trails take a lot of the oxygen out of the air. And when he leaves the room there's no more light."

In November 1982, Commodore received a new president, Robert H. Lane. Many within the company thought Irving Gould had hired Lane behind closed doors. Lane started his career as Product Manager for *Good Humor Ice Cream* in Canada and later became company president of Northern Telecom (now Nortel) in North America and Europe.

Many people thought Lane began making changes within the company too soon, without first studying the company and finding out its strengths. One of the first decisions Lane made was to replace Kit Spencer with another Commodore employee, Myr Jones. With Myr Jones now vice president of sales and marketing, Spencer lost most of his responsibilities.

"Once the C64 became successful, the whole company started blowing up as far as personnel," says Russell. "They started doing magazines and stuff like that. Kit was getting shuffled around."

Russell felt sympathy for Spencer. "The company got bigger and there got to be more politics," says Russell. "People like Kit and me were doers; we weren't politicians. We didn't want to go up the corporate ladder and fight politics; we wanted to do what we liked to do."

Despite his key contribution to two of Commodore's greatest successes, events pushed Kit to the sidelines. "That happens at lots of companies where the original people do things," explains Russell. "Sometimes they reach burnout, sometimes they need a cycle and somebody gets put in their place, and sometimes they just don't want to play the politics anymore. They get tired of, 'Why do I have to argue with these idiots who came in yesterday about how things should be done. Let them go fail and I'll go do something else.' It happens all the time and sometimes it's not worth the battle."

Spencer came dangerously close to leaving Commodore. He felt that if he stayed in the current Commodore environment it would begin to change him. He wanted to stay at Commodore, but not at the cost of corrupting his spirit. He had a family that depended on him.

Spencer was financially secure after building up Commodore stock since the seventies. "He made a fortune in Commodore stock and he said that's enough," says Leonard. "He said, 'I'm going to play tennis now.'"

Rather than allowing one of their best employees to depart Commodore, Jack and Irving offered Kit a minimal job in the Bahamas. According to Charles Winterble, the official company headquarters in the Bahamas was a front. "I used to go there once or twice a year, but there was nothing there but an office," says Winterble.

In his new position, Kit held little power. "Kit could get out of there and go hide in the Bahamas and enjoy the life there," says Russell. "He occasionally showed up for meetings and then he wrote the Commodore company newsletters that he published out of the Bahamas."[8]

Kit Spencer's marketing reign lasted 15 months. Before Spencer, Commodore advertising was deplorable. The loss of Spencer was one of the biggest blows to Commodore, who could have used his talents launching their other computers.

Though no one seemed to realize it at the time, Spencer's superior marketing had gained Commodore an unbreakable lead. He made a success out of the PET, even though it sold for double the price in the United Kingdom. The VIC-20, a modest piece of technology, was the first computer to break a million units. Now with the C64, Commodore would have years of successful sales ahead. He had the ability to turn almost any Commodore product into a marketing success. Unfortunately, the advertising reign was at an end.

The Pinnacle of Commodore

The Commodore 64 entered the computer market at an opportune moment. The recent video game crash resulted in the disappearance of the Atari 2600, Intellivision, ColecoVision, and other consoles, but video games remained extremely popular. With no heir apparent in game consoles, the Commodore 64 filled the void.

The Commodore 64's strongest year was 1984. It won awards as home computer of the year and dominated sales of every other system. The Commodore 64 was one of the most important systems for colonizing

---

[8] According to Russell, Kit Spencer published the company newsletter until the early 1990s.

homes with computers. Wired magazine frequently compares the C64 to the Ford Model T, as the first home computer for the masses.

The designer of the C64, Bob Yannes, witnessed the success of his creation from afar. "I felt good about it because it was something I designed and obviously a lot of people really liked," says Yannes. "Over the years, there's been a lot of people who say, 'That was my first computer and I really learned a lot.' I meet people that are presidents of high-tech companies and they say, 'The reason I got into computers was because I got a Commodore 64.' I find that very satisfying."

The great shakeout proved Jack's skill as a company leader. While other experienced companies folded around him, Jack thrived. Commodore went from a $50 million dollar a year company during the PET era to a billion dollar company in the space of four years. In 1978, Commodore sold 4000 PET computers. Now they sold 5000 Commodore 64 computers in a single day.

No one enjoyed the success more than Jack did. Despite his uneasiness with the press, he gave an interview to the *MacNeil-Lehrer Report*. Jack offered one of his favorite sayings, "Business is like Sex. You have to be involved." Jack subsequently watched the report in his office with over two dozen people. When they showed his quote, everyone burst out laughing except Jack, who was visibly embarrassed.

Irving Gould, the top shareholder in Commodore, should have been delighted with Jack's performance. His 17.9% holding in Commodore stock, which cost him $500,000 in 1966, was worth almost $200 million by 1983.

In December 1983, Commodore celebrated their 25th anniversary as a company. For the occasion, Jack, Irving Gould, and top Commodore executives returned to the birthplace of Commodore, in Toronto Canada. Commodore celebrated with style, hosting *The World of Commodore*, with over 38,000 attendees. Jack had left Canada in disgrace years earlier after a financial scandal and now he returned a hero. Government representatives welcomed Jack.

It should have been a momentous time but it was not. Somewhere between the release of the C64 and 1984, things had gone horribly wrong. January would be Jack's final month with Commodore.

CHAPTER

Ted

1983

In 1983, Commodore was set to release the high-end P & B computers. However, the C64 success gave Commodore no reason to release them. Jack abandoned the systems to the European market, where they fared poorly.

The same year, Commodore released a portable Commodore 64 computer, called the SX-64. It was the first *color* portable computer, which featured a small cathode ray tube and built in disk drives. The machine met with moderate success. Aside from this system, Commodore released no major products in 1983. It made more sense to keep pushing the wildly successful Commodore 64 for now.

This left Commodore with no serious business computers. The PET and CBM line of computers were in their twilight years and Jack needed a replacement. He needed a product to fight IBM.

Chasing IBM

In January 1983, Compaq pioneered a new industry by releasing an IBM PC clone. The move was legal because the IBM PC used widely available parts with no custom semiconductor chips. The BIOS code was the only copyrighted part of the IBM PC, so Compaq had their programmers legally reverse engineer the code.

Soon after, Commodore began producing IBM PC clones, but not in North America. Harald Speyer of Commodore Germany entered the PC clone market on his own initiative. "He built the factory in Braunschweig without asking Jack or Irving or anybody," says Peddle.

In early 1984, Speyer released the Commodore PC-10. The machine captured a large portion of the European PC market, largely due to competitive pricing over IBM PC computers. "He really did this brilliant job of marketing," says Peddle.

The fact that Commodore was producing PC compatible machines seemed like a major concession in the computer wars by Commodore. In truth, the move allowed Commodore to take profits away from IBM and further their own brand of computers.

Meanwhile, Commodore engineers began work on a PC competitor. To create a high-end business computer, Jack needed a 16-bit microprocessor. Due to apathy, MOS Technology had failed to produce a 16-bit processor to compete with Intel and Motorola. "At that point in time we were still butting heads with Motorola, so Motorola wasn't an option, which is what we really wanted to design with," explains Russell.

Instead of hiring engineers to develop a 16-bit processor, Jack looked to acquire the technology elsewhere. He found a potential replacement in the Z8000, a 16-bit microprocessor by *ZiLOG*. "The only reason I ever got involved in designing for the Z8000 project was because we were going to buy ZiLOG," reveals Russell.

Federico Faggin, one of the original engineers on the Intel 8080, founded ZiLOG in 1976. ZiLOG's first microprocessor was the 8-bit Z80, followed by the 16-bit Z8000. "We went and did a lot of meetings with ZiLOG," recalls Russell. "The idea was that Commodore was going to purchase them, so we started designing a business computer around the Z8000."

The Z8000 based computer would use UNIX, one of the most acclaimed operating systems ever and still widely used today. At the time, *AT&T* owned the most popular commercial version of UNIX, but Jack made a deal with a smaller company for a UNIX operating system, which they called *Coherent*. "There was some work done with a company in Chicago called Mark Williams," says Leonard Tramiel. "The *Mark Williams Company* had a knockoff of UNIX, and there was some work done on a computer with them. There was also some other stuff done looking at regular licensing from AT&T."

According to Russell, the deal to acquire ZiLOG fell through. "I remember being in meetings with the top management of ZiLOG while the Commodore guys were negotiating," he recalls. "I think it must have been an issue about price."

According to Byte magazine, Commodore acquired a license to manufacture the Z8000. "We were trying to leverage MOS Technology chips," says Russell. "The goal was to do vertical integration. They let me keep the project because they basically negotiated parts at cost for us to continue on with the technology." Commodore announced the UNIX machine in Byte magazine, calling it *Next Generation*. Unfortunately, the machine lingered in development hell for years.

Looking for an Encore

Commodore gained a dedicated following with the release of the C64. Users were eager to see what would come next. Most hoped for a more powerful C64 compatible system.

Jack understood the rules of business like no one else in the computer industry. His philosophy was simple: low prices sell more merchandise. Nevertheless, Jack still thought of computers as calculators. "He felt that the marketplace would go for lower cost, mixed function computers," says Al Charpentier. "Jack 'grew up' in the calculator market and he looked at the computer as just another big calculator. That's why the follow-on versions were somewhat crippled." Unfortunately, computer software and calculator functions were not the same thing. "That's what he didn't understand."

Jack's failure to realize the importance of backward compatibility and software was about to fail the company. Commodore 64 owners spent a small fortune building up a software collection, as well as creating programs and documents. The last thing users want to do is start their software library from scratch by buying an incompatible computer.

With Jack's most trusted engineers gone, Robert Russell and another ex-California engineer named Shiraz Shivji moved up in the ranks. The engineers met with Jack to decide their next product. "Me, Shiraz, and Jack were working on how to go forward with engineering at that point in time," says Russell. "I was in a lot of the meetings, strategizing, trying to come up with it."

The obvious follow-up would be a backward compatible C64 with more memory, a faster CPU, more sprites, more voices on the sound chip, and higher screen resolutions. At least, that was what the market wanted.

However, Leonard Tramiel disagrees with following the market. "If you ask the market what they want a product to be, they will never, ever, ever come up with something new because they don't know what's available," says Leonard.

Commodore's products always originated with the engineers. "Over the years, Commodore was unusually engineering driven," says engineer Dave Haynie. "The people who were around us were not doing all that much marketing. Those who we had the most direct contact with didn't have a whole lot of input."

Al Charpentier believes Commodore engineering possessed talent but they were missing a long-term strategy. "They had some designers, but it's the vision that they lost," he explains. "Where we wanted to go and where Jack wanted to go were not in line. It was just misunderstanding the market. In 1983, the PC comes out and the market changed drastically, and Commodore didn't recognize the opportunity."

Robert Russell acknowledges that he did not have visionary aspirations. "My whole goal as an engineer was always to accomplish a product, not to be the furthest out into the future," he says.

Curiously, Jack was not listening to the market or his engineers. He wanted a computer to compete with the Sinclair. The mere fact that a cheaper computer existed worried him. "I was involved with that project real early on because I helped specify it," recalls Russell. "We were supposedly doing an anti-Sinclair device, trying to beat out the color Sinclair. It wasn't to be compatible or the next generation of C64. It was supposed to be a less than $100 computer to compete against the Sinclair. It had to be made for $50."

According to Robert Russell, software compatibility with the C64 was not in Jack's mind. "They were thinking about it but Jack was still like, 'They'll just throw away the computers,'" he says.

Jack felt confident a cheap computer was right for the market. He ignored previous objections over the VIC-20 and witnessed incredible success. The VIC-20 had only 5 kilobytes of memory when Commodore had been selling 32-kilobyte PET computers. He had little reason to doubt he could make another success.

Russell had little enthusiasm for the Sinclair-killer, but he was more inclined to go along with his boss rather than resist. Both he and Shiraz Shivji were both young and mild mannered, so there was little chance they would stand up to Jack, even if his ideas were ill conceived. "It was a less than a hundred dollar computer. What did I care? At that time I was trying to get something more advanced together," says Russell.

Inconceivably, Commodore was now on track to build a computer with fewer features than their previous entries. To Commodore engineers, it seemed obvious the proposed computer had no place in the market.

The Animal

Commodore had a problem. How could MOS Technology go forward after their sound and video chip designers abruptly departed?

Robert Russell attempted to reawaken technology from the Chuck Peddle days. "We had really neat stuff that [Bill] Seiler did, like the high resolution board that he just kind of walked away from," says Russell. "That was one of the things he was working on in the TOI era. I was trying to get it resurrected as a project."

Jack attempted to change the structure of Commodore engineering so MOS Technology no longer designed the systems. "Before the new Commodore, everybody was working for MOS Technology in the chip group," says engineer Dave Haynie. "This was as things were changing into their modern form, where you had separate groups for software, systems, and chips. At that point, every director reported to the vice president of technology, Joe Krasucki."

Although Jack wanted a Sinclair-killer as Commodore's next major release, he was now so busy managing the company that he rarely visited his engineers. Instead, he relied on Shiraz Shivji to carry through with his instructions. "Shiraz was his mouthpiece back then," says Herd.

MOS Technology would develop a new video and sound chip for the computer. "We had a VIC chip, and this was the TED chip," says Haynie. "It did slightly better graphics, worse sprites, and the sound was pretty basic.

The TED project initially languished. "When I got there, the Plus/4 was called the TED, which meant Text Display," says Herd. "It had a rocky start in that there was no real ownership of the design. They had spent five months trying to emulate it using a VIC chip, which was stupid because the TED chip had nothing to do with the VIC chip."

The first engineer on the TED project did not last long when Jack realized he was making little progress. "He was too conservative for Commodore," says Herd. "All he ever tried to do was prove that it wouldn't work. You can't exist at Commodore trying to figure out why it won't work; you've got to figure out a way to make it work."

After the lead engineer left, TED passed to various engineers who were apathetic towards the project. "They weren't very aggressive engineers," recalls Herd. Eventually, a new engineer began work at Commodore who showed genuine enthusiasm for the TED. "Basically it got handed off to Herd's organization," says Russell.

Bil Herd was yet another Midwest Commodore engineer. "I was born in Ames, Iowa in 1959," he recalls. He was 23 years old when Commodore hired him.

Herd first became interested in electronics after his father brought home a gift. "My dad had bought me one of those 150 in 1 electronic kits," recalls Herd. "In the third or fourth grade, I was making electronic circuits. I taught myself as much as I could with that."

The inquisitive young Herd began taking apart other electronics devices in the house, such as his father's strobe light. Herd recalls, "He handed me four dollars and I said, 'No, no, I don't need your money.' He said,

'Son, you should be paid for your talent.' I thought, 'Maybe this is something that I could do.'"

The rock group Emerson, Lake, and Palmer influenced Herd in his teen years. "Listening to [Keith Emerson's] music gave me the drive to design a synthesizer to replicate what I was hearing him play," says Herd.

With encouragement and financial support from his father, the longhaired teenager began building his own synthesizer. "He subsidized the build a few bucks at a time," recalls Herd.

Herd's education came to a premature end when his high school denied him entry into an electronics class. "I was from a small town in Indiana and I was having problems staying focused in school," he recalls. "When I wanted the TV repair class, they wouldn't give it to me. They felt I wasn't academically inclined enough. So I dropped out. I'm a high school dropout."

Herd also left home, determined to support himself with his electronics knowledge. "I was one of those people who went off to see if I could make life harder on myself. I don't know of any better way to describe it," he says.

The teenager improved his knowledge of electronics on the streets. "I raised myself literally," he says. "At the age of 16 or 17, I had my TV repair license and was fixing electronics for my dinner, literally. I would hang out in a park and fix tape players for enough money to get myself something to eat. You learn to be good when your dinner depends on it."

Herd followed the path of Chuck Peddle and Jack Tramiel before him by enlisting in the armed forces. "One day I actually walked in and signed up for the National Guard," he recalls. Herd subsequently had his trademark mane shaved off. "I went through basic training and got trained as a teletype repairman at the age of seventeen."

During this time, Herd's father remained supportive. "He didn't hassle me when I took off from school to work on it, nor when I dropped out, nor when I joined the National Guard in lieu of high school," says Herd.

After six months of basic training, Herd returned home and received a new offer from his high school. "When I got back they said, 'Well, we can get you in that electronics class now if you want.' So I went back and ended up dropping out again," says Herd. "After you've been in the army it's hard to put up with the rules of high school. With all that said, they did send my diploma home three years later with my sister."

Herd soon found other ways to combine his love of music with electronics by becoming a roadie. "After I had gotten back from basic training, I did lights for a local rock group in Indiana called *Primo*," he recalls. "They were well known throughout central Indiana. Back when you could not buy light controllers, I had built my own. I made my own

PCB boards and I had an organ keyboard where each key was a different string of lights. The ones on the end were flash pods, so you had to be careful with those. That was a cool time."

Herd received his first technical position helping to manufacture digital weight scales. "I had taken a job at *Pennsylvania Scale Company* out in Leola," he recalls. "We made digital scales, and the guy who had first designed that had been a pioneer in his own right. We used a chip called the 6530 ... made by MOS Technologies. We were one of the first customers for it."

Herd worked with two future Commodore engineers at Pennsylvania Scale: Hedley Davis, a programmer and hardware designer, and Terry Fischer, who created printed circuit board layouts.

Herd made a rapid ascent within the company based on his engineering prowess. "I had been working on the factory floor as a technician then I worked my way up repairing them," he recalls. "We had some problems with the circuits out in production. Rather than just complain about it, I bought data books from Radio Shack and learned enough that I wrote a paper on what was wrong."

The paper earned Herd recognition in the company and he soon moved to design engineering. "I actually got sucked into engineering as an associate design engineer, so that's how I got into the biz of put up or shut up," he explains. "Then I worked my way into full engineer. We had a scale with a seven-segment LED display that was just [incredible] in the late seventies, early eighties. I was the guy in charge of trying to bring green LED technology to Penn. Scale."

Herd also had an opportunity to program. "At Pennsylvania Scale, we did both hardware and software," explains Herd. The digital scales relied on a small amount of code, which the engineers developed on a popular computer. "They had done the first one on a KIM-1," he says.

On their next project, Pennsylvania Scale acquired an AIM-65 development system by Rockwell. "It's like a big KIM-1 with almost the same kind of circuitry except it had a dumb terminal, so you could actually type your commands in," explains Herd. "You would hit compile and it would compile your 2K of code in a couple of hours, and it was great!"

The AIM-65 captivated Herd and he began spending more time with it. "I started dragging it home at night and bringing it back every morning," he recalls. "They weren't small." The late-night sessions made Herd an expert in 6502 machine code.

Bil Herd now held much of the necessary knowledge to develop his own computer systems. In many ways, Herd was an engineering version of Jack Tramiel. He was unschooled in his field but in some ways more impressive than his college-educated contemporaries. "I think there is probably a little Jack Tramiel in me these days," reflects Herd.

He also continued his National Guard duties during his early career. With his unruly hair and even more unruly behavior, he received a nickname. "My handle when I was in a tank unit in the National Guard was Animal," recalls Herd. "I had it painted on my CVC helmet. It had started as a derogatory reference that I took as a compliment."

In March 1983, Herd's position at Pennsylvania Scale grew tenuous. "I had a falling out with my boss," he says. "[Hedley Davis] was reading the paper and he said, 'Hey, do you want to go get a job interview?' I said, 'Where?' He said, 'Commodore.'"

After the release of the C64, Robert Russell and engineering manager Frank Hughes were desperate to find new engineers. "They would go to these head hunters, and the head hunters would put eight or ten people in front of them every night," says Herd. "They would go up and down Highway 202 combing these different places looking for talent. We used to call it Silicon Valley East."

Herd was one of many candidates interviewing for a job. "That night, Bob Russell and Frank Hughes were there," recalls Herd. Herd interviewed with Frank Hughes first. With a lack of formal education, it was easy for Hughes to dismiss Herd as a wannabe engineer.

Herd feels a personality clash made his first interview fail. "Frank didn't like to feel like he wasn't the most important person in the room," says Herd. "I ended up talking about how this thing called a magneto-optical drive was on the horizon and how exciting it was. He was like, 'Yeah, uh-huh. Okay, I'm done.' I was like, 'Crap, I blew it!' I was so excited and I wondered, 'Why couldn't I talk to this guy?' I thought he would be a good electronics guy."

Herd sensed his interview went poorly, but he had one more chance. "All you needed was one of the two guys to invite you in," he explains. "I was done with Frank Hughes and it was a no go. I interviewed with Bob Russell next and he was just beat-up from interviewing people."

Russell discussed a project at Commodore and mentioned several op-codes from the 6502 chip. Each time he mentioned one, Herd parroted the hexadecimal instruction. "I was repeating the machine code to the instructions he was saying, under my breath," says Herd. "Bob was a pretty observant guy and he caught on to it, and the interview was over." It was obvious Herd knew assembly cold. This was enough to persuade Russell to set up another interview.

Herd was now on his way to visit MOS Technology. "They made an appointment for me to go to King of Prussia and actually interview at

Commodore," explains Herd. "They brought me into Commodore and had me interview with Shiraz Shivji."

Herd made a poor first impression. "I jumped into Shiraz's chair because he had his desk facing the opposite way that I was used to," he says. "He walks in and says, 'Excuse me, you are in my chair.' He was holding it against me! I thought, 'Oh no! I've blown it again.'"

Herd also appeared unprepared. "Shiraz says, 'Do you have a resume?' and I said, 'No, I didn't bring one in with me.' They hadn't told me when I was coming in, so I didn't bring resumes," explains Herd. "The way Bob [Russell] was so nonchalant about it, he said come in to talk to me or something, and he already had my resume. Frank came to my rescue and brings in a resume from a couple of nights before."

Herd began talking with the engineers about a personal electronics project. "I showed my ingenuity and love of electronics, and that's what finally got across to them, and that's what got me hired," says Herd. He was now a Commodore employee.

Although Herd was among people with engineering degrees, he did not feel like any less of an engineer. "I had never been to college, but by the age of 22 I actually had about four years of experience as an engineer, which felt like a lot back then," says Herd.

Shivji hired Herd as a mere technician to aid the design engineers. "I started at the MOS building in King of Prussia where the walls were this bright blue color and there were three of us to a room," recalls Herd. "When I got there, there were literally only the holdovers like Yashi Terakura and Bob Russell and some of those guys from the California Commodore days."

Herd got along great with Terakura and vowed to learn Japanese. "Yash's real name was Yasaharu but I was the only Gaijin that could pronounce it correctly," says Herd. "The Japanese had a hard enough time with it, according to Yash."

Herd initially approved of the casual atmosphere of Commodore, where employees were addicted to C64 games. "My first day I noticed people playing games in their offices as you walked by and no-one saying anything," recalls Herd. "I liked the thought that you would be judged on your work output and not the appearance of work. Later, I found out that a good number of the people I saw playing games didn't really do anything useful. So much for the real version of utopia."

On his first day working at Commodore, Herd sat in a room with an engineer named Benny Pruden, the ROM programmer for the Pet 4040 drive. "When I got there, they didn't know what to have me do, so they were going to have me do code for one of the disk drives," recalls Herd.

Shivji had decided on a software role for Herd because of his knowledge of assembly code. It was a disappointing appointment for someone who loved hardware his whole life. Herd had a momentary reprieve when Pruden departed on a business trip. "The guy who was supposed to show me the boring software wasn't there that week," says Herd. Instead, Pruden left him with a stack of books to read.

With his lead engineer gone, Herd decided to wander around MOS Technology. He stumbled on the lab where the 6502 originated. As Bil looked around the empty room, he felt saddened. "I had just missed them. The cigars were still burning in the ash trays, the seats were still warm, but there was no one around anymore," he says.

On the wall, Herd spotted a curious photograph. "There had been a picture of the PET design team hanging up and they would black out the image of everyone that was no longer with Commodore," recalls Herd. "In the end, there was only Yash Terakura and Michael [Angelina] left amongst spooky black outlines."

Eventually, Herd wandered into the systems lab where engineers were busy with Jack's latest low-cost project. "I asked, 'What's this?' They said, 'This is the TED.' I'm like, 'Cool! Are you doing bus sharing?' I just did something at home like that. I wire wrapped my own 6502 board with bus sharing. I think eyebrows went up as I'm peering into it and poring over the schematic. That's how I got picked to be the project leader for it."

"Bil was originally hired as a super-tech and he just fell into this job of being the chief systems guy at Commodore," marvels Dave Haynie.

Herd was no longer in software engineering. "The first week I came off of doing code for the disk drive to being in charge of the TED line," says Herd. When Benny Pruden arrived from his business trip, he must have been shocked to find his new hire in charge systems engineering. "I took the hardware path, thank God, because that's my favorite part."

Herd now had the responsibility of delivering Commodore's next consumer product. With no formal education and lots of bravado, Herd now held one of the prime jobs at Commodore. It was a rapid ascent for a new engineer.

The Making of TED

The first thing Herd noticed on the TED was the lack of a circuit to reset the computer. To make the reset work properly, Herd needed one more chip. "The TED had one stipulation; they said you need to do it in nine chips," recalls Herd. "Nobody wanted to go tell Jack that they needed to add a chip. Well, I didn't care. I said, 'You almost did it in nine, we need ten.'"

Shivji reluctantly passed the news to his boss. "Somebody went to Jack saying, 'We added one last chip to make the reset work right,' and I'm told he just said, 'Fine.' In other words, he didn't care," explains Herd. "He got them to do what he wanted them to do, which was make it in nine chips, not 28 or 30 or some number like that."

Robert Russell was curious if his new hire had the ability to design a complete system. "Honestly, I wasn't too sure about Herd to begin with, but he knew his stuff," recalls Russell. "Once he came in and started working, geeze! He's a guy that gives 200% and then has a good time in between."

Herd now reported to engineering manager Joe Krasucki, who gained a callous reputation. "He came in before we moved and he was stuck in my office, smoking a frigging cigar the first day he was there, which I never liked," says Russell. "He was an asshole manager who may be able to do some hardware design."

Krasucki held a powerful position within Commodore, managing new products. "Joe Krasucki was the head of the systems group there," explains Haynie.

Bil Herd formed an agreeable working relationship with Krasucki. "I was the one guy who got along with him," says Herd. "When he came in, everybody hated him. I heard him coming down the hall, asking people what they were working on and they would be like, 'Why are you asking that? What do you need that for?' Well, I had all morning to hear what he was after, so by the time he walked into my office, I had it all ready to go. That helped me advance because I didn't fight him."

Most managers at Commodore had a difficult time retaining their jobs with Tramiel around, but Krasucki held on. "If he didn't have people like Bil Herd and Greg Berlin to slug it out and make it work, he never would have got anywhere," says Russell.

"I was his cash cow," adds Herd.

Predictably, the rapid ascent of Herd to lead engineer perturbed other engineers who had been with Commodore longer. "There was some resentment from some other people," says Russell. "Some people said, 'Oh, he's just a favorite of Joe Krasucki.'" However, Herd was quick to win over these detractors with his disarming sense or humor and fierce work ethic.

Herd did not back away from a conflict, even with the upper echelons of Commodore management. Sometimes the conflicts turned physical. "[Krasucki] worked for Lloyd Taylor, who was the vice president under Jack," says Herd. "Lloyd Taylor was this big strapping guy, kind of obnoxious and rude. His name had been Red but he had grey hair by then. Everybody was afraid of him."

'Red' Taylor was one of Tramiel's inner-circle cronies. "When he wanted his secretary, he had this old car horn and he would reach down and honk the rubber ball to the horn to call her," recalls Herd. "She'd roll her eyes and walk in there."

The chalkboard walls at the West Chester facility barely stood a chance when Herd was around. One day, the engineers heard a series of loud thumps. "Three heads stuck around the corner into the hallway to see what was going on, and me and [Lloyd Taylor] were literally wrestling in the hall," says Herd. "I've got hold of his leg by the knee and I'm slamming him into the wall. So much for being afraid of the vice president."

To the Z8000 engineers, it looked like an Alpha-male Klingon ritual. "He was kind of one of those brutish guys, so at some point our personal zones crossed each other and we got into a wrestling match," explains Herd. "He pushed and I pushed back. I wasn't afraid of him."

The altercation had no ill effects on Herd's career. "We were laughing while we were doing it," he recalls. "After that, we got along great because I think he respected somebody who stood up to him a little bit."

Herd recruited two of his former coworkers, Hedley Davis and Terry Fischer. "They came after I did, from Pennsylvania Scale Company," recalls Herd. "Hedley Davis, who now works at Xbox, was a well known programmer and designer. He came out of school with an electronics engineering degree." Terry Fischer, a technician, created printed circuit board designs.

Herd later brought in a young engineer named Dave Haynie. "In 1983, I was brought in to work on what we called the TED project," recalls Haynie. "Bil Herd was the chief engineer on that project and he was looking for somebody who could work under him who knew things he didn't know."

Haynie met Herd just before his interview while waiting in the lobby. "I met him for the interview before I knew he was one of the guys I was going to be talking to," says Haynie. "I liked him right away."

Herd was impressed with Haynie's skills and knew they would help augment his own. "Haynie was definitely the kid of the group," says Herd. "The closest I found [to a systems engineer] was Dave Haynie, who had two math degrees from Carnegie-Mellon."

Herd believes Universities at the time were capable of teaching theory, but often overlooked practical aspects of hardware design. "What they weren't teaching in school was how to tell how hot your part would run and the real life situation of it," says Herd. Surrounded by engineers grounded in theory, Herd was a powerful force, respected because he knew practical electronics like no one else. Day by day, Herd proved his value to the team.

Herd's unending source of energy amazed his engineers. "He was a wild-man back then," says Haynie. "He would be working for days straight and hoped everybody else would be along for the ride too. It was one of those things where you're young, you're single, you've got no kids, and you would party as hard as you worked. He basically did a little bit more than everybody else and eventually burnt out."

Unlike many engineers, Herd was a genuine extrovert who spent as much time interacting with the people he worked with as with electronics. "Herd got along with people," says Russell. "He fit the loose Commodore culture but he worked his butt off if he wasn't drunk or high on something."

At the heart of the TED computer was a processor with a new name, the 7501 8-bit microprocessor. The 7501 contained the 6502 core, but it used the new HMOS design (High-speed NMOS). The processor would now run at 1.76 megahertz.

With Al Charpentier and Bob Yannes no longer at MOS, the title of resident semiconductor genius fell to Dave DiOrio. "DiOrio was great. He was my counterpart in the chip designers as far as nailing this stuff," says Herd. "On the Plus/4, I knew I was working in a cool place."

DiOrio's goal was to reduce the number of chips inside the TED. He set out to design the TED chip as a low-cost graphics and sound chip similar to the original VIC-I chip, but with higher resolutions and more colors. This was one of the last chips to follow in the grand tradition of friendly three-letter names.

Originally, the MOS Technology designer attempted to create a prototype of the TED chip using a VIC-II chip. "They dicked with a wire-wrap board based upon the VIC chip which didn't relate to the TED design at all," recalls Herd. "I threw the wire-wrap away without ever turning it on."

Most observers recognize the TED chip as an excellent chip for the time and one of the best manufactured by Commodore. The TED could display 128 colors; 16 colors in eight different shades. In effect, TED eliminated the need for five separate chips. Perhaps the only complaint was the lack of sprite capabilities and inferior sound.

As with any new semiconductor chip, Herd had to deal with problems in the early revisions. "The TED chip had to go through many revs before it was usable, mostly due to the lack of checking tools," recalls Herd. "I remember the day we got TED up with a processor. The system would come up and then puke on the screen. I sat and stared at this thing for a couple of hours. There really wasn't a lot of tools at my disposal so I had to think about what, if anything, was fixable in the mess."

Terry Ryan, who saw Herd staring at the screen, later said, "He just stared at it. It was scary."

Herd was still thinking about the problem as he drove home. "Later that night, with my mind still on work, I drove my [Datsun] 280Z between a guy wire and the telephone pole in order to miss a car," recalls Herd. "The whole time I was still thinking about work. I just backed up and kept driving."

The engineers gathered at Terry Ryan's house for a casual get together. "That night was a bad beer and bad movie party at Ryan's featuring *Schmitz* beer, *Plan Nine from Outer Space*, and *Attack of the Killer Tomatoes*," says Herd. "Unfortunately, I took out my frustration by challenging a couple of people to keep up drinking with me."

Herd, a self-described alcoholic, had an unfair advantage over the other engineers. "At one point, a junior programmer named Mike Isgar went running for the back yard to throw up, only he didn't get the screen door open before going through it," says Herd. "I heard a story about my first 'programmer kill' that night and went with that as a theme of the differences between men and programmers."

After his first programmer kill, the engineers began to look at Herd as a carnivore thinning out the pack of programmers. Terry Ryan told Herd, "Try not to kill more than you can eat."

Herd functioned much like Chuck Peddle, who found parties to be the best atmosphere for coming up with creative ideas. "That night I figured out what the problem had to be," explains Herd. "I walked in the next morning, moved the wire, and had it working in five minutes. Alcohol and problem solving seemed to go hand in hand for me. That's the problem with being an alcoholic."

Terry Ryan developed most of the ROM software for the TED computer. A friendly rivalry developed between the software and hardware engineers. "Terry Ryan was the programmer who wrote Basic version six," recalls Herd, who found the programmer standoffish at first. "He was like, 'Leave me alone, I'm working.'"

Herd later grew to appreciate the programmer. "This guy is so cynical it cuts like a blade," says Herd. "Most of the time you don't even know if you're being insulted."

Ryan employed a creative system to help navigate the confusing halls of MOS Technology. "There were all these blue rooms and blue hallways all shoved together," recalls Herd. "He put a picture of a bunny rabbit outside his door so he could find his office."

The Commodore engineers employed sophomoric pranks to dispel the tension. "I took the picture of the bunny rabbit off his door and made about 200 photocopies," says Herd. "I spent a good couple of hours hiding these in everything he owned. I had them in his Kleenex box halfway down. I had them in his shoe under the tongue. Two years later, we're talking and he pulls a file, and there's a bunny rabbit."

Herd decided to use the new 16-kilobyte DRAM chips that just appeared on the market. MOS Technology bought the process from a company called *Micron* but manufactured the chips themselves. "I remember they couldn't get this one spec down, and when they called Micron about it and they were like, 'Yeah, we couldn't either.' So they ended up buying a bad DRAM process," says Herd.

Tramiel sued. "We had sued Micron and a lot of other companies," says Herd. "Part of it was because Micron made them wrong and part of it was because we didn't use them right. That's what happens when you have chip designers doing hardware design. But Jack Tramiel got the lawsuit to stick. It was pretty cool."

Ira Velinsky, the engineer responsible for the P & B series cases, created the TED case. Tramiel called him his Jewish-Japanese engineer. "He worked out of Tokyo for Sam [Tramiel]," says Herd. "He looks every bit Jewish, he speaks enough Japanese to get in lots of trouble, and he was a real character. I'd go over there and he'd get me in trouble. You had to learn not to trust what he told you the Japanese meant at first."

The TED computer received a proprietary joystick port, despite the popularity of the standard D-Shell connector by Atari. "The reason given to us by Ira Velinsky was that it was the only place it would fit," says Herd. "Sure enough, if you look at the case you would not have room for two of the D-shell connectors."

The small TED case was reminiscent of the computer it sought to overthrow. "The original case was this tiny sloping little Sinclair case," explains Herd.

Velinsky presented a new joystick for the TED. "Ira Velinsky had designed another joystick and brought it in," says Herd. "This was from a soft-tool, so it was a $40,000 [prototype] joystick. It had a handgrip which was pretty cool but it came down to a real skinny 3/16 of an inch diameter before it went into the base of the joystick."

Herd disagreed with the design. "Everybody is saying, 'This looks like it will break.' And Ira is saying, 'No no, that will never break. It's been *designed*.' That was the word he was using."

"Everybody is saying, 'Ira, this is going to break. Kid's are rough. It's got to last a year.' He said, 'No, no, It'll never break. I guarantee it.'"

Velinsky held his ground, so Herd took the argument to a new level. "Then we got onto something else and I've got the joystick in my hands," recalls Herd. "And you heard, 'Snap!' You can see me pushing this broken joystick back into the middle of the table. It's true, I had to bend it a little harder than I thought I would but the point was if I could break it sitting there, it was going to get broken a lot. So I broke a $40,000 soft-tool prototype to prove a point."

As summer approached, progress on the TED slowed down. "TED slumbered for many months until the summer before the CES show," says Herd. Commodore was about to undergo a drastic reorganization.

Mega-Headquarters

Prior to the departure of Charles Winterble and his team, Jack decided he wanted to organize the company into one centralized location on the East Coast. "We were just getting ready to move down to the new facility," says Winterble.

Jack had his reasons for the move. "He just recognized that it was a lot less expensive to get people in Pennsylvania than it was in California," says Al Charpentier. "I think he also was thinking that he was going to use the big facility for manufacturing."

The new premises relieved the cramped conditions in the MOS Technology building. "We were at the limits of our building," says Russell. "We had two years where we were on top of each other after the VIC-20. There was no more space for anybody. When the C64 became real popular, all they did was put more people in the same office space. West Chester was really the thing that relieved the pressure."

Up until 1983, CBM had been a diffuse collection of operations dispersed across California, Pennsylvania, and even Arizona. Now Jack moved his company into a massive facility in West Chester, Pennsylvania at 1200 Wilson Drive. "Jack's idea was to consolidate everything in the West Chester facility," says Winterble.

The facility had a history of manufacturing. "It was an old Zenith TV tube manufacturing facility," says Charpentier. "That was an expensive building. Commodore went in and gutted it and renovated it."

According to Russell, a greeting card company resided in the building after Zenith. "I went there when it was clear full of frigging greeting cards because it was a greeting card manufacturing plant," he says.

In the summer of 1983, Commodore employees moved into the massive building. "It was a two story building and 585,000 square feet," says Russell. "It was mostly production. In the front of the building they put engineering, corporate, software, and those things."

Commodore used most of the building for manufacturing and warehousing. "It was assembly line and it had huge amounts of storage space," says Haynie. "They did all of the final assembly for the America's there."

"That building was so huge compared to what we were used to," says Russell. "We opened up some warehouse doors and there was a whole atmosphere environment and rain clouds in some of those huge rooms."

The move to West Chester was hectic, especially with C64 production at a peak. "We had just a lot of irons in the fire at that point in time," says Russell.

The move also disrupted system designers like Bil Herd. "In the summer to late fall I remember trying to get prototypes built while we were moving," says Herd.

Compared to the Commodore of old, the new Commodore was about to go large. "Teams were real small up until the C64 started expanding things," says Russell. "There weren't that many engineers. I mean, Bob Yannes and Al Charpentier were the main chip engineers."

Russell and Shivji continued their hiring spree to restock the Commodore talent pool. "Shiraz and I just interviewed everybody in creation," says Russell. "From 1982 until 1985, I hired about 80 people. We had a full boat at West Chester. We were always trying to get personnel but it was hard to find anybody who knew anything."

Jack put Russell in charge of moving mainframe computers. "I was in charge of moving the VAX computers out of the MOS facility to the [West Chester facility]," says Russell. "I guess I was the highest low-guy on the totem pole."

Dave Haynie, fresh out of University, desperately wanted to use UNIX. "We had one UNIX machine, which was pretty much there because a lot of the programmers and other people demanded a UNIX machine," says Haynie. "So we were running DEC Unix on a small VAX 11750. That had all the email and everything."

The engineers were stuck using PET machines to compile code for the system ROM's. "I had had it with that stupid PET they had given me to work on," says Herd. "I wasn't in the mood for the problems it was throwing. It wanted to see two different floppies in the same drive at the same time if I recall. I grabbed it off my desk and stepped into the hall with it over my head shouting profanities. I said, 'Take it or I am throwing it.' I didn't really want to throw it but I would have. Someone who hadn't rated a PET of their own rather quickly liberated me of the load."

Haynie convinced Herd to go for VAX access. "I had used UNIX systems in college and at Bell Labs when I did two summers there," says Haynie. "So I knew what it was and said, 'Yes, we must have this.'"

Herd set his sights on the VAX system. "I went and asked for a hookup to the VAX," recalls Herd. "They said, 'Oh gee, no terminals.' It was a lie, since they bought eight terminals. I said, 'No problem, I have several at home.'"

When a barrier existed, Herd either smashed through it or went around it. "It was all attitude," says Herd. "Everybody that worked there, it was just, 'Get the fuck out of my way, we're coming through.'"

"They were like, 'Well, I guess you can get on it but you have to hook it up yourself.' They were acting like I would never know how to do that. An hour later I'm in there and they were asking, 'What are you doing?' I said, 'That's the last of the wiring.' We had already run the wires and everything. I brought a terminal in from home and we were up!"

"I was the eighth person on the first VAX and the only person not in the chip design group," says Herd. "Dave Haynie and I put it to good use, though he had to sit in my office originally to use the terminal."

Herd's aggressive attitude did not make him popular with some. "We had people who were in charge of our VAX system who weren't there to serve us," says Herd. "They were just there to keep their jobs."

Herd often clashed with the VAX administrator. "He called his cubicle the Operations Center when he answered the phone," laughs Herd. "The manager in charge of users working on the VAX was into telling me what I couldn't do and I replied I could be on the highest level of the system in a few minutes if I needed to. He made that bet."

It was unwise to bet against the cocky young engineer. Herd used a simple method to spy on the manager's keyboard commands. "I took out my screwdriver and moved the wire from my terminal to his, back at the wiring block, and simply watched him type his password to logon," recalls Herd. "It actually took less than five minutes as he got [curious] and wanted to see what I might be trying on the system level."

Breaking into the VAX system became something of a sport to the engineers. "Late one Sunday night, I stick my head into the printer room outside the VAX room and see the door to the computer/VAX room lying on the floor," recalls Herd. "Peering into the gloom I was met with the sight of Hedley Davis sitting at a terminal, literally illuminated by the lights from the tape backup machine. The machine is whirring and Hedley was looking somewhat excited at the aspect of [loading] the tape of VAX games that ships with VAX. I remember seeing the screwdriver laying there which was the only tool he had used to overcome our multi-thousand dollar card pass door lock system management had installed to make sure we couldn't reboot any computers late at night if we needed them to do our work."

The new West Chester facility created a small community. It even contained a small electronics store to sell Commodore products to employees at discount rates. "They would sometimes sell liquidation things as well as just the normal everyday Commodore stuff," says Haynie. "You could buy Commodore calculators there, which was pretty much the only place in North America that still sold them. Anything that was being discontinued or liquidated would show up at the Commodore Employee Store."

During the move, Jack also shut down the production group of 35 people, which had fumbled the C64 production schedule. He terminated most of the employees in the group, while he reassigned others within the company. The move shocked employees.

How They Built the Bomb

After the interruptions and distractions of moving to a new location, the TED project fell behind schedule. With the January 1984 CES approaching, the engineers had all the motivation they needed to complete the project. "In late summer we kicked it into gear," recalls Herd. "I don't think we knew how to make good use of our time when we weren't in imminent peril of CES." Unfortunately, the project was about to get a lot more complicated.

Dave Haynie feels Herd and his team accomplished the goal Jack set for the TED computer. "There were a lot of good ideas in everything that was done there, both the hardware and the software," says Haynie.

The move to West Chester brought the engineering group into closer contact with marketing and software people, such as Sig Hartmann and Michael Tomczyk. Soon, marketing and others in the company began lobbying for changes to the TED computer.

Leonard Tramiel felt marketing should have stayed away from computer design. "They don't know what can be done," he says. "If they knew, they would be product developers. As soon as you have product design being done by people who don't know how to design products, you can't progress."

Hartmann and Tomczyk proposed adding permanent applications to the computer in ROM memory. They wanted to see built in word processing, spreadsheet, database, and graphing software, much like the popular Lotus 1-2-3 suite. They renamed the computer the 264, and later Plus/4. "The Plus/4 got horribly mutilated by the people in marketing of all places," recalls Herd.

The idea of built in software was ill conceived. It defeated the very purpose of a computer, which is to run an unlimited variety of programs. Users would be unable to update the built in software, which would quickly become outdated as other software programs continued evolving.

Surprisingly, Jack backed his marketing people. Herd was at odds with his employer, but he had little recourse. "I respected his decision-making capacity, if not his decisions every time," he recalls.

With support from Jack, marketing began requesting even more features. "Sometime during the summer of 1983, it started growing features," explains Haynie. "By the time I came along, all these features were set and it was just a matter of getting them to work."

Haynie thought it was a mistake to allow others to step in and change the course of the TED computer. "You see that from time to time in management," he says. "Whether it was due to ego or something else, these things happen."

The relatively new engineers felt they were obliged to listen to marketing managers rather than chart their own course with the computer. "As it was happening, I was still kind of new at this," says Haynie. "It wasn't necessarily Commodore engineering's job to decide what kind of model should be made."

Robert Russell felt it was pointless to attempt to improve on the minimalist system by adding features. "None of the engineers liked it because we all knew that fundamentally it was meant to be $50 computer that we would sell for a hundred bucks," he says. "For them to add software and call it a Plus/4 was wrong."

However, Commodore would still release the original Sinclair-killer TED computer, now called the C116. "The 116 was the original design meant to compete with the Sinclair," says Herd.

Both the C116 and the 264 would receive a calculator style keyboard, similar to the original PET 2001. "The reason it had the crappy keyboard was because that was what a Sinclair had," explains Russell. Jack knew from experience that a substandard keyboard could kill a new product, yet he went along with the decision anyway.

Programmer Terry Ryan, who developed the Basic software for the TED series, received interference from his manager. "When he wrote structured Basic, which went into the Plus/4, he got in trouble for doing it," recalls Herd. "He was told, 'Do not put LOOP-WHILE and these instructions in there,' and he got a bad review for making great code. The good news was his boss got fired weeks later."

Ryan also included powerful new commands, making it easier for users to program graphics and sounds. It was an improvement over the POKE commands of the VIC-20 and C64.

Perhaps the greatest potential for the TED computers was the inclusion of a graphical operating system. John Feagans, who previously created the Magic Desk cartridge for the C64, was still passionate about graphical user interfaces. Feagans joined the project to develop Magic Desk II. Press releases claim the "menu system uses icons, or picture-symbols, rather than words to convey the different functions (similar to Apple's more complex business-oriented Lisa)."[1]

As CES approached, marketing decided to request even more features. "TED had been mutilated, decimated, and defecated upon," recalls Herd. "Management decided to kick the body one last time."

Commodore had managed to acquire two of the best minds in speech technology at the time, the makers of the incredible *Speak & Spell* educational tool. "We hired the guys who made the Ti Speak & Spell, Tom Brightman and Richard Wiggins," recalls Herd. "Rich has a PhD and Tom is just extremely bright. Back when the Ti Speak & Spell came out, there was nothing like that! My God, they made a movie about it."

The two pioneers worked out of a Commodore research office in Texas. Commodore gave them a mandate to create a speech cartridge for the C64 called *Magic Voice* and built in speech capability for yet another TED model they would call the 364. "That was basically just a 264 with a numeric keypad and a Magic Voice speech synthesis built in," says Haynie.

Adding Magic Voice to the TED was not difficult. "The software was already done for it, because it had been the Magic Voice add-on, or as we always called it, Tragic Voice," says Haynie, in reference to the monotone voice, which sounded like a depressed robot.

The software was somewhat limited. "It was a fixed vocabulary of about 260 words and that was pretty much it," says Haynie. "It didn't have a phonetic language so it was real hard to get it to say the stuff you wanted to."

Herd loved the technology. "It was literally the first talking computer I knew of, and I didn't care how it talked," he says. "It said 'gerple' instead of purple."

The Magic Voice software amused the engineers during their daily routine. "I was working on that one day and somebody brought in a thing called *S.A.M.* which was a thing for the Commodore 64 that had speech," recalls Haynie. "You could construct an amazing array of words. We were trying to say dirty things about each other and I was extremely

---

[1] Compute!'s Gazette magazine, "Commodore's New Computer Family" (April 1984), p. 20.

limited with the 364 vocabulary. I was just totally destroyed by S.A.M. when we were having a laugh one day."

After months of development, the 264 was obviously evolving beyond the cheap Timex-Sinclair killer. It stood little chance in the marketplace. "Once we left, the company marched down the Plus/4 path, which was wrong. It was just wrong," says Charpentier.

With CES closing in, the magnitude of the workload became clear. "We went like nuts for the fall through CES," recalls Herd. "We hit time compression in the fall when the 264, 364, and 116 were all parallel developed to some degree."

Russell's project engineers impressed him with their work ethic. "There were certain people like Greg Berlin and Bil Herd who were core engineers," says Russell. "They worked their butts off to try to fix the problems and get it running. ... They are friends for life after you go through that type of war."

Like Chuck Peddle before them, the engineers used cots in the workplace. "These are the guys who gave 199% working 20-hour days," recalls Russell. "They would be in there sleeping because they wouldn't go home. We had these real long cubicles and we had enough space to go under the desk and sleep. It was an intense environment."

Herd was disappointed some of the engineers were less than dedicated. "The 'second shift' guys - meaning the guys that showed up only after management had left - basically gave up any pretense of working that we could discern," he says. "The true workers were there both during the day and night."

To defeat the mounting pressure, Herd and his engineers frequently turned their attention to video games. "In that same room we also had a racecar game. It was one of those ones with the old Atari Pong paddles. When you would get all whacked out from the stress and the pressure, you would go play this game," explains Herd. "You would walk in there and somebody would be standing there slack-jawed with foam coming out of his mouth just playing this racecar game. It didn't require any thinking, just twisting a knob. After about an hour of that, you would be ready for Commodore again."

A few weeks before CES, Herd began running into unforeseen obstacles. "The security guards started locking the door," recalls Herd. "They got a rule that said all lockable doors should be locked on Friday nights. So Saturday I walk in, and I can't get in my office. There is no key for this door because it's new construction, and the contractors hadn't dropped the keys off yet."

With the deadline near, Herd decided to go around the problem. "I had to get back to work," says Herd. "You can't keep me from working. So I climbed over the ceiling and got all gucky doing it, and cut myself, but I opened the door and got back to work."

To prevent the incident from reoccurring, Herd posted a friendly notice on the door. "I put a sign up that said, 'Please do not lock this door. There is no key for it,'" he recalls. "Well they locked it again. We went through three layers of notes. The first one was real polite, the second one said, 'Look, you locked it again. We can't get in to do our jobs. Don't lock this door, there is no key.'"

Herd thought his notes explained the situation clearly, but the instructions from management overruled Herd's pleas. "Well, it got locked again," says an exasperated Herd. "Somebody came and got me and said, 'I can't get in the room. It's locked again.' This is the room they had given me to do the project, so it's my room as far as I'm concerned."

Herd stormed towards the locked door in a rage. The previous times, he had gone around the problem. Now he decided to go through the problem. "I punched a hole through the wall to where you could reach in and unlock the door," recalls Herd. "I just barely missed a light switch on the other side, which would have split my knuckles wide open."

Herd thought the faceless battle of wills had come to a climax, but it continued. "They locked the door again!" says Herd. "You had to reach through the hole to unlock the door and you would get your arm all chalky and everything. Finally, I had to write a note that said, 'Look, assholes. There's a fucking hole in the wall next to the door. You can stop locking it now.'"

When Herd came in on Monday morning, management was not amused. "It happened over Friday, Saturday, and Sunday," says Herd. "On Monday morning, Bob Shamus, the QA engineer, said, 'They're looking for whoever put the hole in the wall. They're in big trouble!' He's walking around saying that, and somebody said, 'Bil Herd put that hole in the wall. There's a sign there you should read,' and he shut up."

CHAPTER

16

Dismissing the Founder

1984

Jack Tramiel had come a long way after arriving in America. Since his days in Poland, he dreamed of running his own factories. Now, his worldwide factories turned out thousands of computers each day. His efficient, frugal way of life was present at every level of Commodore, from the boardrooms to the factory floor.

Jack enjoyed the simple pleasure of touring his manufacturing facilities and talking with his workers. He had lived in small apartments and driven a taxicab to make his dream come true. Now, analysts mentioned his company in same breath as IBM, the company he sought to emulate since the 1960s. Nothing gave him more satisfaction than watching computers roll off the assembly line, except perhaps watching his own boys grow into men.

Jack's sons were the most important part of his world. "My family became very, very important to me," said Jack in a 1986 interview with German *Data Welt* magazine. "I believe that in life you have to help one another, you have to trust one another, and you have to develop continuity in all things, which I strive for." Jack harbored a dream of handing Commodore over to his three children, fighting the corporate war together as a family business.

The Tramiel Sons

Over the years, Jack had subtly guided his sons on a path that would allow them to run a business together. He knew there were three important roles in any successful technology company: a business leader, a technology guru, and a financial analyst. In the past, it had been Jack Tramiel, Chuck Peddle, and Irving Gould. More than anything, Jack hoped to continue his legacy at Commodore using his sons in all three key roles.

At first glance, Jack's sons did not resemble their father. Jack was clean-shaven, but all three boys resembled grizzly bears with their full, bushy beards and moustaches. Jack was rotund, while his sons were taller and thinner. Individually, his sons could not match Jack's ambition and determination, but perhaps together they could run Commodore.

Sam was the most similar to Jack physically. He had the same bulging eyes and intense stare. Sam also shared the same tough management style, though he was less abrasive than Jack. Trained at York University in Canada, Sam was destined to handle business affairs at Commodore.

Although he had exiled Sam to the Far East after his wife passed away, Jack welcomed Sam back after the release of the Commodore 64. According to Chuck Peddle, "He meets this girl that he's totally in love with … but the parents don't necessarily agree. He finally just marries her and she does the right thing: she makes a couple of babies. At that point Jack and Helen circle back in."

Leonard, the middle child, would be leaving Columbia University in 1984 after receiving his PhD in astrophysics. According to Peddle, Jack was upset his son did not go into something practical, such as electrical engineering. Despite his chosen vocation, Leonard received work experience in Commodore's engineering labs over the years. He helped with the original Pet and occasionally helped troubleshoot other computers. According to Jack, "I always strove to show them what I do, and to involve them with what I do and discuss our successes and failures." (Data Welt)

Gary, the youngest in the family, was the moneyman. He received financial training at Manlow Park College. After college, Gary briefly worked for *Merrill Lynch* as a stockbroker. He also managed the Tramiel's multimillion-dollar investment portfolio.

There is little doubt Jack wanted his sons in key positions at Commodore, for simple reasons. "I don't think Jack really trusted anybody except his family," says Yannes.

Jack let his feelings about his sons known in an interview. "My dream was that my sons continue to try to be the best, exactly as I have tried to be the best in my area, however not to force them to work in the same industry." He also doubtfully added, "By the way, all three specialized in different aspects of the company without any planning." (Data Welt)

With his sons' educations ending, Jack planned to assimilate them into Commodore. Some employees doubted Jack's sons and wondered if they could produce the same magic as their father. Jack was truly a unique individual and it was unfair to expect his sons to match up to his larger than life image. As Commodore engineer Dave Haynie says, "They were no Jack juniors."

Unfortunately, Irving Gould also had no faith in Jack's sons. As Haynie recalls, "Gould, being the principle stockholder and usually chairman of the board, wasn't happy with Tramiel's plans to bring his boys up as his successors." A disastrous clash of wills was now on an unalterable path.

Jack and Irving

To casual observers, it looked like Jack was completely in charge of Commodore. However, despite founding Commodore and holding the CEO position, Jack did not hold the most power within the company. The real power belonged to Irving, who owned 17.9% of Commodore stock; more shares than any individual.

Irving Gould held residences in three locations: New York (where his wife lived), Toronto, and the Bahamas, ostensibly for tax purposes. "He had a whole schedule set up of how many days he could spend in the United States and how much time he had to be out of country," explains Russell. "Irving would show up unexpectedly because it was time to put some time in the United States."

According to Chuck Peddle, Gould relished the fame brought to him by Commodore. "Irving was rich," says Peddle. "He started a container business and he sold his container business. But being rich in New York wasn't enough. Being the top dog in a hot company put him in a totally different social structure. Irving liked being the owner of this hot company whose stock was running."

Rumors floated that Gould thought Jack was getting too much credit for Commodore's success. The financier is an important part of a company and perhaps Irving felt he should share more of the spotlight.

Through the years, Irving earned a reputation among Commodore employees for living an ebullient lifestyle. "Irving was the guy who flew in the jet with this gorgeous babe for as long as I worked at Commodore," says Russell. "That's what Irving was. I never saw Irving with what was identified as a wife but he would show up with this gorgeous babe every now and then."

Irving's vast wealth allowed him to do anything he wanted. One of Irving's passions was collecting expensive oriental carvings and vases. The *Toronto Star* even featured an article on his famed collection. Irving's other passion was his seventy-foot yacht, which was manned 24 hours a day with a captain and crew.

Leonard Tramiel visited Irving's lavish residence in the Bahamas. "People with a lot of money like to travel a lot, and he certainly liked to travel and had a lot of nice places to go," says Leonard. "I had been on his boat in the Bahamas and seen his house down there. He certainly had nice stuff."

Despite his regular visits to the United States, Irving remained a cipher to those who worked with him. "Even though we were important to Irving, Irving was never close to any of us," says Peddle. "He was a very cold, distant guy. I liked Irving, but Irving was the kind of guy who could reach across the table, cut your heart out with a penknife, and never crack a smile or feel bad about it."

"I'm not saying he didn't have the ability to be socially gracious, but underneath it there was nothing," explains Peddle. "He literally does not have emotions. There's just nothing underneath that front layer. He was one of the most absolutely ruthless, focused people I've ever met."

Engineer Robert Russell spoke with Irving on several occasions, but was unable to pierce through his veil. "Irving was always a really tough guy for me to read," recalls Russell. "He was more the type of guy who nodded his head."

Leonard Tramiel found it difficult to know Irving. "I certainly met him a few times but I never really spent any time talking to him and didn't really know the man," he explains.

Charles Winterble had similar experiences with Irving. "I used to do the financial presentations," he recalls. "I'd give presentations to stock analysts [in New York and San Francisco]. He was always nice to me and complimentary on the stock presentations. He would have his Roll's Royce pick us up in New York and drop us off, which was rather nice. But I would not even pretend to know him very well, if you know what I mean."

Irving met Jack in 1966, when a financial scandal in Canada threatened to destroy Commodore. "That was big time shady stuff, but I think that was more Jack's partner," says Russell. "Irving didn't really let that type of stuff happen, as far as I knew."

For eighteen years, Irving and Jack operated the company in relative peace. There was no doubt they were responsible for each other's success. Jack was responsible for transforming Irving's $500,000 investment in 1966 into over $200 million dollars by 1983. For his part, Irving was chiefly responsible for saving Commodore when no one would loan money to Jack. In fact, after the scandal, Gould had to guarantee every loan Commodore received.

After Jack turned Commodore around, Gould rewarded him. As a gesture of gratitude and trust, Gould sold Jack 8% of Commodore at cost. This was an enormous gesture, worth $90 million by 1983.

As a publicly traded company, Irving Gould wielded his power as Chairman of the Board. If push came to shove, the board would support Irving over Jack. Jack might run Commodore, but Irving was the final word on any decision. As Commodore approached $1 billion in annual sales, Irving felt the company should operate more like a Fortune 500 company.

Bob Yannes believes Jack's management style did not suit Commodore after it expanded. "You're talking about a company that was run as if it was a small garage shop," says Yannes. "He was in charge and he made all the decisions. The fact that it became a billion dollar company was almost a fluke. Left to normal circumstances, a company run that way would never have gotten that large or that successful."

In January 1983, a curious article, titled *Albatross*, appeared in Forbes magazine. The teaser read, "Jack Tramiel's cloudy past and autocratic personality mar the otherwise bright future of Commodore International." It was a strange article to appear during Commodore's best year ever. It seemed like someone was intent on eroding Jack's leadership position and preparing the way for a new leader.

Significantly, Gould had nothing positive to say about Jack in the article. In fact, Irving's quotes bolstered his own contribution to Commodore. The article read, "[Irving] kept Tramiel on a very tight financial leash. 'I wouldn't give them enough money to take any real risks,' Gould says." It seemed to be a first strike to remove Jack from the company.

The negative article in Forbes did not surprise Yannes. "The financial community did not like Jack at all, supposedly because he was really unpredictable and he was totally in charge of the company," he explains. "If he made a bad decision, there wasn't anything to temper his decision."

Tramiel received other negative news coverage. "There was a horrible write-up of him in Barron's magazine that just made him livid," recalls Yannes. "They were pretty scathing."

Al Charpentier believes Jack had some big faults. "He didn't listen real well," says Charpentier. "He made up his mind and it was very difficult to change his mind. That's not unusual for people who are running companies because they believe in what they are doing, but that led to most of his problems."

The quirkiest aspect of Tramiel's business style was not allowing budgets on projects. "He didn't believe in budgets because he believed budgets were a license to steal," explains Yannes. "If you said you needed fifty million dollars to do something then you were going to spend fifty million regardless of whether you needed it or not. So he didn't let his people have budgets. How can you run a business without having budgets?"

Jack personally signed all company expenditures over one thousand dollars. "You would tell him what you were going to spend and he would either approve it or disapprove it," explains Yannes. "How can you get your work done under those conditions?" Spending came to a halt when Jack was away on business trips. "He was all over the place. We had stuff in Japan, the Bahamas, California, Pennsylvania, and Europe, plus he took a lot of time off for himself. You just can't run a big business that way."

Two months before the Forbes article, in November 1982, Bob Lane entered Commodore as company president. Many suspected Jack did not support his appointment and felt Irving Gould was behind it. While Jack visited Asia for a few months of rest, Lane persecuted employees loyal to Jack.

Peddle believes Jack felt insecure bringing in competent leadership. "In order to make it work as well as he could have made it work, he had to bring in all these people that were better at things than he was," explains Peddle. "If you read entrepreneurial 101, you hire people better than you at everything. That's the way to be successful, because they'll take the company places you couldn't take it. A lot of entrepreneurs miss that step, and that's why they fail."

Jack made sure he was the only one in Commodore with real power. "Jack never brought in anybody that would have even conceivably been any threat to Jack," says Peddle. "Sometimes he would bring in some guy and say, 'I'm going to start taking time off and give this guy part of the action.' We would say, 'Ho-hum,' because we knew it wasn't true. Then Jack would give the guy some rope, he would hang himself, and then Jack could kill him."

Commodore executives rarely lasted for more than six months. In the Forbes article, Jim Finke claimed, "five key executives have departed in the past few months." It might have been impossible for anyone to last near Jack. It seemed like the constant rotation of executives and managers had more to do with Jack keeping control of the company rather than decisions that would benefit Commodore.

The situation produced poor leadership. Commodore needed seasoned managers and executives who could take on the microcomputer industry. Instead, executives barely had a chance to learn about Commodore before they were out the door.

As a result, Commodore always had inexperienced managers who could not possibly grasp the situation. Ex-Commodore president Jim Finke expressed his frustrations with weak top-level management at

Commodore. "Remember Machiavelli? The strongest kingdom had the strongest barons and a strong king. There are no strong barons in Jack's kingdom. There is only a strong king." (Forbes)

Engineers lasted longer than managers did, but rarely stayed for long at Commodore. In the short history of Commodore computers, there had been frequent mass exoduses of the best engineers, including Bill Mensch and the 6502 engineers, Chuck Peddle, Bill Seiler, Al Charpentier, and Bob Yannes. Commodore undoubtedly could have achieved greater success if they could retain their key engineers.

Jack's business philosophy included trapping, suing, and ripping off other companies rather than establishing long-term working relationships. As a result, very few companies wanted to do repeat business with Commodore if they could avoid it.

Jack's devotion to cutting costs often came dangerously close to alienating important partners. As Steve Jobs said in reference to research he did on Commodore, "I couldn't find one person who had made a deal with them and was happy. Everyone felt they had been cheated."[1] The only people happy with Commodore were their end customers.

While others lamented his leadership, Jack continued his obsessive drive towards total vertical integration. Due to the incredible number of computers produced and sold during 1983, a worldwide RAM shortage occurred, causing prices to increase.

Jack once again tried producing RAM internally. He bought the manufacturing rights for a 64-kilobyte RAM chip from an Idaho company. In late 1983, he set up a manufacturing line in the Costa Mesa, California production facility. Commodore was now on its way to being the most lethal computer company in the industry.

Peddle believes Jack developed his tough business strategy when Commodore went through turbulent periods. "There was a definite period of time when Commodore was cash poor and Jack was using that as an excuse to do all kinds of jerking around, 'Sue me,' and all that to stay alive," says Peddle.

Jack's ruthless tactics continued, even in profitable years. "Clearly there was a period of time when Commodore had lots of money, and they still didn't take care of those guys," says Peddle. "During the C64 and VIC-20 times, they had tons of money."

Yannes felt Jack's short-term tactics could not go on forever. "The whole philosophy, the whole corporate culture at Commodore was

---

[1] Michael S. Malone, *Infinite Loop* (Currency, 1999), p. 102.

something that couldn't be sustained. The company had to be run differently," he says.

Jack was tough, but he was also charismatic. Employees felt a keen sense of purpose when he was around. Their lives and actions seemed more real, as though what they did really mattered. There was no arguing with success, and Jack delivered it to his employees.

Tramiel felt like an equal among his employees. Jack told an interviewer, "If you ask the people who worked with me, they will say that I have not changed in the last 25 years. I was always one of them." (Data Welt)

Bil Herd felt he understood the source of Jack's drive. "There was this presence and everything, but right on his arm was that tattoo," recalls Herd, referring to his concentration camp identification number. "You would look at that, and you would know what that was and just know a little bit more about that man when you saw him."

With Commodore becoming a billion dollar company, Irving Gould was in a dilemma. Did Jack's good points outweigh his bad? Would Commodore do better without the founder at the helm?

In June 1983, Commodore lost another company president, Robert H. Lane, the latest in a string of presidents that lasted only a year or two. Gould saw Lane as a way to inject professionalism into Commodore. It was his hope that he could keep Jack *and* use Lane to transform Commodore into a Fortune 500 company. A temporary president, Don Richard, took over while the board searched for a replacement.

Yannes recalls the general feeling about Tramiel. "People were wondering, 'What do we do about Commodore? Here's this company that's really successful and they're really on the cutting edge, and they are really growing, but what do we do about this guy Jack?'"

Jack came forward with a solution to the revolving door problem of Commodore presidents. He suggested Sam Tramiel, his son, as the new company president. Irving had different plans.

The Commodore Curse: Part VI

The clash between Gould and Tramiel culminated when Jack began placing his sons in key positions at Commodore. "Jack looked at this as his family business and wanted his sons to take over," explains Dave Haynie. "From everything we ever heard, Gould would have nothing to do with that."

Jack let Gould know about his intentions at the summer 1983 CES show in Chicago, where Commodore rented a lavish 300-foot boat to display their new software. "That was where the initial seeds were sewn," says Russell.

Soon after, Jack appointed Sam Tramiel as the General Manager of Commodore Japan. He gave his younger son Garry a job in finance. "Between June and January is when his two sons were appointed positions," recalls Russell. "I was told we have to find a place to accommodate Leonard, and we were trying to figure out how to do that."

Leonard was preparing to graduate at Columbia University. According to Leonard, he held no firm plans for his career at the time. "I wasn't sure, actually," he recalls. "I was a PhD student in Physics at Columbia and I would have been perfectly happy going to work for Bell Labs or doing some research thing, or going to work for Commodore."

"Leonard was the only one who wasn't really locked into anything," says Russell, who was more than happy to find a place for Leonard within Commodore. "We got along because we were both software types. We talked about stuff and I sent him information when I was asked or when I was feeling like it."

By late 1983, Russell was ready to welcome Leonard to the Commodore engineering group. "He was coming over into my side of things, which was the engineering software," says Russell.

Leonard claims he would not immediately have received a management position like his older brother Sam. "If I had gone to work for Commodore, I would not have initially taken on a leadership role in engineering because there was already an engineering group there," says Leonard. "I would have to work my way up. I would have maybe worked as an engineering manager of some sort, but more likely as a programmer."

On December 13, 1983, Jack celebrated his 55th birthday. The family gathered at Jack's ranch in California and presented him with a new sports car. Jack put away the tensions of work and spent a day of happiness and contentment with his family.

For the past six months, Commodore had been without a permanent president. Jack wanted Sam in the role. Irving wanted Marshall Smith, the former president of *Thyssen Bornemisza Incorporated*, a major player in the steel industry. Neither Jack nor Irving would budge.

Later in the month, Jack triumphantly celebrated the 25th anniversary of Commodore in Toronto. It was an amazing experience for Jack, who rarely looked back. The display included calculators, typewriters, and even the original wooden PET. It was Jack's opportunity to appreciate how far he had taken Commodore.

January 10th was the start of CES in Las Vegas and Commodore's annual debut of new products. This year was the biggest show ever, with over 90,000 attendees. Commodore presented their most ambitious booth yet. In the center of the booth, writer Jim Butterfield demonstrated the 264. "The CES show centered on the 264 version with Magic Desk," says Herd. All around were Commodore's new software packages, mostly for the C64, including Magic Voice.

According to Herd, when he demonstrated the 264 people asked, "Why isn't it C64 compatible?" Herd gazed at months of hard work and replied, "What can I tell you? I made it work! Doesn't that count for something?" It was a let down for Herd, who hoped his computer would be well received. Afterwards, he says he felt beat up. The request for backward compatibility surprised Herd, since backward compatibility was not at all on his mind as he designed the 264.

Bil Herd at CES in 1984 (photo courtesy of Dave Haynie).

Dismissing the Founder – 1984

Herd had a chance to meet the Commodore Texas engineers who created the speech capability for Magic Voice. As usual, Herd pulled them into his hard-living lifestyle. "It was really cool running into people like that back then and having a beer with these guys," says Herd. "Me and the one guy nobody talked with, we went out terrorizing the bar one night together in Vegas."

The biggest display in the Commodore booth was an arcade, which displayed 30 different C64 games. It was located in a darkened room where attendees could play the latest games like *Satan's Hollow*, *Zork*, and *Wizard of Wor*, which included Magic Voice capability. There were also some unconventional titles, such as *Dancing Monster* and *Buffalo Roundup*.

Jack and Irving gave a joint press conference, where they announced Commodore sold over three million computers in 1983. In total, Commodore sold over a billion dollars worth of product for the year. Afterwards, Commodore sponsored a dinner party for employees and industry insiders.

The booth also contained a large meeting space above the arcade. "We had a booth at the January CES that had a second level office space; a demonstration room to show the retailers," explains Russell. The meeting space also contained several relaxing sofas for the tired employees. There was also a small room for closing deals with distributors and a plush office for Jack.

As Robert Russell and other engineers prepared demonstrations for the show, they began to hear a rising level of noise coming from Jack and Irving. "We were doing setup early in the show," says Russell. "That was where the blowup happened that I overheard. I was setting stuff up next to the door where they were going at it."

Russell clearly heard the reason for the argument. "The blowup I heard about was about the sons. Jack had kind of thought his sons were going to be in positions in the company, and Irving said, 'No, I've rethought having your sons in these positions in the company.' Jack said, 'You know that's what I want.' Irving was like, 'No.' He started ranting and raving."

For the first time ever, Russell saw Irving Gould display emotion. "He got heated during that. That was the only time I actually saw him upset," recalls Russell. "I've been to board meetings with Irving where there was much worse news and he didn't even flinch."

Gould felt Jack would gain too much power with his sons in key positions. "It was definitely the sons and Jack's effective control of the company by putting his sons in all the power," recalls Russell. "You've got to realize, Sam was [already] running a big part of the company."

Throughout the argument, Jack remained uncharacteristically calm. "Jack was trying to offer his case rather than attacking Irving," says Russell. "He was arguing and Irving was going, 'No.' It was like seeing something blow up."

Russell, who was used to seeing Jack in full control of every situation, felt startled by Irving's sudden domination. "I was more in shock that it was coming apart before my eyes," recalls Russell. "Irving was like this guy who flew in with cute broads on his jet. It wasn't like he was part of the company."

From the tone of the argument, Russell sensed the relationship between Irving and Jack was at an end. Russell was also about to lose his most valuable asset, the Jack card. "You played a Jack card and said, 'If you don't believe me, go ask Jack.' All of a sudden, my whole source of power was walking out the door. It was pretty shocking to the people who were there."

The argument abruptly ended when Jack drove away in the car his family gave him for his birthday. "Jack came up in the car and drove away, and wasn't coming back. That was that," says Russell. "His sons were kind of standing around there. Everybody asked, 'Is Jack coming back?' We said, 'I don't think so if you heard that conversation.'"

On Friday January 13, Jack met with the board of directors in New York behind closed doors. Those who attended have not revealed what took place. "I know exactly what happened, but for personal reasons that I don't really understand, neither my father nor Mr. Gould has ever been interested in documenting or revealing the actual events," says Leonard Tramiel. "I wish there was some way to convince my dad to tell you the real story, but he won't."

In an interview with a German magazine, Jack revealed, "To put it briefly, our philosophies were different. It came to the point where I said to him, 'Either I lead the company my way, which I think is correct, or I must go.' He [Irving] was completely friendly and said to me, 'If you will not do what I want, then go.' And I went." (Data Welt)

According to Commodore employees, Jack walked out in the middle of the board of directors meeting. According to Herd, "I think he had made a billion that year. The comment I heard at the time was they said, 'Yeah, but you're not the guy to take us to 10 billion.' I don't know if that was true or not, but Irving Gould was the CEO at the time."

According to Yannes, Irving told Jack, "You are a detriment to the growth of the company." Yannes thinks it was the correct decision. "I think the market analysts were correct in that he was not the person to be running a $500 million or bigger company. You just can't run it like your own little shop," he says.

Jack Tramiel claimed spending issues were part of the disagreement. "Just because we were a billion-dollar company, we did not have to throw money out the window like a billion-dollar company. Because if you spend more, you must increase prices. The man I had worked for was of another opinion. When business was good, he wanted to spend more. That is one of the points in which we had a different opinion." (Data Welt)

Gould's stubborn refusal to use public stock to raise money for Commodore also aggravated Tramiel. "We were also in disagreement about the question of financing. I was of the view that we should have made a new stock offering when our shares were highly traded; particularly since we had never increased the number of shares since we had listed on the stock exchange in 1962. With the 120 million dollars, which we would have earned by offering two million new shares, we would have paid back all of our debts to the banks and strengthened the position of our company. We could have survived the storm, without having to rely on the banks. The man I worked for thought this would water down his portion of the company and he would lose influence - that was absolutely wrong." (Data Welt)

Although the CES disagreement stemmed from Jack's plan for his sons, Leonard Tramiel does not believe it was the central issue. "The most persistent story was that my father wanted his sons to be the leaders of the company and Mr. Gould wanted it to be professional management, and that the disagreement was the foundation of my father's departure from the company," says Leonard. "That is 100% not true. That had absolutely nothing whatsoever to do with it."

Dave Haynie believes his sons were part of the issue. "As a worker bee at Commodore, we weren't in the boardroom then, but neither were Sam or Leonard," he says. "It's impossible to say if that was ultimately the reason why Jack left, but I think it was definitely on the table."

Chuck Peddle also believes his sons were at least part of the issue, despite Leonard's denials. "I'm not saying he's wrong, because Leonard is a very truthful guy," says Peddle. "But to some extent, Leonard is biased because he needs to protect his family position." Jack clearly wanted to see his sons join Commodore, talked about it often, and he was making it happen.[2]

---

[2] After Tramiel left Commodore, he and his sons ran their next company together. This might be the best evidence of his intentions.

Chuck Peddle felt Jack always believed Commodore was his company, even though Gould owned more shares. "I think he just never got over the fact that it wasn't his company anymore," says Peddle.

Tramiel later said of his resignation, "Naturally, that was very, very hard for me. But if I cannot lead the company in the way I consider correct, then it is no longer my company." (Data Welt)

Within days, the *Philadelphia Inquirer* reported Tramiel's resignation. A press release issued by Commodore stated it was due to personal reasons. The official line from Commodore stated, "He had been thinking about it for some time, and each landmark that Commodore achieved brought the day closer when Tramiel felt he could go on to other things."[3]

Jack was out of Commodore for good. Over the last 25 years, he had been all over the world on business trips, but he never had time to see the sights and take in his surroundings. Now, he planned to revisit those people and places, and to do some soul searching. He planned to spend the next year touring the world with his wife Helen on a cruise ship.

Following the departure of Tramiel, newspapers were buzzing with speculation. The day after the board of directors meeting, the New York Times headline read, "Founder of Commodore Resigns Unexpectedly." A few days later, another headline appeared, saying, "Rift Denied in Tramiel Departure."

Irving Gould knew he wanted to turn Commodore into a professional, business oriented company, however he was not sure how. "He never really thought about a 10-year technology company. He never thought like an HP," says Chuck Peddle. "He never had to do that before and it wasn't in his background. It wasn't in Jack's background either."

Less than a week after Tramiel's departure, the New York Times declared, "Commodore Fills Tramiel's Position." Irving chose 54-year-old steel industry executive Marshall Smith. Smith recently completed 17 years at Thyssen-Bornemisza Incorporated, with eight years as CEO. Irving began making his presence felt at Commodore. "I didn't really see Irving do anything until he brought the guy in from the steel industry after Jack left," says Russell.

Most Commodore employees doubted Smith's ability to lead a computer company. "I think Marshal Smith had his heart in the right place, but he was not a person who should be in the computer business,"

---

[3] *RUN* magazine, (March 1984), p. 6.

says Haynie. "He wasn't used to an industry that moved that fast. He came from steel, which changes every generation, not every six months."

Curiously, Sam and Gary retained their positions with Commodore. "[Jack's] sons stayed on," recalls Haynie. "They were there for at least six more months."

The Plus/4

Commodore's marketing arm convinced Smith to release only two 264 computers: one with 64 kilobytes of memory and one with only 16 kilobytes.

The 16-kilobyte version of the 264, now called the C116, represented Herd's original goal. Commodore was about to repeat an old mistake by using a low quality keyboard similar to the original PET-2001. "It was tiny, but not quite as bad as a Timex-Sinclair membrane keyboard. It was more like a calculator keyboard," says Haynie.

Commodore also wanted to produce another 16-kilobyte version of the computer called the C16. "The C16 came after CES," says an obviously disgusted Herd. "The C116 became a C16 abomination. They stuck it in a C64 case." The C16 looked remarkably like a VIC-20, except the case was black with light-gray keys.

The Plus/4, complete with Sinclair-style case and calculator keyboard, included 64 kilobytes of memory and built in software.

The most fanciful computer in the TED line, the talking 364, did not make it very far after CES. "I was in charge of that for about two weeks between the time it was handed to me and the time it was cancelled," says Haynie.

Commodore scheduled the release of the TED computers for May 1984, but they met with inevitable delays due to RAM shortages and problems with their supplier, Micron. "We had to wait on the 16K DRAM's which were brand new back then," says Herd. "All of this wouldn't have mattered as it waited on the TED chip."

Much like the VIC-20, the final production design for the C116 went to Japan, where Sam Tramiel was still General Manager. Irving Gould must have worried, having the son of a disgruntled company founder within his company. "A lot of the different models came out of the Japan office, which is where Sam was working at the time," says Haynie.

The completion of the C116's design was helped by Herd. "They had flown me to Japan to get it ready, which is how I found out some of the things that were going on," recalls Herd.

Herd met the formidable Tony Tokai in Japan. "There's two types of Japanese businessmen. There's what I call the Samurai and then there's the other people. He was Jack's hit man in the Asian market," recalls Herd.

Similarities between Jack Tramiel and Tokai were apparent. "He was born and bred in Jack's shadow, as far as his management style," says Herd. "He was a rough person. You didn't cross him unless you had some pull of your own."

Herd played a game of dominance with Tokai. "I'm a Samurai too. I wasn't raised that way, but I was born that way. When Tony would smack a chair, that was his way of telling his underlings where to sit," says Herd. "I'm in his office in Japan and he smacked a chair cushion with his hand. I looked at him after he did that and I put my feet up on the table. By putting my feet on the table, what I said was, 'I'm an American, I'm Bil Herd, and that shit is not going to work with me.' So then, Tony and I started getting along a little bit. It was like two alpha-dogs."

It was up to Herd to ensure the TED computers passed FCC requirements. "I brought some FCC knowledge with me [from Pennsylvania Scale Company], so I was able to get a handle on that," explains Herd. "It flew through FCC, which was a first."

Herd was determined to improve his communications with his fellow Japanese engineers. "I learned Japanese because that was a way to become a better engineer," says Herd. "Pretty soon I was going over there and moving around at will."

A second language became valuable in other ways. "I spoke enough Japanese that when my boss was being an idiot, I could say in front of a room full of people, 'Ignore him, he's being an idiot.' They would all laugh and he would look at me and go, 'What are you doing?' I'd say, 'He's going to be dead soon. I don't care,' which meant he was going to be fired."

Herd encountered some inexplicable mistakes while in Japan. "We had some mighty funny things happen to the Plus/4 during the time when Jack was no longer with us but his sons were," recalls Herd.

The first anomaly Herd found had to do with the plastic material used for the case. "Suddenly the case, which was supposed to be made of fire-retardant plastic, had been re-specified to be a flameful plastic," says Herd. "We were like, 'Well, we normally keep very good track of these changes to these drawings, and yet this one seems to be erased and penciled in.'"

Earlier on, Herd decided to use the Commodore 64 power supply for the TED computers. Once again, Herd found more anomalies. "The one that really got us was that we had laid out the board for a circular DIN connector so we could use the Commodore 64 power supply," recalls

Herd. "The case drawings were property of Japan. They're going straight to plastics and it had a square hole. I'm like, 'That doesn't fit the board.' Out comes this prototype board, they said, 'No, no. We're going to redo the board with a square connector.' I said, 'We haven't tested with the FCC with that, but I can put a square one back on the master one if you want.' I think we ended up with a square one for a while and went back to circular."

Herd had a third and final surprise when his power supplies arrived. "When we got the power supplies, the round connector was plastic. In other words, it didn't conduct electricity," says Herd. "So we couldn't get through FCC again plus I'm dubious it would not have been breaking a lot. So we had to quickly get power supplies with metal collars on them. That was just the kind of thing that was happening."

Engineer Dave Haynie believes the changes could have been due reducing costs, but does not discount the possibility of sabotage. "It's very possible, but things are always being cost reduced," says Haynie. "Anything that is changed is supposed to go through engineering. We had a complete system for that where a responsible engineer signs off on everything after presumably ensuring it works. Things like that shouldn't get through. So if something like that happens and we find it by surprise, well, there's probably been some monkey business somewhere."

The Backlash

Every successful company has a figurehead who can motivate and inspire. At the time, Microsoft had Bill Gates and Apple had Steve Jobs. Jack was without a doubt Commodore's figurehead. When they lost him, they lost the soul that drove the company forward. "Jack was the whole personality of the company. There was nobody else," says Russell.

Even though Jack treated many of his employees harshly, they were ready to follow him. His shocking departure left his disciples wondering what to do. "Without Jack, they were asking, 'What the hell is Irving going to do?' Once you saw somebody like Marshall Smith, you were like, 'You've got to be kidding me,'" says Russell.

True to his word, Irving Gould expanded Commodore. He did not want the lean, perennially understaffed company of the past. "Commodore at that time was ballooning with all these guys being brought down from Northern Telecom [Nortel] up in Canada, like Martin Shibilski," says Russell. "They were big-company guys building empires."

Under Jack, Commodore had an emphasis on results. That began to change after he left. "All of a sudden titles became important," says Russell. "A lot of the time you just went around as a member of engineering on your business card, which was fine. Then all of a sudden, you had to be a manager of this or something of that."

Without a 'Jack card' to keep managers from overstepping their authority, engineers like Russell found it difficult to do their jobs. "The engineers that I hired were guys like me who thought, 'This is bullshit.' Guys like Shiraz that were like, 'We're here to do things, we're not here to go fight in meetings and sit across the desk from Martin Shibilski and Joe Krasucki, and argue to try to get things done the right way."

Meanwhile, Jack and Helen continued touring the world. They only got as far as Sri Lanka and Hong Kong before Jack realized it was not the life for him. In early 1984, Jack ended his worldwide tour and returned to New York to get back to doing what he loved best: business. While in New York, Jack began visiting old Commodore employees.

Jack formed a company called *Tramel Technology Limited* (using Tramel instead of Tramiel so people would pronounce it properly), more commonly called TTL. Jack explained the mysterious entity as "a technology holding company." In reality, Jack wanted to get back into the computer market and destroy Commodore.

In the middle of May, top managers began resigning from Commodore. Sam Tramiel was the first. Next was Tony Tokai, Vice President of Commodore Japan. Something was happening behind the scenes and Jack Tramiel was likely behind it.

Jack began planning a C64 killer. He gave the task to his Commodore engineers, headed by Shiraz Shivji. According to Robert Russell, much of the design came together at Commodore. "Shiraz and I were doing lunch all the time, working on what we wanted to do for the next generation computer," reveals Russell.

The engineers designed their computer based around the Motorola 68000. The computer was definitely not intended for Commodore, since using a Motorola chip was unthinkable at the time. "We were still butting heads with Motorola, so Motorola wasn't really an option," says Russell.

Russell's Z8000 UNIX engineers helped design Jack's new computer. "My engineers were working on the Z8000, mostly hardware guys, and then with Shiraz, we'd all go out and have lunch together," explains Russell. "Those were done during Commodore lunch hours at a cheap fish restaurant."

"We were choosing our chipset and talking about how we were going to design it and build it," says Russell. "We were sketching it on a napkin."

Soon, Commodore engineers began leaving. "Shiraz Shivji left," recalls Russell. "A bunch of my hardware engineers left, including my best friend at that point in time." Shivji took three of his engineering staff:

Arthur Morgan, John Hoenig, and Douglass Renn. "It was mostly my engineering group that left as far as hardware engineers."

To Russell, it was obvious why his friends and coworkers wanted to leave with the engineer-friendly Jack. "It was an opportunity to finally go break out and do something new," explains Russell. "Most of these guys were the type of individuals that Jack's personality appealed to. If you were aggressive and wanted to make something happen and create the next generation Commodore 64, obviously you could do that with Jack a lot easier than you could do it at Commodore."

Curiously, once again Russell chose to stay with Commodore rather than leave with his fellow engineers. "I turned them down and said, 'I have learned all I want to learn from Jack. As much as I like you guys, I want to do something different.'"

One of the most critical people to leave Commodore was John Feagans, who was working on the Magic Desk II software for the Plus/4 computer (and for the C64). The graphical user interface for the Plus/4 was now without a programmer. It would be impossible for someone else to carry on Feagan's work.[4]

Others soon followed. Neil Harris, onetime programmer of VIC-20 games, departed. Ira Velinsky, production designer at Commodore Japan resigned. Lloyd 'Red' Taylor, president of technology resigned. Bernie Witter, vice president of finance resigned. Sam Chin, manager of finance in East Asia resigned. Joe Spiteri and David Carlone of manufacturing resigned. Gregg Pratt, vice president of operations resigned.

Irving Gould was alarmed at the impact these resignations would have on Commodore; not on the actual loss of talent, but on the image it projected to shareholders. To counteract this, he issued a vague press statement that indicated Marshall Smith was just cleaning house. It was nothing of the sort. They were joining Jack Tramiel to fight Commodore. Soon, Jack would own Atari.

Release the Bomb

Advanced press for the Plus/4 stated it was supposed to be more high-end than the Commodore 64, which falsely built up expectations. Commodore came surprisingly close to producing a product the market might have desired. If they succeeded in producing a functional graphical user interface for the low-cost Plus/4, they might

---

[4] Feagans obsession with graphical operating systems did not end with Magic Desk, and he went on to port a graphical operating system called GEM for Atari.

have had a popular product to compete with the overpriced Macintosh, which debuted at the same time. However, with John Feagans gone, no one could continue his work on Magic Desk II. Commodore now had to find a suitable software replacement if they were to meet their May release date.

Sig Hartman found a company called *Tri-Micro*, which produced a software package called 3 + 1. It contained a file manager, a word processor, a spreadsheet, and a graphing program. Because there were four applications, Commodore changed the name from the 264 to the Plus/4. The general feeling among the engineers was that the programs were sub-standard, and without the ability to upgrade, users were stuck with them.

During the design phase, Herd concentrated on keeping his target of under $50. "I actually knew the prices in my head of a 7407 gate on Hong Kong that week," says Herd. "That's how sensitive we were to prices." Unfortunately, Herd's dedication was for nothing.

Herd was disappointed with the new software. "We designed it to cost 99 bucks, and we succeeded. Our cost was $49," says Herd. "Then the software management, Sig and those guys, got hold of it, and they put that real bad Plus/4 software in it, and then they left for Atari. I think they were sabotaging it with software."

With all the new additions, the Plus/4 price soared. "They made the cost $299," says Herd. "Well I'm sorry, but it was designed to cost $99 and it would have been a good computer for $99."

Dave Haynie believes the addition of software might have been part of a larger plan. "In retrospect, it seems like that was an ideal way to make Commodore all confused about what they ought to be doing while Jack set up his operations," speculates Haynie. "I don't think you could ever prove it but it seemed that way to a bunch of us. We have this product that nobody wants."

Robert Russell believes it was just poor marketing. "I think it was one of those things where the marketing and sales organizations wanted to run with something because people were starting to make comments that the Commodore 64 was aging," he says.

The difference between Jack Tramiel and Marshal Smith was now evident. Jack brought products to CES, observed the crowd's reaction, and if the reaction was poor he cancelled them. He had done this before with the Max Machine and other computers. The new management continued forward, ignoring the lousy press.

Commodore vice president of marketing Myrddin L. Jones was interviewed about the 264 line. It was painfully obvious Jones did not grasp the importance of software and computers. When assistant editor

Selby Bateman asked, "Why buy a 264 instead of a 64 that has a word processor and, say, a Simon's BASIC? It would be the equivalent of the 264 for less money." Jones replied, "The difference is that the market is changing because the consumer is far more knowledgeable."[5] It was a non sequitur. Irving Gould issued similar unsure statements in the May/June 1984 Commodore Magazine.

After the summer 1984 CES show, Commodore released the Plus/4. "You can see what a bad CES booth looked like because we didn't go all out at the summer CES shows," says Herd. Commodore never could explain the market for their new computers, and the general reaction from the public was, 'Who ordered these?' Compute!'s Gazette called the software, "mediocre compared to the best commercial software for the C64."

Commodore sold the C16 abomination, as Herd referred to it, exclusively in Canada. They sold off their inventory of C116 computers in Japan. The Plus/4 became their main product, which they attempted to sell worldwide. However, the computer cost more than the C64 and did not even contain a real keyboard. Predictably, it fared poorly.

It should have been apparent by early 1984 that there was no reason to release the 264 line due to the continued success of the C64. If anything, the computers would cut into C64 sales and confuse customers. "It was the same problem that everybody else who had gone after the Commodore 64 had run into," recalls Haynie. "The C64 was too popular." Rather than wasting their time working on the doomed Plus/4, engineers could have concentrated on making the next generation Commodore 64.

Bil Herd receives solace knowing that his computer sold well when retailers later dropped the price. "When they sold them through some of the other mail order companies, they couldn't keep them in stock at 99 bucks," says Herd. "You can think whatever you want, but it was a great $99 computer."

The Plus/4 received almost no software support from developers. Al Charpentier blames Jack for the oversight. "Jack didn't understand the power of software," explains Charpentier. "It's a software game, and to win this game, you have to have lots and lots of people writing software for your product. He didn't understand that you had to feed the market and you would have to pay for software to be done up front. His feeling was, 'Let me put a lot of boxes on the shelf and the software guys should

---

[5] *Compute!'s Gazette* magazine, "Some Answers from Commodore" (April 1984), p. 58.

be privileged and happy to write stuff for my boxes'. That wasn't realistic back then."

According to Haynie, there was no competition in consumer's minds. "You had ten thousand programs for the C64 and not one of them would run on the Plus/4. There was no way it could compete," he says.

Commodore took a technological step back and expected interest in their higher priced product. "The sound wasn't as good, the graphics were a little bit better, but the C64 had better sprites and you needed that for games at the time," explains Haynie. "What was better wasn't better enough to offset anything else."

Commodore's reputation suffered in the aftermath. Even though Jack instigated the projects, many thought it was a sign that Commodore could not compete without him. Casual computer buyers wondered why Commodore even bothered. Even the youngest computer users knew it was a bad idea. It seemed like everyone knew except for Commodore management and marketing.

According to Chuck Peddle, Irving Gould blamed Jack for the failure. "He went out and designed this follow-up to the C64, and he built up all this inventory, assuming he was going to go out and get everybody to upgrade their machines," says Peddle. "The product never went anywhere. If you talked to Irving after that, he said, 'Jack almost broke the company. I left him alone and didn't watch him.'"

Commodore's upward trajectory was halted. Only the Commodore 64 allowed the company to continue. Irving needed to find a suitable replacement for the Commodore 64 soon otherwise his shares in Commodore would continue their downward plunge.

CHAPTER

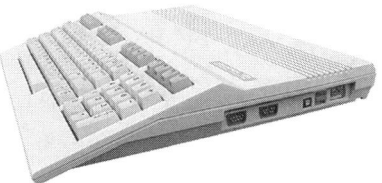

17

The Sequel

1984

The Plus/4 and C116 computers failed to impress the original Commodore 64 creators. "We were disappointed that there were no exciting follow-on products in a [C64] family," says Winterble. "Where is the 128K version?"

After their recent failure, Commodore was desperate for a successful follow-up. It was a realization that they needed to build on the C64's success rather than attempt to compete with it.

The Commodore 64 continued on an upward trajectory well into 1987 and the company still had money in the bank. There was plenty of time. Commodore would soon decide on a true C64 successor.

Backward Compatibility

By 1984, it was apparent the C64 was a major force in the computer industry. Bob Yannes was sure Commodore would attempt to create a sequel. "I would have made something that would have led them to continue the Commodore 64 line; a Commodore 64 that had an 80-character screen that was improved in every area: more memory, better sound, better everything," he says.

Commodore management needed a way to turn the success of the Commodore 64 into a perpetual market. Since users do not want to purchase a new software library when they buy a new computer, the best way was to release a backward compatible Commodore 64 with more memory, a faster processor, and more features.

Marketing at Commodore obviously knew the importance of backward compatibility. The March/April Commodore Microcomputers magazine article starts, "Ask a Commodore 64 owner what kind of computer they would like to see Commodore produce next. They would probably chuckle and say, 'A compatible upgrade of the 64.'"

Bil Herd maintains the idea did not occur to the engineers or management of Commodore. "Nobody thought about doing a C64 sequel," says Herd. "There had been this weird-assed thing called the B128, and it was more like a PET than anything."

Dave Haynie believes they might have attempted some backward compatibility with the C64 sequel. "They had previous failures to make a new, compatible Commodore 64," says Haynie. "There was a C64 sequel by entirely different engineers that had been in development that just never worked right."

The C64 sequel had more in common with the B128 than the C64, however. "They were calling it the D128 but it was really a spin-off of the B128," says Herd. "It didn't have any C64 compatibility."

The D128 had almost the same specifications as the failed P & B series. "The D128 was a version without the [VIC-II] chip in it," says Russell. Like the P & B series, it contained a 6509 microprocessor, a SID chip and a new video chip called the 8563 that had been in development for over 18 months.

Robert Russell led the D128 team. "We were basically taking a C64, putting a [video] chip from the Z8000 [project] in it, and doing an add-on processor card slot to make it more standardized," explains Russell. "We were kind of using stuff from the P and B, and blending that together with more C64 compatibility than those machines had."

The D128's lead designer possessed limited practical abilities. "One of the engineers was Dr. Cong Su, a Chinese guy working in the United States," explains Haynie. "He was a very clever theoretical guy who should never have been near an engineering laboratory. He had some good ideas and just couldn't get them to work."

True backward compatibility was obvious to Commodore's competitors in the computer industry, such as IBM and Apple, who released successively improved versions of their computers. It was obvious to magazine writers. It was obvious to computer sellers. It was obvious to computer users. It was obvious to 13-year-old teenagers with computers in their bedrooms. At CES, it became obvious to Herd.

Herd received his first taste of the importance of backward compatibility when he showed his Plus/4 computer at the June 1984 CES in Chicago. "Everybody was like, 'Why the hell didn't you make this compatible!' They would show me their software they had invested all their time in, and I'm going, 'Yeah, why didn't we make it backward compatible?'" recalls Herd.

During the show, Herd relayed his concerns to Irving Gould. "That day, around the other side of that booth, I got into a conversation with Irving about the Plus/4's compatibility problems," recalls Herd. "I was loud, and I probably had alcohol on my breath." He presented Gould with a scathing critique of Commodore's failure to pursue backward compatibility. "I said, 'Our next computer should be compatible. I'm catching all kinds of shit over this compatibility problem, and compatibility wouldn't have been that bad [to implement].' He tolerated me, but I don't know that he ever did anything from it."

Most of Herd's engineers felt the task would be too difficult without the original C64 engineers. "Nobody thought about C64 compatibility. Nobody even thought we could do it again. Nobody even knew what it meant, because the guys who had done it were gone," explains Herd.

Herd made it his personal mission to convince Commodore to take backward compatibility seriously. "The idea of doing another C64 compatible machine started with me literally because I put up with all that crap at the CES show," he says. "Everybody else, it didn't phase. I swear to God. Nobody else was walking around talking about ever doing a C64 machine again. I'm not trying to grab credit, but I was the one who said, 'Whatever we do, why don't we make it C64 compatible.' They said, 'You can do that?'"

Herd wrote a lengthy memo to Commodore management titled, 'Yes Virginia There is Compatibility'. "It was written a couple of months after the Plus/4 show," says Herd. "I made some fairly brash statements regarding my opinion of product strategy."

The high-school dropout's memorandum was unrefined and strident in tone. "It would have been written in bad English that changed tense. I didn't write good English back then and we didn't have good spell checkers," recalls Herd. "It would have looked like it was written by a maniac to the wrong person. I think I went over edge in a sentence or two and got derogatory at one point. I wrote like I talked, so I had curse words in there. It was passionate and pissed off. I didn't have a lot of patience for people who didn't see the obvious."

Looking back, Herd wonders how he got away with it. "I would hate to try to put up with me now like I was then," says Herd. "When I wrote it, I didn't know what would become of it."

If Herd expected a reaction from his letter, he did not receive one. In the meantime, Herd became project engineer on Commodore's first laptop LCD computer. "I was working on the LCD, which wasn't C64 compatible."

The Laptop Computer

Commodore still had LCD manufacturing capacity in 1984. "There was a group down in Texas which had been *Commodore Optoelectronics*," explains Haynie. "They were the guys who made the LCD panels."

Commodore Optoelectronics was previously Eagle Picture, purchased by Jack Tramiel in the late seventies. "We owned an LCD plant that was in MOS Technology and we still called it *Picture* internally," says Herd. "It fed watches and calculators, which I assume is why we had an early interest in it."

According to Herd, Commodore was unique as a computer company with their own LCD capability. "The thing that Commodore had that nobody else had was glass," says Herd. "There were no American makers of LCD glass, except for Eagle Picture."

When Commodore moved into the massive West Chester facility, Eagle Picture also moved in. "I got involved with them when they were moving into West Chester, and I introduced them to the facility," recalls Russell. "They originally moved in and they had an LCD production line in the front corner of the West Chester building."

Eagle Picture made a diverse range of LCD products for Commodore. "They were doing these specialty LCD's with great big clocks," recalls Russell. "They had ones that were the size of a piece of paper, eight and a half by eleven or so, with big independent LCD sections in it to light up different things. They gave them out as advertising and gifts, handing them out internally."

In the early eighties, computer makers began investigating portable computers. "I was fresh off the Plus/4, I knew what our chips could do, and I knew we could design our own memory management units, so I did the design for an LCD computer," says Herd.

Herd began working on the LCD computer with another Commodore engineer named Jeff Porter. "I did the LCD design on graph paper, got interested in the D128, and he was obviously competent enough," recalls Herd. "At that point we actually handed off the LCD to Jeff Porter."

The engineers liked Jeff Porter, even though he did not quite fit in with them. "Jeff was the only one of us who knew how to tie a tie, so he was destined to be management," says Herd. "You could find him in his tie at ten o'clock at night."

The former AT&T employee's first job at Commodore was to advance their modem technology. "Jeff Porter was originally hired to build us a modem that went faster than 300 baud for the D128 and C64," recalls Haynie. "It took three months to build this modem and then the LCD project came along." Because of his experience, Porter decided to include a modem in his LCD computer.

"When Jeff Porter took over the LCD design, he put his heart into it," says Herd.

The LCD computer required an LCD screen capable of producing thousands of pixels. "We were trying to get into what I would call the dot matrix LCD," says Russell. "Michael North was the guy who originally put together the spec sheets."

Compared to other LCD displays at the time, the Eagle Picture LCD screen was remarkable. It contained 80-columns by 16-rows of text or 1200 characters (compared to 1000 for the Commodore 64). In total, the screen displayed 480 by 128 pixels.

LCD technology was still primitive in 1984 and manufacturing the display was difficult. "They would show me these big panels with so many defects," recalls Russell.

Commodore intended to dethrone Tandy's LCD laptop computers. "It was like the Tandy-100 only on steroids," recalls Haynie. "It had a bigger display, the software was actually pretty good, there was tons of ROM in there, and it had a lot of [RAM] memory inside. It didn't run anybody else's software, but it was pretty cool."

The LCD computer weighed only five pounds. With the efficient CMOS 65C02 processor developed by Bill Mensch, it could operate for 15 hours on four AA batteries. While it lacked a disk drive, it contained 32 kilobytes of battery-backed memory to save data. It also included a serial port, which allowed access to disk drives and printers.

Herd carried forward the Plus/4 idea of built in software for the portable laptop computer. "The most interesting thing about the LCD was that all the productivity software built in was done in-house, and it was excellent," claims Haynie. "It was everything the Plus/4 hadn't been." The software included eight applications, including a word processor, file manager, address book, scheduler, calculator, memo pad, and a telecommunications package for the built in modem.

Commodore estimated the LCD computer would retail for only $500. Marshall Smith told Porter that if he could acquire enough orders at the upcoming CES show, the product could become a reality. According to Herd, "They told him, 'Go get 15,000 and we'll talk.'"

Conceiving the Next Computer

The glacial pace of D128 development began to frustrate engineering manager Robert Russell. "Cong Su was one of those guys who you wondered why he was around sometimes," laments Russell.

Bil Herd also noticed the sharp contrast between Cong's knowledge and lack of practical ability. "He was mathematically brilliant and couldn't get himself into and out of a parking spot," he says. Commodore needed someone with real world experience.

Engineers who failed to perform at Commodore often earned nicknames. "To show you how cruel we were, do you know what a dongle is?" asks Herd. "It's a little add-on piece of hardware that sticks to another machine and makes it work sometimes, like game dongles. Well, there was this other engineer who wasn't very good, and he used to follow Cong around real close. So I coined the phrase Cong Dongle to describe the guy who stuck on Cong."

Herd got involved with the D128 project while working in the same lab as Dr. Cong Su. According to Herd, "Freddy Bowen was sitting there with Cong Su behind me in the lab, and I'm working on my LCD thing, and I keep hearing [Dr. Cong Su say], 'I don't understand how it can be doing that!'"

As Herd listened, he realized the problem was due to a short circuit. "Finally I lean over and say, 'It's because you've got contention,'" says Herd. Dr. Su was reluctant to accept the explanation, telling Herd, "You must be wrong."

Herd delved into the problem. "I looked over and grabbed this photocopy of his PLA. He had photocopied it so close to the edge that he was missing the last row of terms," recalls Herd. "I showed him and said, 'Look, you're missing a row.'"

In minutes, Herd had solved a tenacious problem that had occupied the engineers for most of the day. Even more impressive, the project was unfamiliar to Herd. "Freddy Bowen looked at me and said, 'You know, I need Herd.' I said, 'That looks interesting, but can we make it compatible?'"

Herd received the plans for the D128. "By the time Herd got it, we had already sketched it up several times and gone through several iterations," says Russell.

According to Haynie, Herd discarded the plans. "We really didn't look at it much before getting into the C128," he says. "At that point there was very little left that described what they were trying to do."

Herd shared engineering tasks with Dr. Cong Su and began pushing his concept of backward compatibility. With the brash young Herd around, Dr. Cong Su began to lose his position on the project. "He was who I shared the title of C128 designer for a week with, and then he was kind of on the outs," says Herd. "People who didn't belong there got scorched real fast and would get pushed to the side."

The Sequel – 1984

To incorporate backward compatibility, Herd started over from the beginning. "The D128 had that funny-assed processor and other things, and it used a color 6845 chip. It didn't use the VIC chip at all, and how can you not start with the VIC chip?" says Herd. "I looked at the existing schematics once and then started with a new design based on C64ness."

Herd directed planning sessions with the software and semiconductor engineers. "We commandeered the office all the way to the left of engineering row," says Herd. "It was Freddy Bowen, Terry Ryan, myself, and Dave D'Oreo. It literally started with four of us in a room with a whiteboard, drawing big blocks."

The engineers decided to have two separate modes: a mode with C64 compatibility, and a 128K mode with more memory and features. According to Herd, Fred Bowen believed the advanced 128K mode should not be compatible with the C64. "Freddy Bowen started this thought and I went with it. It made sense to me," says Herd. "He said, 'No, keep it different. Don't try and be a bigger C64, because then you will really fuck with compatibility.' We didn't want a hybrid definition of compatibility, and I applaud that thought that he started with."

After the meeting, Herd created the schematics. "I wrote the schematic from scratch, starting with a VIC chip and starting with a 6510 alias; the NMOS version [called the 8502]," he says.

Herd found himself competing with Jeff Porter and the LCD project for resources. It was a holdover from the Tramiel years. "Jack was gone at this time, but he made it so the departments competed with each other for resources," says Herd.

Dave Haynie began working on the LCD project until Herd stole him for the C128 project. "I actually worked on [the LCD computer] for about a month before Bil asked me to come on the C128 project with him," recalls Haynie.

The engineers gave the computer the obvious name of Commodore 128, or C128 for short. "When we started the Commodore 128, we always knew it was going to be called the Commodore 128," says Haynie. "It wasn't like it was a secret project or anything."

Marketing had a heavy hand in the Plus/4, but they were notably absent from the C128. "Nobody told us what to do, as far as the design. We drove the design, and it was a rare opportunity in history," explains Herd. "This would never happen at IBM or another company."

The unique freedom was due to a power vacuum left by Tramiel. "The reason I think there wasn't that process where marketing reviews everything is because under Jack, it wasn't necessary," says Herd. "Jack called the shots. With Jack gone, the engineers were free to say, 'Hey, look what we've got for you guys.'"

An aggressive engineer who passionately believed in backward compatibility now helmed the C128 project. Commodore would have a C64 successor. Although it was already August 1984, the C128 would have to be ready for the January 1985 CES show. With most computer companies focusing on 16-bit technology, industry analysts wondered if the market was still interested in 8-bit computers.

The 16-bit 6502

Chuck Peddle originally planned to follow-up the 6502 chip with a more powerful version. "The 6502 was never intended to be an end," says Peddle. "The 6502 was to get us into the market and selling cheap controllers but we had always planned on a 16-bit version." The success of the PET sidetracked Peddle.

While Motorola and Intel delivered 16-bit sequels of their chips, MOS Technology lagged behind. "I don't know precisely why they didn't [produce a 16-bit chip], other than Motorola is about a thousand times larger," says Haynie. "Over time, fewer and fewer companies were successful with microprocessors. The only ones who did really well in the merchant market were Motorola and Intel."

With a limited workforce through the early eighties, Robert Russell believes Commodore had higher priorities. "We wanted a 16-bit 6502 but it wasn't as important as fulfilling the computer demands," he explains. "We had a successful VIC-20 and we wanted something else to put on the shelf. We had a successful 80-column PET, the 8032, and it was doing huge gangbusters as a business machine. Nobody was saying, 'I need a faster computer'. They basically wanted more features."

Bill Mensch, the original layout engineer on the 6502, continued the 6502 legacy. When Jack's CMOS project failed, he cut Mensch loose but allowed him to hold onto the Western Design Center. "We moved him from Pennsylvania, set him up in Phoenix, and then abandoned him," says Peddle. "He went to Rockwell and basically got them interested in doing a CMOS version of the 6502, which they did." Mensch subsequently released the 65C02, used by both Commodore and Apple.

While the original 6502 engineers headed back west to Arizona, Will Mathis decided he liked the East Coast and stayed close to Commodore. He eventually came back for a 16-bit sequel. "He wound up getting a consulting job in Philadelphia," says Peddle. "Will consulted for Bill Mensch."

Robert Russell recalls Mathis at MOS Technology. "He was working on 16-bit designs and consultation with Commodore, but nothing really came of it because we were too busy with the VIC product line," he says.

Lack of funding also hindered the 16-bit 6502 project. "I think the amount of investment they put into it wasn't what a chip company really needed to stay competitive," says Haynie. "Microprocessors were just not in the cards."

After the project fizzled at Commodore, Mensch tried Commodore's closest competitor. "Mensch finally did it because Apple wanted it," says Peddle. "Thank God for having Bill there and carrying it on. He took that technology to Apple and created the 65816."

Mensch began his design in consultation with Apple in 1982. He called his chip the 65816 due to its ability to perform in both 8-bit and 16-bit modes. "Mensch was working with [Mathis] and later on went on his own and took what [MOS Technology] did and created the 65816," says Russell.

According to Peddle, "Bill Mensch did all the architecture on his 16-bit chip himself." The 65816 overcame many of the 6502's limitations, including the limited stack size. It could also address 16 megabytes of memory, as opposed to only 64 kilobytes with the original 6502.

At Western Design Center, Mensch did the work of entire teams of engineers. Peddle believes Mensch had a rare ability. "There are few world's great composers and there are a few worlds great artists," says Peddle. "Bill is a great layout guy, and he's a great circuit designer because of that."

Mensch's sister, Kathryn, helped him layout the chip. "His sister is a great layout person just like him," says Peddle. "For his sister to have it, it means it's some kind of inherited gene."

The siblings were able to progress with very little funding. "The WDC was Mensch and his sister," says Herd. "We used to just kid about it being hand crafted chips. By that, we were saying that they probably weren't using the newer tools that were around. They were doing it like they were doing in the old days, just shy of using rubylith and razorblades."

Robert Russell compared the 65816 to the original SY6516 specification sheet. "I was sitting there looking at the 6516 saying, 'Damn, that was pretty good architecture.' But he did even a better job with the real one," he says.

By March 1984, Mensch had samples in the hands of both Apple and Atari. When he approached Commodore, he ran into Bil Herd. "I had a conversation about using it one day," says Herd. "I was in my office and he called me. He said, 'Hey, you should look at building this in. I'm trying to get Apple to build it in and then there will be this common code.' I'm like, 'So you're trying to tell me Bill that because my competitor is using it, I have to use it.' He didn't like that comment."

Mensch's marketing skills failed to impress Herd. "I had tried to treat the call with the reverence of speaking to one of my elders but the logic got lost in the sales attempt," he says. "The Apple comment wasn't a compelling argument to a young engineer looking to do the things the best way, not what's best for the vendor."

Herd was also studying Motorola's 16-bit processor at the time. "We were looking at the 68000," he says. The 68000 design used many registers, compared to the minimal registers in the 65816. "I completely disagree with the attitude that having less registers by design is better than having more," explains Herd.

"His final attempt to get me to use the chip was, 'Well, the 68000 has got those 16 registers, and that's just so much stuff you have to store every time you get an interrupt. My chip has only got two registers, so it's easy.' I couldn't believe that. I'm like, 'So what you're saying is it's less powerful so therefore it's quicker, but if I wanted to I could use two registers on the new chip and it would be just like yours.' He goes, 'Uh, yeah, I guess.' That was the only conversation I had with Bill Mensch about using it."

Herd felt Mensch should have consulted with Commodore engineers during his design process. "If Mensch had talked with Freddy Bowen, he would have got good feedback earlier on in his design cycle," says Herd. "Fred would have read him the riot act on how to make a kernel for a C64 compatible user system."[1]

The C128 Animals

The Commodore 128 was the first project after the mass exodus of key staff to Atari. Six of the seven Plus/4 engineers eventually moved on to develop the C128. Bil Herd, Dave Haynie, and Frank Palaia would design the hardware, while Fred Bowen, Terry Ryan, and Von Ertwine developed the system software. The engineers hoped to redeem themselves to the outside world.

Management realized the tight schedule meant the engineers would have to work overtime, so they did everything possible to keep the engineers busy at Commodore until late hours. "We occasionally got

---

[1] A company called *CMD* later released a C64 upgrade called the *SuperCPU*. The device uses a 65816 chip to upgrade a stock C64 to 20 MHz and 16 megabytes of memory. It was surprisingly backward compatible, drastically speeding up 3D games such as *Freescape*, *Mercenary*, and *Sentinel* while maintaining the correct timing.

bribed," recalls Haynie. "Occasionally, a manager would say, 'We're bringing in beer and pizza at 10:00 or 11:00 [at night]', but it wasn't like we were drinking beer on the job all the time."

Management set the precedent, and soon Herd began bringing his own alcohol to work. "I got the guards used to seeing me walk in with a case of beer on my shoulder," recalls Herd. "My record was 11 days without leaving, and given the fact that I drank a lot back then, I couldn't live at work without a refrigerator with beer in it. They were told to leave us alone on that."

Beer became a constant companion to Herd while he developed the C128. "I had a refrigerator in [Greg] Berlin's office," says Herd. "Anybody was welcome to put their beer in there, but there was a beer tax, which meant we would take as much as we wanted. One time, a guy had shown up with this San Francisco brand beer, and when he came to get one, they were gone. We just said, 'This time the beer tax was 100%. Sorry.'"

The engineering culture changed radically under Herd compared to the days when Chuck Peddle and Charles Winterble ran their respective systems groups. "It was kind of wild," recalls Haynie. "It was the kind of place where you were encouraged by the fact that you could be wild. There was a lot of camaraderie there. We pulled lots of late night hours and I kept a sleeping bag under my desk. It was a very, very creative environment."

The unruly behavior of the C128 team soon earned them a nickname. "We were collectively known as the C128 Animals," explains Herd. "The term Animals was used by the highest management levels I was aware of at the time and described the effort and spirit of the team."

Haynie laughs at the old moniker. "We kind of looked like animals," he recalls. "Me and Bil had the long hair and we sometimes smelled like animals after too many days without going home."

To outsiders, Herd barely appeared civilized. "I walked around without my shirt on a lot and without shoes occasionally," says Herd.

Computer engineers have a reputation for leading staid lives, but Herd feels the C128 Animals challenged the stereotype. "I went into the Plus/4 with wild-eyed enthusiasm and by the next year I was cocky like a Jet fighter pilot," says Herd. "There were no geeks on our team except Terry Ryan. He was the resident vegetarian who wrote Basic 7.0."

After the move to West Chester, Commodore employees became patrons of a local bar called Margaritas. "When we started going there, it was kind of this little biker bar place," recalls Haynie. Margaritas soon prospered due to the close proximity to Commodore headquarters.[2] "We called it the 'house that Commodore built' because they added an extension and it got real fancy."

Herd fit right in. "I could walk right into a biker bar and you would never know I knew anything about computers," says Herd. "If anything, I was probably more dangerous than a normal person and hopped up from all the testosterone we got at work."

Although Haynie restricted his Margaritas visits to Fridays, Bil Herd sometimes worked from the bar. "To get out of the office (this was in the days before cell phones) we would go down to Margaritas," recalls Herd. "Dave D'Oreo and I had the bartenders in the area trained if we showed up in the afternoon. We pushed a couple of tables together and spread our schematics out, and that was how we would work all afternoon. Some of our schematics actually had rings in the corners from the beer mugs holding them down."

Chip designer Dave DiOreo (left) and Bil Herd (photo courtesy of Dave Haynie).

While the C128 Animals enjoyed their freedom, management started building up. "In the C128 days, they had installed a needless layer of middle management that pretty much did nothing, at least that I could

---

[2] A Margaritas bartender amused patrons by stopping a fan blade with his tongue. He later became semi-famous after winning *Stupid Human Tricks* on *Late Night with David Letterman*.

determine," says Haynie. "Rather than reporting directly to the director of engineering, we were reporting to this middle-guy."

Herd grew frustrated seeing resources wasted on unproductive projects. "To give you an idea of how middle managers dog-piled on the department, we got a manager in charge of components," says Herd. "He didn't know anything about the real life aspect of Asian markets or cost and availability overseas that I could detect."

The waste of resources appalled Herd. "He officially had more salary and people to support our ability to use the microfiche than we had designing the C128 computer," says Herd. "He hired a couple of more people and set up a computer-indexed version of data books that used microfiche. The microfiche was sort of out of date and I had several hundred data books anyway that actually traveled well to the local bars."

When the C128 Animals found someone without a purpose, they attacked. "The manager's name was Elroy, and rarely did we ever just say his name," explains Herd. "We usually sang it in a sentence, as in, 'Our Boy Elroy' [from the *Jetsons* TV show]. Whether you were in an intense discussion with management or a meeting, or at the bar, you didn't say Elroy, you sang it."

The middle manager provided one side benefit: access to executive email. "I never complained about the microfiche program as it was my favorite backdoor into the VAX system with manager privileges, since he had installed it incorrectly," reveals Herd. "If you hit Ctrl-C at the right time, it would break to the prompt and you would be logged on as Our Boy Elroy. [It was] great for finding out what managers were up to."

When marketing released promotional material for the C128, Herd's goal was set even higher. "We never said it was 100% compatible. We called it compatible-like," says Herd. "Then we found that Julie Bauer over in the marketing department had put out a brochure that said, '100% C64 compatibility.' So we said, 'Great, I like a challenge.'"

Achieving 100% compatibility became a mission. "The whole thing with the C128 became live or die whether it was compatible or not," explains Herd. "Anytime somebody thought they found a reason that it wasn't compatible, it was, 'Aha! We found why it will fail.' We created the culture that C64 compatibility was a must have, and compatibility meant 100% not 95%."

Herd tried to fixing the problems in the C64, but it inadvertently created new problems. "I started out as one of the only guys who knew where all the glitches were," says Herd. "I designed them out, and you know what? Cartridges stopped working."

The problems encountered while recreating C64 mode originated with the C64 team. "The guys who designed it weren't hardware engineers, they were chip designers," says Herd. "There is a different way of thinking. I have nothing against the guys who developed the C64. They were pioneers and they did it first, so this is not a swing at them or anything."

Herd credits the glitches to Bob Yannes' inexperience with systems design. "The chip designers just didn't know some of the basic rules," says Herd. Because of the delayed 64 documentation, programmers found their own tricks to create software, which often relied on glitches. "The guys who designed cartridges would use the glitches to clock data. It was like, 'No, no! Use the clock, not the address lines changing.' But they had found something that happened repeatedly."

It was disheartening to recreate the problems. "I had to put them back in," laments Herd. "There was a wire on the C128 and next to it, it said, 'Puts glitches back in.'"

Herd's attitude carried the project through. "The whole thing with Commodore 64 compatibility was you couldn't sit there and argue about why something wasn't compatible, and blame the guy that did it," says Herd. "You had to make it compatible."

Dave Haynie became the engineer most responsible for compatibility. "On the C128, I basically turned into the compatibility guy," he says. "I was getting all sorts of add-on hardware and when it didn't work I had to sit there and figure out why, and then figure out if they were doing something I considered legitimate."

Haynie used an old Bally-Midway game to test compatibility. "Our favorite cartridge was Wizard of Wor because that one did all kinds of crazy-assed things," he says.

Herd had very little time to make the 128 project happen. Five months remained until the computer's CES debut. "You'd think if we were smart we would have started in January for next year, but I think I started in August for next January," says Herd.

Building the Herdware

Software developers usually create software for the largest platform available. Since that was the C64, the 128K mode would have to be very similar to the existing C64 standard so that programmers could develop one program that would work on a normal C64 *and* the enhanced 128K mode. Even though the enhanced mode may not run all of the old software, it would run the new C64 software faster and better, encouraging existing C64 owners to upgrade. Call it *forward compatibility*. This was the path taken by IBM and Apple.

Much of the computer press at the time believed the C128 would be a C64 on steroids. Indeed, Herd set out to produce a machine with 128 kilobytes of memory, a 2 MHz processor, and 80 columns. However, would it be attractive to software developers?

Adding an additional 64 kilobytes of memory required ingenuity from Herd, since 6502 processors only addressed 64 kilobytes. "The CPU can only put out 16 bits worth of address, or 64K of memory," explains Haynie. "So no matter how much memory you have, the CPU can only talk to 64K at a time, no matter what you do."

Al Charpentier and his MOS engineers had already included a simple method of allowing more memory on the C64 called *bank switching*. "We handled that in the 6510," says Charpentier. "There was a port register that allowed you to do extended addressing."

By 1984, Charpentier's method of bank switching was outdated. "We didn't use that other banking scheme that was there [in the 6510]," says Herd. "Time had passed, so it was no longer the ideal way."

Herd and his team devised a Memory Management Unit chip, or MMU. "As far as I knew, I was inventing it, although I'm sure I hadn't," says Herd.

The results were impressive. "The way we did it in the C128 was the right way to do it," says Haynie. "You put an MMU in there and let the programmer manage the memory that you are banking between."

The MMU made it more difficult to add features while retaining backward compatibility. "If you change the memory map around at all, you will lose some compatibility," says Haynie.

Herd initially attempted a faster, better C64. "We had uber C64s," reveals Herd. "We had it working at one time. It was a C64 with an MMU. There were all kinds of addressing modes and other things. You could actually go into dual speed mode." The description sounded like the mode most people expected.

The 'uber C64' had less C64 compatibility but more features for programmers. "We could run a C64 program, stop it, and it was really a C128 with all the resources at its command," explains Herd.

Unfortunately, the VIC-II chip could not keep up with the 2 MHz processor. "He was trying to do something faster, but once again, there were problems with MOS getting chips to run faster on the 6502 side," says Russell.

Herd wanted his uber C64 to work with older software titles. "You would be hard pressed to find a game that didn't screw up somehow, because you needed room in the memory for the Memory Management Unit to sit there," explains Herd.

To the engineers, it seemed pointless to attempt backward compatibility with a more powerful system. "The [C64] programmer's reference guide told the users how to do every damn thing and how to get to every bit," says Russell. "People were doing weird stuff with peeking and poking, so to be 100% compatible was too difficult."

Instead, Herd decided to concentrate on a radically different C128 mode that retained very little compatibility. "We not only added a better kernel, and a better version of Basic, but we put a ROM monitor in there and some other things," says Herd. "That's why it's not compatible with the old. None of that crap fit in the bag."

Commodore 64 designer Bob Yannes claims he would have followed a similar path taken by Bil Herd for a C64 sequel. "I probably would have made the C64 a subset of a new machine," he says. "I wouldn't want to cripple the capabilities of the new machine in order to be compatible with the C64."

Programmer Terry Ryan improved almost every aspect of Basic, including better graphics commands and disk commands that were more like Microsoft DOS. The C128's starting screen even displayed, 'Microsoft Basic copyright 1977,' which was a first for a Commodore computer. According to Robert Russell, Microsoft was behind the change. "They came in and demanded that we put Microsoft back on the Basic, even though they didn't contribute anything," he says.

While Herd drove the hardware design, Fred Bowen developed the system software. "Fred was really the hands-on software guy then," says Russell. "Herd and Bowen were much more into implementation and what was really getting done on the product."

The software engineers had a surplus of ROM memory available, so the design team decided to add their signatures to the computer in the form of Easter eggs. Users who typed SYS 32800,123,45,6 received a message:

> Brought to you by...
>
> Software: Fred Bowen, Terry Ryan, Von Ertwine.
>
> Herdware: Bil Herd, Dave Haynie, Frank Palaia.

Terry Ryan also added messages of his own. An early message said, 'Veni Vidi Vici' (I came I saw I conquered). Herd and Ryan attempted to verify the message in the ROM code. "One time we spent two hours looking for a message to come through the analyzer," recalls Herd. "Finally I said, 'Nope, just a bunch of V's.' [Ryan] stopped, looked at me, his moustache twitched and he mouthed the word, 'Shit.'" As it turns out, Herd was not familiar with the saying. "I didn't recognize it as English and it had been working the whole time," he says.

Ryan added other messages that reflected his thoughts during cold-war arms race and Soviet collapse. "He of course was the author of, 'Link arms don't make them,'" says Herd.

Herd often fell into conflicts with other groups in Commodore. One such group was the Quality Assurance team, who verified Herd's work. "Early in the design I thought that the QA department might indeed help us assure the quality of the design," recalls Herd.

Herd openly mocked members of the QA team, and soon it seemed like they were out to get him. "The culture became, see who can poke a hole in the C128," says Herd. "It became a past time for a lot of different groups."

"We had product assurance people running every piece of software on the C128," recalls Haynie. "They came up with this *Island Graphics* paint program, which was a pretty popular program."

Herd continues, "Somebody downstairs had tried a *Koala Paint* cartridge, and I'm glad they did. He sent a runner up to tell me it had failed, so I knew about a minute before everybody else that there was about to be a problem. [The runner] just said the Koala Paint crashed, and I was thinking, 'This could be real serious, but let's see what it is.'"

Herd prepared himself. "I was eating a sandwich at the time," recalls Herd. "I leaned back to get a little Zen-like trance going. Sure enough, they come down the hall looking like the *Witches of Eastwick*. The doors open and in comes one of the managers, and there's the QA guy, there to say, 'I told you so,' and probably three or four others in an entourage. They have one thing on their mind: to prove that the C128 has a problem."

Herd felt under attack but tried not to show it. "I'm still eating a sandwich being cool about it. I said, 'Alright, let's walk to the lab. Show me what you've got.'"

Haynie recalls the unusual bug. "With their startup screen, they would draw a pretty picture using all the Island Graphics painting functions," he explains. "One of the things they did was read the characters out of the ROM, blew them up real big, and then they would paint them."

"We plug in the cartridge and it says, 'Koala Paint,' and it spells 'koala' and then the word 'paint' under it," explains Herd. "The characters are a couple of inches high."

On the C128, programmer Terry Ryan had improved the original C64 font set. "The characters are what's called the Atari font," reveals Herd. "We called it the Atari font because we took it right from Atari. If you look at the early Atari computer, it's 100% the same. Well, guess who we made ROM's for? The rumor is we lifted their font right off their cartridge. If we didn't, we copied it bit for bit, byte for byte."

Ryan attempted to replace the old Atari fonts. "Terry Ryan had put in a real Times-New Roman font so in C64 mode it looked different. You would think the text looking different would not make it behave different," says Herd. The seemingly innocuous change came back to haunt the team.

Herd watched the screen and spotted the problem. "It works its way through all the characters, and when it gets to the 'i' in paint, it missed the dot," he says. "The dot in the 'i' had moved to where it looked better. So instead of painting the dot in the 'i', which would have been very quick, it had missed it and hit the background."

"It proceeded to paint the entire background," says Haynie. "As well as doing that, it erased a bunch of stuff. The next one would come along, and so on. When you ran it on the C128 in C64 mode, it took about half an hour to startup." Terry Ryan's seemingly benign change to the font set rendered the software unusable.

Herd came up with a temporary solution. "I said, 'Grab a C64 ROM and brick lay it on there.' I went back to eating my sandwich, and in less than ten minutes, they have a C64 ROM soldered to the top of a C128 ROM, and it's working," says Herd.

The glitch showed how close the engineers had to stay to the original design for 100% compatibility. "Anything that you could think of on the Commodore 64 was essentially part of the hardware description, even if it was software because somebody somewhere had figured out a way to use it in ways you would never think of," says Haynie.

Herd felt vindicated for solving the problem in front of his detractors. "All the people who were gunning for me again had to go off mumbling to themselves," he says.

Herd's relationships with management deteriorated. "When I was working there, designing the computer wasn't the only obstacle," says Herd. "In fact, that seemed kind of easy compared to trying to navigate the middle management morass that was there."

Herd acknowledges his role in antagonizing the managers. "I would do things and I would piss them off, and if they did something wrong I let everybody know it," explains Herd. "They didn't actually have a lot of power, hence they were ragged at me because they couldn't do anything to me."

Jack's absence contributed to the management problem. "They were rampant at this time. It was like too many deer and they needed to be thinned out because there were no Jack Attacks," says Herd. "There really wasn't any accountability for bad management. They had completely broken the cycle of, 'Do a good job and you'll stay, don't do a good job and you'll leave.' Instead, it was open ended."

A former Nortel executive was responsible for evaluating the managers. "Adam Chowaniec was a French-Canadian and he worked for Northern Telecom [Nortel]," says Herd. "He had worked for Lloyd Taylor who was vice president under Jack."

Herd got along well with Chowaniec and often relied on him for support. "Adam Chowaniec had done a real good job of managing the technology," says Herd. "I got along with him great."

Herd felt the Chowaniec needed to get tougher with his staff. "What Adam didn't do until later was fire a bunch of people who needed to be fired where it wasn't like you could redirect their efforts and get them going in a positive fashion," he explains.

Herd's nemesis at Commodore was a software manager named Julian Strauss, who was also Fred Bowen and Terry Ryan's boss. "Julian was one of those managers who said, 'I can see the advantage to deciding not to decide this right now.' I said, 'So you are going way out on a limb in that you're not even going to decide to decide something? Good going, Julian.' I couldn't stand not making a decision. That's what I learned from people there; how to make decisions."

As usual, Herd openly courted confrontations. "One time I dragged in one of the plants and set it next to him, as a reference to which one you could get a better answer out of," says Herd. "I really hated this guy."

Herd also conflicted with the QA manager, Bob Shamus. "At some point the head of the QA department declared that the C128 pretty much wouldn't work," says Herd. "I guess he meant it was a matter of time before we all achieved the same level of enlightenment that he had. He basically hovered about waiting for every opportunity to be vindicated." With so many enemies, it was doubtful Herd would survive at Commodore long enough to finish the C128.

CP/M

CP/M was the first operating system developed for personal computers in 1973. Gary Kildall, the programmer of CP/M, was familiar to many computer users in the eighties as the co-host of the PBS series *Computer Chronicles*. According to host Stewart Cheifet, "Kildall was the rare combination of genius and gentleman."

Software pioneer Alan Cooper said, "CP/M was 5K and it gave you no more and no less than what an operating system should do." It was the most widely used operating system until MS-DOS. In fact, the original

MS-DOS was a direct knockoff of CP/M, resulting in almost identical commands.

Bil Herd wanted to make his C128 compatible with the existing Commodore CP/M cartridge, which used a Z80 processor. The cartridge was designed by an engineer they dubbed 'Shooting Star'. "This guy was supposed to design a Z80 cartridge for the Commodore 64," explains Herd. "One of the things I noticed when I did the C128 was that the Z80 cartridge didn't work in the C128, and it *really* didn't work in the Commodore 64; they just thought it did."

Herd discovered the problem. "I'm going through this pile of papers a year later and I find a schematic for a Z80 cartridge," he recalls. "I open it up and look at it, and low and behold it's the Z80 coprocessor card for the Apple! Shooting Star ripped it off and that's why it didn't work."

Herd studied the problem and realized the CP/M cartridge used more power than the C64 supplied. "I got paid to be cheap and I couldn't afford to pay for half an amp that I would only use if somebody had the CP/M cartridge," he says. "I couldn't afford to add five dollars to the cost of [the C128]." He considered alternatives.

Herd moved CP/M off to the side and tried another cartridge. "Then we got the Magic Voice cartridge in from Texas and it wouldn't work," he says. "I looked at it to see why it was crashing my C128, because until then I had a good record. There were these lines called the game lines in the C64 that would cause the memory map to shift, and they were using it in a new and unpredictable way."

To fix the problem, Herd required the C128 to start at memory address zero, but the 8502 started elsewhere. "One night, everybody left and it was broken," says Herd. "During the night, I said, 'I have no way to fix this, unless we startup by not starting at that address.' I said, 'Hey, Von. The Z80 chip starts from zero, doesn't it?' He said, 'Yup.' I said, 'Cool. I need somebody wire wrapping tonight.'"

The hour was too late to purchase a Z80 chip, so Herd looked elsewhere. "Everybody had doorstops that were actually Sinclairs," he recalls. "I went and tore open my doorstop because we didn't own a Z80 chip in the place."

The C128 Animals spent the night reconfiguring the C128. "By morning, we had written enough of the kernel and wired this other processor in," he explains. "When you turned on the thing, it would wake up at 0000, set up the MMU, and then it would look to see if there was a cartridge before turning control over to the 8502." After the changes, Magic Voice worked.

Herd also used the Z80 to load disk programs automatically when the user turned on the C128. This made a disk-based operating system more viable. Users could also select which mode they wanted by holding down different key combinations when the C128 started.

In the end, Herd had three good reasons for including the Z80 processor in his C128. "One, I couldn't afford the CP/M cartridge. Two, I couldn't afford the black eye from not being compatible with Magic Voice. Three, I ended up using it to boot the thing. So the first dual processor home computer was born," he says.

Employees who came to work in the morning were stupefied at the rapid transformation of the C128. "Everybody left one night and there was one processor in the C128, and they came back the next morning and there were two," says Herd. "The speech cartridge worked and I didn't have to worry about the CP/M cartridge anymore."

Others were unenthusiastic about the additional processor. "Commodore Australia wrote us a telex that said, 'We will tear the Z80 out of every C128 before we sell it!' We thought that was funny. They could try it, but where are they going to get the code to run it, because it boots from the Z80," says Herd.

CP/M also served a tactical purpose in the C128. "We had CP/M in there because we wanted the C128 to hit the ground running with a bunch of software that would be somewhat useful for business," says Haynie. "We understood, especially after the Plus/4 and TED stuff, that it was going to be hard to get people to write new programs."

The engineers were well aware that CP/M was antiquated and losing market share by 1984. "It definitely was," says Haynie. "But we walked into it with our eyes open. We knew that was a transitional thing."

CHAPTER

18

Brawling for the C128

1984 - 1985

After the mass exodus of talent from MOS Technology, it was uncertain if the remaining engineers could continue advancing Commodore's semiconductor designs. At the time of his departure, Bob Yannes recalls, "There weren't very many chip designers there."

Al Charpentier believes MOS Technology had design talent. "There was a hole in the organization after we left, but I think there were still some good people there," he says. While the rest of Commodore moved to West Chester, the MOS Technology engineers remained at MOS headquarters in Norristown, Pennsylvania.

It was up to MOS Technology engineer Dave DiOrio to continue the VIC chip legacy. "He was instrumental in the design and capabilities of the C128," says Herd. While the C64 designers had nine months to complete their chips, the C128 team had only five. However, the design changes were not as ambitious.

For sound, the C128 used the 8580 SID chip, which received no improved functionality over the 6580 SID. "The only difference was we got a 9 volt SID chip instead of a 12 volt SID chip," says Haynie. "We didn't have two chips for stereo, but it was something that had been talked about."

Yannes had plans for further development of the SID chip. "If I had stayed at Commodore, I think I would have had time to refine it and make it a much better sounding product," he says.

Commodore attempted to improve on the SID chip after Yannes departed. "They had a guy named Rudolfsky but he was the wrong guy to try it," says Herd. "He was supposed to be the analog guy, and he was a case. He tried an NMOS version of the SID chip, and the rev I saw was visibly worse. He broke a lot of rules."

The alterations by Rudolfsky created a loud thump sound in the SID chip when it became active. "Capacitors are attached to the sound chip, because it's an analog device," explains Herd. "You have to respect that these things are out there holding charge. So Rudolfsky tried to improve the SID chip, and he really didn't. He moved it backwards for a while. He brought back the thump."

MOS Technology did not even attempt an improved VIC-III chip. "From a design point of view, once Charpentier left, that was a big deal for MOS," says Winterble. "The VIC chip wasn't the most stable thing in the world. It was so complex that after [Charpentier] left, they were afraid to touch it. That was a problem."

Instead, Herd relied on an 80-column video chip called the 8563,[1] designed by a husband and wife team. "Kim [Eckert] was very bright, and so was his wife Anne," says Herd. "They both happened to be red heads from Texas."

Like Peddle and his team, Eckert was from the more formal atmosphere of Motorola. "Kim had come from Motorola and had designed and patented some of the logic blocks in use on the Motorola 68000," explains Herd. "He had great stats on paper."

Motorola ran on a corporate nine-to-five schedule, while Commodore ran on passion. "It was a clash of corporate culture," says Haynie. "We didn't like Kim Eckert too much. He wasn't a typical Commodore chip guy."

Although the C128 would use the 8563 chip, Eckert originally designed it for the C900 UNIX machine. As Herd recalls, "Bob Olik came to me, who was Dave DiOrio's boss and head of the chip designers at this point, and he said, 'I've got a chip for you.' I was going to use the industry standard 6845. I said, 'Hey, this looks cool. This is a 6845 with these additional features,' and they said, 'Yes.'"

"It was my understanding that this part had the same operating parameters as the 6845, a very common graphics adapter," says Herd.

The 8563 chip had features not available in the VIC-II chip, such as 80-column text display and 640 by 200 resolutions. However, it lacked features of the VIC-II, such as sprites. Since the 8563 had no support for VIC-II graphics modes, the C128 required a separate VIC-II chip.

---

[1] The 8563 designation may indicate it was a continuation of the TOI 6563 chip started years earlier by Bil Seiler. According to Russell, "He had a real high resolution display early on."

Herd thought the technology was stable. "The chip had actually already been around for a year and a half," he recalls.

After he added the 8563 chip to his prototype, he began noticing problems. "Not scrutinizing the chip for timing differences the way I normally did any new chip was a mistake I made," says Herd. "I blame myself as this really is the type of mistake an amateur makes."

Prior to Herd discovering the chip, the 8563 project was plagued with problems, even though Eckert had more advanced design tools than Al Charpentier had. By late 1984, the 8563 was far from complete. "The 8563 took nine revs before it could just display some characters correctly," says Herd. "That was a troubled chip."

Haynie felt frustrated by the lack of communication from Kim Eckert. "I always had problems because of lack of documentation because it wasn't like many of our chip designers wanted to write up specs," he says. "They said, 'Here, design something with this chip. Oh, by the way, we're not going to tell you how it works.' They would basically give you the notes they used to design it with, which were sometimes exactly what the chip did, and sometimes they weren't."[2]

Herd became more and more disappointed with the 8563's fundamental design. The video chip's main function is, of course, to draw pixels on a screen. Each time the video chip draws a line, it tells the processor it has finished so it can get the next line of data. Programmers call it an *interrupt* when the video chip notifies the processor, because it interrupts the processor. To his astonishment, early 8563 revisions had no interrupt facility built in.

After complaining frequently about this, Herd sat down with Eckert to find why the chip lacked an interrupt. According to Eckert, an interrupt was redundant because the processor can check the status any time by checking on the video processor. In other words, instead of the video chip telling the processor when it is done, the processor keeps checking to see if the video chip is done.

The explanation amused Herd. In Eckert's mind, it seemed like the system would do nothing else besides talk to his 8563 chip. Herd used the analogy of a phone to describe the poor design. When a phone rings, it is effectively interrupting you to tell you someone is on the line. Eckert

---

[2] After the release of the 8563, programmers discovered undocumented features. "It was funny, because the chip was so lightly documented shall we say, that users found features that nobody knew existed, like the fact you could do an 80-column bitmap mode," says Haynie. "Apparently [Kim Eckert] never mentioned it to anyone."

thought it was better to eliminate the interruption and rely on the user to keep checking the phone by picking it up and saying, 'Hello?'

This became a sticking point between Eckert and Herd. Heated discussions often erupted over the interrupt. During these discussions, someone would stop, excuse himself, and pick up the nearest phone to see if there was anyone on the line. According to Herd, "This utterly failed to get the point across but provided hours of amusement." Whenever a phone was nearby, one of the C128 Animals picked it up and said, "Hello?" This behavior puzzled the owners of Margaritas, who wondered what fixation the Commodore engineers had with their pay phone.

To make matters worse, MOS Technology was having problems producing 8563 chips that even powered up. CES crept nearer and September came and went. Some revisions would literally self-destruct and release a pungent odor. To prevent this, Herd turned to the black arts. According to Herd, "Sometimes, all I had to do was touch the board in a mystical way and then back out slowly, accompanied by ritual-like chanting and humming. This became know as the 'laying of hands.'"

To Bil Herd, it seemed like everything was against the C128 Animals. "These were the middle managers that couldn't or didn't embrace what we were truly trying to do," says Herd. "They either wanted to stake out their territory, were mortified that the rules were being broken, or they simply wanted to be noticed."

Herd continued battling with QA manager Bob Shamus after making a costly mistake. "We didn't have design-checking tools back then and we had hand created the font for the gate array," says Herd. "If you held out the green and white computer paper, it would extend almost to the floor. There was a term on each line. Well, one of them was wrong."

Herd released the set of terms before anyone had verified them. "We had released it aggressively to MOS because I knew that if you slowed them down, it would be us that were hurting when we didn't get the chips on time," explains Herd.

Without realizing the error, the MOS Technology technicians created a half-run of PLA chips, which came out to over ten thousand chips. "If you turn it over to production, it's five weeks before you see your chips," explains Herd. "We had gotten the first half and they were screwed up."

The error resulted in Ultimax mode not working properly while in C64 mode. "Who used Ultimax mode? Well, it turns out the English soccer game did, so when you plugged in the soccer game into the C128, it would actually come up with big black and white checker blocks," explains Herd.

Herd looked into the problem and traced it to the gate array. "I went to go and find out why, and sure enough, on this huge piece of paper where there should have been a one there was an X," says Herd.

The small error turned out to be very costly. "It cost a couple of hundred thousand dollars," says Herd. "Basically it was my fault. Somebody in my group missed it but I took all blame for anything."

The managers summoned Herd. "I go into this meeting and the two heads from QA are there. One was from the QA engineering group, who had never done anything useful in his whole time there," says Herd. "There was also the president of MOS Technology and the vice president of Commodore."

Herd instantly noticed the mood was heavy. "The one guy pushes this little stack of paper forward and says, 'We have proof that you approved the bad font.' I said, 'Yeah, I fucked up,' and those were the words I used in this big meeting. I said, 'Here's how we're going to fix it.'"

Herd was more worried about fixing the problem than losing his job. "There was a plan [to have me fired], but I didn't think for a second I was in jeopardy," says Herd.

The manager cut Herd off before he could continue. "The guy cleared his throat and he says, 'Ahem. No, we have proof that it was you that messed it up.' I said, 'Yes. I – fucked – up, and here's how we're going to fix it,' and I started to outline it."

The QA manager was determined to make Herd squirm. "He starts to do it again!" recalls Herd. Luckily, Herd had an ally in the room. "The president of MOS, who taught me how to make a decision, cleared his throat and the room goes quiet. He said, 'I think Bil is on it and he's trying to tell you how to fix it.'"

Herd had a plan to save the other half-run of the PLA chip by making minor corrections to one of the layers. "We made a mask that we would never use again for layer six, which was metal, and we were able to recover one of the split lots," says Herd. "We corrected it in less than a week and we got half a run out of it."

The dedication to build the C128 by January overrode everything else, including Thanksgiving. The young engineers skipped visits home to family and concentrated on the computer. Herd's manager was kind enough to bring in some turkey and stuffing for Bil and his C128 Animals.

As December began, the only custom chip that worked was the 8502 CPU. Herd waited patiently for MOS to deliver new batches of chips, which always arrived in huge glass jars. He tested the latest batch of 8563 chips and concluded they were worthless. That night, delirious from testing so many chips, Herd devised a little gumball-like contest for his fellow engineers. He placed a sign on the jar reading, 'Guess how many working 8563's there are in the jar and win a prize.' "If the number you guessed was a positive real number, you were wrong," says Herd. The C128 Animals were in real danger of missing CES.

The CES Panic

In December, with five weeks before CES, stress levels peaked among employees. Sometimes it seemed like making the deadline was more important than designing a functional computer. "It was a weird time because you didn't do the product as best as you could," explains Herd. "You had a relatively narrow window to shove the shit into the bag and you spent the rest of the time making the bag a good bag."

However, no one doubted they would make it. "I can honestly say that it didn't seriously occur to me that we wouldn't be ready for CES," says Herd.

Showstoppers were problems that prevented the computer from working. Sometimes the engineers encountered as many as three showstoppers in a single day. With CES nearing, all the C128 Animals cared about were killing showstoppers. If it was a minor problem, they did not address it. "Often we didn't get it right; we just got it done on time," says Herd. "You could not make that date otherwise."

Herd knew they would have to change their attitude if they were going to make it for CES. According to Herd, he frequently quoted Clint Eastwood from *The Outlaw Josey Wales* to his engineers, "Now remember, things look bad and it looks like you're not gonna make it, then you gotta get mean. I mean plumb, mad-dog mean."

The hectic schedule played with the engineers' sleep patterns. "At most places, you're not allowed to sleep but I would sleep in the middle of the day if I was tired," says Herd. "Of course, I had been up all night or been up for two nights in a row. If I really wanted to get some sleep, I had this sign that both Adam [Chowaniec] and Ed Fix had signed that said, 'Do not disturb under the authority of Adam Chowaniec and Ed Fix.' I put that on my door and you had to be at their level or higher to knock and wake me up."

Herd inspired the C128 Animals with his own diehard example. "I certainly stayed for multiple days," recalls Haynie. "I went home, got a good night's sleep, and then came right back and stayed for a few more days."

Herd was perpetually exhausted during the final month before CES. "One afternoon the phone is ringing. It continued ringing in spite of the fact that three people were gathered around a terminal only a couple of feet from it," recalls Herd, who had been fast asleep. "My door opens and I come out with a metal leg I had previously wretched off of a desk, walk to the phone, and do a hard Samurai bash on the phone. This had the effect that the phone stopped ringing immediately. The three people had turned to stare at the phone like it had just appeared there, and I, with the leg of a desk slung back over my shoulder, went back into my office to go back to sleep."

The C128 Animals had little time for family, home-life, commuting to work, eating, or sleeping. Commodore became their life. Bil Herd's personal record was 11 days without leaving the West Chester facility. He kept an air mattress under a table for when fatigue overtook him. Herd is adamant that he kept himself clean, despite the lack of showers at work. "I may have lived there, but I had been in the service and I knew how to stay clean," says Herd. "I would take a birdbath, which is what we called it."

Herd and the engineers kept toothbrushes, sponges, and washcloths at work. "It wasn't unusual for someone to walk into the men's bathroom about six in the morning and I'd be standing there in my red bikini underwear washing myself out of the sink with cold water," recalls Herd.

Birdbaths were especially unpleasant because hot water was not available on the late shift. "At night, the hot water would turn cold because of power saving," explains Herd. To make his birdbath more pleasant, Herd found an alternate solution. "I got this brown bin and I would go over to the vice president's coffee machine, and I would fill it with hot water from the coffee machine. So now I at least had hot water in my birdbath."

As CES closed in, the lack of working chips became a joke among the systems engineers. The 8563 was especially problematic, with a long list of glitches. The latest revision no longer displayed a solid screen. The first couple of characters on each line were either missing or partially formed. When the chip heated up, the characters disappeared altogether while other characters on the screen seemed possessed. According to Herd, "The 8563 also had a problem where the 256 byte transfer didn't always take place properly, leaving a character behind. This ended up having the effect of characters scrolling upwards randomly." Other problems mysteriously appeared. If a pixel was by itself, it became invisible. The problems gave the engineers nightmares.

Incredibly, the two 8563 chip designers went on vacation in December, leaving behind a non-functioning chip. "That was Kim and Anne Eckert," says Herd. "They may not have been married at the time, but they did get married. They were gone, off on an island or something."

"Going into December we had a chip with .001% yield," says Herd. "The yield of chips that even worked this good fell to where they only got three or four working chips the last run." A run produces upwards of ten thousand chips and costs between $40,000 and $120,000 to produce. "It was a pretty expensive couple of chips."

It was up to Haynie and a few managers to find working 8563 chips among thousands. "[We] were going through vast quantities of these to find a handful that would work. They barely yielded," recalls Haynie. "Naturally, we're doing all this last minute stuff between Christmas and New Years."

Even the 'working' 8563 chips had problems. "If they worked at all, they didn't synchronize properly," says Haynie. Herd decided to make a timing circuit and bypass the chip circuit altogether. While Haynie sorted chips, the engineers produced a three by three inch printed circuit board.

Survival at Commodore meant pushing themselves to extremes. "Engineers were like Jet fighter pilots," says Herd. "We were cocky because we needed to be. It didn't matter if they liked you. Either you were good or you were in the way. There was no middle ground."

Herd also clashed with his manager, Joe Krasucki, over the MMU design. "The MMU was designed to go a full 512K," says Herd. Unfortunately, his manager wanted to limit the MMU to 128 kilobytes. "We had gotten an MMU done fast so we could keep developing and I had slated for one more [revision] that had more address lines on it. Joe Krasucki, my boss, pulled the plug on the next rev of the MMU."

Herd was used to going around managers to get things done, but in this case, it would be impossible. "He said, 'Nope. Not authorized.' He told MOS not to do another chip. If he would not authorize the whole transaction between the two companies, who am I to go over there and say, 'Hey, I need you to do another rev of the chip.' So we were stuck with a maximum of 128K."

The decision infuriated Herd. "Even though Joe Krasucki was his boss, Herd had to fight to do what was right," says Russell. "That's where I got respect for those guys. Krasucki would do something stupid and you would wonder sometimes what the hell they were smoking."

The passion of creating a new computer drove Herd and his team on. "I had a drill sergeant who one day said, 'You know, gentlemen, I know it hurts. I know it's pain. Just live with it.' And that's what it was."

Christmas was a minimal affair for Herd and his girlfriend. "We went to Greg [Berlin]'s house," recalls Herd. "Our Christmas eve consisted of stopping at somebody's house on the way home."

By January, some of the chips were still unpredictable. Herd claims the video chip would literally self-destruct and spew bad odors when it attempted to load in the fonts. Engineers began contemplating bizarre solutions to make the chips work during the CES demonstration. According to Herd, "On our side, there was talk of rigging cans of cold spray with foot switches for the CES show."

January 1985 CES

The engineers finally completed the demonstration computers at 2:00 am, just in time for their 6:00 am departure to Las Vegas. As they were packing, they heard the unofficial C128 theme song on the radio, Peter Gabriel's *Salisbury Hill*. Herd took this as an omen that things would go smoothly at CES. "Several hapless programmers were spared the ritual sacrifice that night. Little do they know they owe their lives to some unknown disc jockey," says Herd.

The engineers brought a record number of prototypes to the show. "I guess we had about 30 prototypes by early January," recalls Haynie.

Commodore aimed their CES marketing campaign squarely at the competition. "They were running this campaign where they had arrows going through the Charlie Chaplin hat from IBM, and arrows going through apples," explains Haynie.

Haynie was in for a shock as soon as he landed in Las Vegas. "Bil and I are sharing a cab on the way in from the airport," recalls Haynie. "We see this big billboard about the C128, and guess what it says? It says it's expandable to 512K. We didn't know that! Naturally, when we got back to West Chester, we had to find a way to make the thing expandable to 512K."

Trouble began almost as soon as the C128 Animals stepped into the *MGM Grand Hotel* to claim their reserved rooms. "We showed up in the lobby and you know something is wrong when the line at the desk is only full of Commodore employees," says Herd. "We found out that our hotel reservations had been canceled by someone who fit the description of an Atari employee."

The Commodore employees tried their best to avenge themselves. "We assumed we knew who it was. I heard somebody on the phone saying, 'Hi, this is Sam Tramiel. Cancel my hotel rooms, we won't be needing them.'"

Dave Haynie is not so sure that Atari was responsible for the lack of reservations. "We were always screwing up bookings. Maybe it was just the marketing people playing with the engineers," he says.

Herd was not worried. "Quite honestly, not having a hotel room in Vegas for one night is not that big a thing," he says. "It's hard to tell what time of day or night it is there anyway. I just crashed with somebody who [had a room] or we just partied all night long."

Things got worse when CP/M programmer Von Ertwine arrived at the hotel and spotted Herd. "Von is a heavyset guy himself and he's a wrestler. He's got to be 240 or 260 but not nearly as tall as Greg," explains Herd.

"We're all in this line wondering why we can't get our hotel rooms, and I hear this rumbling noise," recalls Herd. "I turned and this guy had launched himself running across the lobby of the MGM into a flying tackle aimed at me. He hit me so hard that I don't think we hit the rug for a good 10 feet and we came to a sliding halt literally on my face. One of my shoes came off and I had a rug burn on the side of my face for the rest of the show."

One Commodore manager acted on behalf of all the employees to try to save the situation. "He swapped one of the SX64 computers to get us more rooms than we could normally get," recalls Herd. "I think we carried those just as currency. Basically, that went over the counter and more people got rooms for more nights."

After the engineers settled, they presented the C128 computer to Marshall Smith in the Commodore suite. "When we would go to show it to [Smith], I was the guy who was standing right behind them answering his questions," says Herd. "He said, 'Where does the 512K [memory expansion] go?' My boss Joe Krasucki puffed on a cigar and said, 'In the back.' Me and another guy looked at each other and started working our way out the back of the room because we knew we would have to go make the changes that Smith just asked about that my boss said existed, when they didn't exist."

Herd felt frustration with Krasucki, who had previously overruled 512-kilobyte expansion. "It was supposed to be 512K expandable from day one and we were told not to do it," says Herd. "I told him, 'So you are telling us to do what we said we wanted to do all along?' By that time, me and Krasucki were starting to rub each other more and more the wrong way, and he just said, 'Shut up.'"

The Commodore booth was one of the biggest ever. "Commodore had this battleship grey booth that was huge," recalls Haynie. The Commodore 64 occupied most of the space, even though they had launched it three years earlier. "When the C128 was announced, sales of the C64 started up again," says Haynie. "They had the normal stuff, like C64's all over the place, and then they had a special section with the C128 showing off the new things. They also had the Commodore LCD machine."

Marketing people demonstrated the C128's diverse functions. "There were stations set up that would do different things," says Herd. "One would be showing CP/M, one would be running C64 games, and one would be showing 80-column mode and 40-column mode."

The different C128 stations kept the engineers busy. "Normally, it would be smooth sailing and you could have a good time, because you worked hard for it," says Haynie. "There was plenty of that, but it wasn't the whole story."

The fickle C128 prototypes required special attention from their creators. "When you turned the voltage up too high the 80-column chip didn't work, and when you turned it down too low the VIC chip didn't work right in multicolor character mode," explains Herd. "I had made the power supply adjustable, which saved my life, and I carried a little blue tweak tool with me. Some power supplies were adjusted for 5.25 volts and some were adjusted for 4.75 volts and I would match up what you were displaying to your power."

Herd gave the marketing people very strict instructions. "Somebody would come and get me and show me sparkles and I would get in the cabinet and the sparkles would go away, and then I would say, 'Now don't let anybody change what you're doing here without coming to me,'" says Herd. "We crafted what was seen by the public there."

Temperature also played a large role in the demonstrations because of the imperfect 8563 chip. "The way that the 80-column chips were made to work required this phase lock loop circuit," explains Haynie. "The problem with locking circuits like that is that their locking points change when they get warm. You would have to adjust it with this little tweaking tool."

Haynie spent the show running from demonstration to demonstration, adjusting the locking point and keeping the temperatures down. "One of my jobs became instantly clear. I was the guy who ran around with a can of freeze spray and a little tweaking tool," says Haynie. "Anytime a marketing guy shut one of these machines off and couldn't get it to turn back on, I had to spot it, go right over there very discretely, and get this thing back up and running. I had a whole week of that."

Herd disliked the cold-spray solution. "To call me, they would actually just start using their cold spray, because I hated them using the cold spray," recalls Herd. "I'm like, 'You're going to break it one of these days and I'm not going to help you!' So they used it as a hardware engineer call. I'd come running and they would be smiling because they were nowhere near the breadboard with it."

Not all the C128 machines could display every mode properly, but some marketing people were overzealous and attempted to show them off anyway. "You couldn't quite convince these people," says Haynie. "There were also some where the 80-column chip worked well enough to run, but not really well enough to let people look at. Yet you had a really hard time getting the marketing guys to not try to show off the 80-column chip on the machines that we had deemed unacceptable."

With crowds everywhere, the C128 Animals had to attend to the problems covertly; otherwise, the C128 might gain a poor reputation. "I would occasionally have to walk over and say, 'Oh, they need you over there,' and then I would switch it back before anyone saw that it looked like crap," says Haynie.

The Commodore employees were wary of Jack Tramiel. "One of the running jokes became sightings of Sam and Jack in a white truck hanging around where they were unloading our booth," says Herd.

Commodore management officially made it a punishable offence to go near Atari. "During the C128 show, they had an announcement that said, 'Anybody caught over at the Atari booth is going to get fired,'" says Herd. "They didn't tell that to us engineers but they told it to the rest of the people who were working the booth."

Herd was obliged to visit Atari near the end of the show. "I was in the booth upstairs in one of the rooms where we were working and relaxing. The phone rings and I answer. A marketing guy said, 'I want you to go over and check out this one thing in the Atari booth.' I said, 'Well, that wouldn't be a good idea. I'm well known over there and there's no way I can do it clandestinely.' The guy got belligerent with me and said, 'Look, I don't think it's too much to ask. Do you know who you're talking to?' I said, 'Fine. I'll go over there.'"

As Herd predicted, Atari employees spotted him instantly. "I go over and I attracted attention almost right away," recalls Herd. "Tom Brightman, who had gone with Jack, started talking to me. Sig Hartmann starts talking to me. Shiraz was there and a crowd formed. Pretty soon Jack joins the crowd and made me a job offer on the spot."

Although Herd had worked for Jack for almost a year at Commodore and created the Plus/4 under his insistence, it was the first time they spoke. "I didn't meet Jack literally until the year of the 128 as far as actually doing any talking to him, and even then I don't know that he knew my name," says Herd.

Herd did not take the offer seriously. "We were laughing as if it were a joke," he recalls. "Sig then put his big arm around me and started leading me to the side saying, 'No, really, that was real.'"

Herd politely declined the offer. "I was in the middle of doing something. It was hard enough for me to remember to eat, let alone think about changing jobs," says Herd. "I knew where I worked. As Freddy

Bowen said, 'That's when you reach into your jacket and pull the pin on your grenade. One for five – yeah.' We laughed about that."

Shortly after the CES show, management decided the LCD computer's fate. "Jeff Porter did an excellent job of selling that," says Herd. "He had orders in hand from the CES show for 15,000 units. We had this LCD computer ready to launch."

Marshall Smith was less enthusiastic. "The president or CEO of Tandy had a heart to heart with Marshall Smith and they had said, 'Oh, there's no money in this LCD,' and Marshall cancelled the program," says Herd. "Commodore didn't produce an LCD machine after a conversation with our competition telling us not to produce it."

Herd believes Radio Shack lied to Smith. "I had an article hanging on my wall that said, 'Tandy's number one selling product of all Radio Shack products,' and it had a picture of their little stupid LCD machine," recalls Herd. "That was back when it was golden-blue displays and they had 30 columns by eight rows."

The Commodore engineers sensed laptop computers were the future. "I went to the shows and brought home all the literature and put them in individual files, so I knew what the competition was announcing or had out," says Russell. "I knew that there was a glitch [with the Tandy LCD computer] but it was a temporary glitch because they had such an inferior LCD screen. They had a tablet with a tiny LCD display and it was nothing like an LCD computer."

Russell had little influence over the decision. "I was really not involved much with the LCD, other than reviewing it, because at that time my [UNIX] business machine thing was consuming most of my time," he says. "I talked to Marshall about that but it was a done decision. He was adamant that Radio Shack says there's no future in LCD."

Dave Haynie chuckles at the shortsighted decision. "It was one of those things. 'Who needs a portable computer?'"

"That always pissed off every engineering person in the company," says Russell. "I'm still pissed to this day. 'Oh, there's no future in LCD. None at all.' Argh!"

With no need for LCD technology, and no calculator or watch production, Commodore got rid of the LCD division. "Commodore sold off the LCD developer because who's going to need LCD's?" says Haynie. "It's funny when you look back on some of that stuff."[3]

---

[3] Commodore sold off the LCD division sometime in 1985 or 1986, according to Bil Herd.

Final Design and Production

Herd had many enemies within Commodore management, but he could always rely on one executive. "Adam Chowaniec was my guardian angel at that point," recalls Herd. Unfortunately, when Chowaniec disappeared, so did Herd's protection. "He was out for about ten days in Germany and the head of the drafting department had come to see me and said, 'Well, we're going to stop giving such priority to the C128. This has gone on just far too long.' Those were his exact words."

Herd was appalled. "I thought, 'Really? How can I tell you to just fucking do your job? You've decided that the C128 shouldn't be the top priority at this phase of the design.'"

For ten days during Chowaniec's absence, the C128 project fell behind schedule. "Adam got back and wanted to know what asshole stopped the C128," recalls Herd. "It was like, 'As long as you hurt him later, I'll be okay. I'll get this fixed for you, but I want to see him bleed later.'"

Getting the project back on schedule was Herd's main concern. Herd ran three eight-hour shifts of PCB engineers to catch up. The design area became Herd's temporary home. "I took an air mattress, and my army coat because it's very air-conditioned in that area," says Herd. "I just stayed in this room with these guys for the next three or four days in three shifts. They were doing one guy per shift, and there's three designers, but I was there for all three shifts."

The air-conditioned room was great for the computers, but to the humans working there it felt like a refrigerator. "There's something about working like that that makes you like junk food," says Herd. "On Friday I had bought Burger King breakfast biscuits. I bought four or five, and they were sitting on a bookshelf next to me on Friday. It was so cold in that goddamned room that by Sunday they were still good and I ate them for lunch."

"We would have had time to do it in the ten days, but we knocked it out in three. We killed ourselves to catch up for what a manager had done," recalls Herd. "That was an example of middle management just fucking something up." As a remembrance of their efforts, the designers included a small message on the board that only they could appreciate. It said, 'RIP HERD FISH RUBINO.'[4]

---

[4] Inexplicably, the third PCB engineers name did not appear on the board. "It should say Guay on there because he was the third one," says Herd.

"It was the layout guys who put the RIP, rest in peace message," says Herd. "The syntax refers to an inside joke where we supposedly gave our lives in an effort to get the FCC production board done in time."

With the PCB design complete, Japan received the design for production. Herd accompanied the C128 on the trip. "Bil was there for a week, maybe two," recalls Haynie. "He was basically just babysitting. They would make the boards there and ship them off to Europe or America for final assembly."

Communication with the Japanese was mostly in English. "They all knew some English, some more than others," say Herd. "Engineers speak a common language."

However, Herd had improved his Japanese since the Plus/4 days. "He was really trying to learn Japanese," says Haynie. "Every time he went out with the Japanese guys, he'd have them teach him a word or two."

While in America, Herd also had a chance to practice his Japanese with Yashi Terakura and another Japanese engineer. "We went over there and we got them coming over here," says Herd. "One of the guys I call a friend, Katayamo, would come over [to America] and I would put him up at my place."

For Herd, learning Japanese was all for engineering. "It was part of being a better engineer to break down that wall that existed between Japan and us," says Herd. "I took the time to learn Japanese because it was one more thing that increased our chance for success."

During meetings, Herd's colorful descriptions of the 8563 video chip amused the Japanese engineers. "I called it a 'dead piece of shit'," says Herd. "It was a phrase I said in a meeting that just had the Japanese roaring."

Normally, Commodore Japan redesigned the PCB layout to fit their component insertion tools, but Herd gave them a head start. "Instead of designing it to be redone by Japan, I worked with it so the version I was done with could go straight to production, and that hadn't been done before," says Herd. "Every single chip could be inserted with a Panasert machine [made by Panasonic] for the Japanese runs, or a Universal, which is the American machine."

Herd's drinking habits helped him bond with his Japanese colleagues. "One night we were sitting around and everybody was relating what their last names meant. I thought about it and said that my last name meant 'many animals'. The happy drunk Japanese engineers all said, 'So!' in unison. They were quite pleased with the revelation and my Japanese nickname *doobutsu* was born that night, which means animal," says Herd.

Both Herd and Tony Takai had aggressive styles that clashed, but Herd got along with Tokai's next in command. "I liked the guy underneath him, Okuba, who ran the shop," says Herd. "Me and him got to be good friends. He gave me a very touching letter that was very Japanese in that it said, 'With this I wish you well with your life.' You could catch from the letter that he meant it. He gave me a little present that meant a lot to him, which was an ink pen of all things."

Herd embraced his Japanese counterparts, but soon became restless. "There was nothing to do," says Haynie. "That's why Bil wanted to leave, because he said, 'There's no reason for me to be here.'"

Haynie soon found himself on a plane to Japan. "They were insistent upon somebody being there, so he said, 'Dave, come on over to Japan.' I said, 'Okay, great. No problem.'"

Commodore Japan consisted of two facilities: the offices and the production lines. "The place in Tokyo was just an office," says Haynie. "It was exactly what you would expect a Japanese office to be in the mid-eighties. There was a manager at the end of a row of desks. Of course, there were some Americans there who were there full time. They were off doing whatever they wanted to do."

The Japanese engineers excelled in finding cheaper ways to manufacture products. "They occasionally did some serious engineering, like cost reductions on the C128," says Haynie. "Sometimes after you make a couple of thousand of something, you find a problem or you find a better way to do it. After you make a hundred thousand, you find a cheaper way to do it. That's the kind of stuff they did there."

Haynie felt equally unneeded during his stay. "At that time, they were bringing up the C128 into production," says Haynie. "They basically wanted somebody who understood it better than they did to be on hand in case something went wrong. For about ten days, I was there and so was Greg Berlin, who was on the 1571 drive. They would have a few questions, but I think they were just being very polite. We were just waiting for an emergency to break out and it never did."

Haynie and Berlin developed a truncated workday schedule. "We would kind of come in around ten, hang out until lunch time because nothing happened, then we would go to Akihabara," recalls Haynie. "Akihabara is a section of Tokyo where all the electronics are. You could buy components off the shelf and you could buy stereo gear. Greg was outfitting his car, so we were loading up his credit card and then we were starting to load up my credit card with all his purchases."

Although Haynie felt unproductive in Japan, the trip was a needed diversion after working so hard on the C128. "It was just really neat being there and it was kind of like a vacation," he says.

Greg Berlin (left) and Dave Haynie towering over their Japanese hosts. Haynie's shirt reads, "Beer: It's not just for breakfast anymore." (Photo courtesy of Dave Haynie)

Herd continued to battle middle managers right to the end of the C128 production cycle. "The middle managers were all scrabbling to make a name for themselves or clear an area for themselves," says Herd. "[Julian Strauss] had said, 'From now on, you can't release anything to MOS without my approval.' I said, 'If you go fast, I don't have a problem with that. But you need to go at my speed when you do that.' He said, 'Okay, no problem.'"

Herd passed the character ROM to Strauss, as instructed, and waited. "We gave him the font for the character set, and we asked, 'Is it done yet? Is it done yet?' He said, 'No, I'm looking at it.'" The inaction frustrated Herd and he decided to resolve the problem himself.

"There were all these cubicle offices with the managers," says Herd. "They had had some thefts, and there was actually a memo that said, 'Anybody caught breaking into an office will be terminated on the spot. This means engineers too.' They were trying to treat it very seriously."

Herd felt secure because of his critical position on the C128 project and he had no fear of reprisals. When an obstacle blocked Herd's path, he went through it or around it. This time the obstacle was Strauss. "We broke into his office by popping the ceiling out, climbing over his office walls, and dropping down," reveals Herd. "I cut my arm on the top metal thing, got the EPROM out of his desk drawer, put the tiles back in his ceiling, swept up the mess and left."

Strauss was unaware that anything had occurred until the engineers met for a meeting. "Three days later, we said, 'So how's that font coming?' He said, 'I'm almost done looking at it.' I looked at him in the meeting and said, 'I broke into your office, I stole it out of your desk drawer, and I released it to production almost three days ago.'"

The admission had Strauss cornered and revealed to everyone he was slowing down the process rather than helping. "Here I am admitting I had committed a thing that would get you fired," says Herd. "But the point was, this is already done and you're lying about it." Herd survived the confrontation but he was rapidly losing popularity with management.

Soon, it seemed like managers were making decisions merely to thwart Herd. "Later, they would try and tell us what to do as far as being destructive," says Herd. "I built a fuse into the C128 power supply, which I was told not to and I did anyway. They took it out later and somebody rubbed my face in it."

Middle managers were increasingly frustrating Herd. "Near the end, because there hadn't been any Jack Attacks, we were starting to get up to our ears in bad middle managers," says Herd. "They had stopped culling the herd. These people would define their existence if they could mutilate something. That was as good as doing something good as far as they were concerned because they got their mark on it."

It was important for Herd to release an 80-column monitor with the C128; otherwise, users would be unable to take advantage of the advanced graphical modes. However, management significantly slowed down the release of the monitor. "The C128 was one of the first computers to try and sell a monitor to home users," explains Herd.

Commodore rarely adhered to standards. "On the monitor interface, there were no monitor standards because there were barely any monitors out there," says Herd. "On one standard, the syncs were both negative, and on the other standard the syncs were both positive. I was told [by Joe Krasucki] to make one negative and one positive so that only Commodore monitors work with it."

The manufacturer, *Mitsumi*, waited on a final design from Commodore. Herd decided to bypass his manager's instructions and design the monitor interface as he saw best. "We got conflicting information on how to do it, so I made up my mind one night and said, 'Well, we're going to do it this way,' and that's how Mitsumi made the monitors."

Rather than face his boss, Herd chose to deceive him. "A couple of days later, I looked [Joe Krasucki] square in the face and lied to him," reveals Herd. "I said, 'I did it.' Well, I didn't. I actually researched which was the most compatible and which had more monitors out there. So I lied to him and had actually done what I thought was the pure way. I didn't care if I got fired at that point. We were at the end of the [C128] cycle and I was expendable." Today, Herd feels he made the right decision, rather than allowing a bad management decision to stand.

By June of 1985, the C128 was ready for release, including packaging and manuals. Unlike the Commodore 64, the engineers were still around to contribute to the manual. "The manual itself was done in-house by our technical writers," says Haynie. "I wrote part of the technical reference manual and Fred [Bowen] wrote part of it."

Even Herd contributed. "If you ever see a sentence that starts with the word 'additionally', I wrote it," says Herd. "Unfortunately, my English skills weren't quite as good as they are today."

Herd also spent a man-month designing an alternate model of the C128, called the C128D. "We designed the PC board to fit both the regular C128 and the D version simultaneously," says Herd. "It slowed us down and caused lots of grief, but I was intent on having the built in floppy. We showed the D version at the June CES."

The new model did not adhere to the computer-in-a-keyboard design. Instead, it used a PC style case with a detachable keyboard. "They didn't go with the D version right away," says Herd.

The high-school dropout with no college education had succeeded in designing the computer he set out to design, with virtually 100% backward compatibility. "I never doubted," says Herd. "Not because I was egotistical but because I knew that I would do everything in my power to succeed. Looking back, I think that it was that drive that was responsible for the fact we did succeed." Despite management interference, Herd believes he achieved his vision of the C128. "I can't say I would have done too much different."

A Lack of Software

Commodore made an effort to create a software library when they launched the VIC-20 and C64. They accompanied each computer with impressive launch titles that showed the way for other software makers. Under Marshall Smith, the C128 did not receive new software.

A few months before the January 1985 CES debut of the C128, Sig Hartmann, the man who established the software division at Commodore, was having philosophical differences with Marshall Smith. Although the software division previously created launch titles, Marshall Smith wanted to cut his software developers and rely on outside acquisitions of software packages. Predictably, Smith won the argument.

On October 24, 1984, Sig Hartmann resigned. Commodore's software output soon decreased to almost nothing. Hartmann went to work for none other than his former boss Jack Tramiel at Atari.

Software was a high-margin, profitable arm of Commodore. As one high-level source put it, "They want to sell razors but leave the blade-making to other companies - it'll never work that way."

According to Charles Winterble, under Marshall Smith, "Commodore considered themselves a serious computer company, and serious computer companies don't put out games."

Smith replaced Hartmann with a new Director of Software, Paul Goheen, who announced a strategy of less software development. In an interview with Compute!'s Gazette, Goheen expressed concerns over having too many titles. "From a prudent business point of view it makes little to absolutely no sense to have a product line up over 100 titles. You'll end up eating them. I am shrinking the product line, bringing it into the order it should be."[5] While this strategy made sense for business applications, it did not apply to games.

The software division produced thirteen games in 1984 (mostly under Hartmann) and six games in 1985 for the Commodore 64, making it clear Commodore was no longer an entertainment company. Odell Lake was the last C64 title published by Commodore Business Machines but Commodore employees did not develop the title. Without Jack, divisions within Commodore withered and died.

The popularity of the C64 also hurt the chances of anyone developing for the C128-mode. The C128 was really three separate, distinct, and unrelated computers in one case. Most users gravitated towards the C64 mode because of the extensive software library, while C128-mode and CP/M gathered dust.

Had Commodore developed their own C128 titles, users would have had a greater reason to use the C128-mode. Instead, programmers continued developing C64 software because it had the biggest market share.

Bob Yannes believes the computer marketplace changed between 1982 and 1985. "[In 1982], no one was buying computers for the software, other than for games or something like that," says Yannes. "It wasn't important to them whether it ran Microsoft Word or Excel or whatever."

---

[5] Compute!'s Gazette magazine, "An Interview With Paul Goheen" (June 1985), p. 34.

Commodore as a company was mostly hardware driven and rarely focused on software. "That was never the Commodore model," says Yannes. "It was always the lagging element of the machine."

By 1985, software was important. "By the time the C128 came out, software did matter," says Yannes. "People were buying IBM PC's and PC compatibles because they wanted to buy software that was available for them."

A few game companies developed software for the C128. Infocom and Mastertronic tried out a few titles, but separate C64 versions also existed in most cases. *The Rocky Horror Picture Show* was one of the few titles to make full use of the C128 features. Through the C128's entire life, the total number of commercial games developed could fit in a grocery bag.

CP/M mode was the least popular mode for C128 owners. By 1985, CP/M had already lost out to MS-DOS. *Osborne* and *Kaypro* computers were the main platforms for CP/M and Osborne was already in bankruptcy. CP/M software began to look dated.

Although Commodore planned to use CP/M as a way to make thousands of titles available at launch, they hardly used this angle in their advertising. Instead, magazine ads focused on the massive C64 software library, which they estimated to number 3000 titles.

The whole reason for creating the C128 was to allow users to run better software, while remaining part of the C64 line. Unfortunately, since software developers ignored C128-mode, the C64 legacy remained at 1 MHz and 64 kilobytes of memory. Unable to evolve, C64 software would soon look obsolete compared to newer computers.

A Modest Success

Bob Yannes, the designer of the C64, felt the C128 was in keeping with his vision for an expanded C64. "I think the C128 is probably close to what I would have done for a sequel to the C64," says Yannes.

The $300 C128 was a remarkable value for computer buyers in 1985, considering the C64 debuted at $600 three years earlier.

According to Bil Herd, the efficiency of the 6502 processor made the 2 MHz C128 faster than the Intel based IBM PC. "It was faster than the 8088's running at 4.7 MHz," says Herd. "They came out with a 6 MHz 8088 but they would have needed an 8 MHz to take us on."

Dedicated Commodore magazines warmly received the C128. Compute!'s Gazette provided a seven page overview on the C128 that was generally positive, though they noted C64 users had to wait three years for a true encore to their favorite computer.

Run magazine was equally positive about the C128. Reviewer Margaret Morabito was enthusiastic about the price to feature comparison with the IBM PC jr. and the Apple IIc. Though the base price of the C128 was around $300, the C128 with disk drive cost $550. This compared well to the Apple IIc for $1100 and the IBM PC jr. for $1000.

Bob Yannes appreciated the look of the C128, which resembled the case he hoped would enclose his C64. "It seemed like a pretty nice product," says Yannes. "I never had one, and I never really played with it but I saw one and it looked nice."

Yannes' only criticism is the release date. "The C128 should have happened much sooner than it did," he says. "It didn't come out for three years. By then, it was like, 'Who cares?' I would have followed up the C64 with a 128K version within the year, as quickly as possible, just to keep people moving up in the line, and then gradually take it up higher than that."

Charles Winterble was unimpressed with the C128. "What we wouldn't have done is what they did," says Winterble. "They came out with this computer which was a C64, C128, and CP/M. What the heck? Are you out of your minds?"

Perhaps the biggest weakness of the C128 was that C128 mode was not close enough to C64 mode to allow developers to write one piece of code for both computers. "It was only C64 compatible when it was only a C64. The C128 in C128 mode wasn't really C64 compatible," says Herd. "It just shared the same chassis."

At the June CES, Herd received criticism for the C128 mode. "I had a kid criticize me for this at a show one time," says Herd. "This little punk wiped his nose on his sleeve and in a whiney voice proclaimed that if he had designed the C128 he would have found a way to keep the MMU in the memory map in C64 mode. I explained to him that I actually took it out on purpose; I wasn't just so stupid that I couldn't figure out how to map a device in."[6]

Robert Russell, who helped develop three of Commodore's previous hits, has mixed feelings on the C128. "I worked real hard to get a Z80 card in the original C64," begins Russell. "I liked the fact that the [Z80] chip got used, but why couldn't we have done our own piece of silicon that was both 40 columns and 80 columns? That's what I really wanted at that point in time, but we didn't have the design engineers to do that."

---

[6] The 'little punk' would one-day work for Commodore. "This guy's name was Bryce [Nesbitt], who later went on to become a Commodore engineer after I had left," says Herd. "I never did get a chance to backhand him."

In Russell's opinion, MOS Technology lacked the capability to produce a VIC-III chip. "We didn't have the personnel when it was needed," says Russell. "We could do a simple 80-column display chip but we couldn't do an integrated one."

Commodore produced a small commercial campaign for the C128. As Herd recalls, "There was a TV commercial and it had Burgess Meredith[7] for the voice. In one commercial, there was a big drill that was drilling a hole in the side of an Apple IIe, and Burgess is saying, 'You would have to put more voices and better graphics in your Apple to do what the C128 does.'"

Haynie was satisfied with the advertising of the C128. "I thought they did okay," says Haynie. "I think they were pretty ballsy coming after Apple and IBM directly."

Herd felt a connection with the actor, who passed away in 1997. "I always wanted to meet him," says Herd. "I was like, if I ever run into him I'll say, 'Hey, you did the voice for my commercial.'"

Commodore U.K. ads were characteristically clever, showing a weight scale with three computers on one side and the C128 on the other. The caption stated, "When you look at the facts they do seem to weigh rather heavily in our favour."

Herd was pleased with the marketing effort by Commodore. "I think it was fair," says Herd. "I think it filled the hole waiting for the 16-bit [computers] to come. The C128 was really supposed to be a two-year machine. That's another reason it was so important to, 'Don't get it perfect, get it out there.'"

The biggest competition against the C128 was of course the C64. When it became apparent that few games took advantage of the extra speed and memory of C128-mode, there was no compelling reason for most C64 owners to follow an upgrade path, which was the whole reason for C64 compatibility in the first place.

Commodore wanted the C128 to replace the C64 on store shelves. In late 1985, Commodore attempted to end production of the C64. The company planned to sell off the remaining inventory and then concentrate on the C128. Unfortunately, demand did not taper off for the C64. When the inventory ran out, retailers were still clamoring for more C64 computers. The demand forced Commodore to restart C64 production.

---

[7] Burgess Meredith played the trainer Mickey in *Rocky* and the Penguin on the sixties *Batman* TV series.

As Peddle recalls, "The C64 was a victim of its own success. When they tried to improve it, the market didn't bite."

Commodore engineers further improved the design and released the C128D in the hopes of capturing some of the business market. Commodore marketing did not give the C128D a big push and it is very likely it would have failed anyway, given the dominance by IBM PC computers with the more popular MS-DOS.

By the end of 1985, the first year of production, Commodore sold a respectable 250,000 C128 computers. In 1986, Commodore North America General Manager Nigel Sheppard stated, "We estimate possibly 20 to 25 percent of 128 purchasers are people upgrading from a 64."[8]

Over its lifetime, Commodore sold an estimated four million units,[9] making it nearly as successful as the vaunted Apple II line, which sold five million units. The C128 lasted until 1989, when production finally ended. The C128 was the last 8-bit computer released by Commodore.

---

[8] *Compute!'s Gazette* magazine, "An Interview With Nigel Shepherd" (October 1986), p. 28.

[9] This number is from Dave Haynie. He adds, "This info was always hard to get out of Commodore, even when you worked there. We sometimes knew for certain, based on chip deliverys and re-orders."

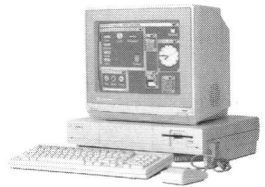

CHAPTER

The Savior of Commodore

1982 - 1985

Commodore failed to capitalize on the unmatched success of the C64, which was a games market. The C128 had virtually no game development and did not transition C64 users into more powerful computers. It was time for Commodore to enter the 16-bit market.

Jay Miner

The man who originated the idea for Commodore's next generation hardware did not work for Commodore. In fact, he was working for Commodore's nemesis, Atari, when he conceived of the revolutionary new computer.

Jay Glenn Miner was born May 31, 1932 in Prescott, Arizona. This made him part of Chuck Peddle and Jack Tramiel's generation, rather than the generation that had created Commodore's most recent hits.

A few years after his birth, Miner's family moved to Southern California. After graduating high school, he signed up for the Coast Guard, which took him to Groton, Connecticut for military training. While there, he met Caroline Poplawski and married her in 1952. Like Tramiel, Miner served in the military during the Korean War.

Miner received his first taste of electronics at Groton in the Coast Guard's *Electronics Technician School*. After completing the six-month course, he joined the *North Atlantic Weather Patrol* where he jumped from island to island by boat and helicopter, repairing damaged radar stations and radio installations. With little to distract him, he immersed his young mind in electronics.

After serving three years in the barren North Atlantic, Miner enrolled at the University of California, Berkeley in engineering. By 1958, Miner

The Savior of Commodore – 1982 to 1985

completed his electrical engineering degree, with a Major in the design of generators and servomotors.

Miner performed contract work for several years until he landed permanent employment at *General Micro Electronics* in 1964. At General Micro, Miner pioneered some of the earliest digital voltmeters and helped design the first MOS calculator chip.

By 1975, Jay had helped found chip maker Synertek, which was the second source for MOS Technology's 6502 chip. When Atari used Synertek to create their custom chips for the Atari 2600, they hired Jay Miner to design the Atari 2600 video chipset at Cyan Engineering (Atari's research lab in Grass Valley). He went on to design the impressive Atari 400 and 800 systems, admired by users for their graphics capabilities.

Miner was an interesting sight at the Cyan labs. People who saw him in the halls often had to take a second look because a tiny black shadow seemed to follow his every move. The shadow was actually a little black Cockapoo named Mitchy that followed Miner everywhere. "Mitchy had a long history of being involved in the computer industry because Mitchy used to go to Atari with Jay and helped him design the systems there," says fellow engineer R.J. Mical.

The dog became a fixture at Atari. Miner had a brass nameplate on his door that read, 'J.G. Miner', and just below it was a smaller nameplate, 'Mitchy'. Mitchy even had her own tiny photo-ID badge clipped to her collar as she happily trotted through the halls. While Miner worked on his groundbreaking systems, Mitchy sat on a couch watching with puzzlement as her master slaved over diagrams and schematics.

Jay Miner and Mitchy (Photo courtesy of R.J. Mical).

By the early 1980s, he was brainstorming the possibilities offered by a new 16-bit computer based on the Motorola 68000 microprocessor, which was not yet commercially available. As an engineer, Miner knew that in order to remain at the forefront of technology, an engineer has to project beyond today's capabilities.

Unfortunately, the naïve Atari management thought they could design tomorrow's computers around today's expectations. They thought the $100 price tag on the 68000 was too much, and apparently could not conceive of a time in the future when the chip would cost less. The management was basking in their present success, unconcerned with the future of technology. It was obvious Miner would not be allowed to advance technology at Atari so he quit.

Miner was now 50 years old and looked like cross between an Amish farmer and Kenny Rogers. He sported a heavy beard on the underside of his jaw and liked to wear pastel blue suits with big collars or loud Hawaiian shirts. With his large frame, Miner was hard to miss.

Though he was always working on a project, Miner spent his free time on other activities. With his wife of 30 years, Caroline, he cultivated bonsai trees and enjoyed square dancing, camping, and backpacking. He even found time to build model airplanes at home.

After Atari, Miner joined a semiconductor startup company named *Xymos* where he designed chips for pacemakers until 1982.

During this time, former Atari co-worker Larry Kaplan contacted him. Kaplan had developed half a dozen games for Atari before starting *Activision* with David Crane, Alan Miller, and Bob Whitehead. At Activision, he designed *Kaboom!*, a bestselling game. However, Kaplan seemed perpetually dissatisfied no matter where he worked and he was unhappy with Activision. Kaplan proposed a new game company to Miner and asked Miner if he knew anyone with money.

Miner talked to his boss at Xymos, Bert Braddock, and they found a group of dentists to invest in the new venture. The dentists noticed the video game craze and wanted to benefit financially. Future employee R.J. Mical believes the dentists were naïve. "These guys were a bunch of dentists in Florida who were just splashing a bunch of money around," says Mical. "They didn't know what was going on, they didn't know the business, and they didn't do all their homework."

Many investors in the early eighties had similar ambitions. "When video games were hot in the early eighties, it was easier to get people excited about video games," says Dave Haynie.

Braddock leased an office space at building number 7, 3350 Scott Boulevard, Santa Clara. Dave Morse, who was previously the vice president of marketing with Tonka Toys, became CEO and president of the company. The entrepreneurs dubbed their video game company *Hi-Toro* in 1982.

The structure of Hi-Toro was simple. Larry Kaplan would design games for the Atari 2600 and other systems, Jay Miner would design chips for cartridges and other hardware, and Xymos would fabricate the chips and cartridges. The dream did not last long. Sometime in 1982, the perpetually dissatisfied Kaplan quit because he felt things were moving too slowly. "He was gone by the time I got there," says Mical.

With their Vice President gone, Dave Morse asked Jay Miner to take Kaplan's place. Miner made sure to add a clause to his contract that said he could bring his dog Mitchy into work everyday. Morse had no objections, so Miner quit his job at Xymos and began working at Hi-Toro full time. Secretly, Miner still harbored the dream of building a 68000 machine. Despite the expectations and desires of their financial backers, Miner would now attempt to steer things his way.

Amiga Corporation

With Larry Kaplan out of the picture, Jay Miner was the only person left with technical knowledge and vision. The financing had been raised for the creation of a video game company, but Hi-Toro was about to embark in a different direction. Miner proposed building a game console to the dentists, who considered pulling out and investing in an ice cream chain. "They weren't sure which they wanted to do," says Mical. "These guys were faced with a laughable choice that I find so amusing. 'Are we going to invest in an ice cream company or will we invest in a new computer?'"

The dentists decided to invest in the game console. If the dentists truly understood the time and expense of designing a console, plus the manufacturing and marketing costs, and the low probability of success, they probably would have balked. However, they knew enamel, not silicon. To them, owning part of a console company for a mere $7 million investment probably sounded good.

Hi-Toro was divided into two parts: the Atari game/peripheral section and the console development section. The games and peripherals would act as a diversion to keep others from guessing what Hi-Toro was really working on.

Jay turned to his old friend from the Atari days, Joe Decuir, to help develop the new computer. Hi-Toro hired Decuir on a contract through his design company, *Standard Technologies,* in October of 1982. The two system architects began working on the concept for their console. It was to be a game machine, yet with a 3.5" floppy drive and a keyboard. This was to be a platform so powerful that game designers could do game development on it directly.

Some time after, the investors decided they did not like the company name, which Larry Kaplan originated. They thought Hi-Toro sounded too much like the Japanese lawn-mower manufacturer, Toro. The group decided to rename the company.

Everyone wanted a name that would come before Apple and Atari in the telephone directory, so they took out a dictionary, turned to Apple, and started browsing backwards. Everyone agreed that the name should sound friendly. Amigo, as it turns out, is one of the few Spanish words in the English dictionary. More importantly, it exuded friendliness, since Amigo means friend in Spanish. However, it was not quite sexy enough, so someone suggested Amiga, the feminine form of Amigo.

Jay Miner did not want a Spanish name for the company. According to Miner, "I didn't like it much. I thought using a Spanish name wasn't such a good move."[1] With time, Miner began to appreciate the name. Dave Morse soon incorporated the company under the new name.

Through the rest of 1982 and early 1983, Dave Morse developed the business while Miner and Decuir developed the technology for the game console. The company now had a clear goal.

Lorraine

When Miner worked for Atari, it was tradition to name prototype systems after wives and girlfriends. Pong was codenamed Darlene, the Atari 2600 was codenamed Stella, the Atari 400 was Candy, and the Atari 800 was Colleen. At Amiga, CEO and President Dave Morse continued the tradition by naming the prototype *Lorraine* after his wife.

Lorraine would feature up to 4096 colors in the most advanced graphics mode, resolutions up to 640 by 480 while in 16-color mode, and an 80-column display. However, the advanced graphics modes would not work on a television set, so users would have to get used to purchasing a monitor with their computer.

The team went through at least seven different concept sketches trying to perfect a unique look for the computer. The computer system would be modular and stackable, like stereo equipment. Early sketches show a base unit, which slid open like a drawer for storing the keyboard. The next unit contained a cartridge port and connectors for other devices. The

---

[1] *Amiga User International* magazine (September 1992), interview by Mike Nelson. All succeeding quotes from Miner are from the same source.

top unit shows two floppy disk-drives side by side. It was a radically different approach to computer design.

The Lorraine was powered by the 16-bit 68000 microprocessor; part of the same family of chips Chuck Peddle pioneered while working for Motorola. According to Motorola documentation, they designed the chip for 'household appliances'. Motorola unveiled the chip in 1980, but samples were not publicly available until 1982.

The sights and sounds of the Lorraine came from the custom chips. "We needed ways to refer to the chips, and I believe it started with Jane," recalls Mical. "The names were supposed to be roughly in the ballpark of the function of the chip. To know the name gave you a sense of what was going on in the chip."

In keeping with the female theme of Amiga Corporation and Lorraine, the engineers used female names for their main chips. "*Portia* was the chip where we had all of the I/O ports," says Mical. The chip produced incredible four channel stereo sound that was much cleaner than the SID chip. Sounds contained no background noise and the chip could play clear digitized sounds and music. A third hire, Dave Needle, concentrated his efforts on Portia.

The engineers appropriately named the Display Adapter *Daphne*. Miner was the chief designer of Daphne. His main inspiration came from his love of airplanes. Miner had recently visited a military flight simulator company called *Singer-Link*, which had innovative display technology for the time. Miner saw the technology and instantly wanted to duplicate it in his machine. As Miner explains, "I had a kind of idea about a primitive type of virtual reality."

Daphne had four different graphics modes, which could display 320 x 200 and 320 x 400 using 32 colors or 640 x 200 and 640 x 400 using 16 colors. This was impressive, especially compared to IBM PC's, which could only display eight colors at once.

The final chip in the Amiga was Agnus, which was effectively a Memory Management Unit (MMU). Agnus was also the *bit blitter*, a mechanism used for producing high-speed animation.

Each of these chips was, in effect, a microprocessor. Many call the Amiga a multiprocessor system, since each chip handles its own load of processing tasks in a specific domain. This meant the 68000 processor was free much of the time, making the computer one of the fastest machines of the time. The 7.16 MHz processor speed did little to describe the actual speed compared to others.

R.J. Mical credits Jay Miner with the vision for the system. "Jay was the whole hardware side of the system," says Mical.

It took the three engineers, Dave Needle, Joe Decuir, and Jay Miner, almost two years to design the custom chips. During this time, little Mitchy patiently watched every move. "I don't know if you know, but Mitchy did most of the design on the system; much more than Jay did," reveals Mical. "She would sit on Jay's lap, and Jay would draw gates, and he would look down at Mitchy and Mitchy would shake her head. Jay would erase it and draw it upside down, and try it a different way and look down and Mitchy would pant. He did design by dog."

In 1983, Joe Decuir's work on the Agnus chip was complete. He left Amiga and returned to Standard Technologies where he would go on to design devices for the upcoming computer.

Once the engineers completed the schematics, they had no way to fabricate the chips. Unlike Commodore, with their built-in semiconductor plant, Amiga Corporation had no access to chip manufacturing. The engineers would have to find another way to test their chips.

Instead of miniaturizing the circuits, they built them full sized using regular components on breadboards. It was as though the engineers used an enlarging ray on their silicon chips. As can be expected, these 'chips' took up a lot of space.

To build Agnus, a technician named Glenn Keller inserted IC chips on a board and wired them together according to the schematic. When the breadboard ran out of room, Keller connected the breadboard to another breadboard around a central core, like a book spine. Each breadboard had up to 250 IC chips on it, with eight breadboards in total, all bundled together with multicolored spaghetti wire. That was just for Agnus.

All three chips were simulated on breadboards and working by September 1983. However, because of the many connections and tangled wires, they were highly error prone, often causing the engineers to search for loose connections or short circuits. According to Miner, "Those were a nightmare to keep running with all the connections breaking down."

According to R.J. Mical, the engineers constructed a special area for the massive chips using anti-static flooring and anti-static walls. The room was just wide enough for one person to fit through, much like a confessional booth. Mical claims they also placed signs saying, 'Ground Thyself', which gave him the impression he was entering an altar to a technology God.

Growing Amiga

In 1983, Morse began hiring a team to begin development. Over the next few months, Amiga hired eight engineers and programmers, including Bob Burns, Glenn Keller, Dale Luck, Robert Mical, Ron Nicolson, Bob Pariseau, and Carl Sassenrath. According to Miner, he hired the engineers based on their enthusiasm for the game console. Miner split his team into two groups: one for hardware development and one for software. Jay Miner led the hardware development team, while Bob Pariseau led software development.

The employees all received a stake in the company. "The best companies that I've been involved with are the ones where everyone owns a piece of the action," says Mical. "Amiga was one of them where, be ye big or little, you've got a stake in the company. Some of the more significant guys were up in the five to seven percent range."

As a new employee, Mical did not receive as much as the others did. "My piece was small, but I'm not sneering at it," says Mical. "It was well worth it to get a chance to come out to California, join up with all these wacky people, and do that company together."

When Mical was hired, he noticed there was some ambiguity about the game console. "It was originally a console but we weren't sure exactly what it was going to look like," says Mical. "They told me when I was interviewing there, 'We're working on a game console. It's going to be a next generation thing; big and powerful and just run circles around the other guys.'"

Mical spotted some odd features for a game console. "I talked to the hardware guys as part of my interview process," recalls Mical. "I'm looking at this whiteboard[2] and there's this port that's marked 'kbdprt', which is like, 'Keyboard port?' And there's this other box, 'extdrv'. External drive on a game console?"

In reality, the engineers were attempting to capture the same market opened up by the Commodore 64. "The original philosophy behind the Amiga was to capitalize on the rising consciousness people were having on computers," says Mical. "Computers like the C64 had become pervasive. There were millions of those things sold. A lot of people were getting used to not just having it as a toy, like the Intellivision and the [Atari] 2600. Instead, it was a system that you actually worked with and it came with a language."

The engineers wanted to have the same power as business computers, but targeted to casual users. "We saw that the usefulness of these things

---

[2] The Amiga engineers immortalized the whiteboard with the original Lorraine design. According to Mical, "Many, many years ago, we put a coat of shellac on it, and while the thing was still wet, we put our thumbprints down in the lower right-hand corner."

in the office was going to end up in the home," explains Mical. "There was a different mentality for what you would do for software in the office and what you would do for software in the home. It was like somehow we became a different human being when we were in the office than when we were in our homes."

The Amiga computer would be accessible to anyone. "We set out to do a computer for the home that was easily understandable and easily usable by anyone," recalls Mical. "You could grasp the concepts of it and interact with it no matter how old you were. It would be a good, powerful computer that anyone could afford."

While the core engineers designed the Lorraine, other engineers worked on games and peripherals for the Atari 2600. According to Miner, the Amiga products were partly to deflect unwanted curiosity away from the Lorraine. "We hired lots of other people to design peripherals which kept the notorious Silicon Valley spies away from the office. All they could see were joysticks and they weren't too much of a threat."

"Keeping it quiet was just because we believed we had an excellent idea," says Mical. "Peripherals were always the smoke screen. It was what we told people we were doing, while meanwhile, what we were really doing was kept under wraps."

The team very quickly developed and marketed several products for the Atari 2600. They released the *Amiga Power Stick*, which was a package of two ergonomic joystick controllers. The controllers became a favorite among Atari owners.

Amiga developed a unique peripheral called the *Joyboard*. The controller resembled a surfboard with a surface area about two feet square. To control a game, the player stood or kneeled on the board and leaned in the direction they wanted to move. Amiga even included a game cartridge for the Joyboard called *Mogul Maniac*, a 3D downhill skiing game. According to Mical, "They sold enough to make money."

In the midst of developing commercial products for the Atari 2600, the market crashed. "The game console sales plummeted and the arcades started to falter," recalls Mical. Suddenly, Atari 2600 products were no longer viable in the marketplace. The games division was losing money.

Amiga completed two unreleased games for the Joyboard. The first was *Off Your Rocker*, a Simon-Says party game. Large quantities of Off Your Rocker cartridges were already produced and Amiga sent them to a company to have labels applied. Since Amiga decided to abandon the Atari 2600, they did not have the money to pay for the labels, so the label company ended up keeping the cartridges. The second game was *Surf's

Up, which featured excellent graphics and simplistic game play. Amiga never manufactured the cartridges.

Amiga abandoned their plans for other innovative products, such as the Power Module, which expanded the Atari 2600 to use cassette tapes, RAM memory, and 3D glasses.

The video game crash frightened the Amiga engineers. "Suddenly we were about to release a game console that no one was going to want," says Mical. With games suddenly out of favor, and many people believing game consoles were just a fad, the dentists suddenly embraced the idea of a computer.

In many ways, the crash was a blessing in disguise. Now the engineers could focus all their energies on a true computer system. "Fortunately for us, it really was a computer and it only took a little bit of extra work to convert it from being just a game system into a full-blown proper personal computer," says Mical.

The Dancing Fools

It was up to the software engineers to develop an operating system for Lorraine. "On the software side was Bob Pariseau, who was the VP of software," says Mical. "The rest of us reported to Bob."

One of the first programmers on the Lorraine was Dale Luck. The former Midwesterner sported typical early-eighties feathered hair and moustache. Members of the Amiga team called him 'Luck Trucking' Dale. R.J. Mical and Carl Sassenrath soon joined the team.

Mical, who was also from the Midwest, got along well with Luck. "Dale is a brilliant engineer and a warm, loving, compassionate, decent, kind, excellent human being," gushes Mical. "He is one of the best humans I've had the pleasure to get to know well in my whole life."

While Jay Miner drove the Lorraine graphics from the hardware side, Dale Luck pushed graphics on the software side. "On the Amiga he was the graphics guru," says Mical.

For a while, as Jay Miner and his engineers decided the architecture and specifications for Lorraine, the software team was content with planning the features of their operating system. They listed the features they wanted on whiteboards and created a design plan. However, eventually they had to start programming their software without any real hardware. That was a serious question. How do you write software when the hardware does not exist?

Ideally, the team wanted to display the computer with a fully functioning operating system at the upcoming CES. However, the hardware would not be ready until late 1983. If the programmers wanted an operating system ready at the same time, they would have to begin programming for the computer before it actually existed.

To overcome the absence of a real computer, the software team created a virtual computer in software. In effect, they wrote an emulator. As Jay Miner and his team created the machine, they would simply tell the software team the register locations in their computer. In this way, the team slowly created an emulated Lorraine.

It was early summer 1983 before the software group had enough information to begin programming their software libraries, giving them only seven months to program everything before CES. During this time, the key programmers sometimes turned in 100-hour weeks.

Dale Luck, graphics guru (photo courtesy of R.J. Mical).

Development took place on an economical Sage computer. "The Sage computer was a remarkable machine," says Mical. "It was a 68000 machine that was an extremely low-cost, wonderfully high-powered multi-user computer. It could support up to four users and it did a darned good job of it."

In the early stages of software development, the computer was ample for the programmers, but things soon changed. "It was a four user computer and we ended up with ten users," says Mical. "If you think four people compiling at the same time made it slow, try five or six or seven."

The programmers soon got into a routine of adding a few lines of code to their program, then waiting for it to compile. "If you changed one of the critical data structures that are at the heart of the system, you ended up having to recompile the whole system in order to make sure everything is fresh," says Mical. "When we did that, it could go five or even ten minutes, sometimes 15 minutes if you were doing a full load. We used to find interesting ways to fill the time when we had to do that."

The hardware engineers like Jay Miner worked for long uninterrupted periods and then took catnaps for a few hours. Dale Luck found it more efficient to work his sleep schedule around the compiler. "We had this program that we created for the Sage called 'beep', and if you typed 'beep' your computer made a loud obnoxious sound," explains Mical. "Our computers had a type-ahead buffer where you could type more instructions than what you could see on the screen. Dale would type the commands to do his builds, then type ahead the command 'beep', so that when the build was done it would execute the command 'beep' and make this loud obnoxious sound."

"Dale had a pillow on his lap, and he would type in the build command, type in the 'beep' command, then put his head down on his pillow and fall asleep for five minutes," recalls Mical. "The computer would say, 'Beep!' and he would sit up and get back to work. It was the most astonishing thing. He would sneak in five minutes of sleep here and there."

The programmers often worked after hours, since there were fewer programmers on the Sage system at night. "We did long late night builds," recalls Mical. "Dale and I would work through the night and just grind non-stop."

The two programmers fought a constant battle against fatigue. "We would need to keep ourselves pepped up," says Mical. "When the going got long and the trade show was tomorrow, you've got to deliver. So we would play loud music to keep us awake. We played Led Zepplin and the two of us would dance and dance to keep awake. We would dance together sometimes or just dance with your computer."

The regular Amiga employees were oblivious to the late night insanity of their programmers until one morning. "One of the sales guys shows up early for work and gets there at seven AM," recalls Mical. "The music is booming out of the software lab and he comes around the corner, and there's the two of us dancing together in the middle of the room. Thereafter, we were known as the dancing fools."

The software development process was strenuous, so Mical developed a method to sooth his nerves using the Joyboard. According to Mical, "There was a Guru Meditation game that we used to play on the Joyboard. You would put the Joyboard up on a chair and then you would sit on it. The game was to attempt to remain motionless for as long as you could stand it."

The designers loved the Guru Meditation game and decided to incorporate it into the Lorraine operating system. System errors were frequent in the alpha code and the programmers rechristened them 'Guru Meditation Errors'. When an error occurred, a 'Guru Meditation Error' flashed on the screen.

One of the key programmers on the Lorraine was Carl Sassenrath. "He wrote the multitasking kernel of our machine," says Mical. "Carl did the EXEC, and that thing was a work of art."

Before working at Amiga, Sassenrath worked for Hewlett-Packard. In 1981, he took a break and joined the Antarctic research team from Stanford University as a research scientist at the South Pole.

Carl Sassenrath (photo courtesy of R.J. Mical).

Upon returning from the South Pole, Carl went to work developing a graphical user interface for a prototype of the *Sun Workstation*, loaned to him by Stanford student Andy Bechtolsheim (cofounder of Sun Microsystems). The features for his user interface were impressive, including a bitmap display, icons, fonts, a mouse, hyperlinks, and remote procedure calls to a database server. Sassenrath was uniquely suited to help develop the Lorraine operating software.

When the team decided to switch from game console to computer, Sassenrath had very little to change. "It was a multitasking OS all along, from the beginning," says Mical. "It really wanted to be a computer."

The kernel, or EXEC as the programmers called it, was the base of all Lorraine code. The EXEC allowed more than one program to run at the same time. Using the Command Line Interface (CLI) users could start and stop programs in memory.

In late 1983, the team was in trouble. They were out of money and rapidly falling into debt, with no means of making money in the near future. However, no one was willing to give up the dream after accomplishing so much. Most managers had to take out personal loans and mortgages on their houses, and even paid for expenses on their credit cards. Dave Morse, CEO of Amiga, took out a second mortgage on his house. It seemed like Amiga Corporation was heading for disaster.

To save Amiga, the team decided to pay a visit on Jay's old company Atari Inc., since they had the necessary funds and resources to help finish the chipset and fabricate chips. In late 1983, Dave Morse went to Atari with a proposal. In exchange for access to the Amiga chip technology, Amiga would receive an influx of cash from Atari.

The two companies settled on a deal that would allow Atari use of the chipset for video game consoles through the first year. The following year, Atari would be allowed to offer a keyboard upgrade to their video gaming system to turn it into a computer, as well as offer a full computer system. Atari Inc. gave Amiga $500,000 to complete the chipset.

Atari planned to use Amiga's technology in an advanced game system to be released in 1985, codenamed Mickey, that would be released as the Atari 1850XLD. This would be a full computer with keyboard, based on the Amiga chipset.

The Boing Demo

The Las Vegas CES opened on January 4th, 1984. The engineers had worked almost non-stop through Christmas preparing the Lorraine for the show. Now they had to disassemble the prototype and prepare it for a short flight to Las Vegas. Transporting the prototype was a nightmare. "There was a core of us engineers who went to every show because the system was so fragile," says Mical. Rather than shipping it separately, the team purchased a passenger ticket for the Lorraine breadboards and stacked them between pillows to absorb shock.

While purchasing the ticket, the attendant informed the team that flight regulations required a name for each occupied seat, therefore the Amiga team had to fill out a name on the ticket. Rather than use the name Lorraine, Dale Luck filled in Joe Pillow. The legend of Joe Pillow, the most mysterious developer of the Lorraine, was born.

Joe Pillow flanked by R.J. Mical (left) and Dale Luck (photo courtesy of R.J. Mical).

Once at the show, Jay Miner had a chance to survey the competition along with the 90,000 other attendees. Commodore, with Jack Tramiel still at the helm, was there to show off their doomed Plus/4 computer. Atari was also there, still showing off the Atari 800XL, which was a small update to the Atari 800 that Miner himself helped design years earlier. Apple was not at the show, but they would debut their comparatively primitive black and white Macintosh in the same month. Looking at the competition, Miner must have felt a degree of satisfaction. His computer was ahead of the competition by at least half a decade.

Despite the video game crash in 1983, Dave Morse decided to bring the Atari 2600 peripherals and games to CES. It was one last attempt to turn their efforts into cash, and to camouflage the Lorraine. "At the first CES, we were concealing what we were really doing, or at least attempting to," says Mical. "There was the external portion of the booth where any casual visitor could see a display of joysticks, Joyboards, peripheral products, and some software that we had created that used these devices."

According to Mical, the ruse worked. "I believe until the end it was a well kept secret," he says.

Amiga rented a simple gray booth in the West Hall at CES with an enclosed space behind the public display to show off the Lorraine. Unfortunately, the enclosure had no ceiling, so crafty attendees could

The Savior of Commodore – 1982 to 1985

sneak a peek at the Amiga by riding up the escalators and craning their necks as they reached the top.

The January 1984 CES Amiga booth. Note the Joyboards on the floor (photo courtesy of R.J. Mical).

"There was a guarded door that let you into the inner sanctum," recalls Mical. "You had to be with one of us to be able to get through the door. On the inside was the computer. It was still in its prototype stage and we had the three chips in their prototype form on a table with a skirt around the table."

The Lorraine hardware was incredible for 1984, especially compared to makers like Apple, Atari, IBM, and Commodore. However, the system required software to show off its capabilities properly. Through the first day and well into the evening, Mical and Luck programmed non-stop. "We never stopped working," says Mical. "We were constantly refining and polishing the demos, making them more impressive and exciting."

The experience was amazing for the two programmers, who finally had a chance to explore the machine in a creative way. Mical was no stranger to flashy graphics and sound, having come from an arcade company. The two programmers planned to create an ambitious demo. They wanted a rotating, checkered polygon ball bouncing on the screen accompanied by stereo sound, running in the multitasking environment. They called it the *Boing Demo*, and it would become one of the most famous demonstrations of a new computer.

"We had stayed up all night working on the Boing demo," says Mical. "The sales and marketing would just love us because everyday they would come in during the trade show itself and there would be the two of us exhausted in one of the back conference rooms sleeping with our heads resting on the table."

Dale Luck (left) and R.J. Mical asleep in the CES booth (photo courtesy of R.J. Mical).

People outside the booth heard the rhythmic banging of the demo coming through the thin office walls, followed by the gasps of those who were lucky enough to see it first hand. The demonstration stunned those who saw it. Not only was there a real-time 3D object smoothly animating on screen, but it was big! Behind the ball was a shadow, perfectly cast onto a purple grid. The illusion was perfect. Where the shadow fell, the grid color darkened appropriately. No one had ever seen anything like it. Every time the ball hit the ground, the Lorraine produced a thunderous sound, in stereo. According to Miner, "The booming noise of the ball was Bob Pariseau hitting a foam baseball bat against our garage door."

The Amiga employees gave choreographed demonstrations of the Lorraine to a succession of groups. "There was a whole presentation that we made," says Mical. "We talked about the machine and [Bob Pariseau] stood up in front and gave the spiel."

The Lorraine looked rough and unfinished to most potential investors, so the engineers had to reassure them the final product would look better. "That was part of the spiel," says Mical. "We had to explain, 'This is the state of it right now but we're going to take all of these big stacks of silicon and chips and wires that you see here and turn it into three chips.

It's going to be a nice little computer that is going to look like these drawings someday.'"

During the presentation, the engineers showed off their best demos. "We had various interesting whiz-bang demos that we put together to exercise the various capabilities of the system," says Mical. "One engineer would sit at the computer console and launch one demo after another to show off all the capabilities."

Mical loved the demonstrations. "We had just a whole wonderful collection of demos," he says. "There was probably a dozen of them that we showed."

Many attendees were skeptical of the Lorraine, believing it was a fraud. "It was wonderfully gratifying because the more savvy people invariably walked up after the demo and gave a good look at the machine," says Mical. "They would get down on one knee to lift up the skirt and look under the table to see where the real computer was. They thought there must be some trick that we were pulling off under the skirt, but it was nothing but power cords."

Mical particularly enjoyed an interactive demonstration of the speech capabilities. "One of the demos was the *Talking Heads* demo," recalls Mical. "It was a couple of robot heads and they were nicely done. The male was Mr. Amiga and the female was a reporter asking questions. The reporter would ask certain questions about Mr. Amiga and he would describe his capabilities and the technology."

Audiences loved the final part of the demonstration. "The most impressive part was where we proved to the audience that it wasn't just good at doing canned speech, but that you could get it to say anything you wanted," says Mical. "We would ask the audience to throw sentences at us, and we would type them in and it would speak those sentences for you right there. It was impressive to people."

When the Amiga team spotted a Sears representative, they tailored the demonstration just for him. "We wanted Sears to carry the machine," says Mical. "When one of the bigwigs at Sears was in there seeing the demo, without warning, the guy who was riding the keyboard typed in, 'I buy all my tools at Sears,' and the place lit up in a great roar of laughter. It was a wonderful little touch."

Amiga hoped that someone attending the demonstration would be interested in investing in the project. "I know Commodore visited," says Mical.

After CES, Amiga sent press releases to the major magazines announcing the features of the new Amiga PC. Byte magazine commented, "Joystick maker Amiga Corp. is developing a 68000-based home computer with a custom graphics coprocessor. With 128K bytes of

RAM and a floppy-disk drive, the computer will reportedly sell for less than $1000 late this year."[3]

Creative Computing took a firmer stand on the Lorraine, with writer John J. Anderson proclaiming, "If there was a hit of the show for me, it had to be my first glimpse of the supermicro code-named Lorraine by Amiga." He went on to say, "As far as I'm concerned, the Lorraine demo was reason enough to have made the trip to Las Vegas."[4]

The enthusiastic response lifted the spirits of the Amiga team; however, they received no concrete investment offers. With the Atari 2600 market as good as dead, Amiga failed to make any serious sales of their joysticks or games. Money would soon become their most pressing issue.

Intuition

Though the engineers changed their console into a computer before CES, they felt the computer was lacking one important component. "We just did an inventory of what a computer needed to have and what ours had, and the user interface was the piece that it lacked," says Mical.

The programmer responsible for creating the Graphical User Interface (GUI) was Robert Mical, or R.J. as everyone called him. "I'm a Chicago boy," says Mical, who was born in 1956. "I got my love of science and math from my parents. Both of my parents were good at math or science and good logical people."

Mical found his calling for science when he read a children's book by author Bertrand R. Brinley. "There was this book that was called *The Mad Scientist's Club* that I read when I was very young," recalls Mical. "It's a delightful tale of these five boys who have a club and they get into all these shenanigans."

Like many electronics engineers, Mical had his first hands-on experience with a kit. "When I was almost a teenager I started loving science," recalls Mical. "My parents got me a toy called a *Heathkit*. Heathkit was an electronics play toy with a simple circuit board and you got all sorts of electronic components: resistors, capacitors, tuners, and variable pots and things. The kits included great instructions for how to build your own radio, how to build your own telegraph set and all this stuff."

Mical branched out and began experimenting himself. "I built my own AM radios and I built my own telegraph systems," recalls Mical. "That

---

[3] *Byte* magazine (April 1984), p.10.
[4] *Creative Computing* magazine (April 1984), p. 150.

was cool, but then I discovered that if you played around with it you could make other interesting electronic toys. My favorite one that I discovered was that if you plugged it all in just right and then grounded one of the capacitors with your finger, the speaker made this eerie squealing noise."

The Mad Scientist's Club inspired Mical to do mischief with his new invention. "I took the speaker and mounted it inside a shoebox and ran the wires underneath the floorboards from the closet in my sister's bedroom into my bedroom, where I hid the Heathkit under my bed," explains Mical. "On a regular basis, I would go and make that speaker in her bedroom squeal. It wasn't quite like a mouse; it was more like a ghost mouse."

The prank confused his family, much to Mical's delight. "It had my parents in there for weeks trying to figure out where that noise was coming from and what was wrong," says Mical. "My sister was terrified. Then finally one day, there's my father standing in the doorway of my bedroom with the shoebox in one hand, holding the wires in the other."

With Mical's hoax exposed, he turned to more benevolent projects. "Then came my first real big project," says Mical. "When I was 14 years old, I built my first computer, a tic-tac-toe playing computer. It was made out of D batteries, flashlight bulbs, and relays."

The young Mical learned how to represent logic in electronic switching relays. "I had just learned about relays and was fascinated by the things," recalls Mical. "A relay is this electromagnetic thing where you put electricity to it and it causes a contact to close. If you take the electricity off it, it opens. It's like a big clunky transistor."

Unschooled in logic, Mical's tic-tac-toe game was not a model of efficiency. "They were so big and clunky, and I used dozens of them to implement the tic-tac-toe logic," recalls Mical. "I was stupid and naïve. There were all these tricks I learned later, and I could have done it with ten transistors to play the whole game."

Despite his lack of understanding, Mical's game performed impressively. "It worked really well," says Mical. "It went through a set of D batteries in three games but it worked! You couldn't beat the thing."

Mical's idyllic childhood shattered when his father left the family. "My dad was trained as a chemical engineer," says Mical. "After my dad split on us, my mom had to get a new life together for herself. She got back into doing office work in a medical place."

Mical attended the University of Illinois intending to earn a degree in English, while harboring ambitions to enter journalism. Despite taking courses in English, Mical gravitated towards technology and computers. "Anyone at the university had access to an account, and if you were a student you could play on this one computer," explains Mical. "At this point, I had already taught myself how to program and by then I knew FORTRAN and Basic."

Sometime in 1977, Mical's natural inclination to create games blossomed "I had an account and I had written a bunch of my own programs," recalls Mical. "I had created my own version of a Star Trek program. Star Trek was really popular then, and there was a Star Trek game on these simple teletype computers where you would give coordinates and your ships would move around. It was clunky and I wanted to do a better one, so I did a better one."

Like many students, Mical was unsure what he wanted to do with his life. "I was having a terrible afternoon sitting in the computer lab," recalls Mical. "I'm trying to figure out what I'm going to do with my life. I'm worrying and fretting over it, and then taking a break from worrying to play with my computer game. Then all of a sudden, it dawned on me. 'I could do this! I would love this!'"

Mical entered engineering. "I had this epiphany to go off and be a computer scientist," he says.

Four years later, in 1981, Mical began working for a Chicago industrial company, *Sciaky Brothers*. "Right after University I got a very nice job but not a game job," says Mical. "It was working with electron beam welding equipment."

The company soon began using Mical for all their computer needs. "I was writing utilities and writing database managers for them, having a grand old time," says Mical. "But the whole time I was doing it, I was feeling like it was just a job. I wasn't doing something significant. I was making money and living for the weekends."

After working for more than a year, Mical followed his feelings. "It nagged at me until I finally decided that I needed to go see the world and get my head straight," says Mical. The young engineer took nine months off to travel around the world, including Japan, the Soviet Union, and Europe. According to Mical, the experience changed his life.

When Mical returned, he sported long, unkempt hair and an even longer *Doctor Who* style scarf. The self-described artist, poet, and musician decided to pursue his dream. "When I got back it was time to change my life and go to the next big thing," says Mical. "I didn't want to just make a living. I wanted something meaningful and significant; something that was good for me that brought together all of my skills and my art and my music and my love of computer science. So I had the idea that I ought to go into video games."

Mical began looking for an appropriate company. "I went to two of the arcades and looked around for who was doing the best games," says

Mical. "By far and away, *Williams* had the best games at the time. They did *Joust* and *Robotron* and *Defender*; all of those wonderful, classic games. I wanted to be part of that."

Mical found it difficult to enter the video game industry. "It's funny, because I was so completely unqualified for that job," says Mical. "No skills, no credentials, no history. I asked if I could get the job and they said, 'No.' I said, 'Please, let me work with you guys. I need a job real bad.' They said, 'No, we can't. There's other people we're hiring. You're not qualified.' I couldn't get through that one person who would say no to me."

Mical felt dejected, but not enough to stop trying. "I knew that if they would give me a chance that I would do well there," he explains. "It was always one of my trademark comments I used to make during interviews. 'Give me a week and a good manual and I'll be the best damn employee you ever had.' So I needed to persuade them to give me a chance at it."

The would-be game programmer found an alternate way to contact employees within the company. "I'm embarrassed to say, but I struck up a relationship with the receptionist of the company," says Mical. "I didn't exactly seduce her but I did my best to be charming and wonderful and offered to take her out on dates in exchange for a copy of the phone list, which she finally coughed up for me."

Mical began systematically calling employees. "I started going through the phone list and calling everyone on the inside, trying to persuade them," says Mical. "Finally, this guy Noah Falstein took notice.[5] He was finally the first guy at Williams to recognize, 'Well, maybe we should give this guy a try.' That's how he offered to let me have a go at working for them."

At Williams, Mical helped create the cult favorite *Sinistar* with Falstein. "He was already involved in the Sinistar project so I jumped in. The project was largely done when I joined," says Mical. The Asteroids style game featured crisp, scrolling graphics. In the game, players try to thwart a group of robots from assembling a giant Juggernaut ship.

The speech was adored by arcade players, who delighted as the ship taunted with statements like, 'I live.' and 'Run coward!' "I did special effects and worked on the voice stuff and some of the underlying code," says Mical. Mical claims Sinistar was one of the most powerful arcade games ever written at the time, and even included a multitasking operating system.

---

[5] Falstein later worked on *Koronis Rift* for *Lucasfilm Games*.

After his stint with Williams, Mical interviewed with Jay Miner and became an Amiga employee in July 1983. Mical became fast friends with Amiga's most important employee. "I was Mitchy's second best friend at that company," says Mical. "I used to keep a bag of dog treats in my drawer. Mitchy would come trotting into my office without warning and jump up onto my lap. I had no family and I hardly knew anyone, and here was this dog that was friendly to me."

Shortly after CES 1984, the Amiga team decided to create a GUI for the Lorraine. At the time, many computer companies were beginning to embrace the GUI paradigm originated at Xerox. "The Mac would have influenced the decision, but less so than some of the more sophisticated machines that we were using at the time," says Mical. "We were using Sun Workstations and they had very powerful user interfaces that were much more powerful than what the Mac had."

Mical called his new interface *Intuition*. "Intuition was the input mechanism for the whole system," explains Mical. "It gave users that experience that we are familiar with now: windows, menus, using a mouse to move a pointer around on the screen, and dialog boxes which we called requestors that would give you options."

Using the Daphne graphical chip, Mical was able to create features that remain unavailable on modern systems, such as displaying different screen resolutions in different windows. "It could interleave those different screens on the same output display in the same way you can interleave windows now and overlap them, but with the different display resolution screens that we had on the Amiga," says Mical.

The software engineer had to forgo things others take for granted, such as having weekends off, going home, and sleeping. "I took on that job and spent seven months of my life working on average six and a half days a week to do that thing," recalls Mical. "Almost every week was a 100 hour week."

The Amiga employees were careful not to put themselves at risk of a lawsuit over their GUI. "We started out passing around design docs. The actual implementation was done completely behind the walls so that there was no knowledge of what anyone else had done," says Mical.

Because of their policy, Amiga did not receive any infringement lawsuits based on their GUI. "Not a one; not from anyone, ever," says Mical. "I attribute that mostly to the fact that once I decided that I needed to do a user interface, I slammed the door and drew the blinds and invented it completely and entirely on my own. I didn't look at any other computer system through that whole period. We wanted it to be as cleanroom as possible."

Mical was even able to secure patents based on his original ideas for the GUI. According to Mical, "Because of that, it turned out that I scored several patents for stuff that I created on the Amiga; one patent of which was violated by Microsoft up until just recently."[6]

Intuition easily outclassed the Macintosh operating system and was more reminiscent of the then non-existent Windows 95. One powerful feature that distinguished the Amiga operating system from the Macintosh was the Command Line Interface (CLI). This allowed users access to powerful DOS commands using command line arguments.

Surviving Tramiel

In 1984, as Amiga Corporation ran out of money, they were on shaky ground both figuratively and literally. On April 24, 1984 at 1:15 pm, the Morgan Hill earthquake hit California. "That was so remarkable for me because it was my first earthquake ever in my life," recalls Mical. "You could tell the difference between someone from California and someone not from California because all of my coworkers, who knew better, dove under their desks, dove into the doorways, and got themselves into protective positions."

Mical was from Chicago, where earthquakes were unknown. As Mical recalls, "I'm standing in the middle of the room, riding up and down on the floor with my arms out to the side saying, 'Wee,' like some kid on a surfboard. All my coworkers are shouting, 'Get under the desk you idiot!'"

Rather than cover for protection, Mical left the building for a better view. "I went running outside past all the plate glass windows and everything," says Mical. "I was so colossally stupid, but I didn't know. I ran out into the parking lot and it was just the most amazing thing I've ever seen in my life. To see the cars all heaving up and down with their burglar alarms going off one by one; to see these rows of stately palm trees crisscrossing each other as the waves went over them; God, it was just so gorgeous. And then I threw up."

Fortunately, the fragile Lorraine survived the ordeal. "Nothing got broken during the Amiga years," says Mical. "It was just a very cool ride."

---

[6] According to Mical, "You go over an icon and press the right mouse button instead of the left, and a menu appears that has menu items. If you select one of those items, it can cause a secondary menu to appear and you have other choices you can make. I got a patent for that technique."

As if one earthquake wasn't enough, Amiga was subject to another earth moving event: a visit from Jack Tramiel. In April, Jack began looking for technology to complete Shiraz Shivji's basic plans for a C64 killer. He eventually made his way to Amiga, on the advice of Commodore executive Lloyd 'Red' Taylor, who once wrestled in the hallways with Bil Herd. "Red Taylor ran across the guys out there, because he liked to go out to California to do stuff," says Russell.

Jack sat down with Amiga CEO Dale Morse to work out a possible buyout. "We mostly met with Sam and on occasion Jack," says Mical. "I only had hands-folded discussions with them across the table about various things. I also met his son Leonard on a few occasions."

To their disappointment, Jack did not want any involvement with the Amiga engineers. He just wanted the chipset. It seemed like they were making a deal with the devil. "They were hard, hard businessmen," says Mical. "They came to understand our situation. The deeper in they got with us and the closer they got to making a deal and understanding our finances and what we had to offer, the more they were able to come to realize how desperate we were."

The desperation was obvious to Jack's finely honed business instincts. "Instead of negotiating in a way to get us to say yes, they started negotiating to see how far they could push us to still say yes as the deal got worse and worse," says Mical.

There were roughly six million shares in Amiga Corporation. Initially, the two groups discussed an offer of three dollars per share. However, after many meetings, the offer fell to under a dollar per share. "Instead of the deal that they were offering us increasing over time, it decreased. It was pathetic and ridiculous," says Mical.

The aggressive moves by Atari threatened to alienate the Amiga team. With the latest offer at 98 cents per share, the talks soon disintegrated. The experience of dealing with the Tramiels left a bitter taste with Dave Morse and the rest of Amiga.

In the meantime, the engineers continued redesigning the Lorraine as a true computer and not a console. One of the most important features yet to add was a disk operating system. Amiga hired a third party to supply the operating system. "It was some engineering shop and we actually saw it running in their labs at one point," says Mical.

The semiconductor designers also refined the chip designs. "Over time, Portia became *Paula*," says Mical. "They redesigned the thing and the decision was made to let it have a different name in order to make it clear that it was the new chip."

The Amiga team demonstrated the Lorraine once again at the June CES in Chicago. This time, Lorraine used actual silicon chips for Daphne, Agnus, and Paula rather than the bulky breadboards. The team also unveiled Intuition. Predictably, the computer received even more praise, with Compute! magazine saying it was "possibly the most advanced personal computer ever."[7]

The June 3, 1984 CES show proved to be an important turning point for Amiga. During the show it was leaked that Jack Tramiel was in talks to purchase Atari. Jack wanted Atari for its large manufacturing facilities and distribution network for his mostly-complete computer.

CEO Dave Morse and the rest of Amiga knew about a clause that had been built in to the Atari Inc. contract when Atari had agreed to advance $500,000 to keep Amiga alive. "Atari at this point had locked us into the terms of a deal and had given us an advance on money so that we could keep making payroll and keep the effort going," explains Mical. "We had a timeline; a month to either say yes to the deal and sign the deal, or say no to the deal and give them their money back."

Amiga would forfeit their technology to Atari if they failed to pay back the $500,000 loan by the end of June. "This was a dumb thing to agree to but there was no choice," said Miner. Remembering Jack's turbulent visit in April, and his disinterest in the Amiga staff, they knew the future looked dismal if he purchased Atari.

Worried about the possibility, Morse worked tirelessly lining up potential suitors for Amiga. He gave presentations to Sony, Hewlett Packard, Philips, Apple, and Silicon Graphics. Unfortunately, most companies were concerned because the Lorraine was not PC compatible. Steve Jobs of Apple even criticized the Lorraine architecture, saying there was too much hardware in the machine.

It seemed like Amiga was destined to go to Atari. Then Commodore entered the picture, again as a result of Lloyd Taylor's involvement. "Red Taylor was really the one who brought that opportunity to the company," says Russell. Red Taylor, a Tramiel loyalist, also previously told Jack about Amiga. In effect, he was responsible for pitting Commodore and Jack Tramiel against one another. (Taylor soon left Commodore to work for Tramiel.)

According to Mical, the call from Commodore came at just the right moment. "The negotiations weren't going well, and all of a sudden Commodore becomes a contender for the opportunity to buy the Amiga," says Mical. "They phoned out of the blue. There had been a relationship

---

[7] *Compute!* magazine, "Software Power!" (August 1984), p. 32.

established already, but the call was, 'We've heard things and we want to know whether or not there is an opportunity here for us.'"

Mical believes antagonism fueled the negotiations. "There was a drama taking place that I didn't know about at the time," explains Mical. "There was a subtext to everything that was going on. Commodore had let the Tramiels go in circumstances that were unhappy for people. The Tramiels went to Atari, and part of their intention was to take over the success of the C64; to take that away from Commodore and to have that success be Atari's success. They wanted the Amiga [chipset] to be the C64 killer and sink the ship of Commodore."

Commodore knew the situation was urgent and they sent a team of engineers to inspect Amiga's technology. "I was told to lead this team of engineers out to do an evaluation of Amiga," says Russell. "So I went out there in this big rush because we have to do this before Atari takes possession by default. I took a bunch of chip designers, software guys, and hardware guys out there."

When Russell arrived, he noticed that Amiga was close to the old Commodore headquarters. "They were actually just across the Street from our Scott Boulevard location," says Russell. "There was this little office park of single story buildings with a ton of little companies in it."

The Amiga executives were forthright with the engineers and described the predicament they were in with Atari. "They were concerned about trying to find sources other than Atari," says Russell. "Atari was just going to take it for the money they had already put into it and those guys weren't going to get anything out of it."

According to Russell, the Amiga engineers tried repositioning the Lorraine yet again in one last attempt to entice investors. "Those guys were desperate when I was out there trying to come up with a way not to sell it to Atari," he says. "They had worked real hard and were thinking real hard about PC compatibility at that point in time. We talked with them about the original design of the product and what it was becoming. We asked why they were changing it. Apparently they had run into [investor] problems with it not being PC compatible."

Russell learned as much as he could about the company, the situation, and the Lorraine technology and presented his findings to his executives. "I called back with the evaluation and said, 'Here's a tentative off the cuff impression. They're doing the wrong thing by trying to make it PC compatible, but they've got exactly what we need as far as a chipset core and features. It's definitely a step up.' The other engineers I was with chipped in on the phone." In Russell's mind, the Amiga technology would be perfect for a low cost Commodore 64 replacement computer.

Marshall Smith and Irving Gould liked what they heard. "On the phone call, it sounded like it was a done deal and we were going to go ahead," recalls Russell. "I even remember talking about how many million dollars we were going to pay to get chip rights, rather than buy the company. They were willing to sell the chip rights for a few million dollars, rather than making us buy the whole company."

Mical believes both Irving Gould and Marshall Smith played an active role in pursuing the Amiga technology. "It was both Irving Gould and Marshall Smith," says Mical. "But it was more Marshall Smith's gig."

Russell was in favor of purchasing computer rights for the chip technology, and leaving the rest for Atari. "The only thing Atari was going to end up with was the right to use that chip in a game machine," says Russell. "We were like, 'Hell, let them have the game machine. We'll buy the computer chip rights for $2.4 to $4 million.'"

Commodore was thorough in analyzing the deal before committing to it. The executives consulted with their key engineers, including Bil Herd. "By that time, I had a reputation for how to make shit work, and how well it works, and whether it's going to work well," says Herd. "I was asked some questions about it fitting the Commodore style of manufacturing, but nothing instrumental. I didn't really change the course of anything."

Herd had some questions of his own regarding the new acquisition, which occurred right as he was starting work on the C128. "Adam [Chowaniec] had shared with me the preliminary stuff," says Herd. "It was funny to have those original documents and see little pictures of Atari tanks all over them. When they asked my opinion of some things, I kept coming to, 'What is it supposed to do?' That was a natural question to be asking but we all knew the next machine had to be 16-bit."

Back in California, the Amiga team awaited their fate. "The last minute negotiations with Commodore were intense," says Mical. "Those were tense and scary tightrope walking days. At the time, it was so terrifying to have the company so close to the brink."

Commodore and Amiga discussed the technology. One of the biggest disagreements occurred over memory. The original Lorraine prototype used only 128 kilobytes, the same as the C128 and Macintosh computers. Over time, the Amiga engineers realized they would need 512 kilobytes. "[Commodore] wanted a 256K machine as the 512 was too expensive," says Miner. "Back in those days RAM was very pricey, but I could see it had to come down. I told them it couldn't be done as we were too close to being finished, it would spoil the architecture."

Miner compromised on 256 kilobytes with an additional memory expansion slot on the front of the machine. "The 256 K RAM was a real problem," says Miner. "The software people knew it was inadequate but nobody could stand up to Commodore about it. We had to really argue to put the expansion connector on the side and this was before the deal was finalized so we were close to sinking everything."

Commodore gave Amiga the money they needed to pay back Atari. On June 30 1984, instead of delivering the chipset to Atari as planned, Amiga delivered a check to Atari for $500,000. Atari would not produce a computer using the Amiga technology.

Warner Communications still owned Atari. By 1984, the company was hemorrhaging money and Warner just wanted to get rid of it. Stephen Ross, Warner's chairman and chief executive officer, approached Jack through his son Gary Tramiel in late June, to reopen the idea of selling off the Atari division to him. Jack unleashed his tough negotiating style in a meeting that began Sunday, July 1. By the early morning hours of July 2, TTL owned Atari for no money down. Deftly, Jack had managed to work out an exchange with Warner whereby Warner would get stock equivalent to 32% of the available shares in Jack's newly forming Atari Corporation (Atari Corp.) as well as a promise of $240 million in long-term notes.

When Warner announced they had sold Atari, Warner shareholders greeted the news enthusiastically and the stock price shot up. Jack was able to pocket several million dollars on the stock surge. It was the type of deal only Jack Tramiel could negotiate. The deal was sweet success for Tramiel, who was largely responsible for bringing Atari to its knees.

Jack immediately installed his sons into key positions at Atari. Haynie believes this proves Jack was intent on having his sons run Commodore. "What did he do? He went and bought Atari, started up a computer company, and put his sons in charge," recalls Haynie. "If he could have done that at Commodore, why wouldn't he? You can draw some conclusions there."

Commodore soon experienced an exodus of employees to Atari. Approximately 35 managers, technicians, engineers, and executives put their faith in Jack and left Commodore. It was a vindication of Jack's magnetism as a leader. They trusted Jack to lead them to success, a large gamble considering the dominant position Commodore enjoyed.

Not everyone departed with Jack. Michael Tomczyk, the original VIC-20 marketing executive, was not asked to join Atari. Earlier in the same year, he left Commodore, feeling it was no longer the same company without Tramiel.

Advertising man Kit Spencer decided to stay with Commodore. Jack wanted Kit to join him at Atari, but by now Kit was a loyal Commodore

The Savior of Commodore – 1982 to 1985

employee and wanted the stability for his family. "He didn't do the Atari gig, which always surprised me," says Russell. "Jack and Kit fell out because Kit stayed with Commodore."

Russell became nervous that he would lose some of his key project engineers, so he made an agreement with Shiraz Shivji. "[Shiraz] called up and we discussed it after he had left the company," says Russell. "He said that he wasn't going to take those engineers." In particular, Russell wanted to retain a Z8000 engineer until he completed his work. "Shiraz promised me that he would let him wrap his stuff up."

However, Shiraz backed out of the agreement. "I was at a board meeting in London when this engineer just left," says Russell. "I got a phone call at the board meeting that he was gone, and that just pissed me off to no end. I thought I had an agreement with Shiraz."

Bob Russell tipped off Commodore lawyers about possible theft of trade secrets. Russell thought it would be a good idea to inspect what the ex-employees were moving out of Commodore. "We put a lawsuit and we opened up their moving vans," recalls Russell. "They were taking peoples 'personal goods'. When the lawyers cracked open the moving truck, we found all kinds of Commodore documentation."

In a suit filed July 10 in Chester County Court, Commodore charged that Shiraz and three other former employees had stolen information on new products Commodore was developing. A Washington Post article soon appeared with the headline, "Commodore Says Four Stole Trade Secrets". Commodore obtained a preliminary injunction against releasing the new Atari computer.

Jack was furious. He was triumphant from negotiating the deal of the century to purchase Atari and now the injunction would stop him from marketing his new computer. To make matters worse, he had no means to fight back immediately.

News of Tramiel's departure, the exodus of top talent from Commodore, and Jack's purchase of Atari had a devastating effect on Commodore stock. If Irving knew how poorly the stock would fare, he likely would not have stood up to Jack at CES or attempt to replace him. Through 1984, the price fell from $60 to $20. It was clear investors thought Tramiel was the true reason for the success of Commodore. They had little confidence in Irving Gould or Marshall Smith.

With Commodore losing so many engineers, they decided to purchase the entire Amiga Corporation. "I came back thinking it was going to be a four million dollar purchase and we would have the rights to use the chips in computers," says Russell. "Then the next day they were like, 'We're buying the whole company for $24 million.' I'm like, 'Say what? We could have got it for a tenth of that. Why did we buy the whole damn company?'"

Commodore now owned 100% of Amiga Corporation. Russell believes Irving and Marshall intended to thwart the Tramiels. "I'm sure part of that $24 million was spite," says Russell.

Commodore purchased Amiga Corporation for $4.25 per share. Commodore would make the official announcement on August 15, 1984. The partners in Amiga, including Jay Miner and Dave Morse, finally found contentment. "If you were in the two to three percent range, you were considered one of the major shareholders in the company," says Mical. "It would be good."

Things also worked out for the Florida dentists, who originally invested $7 million. "I was told that every one of the investors who put any money in all did very well when Commodore bought the company," says Mical.

Mical himself was not a major shareholder. "I was a lowly engineer," he says. "I rose to be director, but I didn't get a commensurate increase in my stock. I was young and naïve back then, and I didn't know to ask for it. I should have asked for it."

Although everyone involved seemed happy, Robert Yannes recalls the frustration of his friend Bob Russell. "When [Bob Russell] found out what they paid for the company, which was some outrageous sum of money, he called me and he said, 'Yeah, it was a good thing to buy but not for that much money! You could have taken that money and divided it up among the engineers and each would have gotten several million dollars. I guarantee you they would have designed something better than the Amiga.'"

The entire Amiga enterprise was renamed Commodore-Amiga and incorporated as a subsidiary of Commodore. Jay Miner insisted on one important clause in his contract. He wanted Commodore to allow Mitchy to become an official member of the Commodore-Amiga development team. "I wouldn't say they were okay with it," says Mical. "They tolerated it because it was Jay and who's going to argue with Jay?"

Jack was still seething from the lawsuit by Commodore, but he soon found a way to counteract the lawsuit. Leonard Tramiel and his staff had found the documentation on the original Amiga deal, and realized Atari had a project called 'Mickey' to use the Amiga chipset.

After absorbing the new information, Jack regrouped and launched a legal assault. He immediately used this information to begin renegotiating the terms of his purchase with Warner, claiming the value of Atari Inc. was diminished because of the loss of the Amiga deal.

On Monday, August 13 (one day before the Commodore-Amiga deal), Tramiel filed a $100 million countersuit against both Commodore and Jay Miner personally, charging breach of contract.

"Atari at that time was lawsuit happy," recalls Mical. "Their legal department was a profit center for the company. I don't know if this is true or not, but we used to joke that half of their business came from their lawsuits, and only half of it came from their actual products. They sued everybody. They just sued and sued and sued. It was laughable."[8]

The suit contended that Atari Corp. owned the rights to the Lorraine's technology. Jack claimed Atari had spent time and money preparing to use the chips in 'Mickey'. He had a point. A week before Tramiel bought Atari Inc., Amiga returned the $500,000 to Atari, saying it was unable to develop the chips. This was questionable, since the technology was obviously working at the recent CES show.

Atari charged that those chips were now being used successfully in Amiga's new computer that Commodore intended to sell. Jack and Atari Corp. requested a permanent injunction to prevent Amiga from transferring the chips to Commodore and also asked for $100 million in punitive damages.

Commodore backed up its newly acquired company by paying for Amiga's defense fees and stepping in to take charge of the case. "Nothing ever came of it," reveals Mical. "There was a little bit of buzz, but it went away because there were no grounds. We didn't do anything wrong. We followed the letter of the agreement with them and did everything right. They were just frustrated and lashing out."

Commodore and Atari settled their suits, but the terms of the settlement are a mystery because the court documents remain sealed. The end result was that Jack was allowed to continue marketing his computer and Commodore and Amiga moved on with their computer.

---

[8] Atari also tried suing Nintendo.

The Amiga

1985-1986

In late August 1984, Jay Miner took his seat as General Manager of Commodore-Amiga. The engineers were thrilled with the arrangement. "Commodore did the best thing they possibly could have done to make sure that the product they bought was successful: they left us alone," says R.J. Mical.

Commodore-Amiga

Commodore-Amiga moved ten miles from the small offices on Scott Boulevard to a spacious rented facility in Las Gatos, California. "It was a nice big facility with a huge kitchen and offices for everyone. It was great," says Mical.

The new location was uniquely suited to Mical's style. "There was a lovely green courtyard in a gorgeous, lush setting," recalls Mical. "It was close to good restaurants and close to a beautiful huge park, which was great for walking. I've always been a walker. My best meetings and my best design thinking sessions have taken place out of doors. It was a beautiful place for that."

The Los Gatos area also had all the cultural necessities for young engineers. "There was this wonderful pizza parlor that we always used to go to and play video games and drink beer and eat pizza," recalls Mical. "We would go there together quite often. We were real close friends with each other, as well as coworkers, so we would regularly hang around and socialize in the evenings."

Dave Haynie recalls the best part about Los Gatos. "I only went out there a couple of times and I really liked being out there in Los Gatos simply because there were no Commodore management types wandering around," he explains.

The Amiga engineers enjoyed their arrangement with Commodore. "They had this brilliant group of engineers who had put this machine together and they just left us to invent the thing ourselves without interference," says Mical. "In the beginning, we were all vastly in love with Commodore and their way of doing business because we were going to be able to finish the Amiga the way we intended."

Commodore gave the Amiga engineers the proper resources and tools they needed to develop the system. "They gave us a huge infusion of cash which allowed us to buy new computers for ourselves and hire some extra people that we needed," says Mical.

The Amiga team finally received adequate computing power for development. "At Amiga, we used the Sage and it was miserable and slow," says Mical. "We instantly went from ten people on one Sage to each guy having his own SUN workstation, with massive power and its own hard disk and its own CPU. Those were heavenly days."

With the tremendous resources available at Commodore, Jay Miner felt they should go after IBM. In his mind, IBM was vulnerable because of their primitive technology. According to Robert Russell, the first thing the Amiga team did when they started at Commodore was undo the PC-compatibility revisions made to the Lorraine. "They had to go back and take some stuff out and repurpose it, and make it once again 68000 based," says Russell.

Between Commodore engineers like Robert Russell, Commodore marketing people, and Jay Miner, arguments occurred over which market they should target. Russell was in favor of a low cost, high performance product to replace the Commodore 64. Jay Miner wanted a high cost, high performance machine for the business marketplace. According to Miner, "This battle of cost was never ending, being internal among us as well as with the investors and Commodore."[1]

Russell had a valid point, since Commodore had their biggest success in the low cost, high performance market dominated by the Commodore 64. "I wanted a cheap Commodore 64-space replacement," says Russell. "That's why I pushed them to buy the computer. It most certainly wasn't the PC compatible they were trying to turn it into and it most certainly wasn't a business machine."

---

[1] *Amiga User International* magazine (September 1992), interview by Mike Nelson. All succeeding quotes from Miner are from the same source.

Russell's assessment of the Lorraine matched the original concept as described by R.J. Mical. "As far as I was concerned, it was a personal computer," says Russell.

Unfortunately, marketing experts previously convinced Commodore management that they did not have to do anything new to retain the low-end computer space. "Later on we had these marketing experts who would come in and say, 'Well you guy's own this space, so you don't need to do anything about it,'" recalls Russell. "As much as people protested, corporate listened to them."

Russell sat through one meeting with the experts in disbelief. "I plainly remember sitting in a meeting and the marketing people came in and started drawing. 'Here's the computer market in four quadrants. You own that space where the C64 is at in that quadrant. You don't need to do product in that.' All the management is saying, 'Okay. Yeah. That makes sense.' We're saying, 'No! No! We own that, but how do we maintain it?'"

Even though Russell patiently screamed that they needed to figure out how to continue their success in retail, management felt they could retain a perpetual lock on the low-end market with the C64.

The Commodore-Amiga engineers began building a new prototype, different from Lorraine. Dave Haynie explains, "The first codename was the Lorraine. That was the one in the black metal cases and they still had the 5.25-inch floppy. Then the next generation of that was called the Zorro."

Although Miner was General Manager of Commodore-Amiga, he continued designing and improving his chips at the lowest levels. "I never met Jay Miner but I have a lot of respect for him," says Bil Herd. "The only thing I ever heard bad about him was that his dog stunk. One of the programmers was like, 'Oh, I hated that dog!'"

Although Mitchy was slowing down, she continued working with Miner developing the chips. "Mitchy was really kind of an old dog during the Amiga days," says Mical.

Miner was a creative man and believed in experimentation, even though it was already late in the development cycle. Sometime in 1985, Miner developed a revolutionary graphics mode called Hold and Modify, or HAM. HAM made it possible to show 4096 colors on screen at once, producing photo-realistic images. It was a first for personal computers, with the potential to revolutionize the industry.

Miner's work amazed Bil Herd, who was surprised to see so many colors displayed on a standard television set; something he thought previously impossible. "I started in the TV repair field, so I actually know why you can only make so much color in a certain amount of time," says Herd. "The color crystal frequency is 3.58 MHz, which means you can only have 40 transitions of that across your screen. If you change the information faster than that, you get that rainbow effect, where one side of a character is red and one side is green."

The rainbow effect had plagued earlier computers from other companies. "The Coleco Adam had those rainbows running through it," recalls Herd.

"On the Amiga, they said, 'Fine. We will change the color as fast as the TV will go, but we can change the black and white part of the signal twice as fast.' They were right," explains Herd. "In TV sets, that's why you can see the little black line between people's teeth. That's the black and white modulation, which is going much faster."

Miner exploited the fact that the black and white signal on a television set is faster than the color signal. "That's what the Hold and Modify for the Amiga was," says Herd. "They would put a color out there, and then you could change the brightness of the color for the next pixel. You couldn't change the color, or else you would get these artifacts, but you could change the brightness of the existing color. It was the first time somebody had broke that barrier about what you could see on a TV set." With the new changes, the Daphne chip became *Denise*.

Over on the software side, R.J. Mical continued developing and refining Intuition. "That gave me the best title I have ever had in my entire professional career," quips Mical. "For a while there at Commodore, I was their Director of Intuition."

Commodore licensed a software package called *SoftVoice* from the same company responsible for the popular S.A.M. (Software Automated Mouth) on 8-bit computers. SoftVoice was a simple text to speech utility, similar to the one used earlier on the Lorraine. "The technology was quite good, but taking it from good to really great was an art form that a lot of us were involved in," says Mical. Mical's experience with the Williams arcade game Sinistar, which also had speech capabilities, helped him on the project.

The Amiga acquisition had a tragic effect on the disk operating system, which the engineers called CAOS (Commodore Amiga Operating System). "What a drag that whole situation was," recalls Mical.

CAOS was the part of the operating system responsible for managing files on disk, separate from EXEC and Intuition. "CAOS was the original file system for the Amiga," says Mical.

CAOS was outstanding. "The original file system that we had designed for the machine was just beautiful," recalls Mical. "It was exactly what you would want a modern multitasking operating system to have."

Mical admired the work done by the third-party engineers, but greed exerted an influence after Commodore bought Amiga. "It was being developed by these guys who I believe were extremely good engineers, but they were also cutthroat businessmen," says Mical. "When Commodore bought our company, these guys saw an opportunity to get a much better deal for the operating system out of Commodore than the deal that they made with us."

In many ways, it was easier to make business deals without Commodore. "We were a tiny little startup of starving artists trying to do something big to change the world," explains Mical. "Now they are dealing with big fat Commodore with big fat checkbooks, big fat guys smoking big fat cigars, and they wanted some of that big fat money. So instead, they tried to extort a bunch of extra money out of Commodore. Commodore tried to negotiate with them in good faith, but the whole thing fell apart in the end."

Today, the incident still upsets Mical. "That was a damnable thing for us," he says. "To have it so tantalizingly close but never get a chance to use it was such a heartbreak. I feel very badly about the evil business thing that they did to try to make money rather than to live up to the commitment they made to us. It was a jerk-butt thing that they did there."

The engineers also wanted Basic in the Amiga. Unfortunately, Commodore could not use the 8-bit 6502 Basic they purchased from Microsoft long ago. They would have to go back to Microsoft and negotiate for a 68000-based Basic. "Microsoft got their revenge when Commodore tried to negotiate a Basic for the Amiga," explains Jim Butterfield. "Not only was that reportedly costly to Commodore, but Microsoft also insisted that the next 8-bit product, the Commodore 128, show the Microsoft name or the deal was off."

Before departing for Atari, Sig Hartmann, the Director of Software, handled the transaction with Microsoft. "Sig was an effective manager and was also effective at bringing things in and dealing with the Microsoft's of the world," says Russell. "They were starting to get to be in a position of power and he dealt with those things."

The software engineers found time to sneak Easter eggs into the system, which users were quick to discover. By holding down both Alt keys and both Shift keys, and pressing one of the function keys a message would appear. Users who pressed F10 while doing this were treated to a message saying, 'Moral Support: Joe Pillow & The Dancing Fools'.

The Choice of a New Generation

Following Jack Tramiel's departure in January 1984, Commodore had their highest revenues ever of $1.3 billion, which landed Commodore on the Forbes International 500 at 380th position for first time ever. Subtracting the costs of doing business, Commodore earned a profit of $144 million. This success was largely attributable to the Commodore 64 and the Tramiel years.

Unfortunately, the failure of the Plus/4 would shortly catch up with Commodore. For the period ending December 1984, profits were down 94%. Then for the quarter ending in March 1985, Marshall Smith reported an embarrassing loss of $21 million.

Most analysts blamed the loss on the Plus/4, which Jack Tramiel conceived. Fortune magazine concluded that under Tramiel, Commodore was "a one product company whose management gave little thought to planning for the future."[2] Tramiel had let research and technology slip while he was at the helm. MOS Technology did not even have a 16-bit microprocessor because Tramiel never pushed for one.

To compensate for the enormous losses, Marshall Smith and Irving Gould began cutting a significant portion of Commodore employees, mainly factory workers. The layoffs amounted to 45% of the company.

Gould also took a hard look at his President and CEO, Marshall Smith, and decided he needed someone more vibrant. Gould included Smith in his search for a new CEO and planned to have him work closely with his replacement to ensure a smooth transition.

In late 1984, Irving Gould hired a search firm, which scouted out the most successful companies of the mid-eighties. Earlier in the year, Steve Jobs hired John Sculley, the former CEO of Pepsi, to head Apple. Gould wanted his own John Sculley.

Gould chose Thomas J. Rattigan, a former Pepsi president, to lead the new Commodore. Rattigan was born in Boston, Massachusetts in July 1937. His father, Thomas F. Rattigan, was a World War II army veteran. "I was brought up during the Second World War and was from a working class family," says Rattigan. "My father, Thomas Francis Rattigan, served in the U.S. army. I grew up in Boston but when my father went into the service we were living in Springfield, Massachusetts."

Rattigan's education prepared him for his future role with Commodore. He attended Boston College and received his degree in Business Administration in 1960. He immediately pursued a master's degree at the

---

[2] *Fortune* magazine, "How Commodore Hopes to Survive" (January 6, 1986), p. 30.

Harvard University Graduate School of Business Administration, graduating in 1962. Rattigan immediately took a job with *General Foods*, where he worked in marketing. "I spent eight years of General Foods from 1962 to 1970," recalls Rattigan.

He then joined *PepsiCo Incorporated* as a marketing executive. In 1982, he became president and CEO of *PepsiCo Bottling International*. Rattigan describes his strategy against Coca-Cola. "We tried to operate like the Viet Cong during the war, where you try to hit them where they weren't and hopefully outflank them. A head on assault would have been disastrous." Perhaps his knowledge of fighting against a larger competitor would help Commodore survive.

In the mid eighties, Pepsi was one of the most dynamic and respected American companies, largely due to brilliant marketing. The slogan, 'Pepsi, the Choice of a New Generation,' was having an impact, and Pepsi was growing fast. Pepsi always seemed to have the latest pop sensation pitching their product. Gould hoped he could bring some of that success to Commodore. It was an inspired decision by Gould and could potentially straighten out the weakness in Commodore marketing.

Rattigan was no longer with Pepsi when Gould began his search. "[Commodore] didn't really lure me from Pepsi because I had left in the spring of 1984," recalls Rattigan.

In 1984, Rattigan was spending time with his family. "We had four children," says Rattigan, who often took his family on ski trips. "There were two places; either north of New England, largely Vermont, or in the west in Utah and Colorado."

When taking time for himself, Rattigan enjoyed reading. "Most of it was non-fiction and a lot of it was biographical and/or historical in nature," says Rattigan. "I'm not one of these guys who walks around quoting books that I've read. I read them for enjoyment."

Rattigan's sabbatical ended with a phone call. "Sometime later in that year, I got a call from a search firm," recalls Rattigan. "Commodore was looking for somebody to run their North American operation, which was the United States and Canada, with the indication that once I came in and did that for a while I would be taking over from Marshall Smith, who was then the CEO."

Rattigan talked with both Irving Gould and Marshall Smith. "We had some discussions in late 1984," recalls Rattigan. "I went into Commodore on that basis; taking over responsibility for the North American operation, reporting to Marshall. We both understood that at some point in time he would be leaving and, assuming I was doing what they hoped I would be doing, I'd move up into that slot." In the meantime, Marshall Smith would continue as CEO of Commodore

International, retaining control of the technology and finance departments. He also retained his vice chairman status on the board of directors.

On May 27, 1985, Fortune Magazine announced Thomas J. Rattigan as the new President of Commodore North America. Rattigan seemed to hold promise for a new Commodore culture. At 44, Rattigan was relatively young, resembling actor Vince Vaughn with a dash of the TV Batman, Adam West.

Most Commodore engineers saw a bright future under Rattigan. "Rattigan really was on the marketing side of things. I thought Thomas Rattigan was a sharp marketing guy," says Russell. "He was definitely more on the ball than Marshall Smith was."

The transition from a soft drink company to technology required a quick education. "It was a new business to me," recalls Rattigan. "The company was in many ways living hand to mouth based on what the economic scenario was. All of a sudden, I've got a fair number of people reporting to me who I don't know. The early months really were just familiarizing yourself with the people and the business as best you could."

His greatest weakness was a lack of familiarity with computer technology. "The closest most of us in those days got to computers was our secretaries buying *Wang* workstations," says Rattigan. "We were pretty much in the dark ages when it came to technology."

What Rattigan lacked in computer experience, he substituted with business savvy. "You have to learn the language and that was part of the equation," explains Rattigan. "You had to try and understand what the problems were and what opinions you might have on them. I was sitting down with Marshall and other people and discussing those kinds of things. It was a quick and short breaking in period, but that's where I spent a lot of my time."

A new era was about to begin for Commodore. If Rattigan could convince consumers to take the *Pepsi Challenge* against the Macintosh and IBM-PC, the Commodore-Amiga could thrive.

The Commodore UNIX Machine

While Amiga development continued on the West Coast, an East Coast Commodore group continued developing a rival to the Amiga. "The other group was the C900 group," says Dave Haynie. The project was a continuation of the 16-bit Z8000 computer started in 1983 by Frank Hughes and Robert Russell.

The engineers attempted to create an entertainment system out of the C900. "At one time we were going to do a gaming version of the Z8000 with the memory mapping chip and everything," recalls Russell. "Once we put it together as a prototype and we were running Basic on it, it was kind of like, 'This isn't a gaming machine! It's not interesting because there's no way to make it compatible. What the hell is this but just a super fast thing that looks like a Commodore 64.'"

Commodore's in-house 16-bit computer was to be a more serious computer, targeting the business world. "With the Z8000, we were trying to run a UNIX like operating system and it was clearly a business machine," says Russell.

Computer pioneers Dennis Ritchie and Ken Thompson developed the UNIX system (originally called UNICS) in 1969, along with the C programming language. The source code for the operating system was freely available and companies quickly began customizing and selling different flavors optimized for different machines.[3]

Commodore named their operating system *Coherent*, which they claimed was compatible with AT & T's *Unix System V*. Coherent even boasted a graphical user interface similar to the UNIX standard, *X-Windows*.

"Frank [Hughes] was in charge of the Z8000 project," says Bil Herd. "He was from the West Coast, like Shiraz and Bob Russell. He was a rebel in his own cause. No boss liked him."

Herd encountered Hughes during his first interview, which went poorly. "I was one of the few people who got along with him later," says Herd. "I liked him. The secretaries realized he was more of a pussycat when he was trying to act like a big belligerent bear."

At the time, engineers called the machine the Z-machine because it contained a Z8000 chip. Herd loved to tease the UNIX group by calling them Z-people. The engineers soon raised the naming convention to absurd heights and began calling the pens they used Z-pens and the food they ate Z-meals. "They were kind of treated as second rate citizens unfortunately," says Herd.

Herd was impressed with the ingenuity of the Z-people and their ability to thrive in the Commodore environment. At the massive new West Chester building, space was abundant and there were many rooms available. One night, the Z-people stole the furniture out of the Commodore lobby and made their own lounge so they could relax and smoke. The unauthorized lounge would obviously not last long once managers found out about it, so the Z-people disguised it as a VAX mainframe repair depot. According to Herd, "I was so amused by this that I stopped teasing them for a week."

---

[3] Much later, in the late 1990's, UNIX popularity surged in the form of *Linux*.

Engineers used the name Z-machine internally but Commodore referred to it as *Next Generation*. In 1984, Commodore chose a new name. "Commodore marketing had decided that their computer was going to be the Commodore 900," says Haynie.

After Tramiel left, titles became more important at Commodore and the executives offered Russell s new title. "They asked me if I wanted to be director of business machines, which is what the Z8000 was," recalls Russell. Unfortunately, the recent exodus to Atari left Commodore devoid of knowledgeable management. "I said, 'I don't want to step up to director because I have no mentors here. I have nobody to show me how it's done.'"

Instead, Russell stepped up into management. "I became management there just because they said, 'You've been around here the longest and you can show the other guys the ropes.' I was already hiring people even though I wasn't a manager, so what the hell. Okay, I'll be a manager."

In 1984, Russell attended a meeting in London where anxious Commodore executives contemplated the threat posed by Jack Tramiel. "We were at a meeting in London. All the big general managers were there, maybe 20 people," says Russell. "I was there because I had the Z8000 project and I was doing reports to the board on engineering. The Amiga was part of it. I knew what was happening with Atari and Jack and their engineers."

According to Russell, Irving Gould held his cool in the midst of bad news. "Shit was hitting the fan all over the place," he recalls. "My engineers were already leaving with Jack and they knew Jack was doing something. Basically the C64 was starting to lose its momentum then. You could see that the company had turned the corner in some respects. It was pretty bad as far as how the regional people were doing. They were getting slammed."

The loss of key engineers to Atari hindered the C900 development. "There were three different teams on the C900 before they got that to work right," recalls Haynie. "The last of those were George Robbins and Bob Welland."

According to Dave Haynie, the engineers improved the graphics capabilities of the 8563 chip. "Bob Welland was designing stuff that was actually very sophisticated," he recalls. "He was trying to get Commodore to leapfrog some of the problems we had with Motorola. He had designed a graphics chip for the C900 that had its own blitter, which was a bit more sophisticated in some ways than the Amiga blitter. They may have actually done a prototype of it, but that was one of the things that was never finished."

The second engineer on the C900 project was George R. Robbins, whom Bil Herd called 'Grr'. "He was a little bit older than most of us at the time," says Haynie. "He lived a bohemian lifestyle."

According to Dave Haynie, when Robbins was not sleeping in his van, he literally lived at Commodore. "In the C128 days, he was the guy on the low-end machines," says Haynie. "He had a green van behind Commodore and he kind of lived [at Commodore] for a while. He just never left."

Herd agrees. "He actually lived there, even when there were no projects going on," says Herd. "He didn't have a driver's license and I think his car was broken."

Engineers often made jests about the distinctive odor that followed Robbins, which were in good fun since most engineers also smelled from time to time, depending on their work schedule. "The difference between George and me was George didn't do the things for hygiene that I did," says Herd. "We all knew it."

When Robbins needed sleep, he nested. "George was different," explains Herd. "George would sleep in bubble wrap. We called it nesting. You could look under a table and see a whole bunch of bubble wrap and maybe a foot sticking out of it. Then he would walk around with these little red circles on his face after he woke up."

Robbins lived on cafeteria food at Commodore and resorted to vending machines when the cafeteria closed. "He was drop kicking the vending machine," says Herd. "He probably had no change and needed to eat or something."

For years, Commodore engineers requested onsite showers due to the odd hours they worked, however management refused. "That was the one thing we could never get," says Haynie, who still sounds frustrated. "Bil had made a deal that if we finished [the C128] on time we would get showers. We were petitioning for years."

Herd remembers the negotiations. "I was always telling people, 'You need showers. Look, I'm here all the time. You want work out of me? Put a fricking shower in. I'm using a brown tub I fill out of the coffee machine.'"

The eccentric Robbins improved the original C900 design, and more importantly, he had the ability to complete the project. One unique feature of the C900 was the ability to act like a shared mainframe computer. "They were going to have terminals to hook into the UNIX machine," says Haynie. "They were developing a multiple port card for the thing so you could use it more like the VAX rather than like the workstations."

The C900 used a Z8001 chip running at 10 MHz. "The Zilog processor, the Z8000, was a 16-bit," says Haynie. The system also contained a reasonable 512 kilobytes of memory and a 20 megabyte hard drive.

Video was produced by the same graphics chip as Bil Herd's C128. "The [8563] chip used in the C128 for high resolution was actually done for the Z8000," says Russell.

The C900 received a professional, compact case design. "All the plastic design, all the case work, and all the molds that had to be cut were being done out of Japan," says Russell. "There was nothing out of the United States."

Ira Velinsky delivered the C900 case before departing Commodore. "We had a US designer Ira Velinsky there but Ira was spending more time dealing with Japan talking Japanese than he was doing much here in the United States," says Russell. "Of course, Ira then went on to Atari too and did case work for them."

Commodore promoted the C900 in Commodore Microcomputers magazine, including photographs of a remarkably complete system.

As the Commodore 900 was heading for production, Chairman Gould decided to pull the plug on the project. Like Tramiel before him, Gould was not afraid to cancel projects that he thought had limited potential. "The Z8000 got canned eventually," says Herd. "It was really a product with no marketing and no interest. It was one of those things being driven by engineers again, but it didn't really go anywhere."

"[The C900 was] basically a victim of the Amiga," says Haynie. "It took some settling time, but once Commodore knew that the Amiga was their future, the C900 was no longer in the books. After they had finally gotten it working, it was cancelled."

Haynie attributes the cancellation to the poor state of Commodore finances at the time. "That decision was made in 1985 and Commodore wasn't doing too well then," says Haynie. "It was clear that they were making survival cuts at that point. They didn't believe they had the resources to launch two separate machines that were incompatible with each other."

Commodore sold off the limited production of C900 machines. "We actually had releases out because we were nearing completion on it," says Russell. The engineers had built approximately 500 machines by the time Commodore cancelled the project. Commodore sold the machines in Europe sometime in 1985 for approximately $4000 each as development systems. It was probably a good business decision since the Z8000 was not the future and neither were terminals.

Finishing the Amiga

In the pre-Commodore days, Amiga stated that they would release the 'Amiga PC' in late 1984. After the acquisition by Commodore, the team pushed back the schedule to late 1985. When news of a rival 16-bit computer from Atari began circulating, Commodore managers began pushing for a mid-summer 1985 release.

The transformation into a business machine caused delays. "It was entirely due to the fact that we wanted to turn it into a real computer," says Mical. "It wasn't just the user interface. Some of the other things were smaller but equally significant. We needed a word processor, we needed a good graphics program, and we needed the basic set of tools that could also do some businessey officey things."

While at Commodore, the computer simply became the Amiga. At the January 1985 CES, where Commodore unveiled the C128, the Amiga was not on public display. "They were showing everything behind the scenes," says Haynie. Commodore rented a suite for the Amiga where they showed it to select individuals. Since the Amiga was incomplete and lacking a disk operating system, the engineers loaded programs into the Amiga using one of their new Sun workstations.

CES was the first real meeting between the Commodore 8-bit engineers and the new Amiga team. "They called a bunch of us who were there into a room and showed us the early demos," recalls Haynie. "This was January 1985 and they hadn't finished the operating system but parts of it were working. We got to see the Boing Demo and RoboCity and some of those famous demos."

Haynie immediately knew the Amiga was a groundbreaking piece of technology. "It was really impressive because nobody had ever seen anything like that on a computer," says Haynie. "It was different enough from anything anybody had done that it was quite profound, especially for people who designed these things."

There was instant chemistry between the West Coast Amiga engineers and the East Coast Commodore engineers. "We got along because we were the same kind of people," says Haynie.

Mical recalls the Commodore engineers. "There were a lot of really brilliant people," recalls Mical. "Bil Herd was great. I hung around with Bil at CES and a lot of other shows as well."

Herd remembers his first encounter with Dave Needle, a chip designer on the Amiga. "He was the kind of guy who always showed up in sandals," recalls Herd. "It wasn't my look, but okay. He was a sandals and a Hawaiian shirt type of guy whereas I was the tight T-shirt and tight jeans type of guy."

"When we first met the Amiga guys, the guy that had done the hardware design had claimed to be from Jupiter," says Herd. "We just looked at him and said, 'We're from Pluto, man. We've got you beat.' He was still in the inner planets as far as we were concerned."

The Commodore engineers received a thorough education on the Amiga when one of the display models broke down. "One of them was broken and we ended up taking the whole thing apart to get it to run at the show," explains Mical.

Dave Haynie and Bil Herd became engrossed in studying the machine as the Amiga engineers took it apart. "One night, Herd and I ended up hanging out with some of the Amiga guys. I think it was Dale [Luck] and Dave Needle, the guy who did hardware and chips," says Haynie. "We went up to the big suite they had rented for them and they showed us the inside of the Amiga 1000."

The Commodore engineers were surprised to see similarities to the C128 they were currently working on. According to Haynie, "It was kind of funny because we looked inside and I said, 'You have one of those too!' We had a problem with the 8563 display chip and it had to have a tower, which was basically a circuit board with a bunch of chips on it that you plug into a socket. You only see those when somebody made a mistake somewhere. Well guess what? They had a tower about the same size as ours sitting in the socket of their display chip, which was called Daphne and later became known as Denise."

As usual with Bil Herd, the night was not complete unless it included alcohol. "After that we went out and got drunk together," says Herd.

During the development phase of the Amiga, Commodore did very little promotion. Compute editor Richard Mansfield called Commodore 'aggressively silent' with respect to the Amiga. This was puzzling because usually companies go out of their way to pre-hype their products. Commodore had the most anticipated computer in the industry, yet they were doing the opposite of what they should have been doing.

As the avalanche of non-news continued, Compute! editor Tom Halfhill decided to force the issue. In early May, Halfhill showed up unannounced at the Los Gatos facility, along with fellow program editor Charles Brannon. Though it was a brash move, the two thought they had a chance at success. After all, Commodore could not turn down free publicity if it showed up on their doorstep. They were wrong.

The editors were lucky enough to run into Commodore-Amiga president Dave Morse in the parking lot. However, Morse was apparently uninterested and drove off hurriedly. The two spoke to the receptionist and asked for someone, but when a manager arrived, all she had to say was, "We aren't saying anything publicly at this point. We aren't saying anything at all." The two asked to speak with General Manager Jay Miner but the manager said he was not around.

Later, Compute! complained in an editorial that Commodore gave a hands on demonstration of the Amiga to a competing magazine, Byte, but denied the Compute! editors.

It seemed like Commodore was shunning free publicity for the Amiga. The old Commodore would have called in someone like Michael Tomczyk, who understood the value of publicity. Instead, the new Commodore seemed to regard the press as a minor annoyance. The incident did little to bring Compute! editors to their side.

Commodore soon made a change to the Commodore-Amiga leadership, which the Amiga team accepted. "They replaced the company head," says Mical. "They took Dave Morse, who is a brilliant guy, removed him from being president of the company, and put their own guy in, Rick Geiger. He was a good guy and I liked working with him."

Throughout 1985, delays with the CAOS disk operating system continued as the third party developers remained uncooperative. "As it was getting worse, and as we were becoming more doubtful as to whether they were going to do the right thing for us, we started working on Plan B," says Mical.

The engineers began looking for another disk operating system for the Amiga. "Plan B was TripOS, the operating system that came out of the UK," says Mical. A programmer named Dr. Tim King originally developed TripOS at the University of Cambridge Computer Laboratory in the late seventies and early eighties. Originally, King developed TripOS for the IBM 3081 mainframe computer. Later, he translated it for the PDP-11.

Mical was understandably disappointed with TripOS. "No disrespect to the guys who invented it, but it was not meant to be on a class of machine like the Amiga," he says.

The system was inferior to CAOS. "That file system had a lot of problems, but its biggest problem was that it had been designed for an 8-bit world, and the Amiga was a 16-bit world," says Mical. "The whole thing was just a mess because of it. All the file system operations had to go through this translation mechanism to get into their code."

Mical also found the institutionally developed code less than efficient. "Their code was University quality code, where optimized performance is not important, but where theoretical purity was important," explains Mical. "We were getting University quality engineering where it was bad and it was slow and it turned out to be buggy too."

After working so hard to create the perfect system, it was a difficult compromise. "Everyone was upset from top to bottom," recalls Mical "The only guys who weren't upset were the TripOS guys."

Dr. King formed a company called MetaComCo, and with amazing speed was able to port the operating system to the Amiga. Commodore renamed the Amiga version of TripOS to AmigaDOS.

The completed operating system used two separate disks. The disk called *Kickstart* essentially contained the system ROM, the equivalent of the PC BIOS (Basic Input Output System). Once the system booted, the user inserted another disk called *Workbench*, which contained the graphical user interface and operating system.

Jay Miner continued development on his chips, including Denise. Though the Denise graphics chip was impressive for 1985, one function of the chip disappointed Miner. Jay's dream of creating a computer capable of producing incredible flight simulator graphics did not quite come true. He was hoping programmers could use HAM to display 4096 colors using polygon graphics. While HAM was great at displaying color images, it was much slower than he had hoped.

According to Miner, "I said that wasn't needed any more as it wasn't useful and I asked the chip layout guy to take it off. He came back and said that this would either leave a big hole in the middle of the chip or take a three-month redesign and we couldn't do that. I didn't think anyone would use it. I was wrong again as that has really given the Amiga its edge in terms of the color palette."

Without HAM, only EHB mode would remain, which could display 64 colors at once. While 64 colors were impressive, it did not produce photo-realism, a key feature that became a major selling point. "There's two things that happened with the HAM mode," recalls Mical. "One was video and the other was frame capture technology that took advantage of the HAM mode."

MOS Technology fabricated all the custom chips for the Amiga. "They brought more people in, especially as we were getting into the Amiga stuff," says Haynie. "We had our share of resident wizard types who were just really, really smart guys. They were transitioning from a chip company where just making a chip made sense, to this company that was supposedly vertically integrated to deliver consumer products."

Commodore eventually funded a CMOS process line at MOS Technology. "They were trying to get a better process when they were doing the Amiga line," says Russell. "They basically cleaned out the side of the building that had the cafeteria and put in a new production line. That was when [Commodore] ran into money problems."

VIC chip designer Al Charpentier believes MOS Technology may have become a burden to Commodore as the years went by. "It is such an extraordinarily expensive proposition to be in the chip business that at the end of the day, it was more of a drag than an asset in my opinion," says Charpentier. "I think it created an environment where they didn't want to look outside the box because they had the fab. It created an environment where they kept saying, 'Well, we've got to buy it out of our own fab.'"

MOS Technology no longer attempted to sell semiconductors to outside companies. "At that time they were only building Commodore chips," says Russell. "It was probably 95% captive. We would sell random parts to people, but not as a sustainable business."

Internally, Commodore was unsure if they should continue relying on MOS Technology. "Everyone was arguing that we can buy it cheaper from other suppliers," says Russell.

Later in the year, Commodore began talking about IBM compatibility with the Amiga. They hoped to emulate the IBM-PC using a software product called the *Transformer*. Jay Miner felt it was a mistake to attempt IBM-PC compatibility. According to Miner, "It's funny but I never really saw MS-DOS compatibility as being that important for the Amiga. I said at the time to Commodore 'Hey, we're different. Try to take advantage of that, not imitate or simulate other people.'"

According to Russell, Commodore decided to recycle the C900 case for the Amiga. "It used my Z8000 keyboard and [case] because it was more of a business machine," reveals Russell. In a nod to the original modular design, the keyboard slid underneath the case in a small compartment, giving the Amiga a tidy appearance when not in use.

With the production model completed, Jay Miner thought it would be appropriate to give credit to the entire Amiga team right inside the case. All 53 team members, including the original Amiga team and the new Commodore engineers, had their signatures inscribed on the plastic mold. "There wasn't any real thumbprint of Commodore's on it except some of the Commodore guys got their thumbprints on the lid, and those were good guys," says Mical. Alongside the signatures was Mitchy's paw print, in tribute to her enduring loyalty. The tiny signature of the mysterious Joe Pillow was also included.

Amiga Launch Party

Commodore held a lavish debut for the Amiga, something they had not done in the past for any of their computers. "The Launch Party came from the Amiga marketing people," says Mical. "The Amiga marketing people were a brilliant bunch."

On July 23, 1985, the official Amiga launch took place in New York. Commodore rented the renowned Lincoln Center for the event. With its modern architecture and vast theater, it was an appropriate setting to unveil a revolutionary computer.

Hundreds of people attended the event, including technology writers, editors, reporters, market analysts, employees, software developers, and even some celebrities. "We had Deborah Harry there," says Mical, referring to the lead singer of Blondie. Irving Gould ensured much of the crowd consisted of Wall Street investors and journalists from business publications.

The scale and grandiosity of the event impressed the Amiga developers. Jay Miner and his entire Amiga team flew down from California for the launch. According to Mical, "We were intensely involved with setting the whole thing up, getting it all organized, getting the software to work, figuring out the plan for how it was all going to flow. It was a gigantic group effort that involved the whole company." Irving Gould spared no expense and flew in the engineer's wives and girlfriends.

The event started late in the day and continued into the night. "As I recall it was late afternoon but I think it was still light when we arrived," says Mical. "We were assembling and getting the whole cast together."

Attendees wore their best attire. "The engineers and the Amiga staff were all elegantly dressed in tuxedos,"[4] says Mical. Attendees packed into the reception area of Lincoln Center, chatting and periodically stepping up to the fully stocked bar for free drinks. A woodwind trio played soothing tunes while a small laser show kept the crowd entertained.

Marshall Smith indulged his thirst for martinis. "Marshall liked to drink a lot," recalls Herd. "There's a film of him doing the Amiga intro and he had already been into the martinis, and it was just kind of sad."

Looking like James Bond himself in his black tuxedo, Thomas Rattigan garnered much of the interest from the press. "It was a hell of a party!" says Rattigan. "We had a good crowd there and we got pretty good press out of it." The press questioned Rattigan on his Amiga strategy. Still new and understandably shaky, Rattigan tried his best to give meaningful replies.

---

[4] Commodore recorded the event and gave copies to Commodore-Amiga engineers and staff. According to Mical, "I had gotten white gloves for the event, which turned out to be amusing because now you can find me in the audience when you go back and look at the video tapes of the launch. You can see where I am because that's me with the brilliantly white hands clapping politely."

After the reception, attendees entered the darkened theater for the Amiga demonstration. After years of effort, it was time for the engineers to unveil their creation. "We were all just so nervous because we needed to exude confidence and professionalism," says Mical. "It was a thin veneer underneath where a bunch of sweating engineers were praying that the demos wouldn't crash and that this whole thing would come off flawlessly."

R.J. Mical in his white gloves at the Amiga launch (photo courtesy of R.J. Mical).

Commodore-Amiga chose one of their own as the master of ceremonies. "The overall presenter was my boss, a guy named Bob Pariseau. He was the VP of software engineering," says Mical. "He was smooth and slick; an excellent presenter and an excellent spokesperson who did a fantastic job at the launch."

Cameras were set up to capture close-up images on the user and computer, as well as a direct feed from the Amiga onto large screens above the stage. "It was a carefully crafted presentation," says Mical. "Pariseau did a brilliant job of getting the material together and figuring out all the dodges they might have to make if things crashed."

Pariseau showed off the glory of Intuition, with emphasis on the revolutionary multitasking capabilities. He also showed the always-popular Boing Demo, which elicited gasps from the audience. This time, however, it was running while multitasking with another program. The window smoothly scrolled to reveal both programs running simultaneously.

To show off the Paula sound chip, Commodore recruited musician Roger Powell of *Cherry Lane Technologies* and Mike Boom of *Everyware Incorporated* to compose music using the Amiga. For many attending, it was the first time they had heard computer synthesized music as it boomed through the auditorium.

For the finale, artist Andy Warhol came on stage, along with singer Debbie Harry, to show off the graphics capabilities and ease of use of the Amiga. Warhol was a curious choice to demonstrate the Amiga, since he did not represent mainstream sensibilities. His most famous paintings were of Campbell soup cans repeated in different colors. As one attendee reported, "Warhol and Harry didn't seem to know why they were there, which probably matched the feeling of the audience."[5]

Left: Bob Pariseau at a CES presentation. Right: In the office. (photos courtesy of R.J. Mical)

Warhol lacked knowledge of computers, which gave the engineers a chill as he approached the Amiga. "Andy Warhol was a lovely guy and a fascinating artist," says Mical. "He had a good grasp of the fact that technology was going to change everything but at that time he was not into sophisticated computing. No graphics artist was because it was a brand new tool."

To offset Warhol's inexperience, Commodore made sure one of their employees was on hand to supervise. "Our chief artist at the time, a guy named Jack Hager, stood next to Andy and made jokes with Andy through the whole thing," says Mical. "He was the perfect counterpoint to Andy Warhol because Warhol is in an odd environment where things are queer and foreign."

For his presentation, Warhol used the mouse and a software program called *Graphicraft* by Island Graphics to paint an image of Debbie Harry. One screen showed Harry live, a second screen showed the Amiga screen

---

[5] *PC Magazine* (January 14, 1986), p. 119.

output and a third screen showed Warhol working away at the computer. Before hundreds of attendees, Warhol created one of his signature celebrity paintings.

"There were some incredibly dicey moments," recalls Mical. "He digitized her and then he was going to paint in her face. He was only supposed to use the paintbrush but the flood fill was known to crash every second time you used it. He went to reach for the paintbrush and grabbed the flood fill. 'Click click clickedy click.' I was like, 'It's going down! It's going down!' And it *didn't*. The engineers in that audience willed that art program collectively. If there is such a thing as the Force, we used it that day to keep that flood fill from crashing."

Luckily, Jack Hager was on hand to politely steer Warhol to the paint tool. "The only time we saw a real crack on [Jack's] face is when Andy starts clicking around with the flood fill," says Mical. "Jack was smooth right through that but you could see, behind the eyes, he was getting ready for the joke that he's got to make when the machine crashes and we've got to reboot the machine."

To the relief of the Commodore-Amiga engineers, the presentation came off flawlessly. "It was a great big party and it came off really well," says Mical.

Subsequent to the launch party, Warhol remained supportive of the Amiga. He used the computer to help create a video for MTV out of Warhol Studios in New York. Warhol had a strict no-interview policy (despite being the publisher of *Interview* magazine) but he curiously sat down for an interview with Amiga World magazine.

The Amiga launch party ensured coverage by magazines and newspapers, many outside of the computer industry. According to Rattigan, "The trade papers were somewhat dubious about the Amiga, given our checkered history with having originally dealt with computer stores and, prior to my time, shifting to mass distributors."

Magazines such as Popular Computing, Fortune, Byte, and Compute! all covered the event. Fortune downplayed the potential impact of the Amiga, stating, "While initial reviews praised the technical capabilities of the Amiga, a shell-shocked PC industry has learned to resist the seductive glitter of advanced technology for its own sake."

Commodore Microcomputers recruited an impartial freelance writer in Louis Wallace to cover the launch for their magazine. Of the Amiga, Wallace said, "To give you an idea of its capabilities, imagine taking all that is good about the Macintosh, combine it with the power of the IBM PC-AT, improve it, and then cut the price by 75%."

Although Commodore successfully promoted the Amiga at the launch party, the Amiga would not appear on store shelves for months after the event. Commodore still had to manufacture and distribute the computer and there were plenty of problems to overcome.

Jack Strikes Back

Within the first week of buying Atari Inc., Jack closed all 8-bit computer projects and froze all other operations pending an evaluation. He also announced his intentions to reduce the size of Atari's staff to just 200 people.

Atari Inc. had already suffered massive layoffs, starting the previous summer when 600 employees lost their jobs, followed by a monstrous winter layoff of about 6,300 from its worldwide staff.

By Thursday, employees received notice that most of the departments outside of the main research and engineering groups would be closed or drastically reduced. On Friday, about 95% of the staff in each department received a notice of termination.

In the meantime, Jack's son Leonard had joined Atari Corp. and, along with Shiraz Shivji, began the process of interviewing engineers from Atari Consumer as well as Atari's old coin-op division (still owned by Warner and renamed Atari Games). Some engineers were asked to stay on at the new Atari while others were offered a severance package.

Atari engineers like Jay Miner were now designing Commodore computers, and Commodore engineers like Shiraz Shivji, John Feagans, and Leonard Tramiel were now designing Atari computers. It was a complete flip-flop.

Although the Amiga team had developed their computer in absolute secrecy behind a veil of deception, they now had Atari threatening to compete directly against the Amiga. "That was the proposed Amiga killer that was in its own rights a good machine," recalls Mical. "It had a lot of good capabilities and there was some good engineering that was done to it, both hardware and software. But the Amiga was superior."

Robert Russell had helped design the computer with Shivji and other engineers while at Commodore. Now, the computer was competing against Commodore. "The guys who did the paper designs with me left and went with Jack," says Russell. "I'm talking about the Atari ST."

Shivji designed the Atari ST quickly using cheap, readily available parts. There would be no customized chips in this computer. The Atari ST had only 512 different colors available compared to 4096 on the Amiga, and the Atari ST could only display 16 colors at once. Denise gave the Amiga a clear advantage.

The Atari ST only claimed superiority in sound. It offered Midi support, which was popular with musicians dabbling in electronic synthesizer music. The Atari ST computer was the first on the market with built in Midi ports (one input and one output) which allowed a keyboard synthesizer to attach to the machine. This allowed the computer to control a Midi instrument or a musician could play on a Midi synthesizer and record the musical notes on the computer for playback.

With the hardware design of the ST mostly complete before the purchase of Atari, Jack now needed an operating system. He turned to Digital Research, the company owned by Garry Kildall, co-host of Computer Chronicles and inventor of CP/M. Kildall had developed his own graphical user interface several years before, called GEM (General Environment Manager). GEM was not a multitasking operating system. It was clear the Amiga had the Atari ST beat.

For Jack, quality was never an issue. Beating his competitors to the finish line and offering the cheapest product were always his most powerful weapons. Consequently, the Atari ST would never win over critics who compared it to the Amiga. "The Amiga was superior largely because of the timing of things," says Mical. "The Atari engineers didn't have time to keep working on it, to refine it, to make it into a machine that would be the equal of the Amiga. They surely had the engineering talent, but Atari couldn't wait for them to go through the whole cycle that we went through."

When CES Las Vegas rolled around in January 1985 (the same show the C128 debuted), to everyone's surprise the Atari ST was on display. Atari proclaimed a new slogan, espousing Jacks lifelong philosophy, 'Power Without the Price'. Atari was able to begin taking dealer orders for the Atari ST (dubbed the *Jackintosh* by journalists seeing it as a full color competitor to Apple's Macintosh), while Commodore was not. Atari now had a definite advantage.

Later in the year, at the fall Comdex in Las Vegas, Atari showed up with dozens of software vendors and displays. It appeared as though the Atari ST had more software support than the Amiga. Meanwhile, as Computer Chronicles pointed out, the Commodore Amiga was conspicuously absent.

Despite the obvious financial trouble at Atari, and despite the shorter development period, Atari was able to get the Atari 520ST on store shelves in late summer 1985, ahead of the Amiga. It was a testament to the drive, determination, and business shrewdness of Jack Tramiel. He made executives of other computer companies look lazy.

The rapid production of the Atari ST garnered both fear and respect from the Amiga team. As Mical recalls, "In the end, it was a contender, and Atari was aggressively pricing it so it was more than a contender."

Macintosh

Since 1984, the Apple Macintosh was the most popular computer with a graphical user interface. A brilliant designer named Jeff Raskin conceived the Macintosh, though somehow Steve Jobs ended up receiving the most credit. "[Raskin] deserves it, but there was a period of time when people were hiding that and saying it was Steve's machine," says Peddle.

After Steve Jobs lost the Lisa project, he took over the Macintosh design. Jobs had a strong but ultimately uninformed view of computer design. He embraced minimalism as the best design philosophy but often at the cost of functionality. For example, Jobs insisted the Macintosh should only have 128 kilobytes of memory and forbid his engineers to include the ability to expand the memory beyond that. They did anyway, which ultimately saved the Macintosh from obsolescence.

In many ways, Apple and Commodore exchanged design philosophies. Apple went from the Apple II, a color games machine, to a black and white business machine. Commodore went from a black and white business machine, the PET, to color computers with an emphasis on games. The Macintosh even resembled Chuck Peddle's PET design by including everything in one unit, including the monitor, data storage, and keyboard.

There were other technical similarities. "If you ever took a look at a Macintosh ADB keyboard, the original Macintosh keyboard, and how they were hooked in with their serial bus, I swear it was a copy of how we did the serial bus," says Robert Russell. "It was exactly the same thing. I ended up doing a lot of Macintosh development and I saw their code and it was like, 'Hmm. You know, it looks real familiar.'"

Compared to the Amiga, the Macintosh seemed antiquated. "The Mac was primitive," says Mical. "The Mac was not a competitor in the beginning because the Mac didn't have color, even for the longest time after that."

Another weak aspect of the Macintosh was the operating system. "Because of the nature of how they did the operating system, it was amazingly slow," says Mical. "It wasn't until they got OSX, but that's different. The very nature of the machine and the way it does all this indirection to protect programmers from themselves just makes the machine slower."

Even TripOS on the Amiga was better than the disk operating system for the Macintosh. "The file system was wrong," explains Mical. "It was a flat file system; it wasn't a real directory file system."

Thomas Rattigan knew he had a technological advantage over his former Pepsi executive, John Scully. "I think it was pretty interesting technology [in the Amiga]," says Rattigan. "You had the same chip that the Mac had in it but you had the capacity for multitasking, which the Mac did not have at that time."

Mical believed the multitasking capability was an important difference between the Amiga and the Macintosh. "Theirs wasn't real multitasking; it wasn't multitasking at all," says Mical. "In terms of technology, the Amiga had the Mac beat hands down."

Disk swapping on the Macintosh often caused suicidal tendencies among users. To run an application such as MacWrite, users had to eject the system disk, insert the program disk, wait for it to load part of the program, then the Macintosh asked for the system disk again. This process repeated four or five times before the application finally loaded, even with the improved 512-kilobyte Macintosh. In the computer holy wars, Amiga users derisively called it the Crapintosh.

The Macintosh was a computer with all the safety features engaged, which made it ideal for people who did not know anything about computers. Users could not open the case, they could not expand the memory of early models, and they could not even press the eject button on the disk drive because it did not have one.

Although Apple tried to promote the Macintosh as a high-end computer, it was clear by the features that it was more low-end than the 'low-end' Atari ST and Amiga. Byte magazine included the Macintosh in the low-end category, despite the high price.

In reality, the Macintosh was closer in performance to the Commodore 128 with a graphical operating system such as GEOS. The Amiga and Atari ST were in a higher technological class than the Macintosh. "I was no fan of the Mac," says Dave Haynie. "It was truly the dumb blonde of the computing world."

Steve Jobs used his reality distortion field to promote the Macintosh to the popular press, which was often unaware of the alternatives. In a quote to the New York Times, Jobs said, "The Macintosh turned out so well because the people working on it were musicians, artists, poets and historians who also happened to be excellent computer scientists." This was a complete reality distortion since their engineers took most of their ideas from other companies like Xerox, including the mouse from inventor Douglas Engelbart.

Apple ran a televised commercial during the Super Bowl that claimed the Macintosh would free users from the tyranny of IBM. The ad was ironic, since in reality the Macintosh was a proprietary, closed system while the IBM-PC was open architecture. Furthermore, Apple overcharged horrendously for their technology. It was the kind of hypocrisy only Apple fanatics could ignore.

"Apple created splash with that 1984 stuff, but that was for dramatic effect," says Rattigan. "The degree it succeeded within the context of their objective, which was to break into the business community, you would have to say in many ways it was marginal."

Buying a Macintosh took away any choice. Apple locked users into a small 12-inch black and white monitor, an undersized keyboard, and a mouse with only one button. Although the commercial imagined a world of row upon row of identical, mediocre PC computers, the truth was that the Macintosh represented a monotonous, dystopian future worse than the PC world of open architecture.

The initial success of the Macintosh in the face of poor technology and high prices impressed Thomas Rattigan. "In the hands of an Apple at that time, [the Amiga] would have been looked upon as a real breakthrough, and the enthusiasm and the success of the machine would have been much more assured than it could have been in our hands," says Rattigan.

Apple acted like big brother by suing Digital Research Incorporated for their GEM user interface on the Atari ST. Byte magazine took Apple to task for the lawsuit, saying, "We at BYTE call on Apple to recognize the long-term implications of its actions and limit itself to prosecuting cases where the alleged theft is not of 'looks' but of actual program code."[6]

Although the Macintosh received some sales initially, they tapered off quickly. Sales of the Apple II easily overshadowed the Macintosh. "The Mac came along and they almost lost it over that. They never did go for the consumer stuff," says Peddle.

The sudden drop-off in Macintosh sales was likely the result of the Amiga and Atari ST. "That was a problem then," explains Mical. "The Mac and the Amiga were like the voting block being split [between two candidates]."

After the lackluster sales of the Macintosh, Apple ran into financial difficulties and began cutting jobs. Much like Jack Tramiel before him, Steve Jobs soon found himself thrown out of the company he helped create.

An Uphill Marketing Battle

Commodore decided to market the Amiga to the high-end business market. It was a risky move considering their strengths lay in the

---

[6] *Byte* magazine, "Editorial" (January 1986), p. 6.

low-end home market dominated by the Commodore 64. "Such a change was needed, Gould said, because business was a bigger and faster-growing market than the home."[7]

Their marketing plan would determine how well they succeeded. To sell the Amiga to businesses, the Amiga would have to appear on store shelves where businesses purchased computers. They would also have to follow up the release with appropriate advertising. The Amiga engineers now became spectators, watching as Commodore carried the fate of their computer.

Commodore gave the Amiga a business price of $1295, without monitor. It appeared Commodore was going after the Macintosh market. The price immediately put the Amiga out of reach of most Commodore 64 owners.

The Amiga engineers believed they had a legitimate chance against IBM and Apple, as long as they aggressively sold the computer. "The biggest thing was marketing," says R.J. Mical.

Mical believed an anti-Microsoft sentiment at the time could help the Amiga. "There was a window when the Amiga could have grabbed a lion's share of that market if things had gone right," says Mical. "People were looking for an alternative to Microsoft and we represented that alternative."

According to Mical, the marketing people were excellent. "The marketing effort was headed up by two people: Jerry McCoy and a woman named Caryn Havis," says Mical.[8] McCoy and Havis did not partake in the engineering decisions on the Amiga but it was up to them to carry out the strategy.

Dave Haynie, who held a positive view of marketing, explains their role at Commodore. "I think they used their job as more of a salesperson rather than a marketing person," explains Haynie. "They were looking to find ways to sell computers."

Since the early eighties, Commodore relied on mass-market retailers like Kmart to sell their low-cost computers. Now, they were jettisoning that strategy in favor of attempting to copy Apple. "It all backfired when the Amiga came along and you actually needed a distributor," says Haynie. "That wasn't a machine that would sell well in Kmart."

Commodore's biggest obstacle to selling the Amiga originated in the Jack Tramiel days. Since the Amiga was too costly for the retail market, only computer distributors could sell the machine. Unfortunately,

---

[7] *The Philadelphia Inquirer*, "A New Strategy" (May 4, 1987), p. E01.

[8] "She sports a different last name these days," says Mical. "Her name is now Caryn Mical and she and I met during the Amiga days." Today, R.J. and Caryn are married with four children.

Commodore had little credibility with computer stores since Jack undercut their prices with the VIC-20 and C64. "I think part of the problem with Commodore was that their US market had been so messed up with the whole C64 thing that there was only so much they could do in the US without a real concerted strategy," says Haynie. "I don't think the C128 changed things that much because of course anybody who sold the C64 could sell the C128."

Even before the Amiga release, the computer industry questioned Commodore's ability to market business computers in North America. Compute!'s Gazette editor Richard Mansfield wrote, "Commodore has a phenomenal computer, the Amiga, but a decidedly obscure marketing strategy for it." He went on to ask, "Is the Amiga so far beyond previous machines that Commodore doesn't yet know its identity and, thus, cannot yet position it or give it the right image?"[9]

Thomas Rattigan was well aware that Commodore had severed ties with the computer distributors. "Prior to my time, Commodore shifted to mass retail," says Rattigan. "All of that was recognized at the time. There was the issue of how do you regain the confidence of computer retail distributors who Commodore had obviously ignored because of the focus on mass merchants."

According to Mical, Commodore even turned down Sears' computer centers in an effort to concentrate on computer stores. "Sears wanted to carry [the Amiga]," reveals Mical. "They could have gotten it into Sears but they didn't get it into Sears. There were all these opportunities that they squandered."

Delays prevented the Amiga from shipping in quantity. "It didn't ship until August of 1985," says Haynie.

When the Amiga finally launched, engineers were still contending with minor changes and bug fixes in the operating system. "In the very beginning, the technology wasn't as bug free and robust as it should have been," says Mical. "It started to get a bad rap for the flaky technology and it didn't get the boost in the public's awareness that it needed because of that."

The crux of the problem was the unstable operating system. "The 1.0 release of the operating system had a lot of bugs in it and it crashed a lot," says Mical. "People would use the machine and start getting something together, an art project or something, and then it would crash and they would lose all their work. The guru meditation error."

---

[9] *Compute!s Gazette* magazine, "Editor's Notes" (November 1985), p. 6.

Magazines featured hands-on previews of the Amiga. In August, Byte magazine featured the Amiga on the front cover. It was rare for a specific computer to make the cover, signifying the Amiga was indeed a revolutionary machine. Inside was a generous 13-page preview. It was a firm endorsement from the industry's top magazine.

The same month, Run magazine launched *Amiga World*. For the first time ever, a magazine launched before the release of the computer. The aggressive launch schedule established Amiga World as the premier Amiga magazine.

Curiously, Commodore seemed to have little confidence in Commodore. Compute!'s Gazette reported, "It has been decided that the Commodore name and company logo will not appear anywhere on the Amiga or its peripherals. Commodore's official comment on this was that they wanted the new machine to stand on its own. This probably means that Commodore is concerned that its name - so long associated with home computing - would prevent the business community from taking the Amiga seriously."[10] If management did not have confidence in the Commodore name, how could their customers?

By October 1985, Compute! magazine reported that only 50 Amiga machines existed and Commodore used them all for demonstration and software development. Finally, in mid-November 1985, Amiga computers began appearing on store shelves in quantity. It was too little too late. Companies typically make 40% of their total yearly sales in the fourth quarter alone and Commodore had missed over half of the fourth quarter. As a result, they only managed to sell 25,000 to 40,000 Amiga computers by early 1986; far less than their projections.

Bil Herd believes Commodore did not put forward a strong marketing effort. "When the Amiga hit, they were sitting around with their feet on the table going, 'At last, a real computer that will sell itself. We're on the gravy train.' Well, of course it didn't sell itself," says Herd. "You've got to go out and sell it."

Bil Herd blames the marketing failure on the lack of clear leadership. "When Commodore lost Jack Tramiel, we seemed to lose our ability to make decisions," says Herd. "We got technology like the Amiga and it lay there like a beached whale. That could have been something."

The Commodore Curse: Part VII

Following the release of the C128 in 1985, Bil Herd and his engineers took a much-deserved break. "After the C128 hit in June/July, I actually made all my guys go off fishing with me and got out of the

---

[10] Compute!'s Gazette magazine, "Editor's Notes" (November 1985), p. 6.

building," says Herd. "New employees would wonder why we wouldn't be there for three days in a row."

Herd continued making enemies at Commodore. "I had hired a new guy and he would bitch about me not being there," he says. Herd also still had to contend with Bob Shamus, the QA manager and Herd's sworn enemy.

Herd had his chance for revenge when Commodore underwent a series of layoffs. "One day Adam [Chowaniec] called me in and said, 'I need to reduce people.' I said, 'I've got a guy for you,'" says Herd, referring to the new hire who complained about his absences. "I pointed at Shamus and I pointed at this other guy and said they should go, and they fired them."

He also lost his manager Joe Krasucki. Herd's immediate manager became Ed Fix, whom Herd got along with. "Ed and I never had a bad word between us," recalls Herd.

Herd had no plans to follow up with another C64 sequel. "The C128 was kind of meant to glue in the last of the 8 bit stuff while we moved to 16 bit, but it was as far as I wanted to push the C64 compatibility stuff," says Herd. "Besides, wasn't the Amiga a C64 on steroids?"

Although Herd later worked with a Japanese engineer to cost reduce the C64, which the engineers dubbed the C64CR, he wondered what his place would be once Commodore released the Amiga. To make matters worse, Herd's protector was gone. "Adam [Chowaniec] had left, who was kind of my guardian angel at that point," says Herd. "I'm really pissing some people off about this time in my career. My alcoholism was really giving me a fit, things had slowed down, and I was convinced that we were not going to do another [computer]."

Herd's friend Dave Haynie recalls the troubled period. "He was burnt out, he was tired, and I think he was kind of frustrated," recalls Haynie. "There were a lot of things that we would have liked to have done differently on the C128 that the management said, 'These are the resources you are getting.' He was tired of that and I guess some of it was the politicking that they had back then. He was just sick of the whole thing."

Life at Commodore became aimless for Herd and his thirst for alcohol increased. "All this activity that was going on at Commodore and all the craziness you hear about, what you are hearing about is a young alcoholic in his prime when things are still working out," explains Herd. "It was obviously getting worse for those around me. What had been, 'Oh, he's a crazy man,' went to 'He doesn't stop. He still isn't stopping.'"

By the end of 1985, Commodore had successfully launched their sequel to the C64, and with the Amiga, they had released the most advanced personal computer on the market. Commodore decided to celebrate Christmas in style. It was the party that got out of control.

In December 1985, Commodore's thousands of employees crammed into the historic *Sunnybrook Ballroom* in Pottstown, Pennsylvania. "There was a Christmas party where everybody was pretty damn looped by the end of it," recalls Russell. "It was probably the biggest, best Commodore Christmas party ever. They were giving away all types of neat stuff and everybody was loaded up on tons of free booze."

Nobody enjoyed the free beverages more than CEO Marshall Smith did. Surprisingly, the former steel industry CEO took part in some impromptu slam dancing on the dance floor. "Marshall Smith is a pretty big guy," says Russell. "All I can say is he was a good drinker and he could body slam with the best of them, as Herd can attest to. Herd and him were slam dancing, and Greg Berlin too. Drinking and body slamming; that's about the only thing I think he was qualified to do."

Bil Herd recalls fraternizing with his CEO. "I punched Marshall one night," says Herd. "I drank a lot and he got drunker through the night. At this time I had my hand in a cast."

Herd was edgy at the best of times but even worse when alcohol impaired his judgment. "He did that slap on face thing when you're talking to somebody," recalls Herd. "I whacked him back. I did it with my cast hand, so what would have been a whack came across harder. It knocked him back a little bit."

Most employees would worry if they punched their CEO in the jaw, but Herd was indifferent. "I figured he probably wasn't going to remember it but that wasn't the important thing at the time," says Herd. "I said, 'Don't do that again.' He looked at me and kind of staggered. We got along after that, sort of."

In early 1986, Commodore assigned Herd to product manager for the European version of the Amiga. "He was there for a little while, while the Amiga stuff was just starting up," recalls Haynie. "He got one of the first books that described the Amiga."

Although Herd was impressed with the Amiga, he felt the project offered little challenge. "That was just paper. I would have changed some timings and told them how to cut a new chip but that wasn't really challenging," says Herd. "My ego wouldn't let me stay doing nothing and they didn't have a project for me to do."

Within his first week on the project, Herd was already looking for a new job. "I was so damn hungry to keep doing what I was doing that I actually quit and took a job as the director of engineering for a startup doing image recognition," says Herd. "There were a lot of Commodore people interviewed there. We all felt like the ship was rocking a little bit. They did a great job of appealing to a young mans ego."

Bil Herd on the night he punched Marshall Smith (photo courtesy of Dave Haynie).

Herd was somewhat of a Lothario and solidified his reputation as an animal on his last day at Commodore. "I was known for biting," explains Herd. "I think the women of Commodore compared who had been bitten where, including the fact that I bit the person doing my exit interview."

Herd had mixed feelings about leaving Commodore. "I was hopped up on being a Commodore engineer. Why else would you sleep 11 days in your office?" says Herd. "It really was a great place to work."

Despite his lack of formal education, Herd made some incredible contributions to Commodore. "He did an exceptional job," says Haynie. "To this day, if you are trying to fix something in hardware, Bil is the guy you want there in the lab with you. I've never seen anybody as good at diagnosing little weird problems as Bil and he learned it on the streets."

Like most former Commodore employees, Herd cherishes his memories with the company. "As my memory fades, I remember the good and forget the bad," says Herd. "Did I mention that Commodore was a fun place to work?"

CHAPTER

21

Dropping the Ball

1985-1987

Jay Miner and his engineers were satisfied with the Amiga and with Commodore. "The Amiga 1000 is almost exactly what we intended," says R.J. Mical. Now it was up to Commodore to tell the world about it.

Un-Advertising the Amiga

The Amiga engineers were ecstatic with Commodore and their treatment of the Amiga until the advertising campaign began. "Something happened when the Amiga stopped being ours and started being Commodore's," says Mical. "Their marketing and sales teams started kicking into gear and they took over the whole thing from us. Somewhere in that organization, someone or some group of people or perhaps all of them were insane. They did unbelievable, shocking, amazing, frighteningly stupid things with the Amiga."

Commodore marketing replaced the Amiga Boing Ball with a logo similar to the classic rainbow C of the Commodore 64. The rainbow checkmark was supposed to convey the vibrant colors of the Amiga. However, the Amiga team felt the new symbol was not nearly as potent as the Boing Ball, which was already well recognized.

On the advertising front, the Amiga should have had a distinct advantage over the IBM PC and Macintosh. Both those computers were bland and did not translate well to a visual and audio medium like television. The Amiga was made for television.

It was obvious to Mical that the producer of the television commercials did not understand the Amiga. "They had the most ridiculous ad campaign for launching it into the public's eye," he recalls. "It was just nuts. It would have been laughable if it weren't for the fact that the machine that we had worked so hard on was being shat upon by these guys that didn't have a clue how to make it a popular device."

The first commercial did little to impress the engineers. "The launch television commercial of the Amiga had people almost zombie like, presumably in some sort of state of ecstasy but maybe it was more a state of mental disturbance, walking up towards this pedestal from which emanates a light," recalls Mical. "You finally see that there's some sort of computer monitor glowing with light."

The point of the ad baffled Mical. "Whatever it was, it did not advertise the machine," he says.

Mical was disappointed the advertisement failed to highlight the groundbreaking Amiga features. "It did not show you the cool graphics, the cool audio, or the multitasking operating system," he explains. "This is a computer for the next generation!"

Bil Herd remembers the ambiguity of a different commercial. "There was this fetus crying and then an old man walking up these white steps. It was kind of like *2001: A Space Odyssey*," recalls Herd. "We were like, 'What the hell are they talking about?' Well, they were trying to get across the dawn of a new generation."

Back in the engineering labs, the fetus became a daily joke. "We saw pictures of how they made the commercial and the fetus literally had a stick in it that they held up in front of the camera," explains Herd. "We got a hold of that picture and stuck it up. It looked like a taste treat for dinosaurs or something. It was morbid actually. I mean, a fetus on a stick, oh my God. What were they thinking over there in marketing?"

The ad agency also produced a commercial with a nostalgic motif featuring black and white stock footage. The commercial showed images of children diving into a swimming pool, graduation, and teenagers doing the twist. The narrator says, "When you were growing up, you learned you were facing a world full of competition."

Commodore print advertising also used nostalgic black and white stock photographs. Each print ad promoted the slogan, "Amiga gives you a creative edge." It was an ironic motto. One of the earliest ads ran in *National Geographic* in November 1985 and targeted the education market. It showed a black and white image of schoolchildren with the caption, "You've always had a lot of competition. Now you can have an unfair advantage."

The second magazine ad (and the first to grace the pages of Byte) came in January 1986. It featured a black and white photograph of boys running to their soapbox cars. The title was, "Today if you come in second, you've lost the race."

In Mical's mind, the old-fashioned advertising was misguided. "It was in sepia tones," says Mical. "Again, this is the message that you want to give people? 'Come get this new computer. It's got true colors!' They were just insane. The mind boggles that somebody out there thought this is a good idea. Let's sell this new, powerful, *color* graphics computer with an ad that shows sepia tones."

The advertising did little to appeal to the target group of computer users. Instead, it looked like Commodore was trying to market the Amiga to the retirement crowd.

Bob Yannes thinks Commodore should have attacked IBM and Apple. "The PC's were boring, mundane machines that were meant for businesses," says Yannes. "They weren't meant for creative stuff. Apple made a lot of hay with that when they introduced the Macintosh. Commodore could have attempted that too."

Dave Haynie wonders how the commercials could have swayed anyone over to the Amiga. "I remember some of the early ads," says Haynie. "I vaguely remember the first ones that were shown here and you didn't know what it was that they were advertising."

Herd agrees. "You could watch an Amiga commercial and not even known you had seen one," he says. "I remember seeing one or two and going, 'What was that a commercial for?'"

The new commercials fell short of the earlier VIC-20 commercials featuring William Shatner. In the past, Commodore's most successful commercials were direct comparisons to their competitors' products. With the Macintosh so vulnerable, the perfect commercial would simply compare the two computers. The Amiga could even use a color printer, which would have made the black and white desktop publishing, the one niche market of the Macintosh, appear limited. If Commodore could get the message out to customers, they could own the desktop publishing market. Instead, the Macintosh outsold Amiga two to one[1], even with a higher price.

Commodore was aggressively silent before the launch to heighten the effect, but because of the botched advertising campaign, barely anyone outside the industry had faith in the product. "They went into this stealth silence mode so they could have some big splash knobby thing or other," says Mical. "Instead it was a splash in a puddle. It was tragic to have the machine do as poorly as it did. In my opinion, it was mostly, but not all, due to the lack of marketing on the machine."

---

[1] According to the Philadelphia Inquirer, the Amiga sold only 100,000 systems in their first year, compared to 200,000 for the first year of the Macintosh.

One of the most famous and strikingly effective print ads appeared later in 1986, showing a full-page screenshot of Tutankhamen. For the first time, Commodore succeeded in showing off the graphics capability of the Amiga. It said, "Amiga under $2,000. Anyone else up to $20,000." The approach was bold and it showed off exactly why the Amiga was different from other computers.

When asked about the commercials, Thomas Rattigan distances himself from the advertising effort by Commodore. "I suspect whatever it is that we did, it was fairly modest dollar wise," says Rattigan, who does not recall any specific commercials. "I was not directly involved in terms of sitting down on the creative side and reviewing storyboards."

Rattigan reveals the true reason for the limited airtime of the commercials. "Basically the company was living hand to mouth," he explains. "When I was there, they weren't doing very much advertising because they couldn't afford it."

The previous year, Commodore spent $25 million for Amiga Incorporated when they could have had the technology for $4 million. Now, they did not even have the money to advertise their acquisition properly. "You had the company going into pretty serious financial straits," says Rattigan. "They had lost maybe a couple of hundred million dollars in the preceding six or seven quarters. Advertising, other than around Christmas time, really wasn't a priority. That was a luxury the company couldn't afford."

Even with limited budgets, Commodore could have produced smarter, more effective commercials by showing off the capabilities of the Amiga. Rattigan attributes this failure to the general state of computer marketing sophistication in the eighties. "When you look at the Proctor and Gambles of the world and General Foods or Kraft or Philip Morris, I think you would have to say that the marketing sophistication was much higher in those firms than it was in a host of other industries," he says. "I don't think you were going to walk into any of those [computer] companies and find five star marketing people by and large."

Commodore marketing needed a word to describe what the Amiga offered that others lacked. The Amiga could play video, it could display true color photographs, and it could play recorded audio clearly. In other words, it handled media from multiple sources - photographs, audio, and video. In a word, the Amiga was a true multimedia computer. Unfortunately, Commodore marketing could not think of a buzzword to describe the computer. Years later, other computer companies would bring the word to the forefront.

In contrast, people remembered the IBM ads with Charlie Chaplin. They were fun, distinctive, and very effective for IBM. Others remember the Orwellian Macintosh commercial, which ran during the Super Bowl. Despite the ineffectiveness of the commercial and the subsequent slow Macintosh sales, people remembered the ad. Nobody, not even the President of Commodore, remembered the Amiga ads.

Looking back, Mical's frustration with the advertising campaign is apparent. "I don't know who it was inside the Commodore organization. Unfortunately, I don't have someone to point the finger at on that one," he says. "There must have been someone inside the organization who approved these ads, but out there somewhere is some ad agency that thought this was a good idea. All across the board, it was massive stupidity. I don't know if Commodore guys told the ad agency, 'Give us sepia tone,' or the ad agency said, 'Oh my God! You've got to have sepia tones.' I don't know where that came from. Someone just go out and dump a bucket of ice water on their heads and then I will be happy." According to Mical, Thomas Rattigan fired the ad agency.

Although Commodore North America was losing their market share once again, Commodore Europe proved as strong as they had been in the past. According to Dave Haynie, "One of the weird things that people never quite understood about Commodore was that every region was responsible for their own advertising and their own advertising plans and the way they wanted to sell computers to their country."

Foremost in Europe was Commodore Germany. "They had very good advertising in Germany because Germany was always one of the best regarded places for Commodore," says Haynie. "You could walk through an airport and see Commodore ads. The first time I went over there I was like, 'This is unbelievable.'"

The Hanover Faire, which later became *CeBit*, especially impressed Haynie. "That was a big show for Commodore," he recalls. "They had a huge two-story booth with a bar upstairs. It was a bigger scale than anything ever done in the United States."

Haynie believes the PC clone business aided Commodore Germany. "Some of the European companies wanted to deal with one vendor for everything," he explains. "They might like Amiga's but if you didn't have PC clones you couldn't get their business, which is why Apple was just doing so well in Europe – they weren't of course. Nobody was buying Apple and they were wickedly overpriced there at the time."

In 1986, it became apparent the advertising campaign was a failure. Marketing director Nigel Sheppard, who replaced the previous director in January 1986, revealed the sales on the Amiga. "On Amigas, we're looking roughly at a run rate of 10,000 to 15,000 a month on a worldwide basis," Sheppard told Compute!'s Gazette.

Round One: Atari

After the Christmas season, it became clear the Atari ST had won the first round. Atari sold more systems and gained a larger software base thanks to an aggressive strategy by Jack Tramiel.

Commodore's lack of marketing muscle became apparent in 1986. At the January CES in Las Vegas, for the first time ever, Commodore was absent. Industry analysts were stunned, especially considering rival Atari was there showing off the 520 ST. Ahoy! magazine reported:

> Understand that the last four CES shows in a row, dating back to January 1984, Commodore's exhibit had been the focal point of the home computer segment of CES, the most visited computer booth at the show - as befitted the industry's leading hardware manufacturer. Their pulling out of CES seemed like Russia resigning from the Soviet Bloc.[2]

The withdrawal from CES was not devastating to the Amiga, since Commodore was not targeting the Amiga to the consumer market. COMDEX was where dealers abounded. However, Commodore was also absent from COMDEX. Though they reserved space, they did not end up using it. Atari attended the same show. An amused Tramiel told journalists, "We sell more Atari 520ST's than Commodore sells Amiga's, and we sure want to sign up more dealers."

Officially, Commodore claimed they were selling all the Amigas they could make and had all the dealers they needed. In truth, Commodore did not have the money to attend COMDEX. They had defaulted on their bank loans and the bankers refused to loan money to pay for shows. Commodore presented a single press conference at COMDEX.

Commodore was also absent from the June 1986 CES in Chicago. Instead, they rented a suite at the show to display C64 and C128 computers. As Robert Lock wrote in Compute!'s Gazette, "The seeming lethargy in market positioning that has stricken Commodore since the introduction of the Amiga is one of the most shocking turnabouts we've witnessed in the modern history of this industry. One wonders whether the bankers have begun the call the strategic shots at Commodore."[3]

Commodore engineers attended CES and gave demonstrations from a rented suite. "Through most of Commodore, until the money got really bad, Irving Gould would of course have a suite at every one of these big shows," recalls Haynie.

Irving Gould never stayed in the United States for long. "He always left a day or two early, so his suite was always empty by the end of the

---

[2] *Ahoy!* magazine, "Scuttlebutt" (April 1986), p. 8.
[3] *Compute!'s Gazette* magazine, "Editor's Notes" (September 1986), p. 6.

week," recalls Haynie. The Commodore employees took advantage of the empty suite. "We would have a party in Irving's suite every year. It was a standard company thing. Everybody would go there."

Although Commodore Business Machines in North America was having financial difficulties, Commodore Europe continued to have strong sales, which saved Commodore for the time being. Commodore Europe did not alienate their computer dealers during the VIC-20 and C64 days and their computer dealership network was intact.

In late 1985, Thomas Rattigan inherited more responsibilities. "It was kind of funny because there was an interim step in there where I became Chief Operating Officer but technology and finance continued to report to Marshall," he says.

In February 1986, Gould finally promoted Rattigan to president and CEO of Commodore International. "There was a board meeting in February 1986 in the Bahamas," recalls Rattigan. "It was decided that I move up and take all of it, and Marshall would be leaving." Rattigan could begin to make a real difference.

The board gave Rattigan a five-year contract, which would expire on July 1, 1991. It seemed like Rattigan represented the future of Commodore.

"Marshall was gone shortly thereafter, and breathing a heavy sigh of relief in my opinion," says Rattigan. "Marshall was working his butt off, working very, very hard with what he had in terms of the people. In certain respects, I think that may have tempered the contribution he could have made."

Rattigan did his best to motivate employees at all levels. "You had to get the right people around you and you had to get them onboard," he says. "Then you had to get people enthusiastic about how we can turn this company around."

Rattigan was impressed with the work ethic of ordinary Commodore employees. "We had people coming in on Saturdays who would work at no pay," says an astonished Rattigan. "I'm talking about the people on the [factory] lines. They would come in and we would be loading trucks to get stuff out so we could build a shipment for that particular quarter."

Rattigan did what he could to reward the employees. "You would buy 20 or 30 pizzas and 20 cases of beer. What you were really trying to do was get them committed to survival and making it happen. Fortunately, we had that."

Rattigan also made his employees full participants in Commodore's success. "After we started getting on the road, one of the things we came up with was the idea that, rather than giving people raises, which they hadn't had for quite a while, I said, 'Let's reward them on the basis of what the stock price does,'" explains Rattigan. "The stock was trading at about five bucks per share at time. We put a big board up in the cafeteria and said for every point the stock goes up, we're going to give a one percent bonus up to a 10% level. It will be a cash bonus payout."

In the Tramiel days, Commodore lost engineers like Robert Yannes because they felt excluded from the success they helped create. Now all employees would share in Commodore's success.

It Lives!

Wall Street analysts labeled Amiga the 'save the company machine', but another computer kept Commodore alive. By early 1986, the company had sold between five and six million Commodore 64 computers. "The C64, in percentage margin terms, was the most profitable piece of equipment we had in the entire product line," says Rattigan.

It was apparent the C64 was the base of Commodore profits, but Commodore engineers did not seem to know how to extend the life of the C64. According to Dave Haynie, the engineers did not intend the C128 to replace the C64. "It wasn't really a replacement, it was more of an upgrade," he says. "I don't think anybody tried to position it as replacing the C64 because the C64 only cost $35 to make, so if people wanted to buy them they were more than willing to make them."

The surprising popularity of the C64 made it even more popular. "It wasn't specifically because the C64 was that great," says Haynie. "It was a good computer that had hit critical mass. It was the same exact factor that made the IBM's popular; only they were cloneable too, which the C64 wasn't."

Commodore jealously protected their monopoly on the Commodore 64. "Those were the days when everything was proprietary and they didn't like people making clones of the floppy drives," says Haynie. "They certainly didn't want people to clone the C64. They didn't want the Amiga to be cloned."

The complex custom chips made it impractical for other companies to create clones. "Commodore didn't want people going out there and making clones of anything so they had to sell the chips at ridiculous prices so that didn't happen," says Haynie. "The actual cost of a SID chip was a couple of dollars or less, but if you wanted to buy one you had to pay Commodore replacement costs, which were twenty to thirty dollars."

The C128 also contributed to Commodore's revenues. "[The C128] was supposed to be sort of a stopgap measure," explains Herd. "It was supposed to have a year of climbing and then die off over the second year and give our 16-bit guys a chance. When they didn't market the Amiga very well, they kept the C128 alive longer." By June 1986, Commodore had sold an impressive 600,000 units.

In 1987, Commodore unveiled a business oriented C128D exclusively in Europe, which featured an Amiga style case. "That's where it had the built in drive," says Herd. "The D version was originally supposed to come out at the same time [as the C128] but it just lagged by a couple of years."

"The C128D was actually something that Europe wanted," says Haynie. "Bil was around for the beginning of that and I kind of finished it up."

Legions of Commodore fans were curious if Commodore would attempt another computer in the C64 line. Inside Commodore, management did not believe there was any reason to attempt to continue the C64 success. "That was really what we tried to do with the C128," says Rattigan. "There was more talk in terms of cost reducing the C64."

At the June CES in Chicago, where Commodore rented a suite to display their new products, Commodore announced a new version of the C64. Users were excited and hopeful.

Instead, Commodore announced a Commodore 64 with the same features and a new case. They called it the C64CR (Cost Reduced). "There was a cost reduced C64 that got made about the same time as the C128," says Herd. "I helped a little with that, but it was mostly done by an engineer from Japan named Katayama."

Herd's experience on the C128 project made him invaluable to Katayama. As before, Herd made sure to reintroduce all the bugs back into the C64CR, otherwise some programs would not work properly.

Commodore marketing renamed the computer the C64c. Although the performance of the C64c was identical to standard C64 computers, there were many improvements to reduce the cost of assembly. "In the Commodore environment, cheap was considered a type of performance," says Herd. The motherboard was smaller, with less components and it now it used the 8510 processor. The old C64 used several different types of screws to assemble, but the new design used only two different types of screws.

Rattigan, who was from the soft drink industry, saw parallels to Coke Classic versus the New Coke. As Commodore magazine wrote, "Unlike Coca-Cola, Commodore kept the classic alive without the necessity of outcry."[4]

---

[4] *Commodore* magazine, "The Year in Computers" (January 1987), p. 71.

Dropping the Ball – 1985 to 1987

Engineers created a new C64c case that looked more professional, with a standard off-white color. "He actually used the case styling that we used for the C128," says Herd. The new case was similar to the wedge-shaped case design envisioned by Robert Yannes and Al Charpentier, which they planned to introduce sometime in 1983. As CBM General Manager Nigel Shepherd described it, "We decided that there should be in appearance more synergy between the 64 and the 128."

In June 1986, production ended on the old C64, and production began on the new C64c. Commodore raised the price of the new computer to $199 in retail, up from $159. The main reason for the price increase was *GEOS*, a graphical operating system that duplicated nearly every function of the Macintosh computer within a 64-kilobyte memory space. The increased price and lower manufacturing cost would make the C64 more profitable than ever for Commodore, but as Nigel Shepherd let slip in an interview, "We needed the extra margin."

In February 1986, Nintendo revived the console market when they released the Nintendo Entertainment System (NES). The original set sold for $249, which included a Zapper light gun and ROB, the Robotic Operation Buddy. Soon, Nintendo released the Action Set for $199, which included the console, two controllers, and *Super Mario Brothers*. It was an instant hit.

Commodore management began to consider options to compete against Nintendo. "There was talk of making [the C64] a game machine, and less computer-like," reveals Rattigan. "That was going on while Gould and I were having differences of opinion."

Robert Russell investigated the NES, along with one of the original 6502 engineers, Will Mathis. "I remember we had the chip designer of the 6502," recalls Russell. "He scraped the [NES] chip down to the die and took pictures."

The excavation amazed Russell. "The Nintendo core processor was a 6502 designed with the patented technology scraped off," says Russell. "We actually skimmed off the top of the chip inside of it to see what it was, and it was exactly a 6502. We looked at where we had the patents and they had gone in and deleted the circuitry where our patents were."

Although there were changes, the NES microprocessor ran 99% of the 6502 instruction set. "Some things didn't work quite right or took extra cycles," says Russell. "I don't know if anybody else figured that out, but Rockwell also had the core at that time, and we thought maybe they got the core from Rockwell."

The tenacity of the Japanese was obviously formidable. Russell offers an opinion on why the Japanese elected not to purchase chips from North

American sources. "They looked at the patents and realized that we weren't going to let them come over and sell against us," he says.

HAL Labs, the company that once created games for Commodore Japan, now created games for the NES. Since the NES used the 6502 processor core, it was easy for their developers to make the transition. "They could do Nintendo games no problem," says Russell.

Many saw the NES as competition to the C64, but in fact, it may have indirectly extended the life of the C64. Consumers often compared the two and decided on the C64. It had a larger game base, cheaper games, a graphical operating system, an optional printer, and you could use it for telecommunications with a modem. To informed buyers, the C64c seemed to be the obvious choice over the NES, especially when parents made the final decision.

The hidden selling point of the C64 was the rampant piracy network among teenagers. A sophisticated piracy network imported the latest games from around the globe, so Commodore 64 owners received the latest hits free. Though ultimately destructive to the C64 market, it gave the C64 an advantage over the Nintendo.

The software market for the C64 peaked sometime in 1987 and 1988. It had staying power and software producers took notice, creating some of the best C64 games ever. Masterpieces like *Maniac Mansion*, *The Last Ninja*, *Pirates!*, *Legacy of the Ancients*, and *The Great Gianna Sisters* appeared in 1987. In total, there were 1,246 games released for the C64 in 1987.[5] The next year, the C64 received 1,319 new games. Only in 1989 did the number of new releases begin to decrease.

The Commodore 64 received conversions of most games released on other gaming platforms, such as *Sim City*, *Tetris*, and *Lemmings*. Computer games always appeared on the IBM PC, Amiga, and Commodore 64. Even technologically impressive games like *Defender of the Crown* and *Faery Tale* came to the C64. Because of this, C64 owners did not feel left out of the latest in software throughout the eighties and into the nineties.

Commodore focused their software development on their newest machines. "The software developers were starting to go away from the C64 a little bit," says Russell. "We had a big problem. All of a sudden, compiling languages were becoming available like C and they were all based on stack operations. From day one, that was my problem with the 6502 and why I didn't like the chip. [Compilers] needed deep stacks in

---

[5] These figures are from the Gamebase library, which includes public domain and magazine games.

order to work properly. The Commodore 64 had an 8-bit stack pointer, but all the others chips could go the length of the memory."

The lack of a good C-compiler meant games were more difficult to code and had to remain relatively simple. "It wasn't efficient, getting a good C compiler," says Russell. "The Apple II was starting to die at that point in time for the same reasons."

The Commodore 64 introduced more people to computers than any other. Users bought 20 million C64s compared to 5 million Apple IIs.[6] It was an impressive result, considering the C64 received no performance increases. One can only imagine what might have happened if Commodore evolved the system using 16-bit technology.

The Commodore Curse: Part VIII

After the bungled Amiga marketing campaign, the Amiga team lost faith in Commodore.. "Everything was great, but there were a lot of choices they were making, both at the engineering and at the marketing and business level, that we disapproved of," says Mical.

Mical does not blame Commodore for everything, however. "Part of it was due to the reputation based on the technology of the first few months," says Mical. "The 1.0 operating system was absolutely miserable and it had that slow disk operating system as well. It had a lot of shortcomings from an engineering perspective, but they were very small by comparison."

Frustration regarding company direction began to grow within the Amiga engineers. According to Mical, "In the end, we were feeling that we had done this beautiful work of art, and then Commodore, for their lack of experience or their lack of knowledge about the computer industry, let us down."

When working on Workbench 1.2, the engineers inserted a message expressing their feelings towards Commodore. "This happened when I was director of the whole effort," explains Mical. "One day, one of the guys showed me with great delight what they had put in there. It was this thing where you had to press a certain number of keys on the keyboard and it would bring up this message that said, 'We made the Amiga, they fucked it up.' I saw that and I made a sort of nervous chuckle."

Mical knew it could not remain. "I said, 'This is cute but we can't really put this in the machine. That's just not acceptable.' They said, 'Aw, come on!' I said, 'No way, man. We're just not putting this in the machine. You've got to take it out.'"

---

[6] Winnie Forster, *The Encyclopedia of Game.Machines* (Gameplan, 2005), p. 18, p. 62.

Mical double-checked before signing off on the code. "The final release of the OS was done, and with great fear I did the keystrokes to make sure that it wasn't there," recalls Mical. "When you put in that keystroke, a line of text came up, but it said, 'The Amiga, born a champion.'"

Unknown to Mical, the offending text remained. "They didn't take it out," says Mical. "All they did was bury it one level deeper and encrypt it. Because they made it harder to get to, it took one of the fans something like two weeks to find it."

The programmers had gone to extraordinary lengths to hide their secret message. "You had to do this keystroke where it took eight fingers and both thumbs to press all of the keys that you needed to get the first message to come up that said, 'We made the Amiga,'" explains Mical. "Then, while you had that message up and while you continued to hold all of those keys down, if you could somehow get the floppy disk inserted into the machine (for instance, if you leaned over and shoved it in with your nose) then for 1/60th of a second, the other message would show up. It would blink up and go away."

The engineers believed the final part of the message appeared too quickly for anyone to see. "Well, it took the guy no time at all to solve the problem," says Mical. "You hooked a VCR up to the Amiga and videotaped it, and there it was for the whole world to see."

The discovery caused havoc within Commodore. "The machine was already being sold and it was on the shelves in the UK when this broke," says Mical. "They took *all* of those tens of thousands of units off the shelf and would not sell the machine until they got new ROM's."

Mical was livid at the devastating financial repercussions of the prank. "The cute joke by one of the engineers hurt us," says Mical. "I know who and I won't tell you his name, but I shake my fist at him even now as I speak. There were a huge number of sales lost in the UK because they wouldn't sell it with that text in there. It took us three and a half months to get the new ROM's out there installed in the machines and the machines back on the shelf."

After the Easter egg fiasco, Rattigan and his executives wanted the Amiga engineering team closer to Commodore headquarters. According to Dave Haynie, "Regardless of what their reasons were, Commodore management ultimately really wanted to have more direct supervision over what was happening there."

Commodore also believed the Amiga engineers should be closer to the fabrication plant at MOS Technology. "They weren't really set up out there to do chip design in modern terms," says Haynie. "Commodore had sent a lot of equipment out there to help, but the fab and everything was out here. I think to a certain extent it was reasonable to at least have the chip people out here."

Rattigan asked the design team to move East. "I liked working for Amiga and working for Commodore was okay, but I hadn't signed on to work for an East Coast company," says Mical. "I had signed on to do wild and exotic things in California; doing startups and inventing all kinds of new stuff."

Mical felt it was time to leave. "I wanted to be free," sings Mical. "I had worked on the Amiga for about four years and there was an opportunity for me to go off and be a contractor, working not only on Amiga stuff but go on with my career and start working on the next thing. It was just the right time in my career to mosey on."

"I left as an employee in January 1986," says Mical. Andy Finkel, the VIC-20 developer of Omega Race, replaced Mical as Software Manager at Commodore-Amiga.

After Commodore, Mical plunged headfirst into Amiga software and peripheral development. "It turned out that I ended up spending a year and a half working on Amiga stuff anyway as an independent contractor rather than an employee of Commodore," says Mical. "I did a bunch of different stuff that all kind of blurs together."

Mical became involved with game development. "I did contract work for *Electronic Arts*," says Mical. "I helped them develop some of their tool technology that they used for the Amiga and I was a consultant for some of the games that they were doing."

Mical even began developing his own 3D game, which he did not complete. "The notorious *Baal* game would have been such a cool title," reveals Mical. "It would have been so much fun to do. My effort got interrupted by another opportunity, so I stopped working on it and never picked it up again."

For months, Mical worked on a *frame grabber*. The peripheral was an early attempt at image scanner technology. Initially, a company called *A-Squared* owned the technology and Commodore made an agreement to distribute the product.

After months of delays, the agreement with Commodore fell apart. Mical stepped in with a plan to finish the product. "There were some interesting scanning devices that were out there that automatically rotated colored filters in front of the lens of a black and white camera," recalls Mical. "There was all this really cool, interesting, mad scientist whizmo-gizmo stuff that people put together."

Along with some partners, he reformed a company called *Grab, Inc.* and began taking orders for the product. Days after demonstrating the frame grabber at Siggraph, Mical left the company, reportedly over artistic differences.

The biggest loss to Commodore was the departure of Amiga visionary Jay Miner. Miner walked out, along with faithful little Mitchy. However, Miner acted as a consultant to Commodore in the following years.

The departure of the Amiga team created a frightening prospect for the remaining Commodore engineers. "I was actually a little worried about it because here we were taking over their baby," says Haynie. "It wasn't as bad a parting as it could have been under the circumstances."

Although the Amiga did not achieve the popularity the designers hoped for, they did succeed in building the machine they originally envisioned. "It was just an amazing thing to see," says Mical. "Those were such cool days; you just couldn't believe it. It was one of the most magical periods of my entire life working at Amiga. God, what an incredible thing we did."[7]

Early Software

The Amiga and Atari ST had been available for just a short time, but within months, the news media criticized the new computers for poor software support. Byte magazine editor Philip Lemmons wrote, "The Atari 1040ST and the Amiga fall short of the Macintosh in both systems software and applications software."[8] This was not surprising, considering the Macintosh had been available a year before the Amiga.

Thomas Rattigan understood the importance of software. "While there was a lot of enthusiasm, I think there was also a realization that we didn't have much software on the machine, and that was going to be a tough sell," says Rattigan. "[Programmers] don't like to write until you've got an installed base. They're interested in making money."

Commodore initially lured many important software developers to create business applications for the Amiga. Autodesk began work on their popular 2D and 3D design tool, *AutoCAD*. Lotus Development Corporation, the company that purchased VisiCalc, began development of the popular *Lotus 1-2-3*. However, when the Amiga sold poorly, the software developers cancelled the titles.

R.J. Mical knew the machine was capable of hosting far better applications than either the IBM PC or Macintosh. "We had the IBM beat hands down," says Mical. "The only thing the IBM had on us was

---

[7] The three custom Amiga chips revolutionized graphics and sound for microcomputers. In September 1995, Byte magazine included all three chips in their top-20 most important chips ever.

[8] *Byte* magazine (March 1986), p. 6.

great business applications so we went after that. We thought we had a roaring chance of taking over the industry with that machine."

To encourage and aid software development, Commodore created a new division called *Commodore Amiga Technical Support*, or CATS. The group worked closely with developers outside of Commodore to develop Amiga applications, software, and hardware.[9]

Mical has nothing but praise for the CATS initiative. "The whole CATS organization was superb," says Mical. "That was a technical support group for the Amiga itself, and those guys really had their act together. They were brilliant assistants to aid the development of Amiga software."

CATS succeeded in spawning high quality software development for the Amiga. "We had every kind of app that you would want," says Mical. "We had a good spreadsheet program. There were good word processor apps. *WordPerfect* was a good one but there were a number of other ones that came together as well."

One technical issue that prevented quality software from running on stock Amiga computers was the lack of memory. Fortunately, the Amiga designers had the foresight to design the Amiga with expansion in mind and Commodore released a 256-kilobyte upgrade. If you owned an Amiga and wanted to use commercial software, the memory expansion was necessary since virtually all commercial programs demanded a full 512 kilobytes.

With the support of CATS, Amiga software began appearing. One of the earliest and biggest supporters of the Amiga was Electronic Arts. Electronic Arts had built their company on the Commodore 64 and they were not about to ignore Commodore's next computer, which was an obvious technological leap.

On the inside front cover of the November 1985 Compute! magazine, Electronic Arts took out a two page spread announcing, "Why Electronic Arts is Committed to the Amiga." Trip Hawkins, the founder of EA, stated, "The Amiga will revolutionize the home computer industry. It's the first home machine that has everything you want and need for all the major uses of a home computer, including entertainment, education and productivity."

Electronic Arts had expertise in games, but they also wanted to exploit the productivity market. One of the first Amiga products they announced was *Deluxe Video Construction Set*. The package aimed to create a new

---

[9] Commodore later gave the group a more fitting name, *Commodore Application and Technical Support*.

market by using the Amiga with a VCR for animations and credits. It was brave new territory for both the Amiga and Electronic Arts.

Electronic Arts followed up with a graphics program. They had previously written a version for the IBM PC called *Prism*. Though it was predictably lackluster on the IBM PC hardware, programmer Dan Silva rewrote it for the Amiga, taking advantage of the superior color palette.

Deluxe Paint launched in September 1985 and quickly became famous for an image of Tutankhamen's mask on the box cover. The startling cover showed off the incredible graphics capability of the Amiga. Colors blended into one another seamlessly, giving a lifelike image no one had ever thought possible on a personal computer. The handicapped *MacPaint* could not even come close to competing with Deluxe Paint.

Mical recalls the impact the program had with graphics artists. "We had the premier paint package at the time and for ten years," says Mical. "The best paint program that you could get was D-Paint on the Amiga; hands down, on all machines, across all platforms."

Despite aiming for the business market, Mical was glad the Amiga received quality games. "Having good games became a secondary thing for us, although to tell you the truth that was never true," reveals Mical. "In our heart of hearts, we always wanted to have good games. And happily, the Amiga always did have really good games."

Even Commodore managed to release a memorable game due to the efforts of the original Amiga team. Having come from Atari, Jay Miner knew many programmers in the field. One former Atari 800 programmer was impressed with the technology and decided to develop an Amiga game for Commodore.

Bill Williams is like the Stanley Kubrick of video game design, known for his startling originality. Born with Cystic Fibrosis, Williams had an intense focus on game design. Williams developed several Atari 800 games, most notably *Necromancer* in 1983.

Williams came to Commodore in 1985 and would eventually design the very first Amiga game, *Mind Walker*. The bizarre premise stated, "You are a physics professor gone mad. Your years of preoccupation with the study of minute particles and obscure formulae have twisted you into a tight knot within yourself, and you seem forever lost in your own internal world." The object of the game was to recover the lost shards of your sanity and put your mind back together.

Bil Herd remembers the offbeat game. "The last game I remember, other than Marble Madness, was this weird game where you help return Sigmund Freud to sanity," he says. "It had this eerie music that just played continuously in the background and could be heard coming from several offices. It was probably still running on my Amiga the day I walked out of the office for the last time."

The game became a favorite among Amiga owners. Williams went on to work for Cinemaware, where he composed in-game music and designed other games such as *Sinbad and the Throne of the Falcon*, *Pioneer Plague*, and *Knights of the Crystallion*.[10]

The Amiga received a powerful boost when legendary computer artist James Sachs fell under the spell of the Amiga. Sachs had previously programmed *Saucer Attack* for the C64, a relatively unknown but beautiful game. He started programming *Time Crystal* in 1985, which was shaping into one of the most graphically impressive C64 titles ever. Unfortunately, according to Sachs, "Rampant piracy drove me out of the Commodore 64 market, and I switched to the Amiga as soon as it was released."

Sachs was one of the lucky developers able to experiment with the Amiga before its release. Using the same Graphicraft software demonstrated at the Amiga launch in New York, Sachs created some impressive drawings of his house and a Porsche. This led to a job with *Master Designer Software Incorporated*.

Master Designer Software touted their games as interactive movies, which they called Cinemaware. Their first release was to be called either Star Rush or Space Rush, with Byte contributor and award winning science fiction author Jerry Pournelle providing the storyline and accompanying novel.

Master Designer Software made a major coup when they recruited none other than R.J. Mical as one of their developers. In 1986, no one was more knowledgeable of Amiga software development than Mical.

Under game designer Kellyn Beeck, the team created a medieval game called *Defender of the Crown*. "It was more than just Defender of the Crown," says Mical. "I invented this whole game system for those guys; a game playing engine. Defender of Crown was built on top of that."

Mical enjoyed working with designer Kellyn Beeck. "Kellyn was one of the better game designers who I've known over the years," says Mical. "I've known a couple of good ones and he was definitely up there with the top two or three that I've ever known."

Mical saw artist Jim Sachs push the Amiga to its full potential. "Jim Sachs, what a God he is," marvels Mical. "Jim Sachs is amazing. These days, everyone sees graphics like that because there are a lot of really

---

[10] After designing 92% of *Bart's Nightmare* for the SNES, Bill Williams became disenchanted and joined a Lutheran seminary, where he studied to become a pastor. He received his master's degree by 1994. In early 1997, his cystic fibrosis caught up with him and he passed away in 1998.

good computer graphics artists now, but back then, 20 years ago, it was astonishing to have someone that good."

The final game was a landmark in video game production values. As game designer Bob Lindstrom recalls, "The shock of seeing Defender for the first time was one of those experiences that changed the gaming stakes for all of us."

Compared to other video games of the time, Defender of the Crown established a new level of quality. IBM had Kings Quest II by Sierra On-Line, a decent but primitive adventure game. The Macintosh had games like Checkers or Backgammon, or board games like Risk. Defender of the Crown had richer graphics than any computer, console, over even arcade game could boast in 1986. It was a revelation.

Unfortunately, Mical has unhappy memories from the final two weeks he spent working on the project. "I did not have a good time doing that title, especially the very end of it," he says. "These days, I'm fond of telling the story that in my entire professional career, I only *worked* for two weeks, and those were two lousy weeks that I hope to never have to work ever again."

According to Mical, Master Designer Software took advantage of their agreement. "They were very greedy, very demanding, and kept insisting that I give them much, much more than I had originally bargained for when I made out this contract," he explains. "It was my first contract after I had left Amiga and I was relatively green. I decided it would be best if I followed through with my obligations with the whole thing and did the whole job, even though they were being grossly unfair."

By the end of the project, Mical wanted to distance himself from the game. "If you notice, you'll find my name on the box because I couldn't stop them from doing that, but if you go and play the game, my name is not in the game itself because I took it off," he says.

Rattigan's Success

When Irving Gould hired Thomas Rattigan in May 1985, he gave him one overriding task; Rattigan was to make Commodore profitable. This was not an easy task for any newcomer, but the Harvard graduate went to work.

"I didn't want to be spending my time on that," says Rattigan. "I really wanted to spend time on how we were going to move the goods, how we were going to reduce our manufacturing costs, and how best to take advantage of the technology we had in hand."

Commodore was in grave trouble. The March 1985 loss of $21 million under Marshall Smith was just the beginning. For the next five consecutive quarters, Commodore continued to report losses and mount debts. By the end of 1985, Commodore posted losses of $184 million dollars. This resulted in some $178 million dollars of unpaid bank loans.

When Commodore magazine asked Rattigan how close the company came to bankruptcy in 1985, he replied, "I guess that depends on your perspective. Close is a funny word. If you're running along the edge of a cliff and it's a thousand feet down, I guess you could find that close. I don't consider it close until you start falling off the edge. We didn't fall off the edge. We may have gotten close, but we didn't fall."[11]

Robert Russell describes how Commodore went wrong after the move to West Chester. "They had gone crazy," he says. "They were this billion-dollar company and they said, 'Let's hire everybody and let's start all these projects.' It was just that we were out of control; it wasn't like we couldn't be profitable."

To make matters worse, Rattigan was facing off against Jack Tramiel in the business arena. It was a challenge that could break almost anyone, but Rattigan was unfazed by his nemesis. When asked of Tramiel, Rattigan replied, "He smokes cigars, so he can't be all bad."

When Rattigan became CEO, he stepped down as General Manager of Commodore North America. "I had moved out of the North American operation and had, over time, met most of the other senior people in the organization," says Rattigan. "I asked Nigel [Shepherd] to come in from Australia to take over the North American operation."

Shepherd impressed Rattigan with his aggressive style. "Nigel made it happen," says Rattigan. "He was the type of guy that, when you asked him to go through a wall, he would just ask you how thick it was so he could decide how fast he was going to run."

Rattigan felt no shame in consulting former Commodore employees. One consultant was Charles Winterble, who had left Coleco after the Adam failure. "I got a call from Commodore and they said, 'Would you come on down and do some work for us?'" recalls Winterble.

Rattigan wanted an experienced opinion on the current Commodore product line. "I went in and I looked at their whole computer line," says Winterble. "They gave me samples of everything and I took everything apart and gave them some inputs on cost reduction. Mostly what Rattigan wanted me for was to reexamine the work their engineers were doing and to give them a second opinion on what they were being told by their engineers."

At this time, Winterble still had a lawsuit against him from Commodore over the Atari 2600 keyboard computer. "It shows the distrust in the company when the management team doesn't even know

---

[11] *Commodore* magazine, "What Next for Commodore?" (May 1987), p. 126.

if they can trust their own engineering team and they bring in somebody from the outside," he says. "Here I am being sued by Commodore, yet they trusted my opinion."

Winterble bluntly expressed his opinion about one new product. "When I saw their version of the C128, I think I didn't make people happy," he recalls. "When they asked about it, I said, 'Are you people out of your mind? What is this piece of crap, the Commodore 128? It's got CP/M and all this crap in there.'"

After the consultation, Rattigan cut back Commodore's diverse line of products. "He laid people off and shut projects down and sold off things that didn't make sense anymore," recalls Russell. "We might have still had steel [furniture] manufacturing up in Canada and those types of things." Rattigan ended the PET and CBM lines, VIC-20 production, and the fabulously unsuccessful Plus/4 and C-16 computers. The company would now focus on the C64c, the C128, and the Amiga, as well as the PC line of computers.

"We had a number of layoffs where people were getting chopped right and left," says Haynie. "The whole 1985 to 1986 was not such a good year because they had spent all this money buying Amiga and all this money launching the product, and then they were waiting for money to come in. Meanwhile the 8-bit stuff was dying again."

Rattigan began three separate rounds of layoffs. "It was just a paring down and actually the first layoff was a good thing," says Haynie. "The second one was questionable. The third one was where they were actually hitting bone."

The first round of layoffs included employees who were not contributing significantly to Commodore. "They had a purging in the 1985 to 1986 years, and if you hadn't proved your worth, you were not going to stick around," says Haynie.

The second round of cuts included Joe Krasucki, who oversaw the creation of the C128. "Joe had left a bit before me," says Russell. "They were going to fire my engineers who I thought wanted to stay with the company; people like Bob Welland."

After Commodore cancelled the Z8000 project, Robert Russell moved onto special projects, such as the NES investigation. "It wasn't like I quit being an engineer," says Russell. "We all got special projects and ended up doing other tasks. Irving knew us and people respected us, but it wasn't necessarily what we had joined the company for or what we were real good at."

Russell sensed the tenuousness of his position. "I got let go later on too," says Russell. "I knew Irving and could have gone to him and saved my job, but you know, I said the hell with it. I'll move on. They're forcing me out because politically they didn't want me around."

The massive cuts made Commodore self-sustaining once again. "[Rattigan] basically got it back under control, but he got it under control by cutting heads," says Russell.

The cuts left Commodore with two engineering groups. "You had your in-house people in West Chester who were largely working on C64 and C128 technology, although they started to do some work on IBM clones as well," says Rattigan. "Then you had technology capability in Germany. They were into IBM clones and much more in the way of business applications on some of the Commodore computers, contrasted to the US where it was largely games."

Commodore Asia also helped with cost reduction redesigns and obtaining parts. "You had a little bit going on in Asia, but that was largely related to the purchasing function that was going on out there," says Rattigan.

Chuck Peddle, who was battling Commodore for the European market with the Victor Sirius computer, credits Commodore Germany with helping Commodore survive. "[Harald] Speyer ultimately wound up saving the company a couple of times," he says. "It kept Commodore in business while they were selling [IBM PC] clones."

By the middle of 1986, it was apparent Rattigan was making a difference. Sales were up 58% from the same quarter the year before and Commodore made their first profit after six consecutive losses. It was only a million dollars, but at least it was not a loss.

In the first half of 1986, Rattigan began to explore other options for the Amiga. "In the hands of Apple at that time, I think the success of the [Amiga] would have been much more assured than it could have been in our hands," says Rattigan. "The best thing that could have happened really, in many respects, was if [Commodore] could have put themselves in the hands of a stronger financial entity in the business."

Rattigan was desperate to salvage the value of Commodore. "There was a real question at that time as to whether or not Commodore could pull itself out of this nosedive," he says. "You had the feeling you were on a Kamikaze plane dodging towards American battleships. So my attitude was, let's explore all of the alternatives."

Rattigan turned to Apple, where his former Pepsi coworker John Scully was in charge. Apple was fearful of the Amiga, which was technologically superior yet cost less. In 1986, it seemed possible the Amiga might usurp the Macintosh. Sales of the Macintosh were slow, and like Commodore, Apple was going through massive layoffs.

Rattigan approached the Commodore board of directors with a new strategy. "I had told the board very early in my tenure, 'The ideal candidate [to acquire] this company is really Apple. Here's what you've got: number one, they have the school market locked. Like it or not, we've got the mass market locked. We've got the same 68000 chip in the Amiga as the Mac. We've got multitasking and they don't. They're buying a lot of their custom chips on the open market and we're producing our chips, so there's significant cost reductions for them on that side.' At that time, we were doing more international business than Apple was. So I told the board, 'I think we ought to explore doing something with Apple.'"

Rattigan knew he would have to convince Irving Gould his investment in Commodore would not be lost. He told Gould, "You've got six million shares and this may be a way to recoup your position and more importantly ensure the viability of the company, granted in the hands of a competitor." Gould agreed.

Years before, Apple tried to sell their company to Commodore. Now, Commodore was trying to sell their company to Apple. "I flew out and met with Scully," says Rattigan.

Rattigan hoped to discuss the proposal in person with John Scully, but the meeting was not what he expected. "We sat down and John brought all of his staff in for some strange reason," recalls Rattigan. It was obvious Scully wanted his team to see their enemy on his knees. Despite this surprise, Rattigan maintained his composure and held back much of his proposal. "We had a general discussion," he says.

After the meeting, Rattigan had a chance to discuss the proposal in depth. "Then [Scully] and I met privately and I said, 'John, here's the things I didn't say in the meeting. We have some trade implications and some competitive implications that would work tremendously to your advantage. Internationally, here's some more.'" Unfortunately, Apple was not interested in an acquisition. "They were just so full of themselves at that point in time," says Rattigan.

There were other reasons the acquisition might have failed had Apple agreed. "Prior to my time, RCA had approached Commodore," reveals Rattigan. "I gather there was some difference of opinion as to what the board composition should be and some other personal things like that. If true, I suspect that even if Apple had been amenable, that particular variable might have resurfaced in that equation."

Although the proposal failed, it showed a lot about Rattigan. First, he felt no loyalty to the Commodore name. Second, if his plan succeeded, he would be out of a job. "What I cared about was what's in the best interests of the company, what's in the best interests of the people, and what's in the best interests of shareholders," says Rattigan. "If that meant I was going to disappear in the equation, I didn't give a rat's ass."

It was probably a good thing the deal did not succeed, since Commodore continued to have success through 1986. Despite the price increase of the C64c, sales soared with the added interest of GEOS. It was one of the last low-cost computers in the marketplace.

Commodore executives realized the C64 had a long life ahead of it, even though it was almost 5 years old. In a magazine interview, Nigel Shepherd predicted the future of the C64. "You're looking at a solid two to three years out of that machine," said Shepherd.[12] He was correct.

In June 1986, Commodore made their first shipments of Amiga computers to the UK and Germany. The European Amiga computers were slightly different from their North American counterparts. The PAL video mode required slightly more memory than NTSC, and in the meantime, RAM prices had dropped significantly. As a result, all European Commodore Amiga computers came with one megabyte.

Europe was always a technologically sophisticated market and the market seemed to recognize the best technology for the best value. The Amiga soon captured a large segment of the 16-bit market. Europe now accounted for 70% of Commodore's Amiga sales, mainly from Britain and Germany.

In the UK, an uncompromising general manager named Bob Gleadow carried the Amiga to success. "Gleadow drove the Amiga," says Peddle. Gleadow joined Commodore UK in the seventies and knew the company well. He was one of the few managers who had dared go toe to toe with Jack in shouting matches.

Commodore Germany, under Harald Speyer, also continued their unabated success. "Germany was a very good market," says Rattigan. According to Forbes magazine, Commodore was a close number two to IBM in the business market and number one in the consumer market until the end of the decade.

Once again, Europe was the only thing keeping Commodore afloat. It was a return to the PET days. However, if Commodore wanted to last into the 1990's, they would need to make the Amiga a success in North America. It was apparent to Rattigan that the Amiga would not succeed in its current form. Rattigan was not ready to give up on the Amiga. He planned to reincarnate the machine to make it more marketable.

---

[12] *Compute!'s Gazette* magazine, "An Interview With Nigel Shepherd" (October 1986), p. 31.

CHAPTER

22

The New Amigas

1986-1987

The IBM PC was about spreadsheets, databases, and accounting software. The Macintosh was about desktop publishing. In contrast, the Amiga was about music, visual art, animations, and incredible games. It was an exciting computer compared to the competition but poor marketing prevented it from earning the market it deserved. It was time to try again.

A New Competitor

The Atari ST and Amiga pressured Apple to release a comparable machine. It was obvious the Macintosh could match neither when it came to color, sound, and most importantly price. In response, the Apple team began developing the Apple II GS, which stood for Graphics and Sound.

Commodore engineers ignored the 65816 processor when it appeared, while Apple II engineers enthusiastically embraced it. They would use it to build a machine with Apple II backward compatibility and a Macintosh-like operating system. The Macintosh's greatest enemy was its lack of applications but the new computer could build on the Apple II library.

The Apple II GS was a quantum technological leap from the primitive Apple II computers. Finally, the machine boasted solid text display without blotchy colors. There was a color palette of 4096 colors, like the Amiga. At 320 by 200 pixels, it could display up to 16 colors at once, and a higher 640 by 200 mode could display four colors at once.

Perhaps of most interest to Commodore 64 fans was the sound chip, designed by ex-Commodore engineer Robert Yannes. At his new company *Ensoniq*, Yannes had developed an improved synthesizer chip called the Ensoniq 32. It used multiplexing to produce 16 stereo voices and even contained 64 kilobytes of onboard memory so it could play music without taxing other system resources. The legacy of the SID chip was now in the hands of Apple.

For Commodore 64 owners, the Apple II GS is an interesting picture of what might have been. It effectively had a next generation SID chip and a next generation processor from the 6502 family. Furthermore, it would build on the success of the popular Apple II line of 8-bit computers, second only to the Commodore 64.

Apple released the system for $999. When adding a color monitor, disk drive, and 256-kilobyte expansion card the cost was $2026.

The Apple II GS outsold the Macintosh initially but it was apparent management wanted the Macintosh to succeed. The computer received almost no advertising and hardly anyone knew about it outside the Apple II user base. Today, it is easy to see that the Apple II GS was superior to the Macintosh, especially considering the seven expansion slots to the Macintosh's zero. Nevertheless, the Mac sold for $2600.

Amiga 500

The Amiga's dismal launch led Thomas Rattigan to consider releasing a cost reduced Amiga computer, called the Amiga 500. Robert Russell blames the marketing team's faulty analysis for not going after the cost-reduced market from the start. "The Amiga 1000[1] came out rather than the Amiga 500, which is what I was fighting for," says Russell.

When Russell first visited the Amiga team and returned to Commodore, he wanted Commodore to use their acquisition for the low-cost market. "I was thinking Amiga 500 level immediately could come out of it," recalls Russell. "It took them a while to move from the A1000 to the A500 but technically there was no reason to take that much time."

When it became apparent the Amiga 1000 was not meeting expected sales, Rattigan changed tactics. He was a quick learner and openly acknowledged previous miscalculations. In an interview in 1987, Rattigan confessed, "I think we banked too much on the software emulator for IBM compatibility, which we saw as a bridge during the

---

[1] Commodore renamed the original Amiga computer the Amiga 1000 to differentiate it from other models that followed.

time Amiga's software was being developed. That obviously, in retrospect, did not pan out to the degree we had hoped."[2]

Rattigan was also acutely aware of the misconceptions about computers and price in the marketplace, saying, "I think the price also confused a lot of people. People seem to think that home systems are under $1,000 and business systems are over $1,000. There tends to be a lot of biases and preconceived notions as to exactly what differentiates home and business computers."

Where Irving Gould and Marshall Smith blindly tried to push the Amiga into the business marketplace, Rattigan formed a realistic strategy. "I don't think the higher end Amiga is going to go into accounting departments, but I do think it is going to go into areas where there is a degree of creativity, if you will." His prediction would pan out exactly as he described it.

Rattigan wanted to bring the massive C64 user base over to the Amiga. A low-cost Amiga was the natural upgrade path. Rattigan's instincts were correct, since many Commodore fans wanted an Amiga, but not at business prices.

Tramiel's Atari had already established their computer in this territory. The Atari 520 ST sold for $999, which included 512 kilobytes, a color monitor, and a 3.5" disk drive. In 1986, Atari released the 1040 ST with 1 megabyte of memory and a built in disk drive for under $1000. It was reminiscent of Tramiel at Commodore, where he constantly destroyed price barriers. As before, his strategy was working. Reports at the time estimate the Atari ST was outselling the Amiga by ten to one. Rattigan had to reverse this trend.

"When I started leaning on them to go with the [Amiga] 500, that was recognition on my part that we better have an alternative," says Rattigan. "Maybe we better return closer to our roots than this pie-in-the-sky concept that we can be a true competitor to Apple."

Dave Haynie gives credit for the A500 to engineers George Robbins and Bob Welland. "[Commodore management] weren't too hot on the idea but they looked at the $1200 or $1500 an A1000 sold for and said, 'This isn't our strong suit,'" recalls Haynie. "When George and Bob suggested the A500, they immediately said, 'Yes, that's what we want.'"

Haynie believes there was no other choice. "Basically, whoever was at the helm at that time was going to push for that," he says. "It was inevitable that someone was going to come up with a lower cost Amiga."

---

[2] *Commodore* magazine, "What Next for Commodore?" (May 1987) p. 76

Rattigan had to choose between the original Amiga engineers and his own engineers. "You had the West Coast group, and of course they were reluctant to fool around with their baby too much," explains Rattigan. "Then you had the West Chester technology group, who I gave the assignment to. I figured they would be more bloodthirsty."

The West Chester engineers were inexperienced with Amiga technology. "There were very few people in West Chester doing Amiga stuff," says Haynie. "Jeff Porter and Andy Finkel were doing an [Amiga] answering machine/modem that never got released."

The Amiga engineers in Los Gatos felt insulted by the move. "There was a lot of resentment about that," says Rattigan. "Obviously the Amiga group on the West Coast was disappointed because the old Commodores transitioned to being the new Amiga."

Rattigan replaced Joe Krasucki with the engineer responsible for the LCD computer. "Jeff Porter was director of new product development during the golden years of the Commodore Amiga," says Haynie.

To ensure the engineers stayed focused on cost reduction, Rattigan employed spies. He reveals, "Without telling anybody, I got to two of the lower level engineers and I said, 'I'm not telling your boss this but you guys are reporting to me directly now. You're going to be my conscience on cost because quite frankly, there aren't enough hours in the day to understand component costs. Every time the primary group working on it comes in, you're going to have a secret meeting with me afterwards and we're going to critique this thing.'"

The lead engineers on the Amiga 500 project were George Robbins and Bob Welland, the two former Commodore 900 engineers who created the failed UNIX machine. After the C900's cancellation, both were scrambling to remain relevant to Commodore. "Bob and George had a problem in that they didn't have a reason to continue existing, so they decided to jump into the Amiga," says Haynie.

According to Haynie, although George Robbins was a good practical engineer, Welland was not. "Bob was a very good theoretical guy but he was one of those guys like Cong Su," says Haynie. "You don't want to let him too near a soldering iron."

Welland was responsible for improving the Amiga chipset. "He came up with the concept of a *FAT Agnus*," recalls Haynie. FAT Agnus allowed 1 megabyte of video RAM, allowing for higher resolutions. The Amiga team did not support the changes. "Los Gatos was bent out of shape about that," says Haynie. "They didn't think it was going to work at all, and clearly it did."

Because of these doubts, Welland created a backup plan. "They did two things: they built the FAT Agnus and they built what they were calling the FAT chip. They built a chip that did all the FAT stuff outside of Agnus just in case the FAT Agnus didn't work."

According to Mical, the original Amiga engineers believed the engineers should have pushed the new chips more. "There were a lot of people that didn't really like the decisions that were made with FAT Agnus because it wasn't enough," says Mical. "They didn't have enough of the extra graphics display capabilities that we were looking for. It was a good step in the right direction but it violated the idea of the BUS architecture and actually slowed the machine down."

Mical was aware that some of their feelings could be misplaced. "We were concerned there was some 'not invented here' going on," says Mical. "We were always watchful that we were not just being emotional little jerks but that our protests were legitimate, and I think they were."

However, Mical reveals that he finally accepted the decisions on the new chips. "In the end, I think it was largely the right choices that were made for FAT Agnes because it was more powerful and it was the next generation," he explains. "It was a careful step rather than a gigantic leap forward. A lot of the old software would still work."

Meanwhile, George Robbins worked tirelessly to cost-reduce the Amiga 500. "They worked out how they were going to make a cheaper motherboard," says Haynie. "Then in combination with Jeff Porter they came up with the actual shape and what it was going to look like."

The Amiga 500 bared a family resemblance to previous Commodore computers. "It was clearly influenced by the C128," says Haynie. The new machine used the same computer-in-a-keyboard design with an external power supply and no cooling fan. Unlike the Amiga 1000, it even sported a Commodore logo. Jay Miner was amazed to see the Amiga fit into such a small case, with a built in disk drive no less.

The new computer impressed Rattigan. "They did an absolutely fantastic job and we got to the price point we wanted," he says.

The original Amiga engineers were initially critical of the Amiga 500. "They started making choices about the Amiga that we didn't like," says Mical. "It was like they took our Amiga and made a C64 out of it. It was a toy version of the Amiga. The A500 came out as sort of a flimsy thing and it wasn't expandable in ways."

However, as the machine started selling, Mical began to realize it was closer to the Amiga's original concept. "I warmed up to the idea because it was continuing the original philosophy that we had with the Amiga, which was to get good computing horsepower into the hands of the masses," says Mical. "It helped the machine be a lot more popular than it would have been otherwise."

The Amiga 1000 could connect to a color television set but the standard Amiga 500 could not. Users had to buy a special adapter, called the A520, or they would have to purchase a monitor. This changed the Amiga 500's market slightly, since users would have to make a costly investment the C64 did not require.

Mical explains the Amiga 500's lack of a color TV signal. "It turned out that a lot of people weren't using the TV anyway because it was giving them a headache," says Mical. "You could do 60 columns and have it look good on a good TV but on a medium quality TV you had to go to 40 columns, and at 40 columns the characters are as big as your head."

In January 1987, normalcy returned to Commodore when they were able to attend CES in full force. For the first time in years, Commodore had a full booth on display. There was now a chance for success.

Amiga 2000

Rattigan wanted a cheaper Amiga but he was not ready to abandon the high-end market. After the Amiga 1000, the Los Gatos Amiga team concentrated on Amiga technical support and bug fixes. They also worked on an improved Amiga. "If you looked at it from the Los Gatos point of view, the A1000 was their cheap product and they weren't going to make it any cheaper because how could you?" says Haynie. "They wanted to move onto something bigger and better, which was codenamed Ranger."

Commodore failed to produce a fast enough IBM PC emulator in software, which they called the Transformer. In 1986, Commodore began talking about an upcoming hardware product for the Amiga called the Sidecar. This expansion would allow the Amiga computer to run IBM PC software, and it would be faster than the Transformer.

Full IBM compatibility was highly desired by Commodore management. Rick Geiger, Commodore's divisional manager who acted as liaison to the Los Gatos Amiga team, promised he would have hardware emulation ready for the Amiga. He hired an outside contractor to design the hardware. Unfortunately, the expansion card never worked and Commodore dismissed him.

Commodore subsequently wanted the Los Gatos engineers closely managed by moving them to the East Coast. Many unhappy Commodore-Amiga employees left, and Ranger was never completed. "There are a lot of mixed stories on just how far they got on that," says

Haynie. "I never saw schematics or anything that claimed to be the Ranger, but of course that's kind of how legends are built. I could never really refute it either."

The Commodore engineers in Braunschweig, West Germany were next to design the IBM PC emulator. Working on the Sidecar, a device that connected to an external IBM PC disk drive, they promised a breakneck turnaround time. They kept their promise.

Compute! writer Sheldon Leemon was amazed, saying, "In what may be a record breaking event for Commodore (or any other computer company), the Sidecar has been delivered in the same year in which it was announced. A scant eight months after I first saw the earliest prototypes at Comdex, one has arrived at my local Amiga dealer."

Shortly after the Sidecar project began, the Braunschweig engineers attempted their own improved design of an expandable Amiga computer. "Germany took the A1000 reference design from a thin white book called the A1000 technical reference manual," explains Haynie. The German A2000 would include an expansion bus using Zorro II slots. "It had the autoconfig[3] and everything, but it was fairly simply based on the 68000 bus with buffer. It wasn't super creative, which is why it worked so well."

According to Haynie, the origin of the strange Zorro name came from the original Amiga team. "In the back of [the reference manual] was a schematic called Zorro," says Haynie. "On the Amiga prototypes, each motherboard had a code name. The first code name that was around when we were there was the Lorraine, and that was the one in the black metal cases and they still had the 5.25-inch floppy. Then the next generation of that was called the Zorro. That's actually how the [expansion bus] was named."

Within months, the Braunschweig team had built their expandable Amiga. They also created an IBM PC emulator card that was both fast and reliable. It could even run *Flight Simulator*, a processor intensive IBM PC game.

Back in West Chester, Commodore management decided the German A2000 was not the leap in technology they wanted. "The Germans basically took the A1000 and put an expansion bus on it and put it in a PC case, and there's the A2000," explains Haynie. "So [West Chester management] looked at that and said, 'This isn't going to work.'"

---

[3] At the time, it was difficult to configure adapter cards in IBM PC computers. The Zorro slots were similar to *Plug & Play* because the Amiga automatically configured the adapter cards.

After the disappointment of the German A2000 and the abandonment of the Ranger, Rattigan looked to his East Coast engineers. "That was largely in-house on the East Coast, with a lot of it being spurred on by this outside consultant that was working for the company at the time," he says. Rattigan's most senior engineer at the time was Dave Haynie, who had previously worked on the C128 project.

Dave Haynie came from a background in electrical engineering. "My dad was an electrical engineer at *Bell Laboratories*," says Haynie. "He was an analog guy from back when analog was important. For at least four months, he was the main guy in charge of all of their fiber optics before he realized it was too much for one department and split it up into three separate projects."

Haynie came from a picturesque East Coast town. "I was born in Summit, New Jersey in 1961," he says. Through the years, his interests varied from black & white photography, electronic music, and finally computers.

Haynie had exposure to technology at an early age because of his father. "I taught myself to program when I was 12 and was writing code for years before I had any formal education in it," he recalls. "The first thing I programmed was for taxes."

Haynie gained programming experience on a calculator so large it even had a monitor. "My dad brought home a huge Hewlett-Packard programmable calculator; one of those desktop things with a CRT [Cathode Ray Tube] and it had magnetic cards," says Haynie. "I was goofing around on it and basically learned how to read the machine code that was stored on the cards."

While still only a child, Haynie learned programming on a timesharing system. "I kept asking him to bring [the calculator] back, and he said, 'I can't really do that because we only have one.' So he brought home a terminal," recalls Haynie. "I had this Ti terminal every weekend and a roller of thermal paper, and I would do whatever I could do on their timeshare system, since nobody used it on the weekends."

A 1972 era *CDC Cyber 72* timesharing system was on the other end of his terminal. "I taught myself Basic and Fortran by taking apart programs that happened to be on the CDC Cyber 72," says Haynie. "That lasted a couple of years."

The Commodore PET was Haynie's first exposure to personal computing. "My best friend got a PET in 1977 when you could go to the island of Manhattan and there was one store that had PETs," he recalls. "It was actually just one room in an office building. PETs were on one side and 4K Apple IIs were on the other side." Haynie was the only teenager in his group with programming experience. He soon created a few games for his friends.

"I got my first computer in 1979, but that was after years of wanting one that I couldn't afford," recalls Haynie. "I ended up getting an *Exidy Sorcerer*. Exidy at the time was a big video game company out on the West Coast and they came out with this computer which was technically cool but had no [software development] whatsoever."

Haynie connected his system to a modified Hitachi TV. He then purchased a 1200-baud acoustic modem and used a technique known as *war dialing* to search randomly for other computers at Bell Laboratories. Haynie soon found a UNIX system and hacked his way in, which provided him with a deep understanding of UNIX.

The young programmer also wrote programs for the Sorcerer and sold four titles to *Creative Computing Software*, which distributed them on cassette tape for $7.95 each. The Sorcerer market numbered only about 5,000 machines and Haynie sold about 500 copies of his software.

In 1979, Haynie entered Electrical Engineering at Carnegie Mellon University in Pennsylvania. "I studied electrical engineering and mathematics/computer science at Carnegie Mellon in Pittsburgh," recalls Haynie. "I taught myself all the computer science stuff." In his last semester, Haynie took courses in Compiler Design and Robotics.

During summer vacations, Haynie worked for Bell Laboratories. He seemed destined to follow his father's example after his graduation in 1983, but it was the year of the AT&T breakup and the company was in a hiring freeze. Instead, Haynie went to work for General Electric in Philadelphia. The Space Shuttle work at GE lured Haynie in but he soon learned 99% of the work was in nuclear weapons. "I was at General Electric for four months and I didn't like it," says Haynie. "I decided I was leaving General Electric and I went to this head hunter and sent out one resume." A week later, Haynie was working for Commodore.

In late 1983, Bil Herd was hiring engineers for the TED project. "I went in with Joe Krasucki, my boss at the time," recalls Herd. "We went back to the same office where I had been hired to do the same thing where they run a dozen people by you every night."

Herd was relaxing in the lobby when an unusual young engineer arrived early. "I'm sitting in a chair reading and this kid comes in and plops down in a homemade shirt," recalls Herd. Most candidates dress up for their interview but the young engineer seemed unconcerned about his appearance. "It was black and he had cut it out and sewn it himself, so it was kind of like a sweatshirt and it wasn't real symmetrical. Picture a sweatshirt without a real good neck hem or without arms on it."

Herd looked too young to be a recruiter. "[Haynie is] excited and wild-eyed. He said, 'So, are you here for the interview?'" recalls Herd. "I said, 'Yeah, something like that. Where you working now?' He said, 'GE aerospace missile division.' I asked, 'Well, why do you want to leave?' He said, 'Oh, I don't want to make missiles that hurt people and stuff.'"

Herd hid the fact that he was from Commodore. "I was asking him all these questions and we're having this enthusiastic heart to heart talk in the lobby," recalls Herd. "He really didn't know who I was at this time. Then they call him in to talk to Joe Krasucki."

Herd took his seat in his office and waited for the candidates to arrive. "When they brought him in they said, 'You'll be interviewing next with Bil Herd.' I looked up at him and I said, 'We've met.' The look on his face was great."

Haynie recalls his shock. "Then I met Bil again," laughs Haynie. "He asked me a few analog questions and things I've never used yet, like Laplace transforms, but he just wanted to make sure that somebody on the team knew this stuff if it ever showed up."

According to Herd, there was no doubt Haynie was the right match for Commodore. "What he didn't know was he was already hired at that point," he says. "He had gotten his whole interview sitting in the lobby."

After the TED and C128 projects, Haynie wondered what to do next. "I played with [the C128] a lot when it first came out, but I have to admit having switched to an Amiga about six months after the C128 started shipping," says Haynie. "My group, which was me and Frank [Palaia], we were trying to figure out what we were going to do to try to stay valuable around here and not disappear. So we had come up with a couple of different dog and pony shows around new variations on the C128."

The two engineers conceived several potential products. "During many parts of this company's existence, engineering was bottom up as far as what the product would be," recalls Haynie. "I would build something and show it off to the bosses and they would say, 'Okay, that's very nice, maybe you could try something else,' or, 'We'll think about it.'"

After Haynie completed work on the European C128D, the Europeans tried their own modifications. "There was the C128D and those actually shipped," says Haynie. "Then they cost reduced it in Europe and put it in a slightly more PC-ish metal case."

The pair attempted to evolve the C128 line, in case it enjoyed the same success as the C64. "Frank and I each took half the problem," says Haynie. "He made a version of the C128 that ran a 4 MHz Z80. I made a version of the C128 with a slightly different MMU that gave 256K of built in memory." Haynie called his proposed system the C256.

The engineers even considered using Bill Mensch's 16-bit chip. "We were looking at maybe using a 65816 or something like that, but it was pretty much flogging a dead horse at that point," says Haynie. "Once the Amiga was there, nobody was interested in more C128s."

A wild-eyed Dave Haynie in 1985.

Haynie ended up on the Amiga 500 project. "I got into Amiga simply because George Robbins and Bob Welland needed some help on the A500," he says. "Everybody thought, 'Well, you're not getting very far with anyone wanting to do any more C128 stuff so maybe it would be a good idea to learn the Amiga. And I said, 'Yes, it would!'"

Haynie was well acquainted with the Amiga technology. "I had already been programming it for nearly a year," he says. "I went out and got one as quickly as I could and then I was writing programs on it before I was actually doing any work for Commodore on it."

Once it was apparent Haynie could contribute to the Amiga technology, management began contemplating a project for him. "They also thought I was the senior ranking low-end guy after two years at Commodore because there had only been three of us and I was the top guy left," he recalls. "Of course, George and Bob had been the high-end guys because they did this little UNIX workstation."

Commodore management thought it appropriate to move Haynie, their low-end engineer, onto the low-end Amiga 500 project and promote Robbins and Welland to a high-end Amiga project. "The idea was I was going to learn the A500 and take it over," says Haynie. "The thing was, this was George's baby."

Although George Robbins was protective of the Amiga 500, Bob Welland was not. "Bob didn't really want to be at that level," says Haynie. "He didn't want to be in charge of a system. He wanted to be the 'new idea' kind of guy working with the chip people."[4]

Haynie was suddenly in charge of Commodore's next high-end product by default. "It basically turned out that somebody was going to take over this A2000 project and you couldn't very well kick George off the A500 if he didn't want to because he started the whole thing," explains Haynie. "So they put me on the A2000, which suited me just fine. It was a little scary because, other than conferring with George on various things, that was pretty much my show."

Irving Gould also brought in an acquaintance named Henry Rubin to develop a marketing strategy for the Amiga product line. "When Commodore was faltering, Irving brought Henry in to help try to figure out what should be done from an engineering perspective," says Mical.

R.J. Mical left Commodore in January 1986, but he continued consulting with Commodore, along with other former Commodore-Amiga employees. "Shortly after I stopped working there I became a contactor," he says. "We dealt with the engineering people from the company; Henry Rubin and guys like that on downward."

Mical got along well with the bowtie wearing Rubin. "I liked him," says Mical. "He was very interesting to work with."

Although Mical no longer worked for Commodore, he enjoyed significant influence over the Amiga through Irving. "[Irving] had put a lot of trust and a lot of faith in Henry Rubin and Henry and I struck up a good relationship," explains Mical. "That led to me spending a lot of time with Irving through Henry. For a while there, I became one of the guys he was asking a lot of advice about. Those were some fun days."

Mical found his influence increase with time. "Very early on, after a lot of the original guys' relationships were falling apart with Commodore, there were a magical couple of months where I had the ear of the powers that be at Commodore," says Mical. "I had them convinced that it would be a good thing to spend the money to go back and hire Carl Sassenrath, the OS guy, to come in and redo the file system."

---

[4] Welland eventually moved onto other companies after Commodore. "He went on to Apple and Microsoft, so I guess he's done the computer company hat trick," says Haynie.

It was a lofty proposition but Commodore listened. "Commodore saw the wisdom in it and they were willing to at least fund the research into it," recalls Mical. "But I couldn't talk Carl into it. Carl was so disheartened with the entire Commodore experience and the way the whole thing had gone. He declined that opportunity. It was really a shame because it might have made a big difference in the final success of the Amiga."

TripOS remained an integral part of the Amiga operating system. "That was one of the things that sorely crippled the Amiga until the very end because they kept using that old file format," says Mical.

Thomas Rattigan felt Irving Gould's outside consultants resulted in 'design by committee'. "That got to be fairly convoluted," he says. "We had one outside guy [Henry Rubin] working on that technology with us. Some of that led to there being a lot of cooks in the kitchen as to what those machines should be."

Too many people were attempting to exert influence on the Amiga products. "Everyone was willing to give advice at that point," says Mical.

Rattigan had a hard time steering Commodore. "It's very, very hard to have a meeting and get uniformity on technological decisions when you have a crowd of more than one," explains Rattigan. "Everybody is an instant expert and everybody has their own axe to grind, and that really slows the process down."

Rattigan tried to force a different management style in opposition to Irving Gould. "You just say, 'The hell with it! This is not going to be the normal corporate thing where we all sit around a table Japanese style to effect consensus, but rather we'll create an in-house competitive situation and hope for the best,'" says Rattigan. Not surprisingly, Rattigan's relationship with Gould began deteriorating while the A2000 project developed.

The Amiga technology gave Haynie a feeling of euphoria. "The designs, as done by the Los Gatos group, were just so radical for the time," he says. "They made me think about things better."

He wanted to provide expansion for the Amiga. "I took the FAT Agnus architecture and put that together with my own chip, the Buster chip, that did the expansion bus," he says. "It also enabled this CPU slot idea that I came up with that would allow you to plug in a card that had a different CPU on it without pulling chips out."

The programmer and systems architect now added chip design to his list of skills. "I was probably the only one who had hardware, software, and chips all in one of the computers because I did a little bit of software and a tiny bit of gate array chip design," says Haynie. "The Buster chip was my first gate array."

A dedicated video card slot, something common today, was an idea evolved by Haynie. "The Germans had the idea for a *Genlock* slot," says Haynie, referring to a method of outputting computer images over video. "They basically took the signals that went to the external video connector and ran it through an internal connector."

Haynie pushed the Genlock concept and concluded that his machine should have a dedicated video slot. "George Robbins and I talked about that a little bit and said this is not right," he recalls. "We should run every signal to that connector. That's what the video slot was for."

Haynie was the lone hardware engineer on the project. "I *was* the design team for the A2000," says Haynie. "That's kind of the way things were there because we had had a lot of layoffs. I was working day and night and there still wasn't enough time to do everything."

His only respite was Margarita's. "That was on Friday's depending on the week," says Haynie. "I got into a habit of working all Thursday night, pretty much every Thursday night, and going to Margarita's on Friday and then going home."

The Amiga team's departure forced Andy Finkel to create a software group to refine and develop the operating system. Compared to the one-man hardware 'team', the software group was very large. "The thirty people in the software group were all for the operating system," explains Haynie. "That's a lot of work. It wasn't like the C64 where you had two guys doing pretty much the whole thing. There were just countless pieces for this very sophisticated operating system."

R.J. Mical was impressed with the Commodore engineers who took over Amiga development. "There were a number of Commodore engineers that were brilliant people who were a real treat to work with," says Mical. "Not all of them were brilliant; some of them were real clunkers but you could say that about the original Amiga guys. There were a whole bunch of them, but Andy Finkel and Dave Haynie were guys that really stood out as the heroes."

The final Amiga 2000 contained a hard drive and space for two 3.5" floppy drives and a 5.25" floppy drive or CD-ROM. It also had incredible expandability. Inside the case were slots for five Amiga cards, four IBM PC cards, a faster processor, or a video card. To fit the massive amount of expandability, the case was noticeably taller than the Amiga 1000 but it had approximately the same footprint.

Reviews for the Amiga 2000 were favorable. Compute! magazine wrote, "Commodore answers those critics who have said that the original

Amiga was too expensive to be a home computer and not powerful enough for a business machine."[5]

Mical was initially dissatisfied with the Amiga 2000 appearance. "The A2000 was a good idea in all respects except it turned our sweet little delicate hi-tech box into this big industrial strength metal clad tank of a computer," he says. "It was contrary to what we wanted in terms of the cool sex appeal of the original Amiga."

Mical hoped for more from the Amiga 2000. "We thought it was going to be more powerful, a better bus, faster RAM, a faster CPU, and with more features in the graphics chip," says Mical. "That probably was a good choice in the end, all things considered, because it was less ambitious and therefore it had better performance and better [backward] capabilities."

Dave Haynie sensed the backlash from the Amiga engineers against the new appearance. "After years and years, I don't think anybody thought I was part of the evil empire just because I built the Amiga 2000, which wasn't the shape that the Los Gatos people wanted of course," says Haynie.

Gould and Rattigan

Rattigan achieved Irving Gould's goal of making Commodore profitable and he continued to increase profits. For the quarter ending December 1986, Commodore posted $22 million in earnings. Revenues for the quarter were $270.8 million, down $68.4 million from the same quarter a year earlier, but that was understandable considering it had been over a year since Commodore had released new products. Commodore had even reduced their bank debt by $110 million in the last 10 months. Soon, Commodore would be a profit machine capable of full-scale advertising.

Rattigan also turned Commodore into a strategic success. When Rattigan took over, Commodore was still suffering from the short term strategies of Tramiel, who delivered diverse, incompatible computers as though they were calculators. Now Commodore could concentrate on evolving their core technology, the Amiga. He targeted both segments of the market, with the low-end Amiga 500 and the high end Amiga 2000. The original Amiga, now dubbed the Amiga 1000, would be soon be

---

[5] *Compute!* magazine, "Commodore's New, Expandable Amiga 2000" (March 1987), p. 8.

phased out. The C64 and C128 were now remnants of the old ways, helping to pay the bills until they died.

For a man who did not use computers, Rattigan's vision of the computer industry was clear and far-reaching. In an interview with Commodore Magazine in early 1987, he displayed an uncanny degree of accuracy in predicting the digital communications industry that culminated with the Internet. When asked if he included *QuantumLink* with the C64c because he thought telecommunications was the future of computing, Rattigan started his reply by saying, "Most of the services are a step ahead of their time."[6]

Rattigan was even garnering software support from some of the biggest software makers of the day. *Word Perfect* was indisputably the most popular word processing package in the eighties and into the nineties. By early 1987, Rattigan lured the Word Perfect Corporation into developing their flagship product for the Amiga.

Commodore stock was now on a rapid climb from 4 7/8 a year earlier to 11 ¼. Rattigan's stock plan paid off for every employee at Commodore. According to Rattigan, the price continued rising. "We got it to 15 bucks and I think everybody got 10% of their pay," says Rattigan.

Irving Gould watched Rattigan's every move. According to R.J. Mical, Gould was an astute financier. "He surprised me because in the beginning he struck me as someone who was just the money guy, who was out of touch with what was actually going on with his company," says Mical. "But that turned out to be wrong. He was a lot more in touch with what was actually happening with the company, where the engineering was going, and what sort of steps the company needed to take to become profitable."

Since handing over the company to Rattigan, Gould rarely visited Commodore headquarters. "He had a small suite of offices in the *Seagram* building in New York," says Rattigan. "In my tenure at Commodore, he was only down to West Chester once and I literally had to insist that he come down."

Instead, he monitored the company through phone calls with select employees, a practice that irritated Rattigan. "He used to spend a lot of

---

[6] Commodore not only distributed QuantumLink, but also made a sizable investment in the company. QuantumLink founder Steve Case eventually changed the name to *America On-Line* (AOL). In late 1999, his company was worth more than any other technology company was. If Commodore kept their original investment, they would have gained billions of dollars.

time on the phone talking to people," says Rattigan. "If he happened to talk to you, and you said something he found particularly insightful, then my phone would ring and I never knew where this was coming from."

Most engineers held a positive view of Rattigan. "I met him a couple of times and he seemed like a good guy to me," says Haynie. After the financial turnaround, Commodore employees were impressed with their CEO. Commodore magazine gave an in depth interview with Thomas Rattigan, celebrating the recent successes. Rattigan was clearly becoming a hero to management and employees in the company.

According to R.J. Mical, one of the few people who frequently spoke with Gould, the opinion was not uniform throughout the company. "He was always the solid business guy when our business guys dealt with him," says Mical. "I know that some people thought he was pretty strong while others thought he was pretty weak and had to go."

Unfortunately, the relationship between Gould and Rattigan had deteriorated rapidly since Rattigan received his five-year contract in early 1986. According to a report in the Philadelphia Inquirer, "Despite his success, Rattigan's high-profile manner was said to have annoyed Irving Gould..."[7]

Gould's perception seemed at odds with reality. Rattigan clearly remained focused on business and, if anything, he ignored the spotlight. When asked if it bothered him that Jack Tramiel and John Scully were media celebrities and not many people knew Rattigan's name, Rattigan responded, "When you have lost something in the range of $270 million in five quarters, I don't think it's time to be a media celebrity. I think it's time to get back to your knitting and figure out how you're going to get the company making money."[8]

When asked if he sensed any jealousy from Gould, Rattigan replies, "Other people have said that. There was an article in Business Week or the Wall Street Journal where Irving was quoted as saying something that led you to believe he was spending a lot of time getting involved with me." In truth, Gould spent most of his time traveling.

It seemed like Gould wanted to claim some of the recent success as his own. "Maybe it just had a lot to do with getting credit," says Rattigan. "I think it was difficult for a lot of people to understand. Here he was, Chairman of the Board and I think when things were going well, it may have caused him some angst in terms of 'where do I fit into this?'"

---

[7] *The Philadelphia Inquirer* newspaper, "In the Executive Suites, the Pink Slip is Showing" (May 3, 1987), p. A01.

[8] *Commodore* magazine, "What Next for Commodore?" (May 1987), p. 80.

The New Amigas – 1986 to 1987

Rumors began to spread through Commodore about tension within the top executives. "Everyone talked about it, but I never saw it," says Mical. "People knew that there was a lot of heavy hitting going on up in politics land at Commodore but we weren't privy to the actual details of it."

Dave Haynie believes Rattigan's increased control of Commodore bothered Gould. "From what I recall, [Rattigan] was definitely trying to increase his power base," says Haynie. "It wasn't like you could actually get rid of Gould, but you could certainly make sure that the people who reported to you were loyal to you and put your own people in place and take over from a functional point of view."

Rattigan had built a loyal team around him, including his right hand man in North America, Nigel Shepherd, and chief financial officer Mike Evans. According to Haynie, Rattigan even tried to bring his own son into Commodore, a move echoing Jack Tramiel. "I originally thought his son was going to be some sort of rich daddy's boy thrust upon us, but the guy was actually a good guy," says Haynie. "He was just one of the guys, but you did kind of have to behave."

Haynie believes Rattigan wanted his son in a marketing role. "He seemed like he was in there and really wanted to learn this stuff," he recalls. "He was just kind of in there walking around learning. I guess he was going to be a marketing guy. He was *really* trying to learn every detail and that's what a marketing person should do."

To reform Commodore, Rattigan had to take control. "In all fairness to Rattigan, I think that was absolutely something that was necessary in order to change the way things had worked," says Haynie. "I think [Rattigan] was doing the right thing."

For his part, Thomas Rattigan was well aware of Irving's unbreakable hold on Commodore and the reasons for Jack Tramiel's dismissal. "He had about six million of the 30 million shares," explains Rattigan. "In the public company sense, that really put him in the control position. That eventually led to he and Jack having a falling out."

Rattigan did not intend to usurp control from Gould. "In the final analysis, he was still chairman of the board and he controlled the board, so there was no way I would be answerable other than to the board," says Rattigan. "If you didn't recognize that you had an IQ less than 60. That's not a fight you pick unless you have a death wish."

According to newspaper articles, Gould was impatient with delays in the Amiga 500 and Amiga 2000. "By November, Gould was telling a securities analyst that he was unhappy at the slowness with which the company was getting off the ground with two new models of the

Amiga."[9] After the disastrous Amiga 1000 strategy, devised by Marshall Smith and Irving Gould, it seemed like Gould wanted instant success.

Rattigan dismisses the comments. "That was a manifestation of a whole host of things rather than the singular comment about the timing," says Rattigan. "The one thing I walked away from that industry knowing was that optimism in terms of due dates was often misplaced."

The Curse of Commodore: Part IX

In early April 1987, Irving Gould brought in consultants from *Dillon, Read & Co.* to examine management practices. It was an ominous sign, considering the rebound under Rattigan, and was likely a pretense to changes Gould wanted to make. According to Gould, the New York investment-banking and brokerage firm was working with Commodore to help the company find additional equity. The next seven days defied belief.

Thomas Rattigan heard the results of the examination, compiled by a Dillon, Read consultant named Mehdi Ali. "It was discussed internally," says Rattigan. "What Dillon, Read may had said in addition to what was discussed with operating management, God only knows. I suspect some of those discussions might have been somewhat richer than what people like myself were hearing at the time."

Rattigan was understandably suspicious of the consultant. "The job of any consultant is, 'How do I get my next consulting assignment?' It's self preservation. That's just the history of the industry," he says.

Rattigan detected something amiss when Gould scheduled a special board of directors meeting without extending an invitation to Rattigan. "Everybody that was asked to attend gets notification," says Rattigan. "I just heard through the grapevine that there was going to be a meeting."

Since Rattigan was a board member, he had a legal right to attend the meeting. "My lawyers at the time said, 'If there's a board meeting, let's just consider it an oversight. You should attend that meeting.' It was obviously said tongue-in-cheek on their part."

Commodore had five board members, including Rattigan and Gould. "It was a relatively small board," says Rattigan. "There were five or six. Besides Irving you had at least two other Canadians; one was from the *Royal Bank* and one was from the *Bank of Montreal*."

---

[9] *The Philadelphia Inquirer* newspaper, "A New Strategy May be needed for Commodore" (May 4, 1987), p. E01.

The most high profile Commodore board member was Alexander Haig. He was a former Chief of Staff for the Nixon Whitehouse during the Watergate scandal[10] and former Secretary of State under Ronald Regan.

Rattigan had attended many board meetings in the past and felt comfortable with the members. "There were meetings in New York, there was one in Toronto, and there was at least one meeting in the Bahamas," says Rattigan. "There may have even been one meeting in Germany at a trade show at one point in time."

The day of the meeting, he surprised the board members by his unexpected arrival in Toronto. Gould was prepared. "They had an outside lawyer there as well. It was all orchestrated," says Rattigan. "As soon as I saw the lawyer, I knew what was happening at the board level and how they had been instructed to handle themselves."

Rattigan did not have a chance to address the board. "When you know there's a meeting that you haven't been invited to, what are you going to say?" he recalls. "The meeting that I sat in on lasted 30 nanoseconds."

"They immediately called an executive session," explains Rattigan. "I was not a member of the executive committee. That was just people going through set motions on a game board that had been pretty well determined in advance. The board members loyalty at that stage was to [Gould]." The meeting would reconvene the next day, without Thomas Rattigan.

"Shortly after that I was on a plane back to the US of A," he says. The next day, Rattigan contemplated his options. "I talked to my lawyers."

On Thursday, April 16, one of Commodore's lawyers, Joseph C. Benedetti, sent a letter to Rattigan informing him Commodore had suspended his duties. Furthermore, the letter stated, "the board of directors will make a determination as to the termination of your employment for cause at a special board meeting."

Even today, Rattigan struggles to understand the reasons for his termination. "Some people have the belief that a manager is a manager is a manager," he says. "If I can hire this guy and he was good in certain respects but for whatever reason we fell apart, I can go out and hire a guy just like him if not better."

Haynie offers a different insight. "He got crushed by Gould because Gould was always going to be the guy who was pulling the strings when he wanted to be able to pull the strings," says Haynie.

---

[10] Many commentators believed Haig was the infamous 'deep throat' who revealed sensitive information to the press. This was disproved in 2005 when the real deep throat stepped forward.

On the same day, Nigel Shepherd learned from a phone call from Gould that he was terminating four top executives, all of whom reported directly to Shepherd. These included the Chief Financial Officer, the Company Controller, the Treasurer, and the Computer Systems Director for Commodore North America. Shepherd objected and asked if he could talk with Rattigan before the firings went through. Gould told him that Rattigan was no longer involved with Commodore.

Once off the phone, Shepherd talked with Rattigan. "I had lunch with Nigel Shepherd," recalls Rattigan. "He and I had a long conversation and drank a few beers."

Gould learned of Shepherd and Rattigan's meeting, and Shepherd ended up in Gould's cross hairs. "He got questioned on that and I think Nigel told him to stuff it," says Rattigan. Gould immediately terminated Shepherd. The situation had all the similarities of a third-world coup.

"Nigel was very loyal to the company and he was loyal to me, and I think he could have been equally loyal to Irving," says Rattigan. "But I think [Nigel] saw this as an injustice, and he was the kind of guy who wore it on his sleeve and told it like it was."

Rattigan refused to give up. On Monday, April 20, Rattigan drove to work in the morning as usual; after all, he had a contract that said he was the President and CEO until 1991.

Things were noticeably awkward as soon as he entered the building. "The guards had been told not to let me on the premises," says Rattigan. "However, they did not stop me from entering." Rattigan had cultivated friendly relationships with people at all levels of the company and the guards refused to carry out their orders. One of them commented, "What the hell am I going to do? The guy is running the company and turned it around, and I'm going to stop the guy from entering? Are you crazy?"

Rattigan continued up to his office on executive row. "When I went to my office, they had changed the locks on the doors so I couldn't get in," says Rattigan. The lawyers soon noticed him. "They asked me to leave, and I said, 'On what basis?'" The lawyers proceeded to give robotic declarations to the CEO. "It was sort of statement kinds of things; they weren't conversations."

Things turned for the worse when Rattigan took a stand. "I said, 'Well, I'm not leaving,'" recalls Rattigan. "So they called security and asked a couple of the guys to come up."

It was a troubling moment for the guards. "They said, 'Would you mind accompanying me?'" recalls Rattigan. Realizing there was no way to win this fight, Rattigan relieved the tension with humor. "I said, 'Of course I don't mind accompanying you. Just don't throw me down the stairs.'"

Although Gould and his lawyers rejected Rattigan, he felt support from the lowest levels of Commodore. "We were walking down the stairs and both of them said to me, 'This is insane.'" Rattigan assured them there were no hard feelings. "I said, 'Well, that's okay guys, you've got a job to do. Do your job.'"

According to an unnamed Commodore employee, "It was unreal. He couldn't even get the photos of his wife and kids off his desk." Rattigan stood in the parking lot for one last look at the company he helped save, wondering where it all went wrong. "I just got in my car and drove away," he says.

There was one problem for Irving Gould and his board: Rattigan had a legally binding five-year contract with Commodore to expire July 1, 1991. In the characteristic madness that is Commodore, Gould fired Rattigan only eight months into the contract. According to the contract, Rattigan was to be paid $600,000 for the first two years of his service and $400,000 for the final three years. In the third year as CEO Gould would allow Rattigan to purchase $6 million worth of Commodore stock for $5000.

On Wednesday, April 22, Rattigan filed a lawsuit against Commodore for breach of contract. He was seeking lost wages and stock options totaling $9 million. In the lawsuit, Rattigan noted that since January 1987, Gould had steadily diminished his authority and responsibilities. Among the charges, Rattigan accused the board of hiring and firing senior management without telling him.

The outside world found out about the dismissal on Thursday, April 23 when the New York Times, the Wall Street Journal, and the Philadelphia Inquirer broke the story. According to the Inquirer, it was "...a move that has astonished and confused both employees and investors."

The newspapers also revealed that Gould named himself CEO. The intrigue affected Commodore's stock price. The day Rattigan filed suit, the stock started a slow dive that would last for years. At first, the stock dropped $0.50 from $12.37. Then when the news broke publicly, it dropped a further $1.50 to $10.37.

Gould went to the press to state his case. He claimed he had dismissed his top executives because of his disappointment in Commodore North America sales. According to Gould, European sales accounted for 70% of Commodore International revenue at the time.

Days after Rattigan's departure, Gould began cleaning out the Rattigan faithful. As Rattigan recalls, "Anybody that I brought in or was high on was in some state of imminent danger." On Friday, April 24, Gould laid off 50 white-collar Commodore workers in administrative positions. Anyone who supported Rattigan was out. The purging of Rattigan supporters continued for the next month.

On May 29, Gould eliminated Michael Evans, vice president and chief financial officer of Commodore North America. "Two gigantic mistakes they made were getting rid of Nigel [Shepherd] and the second one was when they got rid of Mike Evans," says Rattigan. "I heard subsequently that Irving said one of the biggest mistakes he made was letting Mike go. It was absolutely foolish. The guy was indispensable on the administrative side and on the financial side."

Rattigan believes many of the dismissals were due to the Dillon-Read consultants. "You have to ask, did Irving make the decision, or did somebody else influence him to make the decision?" he says. "I think that was probably the outside consultants figuring they had to hit a double or a triple to show that they knew what they were talking about and get the extension on whatever contractual deal they had."

Ironically, an upbeat interview with Rattigan appeared in the May issue of Commodore Magazine, just after the turmoil. The company magazine operated on a three-month lead-time for articles and was already in print by the time Rattigan departed. The article gave Rattigan credit for the turnaround, something Irving could not abide.

Commodore Magazine publisher Diane LeBold, who previously ended her editorial column after mentioning Jack Tramiel's legacy, was in trouble again. With the three-month publishing delay, Diane's last issue was August 1987. The long time publisher of Commodore Magazine departed the company.

On June 12, 1987, Commodore filed a $24 million countersuit against Rattigan. In the lawsuit, Commodore claimed that 'willful disobedience' by Rattigan cost the company millions in needless expenses. Gould claimed Rattigan behaved antagonistically and therefore was not entitled to the benefits in his contract. Today, Rattigan is amused by the countersuit. "I still have that on the top of my bills here. One of these days I'll write them a check," he says.

Rattigan feels Gould wanted to intimidate him into a lower settlement. "That's all posturing and nonsense," he says. "I guess the average person who got notification of something like that would reach for their chest and be in the throes of a heart attack."

Both sides made their claims to the US District Court, Southern District of New York. "There had been a series of depositions that were taken on both sides," says Rattigan. "I think they had me in for deposition for five days. [Nigel Shepherd] turned out to be an unbelievably helpful witness in the trial."

Commodore lawyers dragged the lawsuit out as long as possible. "In that four year period, there was movement of paper back and forth and a few things like that," says Rattigan. "That's a pretty typical strategy."

Four years later, the trial came before a judge. "Court appearances didn't take place until 1991," says Rattigan. He eventually won his $9 million lawsuit and Commodore lost their $24 million countersuit.

Although the lawsuit undoubtedly hurt Commodore, Rattigan left the company with good finances. "When I left, which is just a kind way of saying I was thrown out the door, we had built a very substantial eight-figure number on reserves and accruals that we had on the balance sheet," claims Rattigan. "When I say substantial, I mean very substantial." When pressed for the figure, Rattigan replies, "You wouldn't be wrong in saying it was greater than $50 million."

Commodore had money in the bank and could afford to advertise their upcoming computers, the Amiga 500 and Amiga 2000. "When bringing the company out of near bankruptcy, and then earning profits behind all of that, we had created an impeccably conservative balance sheet," says Rattigan. "It set them up for a long while."

The Battle against the Tramiels

After winning round one, the Tramiels continued their attack on Commodore with the Atari ST. "They tried to hype it, saying that it was better than the Amiga with more power, more this, more that, and less expensive," recalls Mical. "It was less expensive but it wasn't more powerful. It didn't have the right operating system and it didn't have good graphics."

Mical blames the Atari ST's shortcomings on Jack's crippling schedule. "The Atari ST had a lot of good features and the engineers that worked on it were a brilliant lot of guys," he says. "They did a good job based on what they had but what they didn't have was time. That's why they had to cut a lot of features and make it not as powerful as it might have been."

By 1987, many 8-bit computer owners were ready to upgrade to the 16-bit market. Unfortunately, the Amiga 1000 was too expensive. The Atari ST dominated. With the creation of the Amiga 500, Commodore had a new weapon to face off against Atari. It was now up to CEO Gould to carry out the plan.

Thomas Rattigan had set the price of the Amiga 500 at $649 and the Amiga 2000 at $1,495. Irving immediately raised prices. The Amiga 500 went to $699 while the Amiga 2000 went to $1,995. It was a peculiar move at a time when the Amiga needed market penetration.

In June 1987, Commodore released the Amiga 500 to dealers. Although Rattigan had planned to market the Amiga 500 to the retail consumer market, Gould chose to ignore the June 1987 CES show, and instead brought the Amiga 500 to Comdex. It was a strange move. How could Commodore sign up large retail stores without attending CES?

Gould met with over 200 Commodore dealers at the spring 1987 Comdex in Atlanta. His executives promised Commodore would finally do some advertising for the Amiga. Despite the promise, years passed without any proper advertising. Dealers promoted the Amiga themselves with in-store demonstrations.

"The best Commodore ever achieved with distribution was what I would call second tier computer dealers, as contrasted to really being where the action was in terms of the higher end computer retailers," explains Rattigan.

Kmart was a major reason for the success of the Commodore 64. Now, Commodore Business Machines chose to ignore Kmart. "They got real ballsy and rejected some of [Kmart's] return policies," says Haynie. "Kmart had the same kind of policy that Walmart has now: 'We can return this item any time we want in any condition and you have to take it back'. Commodore said no. That's when they were going into Sears only and not Kmart."

Other regions marketed the Amiga differently. Jim Dionne, the General Manager of Commodore Canada, chose to sell the Amiga 500 in Kmart stores where he met with the same kind of success the C64 enjoyed earlier.

For their part, Commodore developed two infomercials to promote the Amiga, which they distributed to dealers on videotape. Despite the tacky music and production qualities, the infomercials powerfully displayed the features of the Amiga 500. The first video, at nine minutes long, highlighted the technical features of the Amiga, including Intuition, true multitasking, graphics and sound. The second 14-minute video highlighted the remarkable diversity of software.

Live demonstrations provided the most powerful promotional tools. The Boing Ball demo was always a favorite, as well as RoboCity. With the advent of ray traced 3-D images, Commodore developed a new demo featuring a juggler. The Juggler demo was incredible for the time and highlighted the animation capabilities of the Amiga. It featured an abstract juggler with three glass balls, each perfectly refracting the light within the spheres. Most people had not seen pre-rendered graphics in 1987 and the effect was astounding.[11]

The failure to market the Amiga 500 through mass-market retail stores affected the company stock price. By October 1987, shares were down to $8.50. It was obvious the market was not confident in Irving Gould's strategy.

Even so, the Amiga 500 soon surpassed the Atari ST in sales. In late 1986, magazines revealed that Atari was not as successful as people first thought. Atari filed a prospectus with the Security Exchange Commission, which revealed the company had only sold 150,000 units as of June 30, 1986. This compared to about 25,000 Amiga units sold by early 1986. The Atari ST had not outsold the Amiga 1000 by ten to one, as first reported.

R.J. Mical recalls the battles between Atari ST and Amiga users. "[The Atari ST] was really attractive to a lot of people," says Mical. "The religious wars flared over which machine was better and I'm sure you could find any number of former Atari ST believers who strongly disagree with me that the Amiga was the superior machine. History agrees it was the inferior machine."

The Amiga was initially second to the Atari ST with game releases. When sales of the Amiga 500 improved, Atari ST software support faded away in favor of the Amiga. Soon, the Amiga software market overflowed with games. "They gave it the old college try, but the Amiga won," says Mical.

In the first half of 1989, it was apparent the Atari ST was dying. Atari earnings fell sharply in the first half of 1989. By 1992, Atari began to see staggering losses, which spelled the end for Atari.[12]

Amigas Everywhere

As the years passed, the Amiga began to attract graphical artists. Before flatbed scanners, hardware developers pioneered scanner

---

[11] The Juggler demo is seen in Tom Petty's 1987 video, "Jammin' Me"

[12] The end of the Atari ST was also the end for the GEM operating system from Digital Research. Gary Kildall, CP/M inventor and television co-host of Computer Chronicles, had to contend with a lawsuit by Apple against the supposed similarities of GEM with the Macintosh. It was a slap in the face to Kildall, who invented the personal computer operating system. Kildall quit Digital Research in 1991. In July 1994, the ex-Navy man had a fight at the Franklin Street Bar and Grill in Monterey, California. Three days later, he died of head injuries at the age of 52.

technology on the Amiga. The early scanners consisted of a pole with a digital camera on top. To scan an image, the user moved the camera up and down to center the image and focused it manually.

Scanner technology allowed users to import photographs into the Amiga. Graphic editing software, such as Electronic Arts' Deluxe Paint, allowed users to modify and touch up their digital art. Games such as *The Pawn* included digitized loading screens that looked as good as the box cover. The Amiga started a revolution in digital images.

The Amiga technology found its way into arcade machines as well. Bally, which had a relationship with Commodore stretching back to the VIC-20 days, used the Amiga motherboards and chips in their arcade machines in 1987.

With Virtual Reality becoming a common buzzword, the Amiga hardware became the center of many VR systems. A company called *Virtuality* created an Amiga based VR system that appeared in arcades and shopping malls.

The original Amiga engineers knew the Amiga was capable of playing and editing video, something no other personal computer at the time could match. "We were trying to pitch the Amiga as the premier video editing platform in the industry," says Mical. "Commodore saw the wisdom in using that as one of the main selling points of the machine."

This unique ability made it appropriate for laserdisc games. A company called *American Laser Games* used the Amiga hardware for their games, including *Mad Dog McCree, Bounty Hunter, Crime Patrol, Gallagher's Gallery, Mad Dog II - The Lost Gold, Space Pirates,* and *Who Shot Johnny Rock?*.

Third party developers created Genlock cards, which plugged into the special video card slot developed by Dave Haynie. The premier hardware and software combination was *Video Toaster*, developed by a company called NewTek. The company began work on their application in early 1987, and it finally shipped in October 1990.[13] The Video Toaster allowed users to add wipes, fades, and credits over their existing video. It also allowed special effects, such as the 'Star Trek transporter' effect. The second part of the software package was a full 3D rendering suite for professional logos and introductions.

The Amiga quickly captured the video editing market. "For the longest time, the Amiga was regarded as *the* machine to do desktop video," says

---

[13] Brad Carvey, brother of Dana Carvey from *Saturday Night Live*, was one of the NewTek engineers. It was rumored that Saturday Night Live used the Video Toaster to generate effects for *Wayne's World* skits.

Mical. Major Hollywood pictures used it for special effects. Films such as Warlock, Robocop 2, and Back to the Future Part II used the Amiga. Science fiction television shows also used the Amiga to render special effects sequences, such as Babylon 5, Seaquest DSV, and Star Trek: Voyager.

The digital video and graphics market was not large enough to sustain Commodore. Mass storage mediums, such as CD-ROM's, were not widespread yet, and the Internet was not in widespread use to facilitate the distribution of videos. In many ways, the Amiga was too far ahead of its time for even Commodore to understand and realize its potential. "The long-term vision of the company was wrong," says Al Charpentier. "The Amiga was a good product, but that was too little, too late."

CHAPTER

23

A Radical New Direction

1988-1992

When Irving Gould took over as CEO of Commodore International, many believed he did not possess the drive or charisma to lead his employees to victory. Jack's battle cry was, "Computers for the masses, not the classes." Irving did not have a battle cry. As Forbes magazine writer Evan McGlinn remarked, "Maybe the jet-setting Irving Gould should let someone else call the shots."

Toy, Copperman, and Ali

Gould's constant jetting around the globe meant Commodore needed a competent president to run the day-to-day operations at the U.S. headquarters. More importantly, Gould needed someone who could recapture the US market. After Thomas Rattigan and Nigel Sheppard departed, it took seven months to find a replacement.

In October 1987, Gould named Max Toy as president and Chief Operating Officer of Commodore Business Machines in North America. The president came to Commodore with more computer industry experience than any before him did. Toy started at IBM where he worked in a variety of sales and marketing positions, then he moved to the highly successful Compaq Corporation, where he was vice president of sales.

Gould instructed Toy to lead "the company towards our goal of recapturing our market share in the United States." His tenure depended on the success or failure of this goal.

Industry observers liked the forty-something president's straightforward, honest approach. Most importantly, Toy was a true believer in the Amiga. He previously worked for IBM and Compaq and knew the Amiga stood above the other PC clone computers.

A Radical New Direction – 1988 to 1992

For a Commodore executive, Toy kept a high profile. He gave a full interview to Compute! magazine in their August 1988 issue. A month later, Toy began appearing in print advertisements for Q-Link, the online service Commodore invested in under Thomas Rattigan.

Commodore employees were generally favorable towards Toy. "He gave good talk and he sounded like he had some plans on what he was going to do," says Dave Haynie.

Commodore showed a profit of $6.3 million for the quarter ending September 1988; not outstanding but at least it was not a loss. Unfortunately, Irving was expecting a larger turnaround and began losing patience with Toy. "He didn't last too long," says Haynie.

In 1989, Irving Gould found a potential replacement in a former Apple executive. "Jean-Louis Gasse was approached to run Commodore," says Haynie. "He had been the head of technology at Apple."

According to Haynie, Gasse was enthusiastic about running Commodore. Unfortunately, he wanted more control than Gould was willing to give him. "They wanted him to run engineering," recalls Haynie. "He basically said, 'I'm going to need to be in charge of everything for three years to turn this company around.' He was happy to do it." If Gasse joined Commodore, he would be the first person to run the company with technical knowledge and vision. "Of course, they said no," says Haynie.[1]

Gould hired a former Dillon Read investment banker by the name of Mehdi Ali as president of Commodore International. Ali intended to work out of Gould's New York offices. Dave Haynie believes Gasse would have been a far better choice. "It's hard to imagine [Gasse] could have been any worse than having the nineties management team in charge," he says.

Ali acted as the day-to-day man for Gould while he was away in his jet. According to those who knew him, Ali did not particularly care about the Amiga or computers. His main goal was to keep Gould happy.

In late April 1989, Gould announced that Max Toy left the company to pursue other interests. The departure did not have the drama of the Tramiel or Rattigan departures. On the same day of his resignation, Gould announced a new North American president.

The replacement was Harold Copperman, a 42-year-old former vice president and General Manager of Eastern Operations for Apple. Before that, Copperman served for 20 years at IBM. Gould wanted someone

---

[1] Gasse went on to create the *BeBox*. According to Haynie, "[The Commodore talks] got him interested in starting up a computer company and doing in the nineties what Amiga had done in the eighties. That's the catalyst of where *Be Incorporated* came from."

who knew advertising and Copperman seemed a logical choice. Perhaps he believed Copperman could bring the Apple salesmanship to Commodore.

Employees were more favorable towards the relatively young Copperman. "I actually had a conversation with Harry Copperman," says Haynie. "I liked him a lot. I liked that he was actually planning to organize different sales divisions in the United States."

Back in late 1987, Gould had promised a major television advertising campaign for the Amiga 500, which never materialized. For the quarter ending June 1989, Commodore reported a loss of $10.1 million dollars, the first loss since 1987. It was clear Commodore needed to do something to stop the bleeding. Gould finally authorized a major advertising campaign for the Amiga 500 worth $15 million dollars.

Copperman was in charge of the campaign. He hired advertising agency *Messner Vetere Berger Carey Schmetterer* to produce the commercials. Steven Spielberg's *Amblin Entertainment* would film the commercials. RJ Mical was enthusiastic about the long overdue ad campaign. "A long time later, they finally got around to doing these really cool ads where they invited Spielberg," says Mical. "They did a really cool set of commercials."

According to Dave Haynie, it was a first for Spielberg. "They got Spielberg involved doing his first commercial ad campaign ever because he liked the Amiga so much," says Haynie. "It was just so much more than we were ever expecting."

Amblin hired George Lucas' *Industrial Light and Magic* (ILM) to produce the special effects. ILM had previously used the Amiga for Back to the Future II. Amblin also contracted a company called *Silent Software* to produce Amiga animations for the commercials.

The $15 million advertising blitz would feature three commercials directed by Matthew Robbins, who previously directed *Batteries Not Included* (1987) for Amblin. The commercials featured Stevie Palmer, a true eighties teenager who used a lot of mousse in his hair.

The first commercial depicts three girls watching a music awards show. Suddenly the image flickers and next-door neighbor Stevie is on television winning an award. Stevie and his friends are using Genlock and a video camera to produce the illusion.

The second commercial, slightly more ambitious, shows Stevie creating a 3D model of his house using a CAD program. "It's just so cool!" says Mical. "The whole house takes off and lifts up off the foundation and goes into the air." Stevie's parents are startled awake as their bed shifts. The commercial, which featured composer Dave Grusin's musical score from *The Goonies* (1985), obviously represents a higher budget compared to the original 1985 Amiga commercials.

The final commercial shows a succession of grey haired or minor celebrities coming to the Palmer residence and asking for Stevie. These include astronauts Buzz Aldrin, Gordon Cooper, and Scott Carpenter, who ask for Stevie's help with a space station. "There's this kid playing in his bedroom and the astronauts come over and he's showing them stuff on the computer and they're all like, 'Ooh-ah,'" describes Mical. "They are real honest-to-God astronauts in the commercial." Next, the *Pointer Sisters* arrive asking Stevie for some help with a song. Tommy Lasorda of the *Los Angeles Dodgers* arrives for some statistical help. Finally, former house speaker Tip O'Neil comes to the door.

According to Dave Haynie, the commercials aired frequently but not as much as the competition. "Nintendo's first year with the Nintendo 64, they spent more on commercials in the United States than they spent on developing the thing," he recalls. "Commodore never hit that peak but it was pretty regular. It would be hard to miss it."

The commercials arrived prior to the Christmas 1989 season, two years behind the launch of the Amiga 500 and four years behind the launch of the Amiga 1000. "Is that pathetic or what?" says Mical.

Bil Herd recalls his reaction to the belated campaign. "When I'd see years later they tried an Amiga commercial, it was sad," says Herd. "It was already too late by this time."

Commodore also produced a series of stylish print ads featuring celebrity Amiga users. Included in the ads were blues guitarist B.B. King, Los Angeles Dodgers manager Tommy Lasorda, and former House Speaker Tip O'Neill. The ads appeared in major print publications, including Time magazine.

The advertising blitz had a positive impact on sales. For the previous quarter ending September 1989, Commodore lost $6.5 million on sales of $165 million. After the ad campaign, sales were up to $200 million with earnings of $7 million for the same period. Overall, Commodore estimated a 50 percent growth in sales of the Amiga product line. Unfortunately, it would be the last major advertising campaign from Commodore.

The Amiga Evolution

While Commodore marketing took hold of product development during the Plus/4, the Amiga years were engineering driven. "In the Amiga days, marketing didn't know what they wanted so we had to tell them," says Haynie.

After designing the Amiga 2000, Haynie continued evolving the system with faster Motorola processors and more memory. "We had the A2000/20 in 1988 and we had the A2000/30 in 1989; that was the A2000 with the 68020 and 68030 processors," recalls Haynie. "They went from 7 MHz to 14 MHz, then to 25 MHz. You had 2 or 4 megabytes of fast memory as well."

Haynie developed a new motherboard for each revision. "I started doing the A2620 board which was our first 68020 board, with Bob Welland," says Haynie. "Halfway through the project he left to go work at Apple[2] so I finished up the A2620 and then I did the A2630. Then I went right into the A3000."

The engineering teams remained small. "Over the years, we were doing the work of entire organizations within the PC industry," says Haynie. "We had maybe 40 people working on all this stuff versus a company the size of Apple which has 40 people per project."

Designing the new Amiga 3000 were Dave Haynie, George Robbins, Greg Berlin, and Hedley Davis. Everyone worked under the vice president of engineering, Dr. Henri Rubin. Rubin regularly came to work with buttons missing from his shirts and habitually wore a bow tie. "He was a little crazy, but other than that he was great," says Haynie.

Most engineers felt affection for their leader because he was one of the few executives who truly believed in the Amiga. "He had to have the fastest, best Amiga that you could get on his desk and he tried to do everything possible on it," says Haynie. "That made him aware of what was possible and what wasn't. In other words, he was doing exactly what a manager should do."

The other manager who used an Amiga was Jeff Porter. "Jeff Porter always had some sort of Amiga on his desk," recalls Haynie. "You could go to other parts of the building and there would be nothing but PC's in some of the financial departments; probably Commodore clones."

Haynie had ambitious plans for the Amiga 3000. "There's a lot of stuff I could do at the system level for the high end because it didn't have to be quite so cheap," says Haynie. The Amiga 3000 would be a powerful graphics workstation designed to fill the video production niche. It would also use the new Amiga OS 2.0.

At the heart of the Amiga 3000 was the 32-bit Motorola 68030 processor, described at the time as a mainframe on a chip. The new Amiga ran at a then amazing 25 megahertz, over three times the speed of

---

[2] According to Haynie, "He was one of the guys on the Newton. He apparently came up with the concept for their operating system."

A Radical New Direction – 1988 to 1992 515

the original Amiga 2000. It would also include a fast SCSI hard drive, two megabytes of RAM, and the new Zorro III expansion slots.

MOS Technology chip designers Bob Raible and Victor Andrade had improved the Original Amiga Chipset (OCS) with an Extended Chipset (ECS). Among other things, the improved Super Denise chip could now display resolutions of 640 by 480 non-interlaced, 1280 by 200, or 1280 by 256.

"I would usually deal with one chip designer at a time when I'm building a new system," says Haynie. "Occasionally we'd have meetings and we'd hash out all the details between the systems people and software people and chip designers. Then they'd be gone for six months or a year and come back saying, 'Here's your chip!'"

By 1990, the IBM PC and Macintosh were catching up to the Amiga in graphics capability. "You had VGA by then, which was really slow but it gave a lot more colors," says Haynie. "You had the Mac II, which also had a slow 256-color card."

According to Haynie, several factors allowed the competition to catch up with the Amiga graphics. "The first reason was that the chip group didn't get enough resources so they couldn't advance the chip technology fast enough," says Haynie. "It really was a matter of not reinvesting enough money in the technology. We had plenty of hard work, which is why we kept up as well as we did."

"The second reason was that I couldn't solve it at the system level by putting in somebody else's graphic chip or designing my own, because the software didn't permit what we called retargetable graphics," he explains. "We had huge powerful graphics rather than fairly simple graphics, which was a little bit too close to the hardware."

To make the graphics retargetable, the engineers had to modify the original operating system. "It needed work and work was being done," says Haynie. "The changes that went into OS 2.0 and OS 3.0 were basically the prerequisites you needed to support retargetable graphics."

Haynie enjoyed working for Henri Rubin. "[Jeff Porter] and Henri were running [engineering], but Henri was this guy that you had to look after a bit," says Haynie. "He had been an engineer and he understood the engineering process. I was perfectly happy working with him even though he did have his crazy points."

The engineers invented a term called 'being Henried', which essentially meant your day was ruined. "I think he sometimes drove his software people to want to kill him," says Haynie. Engineers sometimes came into work with their agenda set for the day, only to run into Henri in the hall. After a few words, the engineers suddenly had to carry out a new directive. They had been Henried.

As the Amiga 3000's deadline neared, Rubin decided to motivate his engineers. Normally, management gave engineers free frozen dinners, soft drinks, and pizza to entice them to stay longer hours. This day Henri felt they needed spiritual motivation.

According to Director of Software Andy Finkel, Henri called Finkel into his office and said he was going to give the engineers a pep talk. Finkel nervously told his boss, "Henri, I don't think this is a good idea."

Henri replied, "Andy, I'm glad you agree. Now let's do it!" and marched into the engineering area. The engineers tore themselves away from their work and assembled around their leader.

For the next fifteen minutes, Rubin gave a motivational speech more suited to a football locker-room. According to Finkel, he used every available cliché to motivate them. "Win one for the gipper. Go for the gold. There is light at the end of the tunnel. It is always darkest before the dawn." The favorite of the engineers was, "We need an effort like we've never seen before... *again*!"

At the end of his speech, the deflated engineers stood in stunned silence. It was the most uninspiring talk they had ever heard in their lives. After some uncomfortable seconds, Henri offered his assessment, "I take your silence as a vote of commitment."

In 1989, Henri joined the board of directors, giving the engineers greater influence within Commodore. While the high-end Amiga evolved, the low-end Amiga 500 had no significant changes from 1987 to 1990. "They did some revisions to the A500 during that time," says Haynie. "They revised it to take more chip memory and use some newer versions of the FAT Agnus."

With the introduction of the new ECS chipset, the Amiga 500 would receive a chip upgrade. Commodore named it the Amiga 500+.

Commodore released the Amiga 3000 on April 24, 1990. Reaction was positive and small news items appeared in dozens of magazines. As usual, Commodore North America failed to advertise the computer, even in print. The machine was on its own.

Things were better in Europe. The Europeans hosted a developer's conference in Paris, which Commodore used to unveil the Amiga 3000. "We would have a developer's conference every year in Europe," says Haynie.

Haynie received the ultimate tribute when he met with Jay Miner in Paris. "Jay was invited out to give a talk at the conference," recalls Haynie. "Before then, we crossed paths and never really had anything to say, but when we introduced that in Paris he kind of liked it. I think I actually got a smile or two out of Jay when he saw the Amiga 3000. We had a few diners together and talked about it."

C65

After Bil Herd's departure, further development on the Commodore 64 line stalled. "I can only speculate, but I think they couldn't get themselves in gear," says C64 project manager Charles Winterble. He was correct.

Sometime in the middle of 1989, Commodore ended production on the C128. Hardly any commercial software took advantage of the advanced functionality of the C128 and it failed to extend the C64 legacy.

The C64 remained popular, however. Software makers continued releasing games that pushed it to the limit, including *Times of Lore* (1988), *Myth: History in the Making* (1989), *Project Firestart* (1989), *Rick Dangerous* (1989), *Turrican* (1990), and *Creatures* (1990). The aging hardware also hosted three dimensional polygon games such as *Total Eclipse* (1989), *Mean Streets* (1989), *Space Rogue* (1989), and *Stunt Car Racer* (1989).

Commodore continued experimenting with new products to leverage the success of the C64. According to Thomas Rattigan, "At one point in time, there were talks of making it more of a game machine and less computer-like. That was going on as I was in the midst of Gould and I having our differences of opinion."

Long after Rattigan departed, in late August 1990, Commodore UK released the Commodore 64GS (GS stood for game system). Though it had the same initials as the Apple II GS, it was not an improvement over the C64. In fact, it was a step backwards. The 64GS was an attempt to capture the console success of the Nintendo Entertainment System. To accomplish this, it had no keyboard, two controllers, and a cartridge slot. It was a Max Machine, only four to eight years too late.[3]

Commodore attempted to end C64 production in 1986, 1988, and 1990. Each time, they hoped buyers would migrate to the Amiga and C128. However, the impressive C64 software library was far too compelling for users to abandon. By 1990, the C64 market finally started to fade.

IBM PCs and clones were always the undisputed leader in the office, but now they were selling well in homes. One of biggest reasons for the PC's success was because all through their evolution, users could retain their old software library. This meant IBM kept their old users and consistently added new users. In contrast, each time Apple, Commodore, and Atari made a new computer, they lost their old user base.

---

[3] Of approximately 80,000 GS systems produced, only 25% sold. Commodore cannibalized the remaining stock and used the motherboards in standard C64c computers.

By the late eighties, two things became so obvious even Commodore management could not ignore it. First, the Commodore 64 was a lasting success and the company's biggest profit center. Second, they needed to build on the C64's success.

The strategy was simple. Commodore engineers would increase the speed of the C64 processor and add more memory, while retaining some backward compatibility. The C64 would evolve with the times, as the IBM PC had. Perhaps one day the C64 could even use Bill Mensch's 16-bit and 32-bit processors.

The C64's popularity crested in 1987, so an improved C64 was still very relevant in 1988. In fact, 1988 would have been an optimal year to introduce an improved C64. Development of the C65 started in January 1988. Over a year later, in the spring of 1989, Irving Gould revealed to a South German newspaper that Commodore was developing a machine with functionality between the Amiga 500 and Commodore 64.

A small group of engineers designed the system. Commodore Semiconductor Group would design several custom chips, including a new VIC-III chip and a new microprocessor. A semiconductor engineer named Bill Gardei led the team. "He was one of the chip designers and not a real friendly guy," recalls Dave Haynie. "People didn't like to work with him."

According to Haynie, Gardei sometimes lorded his control over his chip people. "I never really worked with Gardei but I ran into him at one point," he recalls. "It seems that there was a simulation package that ran on one of the VAX [systems] that everybody used for chip design. However, whenever he got pissed off at somebody, you would lose access to that."

Haynie accidentally took away Gardei's source of control. "I didn't know any of this," says Haynie. "I played with the terminal and thought, 'This is way too slow. I'm going to fix it.' At the same time, I was writing a magazine article for Amiga World on the new SAS C++ compiler. So I combined these two jobs and wrote my own viewer using the new C++ compiler."

Haynie's program simultaneously improved on Gardei's old VAX software and freed his chip designers from his grip. "Apparently Bill Gardei did not like that too much," says Haynie. "I built this display program that solved an issue I didn't know existed in this little power struggle that was going on in the chip department."

Engineers were more than happy to indulge in Gardei's wish to make an improved C64. "I think the main reason that the C65 got done is because Bill Gardei was doing it and everyone was happy to not be working with him, so they let him do it," says Haynie.

A Radical New Direction – 1988 to 1992

A new systems engineer named Paul Lassa would design the hardware. "He was basically the systems guy on the C65, with Gardei doing the chips," says Haynie. "Paul Lassa was basically a junior engineer we hired during the Amiga years. He was working for George Robbins for a while on some of the A500 peripherals and he was becoming the senior engineer at that time."

The software engineer on the project was Fred Bowen, who had been with MOS Technology before Commodore. "Fred Bowen was always on the East Coast," says Robert Russell. "Fred was the oldest timer of anybody around. He sat there and cut the lithographs on the floor to make chips."

Bowen also worked on the C128 project with Bil Herd. "Freddy's a little on the short side and more respectful," says Herd. "He was the oldest of us."

The engineers initially dubbed the project the Commodore 64DX (not to be confused with the DX-64 portable), but they later changed the name to the Commodore 65. In the past, Jack often assigned 8-bit projects late in the year, with prototypes expected for the January CES. Ominously, the Commodore 65 project had no apparent deadline.

According to Dave Haynie, the project remained low profile, even within Commodore. "I was entirely 100% uninvolved with the C65 other than knowing it existed," he says. "By the time I knew about it, they were already getting ready to do prototypes."

In a preliminary manual, Fred Bowen, the engineer who steered Bil Herd away from attempting limited C64 compatibility in the C128-mode, describes the C65 concept:

> The C65 microcomputer is a low-cost, versatile, competitive product designed for the international home computer and game market.
>
> The C65 is well suited for first time computer buyers, and provides an excellent upgrade path for owners of the commercially successful C64. The C65 is composed of concepts inherent in the C64 and C128.
>
> The purpose of the C65 is to modernize and revitalize the 10 year old C64 market while still taking advantage of the developed base of C64 software. To accomplish this, the C65 will provide a C64 mode of operation, offering a reasonable degree of C64 software compatibility and a moderate degree of add-on hardware and peripheral compatibility. Compatibility can be sacrificed when it impedes enhanced functionality and expandability, much as the C64 sacrificed VIC-20 compatibility.

It is anticipated that the many features and capabilities of the new C65 mode will quickly attract the attention of developers and consumers alike, thereby revitalizing the low-end home computer market. The C65 incorporates features that are normally found on today's more expensive machines, continuing the Commodore tradition of maximizing performance for the price. The C65 will provide many new opportunities for third party software and hardware developers, including telecommunications, video, instrument control (including MIDI), and productivity as well as entertainment software.

A MOS Technology engineer named Victor Andrade, along with Bill Gardei, would design the C65's special microprocessor. The 4510 CPU, known as 'Victor', was an 8-bit Commodore 6502 core running at 3.54 megahertz. "[Gardei] was pretty clever because the C65 had a lot of what we wanted to put into the C128 back in the day," says Haynie. "The 4510 was an improved 6502 core, which had some or all of the GTE extensions, and some extensions that Hedley Davis came up with."

Curiously, the engineers chose to ignore existing 16-bit technology. "Which 16-bit chip are you going to use, the Mensch chip? The 65816 was kind of a weird chip," says Haynie. "I suggested using it one time and I don't think Fred liked it at all."

"The other problem was that they were very expensive," continues Haynie. "They cost quite a bit more than the 68000 and there was some question about whether there was any quantity available. The other simple reason is that Commodore had finally built their own CMOS 6502 compatible, so why not use it?"

Bill Gardei designed the 4567 VIC-III chip, which engineers referred to as 'Bill' during development. The Vic-III retained all of the original C64 video modes, allowing backward compatibility with C64 software. It even exceeded the Amiga capabilities by producing 320 x 200 with 256 colors, 640 x 400 with 16 colors, and 1280 x 400 with 4 colors. The 256 colors were programmable from a palette of 4,096. The VIC-III could also display 80 columns of text.

The enhanced features of the VIC-III along with backward compatibility impressed Dave Haynie and the other engineers. "I remember getting some flack for the fact that it had more colors onscreen than the A3000 did," recalls Haynie.

The engineers moderately improved the sound. The C65 used the same sound chip as the C64c, the Commodore 8580 SID chip, but they included two of them for stereo sound. Overall, the sound would not be as clear as the Amiga.

A Radical New Direction – 1988 to 1992   521

In C64 mode, the computer ran at 1 MHz with Basic 2.2. The C65 was not as backward compatible as the C128, running about 80% of the C64 software library. Programs that strayed outside the kernel, such as hacker demos and copy-protection schemes, either crashed or acted strangely.

The C65 case resembled a C128 keyboard, with a built in 3.5-inch Shugart disk drive in the number pad area. The computer came loaded with 128 kilobytes of RAM, expandable internally to an amazing 8 megabytes. A trap door on the bottom of the keyboard opened to reveal an expansion slot, much like the Amiga.

Rumors began circulating in Compute!'s Gazette about a new 16-bit C64, which they incorrectly dubbed the C64GS. The machine would reportedly go on sale in November 1989 in the $300 to $350 range; about half the Amiga 500's price.

The next month, Gazette reported that Commodore cancelled the machine. It was only a rumor, and development continued. The engineers missed the Christmas 1989 season. Commodore could not realistically release the C65 in 1990 and expect success without an advertising miracle. "There really wasn't much of a place for an enhanced C64-class machine in the early 1990s," says Haynie.

Bil Herd maintained contact with Commodore engineers and kept track of the troubled C65. His harshest criticism is towards Bill Gardei. "The C65 was doomed to failure," he says. "To begin with, they didn't know what they were doing or how to get there. There was a chip designer who didn't know anything about hardware design. This guy didn't take input and didn't know what he was doing. Freddy [Bowen] tried hard to make it into something and he couldn't push this guy. I've got nothing good to say about the C65."

Part of Herd's frustration with the project stems from his unrequited desire to join the project. "I could be accused of being jealous that nobody would let me come back to fix it," says Herd. "At the time, I was actually between jobs, and at one point I said, 'Hey, can I come back?' By that time the regime had said, 'That wouldn't be a good idea.'"

Herd believes Commodore management refused his reentry due to his past treatment of managers. "I'm basically a threat to anybody that has any authority," he says. Despite his pugnacious attitude, Herd was the best engineer Commodore ever had for fixing problems and getting projects out the door. "I heard one time somebody came out and said, 'Yeah, they admitted today that they wished you were here to fix this problem.' I was like, 'Yeah, but that's not going to get over my shortcomings, is it?' He said, 'No.'"

The C65 project entered development hell, mainly due to costly problems producing the VIC-III chip. The March 1990 issue of

Compute!'s Gazette reported once again it would not be delivered. Amazingly, as Christmas 1990 came and went, Commodore did not even show the C65 privately. In March 1991, Fred Bowen created the first and third chapters for the C65 manual. In it, he acknowledged Commodore was now targeting the C65 to the international market - in other words, anywhere but the United States. It was an acknowledgement they had missed their opportunity.

Herd watched the project sink from afar and wondered what might have been. "I don't mean to sound glib, but I would have handled it correctly," he says. "I don't know sitting here what the correct answer would have been, but I would certainly have figured it out."

By 1991, Commodore had produced at least 205 C65 machines. However, Gould decided the project was no longer viable and he closed the costly project by the end of the year. "The only reason they are rare is because they weren't worth making," says Herd. "It would not have made production quantities. It wouldn't have made the cut with the users. It just wasn't going to fly."

In 1992, C64 production ended and Commodore gave up the 8-bit line of computers. Even in the UK and Germany, sales of the C64 were slow, forcing Commodore to repackage it with software bundles to sell. Dave Haynie wonders if the 8-bit C65 would have been viable. "I don't think there was any real demand for any 8-bit machine in those days, sorry to say, other than nostalgic purposes," says Haynie.

For software makers invested in the success of the C64, it was a disappointment. Perhaps no one was more disappointed that Geos creator Brian Dougherty. The Geos operating system would have benefited the most from faster processor speeds, better resolutions, and more memory. The technology of Geos was so impressive it quite conceivably could have stayed ahead of Microsoft Windows. Unfortunately, the failure to extend the C64 line meant that Geos never had a chance.

CDTV

In the spring of 1990, rumor spread that Commodore was creating a revolutionary new consumer device for the living room. It would take full advantage of the new CD-ROM technology. The strategy suited Commodore because they excelled at mass-producing consumer goods at low cost. Internally, Commodore called the project 'Baby'.

The project director for CDTV was Atari founder Nolan Bushnell, with in-house Commodore engineers designing the system. Bushnell was a strong believer in the product and had a clear vision of CDTV.

On the outside, the CDTV looked almost exactly like a DVD player, which would not appear until 1995. It was a VCR-sized black box and it even had a digital clock on the front. Inside, however, it was a regular Amiga 500 motherboard with a CD-ROM drive. According to David Rosen, Commodore's director of international marketing, "We've taken a Trojan Horse approach by putting computer capabilities into a familiar box."[4] In place of a keyboard and mouse, the system came with an infrared remote control that contained audio CD buttons and a flat game controller with two buttons.

CDTV stored the Kickstart 1.3 operating system on ROM chips. Within seconds of turning CDTV on, it displayed a beautiful rendered title screen. The stylish menu allowed users to choose audio CD tracks or change system settings.

What would home users do with the CDTV? Not even Commodore seemed certain. Rosen saw it as an advanced audio CD player that could also play multimedia software, educational programs, and of course games. It could also play the CD+G (graphics) standard of music CDs, and Commodore promised it would play VCD and CD-i videos once the standards were finalized. Rosen added, "We don't know what we will be doing with the technology two years from now."

Commodore planned an expansion pack called the CD-1500, which included a black keyboard, a black wireless mouse, a black external floppy disk drive, and Workbench 1.3 boot disks. This would allow owners to use the CDTV as a more expensive Amiga 500. Commodore also produced credit card sized memory cards that plugged into the front of the machine to save game locations.

The CDTV was unveiled at the summer 1990 CES in Chicago. The main booth displayed Amiga 500s, IBM PC clones, and even PC notebook computers. Inside a side room, Nolan Bushnell demonstrated *Baby*. Unfortunately, most of the software was not quite stable and the CDTV gave three guru errors during one demonstration. Despite this, industry watchers were impressed.

Press releases from the show claimed the CDTV would launch in November 1990, in time for the lucrative Christmas season. Commodore officials also promised over 100 launch titles, a dubious claim given Commodore's previous record. This time Commodore was serious about ensuring software support for their new system.

Major software companies like Accolade, Cinemaware, Data East, Origin, Lucasfilm, and Sierra lined up to develop software for the new system. Others, like Broderbund and Strategic Simulations, showed strong interest. Even Grolier's was developing an electronic encyclopedia

---

[4] *Compute!* magazine, "Tomorrow TV" (December 1990), p. 16.

524 THE SPECTACULAR RISE AND FALL OF COMMODORE

on CD-ROM for the CDTV. It was an impressive lineup. Unfortunately, software giant Electronic Arts was taking a wait and see attitude.

The press liked what it saw. *Amazing Computing* and *Infoworld*, among others, gave positive coverage. Compute! contributor Shay Addams said, "CDTV stands a good chance of finally coaxing the mass market into accepting computers, which hasn't happened so far because 98 percent of the public has trouble setting digital clocks and VCRs. Commodore hopes to achieve that acceptance by getting rid of the keyboard and not calling it a computer."[5]

As many predicted, Commodore did not meet their aggressive November 1990 release date. Christmas came and went and CDTV was not on store shelves.

At the January 1991 CES in Las Vegas, CDTV was prominently displayed to the public. The new design included MIDI ports. Commodore even promised the CDTV could play full motion video using the upcoming MPEG standard.

Despite missing the Christmas period, Commodore stock went from a low of 4 ½ in October 1990 to around 11 by early 1991, the highest since Rattigan departed. At the time, 20% of U.S. homes had computers, while 75% had VCRs. Investors presumably believed CDTV could capture the rest of the market. Rumors spread about a possible Commodore takeover by Hewlett-Packard, Apple, Sun, and even Disney. None of these rumors panned out, but they helped the stock price.

Although most people assumed CDTV meant Compact Disk Television, Commodore marketing stated it stood for Commodore Dynamic Total Vision. People started calling it exactly how the name sounded: *Seedy TV*. In early 1991, CDTV finally arrived. Commodore marketing wanted to distance CDTV from the Amiga and promoted it as a next generation VCR. They instructed retailers to display it away from other computers.

The 50 launch titles were fewer than the 100 Commodore had promised, but many were impressive. Most were direct Amiga ports by Maxis, Lucasfilm, Cinemaware, Accolade, Psygnosis, and Interplay. Disney delivered classic stories and educational titles for children.

To market the CDTV, Commodore produced an infomercial on videotape for distributors. It emphasized reference libraries, like Grolier Encyclopedia, World Atlas, the King James Bible, a dictionary, and the complete works of Shakespeare. They also prominently displayed educational and children's titles. The infomercial even touted Genlock

---

[5] *Compute!* magazine, "CDTV: The First Wave" (December 1990), p. A-28.

capabilities, explaining how CDTV could add titles and screen effects to home movies.

Commodore intended to sell the CDTV for $999, but the price fell to $599 by the release date. In the U.K., the system sold for £699. The CD-1500 Professional Pack with keyboard, mouse, floppy drive, and Workbench disks sold for approximately $200.

Philips released the CD-i for $1000 that October. CD-i dominated over CDTV, largely due to its movie playing abilities. It also had two killer-app games: *7th Guest* and *Myst*.

Commodore sold 25,800 CDTVs in Germany, under 30,000 in the UK, and a small number in the US. Commodore UK's Kelly Sumner summated its failure. "We got the basics wrong. Wrong price, wrong spec, no support. It came out with Workbench 1.3 when we were launching Workbench 2.0 so the operating system was out of date. It could have done with a bit more RAM and I think it should have come with a built-in 3.5" floppy disk drive."

The failure of CDTV hurt Commodore badly. They had spent millions designing, marketing, and manufacturing the risky machine and it did not pay off. Commodore, like Philips, was too early.[6]

Speed Bumps

Speed bumps are objects that lie in your path and slow you down. Commodore had both real speed bumps made of asphalt in their parking lots and they had figurative speed bumps that the engineers encountered at work.

Joe Mecca, the facilities manager at 1200 Wilson Drive, created the real speed bumps. There were strange rivalries between Commodore departments, none stranger than the rivalry between the facilities department and the engineering group. The saga eventually reached the absurd heights of a Stanley Kubrick movie, causing Dave Haynie to dub it, 'Dr. Strangemecca or: How I Learned to Stop Worrying and Love Giant Speed bumps'.

The rivalry began one morning when Mecca observed an Amiga hardware engineer, Joe 'Augie' Augenbraun, speeding recklessly in the parking lot as he came into work. Rather than ask Augenbraun to keep his speed down, Mecca decided to be more inventive.

Within weeks, he installed asphalt speed bumps in the parking lot. These were not supermarket speed bumps; these were genetically altered, steroid-enhanced speed bumps. The worst were like half-barrels sticking

---

[6] Philips CD-i players lasted until June 1999. By that time, the DVD player had supplanted CD-i.

out of the pavement. "We didn't like them. We all had sports cars and we wanted to drive 60 or 70 miles per hour in the parking lot and there should be no reason that we couldn't do that," quips Haynie. To aggravate employees further, they were only spaced 20 feet apart.

At first, people tried to go around the speed bumps by driving on the grass. Unfortunately, there was a swampy area next to the parking lot dubbed *Lake Mecca*, and drivers inadvertently became stuck. There was no way around the speed bumps. Even the hardiest struts and shock absorbers had trouble overcoming them. Some engineers claimed they had nightmares where they were in hell, forced to drive through the parking lot searching for a parking space for all eternity.

The final insult to the engineers came when Joe Mecca gave himself his own personalized parking space. According to Amiga OS 2.0 developer Bryce Nesbitt,[7] "He had the only reserved parking space in the whole company, and being a modest guy it was spot number one." Commodore engineers could not abide the injustice without taking action.

At 2:00 AM one night, long after the managers and staff had departed, engineers Bryce Nesbitt, Keith Gabryelski, and Mike Sinz went to work. They removed Joe Mecca's parking sign and replaced it with a handicapped sign they 'borrowed' from a parking lot in the West Chester area. With extreme care, using masking tape, they painted over the orange parking lines with bright blue spray-paint, and even painted a wheel-chair icon in the center of the space. It was indistinguishable from the real thing.

The next morning, the engineers positioned themselves strategically so they could witness Mecca pulling into the space. Several could barely contain themselves as the brown Cadillac approached the parking lot, carefully navigating the speed bumps. As he turned into his spot, his car screeched to an abrupt stop.

Mecca swore profusely and began frantically calling departments in Commodore, trying to find who was responsible. Within hours, a work crew repainted the lines orange, sandblasted the wheelchair icon, and carted off the handicapped sign. The Commodore engineers, who were used to long delays while Commodore bureaucracy functioned, were amazed with the speed the situation was handled. Mecca never found the culprits.

Though the prank gratified the engineers, they still searched for a more permanent solution. Pennsylvania receives a large snowfall each winter, and this often brought out snowplows. Sometimes, if snow covered a

---

[7] Bryce Nesbitt is the aforementioned 'little punk' who criticized Bil Herd's C128 at a CES show.

A Radical New Direction – 1988 to 1992

speed bump, the snowplows inadvertently wiped them out, usually ripping out chunks of the paved surface. The engineers grew wise to this, and soon started bringing shovels to work to disguise the speed bumps, hoping the snowplows would annihilate them. This frequently worked, and in celebration, Augenbraun sent a chunk of asphalt to manager Bob Greg through his mail slot, with a note attached saying, "I believe this is yours."

Unfortunately, once the snow melted, crews replaced the speed bumps. Commodore employees saw the cycle as natural as the seasons. Every winter, the snowplows wiped out the speed bumps, then in the spring the road-salts, melting snow, and constant abrasion by vehicles caused the pavement to deteriorate and create massive potholes in their place. Once dry, crews arrived to fill in potholes and replace speed bumps.

The speed bump saga became an ongoing source of friction. Some managers tired of the open defiance of their rules. One day, Augenbraun and some engineers were dropping off some hardware when they noticed Joe Mecca and a paving specialist standing beside the parking lot, surveying the situation. Augenbraun began speeding up between each speed bump, from 0 to 60 miles per hour, and then coming to a quick stop before overcoming each bump. The constant revving and screeching caught Mecca's attention, and he stared down the group with arms folded as they unloaded their hardware.

Undaunted, the group returned to the car and departed in the same manner. Mecca was not happy about people mocking his speed bumps. According to Augenbraun, the next day the speed bumps were four inches higher.

Deciding things were not quite absurd enough, Bryce Nesbitt wrote a memo on official Commodore letterhead lampooning the situation:

> To: All Employees
>
> From: The Facilities Department
>
> Subject: Speed bump rotation plan for early July
>
> Starting on Monday, July 3rd, the facilities department will begin daily reconfiguration and expansion of the important speed bump network at the West Chester facility. Work will be arranged to maximize the disruption and discomfort to all employees. Each day the executive committee will meet to determine pleasing geometric shapes for the day's speed bumps.
>
> The current record for changing the bump network is two hours. This time should drop to under 30 minutes for the planned national championships. Points are gained in the nationals for lowering employee morale, delaying critical

engineering projects, and destruction to suspension complements. The Commodore team is expecting stiff competition from a group of former Pennsylvania Department of Transportation pothole diggers.

Committee chairman Robert Greg said that employees have been "laughing at our efforts to strictly enforce the new totalitarian parking lot regulations." and "It is impossible to overemphasize the importance of parking enforcement."[8]

Mr. Greg is on the record with the statement, "If I had my way, there would be ten more speed bumps in the parking lot. Employees attempting to evade the bumps by parking out front will have their tires slashed. A newly designed stealth paint will be used to conceal the location of bumps to prevent naughty employees from slowing down. In August, existing white lines in the front lot will be further widened to reduce available employee parking space and starting in September the death penalty will be used to deter violation of the 15 MPH speed limit.

Nesbitt distributed the memo around Commodore on bulletin boards in the halls and the cafeteria. Soon, a directive came down from Commodore management that employees could no longer place memos on the official bulletin board without approval. In response, the engineers bought their own bulletin board and placed it next to the official bulletin board. Above it, Nesbitt placed a sign saying, 'Unofficial Bulletin Board'.

Deciding Commodore management might respond to outside pressure, Augenbraun leaked a rumor on Q-Link stating that the cause of loose chips in the Amiga 500 was due to shipping trucks bouncing over the giant speed bumps in the Commodore parking lot. "That was a rumor that was intentionally spread, I'm sure," says Haynie. The rumor was completely unfounded. However, much to the delight of Commodore engineers, the press picked up the rumor and it made its way into the pages of Amiga World and .Info magazine. Augenbraun, the engineer who started the chain of events with his reckless speeding, had the last laugh on everyone.

The asphalt speed bumps were an amusing diversion, but figurative speed bumps at Commodore caused engineers to lose sleep. Irving Gould was losing patience with his management. In late 1990, Gould laid off six high level executives. The Copperman team was in trouble.

---

[8] The latter was a real quote from Robert Greg.

A Radical New Direction – 1988 to 1992

Dave Haynie feels Gould was too impatient. "Nobody lasted too long," says Haynie. "The job you were given in any of those positions, whether you were head of all of Commodore or head of US operations, was that you had to turn it around in a year. If you didn't do that, Gould was going to fire you and bring in the next guy. But it was a three year job."

Aside from the Amiga 500 advertising campaign, Copperman shut down the still profitable Commodore magazine. Copperman felt Commodore should stay out of the publishing trade, saying, "Commodore's a *computer* company."[9]

In early 1991, Copperman was relieved of his duties. In an effort to avoid another costly fiasco like the Rattigan lawsuit, Copperman was 'promoted' to the position of vice president of Commodore International.

With Copperman, the situation at Commodore was passable, with yearly sales close to a billion dollars worldwide. Things were about to change. "Things went from 'not great, but we're making due' to 'this sucks' sometime after the A3000, around the spring of 1991," says Haynie. "That's when [Mehdi] Ali grabbed the ropes, and one-by-one, group by group, starting making the company his." Though Gould resisted Rattigan's power grab in 1987, he allowed Ali to do the same.

Perhaps Gould saw Ali as a person he could agree with. Like Gould, the former investment banker came from the world of finance. "They became good friends, for whatever reason during the whole Prudential[10] thing," says Haynie. "He had been an investment hatchet man or fixit guy, depending on your perspective, for Prudential Investments and that's where they met. By the time he was put in charge of Commodore, Gould's kids were calling him uncle Mehdi."

The pair helped maximize each other's personal earnings. Commodore stockholders were upset after finding Gould gave himself a raise from $500,000 in 1988 to $1,250,000 in 1989. When Ali became President of Commodore International, Gould set his salary at $1,380,769. Considering Commodore's poor health, it was a strange time to give raises to top executives. To dodge investor complaints, the board voted to move the shareholders meeting from New York to the Bahamas, where very few shareholders could attend.

Most people thought Ali ran Commodore with very little long-term planning. In 1989, Ali began a five-year crusade of budget and staff cuts. Some were necessary but, considering Commodore's poor advertising and marketing operations, there was a danger of cutting too much and

---

[9] *Compute!'s Gazette* magazine, "What's Going On?" (October 1989), p. 60.
[10] Commodore had received loans from Prudential that allowed them to continue operations.

destroying any chance of success. Engineers felt he was stealing the Amiga's future to pay for the present.

Dave Haynie explains Ali's mindset. "I believe he was a guy who thought every solution was basically a matter of cash flow," he says. "If he could cut expenditures then the company would magically become profitable."

Ali knew the real power resided with Gould. "He wasn't around the West Chester office that much," says Haynie. "He spent most of his time up at the New York office. Apparently he fired just about everybody in the New York office and brought in his own people."

Haynie compares Gould's treatment of Ali with Rattigan. "It's ironic that [Rattigan] got tossed out of Commodore for trying to basically take over real leadership of Commodore, which is exactly what Medhi Ali did a few years later," he says. "Ali was just more Shrewd about it and he became good pals with Uncle Irving before making the attempt. When Rattigan tried that it caused big friction."

Ali cared little for computers. "I don't think he understood a thing about engineering and I don't think he understood a thing about the computer business," says Haynie. "He was actually quoted, asking, 'Why in the world is it important for computers to talk to televisions?' This was a guy who didn't watch television and didn't use computers."

"You could hire a guy from Pepsi that didn't know anything about the computer business," says Haynie. "A good manager who is hired for that is hired for his management skills. He will come in and learn as much as he possibly can about the business and he will listen to the people who work for him that tell him about what's going on in the business. Well Mehdi Ali thought he knew everything as far as I was able to tell, and the sentiment was reflected by everyone I talked to."

Mehdi Ali wanted no dissension. "He didn't really want anyone telling him he was wrong," recalls Haynie. "In fact, you could get fired for telling him he was wrong. He liked people around him who basically did what he told them to do."

Early 1990's Commodore began to resemble *The Hudsucker Proxy* (1994), where board members sell their company stock short and try to sabotage their own company for quick profits. "There were many, many deals that were screwed up by Mehdi Ali," says Haynie. "Epson wanted to deal with Commodore. They wanted to sell Amiga's in Japan. At the time, the PC really didn't have the stronghold it had in the US because it was split between PC's and between NEC machines."

Amiga sales in Japan at that time were unimpressive. While Commodore released every new model of Amiga in Japan, the installed base was less than 10,000 compared to over 500,000 Macintosh computers. If a major Japanese company like Epson properly marketed the Amiga, market share could increase dramatically.

Engineers and managers worked to make the deal happen. "The deal had been put together," recalls Haynie. "All the underlings had drawn up all the agreements and they were going to be putting Amiga's into Japan. We had already been working on Asian character sets for the Amiga."

Things went bad when Mehdi Ali entered the picture. "The story is that there was a final handshake kind of thing at dinner," explains Haynie. "It was a very Japanese sort of thing where the bosses meet. Mehdi Ali came into that and started demanding that they change things and just being his old ballsy self. That was a huge slap in the face based on their culture, so the guy said no."

It looked like the deal was dead, but Commodore received a second chance. "Apparently, whatever manager that was in Epson left," recalls Haynie. "His replacement came in, looked over the agreement, looked over all the paperwork, learned about the Amiga and said, 'This is a crazy thing to have lost. We need to go back and get this deal signed.' So they did and the same damn thing happened again! They called up and said they wanted the deal. [Mehdi] apparently met with them to finalize it and screwed it up again. There was no deal with Epson and no Amiga's in Japan."

In a grab at more power, Ali eliminated the president position of Commodore Business Machines. Now, Commodore US operated like other international regions. Harold Copperman was replaced by Jim Dionne, the successful general manager of Commodore Canada. The same month, Ali chopped 10 to 15% of the 600-person US workforce, mostly from the sales and manufacturing divisions. Commodore consolidated manufacturing in Hong Kong. The US and Europe no longer manufactured computers.

After 1991, Mehdi became the biggest speed bump in the eyes of the engineers. "There was a lot of ego involved," says Haynie. Short and stocky, he was like Jack Tramiel but without the success. Ali quickly earned the nickname 'little brown man' or, when managers were around, LBM.

The Amiga Junior

Commodore quickly followed up the Amiga 3000 with the release of the Amiga 3000T. It used the Amiga 3000 motherboard but added a larger 200-megabyte hard drive and 32 megabytes of RAM within a large tower case. Commodore marketed it as a high-end graphics workstation and sold it for just under $5000.

MOS Technology engineers worked on the next generation Amiga chipset, called AAA. "AAA stood for Advanced Amiga Architecture," explains Haynie.

In 1989, Haynie began work on a less ambitious chipset for the current generation called AA. "There was AAA and this was a little bit less that AAA so it was two A's, which didn't really stand for anything," he says.

The public would later know AA as AGA. "What became AGA was originally called Pandora, then it was called AA," says Haynie. "AGA stood for Advanced Graphics Architecture. The marketing department wanted to make it sound something like VGA." AGA displayed up to 1280 x 512 pixels interlaced with 256,000 on-screen colors, from an available palette of 16.8 million colors.

Dave Haynie, along with Jeff Porter and Eric Lavitsky, began work on the first system to use the AGA chipset, called the Amiga 3000+. "It was an Amiga 3000 with the AGA graphics and with the DSP coprocessor. If I had the time and support to get it in there I wanted the 68040 instead of the 68030. With a few small modifications to the sheet metal, it was going to drop right into the A3000 casework," says Haynie.

The original Amiga team continued consulting. "Dale [Luck] was consulting on the software," says Haynie. "Jay [Miner] and a couple of other guys were doing chip consulting."

According to Haynie, progress was slow. "The chip designs were just taking too long because they weren't funding it at the level they should have been," says Haynie.

Other engineers continued developing the low-end Amiga market. "George Robbins was working on a cheaper computer, which we were calling the A300," says Haynie. It was an attempt to reestablish the low-end consumer market. The computer, codenamed *June Bug*,[11] was about the size and weight of a C64, including a built in floppy drive.

Joe Augenbraun was also at work on a project to build the Amiga 1000+, an $800 AGA-based, 25-megahertz entry-level machine. It was set for an April 1992 release.

The A300, A1000+, and A3000+ were highly anticipated by Commodore International sales managers, especially in the UK and Germany. Then Mehdi Ali began his takeover. In the summer of 1991, Ali unexpectedly dismissed the engineering management team, including Henri Rubin and Jeff Porter.

To eliminate Rubin, Ali moved him to an inconsequential position in the multimedia division. "There was this running joke that when you

---

[11] Robbins named his motherboards after B52's songs. He previously named the Amiga 500 motherboard *Rock Lobster*.

A Radical New Direction – 1988 to 1992 533

were promoted to be the head of multimedia that meant you were fired but you weren't actually fired," says Haynie.

The engineers were sorry to see Rubin leave. "He was part of the process and he was a positive factor," says Haynie.

Ali also took control away from Jeff Porter. "Jeff had essentially been running engineering for a while," explains Haynie. "Jeff Porter was sort of pushed aside."

A former IBM executive, Bill Sydnes, replaced Rubin. Sydnes was the manager in charge of IBM's battle against Commodore to dominate the home industry. "Sydnes had been the PC Jr. guy, which at the time was one of IBM's greatest failures," recalls Haynie. "After the PC Jr., he had been the guy at *Franklin Computer* who thought it would be okay to copy the Apple II ROM and not tell or pay Apple anything. He almost brought them to their knees." Sydnes was a questionable choice by Ali.

Sydnes controlled the engineering projects while Gould and Ali spent their time in New York. "I never saw [Irving Gould] around," says Haynie. "Maybe he came and talked to the bosses and we just weren't involved in that. Mehdi spent a lot of time in New York too and Sydnes was down here doing his dirty work."

Sydnes began to exert his hold over engineering management. "Sydnes was a PC guy, so he immediately promoted PC guys," recalls Haynie. "His first mission was to destroy the appearance that the former administration, Henri Ruben and Jeff Porter, were as organized and far along as they were."

Sydnes put AGA chipset development on hold and cancelled the Amiga 3000+. "It was cancelled after three months," says Haynie. "By the second revision of the board I was ordered to not make it into a product."

Commodore sold the 50 existing Amiga 3000+ machines they had built as development systems for programmers. "I had been forced to take out some of the features just to get the thing out the door," says Haynie. Sydnes also cancelled the Amiga 1000+ project.

Predictably, the engineers disliked Sydnes from the start. Dave Haynie describes Sydnes in engineering terminology as a *human bus error*. "Sydnes didn't have the chops to run a computer, much less a computer design department," says Haynie. "The software people had the expression, 'human no-op'. In programming it's 'No Operation'; it's an instruction you stick in there that does nothing. So a person who sits around and does nothing is a human no-op, but a person who causes problems everywhere they go must be a human bus error."

Sydnes changed the Amiga 300 design goals. "Sydnes came in and said, 'We're going to cut $50 off the price of the A500 and come out with this new computer,'" recalls Haynie. "They took over what George

[Robbins] was working on and said, 'We have to change this.' The result was the Amiga 600, which cost $50 *more* than the A500."

Haynie describes the added features to the A600 as bloat. "They wanted new features but the A600 didn't give anybody any new features that anybody would consider useful," says Haynie. "It didn't work with the Amiga 500 peripherals. It cost more. It took away the keypad. There was this whole list of things that were wrong with it."

"There was no correlation between the act of selling, the needs of the marketplace, and what got designed," says Bil Herd.

The engineers took their frustration out on the Amiga 600 by calling it the *Amiga Junior*, in reference to Sydnes' previous bomb. Bil Herd, who remained friends with Greg Berlin, recalls the period. "Supposedly there was a memo from Sydnes that said, 'The next person that calls it the Amiga Junior gets fired,'" he says.

To ensure demand for his A600, Sydnes cancelled the most popular computer in the Commodore lineup. "The Amiga 500 was still popular," says Haynie. "They cancelled the Amiga 500 and put out the Amiga 600."

Under the Tramiel system, Commodore regions had the freedom to order whatever machines they wanted. "Usually it had been, 'Commodore, here's a new product,' and then the marketing departments would order it or not order it," says Haynie. "It was natural selection; it was survival of the fittest and I think it worked well. That's the only time I know that they circumvented that and the results of course were disastrous."

Mehdi Ali and Bill Sydnes radically changed directions. "They got there and between the two of them they decided that nobody needed Amiga's; they wanted PC's," says Haynie. "They spent the first six months pretty much deciding that they should get out of the Amiga business, so they weren't doing anything but the Amiga 600."

For six months, Amiga development stopped. "Then they came to the realization that Commodore couldn't make PC's for less than anybody else," says Haynie. "All of a sudden the Amiga was on again but they had been dragging their feet on the whole AAA and AA stuff."

Around this time, the normally reserved engineer Hedley Davis lost his temper and hurled a floppy drive into the wall. When Haynie entered the product development area one day, the first thing he noticed was a disk drive half-embedded in the chalkboard. Haynie liked what he saw and immortalized the drive with a tasteful frame and a plaque below reading, 'The Hedley Davis Memorial Disk Drive'.

Sydnes and Ali soon decided they wanted a mid-level Amiga. Rather than revive Joe Augenbraun's cancelled Amiga 1000+ project, which

A Radical New Direction – 1988 to 1992

could be ready for April 1992, Sydnes decided to start from scratch. He asked Greg Berlin to take the Amiga 3000 and cut back some features, such as the AGA chipset, and use the outdated ECS chipset instead. The Amiga 2200 was ready in April 1992. Not one division ordered it.

Sydnes was alarmed at the failure, so in May 1992 he went to Greg Berlin to begin a new Amiga computer, the Amiga 4000. However, Sydnes wanted the impossible. He gave Berlin five months to produce the machine, which would ship in September. Naturally it would be a rush job. Berlin took the Amiga 2400 design and added the AGA chips as well as cannibalizing parts from Dave Haynie's Amiga 3000+ design.

"I heard about the decisions coming out of there because I kept in touch with Greg Berlin," says Herd. "Greg was talking about how he had worked on his next rev and made it cheaper and more powerful, and he got told to take the thing out that made it more powerful. He said, 'So here I am going to market with a machine that sucks worse than the old one and costs more.' He used to get pissed."

In the summer of 1992, Ali realized Sydnes was not the right person to run Commodore engineering. "Sydnes was fired shortly after that," says Haynie. "I think he had been there for about a year at that point."

With AGA suspended and restarted, the engineers lost six months of development time. Their chipset was ready in August 1992. MOS Technology released Alice, Paula, and Lisa in time for the A4000. The Amiga 4000 shipped in September, right on schedule.

The engineers also created the Amiga 1200, an AGA based system, which would be the Amiga 500's successor. The A1200 was remarkable for including an optional hard drive inside the keyboard. Commodore released the A1200 in October 1992, just in time for Christmas. Sales of the A1200 were strong.

Despite the heroic efforts from Commodore engineers, they had conceded the North American market for the Amiga by 1992. Though customers could still purchase the machines in North America, IBM PC and Macintosh systems overshadowed them. "Commodore was in a death spiral at that point," says Herd.

A sure sign of the dismal state of the Amiga in North America came in February 1991, when Compute! Magazine, the magazine spawned by PET users, no longer provided coverage of the Amiga. Compute! coverage fell squarely behind the PC market.

Europe remained strong enough to keep Commodore alive, especially in the UK and Germany. However, Amiga game development began to slow down towards the end of 1993. Even Lucas Arts, a long time supporter of Commodore computers, ended support for the Amiga. Without games, the Amiga market could not survive.

CHAPTER

24

The Fall of Commodore

1992-1994

Shortly after Thomas Rattigan saved Commodore from bankruptcy, he remarked, "We didn't fall off the edge. We may have gotten close, but we didn't fall."[1] Since the departure of Rattigan, Commodore had wandered dangerously close to the edge again. This time, they were starting to fall.

"Whatever it was that they tried to do, it just didn't work," says R.J. Mical. "I don't believe it was because of the technology."

Despite the gains made by the Amiga 500, by the end of June 1989, Commodore was again losing money. Losses continued to mount despite strong revenues from Europe. The computer world was about to lose the most colorful company in the business.

Chairman Gould

Irving Gould had many fine points. He recognized Commodore's potential in 1965 when he made a sizable investment in the troubled company. He also knew good leadership when he saw it, in the form of Jack Tramiel.

Sitting in on board meetings, Rattigan saw the real, uncensored Irving Gould. "His favorite expression about people he didn't like was, 'He wanted to live long enough to [piss][2] on the guy's grave.'" As Atari posed the largest threat to Commodore at the time, he was likely talking about Jack Tramiel.

The financial world had many criticisms of Commodore's chairman. A Forbes article titled 'Lost Opportunity?' blamed Gould for his "absentee-

---

[1] *Commodore* magazine, "What Next for Commodore?" (May 1987), p. 76.
[2] Rattigan actually used the word urinate, but he was obviously being polite.

landlord management style." In it, analyst Lee Isgur, who knew Gould for over five years, summed up his management style. "Irving tries to minimize taxes, hates the day-to-day stuff and doesn't like to push the product, so he hires people to do it for him."[3]

In his quest to avoid taxes, the 70-year-old jetted around the world several times a week, from the Bahamas to Canada to the United States. According to Forbes, "Gould can only spend on average three days a week in the U.S. before he may be subject to taxation by the Internal Revenue Service." The dramatic effort to avoid taxes was almost pathological.

After the big advertising push in 1989, Amiga advertising in North America all but stopped. It was even difficult to find print ads in Commodore magazines. In 1990, not a single Amiga advertisement appeared in the official Commodore Magazine.[4]

While he did not use computers himself, Gould should have been well aware of his target market due to his son. Between 1988 and 1991, Jason Gould ran a bulletin board system from his home in Toronto, called the Star Trek BBS. Jason was representative of the typical Amiga 500 user.

Dave Haynie believes Irving Gould's key weakness was a lack of patience with his CEO's. "He would hire someone, expect a miracle, then fire them long before any chance of such a miracle working could have happened," says Haynie. "Problems take time to solve and Uncle Irv apparently didn't understand this. They had some potentially good guys in the power seats at Commodore International and Commodore Business Machines but they didn't get their chance to prove it."

When Gould dismissed Tramiel and Rattigan, he thought they received too much credit. Gould thought of Commodore as his company and felt he should receive the credit. As soon as his President and CEO became too successful, Gould became insecure and pushed them out.

To outsiders, they saw an incredible company emerge around 1981 then suddenly fade from dominance after the departure of Tramiel in 1984. In 1987, they saw Commodore reemerge with the Amiga 500, and again fade away to nothing after Gould dismissed Rattigan. Each time that Gould exerted his control of the company Commodore faded.

Attack of the Clones

In the eighties, many computer users vowed not to buy another computer until there was a clear winner. In 1987, the Amiga looked like one. The price was low, it was technically impressive, and software

---

[3] *Forbes* magazine, "Lost Opportunity?" (November 13, 1989), p. 288.

[4] Commodore magazine had merged with RUN magazine by 1990.

538 THE SPECTACULAR RISE AND FALL OF COMMODORE

support was building. "It was successful in spite Commodore's efforts to un-advertise it," says Mical. "It just didn't hit the critical mass that it needed to. They sold a lot of them; I think the final numbers were close to seven million."[5]

Meanwhile, IBM PC compatibles had built a steady base since the early eighties. With the emergence of clones, such as Compaq, Gateway, and Dell, market competition began to exert a positive influence and prices fell rapidly. Unfortunately for Commodore, the home and business markets became unified.

"The C64 was a game machine," says Chuck Peddle. "It was never intended to be what the PC was. The PC was a serious computer and it had everything. So what happened was a lot of people started buying them for themselves so that they would have a more serious computer and do word processing and everything else."

Commodore and Atari joined the PC revolution by creating their own IBM PC compatible computers. Atari even included the GEM graphical interface by Digital Research and Commodore users could use PC Geos by Berkeley Softworks.

Commodore's move to sell PC compatible computers mystified Robert Yannes. "They lost their vision," he says. "They really didn't know who they were as a company and what people expected from them. They had made a name for themselves doing home computers. For them to go into the PC compatible business with a PC compatible that really had no advantage over any other PC compatible just didn't make sense."

Yannes believes they should have concentrated their energy on the Amiga. "They could have been doing things like the Macintosh and multimedia machines," says Yannes. "The Amiga really was the first multimedia computer and they really had no idea what to do with it or where to go with it."

Microsoft chose to ignore the Amiga, probably because of low sales. Without support from the largest software maker in the world, the Amiga had no chance in the North American business market.

In the early nineties, most users just wanted a computer that could play games, dial BBS systems, and perform word processing. This meant Amiga, Macintosh, and Atari ST owners were quite satisfied with their machines. Unfortunately, this comfortable situation was about to change rapidly.

PC graphics and sound cards made games technologically competitive with the Amiga and game developers began to look seriously at the PC

---

[5] Company records show the Amiga line sold 5,292,200 units worldwide.

game market. On May 5, 1992, id Software released their shareware game, *Wolfenstein 3D*. This game alone made up the minds of many computer buyers. The release of *Wolfenstein 3D* came at a critical juncture and game players shifted to the PC.

The 3D game revolution swept in with games like *Ultima Underworld* (1992), *Doom* (1993), *Alone in the Dark* (1993), and *Under a Killing Moon* (1993). Game companies embraced the PC as a development platform, leaving the Amiga and Macintosh behind.

"As PC's began to play videogames, and as Mac's started to play videogames, that took away the 80% of unit sales that was the [Amiga 500] videogame market," says Haynie.

The industry acknowledged that games were the top reason people upgraded their computers. In 1993, CD-ROM's became standard in PC's. Visually stunning CD-ROM best-sellers like *Myst* (1993) and *7th Guest* (1993) set new standards in software sales.

Then the Internet arrived. Although it had been around since the late sixties, the Internet became a mass phenomenon in 1993 when Marc Andreessen released a World Wide Web browser called *Mosaic*. In 1994, he released the *Netscape* browser, which became the standard. Unfortunately, Andreessen did not support the Amiga and Macintosh initially. People wanted the Internet now and many people saw Netscape as the Internet. The PC had Netscape and other computers did not, so buyers went with the IBM PC and Windows.

Yannes believes it would have been difficult for Commodore to survive in the PC clone market. "There aren't that many [companies] that are doing great profits," says Yannes. "If you are a Compaq or an HP, you are so tied to the bottom line all the time you can't do anything. The margins are terrible and at any given moment you are either one-month away from being a major success or out of business."

CD32

In October 1992, after the Amiga 1200 and 4000 began shipping, engineer Jeff Porter merged the AGA chipset with the CDTV to make a dedicated game console. Commodore was going head to head with Sega and Nintendo with a new console, named CD32.

The decision was ironic as the Amiga was a game console in the early eighties, before it became a computer. "Quite honestly, they could have made a video game version if they wanted to [circa 1984], just like they did later with the CDTV and CD32," says Haynie. The Amiga had come full circle.

CD32 used the Motorola 68EC020 32-bit processor running at 14.28 megahertz. It was the first 32-bit console. The console used the AGA chipset, providing incredible graphics. CD32 also boasted a video chip called *Akiko*, which produced chunky texture mapped polygons in 3D games. "At the time, it was not really competitive with some machines in some ways, but in other ways it was pretty good," says Haynie.

The outward appearance of CD32 was radically different from CDTV, even if the functionality was similar. CDTV resembled a VCR and CD32 was a pure game console. It was compact with round molded plastic, a top-ejecting CD player, and colorful hand controllers. "It looked just like a Sega or something," says Haynie.

The CD32 could play digital videos from CD using a separately released MPEG video decoder card, which played the popular Video CD format (VCD). Engineers snuck in the ability to play CD-i digital movies, which included late eighties and early nineties CD-i films like *Black Rain* and *Hunt for Red October*.

By February 1993, Jeff Porter and his engineers released 15 prototype units to game developers. Commodore knew they had to gain early support for their machine. They unveiled the CD32 at the June CES in Chicago, garnering major retail interest.

Manufacturing took place in a Philippines government owned factory. By September 1993, CD32 appeared on shelves. The £250 UK package included six bundled games.[6]

Despite the usual lack of marketing, CD32 dominated the early CD market, beating PC CD-ROM sales. Over 100,000 units sold in the first three months in Europe.

CD32 debuted in North America at the January 1994 CES show, retailing for $399. Everyone was confident - confident Commodore's lack of marketing in the US would quickly relegate the CD32 to insignificance. "This wasn't the market for them because we didn't have established relationships with dealers and distributors here for any sort of product really," says Haynie. "Commodore had burnt the bridges with the small retailers, and then they basically stopped selling the computers that play in Kmart."

In the end, most CD32 games were merely Amiga ports. This frequently meant the games only occupied a few megabytes of space out of CD-ROM's 700-megabyte storage capacity. Rarely were games larger than ten megabytes in size. Developers often included impressive full motion video introduction sequences to fill the CD. The CD32 even had the first 3D shooter for a console, called *Gloom*. In total, there were

---

[6] The bundle included MicroCosm, Chaos Engine, Dangerous Streets, Oscar, Wing Commander, and Diggers.

about 100 dedicated CD32 titles, the average for failed gaming platforms.

The CD32 was to be the last consumer product from Commodore engineers. In the end, the *Sony PlayStation*, released in 1995, succeeded where Commodore hoped to dominate.

The End is Near

Though Commodore was in a downward plunge by 1993, the engineers slowly improved Amiga technology. At MOS Technology, Dr. Ed Hepler headed the design on the AAA chipset. "He taught at Villanova [University] back then," says Haynie. "He doesn't like to fly, so he was pretty happy to be with a local company."

Work on the AAA chipset predated the AGA chipset. "AAA was started in 1988 and AGA was started in 1989," says Haynie. "That was the 64-bit chipset. AGA was hybrid 16/32-bit." At the heart of the new chipset was Andrea, a graphics chip. Along with improved resolutions, the chipset also provided simple 3D acceleration.

The engineers even had plans for a sophisticated 3D chipset. "There was a follow-on to AAA called Hombre," says Haynie. "That had its own RISC processor built into the graphics chip, which was the Agnus replacement chip. There were only two chips in that chipset and that could give you an entire game machine or you could use the graphics processor in a regular computer."

Hombre included 3D instructions such as hardware accelerated texture mapping and Gouraud shading. OpenGL drivers would support the chips. A Commodore software engineer created an impressive simulation of the texture-mapping algorithm, which wrapped an angelfish picture around a rotating cylinder. According to Hepler, "It would have been competitive with any of the game consoles currently available." It would also be cheap, with a $45 target for the two chips.

Money became a problem for Commodore. In the eighties, MOS Technology lacked the funding to complete their 16-bit microprocessor. Now, graphics chips were becoming a difficult burden. "You could sort of see the same thing happening again in the nineties with the graphic chip," says Haynie. "Commodore certainly had the engineering talent, but we didn't have enough people and enough money to apply that talent in a timely fashion."

Part of Commodore's financial problems stemmed from lawsuits. "I spent a year with our lawyers on and off as a technical adviser on an IBM lawsuit," says Haynie. "IBM had this habit of coming after every computer company individually, slapping a big stack of patents on them, and getting cross licensing and royalties back from them because they had about 20 or so PC patents."

According to Haynie, much of IBM's actions were preemptive. "IBM, being extremely big at that time, was very nervous that somebody was going to get a patent on them that they didn't have a license for," he says. "So one of the main reasons they did this was to get a cross license with you." With cross licensing, if IBM unintentionally violated a patent, they would not be liable to pay royalties on it.

IBM wanted protection from possible Amiga patents. "There was this whole argument about the Amiga," says Haynie. "We knew they wanted a license on the Amiga patents to keep them out of trouble if we came after a patent on them and wanted royalties on several million machines made that year. It was just one of those general purpose cover your ass and get some money out of everyone else in the business."

Haynie believes IBM sometimes used their lawyers for profit. "We went down to their office. Their legal department in Boca Raton, Florida was actually larger than the engineering part of Commodore's building," says Haynie. "They ran it as a profit center. They had some engineer lawyers there who were whoring themselves defending some of the worst patents you have ever seen."

Rather than fight IBM, most companies settled out of court. "They have ridiculous amounts of patents they can go against you with," says Haynie. "When you've got a stack of 20 and you know IBM will come after you with 20 more after that and 20 more after that, you settle. They came after Commodore and said, 'You make PC's, which is pretty straight forward. You're not going to win. You're going to pay us a royalty for PC's.'"

Though Commodore Business Machines' United States operations were not doing great in 1993, they came to an abrupt halt due to a questionable lawsuit. It started in the early eighties. The US Patent Office could not decide which software patents were legitimate. One fundamental concept of patent law says a patent must be a real invention, and more specifically, something 'not obvious to one skilled in the art'. Back then, the U.S. patent office did not have any patent officers with software engineering skills, so they were unable to determine if a software patent application was obvious or not.

This led to outrageous situations, such as IBM receiving a patent for programs that cut and paste text between two buffers, which UNIX had been doing since the late 1970's. They granted software patents as long as a patent search turned up no similar patents.

Meanwhile, a company called *CADtrak* received a patent for a programming technique called the XOR cursor. This small piece of code

The Fall of Commodore – 1992 to 1994

used a very basic logical operation to display a cursor overtop of other graphics on the screen. Programmers usually discovered the algorithm on their own when they begin programming. The patent office considered it a new invention. "Fred Bowen was working on that," says Haynie. "They had a patent on exclusive-OR. As Fred said, 'Damn, I should have patented AND, OR, and NOR.'"

CADtrak produced hardware but realized it was more lucrative to sue other companies over their perceived invention. They cut their personnel to almost zero and effectively became a litigation company. "CADTrak was just lawyers," says Haynie. CADtrak's rampage began pulling in millions, mostly through settlements with other companies. Commodore fought and the lawsuit dragged on into the 1990's.

CADtrak's lawyers knew what they were doing. The jury and judge knew little about technology, but they understood a picture the prosecution held up showing both Amiga and CADtrak screens. The cursor looked the same. While that was not the heart of the argument, it was the most powerful piece of information they could grasp. Commodore lawyers tried to undo the damage but the jury did not agree, ordering Commodore to pay $10 million in damages. Commodore refused to pay, which led to further ramifications.

In late 1992, just before the busy Christmas season, Commodore ran short of crucial chips. "The Mehdi/Sydnes team dragged their feet on the AGA chips, then when it was time to ship them, they didn't order enough because the chips weren't made at Commodore, they were made at Hewlett-Packard," says Haynie.

"We had the A1200 and they couldn't make enough of them because they had no chips," laments Haynie. "They had all the A600's you wanted, but nobody wanted that. They might have taken an A500 but it wasn't made anymore, so that was a bad year." As a result, Commodore missed major revenues.

Haynie compares the devastation to the famous downfall of Osborne computers. "We in a sense Osborned ourselves in the end," says Haynie. "For the Christmas of 1992, you had this new product [Amiga 1200] that everybody wanted and no one could get, and you had the old product [Amiga 600] that was in plentiful supply and no one wanted."

In the summer of 1993, Commodore went through a series of massive layoffs. The building at West Chester, which once housed thousands of employees, now held only a few hundred. The layoffs meant Commodore could pay salaries and continue to operate, but with less staff, there was no chance of a rebound.

In late 1993, Commodore had difficulties paying their parts suppliers. When too much money went unpaid, they stopped sending parts to Commodore. "The problem was, Commodore at that point owed so many people so much money, they were having to pay cash for everything," explains Haynie. "And they just didn't have that much cash."

This had devastating consequences for Commodore and they could only buy enough parts to make approximately 100,000 CD32 units for Christmas of 1993. "By the time the fall of 1993 rolled around, and the CD32 was coming out, they couldn't make enough CD32's because they didn't have enough money," says Haynie.

Haynie estimates Commodore needed to build about 400,000 to survive. "They could make something like 125,000, but they had potential orders for double that," says Haynie.

The CADtrak lawsuit also came back to haunt Commodore. Since they refused to pay the $10 million lawsuit, the US government prevented Commodore from importing products into the country. The CD32 units from the Philippines could not make it past customs, and Commodore had nothing to sell in North America. According to Haynie, the customs problems probably would not have hurt Commodore anyway. "There was so much demand for them they probably could have sold them in Europe," says Haynie.

In the autumn of 1993, the AAA chipset was completed. Unfortunately, there was not enough money. "AAA never got to production," says Haynie. Commodore now lacked the funds for future product development.

During this period, employees and industry observers could not help but notice the disproportional pay the top executives received. Gould's yearly salary was approximately $3,500,000. Mehdi Ali was receiving over $1,000,000 annually. It was a clear indication the top executives were content to bleed the company dry. Engineers could only wonder what might have been if the executives used some of this money on parts or advertising.

Losses continued to mount. Expensive failures like CDTV, the Amiga 600, and the Amiga 2200 devastated Commodore's financial prospects. By December 31, 1993, Commodore lost more than $374 million in the past 18 months alone. It was obvious to everyone Commodore would not be able to operate much longer.

Hopes for a company buyout faded when it became obvious Commodore was no longer an attractive acquisition. Debts were too large and the technology was not as cutting edge as it once was. Employees saw there would be no miracle. In the winter of 1993 and

1994, they began departing for other companies. Management put project development on hold, instructing engineers to design but not build. The only active projects were the CD32's MPEG module, the Amiga 4000T (tower case), and Amiga OS 3.1.

By April 1993, work was at a standstill. Approximately 80 people remained in the huge building. The massive, now quiet spaces almost seemed to mock the remaining employees. It was eerie to walk through the once bustling corridors.

On April 22, Commodore quietly laid off 47 additional employees. Each employee received an exit interview in the near-empty cafeteria by the personnel director. The interviews were more out of tradition than necessity. When asked what they disliked most about Commodore, employees invariably mentioned Mehdi Ali.

At noon, everyone headed to Margarita's Evergreen Inn for the customary layoff-lunch. Margarita's was almost an extension of Commodore by this time. Back in 1983, it was a run-down biker bar. After ten years of constant patronage by Commodore employees for lunches, parties, retirements, and layoffs it became prosperous.

Though it was a somber occasion, the mood was one of giddy defeat with plenty of shared laughter. When engineer Dave Haynie came around with his video camera, employees let out their pent-up feelings. Haynie pointed the camera at the engineering managers and Lew Eggebrecht summed it up saying, "We're fucked!" Employees singled out Mehdi Ali as the cause of Commodore's early demise.

Dave Haynie clearly believes the failure of Commodore was a result of poor management decisions. "You have to actually have a business that's viable, and when you don't understand the business it's hard to run it the right way," he says. "You had some of the hardest working people and some of the smartest people in the industry, but that doesn't get you 100% of the way there alone."

The North American operation's failure was perhaps the largest factor. "If they could have sold a lot more in the United States they might have made it," says Haynie. "It really turned out to be the low-end machines sold in Europe and the high end machines sold here for video purposes, but that wasn't going to last forever if we didn't advance the technology."

On Wednesday, April 27, 1994, Dave Haynie drove to the West Chester facility as usual. Today, there were only about 30 people remaining in the whole building. It was surreal. As he drove up, he noticed the US flag on the front lawn flying at half-mast.

Unable to continue operations, Irving Gould called it quits. "To the bitter end, it was Irving's company. He was truly in charge," says Mical.

On April 29, 1994, Commodore International Limited filed for liquidation in the Bahamas Supreme Court. Within hours, the company released their employees and locked the doors.

Word reached Commodore's US headquarters before the day was out. Suddenly, managers began racing up and down the halls trying to tie up loose ends before the creditors vacated them. Managers hurried to the bank to secure cash for the employees before accounts were frozen. The remaining employees would at least get their last paycheck.

Commodore factories around the world had manufactured products with no one to pay for them. In the Philippines, the government seized hundreds of unshipped CD32 units as payment for the use of their factory.

On April 30, 1994, the Philadelphia Inquirer broke the story that seemed incredible ten years earlier. The headline proclaimed, 'Commodore Goes Out of Business'.

Al Charpentier was surprised Commodore lasted as long as they did. "After the Commodore 64, they took a wrong turn, so they lost almost two to three years where they could have been competing with IBM and Apple, in terms of coming up with a more powerful computer," says Charpentier. "That was a significant loss of time. In the computer world, if you miss a generation, you can die pretty quickly."

The announcement caught R.J. Mical by surprise. "I guess they just couldn't get it together enough to get Amiga sales up high enough to cover the cash flow of the corporation," speculates Mical. "I didn't think they would go all the way down the way they did. I was shocked they went completely belly up like that."

Bil Herd was less surprised. "It took them eight years to die. I recognize that what had been driven under Jack Tramiel got a little worse without Jack," says Herd. "Commodore was in search of a CEO, but none of them understood the marketplace. The failure of Commodore was not a surprise to any single one of us who worked there."

Chuck Peddle believes it all went wrong when Jack closed down his R & D centers. "Breaking up Moore Park was the death knell for Commodore," says Peddle. "It effectively put him out of the computer business. ... The problem is, the consumer computer didn't have legs. It was a great idea, it made tons of money, but it didn't have legs. The business computer market, as you can see, had big legs."

A Party at Randell's

That evening, software engineer Randell Jesup held a party for Commodore employees. About 50 former employees attended. Dave

Haynie attended with his video camera, recording the event.[7]

The party was a wake. They were there to remember Commodore. Flowers arrived from Amiga engineers Dale Luck and R.J. Mical, who were now at 3DO. Technician Mike Rivers added to the funereal mood by providing peaceful background music with his harp. Like any wake, there was plenty of drinking.

Once the sun dipped below the horizon, the engineers took out their frustrations on a pile of PC keyboards. They swung the keyboards by their cables, pounded them with hammers and boards, and one particularly frustrated engineer resorted to head butting a keyboard. Finally, an engineer backed his car over the whole pile.

Engineer Mike Colligan produced a small effigy with a nametag on it. At first glance, it looked like the nametag read 'I.B.M.' in commemoration of the company that drove all others into the ground. A second look revealed that it read L.B.M.; Little Brown Man.

Mike Rivers switched over from the harp to electric guitar and played the Star Spangled Banner while Colligan set the effigy alight. As the little figure burned, CATS manager Gail Wellington commented, "This is about the only warmth we ever got out of the man." With five years of pent-up frustrations purged, the former Commodore employees got on with the task of celebrating Commodore.

Mike Rivers performed an improvised song he called 'Chicken Lips Blues', along with Keith Gabryelski on harmonica. The rambling, nonsensical song went as follows:

> I got the chicken lips blues, I got a computer I can no longer use.
>
> I got the chicken lips blues, I got a computer I can no longer use.
>
> (Except for those of you who know how to do something with it.)
>
> Well, in the last days of Commodore, there were creditors roaming the halls.
>
> And in the last days of Commodore, they got creditors roaming the halls.
>
> They got accountants all over Commodore, and the taxmen and the creditors roaming the halls.
>
> (I'm ad-libbing here folks, thank-you.)
>
> Hell Mehdi, there's a rock lobster attached to my balls.
>
> Well, where the heck am I gonna go? I guess I'll go call 3DO.

---

[7] Haynie compiled his footage of the last days of Commodore and released a DVD called *The Deathbed Vigil*. Appropriately, he edited the material and added effects using his Amiga 3000+.

Where the heck am I gonna go? I guess I'll go call 3DO.
But you know, I just don't know how they're going to pay their CEO.
Well, plain and nothin, and just about three, that strange kind of genius, that Mehdi Ali.
I got the chicken lips blues, I got that computer that's got no use.
(Except for those of you who know how to use it.)
Well, what do I do when my 8520's blow?
Well, what do I do now, now that my 8520's have blown?
Oh God, I got to buy a PC! Oh, no.

Afterwards, employees gathered around the fire, recalling their favorite Commodore stories. Employees recalled the speed bump saga, a *Lemmings* skit put on by the CATS team, and the trials of property passes. For those who had been with the company, it was magic to hear accounts that had only been rumors.

It was hard for the former employees to leave Randell's party that night. Many, such as Dave Haynie, joined Commodore as teenagers and learned their most important lessons while working there. Commodore was their life. Sometime in the early morning, the former Commodore employees began dispersing one by one. A few remaining engineers found it too hard to leave and wanted one last adventure. They decided to go back to Commodore headquarters.

Bryce Nesbitt, Keith Gabryelski, and Dave Haynie arrived in the Commodore parking lot in darkness. The creditors had already locked and chained the doors to the West Chester facility to prevent ex-employees from walking away with company property.

The trio pulled out a few cans of spray paint and masking tape. Carefully, they masked out the names of infamous managers from Commodore's past. Appropriately, they spray painted their names onto the speed bumps. Among the names were Mehdi, McCook, Toy, Sydnes, Archie, and Irving. Mehdi appeared on the largest speed bump. Not satisfied, they spray painted his name on a second speed bump.

Their work done, the three stood in silence before the building that had been their home for so many years. The building that was once Commodore stood vacant. It seemed like it deserved a better fate. Eventually, the three went home. It was over.

Epilogue

"Obituaries customarily focus on the deceased's accomplishments, not the unpleasant details of the demise. That's especially true when the demise hints strongly of self-neglect tantamount to suicide, and nobody can find a note that offers some final explanation. There will be no such note from Commodore, and it would take a book to explain why this once-great computer company lies cold on its deathbed. But Commodore deserves a eulogy, because its role as an industry pioneer has been largely forgotten or ignored by revisionist historians who claim that everything started with Apple or IBM." – Tom Halfhill, Byte Magazine, August 1994

After Commodore, **Dave Haynie** (Amiga 2000, Amiga 3000) joined *Scala*, a company that made Amiga-based multimedia set top boxes, along with former Commodore employees Jeff Porter, Peter Cherna, and Randell Jesup. He now works for *Nomadio* where he is improving radio control technology using microprocessors.

According to Haynie, the West Chester bar Margaritas closed down in 2003. Dave Haynie notified ex-Commodore employees, who gathered for one last time at their old hangout.

George Robbins (C900, Amiga 500) joined *Net Access Corporation*, an East Coast Internet Service Provider. "He ended up having 20 or 30 employees under him," says Herd.

On April 26, 2002, Robbins passed away at the age of 48. "He died at work," says Herd. "He had a heart attack sometime during the night."

Many of Robbins' close coworkers from the Commodore days gathered to say farewell. "They had a memorial for him, and we filled a whole auditorium," says Herd. "I got up and talked about his days at Commodore and the people had no idea. Hedley [Davis] got up and told some stories. People who worked for him told some stories, and we were going, 'George did that?' It was really interesting to hear this man's life throughout his career."

Commodore engineers teased Robbins for his hygienic habits. According to his employees at Net Access, his habits continued. "It was funny to hear in this auditorium how people would talk about it in various ways," says Herd. "We all laughed at the references because at Net Access, they would always order extra T-shirts and they would give them to him. He would never wash them but he'd have fresh shirts at least. They were talking about doing some jeans too and maybe a jacket so they could get George to change some clothes. It was all very loving and cool."

Robbins lived at Commodore and rarely left for home. "The same was true when he died," says Herd. "He had some place he rented above a train station. I don't know if there was running water, but he didn't go too often. Supposedly it was full of Z8000 machines. Unisys made them and never sold them and he bought a whole bunch of them. His motto was, 'Little UNIX boxes that take over the world.'"

"His family went to where he had a rental property to clean it out. They found books and servers but no real condiments of life. They went in and they found this stack of science fiction books. He had taught himself German it turns out."

Net Access also discovered a large part of their infrastructure in Robbins' home. "There were a couple of servers from Net Access and Net Access didn't know where the servers were," says Herd. "It's not like he had stolen them. He set them up there and got them working and never moved them. So here's part of the Net Access internet service provider servers found running at his house through a T-1."

Dave Morse, Amiga's original President and CEO, went to *Epyx* as Chairman and CEO. In August 1987, **R.J. Mical** (Amiga 1000 Intuition Programmer) and **Dave Needle** (Amiga 1000 Chip Designer) met with Morse to discuss a new portable game system. The two engineers developed the *Lynx*, a 16-bit game machine that was ahead of its time.

Out of all the people interviewed for this book, R.J. Mical stood out for his dislike of Jack Tramiel. "There's a guy I would be happy to never do business with again," says Mical. "He destroyed everything in his path, even people that were his friends. For me, there is a dark way of doing business and a light way of doing business, and he chose the dark path. Maybe he's a very happy guy and he doesn't sleep badly at night."

According to Mical, Tramiel's reputation finally caught up with him during the Atari years. "At least once in his life, his way of doing business came back to bite him, and that was when they bought the Lynx from us," says Mical.

"When we were doing the Lynx, before Atari bought it from us, we had these carefully arranged deals with all of the suppliers," recalls Mical. "We said, 'It's us. Give us a break! Do us a favor here and then when the machines start to sell we'll up how much we're paying and everyone will be profitable together.' So we had put together this thing where we were going to be able to launch the machine at $109 and in half a year to a

Epilogue

year to drop the price to $99; that magical below $100 price tag that you need."

Epyx, a game development company, made numerous deals with other game developers. "We had lined up all of these software people that were all ready to get behind the Lynx and start developing software for it," says Mical.

In 1989, Epyx began negotiating with Atari. "Dave and I didn't want to have anything to do with that deal," says Mical. "We assured Epyx that Atari would find a way to drive them out of business and then pick up the company for ten cents on the dollar. They didn't believe us. Dave and I wouldn't have anything to do with it so we quit rather than having any part in the Lynx being owned by Atari. We walked from it."

Mical's prediction was too accurate. "After we quit, Atari got their hands on Lynx and they drove Epyx out of business," recalls Mical.

Ironically, Atari had to use Commodore computers to develop the Lynx. "Sadly for them, the entire development environment was all on the Amiga," says Mical. "All of the tools: the debuggers, the art tools, the audio tools, the assemblers; it was all Amiga based."

Mical and Needle attended one of the Epyx auctions. "After it went bankrupt, Atari went to the auction to buy Epyx gear that Atari could use," recalls Mical. "We went to the Epyx auction after they drove Epyx out of business and tried to pick up some of the gear ourselves. The Atari guy, who was actually a friend of ours, was also there to try to buy Amiga computers, trying to get them for ten cents on the dollar from poor Epyx."

The two Lynx designers decided to exact their revenge on Atari. "We too bid for them," says Mical. "We didn't want them at all. We just wanted to drive the price up. So machine after machine, we drove the price way up and then let him buy it. It was a stupid, cheap, moronic, sophomoric little bit of revenge but it made us laugh."

The Lynx hardware suppliers also exacted revenge on Tramiel. According to Mical, "When Atari got their hands on [the Lynx] and these people then had to deal with the Tramiels, all the hardware suppliers said, 'You're the guy who screwed us last year. I remember. Now we're not cutting the price and if you want any parts from us you have to pay cash up front. We're not going to trust you anymore.'"

Software development for the Lynx also vanished. "We had a legion of software developers that were going to sell software for the Lynx," claims Mical. "They all said, to the one, 'We remember you. You're the guy who screwed us last year. Well, have some screwing back.' They all backed out of the deals."

The sudden reversal of the suppliers and software developers ruined the Lynx and Atari. "They wouldn't cut the prices the way he needed them to cut prices," says Mical. "Instead of $109, they were going to have to retail it for $179, and instead of having 100 titles at launch, they had the small number they had."

For Mical, the Lynx's failure was bittersweet. "All of those evil business practices for all those years finally came back to haunt these guys. Sadly, it also meant the ruin of this wonderful technology," sighs Mical. "It was such a shame, but it was one of those little satisfying moments in life."

After the Lynx, all three ex-Amiga team members joined Trip Hawkins, the founder of Electronic Arts, to design the *3DO* game console. "[Trip Hawkins] wanted to do a software company again and get into the console business," says Mical. "He used to say, 'The sad thing is you never develop a software title, but you always have to develop 17 versions of the same software title to take into account all the different graphics modes and different configurations of the PC.' So his dream was to invent a game system that would be the end-all game system. It would be expandable and extendible into an ever more powerful machine forever into the future. Instead of having to develop 17 titles, you develop it just once and it will work on this great machine. We all locked arms and goose-stepped together into the entertainment future."

Unfortunately, the 3DO failed to compete with Nintendo or Sega. "It was a noble idea. It would have been good if it could have worked but in retrospect, that could never have worked," says Mical.

Jay Miner (Amiga 1000 Inventor) lived his life with weak kidneys, which often caused his complexion to appear spotty. In the late eighties, his kidneys grew worse, forcing him to live with dialysis, an intrusive procedure where machines filtered his blood. In 1990, his sister, Joyce Beers, gave him one of her kidneys. The operation extended his life, allowing him to continue his career in electronics. He designed a microchip for the *Ventritex* implantable cardiac defibrillator. This was to be his last project. On June 20, 1994, shortly after the Commodore bankruptcy, Jay Miner passed away.

Miner's closest friends attended his memorial. "We had a very lovely gathering of friends who all stood up and took a turn remembering Jay," says Mical. "It gave everyone a chance to find some peace in their hearts and celebrate a good person one more time. I was glad to be a part of it."

After winning his ten million dollar lawsuit against Commodore in 1991 (the year his Commodore contract would have expired), **Thomas Rattigan** became Chairman and CEO of *G. Heileman Brewing Company* of Rosemont, Illinois.[1] Mike Evans, former Commodore Chief Operating Officer, also joined Heileman.

Rattigan served as a trustee at Boston College from 1995 to 2003. He donated a substantial amount of money to the college to establish the *Thomas F. Rattigan Professorship in English*, named in memory of his father.

According to Rattigan, "When I finally retired, I said to my wife, 'There's three things I can do, based on what I see my friends doing. That's either play golf, buy a boat, or get myself a mistress.' She said, 'Well if you get a mistress, you better be rich because you're not going to have any money when I'm through with you.'"

Today, Rattigan is retired and enjoys playing golf. He still talks to former Commodore General Manager Nigel Shepherd every Christmas.

Bil Herd (Plus/4, C128 Systems Designer) did not fare well at the startup company he joined after Commodore. "It was a real bad mistake," says Herd. "I found out that I had been spoiled by Commodore. I had been handled with kid gloves to an extent. I had a chip fab at that place and I had these resources available to me that other people can only dream of. I thought all companies could do the things we did at Commodore and was severely surprised. I shouldn't have left."

Herd's new employers were not as accommodating as Commodore management had been. "They were shocked by what they had got with me," says Herd. "I thought they knew what they were getting. I would take the entire department out on Fridays and we didn't come back. We would go to the bar and that blew them away, so I didn't last seven months there before they let me go."

Herd addressed his alcoholism and is sober today. "Now I'm actually a recovering alcoholic. I haven't had a drink in 14 years," he says.

While dealing with his personal problems, Herd used his National Guard medic experience as a volunteer. "I worked in a trauma center," he says. "I started as a volunteer until they said, 'Look, we have to hire you according to insurance once you've been here for so long.' I've done thousands of ambulance calls all times, day or night. So I gave back all that I had spent from those days."

---

[1] In 1996, Heileman sold to Stroh Brewery Company, which Pabst later acquired.

Herd spotted the Internet as a business opportunity in the early nineties. "At that point he was getting into an ISP [Internet Service Provider] that he started, *Interactive Network Systems*," says Haynie. Today, Herd manages his ISP. "He's big. He's got one in Philadelphia and he's up in North Jersey as well as most of South Jersey."

The engineers still gather to remember Commodore. "Once a year we pretty much see each other," says Herd. "On September 11th, 2004 we got together at Greg Berlins for an end of summer thing. It's Bob Russell, Greg Berlin, Dave Haynie, Fish [Terry Fischer], and Andy Finkel."

Bob Russell (VIC-20, C64 ROM Programmer) is head of engineering at *Quadrant International*, a major supplier of DVD and video products to the PC market. According to Herd, "Bob Russell looks exactly like he did 20 years ago. You couldn't look at him and tell how old he was."

No one interviewed knows what happened to **Kit Spencer**, the man who launched the VIC-20 and Commodore 64 to major success in North America. Most believe he stayed with Commodore in the Bahamas until the end, writing the company newsletter and playing tennis.

Al Charpentier (VIC, VIC-II Chip Designer), **Robert Yannes** (SID Chip Designer, C64 Systems Designer), and **Charles Winterble** (VIC-II, SID, C64 Project Manager) received one million dollars from Atari for *My First Computer*. The product languished at Atari. By 1984, it was no longer commercially viable for release.

Their profits were supposed to fund a new computer. "When we left Commodore, our plan was to design the next great computer with better graphics and better sound," says Yannes. "We had a real good plan. We were going to talk to the game companies like Electronic Arts and find out what they were really looking for. [It was going to be] a computer that could play games, with graphics acceleration and a bit blitter. We were going to do sampled sound; a lot of the stuff that ultimately ended up in the Amiga."

The computer they previously created derailed their ambitious plans. "We were well on our way to doing that but the Commodore 64 became such a steamroller that no one was interested in financing a company that was trying to compete against it," says Yannes.

Instead, the trio started sound company *Ensoniq*. "We ended up going into the music business because we were very far along on the design on the sound chip," says Yannes. Commodore engineer **Bruce Crockett** also joined Ensoniq.

The resulting chip found its way into a rival computer. "At one point we were trying to raise some money for the company and we contacted Steve Wozniak directly and wondered if he would be interested in this chip," says Yannes. "He ended up telling Apple they should look into this. So our sound chip ended up going into the Apple IIGS."

In 1997, Singapore based *Creative Technology* bought Ensoniq for $77 million, making the trio multimillionaires. Al Charpentier is still an active entrepreneur and engineer. While interviewed for this book, he was marketing a body-scanning device called *Intellifit*.

Yannes believes the media has treated Commodore badly. "I'm not speaking for myself here, but I think Commodore the company deserves more credit than it gets," he says. "Based on the people I've met in the last 20 years, the Commodore 64 and the VIC-20 had a huge impact on people that it really isn't given the credit for. It's not like tens of millions of people bought them and threw them in the closet. They played with them for a while. It really helped a lot of people get comfortable with computers, to enjoy computers and appreciate computers. I'm not sure that the PC market could exist as it does now if something like Commodore hadn't paved the way for it."

John Feagans (PET, TOI, VIC-20, C64 Kernel Architect, Magic Desk Programmer) went to Atari and worked for Jack Tramiel where he helped develop the GEM GUI for the Atari ST.

Bill Mensch (6502 Layout Artist, 65816 Designer) sold his 65816 chip for use in the Apple IIGS and Super Nintendo console. The Western Design Center still markets 6502-based technology. According to their website, "Over 5 billion 65C02-based micro-controllers are the heart of such diverse products as appliances, automobiles, audio/video equipment, cell phones, modems, medical devices, manufacturing robots and instrumentation, and automated test equipment."

On November 20, 1996, Peddle celebrated the 6502 along with the founders of the microprocessor revolution. "Comdex did an awards show for the 25th anniversary of the microprocessor," recalls Peddle. "All the people who had done key microprocessors were getting awards, and I got an award for the 6502."

Peddle finally had a chance to express his gratitude to Mensch. "I complimented him in public. I said, 'I dropped my microprocessor and I gave up my dream. Bill carried it on and I'm proud of him.' Bill did a wonderful job of carrying on the concept. He did it all on his own with no help from anybody."

Chuck Peddle (6502 Inventor, PET Designer), **Bill Seiler** (PET, TOI, VIC-20 Systems Engineer), and his team of engineers went on to produce the state of the art *Victor 9000*. The machine turned out to be remarkably similar to the IBM PC released a year later. The Victor 9000 dominated business sales in Europe for a short period before the IBM PC overtook them in the late eighties.

Peddle believes if Commodore had produced and marketed his computer, it might have dominated the business market. "If we had done a similar product to what we did, I'm not sure the IBM PC would have ever gotten off the ground," he says. "We did pretty big damage to IBM with no resources. Having Commodore's resources and the ability to raise stock money, I think it would have been a totally different world today."

Years later, Peddle attended an event commemorating the anniversary of the personal computer. The event gave Peddle some perspective on his experiences with Jack Tramiel. "I got to make the world have personal computers because of Jack Tramiel," he says. "He destroyed me, he destroyed my family, he did all kinds of terrible things, but he gave me a chance to do something nobody else would give me necessarily. I can remember that and I thank him for it."

A year later, Peddle ran into Jack at a company named *JTS*. "I asked for an audience with him privately," reveals Peddle. "I basically told him, 'I think you cheated me, I think you did some bad things to me, but you gave me a chance to be somebody that nobody else could be, and I appreciate that.'"

Bob Yannes, the Commodore engineer who was partly responsible for Peddle's downfall, says, "I respect what he did. He did a lot of work on the 6502, which is a great processor, and he was responsible for the PET. Commodore wouldn't have been in the computer business if it wasn't for the PET."

Although Apple revisionists try to paint their founders as the innovators, it is clear Peddle and his 6502 had much more to do with the personal computer revolution. Steve Wozniak built his computer by assembling it from parts available on the market but Chuck Peddle built his machines starting with raw sand.

Byte magazine, which documented the history of personal computers, wrote of Peddle, "More than any other person, Chuck Peddle deserves to be called the founder of the personal computer industry."

Although Peddle's experiences at Commodore were devastating, he feels it was worth it. "I got to live a life that nobody else has gotten to live," he says.

Today, Peddle lives in California with his girlfriend and spends time with his kids and grandkids. He is a running enthusiast, a cat aficionado, enjoys reading science fiction (including works by former Byte magazine contributor Jerry Pournelle), visits CES every year, and travels the world working as an engineer for *Celetronix*. "Everybody keeps looking at me and saying, 'You made all these people rich. Aren't you rich?' The answer is I'm not."

Irving Gould (Commodore Chairman and Financier) remained an enigma until the end. He passed away in December 2001 at the *Mount Sinai Hospital* in Toronto. His family donated a large sum of money to the hospital in his name.

After the failure of Atari, **Jack Tramiel** retired and sold his remaining Atari assets to *Jugi Tandon Systems* (JTS). Today, Jack lives in Mont Sereno, California and travels the world. "His willingness to take chances is what made it happen," says Chuck Peddle. "His unwillingness to grow with the business is what killed him."

Chuck Peddle, arguably the greatest victim of Jack's pugnacious style, wants to remember Jack in a positive light. "When you were with Jack and things were right, he was charming and helpful," says Peddle. "He did some wonderful things for me."

Peddle believes Jack was no worse than other industry titans were. "He was a believer in making things happen," says Peddle. "If you go back and study the history of Rockefeller and those guys, you will discover there were no good guys there. Sometimes people expect movers and shakers to have halos. I don't think most of them do."

Without his ruthlessness, Peddle feels Jack would not have made an impact. "You need a fanatic," he says. "Gates is truly a fanatic. Jack, to some extent, was that fanatic. The business doesn't have any fanatics left. It's just business. There was a time when the Jack Tramiel's were the guys who made the business. He helped build a big business called the Personal Computer business."

As of 2005, Jack Tramiel is a nominee for the *Computer Hall of Fame* at the *San Diego Computer Museum*.

Bibliography

Allison, David. Smithsonian transcript. "A Video History Interview with Mr. William "Bill" Gates" (1993)

Bagamery, Anne. Fortune magazine. "The second time around" (October 8, 1984) p. 42.

Bateman, Selby. Compute! magazine. "Software Power! The Summer Consumer Electronics Show" (August 1984) pp. 32 – 41.

Bateman, Selby. Compute! magazine. "An Interview With Nigel Shepherd" (October 1986) pp. 22 – 31.

Beach, Bruce. The Best of The Torpet. (Toronto: Copp Clark Pitman Ltd, 1984)

Benford, Tom. Ahoy! magazine. "Commodore Software President Resigns" (February 1985) p. 9.

Bennett, Chris. TPUG Magazine. "New Computers At The CES Show" (February 1985) pp. 16 – 17.

Byte magazine. "Commodore Plans UNIX-Like Operating System for Z8000-Based Computer" (February 1984) p. 7.

Byte magazine. "Commodore Exhibits Computer Series" (June 1985) p. 39.

Chakravarty, Subrata N. Forbes magazine. "Albatross" (January 17, 1983) pp. 47 - 48.

Commodore Magazine. "Commodore Appoints President" (January 1988) p. 8.

Data Welt magazine. "An Interview with Jack Tramiel" (March 1986)

DeMott, John S. Time magazine. "A New Pac-Man: Jack Tramiel gobbles Atari" (July 16, 1984) p. 50.

Barney, Douglas. Amiga World. "Chief Concerns" (November 1991) p. 6.

Elko, Lance. Compute!'s Gazette magazine. "The Winter Consumer Electronics Show" (April 1986) p. 22.

Elko, Lance. Compute!'s Gazette magazine. "1987 Winter CES" (April 1987) p. 22.

Elko, Lance. Compute!'s Gazette magazine. "Editor's Notes" (July 1986) p. 6.

Elko, Lance. Compute!'s Gazette magazine. "Editor's Notes" (September 1989) p. 4.

Elko, Lance. Compute!'s Gazette magazine. "Editor's Notes" (November 1989) p. 4.

Elko, Lance. Compute!'s Gazette magazine. "Editor's Notes" (March 1990) p. 6.

Faflick, Philip. Time magazine. "The Hottest-Selling Hardware" (January 3, 1983) p. 37.

Ferrell, Keith. Compute!'s Gazette magazine. "CES: Commodore Software Comes of Age" (September 1987) p. 16.

Ferrell, Keith. Compute!'s Gazette magazine. "Editor's Notes" (January 1988) p. 6.

Ferrell, Keith et al. Compute!'s Gazette magazine. "Tomorrow TV" (December 1990) p. 14.

Fortune magazine. "Can Amiga find friends?" (August 19, 1985) p. 10.
Fortune magazine. "Jack Tramiel: Survival and Starting Over" (April 13, 1998)
Fortune magazine. "The house that Jack rebuilt" (March 16, 1987) p. 10.
Freiberger, Paul and Swaine, Michael. Fire in the Valley: The Making of the Personal Computer, Collector's Edition. (McGraw-Hill Companies, 1999)
Fylstra, Dan. Byte magazine. "User's Report: The PET 2001" (March 1978) pp. 114 – 127.
Golden, Frederic. Time magazine. "Jack Tramiel: Survivor's VICtory" (January 3, 1983) p. 29.
Gracely, Jim. Commodore Microcomputers magazine. "Commodore Announces its LCD Lap Computer" (March/April 1985) pp. 74 – 75.
Gutman, Dan. Commodore Microcomputers magazine, "What Next for Commodore? Things look bright with Tom Rattigan at the Helm" (May 1987) p. 76.
Halfhill, Tom R. Compute!'s Gazette magazine. "Commodore 64 Video Update" (July 1983) pp. 40 - 44.
Halfhill, Tom R. Compute! magazine. "Editors Notes" (July 1985) p. 6.
Hawkins, William J. Popular Science magazine. "New home computers can change your life-style" (October 1977) pp. 30 - 36.
Heimarck, Todd. Compute!'s Gazette magazine. "Changing Your Computer's Personality" (October 1986) p. 83.
Henry, Gordon M. Time magazine. "Adios, Amiga?" (February 24, 1986) p. 52.
Herrington, Peggy. Compute! magazine. "CDTV Goes Prime Time" (April 1991) pp. A-15 – A-22.
Info magazine. "Rumor Mill (Gould pay raise)" (January/February 1990) p. 28Knox, Andrea. Philadelphia Inquirer newspaper. "Commodore Ousts 6 Top Executives" (April 24, 1987), p. A01.
Knox, Andrea. Philadelphia Inquirer newspaper. "A New Strategy may be Needed for Commodore" (May 4, 1987), p. E01.
Kupfer, Andrew. Fortune magazine. "People to Watch" (May 27, 1985) p. 118.
LeBold, Dianne. Commodore Microcomputers magazine. "Commodore Announces UNIX-Compatible Business System" (September/October 1985) p. 10.
Leemon, Sheldon. Compute! magazine. "The Latest in Pictures and Words" (November 1987) p. 74.
Leemon, Sheldon. Compute! magazine. "The Great Amiga Reboot" (September 1987) p. 76.
Leemon, Sheldon. Compute! magazine. "You're Out, He's In" (March 1991) p. A-4.
Leemon, Sheldon. Compute! magazine. "Goofy Rumors" (November 1990) p. A-4.

Lemmons, Phil. Byte magazine. "Chuck Peddle: Chief Designer of the Victor 9000" (November 1982) pp. 256 – 271.

Lemmons, Phil. Byte magazine. "Victor Victorious: The Victor 9000 Computer" (November 1982) pp. 216 – 254.

Levitan, Arlan. Compute! magazine. "Things Are Getting Weird" (January 1991) p. A-14.

Libes, Sol. Byte magazine. "Personal Computers Going Great in Europe" (March 1979) p. 108.

Libes, Sol. Byte magazine. "Radio Shack Sales Over $100 M for 79" (April 1980) p. 116.

Libes, Sol. Byte magazine. "The Japanese Are Coming" (December 1980) p. 216.

Libes, Sol. Byte magazine. "Tandy, Apple, And Commodore Are Top Personal-Computer Performers" (November 1980) p. 242.

Libes, Sol. Byte magazine. "Commodore Status Report" (November 1982) p. 540.

Libes, Sol. Byte magazine. "VIC-20 Tops a Million" (April 1983) p. 458.

Libes, Sol. Byte magazine. "Random Rumors (65000 Processor)" (November 1982) p. 540.

Libes, Sol. Byte magazine. "Price War Develops" (December 1982) p. 500.

Lock, Robert C. Compute! magazine. "Editor's Notes" (December 1983) p. 6.

Lock, Robert C. Compute! magazine. "Editor's Notes" (November 1986) p. 6.

Lock, Robert C. Compute! magazine. "Editor's Notes" (May 1983) p. 8.

Lock, Robert C. Compute! magazine. "The Editor's Notes" (November 1982) p. 8.

Lock, Robert C. Compute!'s Gazette magazine. "Editor's Notes" (February 1985) p. 6.

Lock, Robert C. Compute!'s Gazette magazine. "Editors Notes" (August 1985) p. 4.

Lock, Robert C. Compute!'s Gazette magazine. "Editor's Notes" (September 1984) p. 6.

Lock, Robert C. Compute!'s Gazette magazine. "Editor's Notes" (December 1986) p. 6.

Lock, Robert C. Compute!'s Gazette magazine. "The Editor's Notes" (December 1983) p. 6.

Loos, Barbara C. and Moulton, Dennis J. Fortune magazine "International 500" (August 19, 1985) p. 182

Machan, Dyan. Forbes magazine. "Cheap didn't sell" (August 3, 1992) p. 52.

Malone, Michael. Infinite Loop: How Apple, the World's Most Insanely Great Company, Went Insane. (Currency, 1999)

Mansfield, Richard. Compute!'s Gazette magazine. "Editor's Notes" (June 1987) p. 6.

Mansfield, Richard. Compute! magazine. "Editor's Notes" (March 1985) p. 6.

McGlinn, Evan. Forbes magazine. "Lost Opportunity?" (November 13, 1989) pp. 288 - 292.

Bibliography

Morgan, Chris. Byte magazine. "The NCC: A Dallas Delight" (October 1977) pp. 54 – 56.

Moritz, Michael. The Little Kingdom: The Private Story of Apple Computer. (William Morrow & Co, 1984)

Olafson, Peter. Amiga World magazine. "CD32 Rollout at CES" (April 1994) pp. 6 – 8.

PC Magazine "Amiga Launch Party" (January 14, 1986) p. 119.

Perry, Nancy J. Fortune magazine. "A Big Loss at Commodore" (September 16, 1985) p. 11.

Petre, Peter. Fortune magazine. "Jack Tramiel is Back on the Warpath" (March 4, 1985) pp. 46 - 50.

Philadelphia Inquirer, "Commodore Reports Lower Sales" (April 30, 1987) p. E10.

Philadelphia Inquirer, "Commodore Countersuit" (June 13, 1987) p. D09

Pournelle, Jerry. Byte magazine. "Survival" (January 1984) pp. 62 – 66.

Pournelle, Jerry. Byte magazine. "Jerry's Best of 1985 Awards" (April 1986) pp. 279 – 299.

San Jose Mercury News. "Obituaries: Jay Miner" (July 22, 1994)

Sherrid, Pamela. Forbes magazine. "Faces Behind the Figures" (June 17, 1985) p. 190.

Sullivan, Nick. TPUG Magazine. "Inside Information" (August/September 1985) p. 2.

Tomczyk, Michael S. The Home Computer Wars: An Insider's Account of Commodore and Jack Tramiel. (Greensboro, North Carolina: Compute! Publications, Inc., 1984)

Torvalds, Linus and Diamond, David. Just for Fun: The Story of an Accidental Revolutionary. (Collins, 2002)

Walker, Rob. Silicon Genesis: An Oral History of Semiconductor Technology, "Interview with William Mensch" (Atherton, California, October 9, 1995)

Wallich, Perry. IEEE Spectrum. "Design case history: the Commodore 64" (March 1985) pp. 48 - 58.

Wideman, Graham and Czerwinski, Mark. Electronics Today magazine. "Inside the Commodore Pet" (February 1978) pp. 10 - 16.

Willard, Lawrence F. Byte magazine. "Random Observations and Conversations at the First West Coast Computer Faire" (July 1977) pp. 25 – 30.

Williams, Bobby. Compute!'s Gazette magazine. "Using A 1540 Disk Drive And Commodore 64" (August 1983) p. 90.

Williams, Monci Jo. Fortune magazine. "How Commodore Hopes to Survive" (January 6, 1986) pp. 30 - 32.

Yakal, Kathy. *Compute!* magazine. "The Christmas Of The Computer?" (December 1983) p. 32.